LIBRARY-LRC
TEXAS HEART INSTITUTE

D1714681

American Indian Health

American Indian Health

Innovations in Health Care,
Promotion, and Policy

Edited by
Everett R. Rhoades, M.D.

Adjunct Professor of International Health
Center for American Indian and Alaskan Native Health
Johns Hopkins University School of Hygiene
and Public Health / Baltimore, Maryland

Adjunct Professor of Medicine and
Associate Dean for Community Affairs
College of Medicine and College of Public Health;
Director, Native American Prevention Research Center
University of Oklahoma Health Sciences Center /
Oklahoma City, Oklahoma

Former Director
Indian Health Service / Rockville, Maryland

The Johns Hopkins University Press
Baltimore and London

© 2000 The Johns Hopkins University Press
All rights reserved. Published 2000
Printed in the United States of America on acid-free paper
9 8 7 6 5 4 3 2 1

The Johns Hopkins University Press
2715 North Charles Street
Baltimore, Maryland 21218-4363
www.press.jhu.edu

Library of Congress Cataloging-in-Publication Data will
be found at the end of this book.
A catalog record for this book is available from the
British Library.

ISBN 0-8018-6328-7

The comments expressed by the following authors are not to be construed
as official policy of the U.S. government:
Kelly Acton, Indian Health Service
Brenda A. Broussard, Indian Health Service
Anthony J. D'Angelo, Indian Health Service
William Freeman, Indian Health Service
Aaron O. Handler, Indian Health Service
Gary J. Hartz, Indian Health Service
Candace M. Jones, Indian Health Service
Stephen F. Kaufman, Indian Health Service
Jeffrey C. Long, National Institute of Alcohol Abuse and Alcoholism
Joseph G. Lorenz, National Institute of Alcohol Abuse and Alcoholism
Robert F. Martin, Indian Health Service
Kenneth M. Petersen, Centers for Disease Control and Prevention
Richard J. Smith III, Indian Health Service
Karen F. Strauss, Food and Drug Administration
Thomas Welty, Indian Health Service

Contents

Part III. Major Diseases and Health Conditions Affecting Indians

Part IV. Special Cultural and Ethical Considerations

Contributors

Kelly Acton, M.D., M.P.H., FACP, Director, National Diabetes Program, Office of Public Health, Indian Health Service, Albuquerque, New Mexico

Edwin Asturias, M.D., Research Associate, Division of Disease Control, Department of International Health, Johns Hopkins University School of Hygiene and Public Health, Guatemala

George R. Brenneman, M.D., FAAP, Assistant Scientist and Associate Director, Center for American Indian and Alaska Native Health, Johns Hopkins University School of Hygiene and Public Health, Baltimore, Maryland

Brenda A. Broussard, R.D., M.P.H., M.B.A., CDE, Clinical Research Lecturer, Department of Internal Medicine, University of New Mexico School of Medicine, Albuquerque, New Mexico

Robert J. Collins, D.M.D., M.P.H., Deputy Director, International and American Associations for Dental Research, Alexandria, Virginia

Anthony J. D'Angelo, M.S., Principal Statistician, Program Statistics Team, Indian Health Service, Rockville, Maryland

Raymond J. DeMallie, Ph.D., Professor, Department of Anthropology, and Director, American Indian Studies Research Institute, Indiana University, Bloomington, Indiana

William Freeman, M.D., M.P.H., Director, Research Program, Indian Health Service, Albuquerque, New Mexico

Tim J. Gilbert, M.P.H., R.D., Hospital Administrator, Maniilaq Health Center, Kotzebue, Alaska

Dorothy M. Gohdes, M.D., FACP, Clinical Assistant Professor, Department of Medicine, University of New Mexico School of Medicine, Albuquerque, New Mexico

Alan H. Goodman, Ph.D., Professor of Biological Anthropology, School of Natural Science, Hampshire College, Amherst, Massachusetts

James W. Hampton, M.D., Clinical Professor, Department of Medicine, University of Oklahoma College of Medicine, and Medical Director, The Troy and Dollie Smith Cancer Center, Integris Baptist Medical Center, Oklahoma City, Oklahoma

Aaron O. Handler, B.A., Senior Statistician, Program Statistics Team, Indian Health Service, Rockville, Maryland

Gary J. Hartz, M.S., P.E., Chief, Environmental Health and Engineering, Indian Health Service, Rockville, Maryland

Mohamed Hashem, M.D., Research Associate, Center for American Indian and Alaskan Native Health, Johns Hopkins University School of Hygiene and Public Health, Baltimore, Maryland

Matthew O. Howard, Ph.D., Assistant Professor, George Warren Brown School of Social Work, Washington University, Saint Louis, Missouri

Emery A. Johnson, M.D., M.P.H., former director, Indian Health Service, Rockville, Maryland

Candace M. Jones, R.D.H., M.P.H., Director, Dental Disease Prevention Program, Indian Health Service, Rockville, Maryland

Stephen F. Kaufman, M.S., Leader, Patient Care Statistics Team, Program Statistics Team, Indian Health Service, Rockville, Maryland

Charles R. Key, M.D., Ph.D., Professor, Department of Pathology, University of New Mexico School of Medicine, and Medical Director, New Mexico Tumor Registry, University of New Mexico Cancer Research and Treatment Center, Albuquerque, New Mexico

Kirke Kickingbird, Esq., Director, Native American Legal Research Center, Oklahoma City University, Oklahoma City, Oklahoma

Jeffrey C. Long, Ph.D., Chief, Section on Population Genetics and Linkage, Laboratory of Neurogenetics, National Institute on Alcohol Abuse and Alcoholism, Rockville, Maryland

Joseph G. Lorenz, Ph.D., Postdoctoral Fellow, Laboratory of Neurogenetics, National Institute on Alcohol Abuse and Alcoholism, Rockville, Maryland

James F. Maher, Ph.D., M.D., Resident Physician, Department of Internal Medicine, Jewish Hospital, Cincinnati, Ohio

Spero M. Manson, Ph.D., Professor and Head, Division of American Indian and Alaska Native Programs, Department of Psychiatry, University of Colorado Health Sciences Center, Denver, Colorado

Debra L. Martin, Ph.D., Professor of Biological Anthropology, School of Natural Science, Hampshire College, Amherst, Massachusetts

Robert F. Martin, D.D.S., M.P.H., Chief, Dental Program, Indian Health Service, Rockville, Maryland

Scott H. Nelson, M.D., M.P.H., former Chief, Mental Health Programs, Indian Health Service, Washington, D.C.

Kenneth M. Petersen, M.D., Consultant, Arctic Investigations Program, Centers for Disease Control and Prevention, Alaska Native Medical Center, Anchorage, Alaska

Raymond Reid, M.D., M.P.H., Physician and Research Associate, Johns Hopkins Study Center, Shiprock, New Mexico

Dorothy A. Rhoades, M.D., M.P.H., Assistant Professor, Native Elder Research

Center, University of Colorado Health Science Center, Denver, Colorado; and Clinical Instructor, Department of Medicine, University of Washington School of Medicine, Seattle, Washington

Leon S. Robertson, Ph.D., retired injury epidemiologist, Globe, Arizona

Mathuram Santosham, M.D., M.P.H., FAAP, Professor and Director, Division of Community Health and Health Systems, Department of International Health; and Director, Center for American Indian and Alaska Native Health, Johns Hopkins University School of Hygiene and Public Health, Baltimore, Maryland

R. Hal Scofield, M.D., Associate Professor, Department of Internal Medicine, University of Oklahoma Health Sciences Center; and Associate Member, Arthritis and Immunology Program, Oklahoma Medical Research Foundation, Oklahoma City, Oklahoma

Richard J. Smith III, M.S., Deputy Director, Office of Public Health, Indian Health Service, Rockville, Maryland

C. Matthew Snipp, Ph.D., Professor, Department of Sociology, Stanford University, Stanford, California

Mary Story, Ph.D., R.D., Associate Professor, Division of Epidemiology, University of Minnesota, Minneapolis, Minnesota

Karen F. Strauss, M.S., R.D., Consumer Safety Officer, Office of Special Nutritionals, Center for Food Safety and Applied Nutrition, Food and Drug Administration, Washington, D.C.

John G. Todd, M.S., M.P.H., Dr.P.H., RS, Assistant Surgeon General (retired), U.S. Public Health Service; Former Director of Program Operations, Indian Health Service, Poolesville, Maryland

Patricia S. Walker, Ph.D., Research Assistant Professor, Department of Psychiatry, Oregon Health Sciences University, Portland, Oregon

R. Dale Walker, M.D., Professor and Chair, Department of Psychiatry, and Professor, Department of Public Health, Oregon Health Sciences University, Portland, Oregon

Thomas Welty, M.D., M.P.H., Principal Investigator, Strong Heart Study, Flagstaff, Arizona

Lawrence S. Wissow, M.D., M.P.H., Associate Professor, Department of Health Policy and Management, Johns Hopkins University School of Hygiene and Public Health, Baltimore, Maryland

Preface

Among the reasons for studying the health and health care of American Indians, four are particularly significant. First, through a variety of constitutional, legislative, executive, and judicial circumstances largely associated with the cession of vast tracts of land, the U.S. government assumed a number of responsibilities toward Indian people. Among these responsibilities is the provision of health services. The resulting federal health-care system serving the many distinct tribal groups merits extensive analysis and study. Second, the health status of this population remains among the lowest of any group in the country, a compelling reason for continued examination. Third, the peopling of the Western Hemisphere with many distinct groups has produced a great "natural experiment" that permits comparisons of a variety of biomedical phenomena between diverse populations. Studies of disease processes and manifestations and how they differ between populations have provided an important source of basic biomedical knowledge. Much of this knowledge is beneficial to not only Indians but all people. Fourth, the system of delivering health care that was developed for Indian people is unique. Study of this model can be very useful as the country continues to struggle fitfully for solutions to the various problems associated with the provision of health care to its citizens.

This system has come to be known as the Indian Health Service (IHS), an extraordinarily complex organization of community-oriented, primary preventive and therapeutic care serving members of approximately 550 Indian tribes throughout the country. Some insight into this special program can be gained from a statement made in 1981 by Emery Johnson, the then-recently retired director of the IHS: "The Indian Health Service is an island of tranquility in a sea of turmoil." Indeed, the IHS was at that time relatively free of the stresses being experienced by the medical care establishment, as well as the Public Health Service, resulting from major revisions of American health-care delivery and a re-examination of the role of the federal government.

Dr. Johnson's description of the IHS is not so true today. Efforts to downsize the IHS are accompanied by markedly accelerating shifts of program operations to the tribes, and these movements have resulted in great uncertainty as to the precise responsibilities of the IHS to Indian people generally. However, a dimension of Dr. Johnson's 1981 assessment remains of primary importance. In a larger sense, Dr. Johnson was referring to what I have chosen to term the basic *integrity* or *intactness* of the Indian health programs. By this I mean the soundness of the underlying philosophy and the presence of a specific vision that have guided the IHS through turbulent times. While the country continues its presently inchoate health-care nonsystem, the IHS has remained dedicated to systematic efforts to address the unresolved questions of universal access to care, limited resources, uncontrolled costs of health care, and the resulting zero sum, all of which necessitate making difficult choices among competing priorities.

Interestingly, given the acuteness of present concerns about American health-care programs, the public knows little or nothing about the IHS. The desire to describe the IHS with its many innovations and successes was a major factor in the preparation of this book. Although the IHS's approaches and solutions are not always ideal and should not necessarily be adopted by others, study of the IHS and its approaches should be required for those who propose changes (or, in some instances, no changes) in the present nonsystem.

The background for my opinion is worth explaining. I have had a lifelong relationship with the IHS, beginning with my birth in an Indian health facility. My earliest memory of Indian health is at approximately the age of four, when, following a puncture wound of the foot by a nail in the dirt floor of a barn, I was hastily taken to the "Kiowa" hospital in Lawton, Oklahoma, to prevent the dreaded lockjaw. There an entirely new world presented itself to me. The *gravitas* of the attending physician and the situation, the clean antiseptic smell, the exotic equipment, and the mystery of the hypodermic injection could not have been more strange to an Indian youngster growing up in rural Oklahoma during the Depression. However, I subsequently realized that this invaluable service (which was actually provided by the often-criticized Bureau of Indian Affairs) was available to me but not to my non-Indian peers. This was not an isolated comparison. My childhood took place in a community in which a healthy young student died without medical care for an otherwise readily treatable head injury. That almost certainly would not have happened had she been an Indian person.

Like many Indian colleagues, I eventually moved into other systems of health care (military, for example) and tended not to use the IHS facilities in the belief that others needed them more acutely than I. Later, during my tenure on the Kiowa Tribal Business Committee, I was privileged to take part in an official tribal capacity when the IHS dramatically moved to increase the participation of Indian people in the management of IHS programs. As an internist at an academic health center and as one of the original volunteer physicians at an urban Indian clinic, I had the privilege of serving Indian people directly. This period, occupying nearly a decade, was followed by a tour of 11 years as director of the IHS, where an entirely new experience awaited me. As director, I participated in a vast system of health care involving a host of federal and tribal health workers at the community level and had the opportunity to sit at council tables where national policy was debated. Few opportunities for such a panoramic perspective exist. Subsequent to this tour with the IHS, my official tribal and federal responsibilities have diminished, and I have returned to academia to reflect on the many developments in Indian life and Indian health care during the past decades. The compilation of this overview of Indian health draws on these varied experiences.

The tone of this book is largely that of a reference text, and an effort has been made to present facts dispassionately as they are currently known and understood. But discerning readers may detect other tones. There is a commonly held belief, popular in both print and broadcast media, that the condition of the Indian population is the direct result of malevolent motives on the part of the U.S. government and therefore of the general public. This volume is offered to counter the thesis that Indian ills are the result *only* of governmental neglect. Indeed, I believe this thesis is the ultimate patronization of Indian people. Perhaps another point of view can be held at the same time, that emphasis on the heroic is at least as illuminating and uplifting as is the preoccupation with placing blame. One personal example comes to mind. My great-grandmother, while the Kiowa people were held prisoner at Fort Sill, would quietly and unobtrusively cook during the day and, when night came, would secure a horse and deliver the food to her brothers hiding in the Wichita Mountains several miles away, refusing to surrender. That story seems a powerful counterpoint to the privations suffered by the Kiowas while prisoners at Fort Sill. Thus, my preferred theme, even in what is ultimately a medical text, is that the heroism, not the adversity, is most worthy of our attention.

The opportunity to establish a graduate course, Native American Health, for the Center for American Indian and Alaska Native Health of the Johns Hopkins School of Hygiene and Public Health revealed the need for a single-volume reference text covering the major aspects of Indian health. The editorial board of the Johns Hopkins University Press evaluated a class "work text" and recommended that an expanded and multiauthored text be prepared. This recommendation led to the preparation of the present volume.

The Johns Hopkins course disclosed that thorough examination of Indian health required attention to several broad topics:

1. what one might term the *anthropologic/ethnologic*—that is, the important antecedents, extending beyond recorded history, that characterize the ethnic groups now identified as American Indian;
2. the "civics" of Indian health—dealing with the paramount factor in all Indian affairs, the sovereign nature of most Indian tribes and the resulting

government-to-government relationship between them and the U.S. government and with the tribes' own internal political, organizational, and administrative functions;

3. the various biomedical concerns that have resulted from the special genetic, cultural, social, and historical differences that tend to distinguish American Indians from the rest of the U.S. population;

4. "traditional" Indian medicine and concepts and the special considerations necessary to providing health services to Indian people and, even more important, certain ethical considerations in conducting studies among Indian populations.

The study of the distinct disease patterns among Indians generally uses three major analyses: (1) comparison of overall patterns, such as morbidity and mortality prevalence and incidence rates between Indian groups and other populations, especially the general U.S. population; (2) comparison of disease epidemiology between various Indian groups; and (3) trends in certain prevalence and incidence rates among Indians (again, often compared to other groups) during certain time periods. Such categories and analyses provide the basis for most of the chapters in this book.

A major frustration accompanying all Indian studies is the unsatisfactory ability of available language to be sufficiently precise and discriminating. Terms such as *entitlement, trust status, Indian country,* and even *medicine, Western, traditional,* and many others have multiple meanings. The same is true of certain definitions, including the designation *Indian* itself as applied to the aboriginal inhabitants of the Western Hemisphere. The use of such terms as *Indian, American Indian,* and *Native American* in this volume is discussed in the following section on nomenclature. Further, there is no universally agreed-upon spelling for many names and terms. The reader is likely to note variations in spelling for the same population: Athabaskan/Athapaskan, Ojibwe/Ojibwa, and so forth. Variation also extends to the use of plural versus singular forms for Indian names. For example, one may encounter *the Navajo* and *the Navajos* (or other tribal designations) used interchangeably. Again, there is no generally agreed-upon usage.

The extent and complexity of the many factors related to Indian health far exceed the capacity of any single volume. The present text is based upon the leading causes of death and disability of Indians; the special ethnic, cultural, and political background that helps explain many Indian health conditions; and the nature of their health-care delivery system. A number of diseases and conditions, notwithstanding their prevalence among Indians, are not presented. Rather, attention is given to those conditions on which carefully collected observations have been made or for which differences in disease behavior among

Indians compared to other groups are substantial. For example, gallbladder disease, with its well-known higher prevalence among Indians, is not managed differently and therefore is not included. In a few instances, omissions are occasioned by a relative lack of biomedical/epidemiologic information; for example, homicide, an important cause of Indian deaths, awaits more complete epidemiologic study. Family abuse, a serious problem, likewise awaits further study, as do certain less common metabolic problems encountered among Indian people.

Very few books deal with Indian health generally. The excellent volume by Young (1994) emphasizes biocultural epidemiology and provides important descriptions of the major diseases. Galloway, Goldberg, and Alpert (1999) provided an extensive description of diseases and conditions that is designed for use by the busy clinical practitioner. The present volume differs from these works, especially in its attention to the political and administrative aspects of American Indian diseases and programs designed for their control. Space has not permitted more than an occasional mention of Canadian or Central and South American Indians; their omission reflects the vastness of the materials available and the availability of a volume dealing with Canadian Natives by Waldram, Herring, and Young (1995). Young (1994) also presents considerable information about Canadian Natives, and the excellent summary by Sievers and Fisher (1981) remains a useful survey of North American Indian health.

The goal has been to gather into a single volume as much of the relevant information about the various aspects of Indian health as is possible and practicable. The book can serve as a ready reference for the busy health-care worker or administrator, especially those interested in the broad field of public health. It should prove useful for all workers in Indian health, many of whom have mentioned to me the need for such a volume to serve as an orientation to Indian health, an admittedly complicated field. The book can also provide a ready reference for a variety of policymakers, such as congressional and legislative members and their staffs. As a description of a model for health-care planning for special and disadvantaged populations, this volume can serve as a reference for health-care workers and policymakers in other countries. However, it is hoped that it will be of interest to the general reader as well.

The three chapters in Part I are introductory, providing background information vital to understanding the complex situation of Indian health and health care. In Chapter 1, DeMallie and Rhoades describe the leading considerations regarding the origins of North American Indians, the peopling of the Americas, groupings of certain Indian populations, and their distinctions and affinities. Martin and Goodman, in Chapter 2, describe certain aspects of pre-Columbian diseases and conditions. Their inferences about the health effects of those moving into a "maize economy" and about studies of trauma from skeletal and other remains remind one that the popular conception of a pristine and idyllic pre-Columbian existence is not entirely correct. In Chapter 3, Snipp describes the major demographic aspects of the Indian population necessary for understanding various disease patterns and planning health programs.

Part II discusses the political and administrative bases of Indian Health. Chapters 4 and 5 might be considered the civics of Indian health. Kickingbird and Rhoades discuss the political basis of tribal governments, the exercise of tribal sovereignty, and the resulting all-important federal-Indian relationship in Chapter 4. The continuing evolution of this relationship and the profound influence of the U.S. Congress are felt in virtually all aspects of Indian health. In Chapter 5 Johnson and Rhoades describe the origins and development of federal health services for Indian people and the resultant Indian Health Service. In Chapter 6, Rhoades and colleagues review the major sources of Indian health data essential to analyzing health and disease-related events and describe the various subsets of the Indian population of special concern, especially the population eligible for IHS services.

Part III surveys the leading causes of death and disability among Indian people. Brenneman and colleagues, in Chapter 7, describe the overall vital events relating to Indians and the indices used to examine mortality rates associated with specific conditions in various age groups. In Chapter 8 Long and Lorenz present an overview of the exploding field of genetic studies and their application to Indian populations. Brenneman, in Chapter 9, explores the various parameters of maternal and child health, usually considered to be the fundamental indices of the general health of a given population. Rhoades and colleagues review, in Chapter 10, the major cardiovascular diseases, formerly thought to be relatively unimportant for Indian people but now recognized as the leading cause of death of all Indians and a field that is rapidly progressing. In Chapter 11, Hampton and colleagues summarize the many manifestations of various malignancies among Indian people. In Chapter 12, Story and colleagues review the present state of knowledge regarding the vital subject of nutrition. Diabetes, quickly becoming an even more ominous epidemic among Indian people and a field in which information is rapidly accumulating, is discussed by Gohdes and Acton in Chapter 13. The generally unrecognized importance of the epidemic of injuries and the resultant burden of incapacity on Indian communities and the innovative programs developed by the IHS are discussed by Smith and Robertson in Chapter 14. In Chapter 15, Wissow discusses the issues associated with suicide among the Indian population. Alcohol abuse and its effects among Indians are addressed by Howard et al. in Chapter 16. Rhoades and colleagues, in Chapter 17, discuss the complex situation regarding tobacco use among Indians. In Chapter 18, Nelson and Manson present an overview of the major considerations regarding mental illness and disability. Scofield reviews immunologic and rheumatologic conditions in Chapter 19. Chapter 20 presents an overview of some of the major infectious diseases by Asturias et al. In Chapter 21, Collins and colleagues discuss the usually neglected field of oral health and the special programs designed by the IHS to deal with various problems. In Chapter 22, Hartz et al. examine the development of environmental health programs; equally important, they discuss how the IHS has incorporated this specialty into its integrated program and the pioneering way in which the environmental health programs have developed relations with the various tribes.

In Part IV, Chapters 23 through 26 deal with special topics of concern for those providing health care to Indian people; this section might perhaps be termed the anthropology and sociology of medical practice among Indian people. Chapter 23 briefly discusses some of the similarities and differences between "traditional" Indian concepts and practices and modern "scientific" concepts and practices, especially in what some consider the "postmodern" era. In Chapter 24, Reid and Rhoades discuss, largely based on years of personal experience, important considerations in personally dealing with Indian patients and their respective communities. In Chapter 25, Rhoades et al. analyze the ever more acute considerations that must be taken into account by those who conduct studies among Indian populations. In the concluding Chapter 26, Johnson and Rhoades reflect upon the information in the preceding chapters and offer impressions and inferences about the present and, more particularly, the future of Indian health and Indian health care.

REFERENCES

Galloway JM, Goldberg BW, Alpert JS. 1999. *Primary Care of Native American Patients: Diagnosis, Therapy, and Epidemiology*. Boston: Butterworth-Heinemann.

Sievers ML, Fisher JR. 1981. Diseases of North American Indians. In: Rothschild HR, ed. *Biocultural Aspects of Disease*. New York: Academic Press.

Waldram JB, Herring DA, Young TK. 1995. *Aboriginal Health in Canada: Historical, Cultural, and Epidemiologic Perspectives*. Toronto: University of Toronto Press.

Young TK. 1994. *The Health of Native Americans: Towards a Biocultural Epidemiology*. New York: Oxford University Press.

Acknowledgments

Special thanks and appreciation go to Mathuram Santosham, founder and director of the Center for American Indian and Alaska Native Health of the Johns Hopkins School of Hygiene and Public Health. Dr. Santosham established a graduate course in Native American health, suggested publication of the "work text" prepared for that course, and provided unstinting support throughout the project. Other Johns Hopkins staff supporting the effort include Allison Barlow, Bobbie Gormley, Maha Asham, and Associate Dean Sylvia Eggleston-Wehr. Each contributed time and labor to move the project forward. Generous support from Marianne Gerschel and the Spunk Fund made it possible to establish the course and develop the completed manuscript.

At the University of Oklahoma College of Medicine, first Executive Dean Douglas Voth and then Jerry Vannatta could not have been more generous in providing support and allowing time away from duties so I could carry the work forward. Caylon Coleman, Sally Murphy, and Terry Bahm patiently provided daily support of many kinds, especially with the ever-changing technology of word processing. Nancy Hall provided continuous support and assistance. Edith Schneeberger and the research staff of the Health Sciences Center Library located obscure references with impressive efficiency. Glenn Solomon provided important historical reprints relating to the use of tobacco. The most heartfelt thanks go to Camilla Schumacher and Ruth Jawabira, whose clerical and administrative brilliance regularly and seemingly effortlessly organized the work and resolved endless details necessary in such a collective effort. Their resourcefulness and management of tasks and materials was carried out ingeniously and generously, even with the irregular habits of the editor.

Dr. Elisa Lee, dean of the University of Oklahoma College of Public Health, was likewise unfailingly supportive and encouraging, also providing time away from other duties so the work could move forward. June Eichner, Valeri Shepherd, and Timothy Taylor, of the Native American Prevention Research Center, shouldered many of the editor's other duties to permit attention to this project.

Gratitude is extended to Drs. Stephen Kunitz and Jerrold Levy, who, with their many years of experience and outstanding contributions, generously advised the editor regarding important topics. Two colleagues merit special thanks. Dr. Emery Johnson, retired director of the Indian Health Service and a friend and counselor of many years, drew upon his unequaled personal wealth of information as well as his great wisdom in offering advice. Dr. George Brenneman generously provided references on a variety of topics and provided virtually daily support. Both kindly read all chapters, some more than once, patiently responded to dozens of questions, and provided critiques and insights that helped minimize errors and omissions and clarify many statements.

Among the many experts in the Indian Health Service, the Headquarters Program Statistics Team deserve special thanks for not only the goodwill with which they tolerated interruptions in their busy work, but also the promptness and excellence of their contributions, which were critical factors in completing the volume. Especially helpful were Aaron Handler, Anthony D'Angelo, Stephen Kaufman, and Priscilla Sandoval. In the Office of Public Health, Karen Culloty was unusually successful in obtaining difficult to locate materials and sources. As is the case with so many wonderful colleagues throughout the Indian Health Service, their expertise and dedication are not sufficiently recognized.

At the Johns Hopkins University Press, Wendy Harris patiently guided the editor through innumerable requirements, made suggestions that invariably improved the text, and provided needed support when it sometimes seemed that the task might be too great. Linda Forlifer displayed genius in the copyediting, dealing with innumerable questions, corrections, and clarifications.

A work such as this is, on another level, the result of Indian peoples themselves. Their special existence, with all its vast spiritual and cultural legacy, played no small part in the ultimate production of this volume. It is imperative that in all such studies and examinations Indians are recognized as participants, not subjects. Throughout, this doctrine has guided the present effort. In this context, undying gratitude goes to Bernadine Toyebo Rhoades, an apotheosis of the wife and mother as the central figure in the extended Indian family.

Nomenclature

The peopling of the New World by aboriginal peoples has been associated with the development of thousands of separate and distinct tribal groups, of which there are presently more than five hundred in the United States alone. The need to describe various conditions among such a large number of distinct entities requires nomenclature, classification, and grouping simply for efficient description, discussion, and analysis. The nomenclature for most, if not all, of these entities developed in an inchoate fashion that is often unsatisfactory and ambiguous for present needs. It simply is not practical to list the many individual tribes when attempting to describe common traits, and indeed it would be most desirable to have a descriptive, unambiguous term for the entire group.

The term *Indian,* both succinct and euphonious, continues to be generally satisfactory to identify descendants of those who occupied the Western Hemisphere before 1492, notwithstanding that it was mistakenly applied to what were thought to be inhabitants of the Eastern, rather than Western, Hemisphere. The more specific term *American Indian,* referring to aborigines in the Western Hemisphere, served reasonably well except that certain Alaska groups preferred to be designated *Alaska Natives* rather than *American Indians.* The result is that one nonspecific term was substituted for another. The term *Alaska Native* most precisely designates individuals born in the state of Alaska regardless of ethnic background, as does its companion, *Native Alaskan.* However, continued common usage has led to acceptance of *Alaska Native* (not *Alaskan Native*) and *Native Alaskan* as referring to *aboriginal* peoples and their descendants in the state of Alaska. Because of these ambiguities, in official reports and correspondence the federal government has informally adopted the more complex and awkward *American Indian and Alaska Native,* naturally often reduced to *AI/AN,* still awkward even for an acronym. It will occasionally be used in the present volume. Naturally, the term used by previous authors will generally be retained in citations of their work. Young (1994) employs the term *Native American* throughout his book, perhaps in part because of being based in Canada (where common usage often refers to yet another designation, *First Nations*). Following the frustration and rationale expressed by Fiedel (1987) and in the absence of more precise and acceptable terminology, the terms *American*

Indian and *Native American* will generally be employed interchangeably in this volume, with tribal designations used when more specific identification is required. Occasionally it seems more appropriate to use the more elaborate *American Indian and Alaska Native*. When there should be no ambiguity as to reference, the simpler term *Indian* will be used.

American Indian Health

Part I

The Demographics
of Indian Health

Raymond J. DeMallie, Ph.D., and
Everett R. Rhoades, M.D.

The Aboriginal Peoples of America

As presently understood, the story of American Indian health begins about 20,000–14,000 years ago, when, for reasons obscure but undoubtedly associated with shifts in climate, the first humans known to inhabit the Western Hemisphere made their appearance in North America. Although continuing controversy surrounds questions of routes and the timing of aboriginal migrations (Dillehay and Meltzer 1991), scientific consensus leaves no doubt about the origin of American Indians in Asia. The medical significance of Indian origins derives from the genetic and sociocultural attributes shared by descendants of the aboriginal groups, rather than the exact timing or routes of entry into the New World.

The result is an intersecting series of events that have created a vast natural experiment with far-reaching implications not only for biomedical but also for many other social, organizational, and governmental phenomena. In this natural experiment a genetically related Asian group or groups peopled a pristine hemisphere; over the course of millennia, they developed into a large number of distinct tribes; during the most recent five hundred years, yet another, this time manyfold greater, migration occurred, this one of European groups possessing an altogether different genetic and cultural heritage. Thus, a great number of distinctive cohort groups, each of which has its own biomedical characteristics, now occupy North America. Opportunities for comparisons of various biomedical characteristics among and between the various groups now inhabiting North America have already provided illuminating insights into several disease processes.

This chapter, like most others in this volume, is written from the standpoint of Western science. Many Native Americans today reject the hypothesis of Asiatic origin. American Indians themselves tell tribal stories of autochthonous origins, emerging from under the earth or on or under a primordial sea, descending from the sky, or migrating from an earlier life elsewhere. For such a contemporary Native American critique, see Deloria (1995); Nabokov (1996) provides a comprehensive survey of Native American concepts of the past.

Archaeologic Perspectives on American Indian Origins

As the study of the physical remains left by Native Americans, archaeology is best situated to unravel the question of the origins and routes of population spread throughout North America. (The following discussion draws on Spencer, Jennings, et al. 1977; Fagan 1991; and Snow 1996.) However, the paucity of early archaeologic sites makes interpretation necessarily speculative. On the basis of geological evidence, scientists calculate that Asia and North America were connected beginning about 75,000 years ago by a landmass known as Beringia. Unfortunately, the popular designation—the Bering Land Bridge—offers a misleading image. From 45,000 to 40,000 years ago, as a result of warmer temperatures, Beringia was underwater, and it experienced periodic flooding until 25,000 years ago. Most archaeologists agree that it was during the last cold period, from 25,000 to 14,000 years ago, that humans made their way from Asia to present Alaska (Rogers, Rogers, and Martin 1992, 285). Given the submersion of Beringia since that time, there is no archaeologic evidence for this migration, although paleontologic evidence reveals the migration of large animal species—including elephants and mastodons—from Asia to the New World.

Although most archaeologists in the past believed that humans moved into North America through an interior route, following an ice-free corridor through central Alaska, contemporary opinion seems to favor a route along the Pacific Coast. Supporting this hypothesis is the observation that the Pacific Coast region is one of great linguistic diversity, suggesting longtime depth for American Indians in that area (Rogers, Rogers, and Martin 1992, 288–89).

The earliest archaeologic remains in North America are classified as *Paleo-Indian* or *Big Game Hunters*. The earliest sites (Bluefield Caves and Dry Creek) date from only 12,000–11,000 years ago; their diagnostic feature is chipped stone microblades that appear to be related to a similar technology for big game hunting found in Siberia and dating to 14,000–12,000 years ago. Intriguingly, occupation at the Meadowcroft Rock Shelter site in Pennsylvania is dated to have begun 14,000 years ago, and similar dates are claimed for sites in Washington and Oregon. From this, archaeologists conclude that the spread of these earliest Paleo-Indians south occurred after the end of the Wisconsin glaciation (about 14,500 years ago) and that, by 11,000 years ago, they had settled throughout North America. Recent studies of the oldest Paleo-Indian remains have produced controversy but seem to be pushing back the date of human occupation in the New World. The Monte Verde site in southern Chile, for example, has been dated at 12,000 years ago (Meltzer et al. 1997). Consensus has recently developed around the antiquity of the site, but there is no consensus on its implications for the peopling of the Americas.

In North America, the first defined archaeologic tradition is known as *Clovis,* represented by distinctive stone points (sometimes fluted at the base for ease in hafting to spears), which are found throughout the continent, dating from 12,000 to 11,000 years ago. Hunters whose way of life is known largely from kill sites, the Clovis people apparently centered their activities on the hunting of mastodons, mammoths, and other big game. Significantly, they disappear from the archaeologic record about 11,000 years ago, at the same time that the big game animals experienced mass extinctions. The cause of this major change in fauna is not known; some archaeologists ascribe it to climatic change, while others believe that the Native Americans themselves hunted these species to extinction. However, the latter hypothesis is now considered implausible (Rogers, Rogers, and Martin 1992, 284). (For a modern Native American critique of these ideas, see Deloria 1995.)

Subsequent Paleo-Indian archaeologic traditions include Folsom, dating from 11,000 to 10,000 years ago, a culture also known only from the evidence of hunting *Bison antiquus* with smaller, more finely made spear points than those of Clovis, and a variety of manifestations of Plano cultures, dating from 10,000 to 8,000 years ago, known from their lanceolate points and associated with modern big game species. Evidence from the stone tools of Paleo-Indians reveals that they occupied the entirety of the New World.

Toward the end of the Paleo-Indian period, a new, continent-wide development, which archaeologists have called the *Archaic,* represents technologically more advanced cultures. Beginning about ten thousand years ago and lasting in some areas—the Great Basin, for example—until the nineteenth century, the Archaic period is characterized by the seasonal exploitation of a wide variety of resources, with wild plant foods playing an increasingly important role in the diet. Archaeologic manifestations, with many regional variations, include grinding stones for the processing of seeds as well as the earliest village sites in North America. Chenopods, sunflowers, and squash, among other seed-bearing plants, were domesticated by 2000–1500 B.C. (Cordell and Smith 1996, 234). Domesticated corn spread into the Southwest from Mexico by 1500 B.C. but did not reach the Eastern Woodlands until about 1000 B.C.

Beginning about 1500 B.C., the Woodland archaeologic tradition developed; its diagnostics include pottery making and attention to the burial of the dead. The florescence of the Woodland tradition is represented by the Adena culture (800 B.C. to A.D. 800), localized in the Ohio Valley and characterized by clusters of burial mounds, developed art styles, and political and social complexity. Developing out of Adena culture was Hopewell (250 B.C. to A.D. 750), which spread throughout much of eastern North America and was characterized by extensive burial mounds and rich grave goods representing transcontinental trade networks.

The Mississippian culture (A.D. 700–1700) was the next development in the East. Centered from Ohio to Arkansas, Mississippian influences spread as far as New York and Minnesota and into the Great Plains. A blending of Hopewell culture with influences from Mexico, Mississippian archaeologic sites are characterized by pyramid-shaped mounds that served not for burial, but as foundations for temples or the dwellings of chiefs. Cahokia (A.D. 950–1450), covering six square miles along the Mississippi River east of Saint Louis, is the largest and one of the best-known sites. In the sixteenth and seventeenth centuries, Spanish expeditions through the Southeast met the remnants of Mississippian peoples, who became some of the historic tribes of the region.

However, it is impossible to trace the origins of most tribes back into the archaeologic record. Even when the archaeologic record in an area is unbroken, there is usually no way of connecting sites with the tribes living there during the historical period. Although archaeologists have not hesitated to suggest such connections, in general these sequences are at best informed hypotheses (Eggan 1952).

Biological Perspectives on American Indian Origins

In addition to archaeology, recent developments in the analysis of genetic material are expanding knowledge about the background of American Indians. Each technique has been useful in defining ethnic origins and the grouping of tribes, and both archaeologic and genetic studies permit estimates of the timing of migrations.

Elaborate dentition studies by Turner (1987) identified two distinctive Asian populations, a southern group (sundodont), from which a northern group (sinodont) developed about 15,000 years before the present time (BP). Native American populations "dentally cannot be differentiated from the northern Asian sinodonts" (Steele and Powell 1992, 327), a clear indication of genetic relationship. Turner's research suggests three migrations: Paleo-Indian (before 11,000 years ago), Na-Dene (more recent), and Aleut-Eskimo (most recent, just before the flooding of Beringia). Meltzer (1989, 473), also examining dentition, suggested "a common ancestor for all Native American populations in North China about 20,000 BP, and a divergence of Amerind groups from that population around 14,000 BP."

Schurr et al. (1990), analyzing mitochondrial DNA (mtDNA) sequences, found a high rate of certain rare Asian mitochondrial deoxyribonucleic acid (DNA) in North, Central, and South American Indians and suggested that American Indian mitochondrial DNAs derived from at least four primary maternal lineages. Other investigators applying DNA analysis generally support the concept of three or four migrations (Bailliet et al. 1994; Torroni et al. 1994; Horai et al. 1993; Stone and Stoneking 1993).

However, few of the many questions related to initial migrations to the New World are settled (Szathmary 1993; Weiss 1994). For example, Merriwether, Rothhammer, and Ferrell (1994), examining variation in both ancient and contemporary Native American mtDNA, suggested a single migration into the New World. An excellent and succinct discussion of both the possible timing and manner of first peopling of the Americas and the application of newer genetic techniques to studies of these events was provided by Weiss (1994).

The rapidly growing field of genetic studies will undoubtedly yield new and unanticipated findings that should shed light not only on the origins of American Indians (Hauswirth et al. 1994; Williams et al. 1994), but also on the patterns of disease (Gorski et al. 1994; Lynch et al. 1994; Grebe et al. 1992). Some physiologic traits are more common among or occur exclusively in American Indians (and other Mongolian people) compared to the general U.S. population: a concave inner surface of incisors, the absence of Rh factor hemolytic disease, a rapid blush response to alcohol ingestion, and dry cerumen (Sievers and Fisher 1981). Certain immunologic markers have also been found to a much higher degree among Indians compared to non-Indians, such as erythrocyte and histocompatibility antigens (Williams et al. 1985; Gorodezky 1992).

The Classification of American Indian Peoples

Scientific classifications of American Indian peoples are of two types. First are classifications by language. These are genetic classifications that reveal historical connections among groups; similarities between languages reveal descent from a common ancestor. The patterns of relationship are complex, however, and do not map neatly with geography or culture. Second are culture-area classifications based on similarities between the lifestyles and customs of groups. While they, too, reveal historical patterns of interaction among groups, they are not genetic classifications. Geographical unity makes classification by culture area more intuitive, however, and it is the common means for presenting patterns of similarities and differences among Native Americans.

American Indian peoples comprise a great number of independent tribes and local bands or villages speaking a wide variety of languages. Attempts to estimate the number of political entities that populated North America are stymied by lack of comparability from one region to the next. During the early historic period, for example, the Iroquois living in the New York area were organized as a confederacy of five tribes, each comprising multiple villages integrated by a common clan system. To their west, the Ojibwa living in the Great Lakes area lacked political unity and were organized into a widespread network of independent, local clan–based villages. The problem of trying to place numbers on tribal units ultimately comes down to the problem of the term *tribe* itself, which represents Euro-American, not American Indian, political concepts. In native North America, concepts of political organization were many and varied; only with the imposition of the treaty and reservation system were American Indians forced into a single system of assumed "tribal" identities.

Attempts to estimate the number of native languages fare somewhat better but are also muddied by lack of comparability. The subjective line between distinct languages and closely related dialects (phonologically and grammatically differing forms of a single language, differentiated over time through lack of contact between descendent groups) is often colored by consideration of political units. With this caveat in mind, linguists estimate the number of aboriginal languages in North America at approximately 400; at least half of these are now extinct, and as of 1995 only 46 were still spoken by significant numbers of children, suggesting their continuing viability into the twenty-first century (Goddard 1996a, 3).

Linguistic Classifications

After the pioneering work of Gallatin in the early nineteenth century (Gallatin 1848), linguistic studies were expanded by the Bureau of American Ethnology. Powell (1891) published a new classification of Native American languages divided into 58 families, 26 of which were isolates — single languages not assignable to any other family (Goddard 1996b, 299–308). Despite more than a century of study aimed at refining the Powell classification, the consensus among linguists has not simplified the matter. Today, linguists conservatively recognize 62 language families (Goddard 1996a, 4–8).

Given the assumption of a common origin of Native Americans in Asia, many linguists have sought to reduce the complexity of linguistic classification. The first such classification, based on grammatical as well as lexical comparisons, was published in 1929 by Edward Sapir (reprinted in Sapir 1949). His scheme simplified the Powell classification by organizing the language families and isolates into six major linguistic groups. Reflecting further studies of these groups, Voegelin and Voegelin (1965) published a revised classification that recognizes seven "phyla," each presumed to represent genetic unity, and an eighth phylum that served as a catchall for language isolates and smaller families whose phylum associations were unknown (Goddard 1996b, 314–19).

More recently, scholars have attempted further simplification. Greenberg (1987) divided all American Indian languages into just three groups: Amerind (with 11 subdivisions), Na-Dene (the Athapascan languages plus Haida), and Eskimo-Aleut. This classification is appealing for the way it links with postulated waves of migration from Asia, as well as with dental and genetic evidence (Greenberg, Turner, and Zegura 1986). However, the majority of linguists believe that this classification rests on inadequate linguistic data and, by implication, that it was constructed in part on the very archaeologic and biological data that were subsequently called upon to support it. Further linguistic study over many years will confirm or disprove Greenberg's classification, and in the meantime, while highly suggestive, it cannot be considered scientifically valid.

Classification by Culture Areas

Classification by culture areas offers a pragmatic system more useful for purposes of comparing and generalizing about American Indian peoples and their disease patterns. Assessing the relationship between environment and culture, Otis T. Mason, first curator of ethnology at the Smithsonian's U.S. National Museum, defined 10 "culture areas" in Native America north of Mexico (Mason 1896, 646). This work was subsequently refined (Mason 1907; Wissler 1917, 205; Kroeber 1939, 1).

The modern classification of culture areas builds directly on the work of Wissler and Kroeber (Figure 1.1). Harold E. Driver, one of Kroeber's students, devoted his career to the statistical analysis of cultural trait data to refine the definition and boundaries of culture areas (Driver 1961). Driver's final synthesis enumerates 10 culture areas north of Mexico, and his work stands as the basis for contemporary anthropology. The definitive system of culture area classification, however, has been set by the multivolume *Handbook of North American Indians,* published by the Smithsonian Institution under the general editorship of William C. Sturtevant. The *Handbook* has made adjustments in Driver's boundaries and has joined two of his culture areas, Plains and Prairies, into one.

The following survey of culture areas draws on Driver (1961), Eggan (1968), and Spencer, Jennings, et al. (1977).

The Arctic

Stretching from Alaska, including the Aleutian archipelago, across northern Canada to Greenland, the Arctic is an area of tundra and coastline. North Alaskan Eskimos focused on the hunting of whales, while Central Eskimos depended seasonally on caribou and seal. Local groups were organized as bands

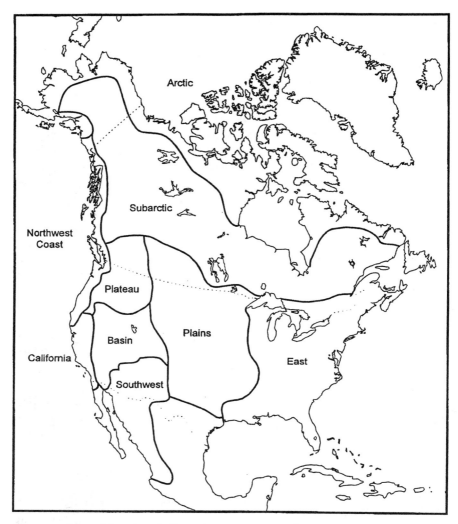

Figure 1.1 Map of American Indian culture areas in North America. *Source:* Data from Driver 1961, Knoeber 1939, and Wissler 1917

based on bilateral kinship, with the nuclear family as the basic unit. Larger units were based on geographical proximity, reinforced by ties of blood and marriage. Society was organized in terms of kin relationships, with no development of political institutions. The Arctic area is distinctive for the coincidence of culture, language, and physical type. There is, therefore, a sharp division between Arctic peoples and American Indians to the south; in fact, the distinction between the Arctic and Subarctic culture areas is the sharpest boundary between any areas in North America.

The Subarctic

Stretching from central Alaska eastward across Canada, the Subarctic is a forested area with many lakes and streams, broken in places by tundra. Driver (1961) divided the area into three geographical subregions: (1) the Yukon Subarctic, defined by the drainage of the Yukon River in central Alaska and western Canada; (2) the Mackenzie Subarctic, defined by the drainage of the Mackenzie River from northern British Columbia across Alberta, Saskatchewan, and Manitoba; and (3) the Eastern Subarctic, from eastern Manitoba across Ontario and Quebec to the Labrador coast. Subsistence throughout the area was based on caribou hunting, fishing, and wild plant gathering. In the west, moose and salmon were available. Culturally, the Subarctic was relatively homogeneous, although in the west there were influences from the Northwest Coast. The inhabitants of the Yukon and Mackenzie subregions were speakers of Athapaskan languages, while those of the Eastern subregion were speakers of Algonquian languages. Tribal names customarily used in the Subarctic refer to groups defined on the basis of differing dialects. Local groups were amorphous bilateral bands comprising extended families that congregated for cooperative fishing and hunting and dispersed during the winter to maximize access to resources. Nuclear families were the basic subsistence units. There was little development of political institutions.

The Northwest Coast

This area embraces the region from southeast Alaska along the coast of British Columbia, Washington, and Oregon, extending into northwest California. It is an area of considerable linguistic diversity but general cultural similarity. Subsistence was based on fishing, particularly for salmon, and on marine resources, including sea mammals, supplemented by wild plants and game animals, which were hunted in the mountains. Large tribal groups were divided into smaller local groups, each centered around a permanent winter village. Cedar formed the resource from which plank houses were constructed in the villages, and during the nineteenth century, with the introduction of metal tools, a distinctive art style developed, most popularly represented by carved cedar poles and elaborate masks. Also characteristic of the area were potlatches, formally structured public distributions of wealth that validated social status and encouraged competition among families. Throughout the area a basic social distinction was made between nobles and commoners, who constituted the status hierarchy, and slaves, who were outside it. Slaves were generally war captives whose relatives had failed to ransom them. In terms of social organization, the area was diverse, including matrilineal clans organized into moieties (dual social structures) among the Tlingit, Haida, and Tsimshian in the north, while the Kwakiutl and Nootka in the center of the area were bilateral, and the tribes along the Oregon coast tended toward patrilineality.

The Plateau

Named for the plateau drained by the Columbia and Frazer Rivers, the Plateau area stretches from the Subarctic in British Columbia southward through eastern Washington and Oregon, Idaho, and western Montana. It is a region of great ecological and linguistic diversity. The most important subsistence resources were salmon, camas (a starchy tuber), and the big game found in mountainous areas. Tribal groups reflected linguistic divisions. There was no tribal political organization: the village was the largest political unit. Permanent winter villages were small, comprising semisubterranean earth lodges, each of which housed an extended family. During other seasons, the extended families dispersed in smaller groups to fish, gather roots, and hunt. The kinship system was bilateral. By the time ethnographic studies were carried out among the peoples of the Plateau, those in the northwest had been heavily influenced by Northwest Coast cultures and those in the east had adopted many of the characteristics of the Plains. Groups along the middle Columbia River, such as the Sanpoil and Nespelem, have been taken as representative of early historic Plateau culture. Cultural traits that seem distinctive to this area are strong commitments to pacifism and to the equality and autonomy of individuals.

The Great Basin

This area comprises the desert and semidesert interior drainage areas between the Sierra Nevada and the Rocky Mountains and from the Plateau on the north to the Colorado River on the south, including Nevada, eastern California, and northern and western Utah. Most of the peoples living in this area were speakers of Shoshonean languages. Subsistence was based on wild grass seeds, piñon nuts, and roots as staple foods, supplemented with rabbits and other small game. Communal rabbit drives, as well as occasional antelope drives, were characteristic of the area. Social organization was based on very small, autonomous bands, which came together in winter villages. Kinship was bilateral, and networks of marriages, together with a tendency toward matrilocality, created ties between bands. More favorable ecological conditions around the margins of the area allowed the development of larger, tribal organizations, such as the Owens Valley Paiute, who sowed wild seeds to increase yields, and the Ute and Eastern Shoshone, who adopted buffalo hunting and many characteristics of Plains culture. One group of Shoshoneans moved permanently onto the plains and became the Comanche.

California

Comprising much of the state of California and extending into northern Baja California, this area was linguistically diverse. Resources, which were varied and abundant, included acorns as the staple food, as well as roots, fish, marine resources, and small game. Throughout the area small groups adapted to specific local environments. As in the Great Basin, there was a general lack of tribal organization. Local groups were relatively sedentary, with clearly defined territorial boundaries. Winter villages were characterized by a tendency toward patrilocality. Patrilineages developed in some areas, organized in moieties. Like Great Basin cultures, California cultures valued pacifism and lacked the social differentiation characteristic of the Northwest Coast.

The Southwest

Encompassing most of Arizona and New Mexico and extending into northern Mexico, the Southwest area can be divided into two cultural types: sedentary horticulturalists and hunter-gatherers. The area is ecologically diverse, ranging from desert to mountains, and the peoples living there were linguistically diverse.

The Pueblos, whose permanent, multistoried villages were spread in a great arc from the Rio Grande valley on the east to the Hopi villages at Black Mesa on the west, depended for subsistence on corn horticulture, supplemented by hunting. In the west, tribes like the Hopi and Zuni were organized in matrilineal clans; among the Rio Grande Pueblos in the east, social systems were bilateral, with patrilineal ceremonial divisions. There were complex organizations of priesthoods and men's sacred societies (kivas), but little development of political institutions until a system of officials was introduced by the Spanish. The lifestyle of the Pueblos represents a fusion of older elements with influences from Mexico, including horticulture, pottery making, and irrigation.

The Upland Yumans in general retained the older pattern of hunting deer and other game and gathering wild plants, although some, like the Havasupai living in the Grand Canyon, adopted horticulture. To the south, the Pima and O'odham (Papago) practiced irrigated horticulture in addition to hunting and gathering. The Athapaskan groups represent a migration, around A.D. 1300, of people from the north who settled in the territory around the Pueblos and became the Navajo and Apache. Although they adopted many cultural characteristics of the Pueblos, including highly developed ritualism, most continued to subsist by hunting and gathering, supplemented by limited horticulture.

The social organization of the hunter-gatherers was diverse. The Yumans were organized in patrilineal bands, although some, like the Western Yavapai, adopted matrilineal clans. The Pima and O'odham were organized in patrilineal clans grouped into moieties. The Navajo adopted matrilineal clans, as did the Western Apache, but most of the other Apache groups retained an older bilateral system of local bands. Political organization among the hunter-gatherers was weakly developed, although the Pima had a tribal chief elected by the various village chiefs. The complexity of the Southwest area suggests the diversity of origins and historical interactions over time.

The Plains

Stretching from the Rocky Mountains to the Mississippi River and from the Subarctic in the Prairie Provinces of Canada to the Rio Grande, this area is divided into two geographically defined subareas, the High Plains west and north of the Missouri River and the Prairie Plains to the east. The tribal groups in both subareas represent a variety of language families. In terms of subsistence, all the tribes of both subareas depended on bison hunting. Characteristic of the Plains as a whole was a highly developed war complex intimately tied to social structure. Acts of bravery in battle and skill in raiding enemy camps or villages for horses were essential for ensuring men's status in society. Among the nomadic tribes, men's status was largely achieved through warfare and raiding, while among the sedentary tribes of the Prairie Plains, access to status was largely ascribed through heredity. Formally organized men's societies provided police functions during the summer encampments and communal hunts.

Located west of the Missouri River, the High Plains is the area of short-grass plains. The tribes of the High Plains were nomadic hunter-gatherers who lived in portable buffalo-hide tipis and who had adopted common cultural and social patterns. Examples of nomads of the north are the Sioux, Cheyenne, and Arapaho; in the south are the Kiowa, Comanche, and a group of Plains Apache. Tribes were composed of bands, with varying degrees of political development. The Cheyenne, for example, had a council of 44 chiefs that symbolized their political unity, but most tribes lacked overarching political institutions. Bands were either bilateral or patrilineal and, throughout much of the year, were autonomous social units. During the summer, tribal bands joined together for communal bison hunts and then, following the patterns of aggregation and dispersion of the bison herds, went their separate ways for the remainder of the year. Tribal rituals, such as the Sun Dance, took place during summer encampments, when tipis were placed in camp circles that visually represented tribal unity and symbolically reflected cosmic unity.

Located predominantly east of the Missouri River, the Prairie Plains is the area of tall-grass prairies. The tribes of the Prairie Plains lived in permanent villages of earth lodges or lodges covered with mats, bark, or bundles of grass, located along water courses. There they grew extensive gardens of corn, beans, and squash, which provided both staple food and a valuable commodity for trade with the nomadic tribes. Seasonally, however, the tribes went on extended buffalo hunts, during which they lived in tipis or other temporary shelters, often arranged in camp circles, and practiced tribal ceremonies parallel to those of the nomadic tribes. Social organization was characterized predominantly by matrilineal (Mandan, Hidatsa) or patrilineal (Omaha, Ponca) clans, although some tribes (Pawnee, Arikara, Wichita, and Caddo) lacked clan organization. Political organization was generally restricted to the village rather than the tribal level, although there were some exceptions (Omaha, Ponca).

The East

Commonality of culture argues for organizing into a single culture area the tribes of the vast area from the Mississippi River to the Atlantic Ocean and from the Subarctic in eastern Canada south to Florida. Subsistence throughout the area was primarily based on a combination of hunting, particularly deer, and corn horticulture. There were some exceptions, such as the Calusa of southern Florida, who did not practice horticulture but depended on rich marine resources, and the eastern Algonquian tribes like the Micmac and Penobscot, who were hunter-gatherers. The basis of social life was the village, comprising houses constructed of poles and covered with bark, mats, or thatch. Villages tended to be politically autonomous. Some groups had developed political organizations, such as the League of the Iroquois, renowned for their system of 50 sachems representing the interests of the village groups of the 5 (later 6) Iroquois tribes in common council. The Iroquois were organized in matrilineal clans divided into moieties. Most of the tribes of the area had either matrilineal or patrilineal clan systems, again with exceptions, like the eastern Algonquians, whose social system was based on patrilocal hunting bands. As in the Plains area, the warfare complex also characterized the East.

Culture areas themselves are artifacts of anthropologists' attempts to group together tribes sharing culture patterns in order to facilitate generalization, and they have no objective reality; with few exceptions (like the sharp division between the Arctic and Subarctic), tribes living on two sides of a culture area boundary share so much in common that drawing the line in a particular place can be only subjective. Using statistical data relating primarily to social organization, Driver et al. (1972) demonstrated that objectively determined ethnic units were not as useful for comparative understanding of Native American cultures as was the scheme of intuitively derived culture areas in general use by anthropologists since the late nineteenth century.

The extent of difference among Native Americans and the amorphous nature of social groups suggest that even the tribal organization of indigenous Americans is often too general for some purposes of classification. In many instances, social divisions representing bands, clans, or extended families within tribal organizations possess characteristics that are distinctive to themselves and influence many present-day behaviors. The significance of this for development of health and other programs is apparent. One can see the desirability of providing some sort of macro-grouping, just to be able to formulate a program. Both the Bureau of Indian Affairs and the Indian Health Service are organized into regional areas that follow, to a considerable degree, the culture-area pattern outlined above. In fact, such groupings have proved to be of considerable importance in studying health and disease patterns, as well as in the administration of health services (Szathmary 1993; Indian Health Service 1997).

The net result of the peopling of the Americas is an extraordinary opportunity to study a variety of human conditions and disease patterns. Continued examination of both genetic and cultural affinities and differences will undoubtedly prove fruitful in future biomedical studies. Indeed, comparative investigations continue to demonstrate the value of studies across tribal groupings (Sievers and Fisher 1981; Young 1994).

REFERENCES

Bailliet G, Rothhammer F, Carnese FR, et al. 1994. Founder mitochondrial haplotypes in Amerindian populations. *Am J Hum Genet* 55:27–33.

Cordell LS, Smith BD. 1996. Indigenous farmers. In: Trigger BG, Washburn W, eds. *The Cambridge History of the Native Peoples of the Americas.* Vol 1, *North America,* pt 1, 201–66. Cambridge: Cambridge University Press.

Deloria V Jr. 1995. *Red Earth, White Lies: Native Americans and the Myth of Scientific Fact.* New York: Scribner.

Dillehay TD, Meltzer DJ, eds. 1991. *The First Americans: Search and Research.* Boca Raton: CRC Press.

Driver HE. 1961. *Indians of North America.* Chicago: University of Chicago Press.

Driver HE, Kenny JA, Hudson HC, et al. 1972. Statistical classification of North American Indian ethnic units. *Ethnology* 11:311–39.

Eggan F. 1952. The ethnological cultures and their archaeological backgrounds. In: Griffin JB, ed. *Archaeology of the Eastern United States,* 35–45. Chicago: University of Chicago Press.

———. 1968. Indians, North American. In: Sills DL, ed. *International Encyclopedia of the Social Sciences,* 7:180–200. New York: Macmillan and Free Press.

Fagan BM. 1991. *Ancient North America: The Archaeology of a Continent.* New York: Thames & Hudson.

Fiedel SJ. 1987. *Prehistory of the Americas.* New York: Cambridge University Press.

Gallatin A. 1848. Hale's Indians of North-West America, and vocabularies of North America with an introduction. *Trans Am Ethnolog Soc* 2:xxiii–clxxxviii, 1–130.

Goddard I. 1996a. Introduction. In: Goddard I, ed. *Languages,* vol 17 of Sturtevant WC (gen. ed.), *Handbook of North American Indians,* 1–16. Washington, D.C.: Smithsonian Institution.

———. 1996b. The classification of the native languages of North America. In: Goddard I, ed. *Languages,* vol 17 of Sturtevant WC (gen. ed.), *Handbook of North American Indians,* 290–323. Washington, D.C.: Smithsonian Institution.

Gorodezky C. 1992. Genetic difference between Europeans and Indians: Tissue and blood types. *Allergy Proc* 13:243–50.

Gorski SM, Adams KJ, Birch PH, et al. 1994. Linkage analysis of X-linked cleft palate and ankyloglossia in Manitoba Mennonite and British Columbia Native kindreds. *Hum Genet* 94:141–48.

Grebe TA, Doane WW, Richter SF, et al. 1992. Mutation analysis of the cystic fibrosis transmembrane regulator gene in Native American populations of the southwest. *Am J Hum Genet* 51:736–40.

Greenberg JH. 1987. *Language in the Americas.* Stanford: Stanford University Press.

Greenberg JH, Turner CG, Zegura SL. 1986. The settlement of the Americas: A comparison of the linguistics, dental, and genetic evidence. *Curr Anthropol* 27:477–97.

Hauswirth WW, Dickel CD, Rowold DJ, et al. 1994. Inter- and intrapopulation studies of ancient humans. *Experientia* 50:585–91.

Horai S, Kondo R, Nakagawa-Hattori Y, et al. 1993. Peopling of the Americas, founded by four major lineages of mitochondrial DNA. *Mol Biol Evol* 10:23–47.

Indian Health Service. 1997. *Trends in Indian Health, 1997.* Rockville, Md.: Indian Health Service, Program Statistics Team.

Kroeber AL. 1939. Cultural and natural areas of native North America. *Publications in American Archaeology and Ethnology* 38. Berkeley and Los Angeles: University of California Press.

Lynch HT, Drouhard T, Lanspa S, et al. 1994. Mutation of an mutL homologue in a Navajo family with hereditary nonpolyposis colorectal cancer. *J Natl Cancer Inst* 86:1417–19.

Mason OT. 1896. Influence of environment upon human industries or arts. In: *Annual Report of the Smithsonian Institution for 1895,* 639–65. Washington, D.C.: Government Printing Office.

———. 1907. Environment. In: Hodge FW, ed. Handbook of American Indians North of Mexico. *Bureau of American Ethnology Bulletin* 30, 1:427–30. Washington, D.C.: Government Printing Office.

Meltzer DJ. 1989. Why don't we know when the first people came to America? *Am Antiquity* 54:471–90.

Meltzer DJ, Grayson DK, Ardila G, et al. 1997. On the Pleistocene antiquity of Monte Verde, Southern Chile. *Am Antiquity* 62:659–63.

Merriwether DA, Rothhammer F, Ferrell RE. 1994. Genetic variation in the New World: Ancient teeth, bone, and tissue as sources of DNA [review]. *Experientia* 50:592–601.

Nabokov P. 1996. Native views of history. In: Trigger BG, Washburn W, eds. *The Cam-*

bridge History of the Native Peoples of the Americas. Vol 1, *North America,* pt 1, 1–59. Cambridge: Cambridge University Press.

Powell JW. 1891. Indian linguistic families of America north of Mexico. In: *Seventh Annual Report of the Bureau of Ethnology for the Years 1885–1886,* 1–142. Washington, D.C.: Government Printing Office.

Rogers RA, Rogers LA, Martin LD. 1992. How the door opened: The peopling of the New World. *Hum Biol* 64:281–302.

Sapir E. 1949. Central and North American languages. In: Mandelbaum DG, ed. *Selected Writings of Edward Sapir in Language, Culture, and Personality,* 169–78. Berkeley and Los Angeles: University of California Press.

Schurr TG, Ballinger SW, Gan YY, et al. 1990. American mitochondrial DNAs have rare Asian mutations at high frequencies, suggesting they derived from four primary maternal lineages. *Am J Hum Genet* 46:613–23.

Sievers ML, Fisher JR. 1981. Diseases of North American Indians. In: Rothschild HR, ed. *Biocultural Aspects of Disease,* 191–252. New York: Academic Press.

Snow DR. 1996. The first Americans and the differentiation of hunter-gatherer cultures. In: Trigger BG, Washburn W, eds. *The Cambridge History of the Native Peoples of the Americas.* Vol 1, *North America,* pt 1, 25–200. Cambridge: Cambridge University Press.

Spencer RF, Jennings JD, et al. 1977. *The Native Americans: Ethnology and Backgrounds of the North American Indians.* 2d ed. New York: Harper & Row.

Steele DG, Powell JF. 1992. Peopling of the Americas: Paleobiological evidence. *Hum Biol* 64:303–36.

Stone AC, Stoneking M. 1993. Ancient DNA from a pre-Columbian Amerindian population. *Am J Phys Anthropol* 92:463–71.

Szathmary EJE. 1993. Application of our understanding of genetic variation in North America. In: Sing CF, Hanis CL, eds. *Genetics of Cellular, Individual, Family, and Population Variability,* 215 ff. Oxford: Oxford University Press.

Torroni A, Schurr TG, Cabell MF, et al. 1994. Asian affinities and continental radiation of the four founding Native American mtDNAs. *Am J Hum Genet* 53:563–90.

Turner CG II. 1987. Telltale teeth. *Nat History* 96:6–10.

Voegelin CF, Voegelin FM. 1965. Languages of the world: Native America, fascicle 2. *Anthropol Linguistics* 7(1):1–150.

Weiss KM. 1994. American origins. *Proc Natl Acad Sci USA* 91:833–35.

Williams RC, Steinberg AG, Gershowitz H, et al. 1985. GM allotypes in Native Americans: Evidence for three distinct migrations across the Bering land bridge. *Am J Phys Anthropol* 66:1–19.

Williams TM, Wu J, Foutz T, et al. 1994. A new DRB1 allele (DRB1*0811) identified in Native Americans. *Immunogenetics* 40:314.

Wissler C. 1917. *The American Indian: An Introduction to the Anthropology of the New World.* New York: Douglas C. McMurtrie.

Young TK. 1994. *The Health of Native Americans: Toward a Biocultural Epidemiology.* New York: Oxford University Press.

2

*Debra L. Martin, Ph.D., and
Alan H. Goodman, Ph.D.*

Health Conditions before Columbus

*The Paleopathology of
Native North Americans*

Information about the health status of the earliest inhabitants of North America provides a chronology of health problems that spans more than a thousand years. Studies of disease in ancient times add an important dimension to our understanding of the life struggles of a largely unknown past. This chapter provides a brief overview of health conditions and quality of life in North America before contact and colonization. Data on health in ancient societies are inferred from the analysis of a wide range of archaeologic materials, but human bones and teeth form by far the largest body of evidence. Although physicians and anatomists began publishing observations on unusual cases of pathology in the mid-1800s (Matthews, Wortman, and Billings 1893), more technical and anthropological analyses began in the 1960s (Wells 1964; Jarcho 1966; Brothwell and Sandison 1967). Employing a more integrated approach, a generation of paleopathologists developed approaches to disease in the past that emphasized population-level analyses and transformed paleopathology into paleoepidemiology (Armelagos 1969; Buikstra and Cook 1980).

New techniques for analysis of ancient human remains employ a wide range of diagnostic methods (Ortner and Putschar 1981), atlases (Mann and Murphy 1990), and procedures derived from forensics (Iscan and Kennedy 1989). For several regions in the United States, there are health chronologies spanning hundreds of years. For example, Walker (1989, 1996), using a multimethodology approach involving analysis of a number of skeletal lesions and detailed reconstruction of the environment, demonstrated that Indians of southern California who lived in marginal island environments (ca. 800 B.C. to A.D. 1150) show greater evidence of health problems than those who lived on the mainland, where food was more abundant and diverse. He also showed that there were changes over time, with increases in infectious disease from 20 percent to 30 percent.

Other regions of the United States for which large skeletal series have been studied include the Georgia coast (Larsen 1987); the Illinois River Valley (Milner, Anderson, and Smith 1991); Ottowa County, Ohio (Lovejoy 1985); and Dickson Mound, Illinois (Goodman et al. 1984). The southeastern United States has yielded abundant skeletal material (Powell 1988; Powell, Bridges, and Wagner-Mires 1991), as has the Southwest (Merbs and Miller 1985; Martin 1994; Martin et al. 1991). Human skeletal remains are relatively less abundant or nonexistent in other areas because of environmental conditions that prohibit preservation (Alaska, Canada, the Northwest, the Northeast, and Hawaii). There has been a shift toward conducting population-level analyses that shed light on epidemiologic characteristics of the health of ancient societies by providing frequencies and patterning of disease within and between populations (Cohen and Armelagos 1984; Goodman et al. 1984). The volume *Human Paleopathology and Related Subjects: An International Bibliography* (Ortner and Tyson 1997) provides a comprehensive, cross-cultural listing of publications dealing with the health status of earlier peoples. Studies of the relatively few mummified remains from North America have provided relatively little medical information, often focusing on mortuary behavior and grave offerings (Cockburn 1980; El-Najjar and Mulinski 1980). Cancers, tumors, skin diseases, and other soft-tissue diseases are relatively rare, although not absent, in the archaeologic record. For example, Ortner and Putschar (1981) listed a broad range of tumors and types of cancers that have been diagnosed in ancient material.

Much of the recent paleopathological literature emphasizes temporal and spatial variability in patterns of disease and the shift in many parts of North America at different times from an economy based on gathering and hunting to agriculture (Cohen 1989). Although not all groups in North America adopted full-blown maize agriculture, many did, and it has been the focus of intense debate and disciplinary convergence (Cohen and Armelagos 1984).

The study of North American archaeologic remains has been under protest by Native groups because historically they have had little say over the excavation and curation of their ancestors' remains (Echo-Hawk 1993). These protests led to legislation passed in 1990 entitled the Native American Graves Protection and Repatriation Act (U.S. Public Law 101-601) (see Rose, Green, and Green 1996). This law ensures that Native Americans have final say regarding the nature of studies that rely on ancestral and historic human remains (Coughlin 1994). In many ways, this legislation has redefined the nature of archaeologic research in the United States and has opened new venues of study as Native Americans and anthropologists have begun working together to re-construct the past (Barrios 1993).

An Analysis of Pathology in Ancient Populations

Because skeletal tissue typically responds in nonspecific ways to disease, the di-agnosis of a specific etiology is often difficult (Ortner and Putschar 1981). For-tunately, what does have greatest explanatory power is not the specific agent, but rather the severity, duration, and temporal course of generalized physio-logic perturbations. These general stressors, as they may be read and deciphered from skeletal lesions, can provide a means for assessing the health status and degree of functional impairment that an individual experienced (Goodman et al. 1988).

To elucidate this general health/stress perspective, we developed a model to apply to studies of health in the past (Goodman et al. 1984; Martin et al. 1991). With its focus on relationships between environment, culture, and biological conditions, this model has proven useful in considering past adaptive struggles and the centrality of health (Figure 2.1). Analysis of past health begins with understanding the environmental context within which people lived. The en-vironment greatly influences how successful groups are at procuring food, as

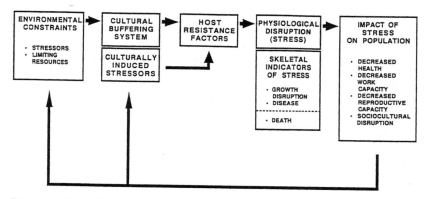

Figure 2.1. Variables that delineate adaptation of prehistoric groups. The feedback loop can be used only when the archaeologic context of the human remains is well documented.

TABLE 2.1
Summary of certain skeletal and dental indicators of disease and mortality

Indicator	Requirements	Subgroups at risk	Comments
Age/sex composition	Well-represented skeletal population	All	Age-at-death represents one of the better overall indicators of adaptation; indicates patterns of mortality.
Porotic hyperostosis	Cranium	Subadults, females	Related to iron deficiency anemia; can provide indication of severity and timing, indicates patterns of morbidity.
Periosteal reaction	Long bones	All	Related to nonspecific infectious diseases; can distinguish localized from systemic infection and provides indication of timing and severity; indicates patterns of morbidity.
Enamel defects	Any teeth	0.5 in utero to age 7	Related to acute or chronic physiologic disruption; can specify age of occurrence and peak occurrence of morbidity.
Subadult size	Subadults with dental age	Subadults	Represents the summation of factors that may affect growth and development; can indicate the timing of greatest stress.
Adult stature	Adult long bones	Subadults	Summation of preadult factors; short stature is often a response to undernutrition or chronic illness.
Osteoarthritis	Vertebrae and joints	Adults	Indication of occupational and biomechanical wear and tear on joint system and the vertebral column.
Trauma	All bones	All	Indication of accidents and violence.
Dental caries	Any teeth	All	Indication of refined carbohydrate diet; can lead to infection and tooth loss.

well as what the constraints may be in terms of providing food, clothing, and shelter. Climate, excess heat or cold, high altitude, parasites, and predators all present challenges in the environment to which successful adaptations must be made if groups are to thrive.

In terms of ancient health, it is important to understand as much about the cultural patterns as possible in order to understand which cultural customs buffered against poor health and which customs may have promoted disease.

For example, enclosed rock shelters in Colorado offered protection from the elements and predators, but they also facilitated the exchange of communicable diseases (Kunitz and Euler 1972). The development of agriculture in North America allowed greater production of calories relative to human expenditure (Wetterstrom 1986) and, thus, would seem to have provided a buffer against undernutrition. However, the resulting increased population density, along with other ecological and demographic changes associated with intensified farming, had a profound influence on health, with statistically significant increases in infectious diseases and iron deficiency anemia (Cohen and Armelagos 1984).

The response to disease stress is often a stereotypic physiologic change that results from the effort to adjust and overcome the stress, and this is frequently manifest in relatively permanent osteologic indicators (Table 2.1). Although the paleopathologist may be limited by the amount of information that can be gleaned from archaeologic remains, a multidisciplinary approach has allowed the integration of forensic, medical, and epidemiologic methods to reconstruct health conditions.

Prevalent Health Problems in Pre-Columbian Times

Paleodemography and Infant-Childhood Mortality

Paleodemography remains one of the primary and crucial sets of data for analysis of general health (Swedlund 1994). Angel (1969) argued that relatively simple statistical procedures, such as calculation of the relative proportion of deaths in infancy and childhood, are informative of the general health of populations. New World pre-Columbian groups (ca. A.D. 800–1300) in general demonstrate ranges of 10–41 percent for deaths under the age of one year (Table 2.2). The wide range of variation in percentage of infant deaths suggests that certain communities were better equipped to buffer infants from early death. The site with the highest infant mortality rate (Tlajinga) is the densely settled

TABLE 2.2
Age composition for pre-Columbian burial populations

Skeletal collection	N	% dying at age (years):			
		<1	1–9	10–18	>18
Black Mesa, Arizona	165	10	24	14	51
Casas Grandes, Mexico	612	10	22	14	54
Pecos Pueblo, New Mexico	1,722	19	14	8	60
Tlajinga, Mexico	166	41	10	10	39
Arikara, Plains	1,487	31	24	10	26
Libben, Ohio	1,239	18	22	14	46

agrarian city of Teotihaocan near present-day Mexico City, and Storey (1992) attributes this to common communicable infectious diseases and to a general undernutrition of many of the people living there. She bases this on a detailed analysis of the infant long bones for signs of periosteal inflammation and porotic hyperostosis, a sign of iron deficiency. Sites with low infant mortality, such as the ancestral Pueblo communities of Black Mesa, Mesa Verde, and La Plata in the American Southwest, suggest that health conditions were relatively improved for infants (Martin et al. 1991).

Lifetable analysis has been used by many paleopathologists to assess the mean age at death or the life expectancy of pre-Columbian groups (Weiss and Smouse 1976; Buikstra and Mielke 1985). Life expectancy for a wide range of North American native populations in general falls between the ages of 15 and 25 (Cohen and Armelagos 1984; Buikstra, Konigsberg, and Bullington 1986; Nelson et al. 1994). What these data reveal most strikingly is not that most people died in young adulthood, but that there was generally high infant mortality combined with an ultimate life expectation of approximately 45 to 50 years (Martin et al. 1991).

Nutrition, Growth, and Development

Variation in size among contemporary groups, at least to the age of 10, depends almost completely on the environment (Habicht et al. 1974). Several aspects of growth and development provide insights into the general level of nutrition. Key among these are measures of subadult long bone lengths relative to age (based on dental development) and signs of growth disruption in teeth (Goodman and Rose 1991). Because chronological age is unknown for archaeologic samples, dental age is used as a proxy, and because sex of subadults cannot presently be reliably evaluated, males and females are averaged.

Several studies examining pre-Columbian growth patterns in children have demonstrated that changes in growth are consistent with changes in environmental conditions (Cohen and Armelagos 1984). Lallo (1973) observed a decrease in growth velocity around the time of weaning in the agricultural groups from Dickson Mounds, Illinois (ca. A.D. 900–1200). Others, such as Cook (1984), Jantz and Owsley (1984), and Mensforth (1985), have also looked closely at patterns of pre-Columbian growth in North America, and all have found evidence for growth dampening around the ages of two to five years. That seems to be a period of increased vulnerability for the growing child in prehistoric communities.

In comparing ancient with contemporary children, variability suggests a role for local conditions in growth and development. Ancestral Plains children appear to be rather close to the modern Anglo standard (Owsley and Jantz 1985),

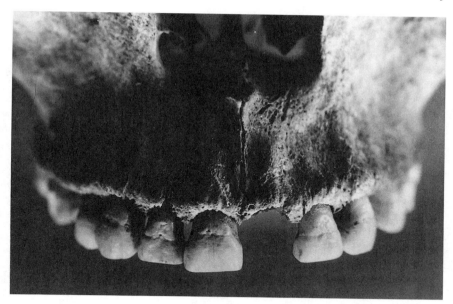

Figure 2.2. Single linear enamel hypoplasias on the upper incisors and canines. These defects formed while the individual was approximately 3 years old. The individual is a 25–30-year-old woman from northeastern Arizona (ca. A.D. 900–1150).

whereas ancestral Pueblo children are smaller (Martin et al. 1991). This most likely corresponds to the more diverse meat and wild plants diet of the Plains children (Merchant and Ubelaker 1977) versus the largely maize diet of the Pueblo children. Goodman and colleagues (1984) compared subadult growth for the Mississippian cultures in Illinois from the earliest hunting and gathering period (A.D. 950–1050) to that from the later intensive agricultural period (A.D. 1200–1300). They demonstrated that the rate of growth, especially in long bone circumferences of individuals at age two years, seemed to decrease in the agricultural group relative to the hunter and gatherer group. By five years of age, the achieved lengths and circumferences of long bones were significantly less in the agricultural groups.

Linear enamel hypoplasias (LEHs) are among the most widely studied indicators of life conditions of past populations (Goodman and Rose 1990). LEHs are caused by a temporary disruption to enamel matrix secretion, resulting in a transverse line or band of decreased enamel thickness (Figure 2.2). Once formed, these hypoplastic areas are relatively indelible because enamel does not remodel (it can be obliterated only by attrition or external forces). Furthermore, the location of LEHs is informative of the time of disruption (Goodman and Rose 1991).

TABLE 2.3
Comparative prevalence of linear enamel hypoplasias

Sample/population	Individuals affected (%)
Homo s. Neanderthalensis (1)	57
Illinois Woodland period (2)[a]	45
Pueblo I period sites (3)[a]	94
Illinois Mississippian period (2)[a]	80
Pueblo II period sites (2)[a]	94
Pueblo III period sites (2)[a]	86
Nineteenth-century poorhouse (4)	72
Highland Mexican children, 1985 (4)	57

SOURCE: Data from (1) Ogilvie and Hilton 1993; (2) Goodman et al. 1984; (3) Malville 1997; and (4) Goodman et al. 1992.
NOTE: Comparative prevalence of linear enamel hypoplasias in the permanent dentition of select samples. Earlier groups are at the top. The North American rates range from relatively low to relatively high.
[a]North American Indian groups.

Epidemiologic studies of these defects in contemporary Native Americans have been reported. In a study of Nahuatl adolescents from highland Mexico, Goodman and colleagues (1992) found that nearly 75 percent had one or more LEHs on permanent teeth and that the peak age for LEH formation was about 2–2.5 years. Infante (1974) found that 19.4 percent of White Mountain Apache children had LEHs on deciduous central incisors that formed about the time of birth, suggesting a peak period of physiologic stress for children in that group.

Hypoplastic defects are common on teeth of ancestral Indian children before colonization. LEHs on permanent teeth have been reported to occur in 50–100 percent of subjects studied (Skinner and Hung 1989). For a sense of the kinds of stress levels in different groups, Table 2.3 provides comparative data for Neanderthals, early transitional agricultural groups, intensive agriculturists, nineteenth-century poor, and contemporary Mexican children. Unlike the data on health derived from long bone growth and stature, these data are highly variable across regions and temporal units, suggesting that LEHs are more sensitive indicators of childhood physiologic disruption and illness.

Iron Deficiency Anemia

Porotic hyperostosis is an additional skeletal indicator of nutritional stress that has been extensively studied in archaeologic populations (Mensforth et al. 1978). Nearly all cases of porotic hyperostosis in North America seem to be due to iron deficiency, and the presence of low iron stores is likely to co-occur with other health problems and nutritional deficiencies (Scrimshaw 1991). Although these lesions can also be caused by hereditary hemolytic anemia as well as other disorders (Ortner and Putschar 1981), iron deficiency is accepted as the primary cause of porotic hyperostosis for the vast majority of documented prehistoric cases (Stuart-Macadam 1987; Walker 1985).

Porotic hyperostosis is a descriptive term for lesions primarily found on the parietal and orbital bones of the cranium, produced by bone marrow proliferation diagnostic of anemia. The lesion generally takes the form of a raised, porous area that develops when the trabecular portion of the cranial bone (diplöe) expands and the outer table of bone becomes thinner, exposing the inner diplöe. Anemias can potentially affect any bone of the skeleton that is involved in the production of red blood cells, but the most frequently affected bones are those of the cranium (Figure 2.3).

Iron deficiency anemia appears to have been widespread and ubiquitous in most ancient populations in the New World (Mensforth et al. 1978; Lallo, Armelagos, and Rose 1977). The general distribution of the lesion corresponds with increasing reliance on agricultural products such as maize, which are low in bioavailable iron. For example, Lallo and co-workers (1977) evaluated changes in rates of porotic hyperostosis for ancient Mississippians in Illinois living in the twelfth century and found that it increased dramatically in the transition from hunting and gathering to agriculture. They suggested that this was due to an overreliance on maize, with its low iron bioavailability, and that the lesions were

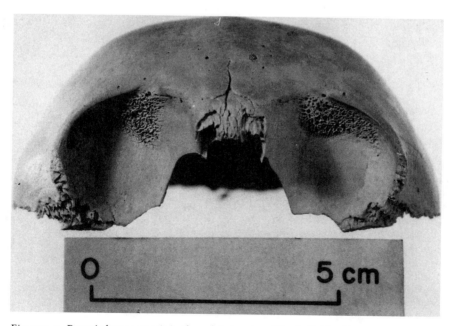

Figure 2.3. Porotic hyperostosis in the orbital region. The individual is a 5–10-year-old child from northeastern Arizona (ca. A.D. 900–1150).

most pronounced in younger children because of diarrheal disease during weaning combined with poor diet.

Palkovich (1985, 1987) studied more than two hundred burials from New
Mexico representing thirteenth-century ancestral Pueblo groups. She found an
early age of onset of porotic hyperostosis in infants (newborn to one year). Her
interpretation is that a chronically poor diet was affecting the pregnant females
and their fetuses. Other studies utilizing human remains from the ancestral
Pueblo populations living throughout the American Southwest have demonstrated similar findings. Walker (1985) provided an extensive review of the
skeletal data on nutritional anemia for many Southwest groups before the four-
teenth century and suggested that lack of iron in the diet, prolonged breast-
feeding, diarrheal and helminth infections, and living conditions conducive to
the spread of disease all seem to have contributed to the prevalence of anemia.

In other regions such as the Lower Mississippi Valley (Rose, Burnett, and
Harmon 1991), the coast of Georgia (Larsen 1987), and the islands off the coast
of California (Walker 1996), rates of porotic hyperostosis are 30–80 percent in
children and 10–45 percent in adults. In general, the skeletal record of porotic
hyperostosis documents a long history of poor iron status as a major health
condition across North America, particularly once maize was adopted as a
primary source of food (Cohen and Armelagos 1984). However, even in marine
and terrestrial environments where maize agriculture was not practiced, iron
deficiency was prevalent. This suggests that local conditions caused parasitism
or diarrheal disease that contributed to iron loss (Walker 1996).

Infectious Diseases

Infectious diseases are among the most significant selective forces in human
evolution (Armelagos and Dewey 1970) and, in combination with undernutrition, continue to be the largest contributor to morbidity and mortality worldwide (Keusch and Farthing 1986). Although most infectious diseases leave no
diagnostic markers, it is fortunate for the paleopathologist that some do affect
the skeleton, changing the morphology of bone tissue (Van Blerkom 1985).
Ortner and Putschar (1981, 106) estimated that the most frequent causes of
infectious disease in prehistory are common microorganisms such as staphylo-
coccus and streptococcus, with conditions such as tuberculosis and venereal
and nonvenereal syphilis relatively rare and more controversial to diagnosis.
The chronic (typically nonlethal) conditions are important to track at the community level because these illnesses perhaps shed the most light on everyday
occurrences of poor diet, transmissible diseases, and the state of waste disposal
and hygiene.

Osteomyelitis results from the introduction of pyogenic infection, and the

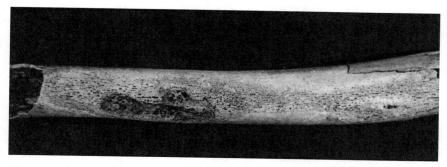

Figure 2.4. Periosteal reaction on the shaft of a femur. The individual is an 11–15-year-old child from northeastern Arizona (ca. A.D. 900–1150).

skeletal response involves the periosteum, cortex, and medullary cavity. Osteitis is another form of this phenomenon, but the reaction is primarily localized within the cortical bone. Periostitis occurs when the reaction is restricted to the outer shaft, or periosteum. It can occur as a direct response to a skin infection, through trauma, through systemic bacterial invasions, or from other soft-tissue infections (Ortner and Putschar 1981). Diagnosis and identification of the cause of the infection are very difficult, and paleopathologists have now advocated using general descriptive categories for classification of the skeletal changes observed (Buikstra and Ubelaker 1994). Referred to as *nonspecific infectious lesions,* the skeletal manifestations are categorized as periosteal reactions because the great majority of the infectious conditions seen on prehistoric bones tend to fall in this category (Figure 2.4). Specific diagnoses are attempted by paleopathologists when there are lesions that seem to fit the pattern reported for treponemal or tubercular infections, although the number of these in pre-Columbian individuals is relatively rare (Fink 1985; Micozzi and Kelly 1985).

Lallo, Armelagos, and Rose (1977) noted that the severity of periosteal reactions among Mississippian burials increased nearly fourfold during the period spanning the hunter-gatherer phase through intensive agriculture. The increase in infectious disease in the intensive agriculturalists was thought to be related to increased population density and sedentism, coupled with low dietary quality and overreliance on maize. Other trends in infectious disease demonstrated that adult women had higher rates than did men and that individuals with infections died at an earlier age. Individuals had a high co-occurrence of porotic hyperostosis and infections, suggesting that iron deficiency may have predisposed children to infectious disease by lowering resistance.

Rose, Burnett, and Harmon (1991) demonstrated that, for the Lower Mississippi Valley and the Trans-Mississippi South, there was a consistent relationship between maize agriculture dependency and increases in the infectious disease rate *only* when aggregated settlement limited the diversity of collectable resources. This suggests that, when the dietary base remained variable, infectious disease rates were lower. Thus, population density itself is not always the single determinant of the rate of infection.

Walker (1996) demonstrated that, for the Native Americans living on the Channel Islands off the coast of California, health status declined over time as people shifted from a generalized maritime hunting and gathering economy to one that focused exclusively on fishing. Despite the increase in protein in the diet, there was a decrease in overall stature and an increase in infectious disease from 10 to 30 percent for the population. Walker suggested that deficiency in other nutrients and microelements may have made the population more susceptible to infections.

Otitis media (middle ear infection) is present in many prehistoric and modern accounts of infectious diseases of children (Titche et al. 1981), and lesions found on the temporal and mastoid bones show generally high rates—up to 50 percent of children under the age of four (Martin et al. 1991). Gregg, Steel, and Holzheuter (1965) cited a rate of 52 percent for prehistoric and historic samples of Arikara, Middle Plains, and Sioux Indians. Rates of otitis media for ancestral Pueblo children from the American Southwest show that this problem was present as far back as 300 B.C., with reported frequencies approaching 80 percent of children under the age of 15 (Martin et al. 1991).

Although tuberculosis affects virtually any bone or articular surface, less than 10 percent of cases develop osseous changes, making the analysis of tuberculosis in prehistoric populations very tenuous (Ortner and Putschar 1981). Lesions thought to be tuberculosis have been identified in numerous prehistoric remains from North America. For many years it was argued as to whether tuberculosis was present in the Americas before 1492. Although the answer is in the affirmative, there are still many problems with differential diagnosis of tuberculosis on skeletal remains. Since the breakthrough study in 1973 of identification of acid-fast bacilli in prehistoric mummified tissue from South America, several seemingly secure cases of tuberculosis have been identified (Buikstra 1981, 15). Then, in 1994, a team of scientists used the DNA-amplifying polymerase chain reaction (PCR) technique to demonstrate that cells from a 1,000-year-old mummy from Peru had a segment of DNA unique to *Mycobacterium tuberculosis*. Stodder (1990) summarized findings in Southwest human remains suggesting that most of the tuberculosis cases occurred after A.D. 1200 in the larger prehistoric population centers in Arizona and New Mexico.

Treponemal infections include diseases such as venereal syphilis, yaws, pinta, and nonvenereal (endemic) syphilis. It has been demonstrated that a mild, chronic, and nonvenereal type of infection existed in precontact North America, but its distribution and frequency are still relatively unknown (Baker and

Armelagos 1988). As in the case of tuberculosis, differential diagnosis is difficult. Key diagnostic traits of advanced syphilis include "saber shin," polydactylitis, and osteolytic lesions of the external nasal vault and nasopalatal region. There are numerous cases in prehistoric North American specimens (El-Najjar 1979; Stodder 1990), but all of these cases are still under intense scrutiny by the medical community.

Dental Health and Pathological Conditions

Dental caries, premortem tooth loss, abscesses, and periodontal disease are all common in studies of prehistoric dentition, although much less so than among present-day Native Americans exposed to refined and soft foods. Edentulism is common in the ancient elderly. For example, in many ancestral Pueblo groups (A.D. 1000–1300) nearly all adults over age 50 have lost all of their teeth, which has implications for their dietary intake and ultimate survival.

The advent of agriculture had a clearly detrimental effect on dental health (Clarke et al. 1986). Costa (1982) reviewed dental disease in the prehistoric Ipiutak and Tigera remains from Alaska and found moderate rates of dental disease. Conversely, the majority of adults in agriculturally based populations have multiple caries (Martin et al. 1991). Frequencies for dental caries range from 10 percent to 80 percent of dentition present (Martin and Goodman 1995).

A key factor in dental health is the grittiness of the diet and the rate of dental attrition. Sand, dirt, and small stones often are processed with maize as well as other food, which increases the rate at which teeth are worn down. A moderate rate of wear may actually protect teeth: abrasion cleans the teeth and may eliminate incipient caries. Severe attrition may expose pulp cavities and lead to premature tooth loss.

Trauma

Traumatic lesions encompass a broad range of pathologies that include fractures, crushing injuries, wounds caused by weapons, dislocations, and degenerative problems such as exostoses, osteochondritis dissecans, and spondylolysis (Ortner and Putschar 1981; Merbs 1989). The cause can sometimes be determined by analyzing the intensity and direction of the force involved as well as the degree to which healing has occurred. These provide a clue to the relationship between the event and the possible contribution of the trauma to morbidity and mortality. Forms of interpersonal violence such as warfare, scalping, mutilation, lacerations, cannibalism, trephination, and amputations can sometimes be specifically identified (Merbs 1989; White 1992). Fractures of the forearm (radius and ulna) can reveal information about the activities of the group. Colles fractures have been found in many specimens. These wrist fractures result when an individual extends the arms to break or soften a fall. More proximally located forearm fracture may result from raising the arm in front of the face to ward off a blow.

Although some studies of trauma have demonstrated that the fractures and healed lesions are indicative of the kinds of daily occupational hazards and accidents to which people are susceptible (Merbs 1983), other studies have focused on the distribution and severity of healed lesions as an indicator of interpersonal violence. Most studies of osteologic evidence of trauma have tended to focus on male activities related to warfare (Wells 1964; Brothwell and Sandison 1967). Injury and risk-group identification that contextualized violence has been reported for a precontact site in Michigan (Wilkinson and Van Wagenen 1993) and for precontact sites along the California coast (Walker 1989). Both of these studies provide models for considering ritualized, institutionalized, or sanctioned violence against women in the Michigan case and men in the California case.

The osteologic and archaeologic literature on ancestral Pueblo Indians of the Southwest (A.D. 1100–1300) provides an example of the health effects of trauma and violence. Wilcox and Haas (1994) provide detailed overviews of archaeologic data that demonstrate evidence of sustained intervillage conflict in the form of fortified villages, palisades, and towers. Skeletal assemblages that are disarticulated, broken, chapped, sometimes burned, and with signs of dismembering have been identified. These collections, which include both children and adult men and women, have been interpreted to represent episodes of cannibalism (Turner 1993; White 1992), witchcraft retribution (Darling 1993), warfare (Wilcox and Haas 1994), or ritualized dismemberment (Ogilvie and Hilton 1993). Whatever the motivation behind these deaths, the evidence suggests violent action directed against certain subgroups.

Evidence for violence directed against women in the tenth through thirteenth centuries comes from ancestral Pueblo sites in the La Plata Valley region of northern New Mexico (Martin 1997). Compared to men, women had a threefold increase in the frequency of healed cranial depression fractures among adults and a twofold increase in trauma of the ribs and limbs. Females also had more cases of infection than males, and they demonstrated higher frequencies of enamel defects, again suggesting that they were possibly members of a targeted group from childhood onward. Although this one case study clarifies the kinds of related studies that are needed to understand trauma in prehistory, local conditions in highly variable settings suggest generally low frequencies of broken bones and sustained injuries (Cohen and Armelagos 1984). Several studies have documented an increase in trauma, particularly at the time of Columbian contact (Stodder 1989).

Osteoarthritis

Osteoarthritis is among the oldest and most commonly known diseases affecting humans. Measuring the amount of arthritic involvement with skeletal remains is sometimes difficult because of the potentially large number of areas to be assessed (each vertebra and all joint systems) and the range of variation in bony response among individuals. Although many factors may contribute to the breakdown of skeletal tissue, the primary cause of osteoarthritis is related to biomechanical wear and tear and functional stress (Ortner and Putschar 1981). Biomechanical stress is most apparent at the articular surfaces of long bone joint systems and is referred to as *degenerative joint disease* (DJD). There may be a relationship between DJD and other health problems. For example, a study correlating the incidence of DJD and infection was undertaken for a Mississippian population from Illinois (A.D. 1000–1200). Individuals with multiple joint involvement demonstrated a statistically higher percentage of periosteal reactions. Both infectious lesions and DJD increased with age, and women demonstrated greater frequencies of DJD in the shoulder and elbows than did age-matched men.

In general, early Native Americans appeared to sustain osteoarthritis at rates comparable with individuals today, although the earlier rate of onset and decreased life span of earlier Native Americans may have served to compress the observable cases into a shorter time frame within the life span (Aegerter and Kirkpatric 1968). Much work in the area of osteologic correlates of occupational stress and weapon use suggest strong associations between lifestyle and patterns of osteoarthritic and other bone changes (Kennedy 1989; Bridges 1990).

Demography and Disease at Contact

There is wide agreement about the effects of diseases and epidemics associated with European contact (Dobyns 1983; Ramenofsky 1987; Reff 1988). The first well-documented, widespread epidemic in what was to become New Mexico was smallpox in 1636. Shortly thereafter, measles entered the area, and many Pueblos lost up to a quarter of their inhabitants (Chavez 1957). After the founding of Spanish settlements and missions, there was substantially more contact, and throughout the seventeenth century, epidemic disease was repeatedly imported.

Osteologic data demonstrate that native groups were most definitely not living in a pristine, disease-free environment before contact. Although New World indigenous disease was mostly of the chronic and episodic kind, Old World diseases were largely acute and epidemic. However, different populations were affected at different times and suffered varying rates of mortality (Larsen 1994, 109). Diseases such as treponemiasis and tuberculosis were already present in the New World, along with diseases such as tularemia, giardia, rabies, amebic dysentery, hepatitis, herpes, pertussis, and poliomyelitis, although the prevalence of almost all of these was probably quite low in any given population (Ortner and Putschar 1981). Old World diseases that were not present in the Americas until contact include bubonic plague, measles, smallpox, mumps, chicken pox, influenza, cholera, diphtheria, typhus, malaria, leprosy, and yellow fever (Larsen 1994). Indians in the Americas had no acquired immunity to these infectious diseases, and these diseases caused what Crosby (1976) referred to as *virgin-soil epidemics,* where all members of a population would be infected simultaneously.

It is important to look not only at the effects of specific events like epidemic outbreaks, but also at longer-term processes that influence the age and mortality structure of populations. Kunitz and Euler (1972, 40) stated that "one does not need to invoke large-scale dramatic epidemics; prosaic entities like malnutrition and infectious diarrhea are more than sufficient to do the job." Neel (1977, 155) likewise cautioned that, to understand the influence of introduced diseases on indigenous peoples, one must first know the longer history and "epidemiologic profile" of the populations. This points to the value of incorporating the information on precontact health as a precursor to understanding the impact of contact.

Lessons from the Past

The importance of understanding health within a broad historical framework is illustrated by the following example, which draws on recent collaborative investigations into endemic health problems of the indigenous groups who call themselves the Pima and Tohono O'odham in southern Arizona. High rates of diabetes, hypertension, and obesity have plagued members of these groups since the 1940s. Recent multidisciplinary efforts to understand the etiology of these patterns have combined oral history, anthropologic, archaeologic, and epidemiologic information on diet and health to better understand the progression of these health problems over time (Smith, Schakel, and Nelson 1991). Some Pima Indians have begun to incorporate traditional foods such as lima beans, tepary beans, mesquite pods, and maize into their diet, with positive health results

(Cowen 1990). Research such as this examines the larger interacting sphere of culture, environment, and biology, and such studies on ancestral menus and ancestral health trends may continue to provide important clues to today's health problems.

Archaeologic remains have value beyond locating disease in time and space. They can aid in guiding current assessment of and decisions regarding health care. For example, at the request of Omaha Indians, paleopathologists analyzed Omaha burials from the late 1700s (Associated Press 1991). It was originally thought that many deaths during that time were a result of epidemic infectious diseases. The analysis, however, demonstrated very high levels of lead isotopes in 50 percent of the skeletal remains, suggesting that many of the deaths may have been due to lead poisoning. This was traced to the use of trade items procured by Indians from colonists, such as casks, paint, and bullets. Dennis Hastings, a tribal historian, stated that "the skeletal remains of our ancestors are speaking to us through science" (Associated Press 1991, F1).

REFERENCES

Aegerter E, Kirkpatric JA Jr. 1968. *Orthopedic Diseases.* 3d ed. Philadelphia: W. B. Saunders.

Angel JL. 1969. The bases of paleodemography. *Am J Phys Anthropol* 30:427–37.

Armelagos GJ. 1969. Diseases in ancient Nubia. *Science* 163:255–59.

Armelagos GJ, Dewey JR. 1970. Evolutionary response to human infectious disease. In: Logan MH, Hunt EE, eds. *Health and the Human Condition,* 101–6. North Scituate, Mass.: Duxbury Press.

Associated Press. 1991. Lead poisoning culprit in Omaha tribe's death. *Albuquerque Journal,* October 4, F1.

Baker B, Armelagos GJ. 1988. The origin and antiquity of syphilis: Paleopathological diagnosis and interpretation. *Curr Anthropol* 29:703–20.

Barrios P. 1993. Native Americans and archaeologists working together toward common goals in California. *Soc Am Archaeol Bull* 11(3):6–7.

Bridges PS. 1990. Osteological correlates of weapon use. In: Buikstra J, ed. *A Life in Science: Papers in Honor of J. Lawrence Angel,* 87–98. Center for American Archaeology Scientific Papers 6. Washington, D.C.: Center for American Archaeology.

Brothwell D, Sandison AT. 1967. *Disease in Antiquity.* Springfield, Ill.: Charles C Thomas.

Buikstra JE, ed. 1981. *Prehistoric Tuberculosis in the Americas.* Evanston, Ill.: Northwestern University Press.

Buikstra JE, Cook DC. 1980. Paleopathology: An American account. *Annu Rev Anthropol* 9:433–70.

Buikstra JE, Konigsberg LW, Bullington J. 1986. Fertility and the development of agriculture in the prehistoric Midwest. *Am Antiquity* 51:528–46.

Buikstra JE, Mielke JH. 1985. Demography, diet, and health. In: Gilbert RI, Mielke JH, eds. *The Analysis of Prehistoric Diets,* 359–422. New York: Academic Press.

Buikstra J, Ubelaker D, eds. 1994. *Standards for Data Collection from Human Skeletal Remains*. Chicago: Field Museum of Natural History.

Chavez A. 1957. Archives of the archdioceses of Santa Fe. *Publications of the Academy of American Franciscan History Bibliographical Series* 8. Washington, D.C.: Academy of American Franciscan History.

Clarke NG, Carey SE, Srikandi W, et al. 1986. Periodontal disease in ancient populations. *Am J Phys Anthropol* 71:173–83.

Cockburn A. 1980. *Mummies, Disease, and Ancient Cultures*. Cambridge: Cambridge University Press.

Cohen MN. 1989. *Health and the Rise of Civilization*. New Haven: Yale University Press.

Cohen MN, Armelagos GJ, eds. 1984. *Paleopathology at the Origins of Agriculture*. New York: Academic Press.

Cook DC. 1984. Subsistence and health in the lower Illinois Valley: Osteological evidence. In: Cohen MN, Armelagos GJ, eds. *Paleopathology at the Origins of Agriculture*, 235–69. New York: Academic Press.

Costa RL. 1982. Periodontal disease in the prehistoric Ipiutak and Tigara skeletal remains from Point Hope, Alaska. *Am J Phys Anthropol* 59:97–110.

Coughlin EK. 1994. Returning Indian remains. *Chronicle Higher Educ* 28:A8.

Cowen R. 1990. Seeds of protection: Ancestral menus may hold a message for diabetes-prone descendants. *Sci News* 137:350–51.

Crosby AW Jr. 1976. Virgin soil epidemics as a factor in the aboriginal depopulation in America. *William and Mary Q* 33:289–99.

Darling JA. 1993. Mass inhumation and the execution of witches in the North American Southwest. Unpublished preliminary paper draft. On file, Office of Archaeological Studies, Santa Fe.

Dobyns HF. 1983. *Their Number Became Thinned*. Knoxville: University of Tennessee Press.

Echo-Hawk RC. 1993. Working together: Exploring the ancient world. *Soc Am Archaeol Bull* 11(4):5–6.

El-Najjar MY. 1979. Human treponematosis and tuberculosis: Evidence from the New World. *Am J Phys Anthropol* 51:599–618.

El-Najjar MY, Mulinski TMJ. 1980. Mummies and mummification practices in the southwestern and southern United States. In: Cockburn A, ed. *Mummies, Disease, and Ancient Cultures*. Cambridge: Cambridge University Press.

Fink MT. 1985. Tuberculosis and anemia in a Pueblo II–III (ca. A.D. 900–1300) Anasazi child from New Mexico. In: Merbs CF, Miller RJ, eds. *Health and Disease in the Prehistoric Southwest*, 359–79. *Anthropological Research Papers* 34. Tempe: Arizona State University.

Goodman AH, Lallo J, Armelagos GJ, et al. 1984. Health changes at Dickson Mounds, Illinois (A.D. 950–1300). In: Cohen MN, Armelagos GJ, eds. *Paleopathology at the Origins of Agriculture*, 271–306. New York: Academic Press.

Goodman AH, Pelto GH, Allen LH, et al. 1992. Socioeconomic and anthropometric correlates of linear enamel hypoplasia in children from Solis, Mexico. In: Goodman AH, Capasso LL, eds. *Recent Contributions to the Study of Enamel Developmental Defects* (Monographic Publication 2 of *J Paleopathol*), 373–80. Termano, Italy: Edigrafital.

Goodman AH, Rose JC. 1990. Assessment of systemic physiological perturbations from dental enamel hypoplasia and associated histological structures. *Yearbook Phys Anthropol* 33:59–110.

——. 1991. Dental enamel hypoplasias as indicators of nutritional status. In: Kelly MA, Larsen C, eds. *Advances in Dental Anthropology,* 279–93. New York: Wiley-Liss.

Goodman AH, Thomas RB, Swedlund AC, et al. 1988. Biocultural perspectives on stress in prehistoric, historical, and contemporary population research. *Yearbook Phys Anthropol* 31:169–202.

Gregg JD, Steel JP, Holzheuter A. 1965. Roentgenographic evaluation of temporal bones from South Dakota Indian burials. *Am J Phys Anthropol* 25:51–61.

Habicht JP, Martorell R, Yarborough C, et al. 1974. Height and weight standards for preschool children: How relevant are ethnic differences in growth potential? *Lancet* 1:611–15.

Infante P. 1974. Enamel hypoplasia in Apache Indian children. *Ecol Food Nutr* 2:155–56.

Iscan MY, Kennedy KAR, eds. 1989. *Reconstruction of Life from the Skeleton.* New York: Alan R. Liss.

Jantz RL, Owsley DW. 1984. Temporal changes in limb proportionality among skeletal samples of Arikara Indians. *Ann Hum Biol* 11:157–63.

Jarcho S. 1966. The development and present condition of human paleopathology in the U.S. In: Jarcho S, ed. *Human Paleopathology,* 3–30. New Haven: Yale University Press.

Kennedy KAR. 1989. Skeletal markers of occupational stress. In: Iscan MY, Kennedy KAR, eds. *Reconstruction of Life from the Skeleton,* 129–60. New York: Alan R. Liss.

Keusch GT, Farthing MJ. 1986. Nutrition and infection. *Annu Rev Nutr* 6:131–54.

Kunitz SJ, Euler RC. 1972. *Aspects of Southwestern Paleoepidemiology. Prescott College Anthropological Reports* 2. Prescott, Ariz.: Prescott College Press.

Lallo J. 1973. *The Skeletal Biology of Three Prehistoric Amerindian Populations from Dickson Mounds.* Amherst: University of Massachusetts.

Lallo J, Armelagos GJ, Rose JC. 1977. Paleoepidemiology of infectious disease in the Dickson Mounds population. *Med College of Va Q* 14:17–23.

Larsen CS. 1987. Bioarchaeological interpretations of subsistence economy and behavior from human skeletal remains. *Adv Archaeol Method Theory* 10:339–445.

——. 1994. In the wake of Columbus: Native population biology in the postcontact Americas. *Yearbook Phys Anthropol* 37:109–54.

Lovejoy CO. 1985. Dental wear in the Libben population: Its functional pattern and role in the determination of adult skeletal age at death. *Am J Phys Anthropol* 68:47–56.

Malville NJ. 1997. Enamel hypoplasia in ancestral Puebloan populations from southwestern Colorado: I. Permanent dentition. *Am J Phys Anthropol* 102:351–67.

Mann RW, Murphy SP. 1990. *Regional Atlas of Bone Disease.* Springfield, Ill.: Charles C Thomas.

Martin DL. 1994. Stress profiles for the prehistoric Southwest. In: Gumerman GM, ed. *Themes in Southwest Prehistory,* 87–108. Santa Fe: School of American Research Press.

——. 1997. Violence against women in the La Plata River Valley (A.D. 1000–1300). In: Martin DL, Frayer D, eds. *Troubled Times: Violence and Warfare in the Past,* 44–74. New York: Gordon & Breach.

Martin DL, Goodman AH. 1995. Demography, diet, and disease in the transitional

Basketmaker III/Pueblo I period. In: Smiley FE, Gregg SA, eds. *Studies in Ridges Basin Archaeology,* 1–48. *Animas–La Plata Archaeological Project Research Paper* 4. Denver: U.S. Department of the Interior, Bureau of Reclamation, Upper Colorado Region.

Martin DL, Goodman AH, Armelagos GJ, et al. 1991. *Black Mesa Anasazi Health: Reconstructing Life from Patterns of Death and Disease.* Carbondale: Southern Illinois University Press.

Matthews W, Wortman JL, Billings JS. 1893. Human bones of the Hemenway Collection in the U.S. Medical Museum. *Mem Natl Acad Sci* 7:141–286.

Mensforth RP. 1985. Relative tibia long bone growth in the Libben and BT-5 prehistoric skeletal populations. *Am J Phys Anthropol* 68:247–62.

Mensforth RP, Lovejoy CO, Lallo JW, et al. 1978. The role of constitutional factors, diet, and infectious disease in the etiology of porotic hyperostosis and periosteal reactions in prehistoric infants and children. *Med Anthropol* 2:1–59.

Merbs CF. 1983. *Patterns of Activity-Induced Pathology in a Canadian Inuit Population. Mercury Series Paper* 119. Ottawa: National Museum of Man.

———. 1989. Trauma. In: Iscan MY, Kennedy KAR, eds. *Reconstruction of Life from the Skeleton,* 161–99. New York: Alan R. Liss.

Merbs CF, Miller RJ, eds. 1985. *Health and Disease in the Prehistoric Southwest. Anthropological Research Papers* 34. Tempe: Arizona State University.

Merchant VA, Ubelaker DH. 1977. Skeletal growth of the protohistoric Arikara. *Am J Phys Anthropol* 46:61–72.

Micozzi MS, Kelly MA. 1985. Evidence for pre-Columbian tuberculosis at the Point-of-Pines Site, Arizona: Skeletal pathology in the sacro-iliac region. In: Merbs CF, Miller RJ, eds. *Health and Disease in the Prehistoric Southwest,* 347–58. *Anthropological Research Papers* 34. Tempe: Arizona State University.

Milner GR, Anderson E, Smith VG. 1991. Warfare in late prehistoric west-central Illinois. *Am Antiquity* 56:581–603.

Neel JV. 1977. Health and disease in unacculturated Amerindian populations. *Ciba Found Symp* 49(n.s.):155–77.

Nelson BA, Martin DL, Swedlund AC, et al. 1994. Studies in disruption: Demography and health in the prehistoric American Southwest. In: Gumerman G, Gell-Mann M, eds. *Understanding Complexity in the Prehistoric Southwest,* 59–112. Reading, Mass.: Addison-Wesley.

Ogilvie MD, Hilton CE. 1993. Analysis of selected human skeletal material from sites 423-124 and 423-131. In: Cohen C, Bunds D, Cella N, eds. *Across the Colorado Plateau: Anthropological Studies for the Transwestern Pipeline Expansion Project,* 18:97–128. Albuquerque: Office of Contract Archaeology and Maxwell Museum of Anthropology.

Ortner DJ, Putschar WGJ. 1981. *Identification of Pathological Conditions in Human Skeletal Remains.* Washington, D.C.: Smithsonian Institution Press.

Ortner DJ, Tyson R. 1997. *Human Paleopathology and Related Subjects: An International Bibliography.* San Diego: San Diego Museum of Man.

Owsley DW, Jantz RC. 1985. Longbone lengths and gestational age distribution in Arikara. *Am J Phys Anthropol* 68:321–28.

Palkovich AM. 1985. Agriculture, marginal environments, and nutritional stress in the prehistoric Southwest. In: Cohen MN, Armelagos GJ, eds. *Paleopathology at the Origins of Agriculture,* 425–61. New York: Academic Press.

———. 1987. Endemic disease patterns in paleopathology: Porotic hyperostosis. *Am J Phys Anthropol* 74:527–37.

Powell ML. 1988. *Status and Health in Prehistory: A Case Study of the Moundville Chiefdom.* Washington, D.C.: Smithsonian Institution Press.

Powell ML, Bridges PS, Wagner-Mires AM, eds. 1991. *What Mean These Bones? Studies in Southeastern Bioarchaeology.* Tuscaloosa: University of Alabama Press.

Ramenofsky AF. 1987. *Vectors of Death: The Archaeology of European Contact.* Albuquerque: University of New Mexico Press.

Reff D. 1988. The introduction of smallpox in the Greater Southwest. *Am Anthropologist* 89:704–8.

Rose JC, Burnett BA, Harmon AM. 1991. Disease and ecology in the Lower Mississippi Valley and the Trans-Mississippi South. *Int J Osteoarchaeol* 1:241–45.

Rose JC, Green TJ, Green VD. 1996. NAGPRA is forever: Osteology and the repatriation of skeletons. *Annu Rev Anthropol* 25:81–103.

Scrimshaw N. 1991. Ecological factors in nutritional disease. *Annu Rev Anthropol* 17:99–126.

Skinner MF, Hung JTW. 1989. Social and biological correlates of localized enamel hypoplasia of the human deciduous canine tooth. *Am J Phys Anthropol* 79:159–75.

Smith C, Schakel SF, Nelson RG. 1991. Selected traditional and contemporary foods currently used by the Pima Indians. *J Am Diet Assoc* 91:338–41.

Stodder AL. 1989. Bioarchaeological research in the basin and range region. In: Simmons AH, Stodder AL, Dykeman DD, et al., eds. *Human Adaptation and Cultural Change in the Greater Southwest,* 167–90. *Arkansas Archaeological Survey Research Series* 32. Wrightsville: Arkansas Archaeological Survey.

———. 1990. Paleoepidemiology of eastern and western Pueblo communities in protohistoric New Mexico. Ph.D. diss., University of Colorado, Boulder.

Storey R. 1992. Preindustrial urban lifestyle and child health. *MASCA, Univ Museum Archaeol Anthropol Univ Pa Phila* 9:31–43.

Stuart-Macadam P. 1987. Porotic hyperostosis: New evidence to support the anemia theory. *Am J Phys Anthropol* 74:521–26.

Swedlund AC. 1994. Issues in demography and health. In: Gumerman G, Gell-Mann M, eds. *Understanding Complexity in the Prehistoric Southwest,* 39–58. Reading, Mass.: Addison-Wesley.

Titche LL, Coulthard SW, Wachter RD, et al. 1981. The prevalence of mastoid infection in prehistoric Arizona Indians. *Am J Phys Anthropol* 56:269–73.

Turner CG II. 1993. Cannibalism in Chaco Canyon: The charnel pit excavated in 1926 at Small House Ruin by Frank H. H. Roberts Jr. *Am J Phys Anthropol* 91:421–39.

Van Blerkom LM. 1985. The evolution of human infectious disease in the Eastern and Western Hemispheres. Ph.D. diss., University of Colorado, Boulder.

Walker PL. 1985. Anemia among prehistoric Indians of the American Southwest. In: Merbs CF, Miller RJ, eds. *Health and Disease in the Ancient Southwest,* 139–63. *Anthropological Research Paper* 34. Tempe: University of Arizona.

———. 1989. Cranial injuries as evidence of violence in prehistoric Southern California. *Am J Phys Anthropol* 80:313–23.

———. 1996. Integrative approaches to the study of ancient health: An example from the Santa Barbara area of Southern California. In: Pérez-Pérez A, ed. *Notes on Populational Significance of Paleopathological Conditions.* Barcelona: Fundació Uriach.

Weiss KM, Smouse PE. 1976. The demographic stability of small human populations. In:

Ward RH, Weiss KM, eds. *The Demographic Evolution of Human Populations,* 59–74. New York: Academic Press.

Wells C. 1964. *Bones, Bodies, and Disease.* New York: Praeger.

Wetterstrom W. 1986. *Food, Diet, and Population at Prehistoric Arroyo Hondo Pueblo, New Mexico.* Santa Fe: School of American Research Press.

White TD. 1992. *Prehistoric Cannibalism at Mancos 5MTUMR-2346.* Princeton: Princeton University Press.

Wilcox DR, Haas J. 1994. Competition and conflict in the prehistoric Southwest. In: Gumerman GJ, ed. *Themes in Southwest Prehistory,* 211–38. Santa Fe: School of American Research Press.

Wilkinson RG, Van Wagenen KM. 1993. Violence against women: Prehistoric skeletal evidence from Michigan. *Midcontinental J Archaeol* 18:190–216.

3

C. Matthew Snipp, Ph.D.

Selected Demographic Characteristics of Indians

The planning and implementation of health-care programs begin with an assessment of the demographic characteristics of the population under consideration. This chapter provides an overview of some of the demographic characteristics of American Indians considered to be useful in understanding disease patterns and planning health programs. It is not intended to be an exhaustive analysis of the factors underlying various changes within Indian populations. Such information includes the numbers of Indian populations and subpopulations, fertility and birth rates, age and gender distributions, recent migration patterns, locations of residence, and levels of economic attainment.

Enumeration of the Indian Population

Enumeration of the Indian population has always been confounded by a number of factors: variations in self-identification, isolation, mobility, and rapid change. The base estimates of the Indian population are derived from the decennial censuses. Several important qualifications should be borne in mind. Continued modifications and refinements of censuses make comparisons between various time periods somewhat problematic. For example, a major shift occurred in the 1960 Census, when race was first designated by the individual rather than by the enumerator. In the 1990 Census, approximately 8.8 million individuals indicated that they had *some* Indian heritage. Of these, 1,959,200 indicated that this heritage was significant enough that they designated their race as American Indian or Alaska Native. The self-identified population that is most appropriate for health planning is thus open to some question. However, the smaller number is the one that has generally been used for health planning.

The dramatic growth in the Indian population since 1960 (an average annual rate of 4.3%) has been attributed to high fertility and improving mortality rates, but especially to changes in the degree to which certain individuals identify themselves as Indian (Passell 1996). The latter has been a major factor in Indian population change in recent decades. That is, changes in numbers over time to a large extent reflect changes in the number of individuals who newly identify themselves as Indian. This phenomenon, considered to be pronounced in the 1990 Census, is discussed at length by Snipp (1989), Harris (1994), and Passell (1996).

Distribution of the Indian Population by Age and Gender

In contrast to the general U.S. population (U.S. All Races), the Indian population contains a greater proportion of young and a smaller proportion of elderly persons (Figure 3.1). Presently, 33 percent of Indians are younger than 15 years, compared to only 22 percent for the general U.S. population. Conversely, only 6 percent of Indians are aged 64 years or older, compared to 13 percent for the general U.S. population (Indian Health Service 1997). However, the age distribution of the Indian population is gradually beginning to resemble that of the general population.

Fertility

Early in the twentieth century, fertility rates for Indians were relatively low (Thornton, Sandefur, and Snipp 1991): the mean number of children ever born to full-blood couples was 4.5, noticeably fewer than that of interracial couples involving either mixed-race or full-blood Indian spouses, with 5.1 and 5.4 children ever born, respectively. Likewise, nearly 11 percent of full-blood couples were childless in 1910, compared to about 8 percent of couples composed of full-blood Indians and Whites and 4 percent of mixed-race/White unions. The lower rates of fertility for those Indians designated as full-bloods led the Census Bureau to predict their eventual disappearance (U.S. Bureau of the Census 1915).

By 1940, a marked shift was noted in the fertility of full-blood Indian couples compared to that of Indian women with non-Indian spouses; the former now had higher fertility rates than the latter. This pattern persisted through the "baby boom" years (ca. 1946–63), and the differences between the fertility rates of the two groups also became larger (Thornton, Sandefur, and Snipp 1991).

In the 1970s, after a noticeable decline (also occurring in the rest of the nation), Indian fertility rates began to rise and now exceed those of both the

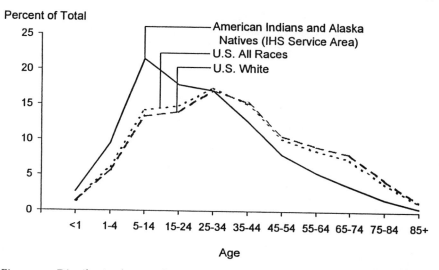

Figure 3.1. Distribution by age of American Indians and Alaska Natives, U.S. All Races, and U.S. Whites, based on the 1990 Census. *Source:* Indian Health Service 1997, Chart 2.4

White and Black populations. In addition, the fertility rates of endogamous Indian couples and Indians residing on reservations have been noticeably higher than those of exogamous couples or couples living in urban areas (Snipp 1989).

Children Ever Born

Children ever born (CEB), or parity, is a widely used measure of fertility. CEB gauges cumulative fertility and allows comparisons of changes in fertility behavior between cohorts of women. The mean number of children ever born to Black, White, and Indian women aged 15 to 44 is shown in Table 3.1. It is readily apparent that the Indian fertility rate equals or exceeds those of either Black or White women. In 1990, the number of children ever born to Black and Indian women, while smaller for both than in 1970, was identical (0.45). Black women appear to curtail childbearing in their late 20s and early 30s, while Indian women continue to have children into later years. In 1990, the mean CEB for Indian women aged 25 to 34 (1.95) was 20 percent higher than the mean CEB for Black women (1.62). This gap persists in the older cohort as well. It is also evident that the mean CEB has declined for all three groups of women, with the largest decrease for Indian women. Among Indian women aged 35 to 44, the mean CEB fell from 4.41 in 1970 to 2.55 in 1990, a 42 percent decrease.

TABLE 3.1
*Mean number of children ever born to women aged 15 to 44,
by race (1970, 1980, and 1990)*

Year	Age	American Indian	Black	White
		No.		
1970	15–24	0.65	0.67	0.35
	25–34	2.93	2.77	2.12
	35–44	4.41	3.54	2.83
1980	15–24	0.53	0.57	0.27
	25–34	2.04	1.86	1.40
	35–44	3.46	3.21	2.54
1990	15–24	0.54	0.54	0.27
	25–34	1.95	1.62	1.31
	35–44	2.55	2.22	1.92

SOURCE: Data from U.S. Bureau of the Census public-use microdata sample.

In the same period, the decrease was 37 percent for Black women and 32 percent for White women. The decrease in mean CEB for Indian women may reflect changes in population composition due to changing racial identities as much as it may indicate "real" changes in fertility behavior. Whether this represents a significant and overall trend requires further study.

As will be seen throughout this volume, firm conclusions about differences between Indian tribes and groups are often hampered not only by absent data but also by small population size of the group under consideration. However, tribal-specific data in the 1990 Census allow comparison of CEB across certain tribes. Among larger tribes, Sioux women are the most likely to begin their families at a young age, while Lumbee women are least likely to do so. However, Navajo women have slightly higher levels of lifetime fertility, with 3.13 CEB. Iroquois women have the lowest levels of lifetime fertility, with 2.05 CEB, nearly one-third lower than Navajo women. Explanations for these differences, undoubtedly related to cultural or socioeconomic differences, are not readily apparent.

The downward trends in fertility rates noted above are present in both metropolitan and nonmetropolitan areas. This decline is somewhat more pronounced in metropolitan areas, but this may reflect the influence of compositional changes over time rather than a real change in fertility. And, as noted in other groups, the fertility of nonmetropolitan Indian women is higher than that of those living in metropolitan locations.

Location of Residence

The distribution of the Indian population was profoundly altered by the arrival of Europeans, certain other general societal changes (e.g., increased employment opportunities in cities compared to reservations), and the actions of the federal government. About three-fourths of the Indian population is concentrated in the western United States; relatively few Indians are found in New England or the Southeast. The tribes in New England were decimated by disease and warfare with colonial settlers (Thornton 1987; Merrell 1989). Indians in the South and the Ohio River valley were forced to migrate early in the nineteenth century, largely as a result of the Indian Removal Act. Eventually, most of the Indian population was resettled on reservations or in the Indian Territory of what is now Oklahoma.

More than any other ethnic minority group, Indians continue to be concentrated in the West and in rural areas. The removal of Indian tribes and the creation of reservations generally placed Indians in sites distant from the mainstream of American society. Indeed, as recently as 1930, only about 10 percent of the Indian population lived in urban areas, while slightly more than half of all Americans were city dwellers (Snipp 1989). By 1990, nearly one-half of the Indian population remained outside metropolitan areas.

Two events, one planned and the other unplanned, were responsible for rapid urbanization of Indians. The first, obviously unplanned, was World War II. During this war more than twenty-five thousand Indians served in military forces, while another fifty thousand worked in munitions plants, shipyards, and other war-related industries (Hagan 1979; Bernstein 1991). The impact of World War II on Indians, especially those in military service, is difficult to overestimate. For many, if not most, the war years were an opportunity to become immersed in non-Indian culture and to adapt to the demands of a new social environment. For some, military service and the resulting benefits of the GI Bill provided job skills that materially assisted in securing subsequent employment (Bernstein 1991, 142–44). Many chose to remain in urban labor markets instead of returning to the poverty and joblessness of reservation life (Fixico 1986; Bernstein 1991).

After World War II, a series of federal policies known as Termination and Relocation assisted Indians to move to preselected urban locations where, it was assumed, they would become employed and assimilate into the mainstream of American society (Fixico 1986). From 1952 to 1972, an estimated 100,000 Indians were relocated to such cities as Los Angeles, San Francisco, and Chicago (Sorkin 1978). Needless to say, not all of these urban immigrants remained in cities; a substantial number returned to their reservation homes (O'Brien 1989). Today, the general impression is that considerable movement between urban and reservation areas continues. Though a few studies showed that some relocatees benefited from the program (Clinton, Chadwick, and Bahr 1975), other studies were more equivocal about the benefits for rural-urban migrants (Gundlach and Roberts 1978; Snipp and Sandefur 1988). Eventually, these policies fell

TABLE 3.2
Regional distribution of the American Indian and Alaska Native populations, 1970–1990

Region and division	Population					Population change (%)	
	1970		1980		1990	1970–1980	1980–1990
Northeast	45,720	(5.8)[a]	79,038	(5.6)	125,148 (6.4)	72.9	58.3
New England	10,362	(1.3)	21,597	(1.5)	32,794 (1.7)	108.4	51.9
Mid-Atlantic	35,358	(4.5)	57,441	(4.0)	92,354 (4.7)	62.5	60.8
Midwest	144,254	(18.2)	248,413	(17.5)	377,899 (17.3)	72.2	36.0
East North Central	54,578	(6.9)	105,927	(7.4)	149,939 (7.7)	94.1	41.6
West North Central	89,676	(11.3)	142,486	(10.0)	187,960 (9.6)	58.9	31.9
South	194,406	(24.5)	372,825	(26.2)	562,731 (28.7)	91.8	50.9
South Atlantic	65,367	(8.2)	118,938	(8.4)	172,281 (8.8)	82.0	44.9
East South Central	8,708	(1.1)	22,472	(1.6)	40,839 (2.1)	158.1	81.7
West South Central	120,331	(15.2)	231,410	(16.3)	349,611 (17.8)	92.3	51.1
West	408,350	(51.5)	722,769	(50.8)	933,456 (47.6)	77.0	29.2
Mountain	229,669	(29.0)	366,291	(25.7)	480,516 (24.5)	59.5	31.2
Pacific	179,681	(22.5)	356,478	(25.1)	452,940 (23.1)	99.5	27.1
TOTAL	792,730	(100.0)	1,423,045	(100.0)	1,959,234 (100.0)	79.5	37.7

SOURCE: Data from U.S. Bureau of the Census 1992; Snipp 1989.
[a]Numbers in parentheses, percentages of total.

into disfavor, and President Nixon's Indian message of 1970 and the passage of the Indian Self-Determination and Education Assistance Act in 1975 marked the first official shift away from these efforts.

The effects of participation in World War II and the relocation programs cannot be judged apart. These events in combination had a major influence on the settlement patterns of Indians, with enormous implications for the delivery of health services. By one estimate, fewer than 10,000 Indians lived in cities in 1926 (Institute for Government Research 1928). According to the U.S. Census, by 1960 about 160,000 Indians were found in urban areas and, within another decade, this number had climbed to 340,000. Between 1960 and 1970, the proportion of Indians in urban areas increased from 30 to 45 percent. However, the de-emphasis of the relocation programs in the late 1960s and early 1970s may have slowed this trend. In 1980, 51 percent of the Indian population lived outside of metropolitan areas, and in 1990, this number had modestly decreased to 49 percent. Again, some portion of this increase was undoubtedly associated with changing patterns of racial self-identification within the Indian population.

Regional Distribution

Table 3.2 shows the geographic distributions across standard census regions since 1970. These changes should be interpreted with caution; some differences may be due to the movement of persons around the country or to differential rates of natural increase between areas. Changing patterns of self-identification may also be responsible for some of these differences. Regional variations in racial self-identification, described as "implied migration," ranged from as little as 0.4 percent in the Mountain division to 37.5 percent in the East South Central division (Harris 1994). Hence, what may appear to be a significant demographic shift may reflect changing ideas about racial identity more than the actual mobility of the population. Regardless, such changes obviously affect health-care planning by federal agencies.

Despite the substantial increase in the number of Indians since 1970, the basic distribution of the Indian population has remained surprisingly stable for the past two decades. In 1990, as in 1970 and 1980, the West had the largest number of Indians. Similarly, the Northeast has the fewest numbers. The area east of the Mississippi River includes the entire Northeast region (the East North Central, South Atlantic, and East South Central divisions) and is home for approximately 488,000 Indians, about one-quarter of the total Indian population identifying itself as significantly Indian.

The rate of growth in all areas was smaller in the 1980s than in 1970s. In the 1980s, the total growth in the Indian population was about 38 percent, with natural increase accounting for about 22 percent. Natural increase was higher in the 1970s, about 28 percent, but changing patterns of racial self-identification generated population growth that raised this number to nearly 80 percent. These intercensal differences are reflected across regions and divisions, with changes ranging from 59 to 158 percent in the 1970s and 27 to 82 percent in the 1980s. Those locations with the smallest numbers of Indians (e.g., the East South Central division) also had the largest increases.

Place of Residence

Urban and Rural Populations

The distribution of the U.S. population, including Indians and Alaska Natives, by metropolitan residence (metropolitan statistical areas, or MSAs) is shown in Table 3.3. Indians more than any other group continue to live outside of urban areas. In 1990, about 78 percent of all Americans resided in MSAs, compared to only 51.3 percent for Indians. Other minority groups, such as Asians or Hispanics, are concentrated in cities at rates of 90 percent or higher. Further, most minority populations who live in metropolitan areas are concentrated in central city locations. This is not the case for Indians — about 55 percent of those who reside in metropolitan areas stay outside the central city.

Table 3.3 also shows the change in urbanization of Indians between 1980 and 1990. These numbers suggest a slight increase in metropolitan residence (49.0% in 1980 to 51.3% in 1990), but it would be a mistake to read too much into this shift. Changes in racial self-identification have an effect on the numbers, as do changes in metropolitan definitions — some places were designated as metropolitan in 1990 but not in 1980. Given the small differences between 1980 and 1990, it is probably more reasonable to conclude that the rapid

TABLE 3.3
Residential distribution of the U.S. population, by race and Hispanic origin, 1990

| | Inside MSAs[a] (%) | | | |
Race/origin	Inside central cities	Outside central cities	Total	Outside MSAs (%)
American Indian[b]				
1990	23.3	28.0	51.3	48.7
1980	20.9	28.1	49.0	51.0
Asian/Pacific Islander	46.5	47.4	93.9	6.1
Black	57.3	26.4	83.7	16.3
Hispanic[c]	51.5	38.9	90.4	9.6
White	24.5	50.3	74.8	25.2
TOTAL	31.3	46.2	77.5	22.5

SOURCE: Data from U.S. Bureau of the Census 1993; Snipp 1989.
[a] MSAs, metropolitan statistical areas.
[b] Includes Alaska Natives.
[c] Hispanics may be of any race. Blacks and Whites are persons with non-Hispanic origins.

TABLE 3.4
Metropolitan statistical areas with 15,000 or more Indians and Alaska Natives in 1990

Metropolitan statistical area	Indian population		
	1970	1980	1990
Tulsa, Okla.	15,183	38,463	48,348
Oklahoma City, Okla.	12,951	24,695	46,111
Los Angeles-Long Beach, Calif.	23,908	47,234	43,689
Phoenix, Ariz.	19,996	27,788	38,309
Seattle-Tacoma, Wash.	8,814	15,162	32,980
Riverside-San Bernadino, Calif.	5,941	17,107	25,938
New York City, N.Y.	9,984	13,440	24,822
Minneapolis, Minn.	9,911	15,831	23,338
San Diego, Calif.	6,007	14,355	21,509
San Francisco-Oakland, Calif.	12,041	17,546	21,191
Tucson, Ariz.	8,704	14,880	20,034
Dallas-Fort Worth, Tex.	5,500	11,076	19,933
Detroit-Ann Arbor, Mich.	5,203	12,372	19,331
Sacramento, Calif.	3,548	10,944	18,164
Chicago, Ill.	8,203	10,415	16,513
Albuquerque, N.M.	5,822	20,721	16,008
Total in metropolitan statistical areas	161,716	312,029	436,218
Percentage of total American Indian population	20.4%	21.9%	22.3%

SOURCE: Data from U.S. Bureau of the Census 1993; Snipp 1989.

urbanization of Indians in the 1940s, 1950s, and 1960s has reached a point of stasis, and there is little reason to believe that the Indian population is significantly more urbanized today than it was 20 years ago.

Although Indians are one of the least urbanized groups in American society, they are nonetheless concentrated in a relatively small number of cities (Table 3.4). In fact, roughly one-half of all urban Indians can be found in as few as 16 cities. These figures reflect the aftermath of the urban relocation programs, as well as spontaneous movement to nearby cities. Seven of the cities shown in Table 3.4 (Tulsa, Oklahoma City, the Los Angeles area, the San Francisco Bay area, Dallas, Seattle, and Chicago) were officially designated Bureau of Indian Affairs (BIA) relocation sites for Indians desiring to leave the reservations. Considerable migration to cities continues, however, unrelated to the BIA relocation program.

Reservation Populations

Reservations, along with the Indian nations of Oklahoma, make up the majority of the territory known as *Indian country*. Reservations are special places because they represent the last remaining lands belonging to people who once claimed all of North America. Reservations are also special places because for most Indians, including many urban Indians, they are the touchstones of cultural identity, places with sacred sites, the location of ceremonial life, and an

TABLE 3.5
Population sizes of reservations with 5,000 or more Indians and Alaska Natives in 1990

	Population			Population change (%)	
Reservation	1970	1980	1990	1970–1980	1980–1990
Navajo	56,949	104,968	143,405	84.3	36.6
Pine Ridge	8,280	11,882	11,182	43.5	−6.0
Fort Apache	5,903	6,880	9,825	16.6	42.8
Gila River	4,573	7,067	9,116	54.5	29.0
Papago	4,879	6,959	8,480	42.6	21.9
Rosebud	5,656	5,688	8,043	0.6	41.4
San Carlos	4,525	5,872	7,110	29.8	21.1
Zuni Pueblo	4,736	5,988	7,073	26.4	18.1
Hopi	7,726	6,601	7,061	—[a]	7.0
Blackfeet	4,757	5,080	7,025	6.8	38.3
Turtle Mountain	3,386	3,955	6,772	16.9	71.2
Yakima	2,509	4,983	6,307	98.6	26.6
Osage	—[b]	4,749	6,088	—[b]	28.2
Fort Peck	3,182	4,273	5,782	34.3	35.3
Wind River	3,319	4,150	5,676	25.0	36.8
Eastern Cherokee	3,455	4,844	5,388	40.2	11.2
Flathead	2,537	3,504	5,130	38.1	46.4
Cheyenne River	3,440	1,557	5,100	−54.7	227.6
Reservation total	128,812	199,000	264,563	54.5	33.0
Percentage of total Indian population	16.3%	14.0%	13.5%		

SOURCE: Data from U.S. Bureau of the Census 1993; Snipp 1989.
[a]Figures for 1970 and 1980 are not strictly comparable because of administrative changes in reservation boundaries.
[b]Not reported for 1970 and not included in reservation total.

essential symbol in tribal life. Reservations were once places where Indians were segregated from the mainstream of the dominant society, but they have become places the importance of which cannot be overestimated.

There are 279 federal and state reservations located around the nation, and, as already mentioned, most are in the West. They range in size from a few acres, such as the small rancherias scattered throughout California, to the Navajo reservation in the Four Corners area. The latter is about the size of Ireland or the state of West Virginia. As important as reservations are to Indian tribal life, it is not true that most Indians live in these places. About 438,000 Indians live on state and federally recognized reservations and trust lands. In absolute numbers, more Indians live on reservations today than at any time in the past; in relative terms, however, the percentage of Indians living on reservation land has declined. The approximately 370,000 Indians living on reservations and trust lands in 1980 represented about 27 percent of the total population; in 1990, slightly less than 22 percent of the Indian population were reservation residents. The population sizes in 1970, 1980, and 1990 are shown in Table 3.5 for a selected group of relatively large reservations.

The Navajo reservation stands out as the most populous (as well as the physically largest) reservation. With 143,405 persons, it is nearly 13 times larger than the next largest, the Pine Ridge Sioux reservation in South Dakota. The total population on these reservations has grown substantially in the past two decades, more than doubling in number. In relative terms, however, they also represent a slowly declining share of the total U.S. Indian population. Evidence of enumeration problems is also noticeable in Table 3.5. In 1980, the Cheyenne River Sioux experienced a very steep (and improbable) population loss, followed by an even steeper population recovery in 1990. Similarly, the Turtle Mountain reservation population was virtually unchanged between 1970 and 1980 but experienced a very sharp increase in 1990. The population decline at the Pine Ridge reservation between 1980 and 1990 may reflect an undercount in 1990, but in the absence of corroborating evidence, this is impossible to determine with certainty.

Economic Well-Being

Indians have consistently been one of the poorest groups in American society. This was first systematically documented by the Meriam report (Institute for Government Research 1928), which demonstrated that Indians were plagued by a host of social and economic ills, including illiteracy, ill health, joblessness, substandard housing, and poverty. The report was also highly critical of the way the federal government discharged its administrative responsibilities for Indian reservations.

Following the Meriam report, the Hoover and then the Roosevelt administrations introduced a variety of reforms to alleviate the economic hardships that burdened Indians (Prucha 1984). The reforms introduced during the tenure of President Hoover had little noticeable effect, but the so-called Indian New Deal introduced during the Roosevelt years transformed Indian country. Perhaps most important was the Indian Reorganization Act of 1934, which restored tribal government on many reservations. Equally significant, the Indian New Deal provided jobs through programs such as the Works Progress Administration and the Civilian Conservation Corps.

Although these programs provided much-needed relief on many reservations, the outbreak of World War II was an even greater turning point in the fortunes of many Indians. One estimate suggested that the average incomes of individual Indian families tripled between 1940 and 1944 (Bernstein 1991, 76). Equally if not more important was the postwar GI Bill, which gave Indian veterans (mostly men) the opportunity to pursue a college education. This program spurred a rise in education among Indians unparalleled in the twentieth century (Snipp 1989). However, these gains were not substantial enough to appreciably change the socioeconomic status of Indians, and they continued to be among the poorest groups in American society (Sorkin 1971; Snipp 1989).

In recent years, the success of some tribes in developing highly lucrative gaming and resort businesses has led some observers to conclude that Indians are no longer an impoverished group. However, most Indians do not reside on reservations with highly successful casinos. Furthermore, as the data for education and income show, Indians are still one of this nation's most economically disadvantaged groups.

Educational Attainment

Compared with other groups, Indians have a significant deficit of human capital. The educational attainment of Indians in relation to that of Blacks and Whites is displayed in Table 3.6. Indians have an excess of poorly educated persons (most likely older individuals) and a shortage of adults who are highly educated. At the lowest levels, Blacks and Indians have about the same proportion of persons with fewer than nine years of schooling, about 14 percent. This is substantially higher (by about 68%) than the 9 percent of Whites with very low levels of education. The proportion of Indians with a high school diploma slightly exceeds that of Blacks: 29.1 versus 27.8 percent. Not surprisingly, the percentage of Blacks and Indians finishing high school is somewhat lower than that for the adult White population.

Perhaps the most significant finding concerns the disparity between college attendance and graduation among these groups. Postsecondary education is not an unfamiliar experience for many Indians. In fact, well over one-third (nearly 37%) of the Indian adult population aged 25 and over has attended college. This figure slightly exceeds the attendance rates for Blacks (35.2%) but is consider-

TABLE 3.6
Distribution of educational attainment by Indians, Blacks, and Whites aged 25 and over, 1990

Completed schooling	Percentage		
	Indians	Blacks	Whites
Less than ninth grade	14.0	13.8	8.9
9–11 years	20.5	23.2	13.1
High school diploma	29.1	27.9	31.0
Some college	27.2	23.8	25.4
Baccalaureate and higher	9.3	11.4	21.5

SOURCE: Data from U.S. Bureau of the Census 1993.

TABLE 3.7
Incomes of Indians, Blacks, and Whites,
1969 to 1989 (1989 dollars)

Year	Median income ($)	
	Family	Household
Indians		
1969	19,722	—[a]
1979	23,440	20,933
1989	21,750	20,025
Blacks		
1969	20,518	15,739
1979	21,517	18,691
1989	22,429	19,758
Whites		
1969	33,687	27,427
1979	35,586	30,197
1989	37,628	31,672

SOURCE: Data from U.S. Bureau of the Census 1993; Snipp 1989.
[a]Not available.

ably below the attendance rate for Whites (47.6%). Nonetheless, only about 26 percent of Indian college attendees also report having a baccalaureate or higher degree, compared with 32 percent for Blacks and 46 percent for Whites. The reasons that Indians are less successful than either Blacks or Whites in obtaining a postsecondary degree are not clear, but certainly this is a decided handicap in a labor market demanding ever higher levels of skill and intellectual ability.

Family Income

Ultimately, the value of education is most directly realized in monetary income, and human capital resources are reflected in the incomes received by Indians, Blacks, and Whites. The deficits registered by Indians are further manifest in their economic well-being relative to Whites. The 1989 median family and household incomes of these three groups are shown in Table 3.7. Family incomes typically exceed household incomes because the latter include single-person households while families may have two or more income earners.

The household incomes of Indians are slightly higher than those of Blacks, while the reverse is true with respect to family incomes. Incomes of Black families may be somewhat higher because African American women are more likely than Indian women to be in the labor force. In either case, the difference between Blacks and Indians is less than one thousand dollars. The family incomes of Whites were about 70 percent higher than those of Blacks and Indians in 1989.

Health Insurance

Indians may be distinguished from other impoverished groups insofar as they have a special agency of the federal government established to provide for their health care, the IHS. Presumably, this should mean that Indians have universal access to health-care services. However, Cunningham (1996) analyzed data from a special sample of Indians and reported that access to health care is less universal for Indians than one might believe. Table 3.8 shows the close connection between health insurance and economic well-being among this sample of Indians. Relatively affluent (high-income) Indians (those living in families with incomes 400 percent or more above the official poverty level) do not rely heavily on the IHS for medical care. In 1987, only about 13 percent of these Indians depended solely on the IHS for health care; 72 percent were insured by private carriers or health maintenance organizations. Conversely, only 6.2 percent of poor Indians were covered by private insurance carriers. Among low-income Indians, 80 percent relied on public sources (IHS or other sources such as Medicare), and of those who depend on public sources, three-fourths depend on the IHS. The percentages in Table 3.8 reflect only persons who had some kind of health-care coverage and do not include persons for whom no coverage whatsoever was available. However, Cunningham (1996, 296–97) also reported that 43 percent of all Indians in his sample had less than full-year non-IHS coverage. In fact, less than one-fourth of all Indians in this survey reported that they had full-year coverage from a private insurance source. Cunningham (1996) also pointed out that 91 percent of those eligible for IHS care identified a regular source of health care, compared to 81.6 percent of the general U.S. population. However, almost one-third of the sampled population identified a non-IHS provider as their regular source of health care.

Among the sampled population in urban areas, 63.2 percent had a non-IHS source of health care; this was true for only 25.3 percent in nonmetropolitan areas with a relatively high population density and 6.3 percent of those living in areas of low population density. Among urban dwellers, 87.5 percent of those with private insurance, 74.5 percent of those with high incomes, and 74.8 percent living in areas with no IHS facility had a non-IHS source of care. Overall, the Indian sample used some health services somewhat less frequently than did the general U.S. population (approximately 82 percent versus 85.3 percent, respectively).

Cultural factors play a role that is difficult to assess and to quantify. Not only are indices of acculturation inexact, but also the process is continually changing and at different rates among different Indian populations. Not surprisingly, Indians whose primary language was not English were less likely to make a non-IHS visit; participants in tribal activities also made more visits to IHS facilities (Cun-

TABLE 3.8
*Family income and proportion of Indians with health
insurance coverage, 1987*

Family income	IHS only (%)		Other insurance (%)	
	All year	Part year	Private source	Public source[a]
Poor	60.0	13.8	6.2	20.0
Low	39.2	19.5	19.2	22.1
Middle	30.0	18.4	44.8	6.9
High	12.9	13.2	72.1	1.7

SOURCE: Cunningham 1996.
[a]Includes insurance such as Medicare.

ningham 1996). Cunningham concluded that, among those eligible for IHS care, many would be seriously underserved without the IHS-supported services. Further, the data suggest that Indians with other ambulatory coverage tend to supplement rather than supplant IHS-provided care. Cunningham (1996) observed that travel times to IHS facilities were actually less for those living in low-density rural areas than in other areas (other nonmetropolitan and metropolitan areas). As demographics continue to change, the challenge will be to ensure that a system is in place to serve Indians who have no recourse other than IHS-supported care.

Discussion

From the arrival of Europeans until the dawn of the twentieth century, the beliefs of many that Indians would disappear were well founded — the Indian population dwindled from perhaps as many as 5–7 million to as few as a quarter million in 1890. However, as the twentieth century progressed, the Indian population staged a surprising comeback. Throughout the first half of the twentieth century, growth of the Indian population gradually increased. Even with rising fertility and declining mortality rates, one would not have predicted the spectacular growth in the Indian population since 1950. In the second half of the twentieth century, the Indian population has increased five-fold, and, at least in the short term, there are few reasons to expect this trend to reverse.

The tremendous growth in numbers and complexity of the Indian population, coupled with the unique legal and political status accorded Indian tribes, requires health workers to increase their knowledge about the demography of this group. There are obvious and compelling reasons why a better understanding of Indian demography is essential for social scientists and policymakers alike — and perhaps even more so for Indians themselves.

The future vitality of the Indian population will depend on more than growth alone. Tribal leaders and others concerned with the future well-being of Indians must find innovative ways to provide for material needs and ensure the cultural survival of Indian people. As Indians move into the next century, meeting the many challenges of preserving cultural traditions and improving economic well-being, more than numbers alone, will be the foundation for sustaining the place of Indians within the mosaic of American society. Further, the dynamic shifts in Indian demography mandate corresponding changes in health-care delivery systems. This has not always been possible, with the result that a substantial proportion of the Indian population, while eligible for federal health services through the IHS, in fact reside in locations, such as metropolitan areas, outside the scope of the IHS and tribal programs. It is likely that detailed studies of different and shifting Indian populations will reveal distinctive health-care needs that will require special attention.

REFERENCES

Bernstein AR. 1991. *Indians and World War II: Toward a New Era in Indian Affairs.* Norman: University of Oklahoma Press.

Clinton L, Chadwick BA, Bahr HM. 1975. Urban relocation reconsidered: Antecedents of employment among Indian males. *Rural Sociology* 40:112–33.

Cunningham PJ. 1996. Health care utilization, expenditures, and insurance coverage for Indians and Alaska Natives eligible for the Indian Health Service. In: Sandefur GD, Rindfuss RR, Cohen B, eds. *Changing Numbers, Changing Needs: Indian Demography and Public Health,* 289–314. Washington, D.C.: National Academy Press.

Fixico DL. 1986. *Termination and Relocation: Federal Indian Policy, 1945–1960.* Norman: University of Oklahoma Press.

Gundlach JH, Roberts AE. 1978. Native Indian migration and relocation: Success or failure. *Pacific Sociol Rev* 12:117–28.

Hagan WT. 1979. *American Indians.* Chicago: University of Chicago Press.

Harris D. 1994. The 1990 Census count of American Indians: What do the numbers really mean? *Soc Sci Q* 75:580–93.

Indian Health Service. 1997. *Trends in Indian Health, 1997.* Rockville, Md.: Indian Health Service, Program Statistics Team.

Institute for Government Research. 1928. *The Problem of Indian Administration* [Meriam report]. Baltimore: Johns Hopkins Press.

Merrell J. 1989. *The Indian's New World: The Catawba and Their Neighbors from European Contact through the Period of Removal.* Chapel Hill: University of North Carolina Press.

O'Brien S. 1989. *American Indian Tribal Governments.* Norman: University of Oklahoma Press.

Passell JS. 1996. The growing American Indian population, 1960–1990: Beyond demography. In: Sandefur GD, Rindfuss RR, Cohen B, eds. *Changing Numbers, Changing*

Needs: American Indian Demography and Public Health, 79–102. Washington, D.C.: National Academy Press.

Prucha FP. 1984. *The Great Father.* Lincoln: University of Nebraska Press.

Snipp CM. 1989. *American Indians: The First of This Land.* New York: Russell Sage Foundation.

Snipp CM, Sandefur GD. 1988. Earnings of American Indians and Alaska Natives: The effects of residence and migration. *Soc Forces* 66:994–1008.

Sorkin AL. 1971. *American Indians and Federal Aid.* Washington, D.C.: Brookings Institution.

———. 1978. *The Urban Indian.* Lexington, Mass.: D. C. Heath.

Thornton R. 1987. *American Indian Holocaust and Survival.* Norman: University of Oklahoma Press.

Thornton R, Sandefur GD, Snipp CM. 1991. Indian fertility patterns, 1910 and 1940 to 1980: A research note. *American Indian Q* 15:359–67.

U.S. Bureau of the Census. 1915. *Indian Population of the United States and Alaska, 1910.* Washington, D.C.: Government Printing Office.

———. 1992. *General Population Characteristics, United States, 1990.* Washington, D.C.: Government Printing Office.

———. 1993. *Social and Economic Characteristics, United States, 1990.* Washington, D.C.: Government Printing Office.

Part II

The Political and
Administrative Bases
of Indian Health

4

Kirke Kickingbird, Esq., and
Everett R. Rhoades, M.D.

The Relation of Indian Nations
to the U.S. Government

The special political status of Indian tribes, the sovereign status of tribal governments, the treaty-making process under which the United States assumed certain responsibilities to tribal governments, and the resulting federal-Indian relationship continue to be powerful influences shaping health care for Indian people. To understand the complexity of Indian health programs, one must be familiar with the political and legal status of Indian tribes. Defining this special tribal political status and various attempts at clarification have resulted in an extraordinarily complex situation, marked often by ambiguity and sometimes by contradiction.

Congress acknowledged the unique character of its relationship with Indian tribes when it charged the secretary of the interior with compiling a published list of tribes with whom the U.S. government maintains a formal relationship. As a preamble to this statute, the *Federally Recognized Indian Tribe List Act of 1994,* Congress noted among its findings that "the United States has a trust responsibility to recognized Indian tribes, maintains a government-to-government relationship with those tribes, and recognizes the sovereignty of those tribes." The resulting dualities in tribal status of dependence under the trust relationship and political independence as governments are often in conflict and have not been completely resolved. Indeed, efforts to resolve the inherent paradoxes mark most intergovernmental discussions and negotiations. As a result, one finds that the most basic definitions of *Indian, tribe, nation,* and *eligibility* often remain ambiguous. Most often, they depend on legislative language devised for a specific, rather than a general, purpose. Further, the context of these considerations, and all relations between Native Americans and their fellow Americans, rests in the legal and political identity of the former.

In analyzing any issue affecting American Indians, including health, one must consider three key factors: (1) the concepts of tribal governments, (2) "Indian country" (which has special implications for Indian health, as noted in Chapter 6), and (3) tribal membership. Each of these is operative at any given time in essentially all Indian activities, especially those dealing with external organizations. A member of the U.S. Public Health Service once remarked that he found Indian health matters most intriguing because, on any given day, one might find oneself discussing the U.S. Constitution.

Who Is an Indian?

The term *Indian* is extraordinarily complex. The definition varies depending on several factors, especially which branch or agency of the federal government establishes the definition and for what purpose. Two considerations underlie the need to determine who is an Indian: (1) questions of legal, judicial, and administrative jurisdiction and (2) the identification of those for whom federal services are intended.

Cohen (1982), perhaps the most authoritative reference relating to Indian law, notes that Congress has invoked its power and defined Indian for a wide variety of purposes, including eligibility for social programs, jurisdiction in criminal matters, preferences in governmental hiring, and administration of tribal property. There is no single statute that defines *Indian* for all federal purposes (Cohen 1982, 23). However, Cohen lays out a rule that forms the general basis upon which most subsequent definitions depend and, indeed, serves as the basis for eligibility requirements for federally provided health services. According to this reference, an Indian may be defined as a "person meeting two qualifications: (a) that some of his ancestors lived in America before its discovery by Europeans, and (b) that the individual is recognized as an Indian by his or her tribe or community" (19–20). Another principle of increasing importance is that a definition of Indian may establish a test whereby a given individual is *excluded* from the scope of legislation dealing with Indians. This exclusionary concept, directed toward those *not* eligible for services intended for Indians, is commonly overlooked but fundamental. In fact, it is the basis for virtually all rules of eligibility. That is, eligibility is not necessarily intended to determine only those for whom benefits are to be granted but is also intended to determine those for whom benefits are not.

Although legislation early in the nation's history, such as the Indian Trade and Intercourse Act of 1790 and its revised versions, often failed to define *Indian,* it ultimately became necessary to define what is meant by the term. The definition contained in the *Indian Reorganization Act of 1934* gives some idea of the complexity involved: The term *Indian* "shall include all persons of Indian descent who are members of any recognized Indian tribe now under Federal jurisdiction, and all persons who are descendants of such members who were, on June 1, 1934, residing within the present boundaries of any Indian reservation, and shall further include all other persons of one-half or more Indian blood. For the purposes of said sections, Eskimos and other aboriginal peoples of Alaska shall be considered Indians. The term tribe wherever used in said sections shall be construed to refer to any Indian tribe, organized band, pueblo, or the Indians residing on one reservation." The question of the degree of Indian blood possessed by an individual, as mentioned in the Indian Reorganization Act, is one of the most difficult to resolve and continues to be of intense concern. Other terms, such as *recognized tribes, Indian descent, Indian blood, Indian tribe,* and *federal jurisdiction,* remain pertinent but incompletely settled today.

Of additional importance for the provision of health services, the U.S. Indian population is divided into two major tribal categories: federally recognized and non–federally recognized. The designation *federally recognized tribe* refers to a tribe that, at some point in the past, had a formal political relationship with the U.S. government by treaty, agreement, act of Congress, executive order, court decision, or administrative rule (Cohen 1982, 6). A *non–federally recognized tribe* is one with which the U.S. government does not acknowledge a political relationship (Cohen 1982). The primary consequence of federal recognition is that services, assistance, and funds are available to recognized tribes through the Bureau of Indian Affairs (BIA) and the Indian Health Service (IHS). Federally recognized tribes are also eligible for certain other federal funds on the same basis as states. According to the BIA, as of November 13, 1996, there were 554 federally recognized tribes, including 223 Alaska Native villages (Indian Entities 1998). Controversy over which tribes are eligible for federal services led Congress to pass the Federally Recognized Indian Tribe List Act of 1994. Under this act the secretary of interior is charged with the responsibility to publish in the *Federal Register* a list of all Indian tribes recognized by the secretary to be eligible for the special programs and services provided by the United States to Indians because of their status as Indians (25 CFR, Part 83).

The U.S. Congress has defined Indian tribes in many laws, generally applying the definition in the Indian Reorganization Act of 1934. For example, the *Indian Self-Determination and Education Assistance Act* (1975) defines an Indian tribe as follows: "Indian tribe means any Indian tribe, band, nation, or other organized group or community, including any Alaska Native village or regional or village corporation as defined in or established pursuant to the Alaska Native Claim Settlement Act (85 Stat. 688) which is recognized as eligible for the special programs and services provided by the United States to Indians because of their status as Indians."

Generally, only Indians who are members of federally recognized tribes are eligible for the special educational, health, or other social services established under treaties or legislation. The *Indian Health Care Improvement Act* (1976) provided this definition: "Indians or Indian, unless otherwise designated, means any person who is a member of an Indian tribe." Tribes themselves establish criteria for tribal membership under tribal law. Although the federal government can establish criteria for eligibility for federal services, the government generally relies on tribal membership as its primary criterion. However, it is entirely possible to be an Indian by ethnicity but not meet tribal membership criteria. For example, a woman member of the Santa Clara Pueblo married a Navajo man, with whom she bore children. By virtue of the fact that tribal enrollment of children was limited to those whose father was a member of the Pueblo, the children were denied membership in the tribe (*Santa Clara Pueblo v. Martinez* 1978). Similar variations for tribal membership are distributed among the many tribes.

Tribal Sovereignty

Throughout the history of the New World, Indians have had to contend with foreign laws. However, these laws often affirmed the special nature of Indian tribes, and attention was often given to Indian tribal customs. One example is the Spanish *New Laws of the Indies* issued in 1542 (Friede and Keen 1971). Over four hundred years later in 1978, the U.S. Supreme Court took a remarkably similar view: "Issues likely to arise in a civil context, will frequently depend on questions of tribal tradition and custom which tribal forums may be in a better position to evaluate than federal courts" (*Santa Clara Pueblo v. Martinez* 1978). These are not isolated examples; among the English shortly after 1600, a system of legal safeguards developed to assure Indians of at least minimal human rights (Trelease 1960; Kickingbird 1976).

More significantly, perhaps, European governments negotiated treaties with the Indians — a practice followed by Great Britain, its New World colonies, and the new U.S. government (Kappler 1904). The more than eight hundred treaties so executed by the colonies and the United States are ample testimony to the recognition of tribal sovereignty. Treaties executed between the United States and various Indian tribes, beginning in 1778 with the Delaware, form the basis for essentially all of the complex Indian law that followed (Kappler 1904; Kickingbird et al. 1980). Treaty making did not *create* tribal governments; it was a means by which the United States *recognized* tribal political identity (*Washington v. Washington State Commercial Passenger Fishing Association* 1979).

See Chapter 5 for a discussion of the point of view that, insofar as many treaty provisions formed the basis for federal responsibility for Indian health,

Indian nations therefore purchased a prepaid health care plan with cession of their lands. Currently, federal Indian law has grown into a mass of statutes, treaties, and thousands of judicial and administrative rulings that have resulted from disputes over what the numerous statutes and treaties mean or require the federal government to do (25 U.S. Code, Indians).

The resulting relationship between Indian nations and the United States is unique in a number of respects. The Commerce Clause of the U.S. Constitution recognizes Indian tribes as one of the governments with whom Congress could regulate trade (Article I, Section 8, Clause 3, U.S. Constitution). The Apportionment Clause provides that Indians not taxed were not counted as part of the state population, indicating that the Indians were outside the political jurisdiction of the states and the United States (Article I, Section 2). Persons unfamiliar with federal Indian law have often concluded that the Constitutional distinction about Indians is of a racial nature. This is not the case. The Supreme Court noted that the distinction was political rather than racial in nature (*Morton v. Mancari* 1973). Indian tribes are distinct political entities — governments with executive, legislative, and judicial powers. Members of tribes are citizens of both their Indian nation and the United States, a fact that has contributed to jurisdictional conflicts. The distinction between the ethnic and political natures of Indians represents another duality that is sometimes the source of confusion. There is no question about the importance of the special genetic, social-cultural, and ethnic Indian characteristics for understanding biomedical phenomena. However, dealing with Indians on a government-to-government basis is political and has little, if anything, to do with ethnicity. In any case, the dominant factor in much of Indian life, affecting the nature of health-care delivery, clearly derives from the sovereignty possessed by tribes and the resulting government-to-government relationship between them and the federal government.

The concept of tribal sovereignty, with its long historical development, was confirmed by the U.S. Supreme Court as early as the 1830s. The sharing of coterminous geography between the Cherokee Nation and the state of Georgia naturally led to conflicts, especially of jurisdiction. The Cherokee Nation sought to prohibit the state from enforcing laws within the boundaries of the Cherokee Nation, asserting that Georgia's laws would eliminate the Cherokees as a political society and seize, for the use of Georgia, the lands of the nation, which had been assured to them by the United States in solemn treaties repeatedly made and still in force (*Cherokee Nation v. Georgia* 1831). The Court noted that the relationship between Indians and the United States is perhaps unlike that of any other two people in existence. Further, while noting that the Cherokee Nation had many characteristics of a foreign nation, the court concluded that tribes residing within the acknowledged boundaries of the United States should more correctly, perhaps, be denominated *domestic dependent nations*. This characterization of sovereign, yet dependent, tribes contributes to the ongoing ambiguity with which tribes are from time to time considered. Interestingly, in its conclusion, the Supreme Court found that the Cherokee Nation had rights and powers of its own as a government, but the Court declined to hear the case on technical grounds of jurisdiction.

Not surprisingly, the Court was faced with a related case the following year. The state of Georgia sentenced a White man, Samuel Worcester, to four years in the penitentiary after he was found guilty of residing within the limits of the Cherokee Nation without a Georgia license, which required an oath of allegiance to the state. Mr. Worcester asserted that the Georgia statute was unconstitutional and sued for redress. The Supreme Court, finding in favor of Mr. Worcester, concluded: "The Cherokee Nation, then, is a distinct community, occupying its own territory, with boundaries accurately described, in which the laws of Georgia can have no force, and which the citizens of Georgia have no right to enter, but with the assent of the Cherokees themselves." The Court went on to state: "The very fact of repeated treaties with them recognized [the Indians' right to self-government] and the settled doctrine of the law of nations is that a weaker power does not surrender its independence — its right to self government — by associating with a stronger, and taking its protection" (*Worcester v. Georgia* 1832). From this foundation the federal courts have regularly concluded that Indian tribes have all the powers of self-government of any sovereign nation except insofar as those powers may be modified by treaty or limited by an act of Congress (House Conference Report 1991).

When critics complained that Indian tribes were not nations in the European sense, the Court responded: "The words 'treaty' and 'nation' are words of our language, selected in our diplomatic and legislative proceedings, by ourselves, having each a definite and well understood meaning. We have applied them to Indians as we have applied them to other nations of the earth. They are applied to all in the same sense" (*Worcester v. Georgia* 1832). It is important to recognize that powers lawfully vested in an Indian tribe are not, in general, delegated powers granted by Congress but are, rather, inherent powers of a limited sovereignty that has never been extinguished.

The question of the duration of the resulting governmental relationship has never been finally resolved. In *Worcester v. Georgia*, Justice McClean pointed out,

But the inquiry may be made, is there no end to the exercise of this (e.g. tribal) power over Indians within the limits of a state, by the general government? The answer is that, in its nature, it must be limited by circumstances. . . . If a tribe of Indians shall become so degraded or reduced in numbers, as to lose the power of self-government, the protection of the local law, of necessity, must be extended over them. . . . The exercise of the power of self-government by the Indians, within a state, is undoubtedly contemplated to be temporary. . . . At best they can enjoy a very limited independence within the boundaries of a state, and such a residence must always subject them to encroachments from the settlements around them; and their existence within a state, as a separate and independent community, may seriously embarrass or obstruct the operation of the state laws. If, therefore, it would be inconsistent with the political welfare of the states, and the social advance of their citizens, that an independent and permanent power should exist within their limits, this power must give way to the greater power which surrounds it, or seek its exercise beyond the sphere of state authority.

While there is no basis for predicting that its duration will be permanent, over the last three decades Congress has repeatedly reaffirmed its recognition of the special relationship and the sovereign status of tribal governments in the Indian Health Care Improvement Act (1976), Indian Health Care Amendments Act (1980), Indian Alcohol and Substance Abuse Prevention and Treatment Act (1986), and Indian Tribal Justice Act (1993). As governments, Indian tribes have the general power to (1) make laws governing the conduct of persons, including non-Indians, in Indian country; (2) establish bodies such as tribal police and courts to enforce the laws and administer justice; (3) exclude or remove nonmembers from the reservation for cause; and (4) regulate hunting and fishing, land use, and environmental protection (Powers of Indian Tribes 1934; Indian Tribal Justice Act 1993; Indian Civil Rights Act Amendments 1990). However, the power to control Indian affairs remains shared between the federal government and Indian Nations, to the exclusion of the states. Many of these diverse, complicated, and sometimes conflicting elements may, at any given time, impinge on the design and implementation of health programs.

The Federal-Indian Trust Relationship

One of the most important doctrines of federal Indian law is the *trust* relationship. The relationship was not created by a single document, nor is its scope defined in any one place. The U.S. Congress's American Indian Policy Review Commission in 1977 defined the relationship as "an established legal obligation which requires the United States to protect and enhance Indian trust resources and tribal self-government, and to provide economic and social programs necessary to raise the standard of living and social well-being of the Indian people to a level comparable to the non-Indian society" (American Indian Policy Review Commission 1977).

Generally speaking, the trust responsibility of the United States is the duty to assist Indians in the protection of their property and rights, the underlying purpose being the continued survival of Indian tribes as self-governing entities. The federal courts have confirmed that the U.S. Congress is the ultimate trustee, which means that *Congress is the only federal entity that may define the scope of the federal trusteeship.* While Congress has placed major trust responsibilities in the Department of Interior, it also has delegated certain duties to other government agencies. The official relationship is between the U.S. Congress and tribal governments, and there are three broad areas in which the trust duties of the United States fall: (1) protection of Indian trust property, (2) protection of the Indian right to self-government, and (3) provision of those social, medical, and educational services necessary for survival of the tribes (American Indian Policy Review Commission 1977, 131).

In protecting Indian property, the United States must meet the stringent standards of good faith and diligence. These standards apply to the federal government in the management of and accounting for monies in Indian trust funds. They also apply to the protection and management of Indian lands and natural resources. The United States' duties toward Indian governments include, for example, an obligation to assist Indians with legal representation, resist taxation of Indian trust resources by the states or other infringements by non-Indians, prevent waste or destruction of resources, and help develop use and management plans (American Indian Policy Review Commission 1977, 136). The application of the trust doctrine to health care is less clear than to, say, natural resources and trust funds. Nevertheless, the Congress regularly admonishes the IHS that its responsibilities are trust responsibilities.

The trust relationship is intimately associated with another concept that also dates back to early Supreme Court cases. While acknowledging tribal sovereignty in *Cherokee Nation v. Georgia* (1831), the Court also stated that the relation of an Indian to the United States "resembles that of a ward to his guardian." Indeed, the Court held that, since the Cherokee tribe was a ward of the federal government, encroachment by the state of Georgia on the Cherokee tribe had the effect of invasion of the United States. This language played a major role in establishing the federal government as trustee for the tribes it had just declared sovereign nations. Subsequent decisions further supported the concept of Indians as wards of the federal government. In *United States v. Kagama* (1886), the Supreme Court noted: "These Indian tribes are the wards of the nation."

The conflict between wardship and trust status on the one hand and self-determination, self-governance, and sovereignty on the other is obvious. Many of the frustrating positions of the BIA and IHS arise directly from these contradictory, or at least conflicting, concepts. Generally, most Indians reject the designation *"ward" of the federal government* while clinging strongly to the concept of the trust responsibilities of the federal government. Among the several dilemmas facing Indian people, this dual situation of sovereignty and self-governance versus trusteeship by the federal government is one of the most fundamental.

That such contradictions have not been satisfactorily resolved is illustrated by the language in the report of the Presidential Commission on Indian Reservation Economies (1984): "The Bureau of Indian Affairs operates in a schizophrenic manner because it has conflicting goals. It is charged with the responsibility of managing all Indian affairs and it is charged with Indian self-determination which seeks to place the management function at the local tribal level. An organization cannot carry out goals which are in conflict with each other." Congress, while pressing for self-determination for Indian tribes, has never made clear the residual responsibilities of either the BIA or the IHS. This single factor more than any other is responsible for the often bizarre policies and regulations of both agencies.

The Movement toward Self-Determination

Indian tribes in the United States continue to function as permanent, ongoing political institutions exercising the basic powers of government necessary to fulfill the needs of their tribal members. There has been a gradual but continual movement in the direction of increased tribal sovereignty with less emphasis on federal executive direction. This movement since at least 1975 has been referred to as *self-determination*.

The Congress has made several attempts to strengthen the sovereignty of tribes. The Indian Reorganization Act of 1934 provided for greater self-governance of tribes and sought to create a situation in which Indian tribes and their citizens could achieve greater independence from the federal government. Although the era of Indian self-determination may be said to have begun with the Indian Reorganization Act, it obtained its real impetus with the 1970 Indian Policy Statement of President Nixon (Nixon 1970). In that statement he called for tribal self-determination and tribal control and operation of federal programs, which were to be achieved with the following actions:

— Repeal of House Concurrent Resolution 108 declaring termination as policy
— Granting tribal control and operation of federal programs
— Restoration of the sacred lands of Taos Pueblo at Blue Lake
— Economic development through the Indian Financing Act
— Increase in financial support for the Indian Health Service
— Assistance for urban Indians
— Establishment of the Indian Trust Counsel Authority
— Establishment of an assistant secretary for Indian affairs

Following that lead, Congress soon passed the Indian Self-Determination and Education Assistance Act (1975). In addition to reiterating the federal government's recognition of tribal sovereignty, this act was intended to strengthen tribal governments by directing the BIA and IHS to turn over to the tribes management of most of the services administered by these agencies, upon formal request by the various tribes. Only three narrow grounds for declination were permitted: (1) if the services provided were not beneficial to tribal members; (2) if a given tribe was deemed incapable of managing the program (in which case the agency was to provide the assistance necessary for the tribe to become capable); and (3) if the trust responsibility were diminished.

The self-determination process, lofty in its goal, suffered from two serious impediments. The agencies were to make available to the tribes an amount of funding that would have been expended by the respective secretary (of Interior or Health and Human Services) for the same program. However, adequate funding to provide for the increased costs was not forthcoming. The underlying assumption that funds would move to the tribes as the BIA or IHS shrank was not in accordance with the reality of increased costs inherent in loss of economies of scale nor with expanding needs for tribes choosing *not* to contract.

Second, an even more intractable difficulty was the fact that the only feasible mechanism for transferring operation of the programs was through government contracting. All parties recognized that the cumbersome government contracting process was not suitable for such a purpose. Indeed, it was a major continuing source of frustration and ultimately led to attempts to move toward an entirely different mechanism.

Self-Governance

In an effort to deal with continuing dissatisfaction with the contracting process on all sides and to move yet further toward self-determination, Congress amended Public Law 93-638 and established the concept of *self-governance* (Tribal Self-Governance Demonstration Project 1988). Self-governance began as a demonstration program limited to 10 tribes in the BIA, later extended to the IHS. There seems to have been no real intention that it be a demonstration project, and in 1995 Congress made the program permanent for the BIA. Under self-governance, Congress has attempted to correct the frustrations inherent in contracting by implementing a new mechanism: the compact. Compacts are designed to avoid the onerous negotiations and the inherently dependent nature of the contractor. However, once again, Congress failed to make clear what responsibilities remained with the agencies. While granting tribes the authority to fashion their own programs, Congress continued to insert language stating that the trust responsibility of the agency must be maintained. It is too early to predict the ultimate outcome of self-governance. However, the uneasy and uncertain relationship between the tribes and the federal government continues, with much dissatisfaction on both sides.

Discussion

The principle overriding Indian health care on a daily basis is the sovereign nature of Indian tribes. The many legal, judicial, and administrative ramifications of this sovereignty have combined to create a most complex and dynamic situation. Basic definitions of such terms as *Indian, tribe, jurisdiction,* and *government-to-government* remain incompletely resolved. The long, tortuous, and complex series of interactions between Indians and the federal government is almost always reducible to the opposing concepts of sovereignty and the granting of ever more autonomy to tribes, on the one hand, and the requirements of the federal trust responsibility, on the other. This paradox has had and continues to have a substantial effect on the design and implementation of health programs. The situation is made more complex by the great and increasing disparity among the tribes with respect to the degree that they may wish to assume management of their programs. Many tribes believe that an expression of their own self-determination is a decision to continue to receive services from the federal government. This concept seems to be receiving less support with the considerable acceleration toward self-governance and the downsizing of the federal government.

The ultimate outcome of these various complexities for the health of Indian people is as yet unclear. It is unreasonable to expect that these paradigm shifts will be entirely free of costs or adverse consequences for at least some tribes. The Congress, with its plenary powers, is the only body capable of clarifying the relationship between the tribes and the federal government. Until this is done, there will be continued frustration, confusion, and occasional chaos.

Since the 1950s, tribes have had an ever-present concern that their special government-to-government relationship could be terminated. This is a fear that has historical justification and is at the center of much of the intensely held desire of Indian people that their special trust relationship be recognized and strengthened in virtually every activity of the federal government. Congress has taken steps to repudiate the earlier termination policy through the Indian Self-Determination Act Amendments of 1988. It has prefaced many of the legislative activities affecting tribal governments in the last three decades with pledges to maintain the trust responsibilities and recognize the inherent power of tribal governments. Indian governments must be equally as bold in charting their future course, whether they are addressing fundamental issues of government or the specific health needs of their tribal members.

REFERENCES

American Indian Policy Review Commission. 1977. 95th Cong, 1st sess, Final Report (Committee Print).
Cherokee Nation v. Georgia, 30 U.S. 1 (1831).
Cohen F. 1982. *Handbook of Federal Indian Law.* Charlottesville, Va.: Michie Co.
Federally Recognized Indian Tribe List Act of 1994, U.S. Code, vol 25, sec 479a (1997).
Friede J, Keen B. 1971. *Bartolome De Las Casas in History: Toward Understanding of the Man and His Work,* 131. DeKalb: Northern Illinois University Press.
Indian Alcohol and Substance Abuse Prevention and Treatment Act of 1986, U.S. Code, vol 25, sec 2401.
Indian Civil Rights Act Amendments of 1990, U.S. Code, vol 25, sec 1301(2) (1990).
Indian Entities. 1998. List of federally recognized American Indian tribes. *Federal Register* 63 (December 30):71941.
Indian Health Care Amendments Act of 1980, U.S. Code, vol 25, sec 1601, note (1997).
Indian Health Care Improvement Act of 1976, U.S. Code, vol 25, sec 1601 (1997).
Indian Reorganization Act of 1934, U.S. Code, vol 25, secs 461, 479 (1934).
Indian Self-Determination and Education Assistance Act, U.S. Code, vol 25, sec 450 (1975).
Indian Trade and Intercourse Act of 1790, U.S. Code, vol 25, sec 177 (1997).
Indian Tribal Justice Act of 1993, U.S. Code, vol 25, sec 3601 (1997).
Kappler C. 1904. *Indian Laws and Treaties.* 2d ed. Vol 2. Washington, D.C.: Government Printing Office.
Kickingbird K. 1976. In our image . . . , after our likeness: The drive for assimilation of Indian court systems. *Am Criminal Law Rev* 675:13.
Kickingbird K, Kickingbird L, Skibine AT, et al. 1980. *Indian Treaties,* 2. Washington, D.C.: Institute for the Development of Indian Law.
Morton v. Mancari, 417 U.S. 535, 553n. 24 (1973).
Nixon RM. 1970. Special message of the president of the United States to the Congress, July 8. In: *Public Papers of the Presidents,* 564. Washington, D.C.: Government Printing Office.
Powers of Indian Tribes, 55 I.D. 14 (1934).
Presidential Commission on Indian Reservation Economies, Executive Office of the President. 1984. Report and Recommendations to the President of the United States, November.
Santa Clara Pueblo v. Martinez, 436 U.S. 49 (1978).
Trelease A. 1960. *Indian Affairs in Colonial New York,* 185. Ithaca: Cornell University Press.
Tribal Self-Governance Demonstration Project, U.S. Code, vol 25, sec 458aa (1988).
25 CFR, Part 83, Procedures for Establishing That an American Indian Group Exists as an Indian Tribe. Section 83.5, Duties of the Department.

U.S. Congress. House Conference Report. 1991. 102d Cong, 1st sess, H.R. Conf. Rep. 261, 3–4.

Washington v. Washington State Commercial Passenger Fishing Association, 443 U.S. 658 (1979).

Worcester v. Georgia, 31 U.S. (6 pet) 515, pp. 559–61 (1832).

5

Emery A. Johnson, M.D., M.P.H., and
Everett R. Rhoades, M.D.

The History and Organization
of Indian Health Services
and Systems

Early Efforts

The development of federal health care for Indian people underwent a gradual evolution throughout the nineteenth and first half of the twentieth centuries. In the early 1800s, while administration of Indian affairs was based in the Department of War, Indians near forts were provided such episodic care as military physicians might offer. Not surprisingly, given smallpox's epidemic nature and the availability of a highly effective preventive, smallpox vaccination was among the first organized health-care efforts. The fact that vaccination of Indians was an important public health measure provided an added incentive to render this care to Indian persons. In 1832, the Congress directed that $12,000 be provided for smallpox immunizations (Bennett 1958). Four years later, the federal government began a program providing health services and physicians to the Ottawa and Chippewa tribes (Sorkin 1971).

In 1849, the jurisdiction of Indian affairs was transferred from the Department of War to the Department of Interior. In subsequent decades, the federal government gradually assumed increasing obligations to provide health care, usually a physician and medications, to tribes. By 1880, the federal government operated four hospitals and employed 77 physicians for the care of Indians. Early support for health was often made available from education funds, emphasizing the desirability of providing health care to students (Bennett 1958). The first separate funding specifically for Indian health ($40,000) was identified in an appropriation act in 1911.

The cession of most of the lands of the United States by the Indians, codified in hundreds of treaties, forms the basis for the federal government's provision of health care to Indians and for the intensely held belief that these services are not provided free. Many treaties identified health services (and certain other considerations) as part of the federal government's payment for Indian land. In effect, the tribal leaders indeed paid in advance for health services for their people, the premium being paid in the form of the land. As a result, members of Indian tribes have a prepaid health program, and the federal government has the obligation to continue its payment (provision of health services to Indians).

While the relationship between the government of the United States and Indian tribal governments is extremely complex, there is a rather simple way to explain the federal provision of Indian health programs. Indian treaties were contracts between the federal and tribal governments. As in any contract, valuable considerations were exchanged; the Indian tribes gave up their land in return for payments and/or services from the U.S. government.

The Snyder Act and Transfer of Programs to the Public Health Service, 1921–1955

On November 2, 1921, the Snyder Act (42 Stat. 208), passed by the Congress to provide continuing authority for federal Indian programs, identified "relief of distress and conservation of health of Indians" as one of the federal functions. However, funding was always a problem, as was the recruitment and retention of physicians and other health professionals. The health status of Indians remained poor, with high infant mortality and excessive deaths from infectious diseases, particularly diarrhea, pneumonia, and tuberculosis. Diseases of little importance to the general population created major problems for Indians. For example, trachoma, an infectious disease of the eye that can cause severe disability and even blindness, was rampant in many Indian communities; in some schools, as many as 95 percent of the children were infected.

Several studies of the status of Indian health were made, including those by the Institute for Government Research (1928), the Hoover Commission (1948), and the American Medical Association (Moorman 1949). Based on these studies, efforts were made to transfer the Indian health program from the Bureau of Indian Affairs to the Public Health Service (PHS). Public Law 83-568, enacted in 1954, provided for the transfer of all functions of the secretary of the interior relating to the conservation of the health of Indians to the surgeon general of the PHS. It was anticipated that improved funding and more efficient operations would result from expertise within the PHS and its relationships with state and local health authorities. The transfer took place on July 1, 1955, when about 2,500 health program personnel of the BIA, along with 48 hospitals and 130 health centers and school infirmaries, came under the jurisdiction of the newly created Indian Health Service (IHS) (named the Division of Indian Health until 1968).

The history of the IHS from the time of the 1955 transfer may be divided into three phases: (1) establishment of the clinical base; (2) emphasis on management, training, and research; and (3) transition to Indian control of health services. None of these divisions is exclusive; they are arbitrary, and elements of the three will be found in each phase. The IHS has always had a broad definition of health—"optimum physical, mental and social well-being, not just the absence of disease" (Johnson 1985, 13). Therefore, when IHS refers to high-quality health services, it includes not just hospital and medical services, but also preventive services, community and social well-being, and environmental improvements.

Phase I: Establishing Basic Clinical Services, 1955–1962

At the time of the transfer, conditions in Indian health facilities were marginal at best. For example, in one hospital where necessary major surgery was performed, there were no laboratory provisions for hemoglobin or hematocrit determinations or for blood counts, let alone for blood chemistries or blood gas determinations (E. Johnson, pers. comm., 1999). The Committee on Appropriations of the House of Representatives, 84th Congress, directed PHS to make a comprehensive survey of Indian health. The PHS established a survey team, including experts from academia and state health departments as well as from the PHS, and, over the next year, this team conducted an extensive survey of Indian health, including in-depth studies of nine reservations. The results of this study were transmitted to the Congress in 1957 as *Health Services for American Indians* (U.S. Department of Health, Education and Welfare [USDHEW] 1957, 174). The conclusions of the study were summarized in the following major points:

1. A substantial Federal Indian health program will be required until gross deficiencies among Indians have been corrected. . . .
2. All plans for increased utilization of community health resources should be developed in cooperation with the Indians and the community, and will need to be on a reservation-by-reservation basis;
3. Federal Indian health program operations should be planned in light of the adequacy of community resources, and the services available to Indians under State and local programs;
4. Efforts should be made to increase State and local community recognition of obligations and responsibilities to Indian residents on a nondiscriminatory basis.

The cost of this program, to be reached in 5 to 10 years, was estimated to be between $60 and $65 million. The operating budget of the IHS reached that estimated level in 1965 ($62.9 million). It subsequently has expanded to $2.24 billion in fiscal year 1999. An additional $45 million would be required for construction and repair of hospitals, clinics, and staff housing, and another $29 million would be needed for construction of sanitation facilities for Indian homes and communities. The report of that study provided an excellent foundation, clearly establishing a baseline of health status indicators and projections with which to compare the actual experience of the succeeding four decades.

The first director of IHS, the remarkable Dr. James R. Shaw, recognized the importance of health statistics and built on this baseline. For those statistics not collected by the National Center for Health Statistics (NCHS), Shaw established a professional unit to provide specialized reports on Indian health (e.g., morbidity statistics, hospital and clinic use data). As a result, there are now four decades of comparable and objective data with which to evaluate changes in Indian health.

The first priority of IHS, then, was to establish reasonably competent and high-quality medical care. Extensive recruitment of health professionals, remodeling and renovation of health facilities, and establishment of clinical laboratories, radiologic services, and surgical teams were undertaken. Funds were obtained to pay for consultation with private physicians and for hospitalization in community hospitals when appropriate care was not available in Indian health facilities. Preventive services included immunizations, prenatal and well-baby care, control of tuberculosis, and environmental sanitation. Notable was the passage of the 1959 Indian Sanitation Facilities Construction Act (P.L. 86-121), which enabled IHS to build, upon request of the Indian community, facilities for the provision of safe water and sanitary waste disposal.

Phase II: Expanding Management, Training, and Research, 1963–1969

With progress being made in establishing basic health services during the first phase, IHS emphasis shifted to concerns for health program management, including comprehensive health planning, health professional and health occupations training for Indians, and formal health management training for IHS administrators. A system of planning based on objective problem delineation, identification of factors that could be modified, consideration of alternative actions, and selection of the most appropriate alternatives became a way of life in IHS. The American Management Association was engaged both to advise IHS in management and to provide specific training to IHS officials. Medical and dental residencies and training programs for nursing, nutrition and dietetics, environmental health, and dental and other health professions and occupations were established, including training for new types of health workers, such as physician's assistants. A major training center, Desert Willow (near Tucson, Ariz.), was established primarily to train community health representatives (CHRs) but soon became the focal point for a variety of training activities — specific skills training leading to new or expanded functions of health workers; management training for health professionals, including training in epidemiology and in health planning; training for tribal leaders in health planning, health program management, and other management skills; and health-related training for Peace Corps volunteers.

Health services research in IHS was also initiated during this phase, leading to the establishment of the Health Programs Systems Center (HPSC) on the San Xavier reservation near Tucson in 1967. The purpose of HPSC was to apply systems analysis to the functioning of the IHS health-care delivery system with the expectation that new technology and new methods would enable IHS to provide more cost-effective and efficient health service. Some of the first studies of the application of telemedicine were carried out here. In 1971, HPSC became a component of a new organizational unit of IHS, the Office of Research and Development (ORD). The basic mission of ORD was to increase the efficiency and effectiveness of the Service Units and to expand the participation of the Indian community in managing its health affairs.

Phase III: Transition to Indian Community Control, 1970 to the Present

The beginning of this transition had its roots in the establishment of the CHR program in 1965, when tribes, for the first time, were able to assume direct management of IHS-funded health-care delivery programs. However, the real turning point came with President Nixon's Indian Policy Statement of July 8, 1970, which was to have the most significant effect on federal-Indian relations since the end of the treaty-making era. The president noted that federal-Indian relations were based on the U.S. Constitution and on treaties between the U.S. government and the governments of Indian tribes — a government-to-government relationship. He stated that the United States honored its treaties and that this relationship was to be maintained. He further advanced the concept of tribal "self-determination," proposing that federal programs provided to tribes be "taken over" and managed by the tribal governments. The Congress, with the support of most Indian tribes, passed the Indian Self-Determination and Education Assistance Act (P.L. 93-638) in 1975. That act established President Nixon's policy of the government-to-government relationship in law and provided that any Indian tribal government could, on request, take over the operation of any BIA or IHS function. The BIA and the IHS could decline to enter into a self-determination agreement only on three specific and narrow grounds: if the services provided by the tribes resulted in harm to individuals (virtually impossible to gauge), if the particular tribe did not have the capacity to manage the program (in which case the federal agencies were to provide the technical assistance necessary to correct any deficiencies), and, notably, if the existing trust responsibility of the federal government were disturbed.

As the tribes gained more understanding of the options available to them, the movement toward tribal management accelerated. As of October 1, 1996, tribes were operating 12 of 49 hospitals and 379 of 492 ambulatory facilities, including 134 health centers, 4 school health centers, 73 health stations, and 168 Alaska Village clinics. Almost all tribes were providing at least some of their own health services (e.g., CHR or Alaska Native community health aide programs), and many were operating significant ambulatory health and preventive health service programs. Many tribes exercise full authority over governmental functions as well as over health, social services, and educational functions.

Although the tribes were initially cautious in assuming operating responsibility, they readily accepted the opportunity to do their own health planning, an important concept included in the second landmark legislation following President Nixon's Indian policy statement, the 1976 Indian Health Care Improvement Act (P.L. 94-437). In this legislation, Congress established two major national goals: to ensure that the health status of Indian people is elevated to the highest possible level and to achieve the maximum participation of Indian people in Indian health programs. The act specified a "benefit package" of health services—inpatient and outpatient care, dental services, preventive health services, mental health and alcohol treatment programs—and established high standards for their delivery.

Public Law 94-437 provided for several important innovations. It authorized the establishment of a personnel-development program built around scholarship support for preparatory and graduate education in several health disciplines, with emphasis on American Indian and Alaska Native students. It authorized appropriations designed to bring the level of health services of Indian people up to that of the rest of the country and for the construction of Indian health facilities and sanitation systems for Indian homes and communities. It provided that the IHS could be reimbursed through the Medicare and Medicaid programs for care rendered to Indians eligible for services under these programs. Funds generated were to be placed in a special account and used for acquiring and maintaining accreditation of the various facilities. Finally, Public Law 94-437 authorized limited support for services to Indians residing in urban areas.

The Strategic Design of IHS Programs

With a clear mandate from the Congress to do more than just provide medical care but, more significantly, also to eliminate the disparity between the health status of Indian people and that of the general U.S. population (USDHEW 1957; P.L. 94-437, Sec. 3), IHS efforts were directed toward developing an efficient and effective health-care delivery system and promoting American Indian and Alaska Native participation in and management of their own health-care systems. As a result, the IHS, over the years, has developed a system of primary care designed to accomplish the following:

— Provide accessible care to each Indian individual, family, and community
— Provide levels of health services competence depending on the size of the population, its geographical circumstances (e.g., isolation), and the health facilities available (e.g., hospital, health center, or clinic)
— Use a team approach to health care, with care initiated by the health-care practitioner who first encounters the patient. This practitioner may be the Alaska Native community health aide (ANCHA), who provides diagnosis and treatment for a limited range of health problems before referring the patient to more highly skilled health professionals; the CHR, who can provide health education, first aid, outreach, and referral; the public health nurse (PHN) in the patient's home; or the clinic nurse or the physician in the field clinic. Alternatively, the patient may present to the outpatient department of the hospital or to the health center, where appropriate medical services will be provided. This provides that the entire *system,* rather than an individual provider, is available to minister to the "whole patient."
— Provide for all levels of acute and chronic health care and preventive and environmental health services, as well as providing staff ranging from paraprofessionals to highly trained medical specialists, including specialists and hospitals under the Contract Health Services program
— Ensure the highest quality of services. This requires regular evaluations, ranging from baseline statistics to continuous collection of disease morbidity/mortality, workload, and demographic information on American Indians and Alaska Natives. It also requires provision of management and health services by appropriately trained individuals and emphasis upon employing local indigenous health providers and managers. Quality of

health care is defined by the highest professional standards, including the Joint Commission on Accreditation of Health Care Organizations, the American Academy of Pediatrics, the American College of Obstetrics and Gynecology, and others. Training of IHS and tribal health workers is provided to meet the relevant standards of accrediting bodies. When such standards are not available, IHS has developed its own set of standards to ensure quality.

—Promote community participation through Indian involvement in planning, evaluation, and operations ranging from health committees involved in information exchange to health delivery systems entirely managed by Indian tribal governments or organizations. The process of involving tribes at all levels began with tribal health committees, who met with the health staff to learn together about the community's health problems, and continued with support for tribal governments and Indian organizations in developing and managing their own health delivery systems and beginning the transfer of IHS Area management functions to intertribal organizations. During the past 25 years, the movement has been increasingly toward Indian management of the health system.

An error common throughout the American health-care establishment and among many politicians is the assumption that health care (and, therefore, the health delivery system) is sufficient to eliminate the disparity in health status between populations. Health care is necessary but certainly not sufficient in itself. The surgeon general recently pointed out that "over half of the deaths that occur in this country in any given year are caused by human behavior" (Satcher 1998). No health agency or practitioner—federal, tribal, or private—can change human behavior to any major degree. All one can do is try to help create an environment conducive to good health and to provide information and encouragement to the population to lead a healthy lifestyle; significant behavioral change depends upon individuals themselves. Therefore, in addition to developing the health service delivery system described above, the long-term strategy of the IHS has been to promote the participation of Indian tribal governments and their people in their respective health programs. Several approaches guided implementation of this system of care.

Health committees formed by individual tribes or intertribal organizations evolved into more formal Area-wide boards in the 1960s and 1970s, created by the constituent tribal governments. In 1972, the National Indian Health Board (NIHB) was formed by the Area Health Boards. NIHB and the American Indian Health Care Association (AIHCA), the latter formed by the urban Indian health programs, were the first national Indian-controlled organizations directed toward their own health-care programs. The Area and national Indian health organizations were encouraged by and received financial support from the IHS. Elected tribal officials and tribal health advocates emphasized that Indian involvement in their health programs was vital to improving the health status of Indian people and that they were determined to play an increasingly active role.

In 1959, the Indian Sanitation Facilities Construction Act (P.L. 86-121) furthered the strategy of Indian participation. This program required Indian tribal governments to request IHS assistance in designing and constructing sanitation facilities for Indian homes and communities, contribute funding or services toward the construction project, and then accept the completed project and operate it (see Chapter 22).

Creation of the CHR program in 1965 with the CHR as a tribal employee provided the tribes with their first significant tribally operated health services delivery programs, operated with IHS funding. At the same time, tribes that had been terminated by congressional action (U.S. Congress, House 1953), abandoned by the BIA before the transfer to IHS, or newly recognized by congressional or BIA action were encouraged by IHS to develop and manage their own health systems rather than to look to the creation of new IHS facilities. With IHS technical and funding support and frequently IHS professional staff, tribes in Alaska, Wisconsin, New York, Maine, California, Louisiana, Oregon, and elsewhere began to create their own community-managed primary care organizations. Urban Indian health centers were also being created by Indian people, again with IHS support. This process began several years before President Nixon's Indian Policy Message (Nixon 1970) and nearly a decade before enactment of Public Laws 93-638 and 94-437. Indeed, it is likely that the several innovations undertaken by the IHS contributed in a major way to the subsequent development of these landmark advances.

Another strategy to assist Indian participation and acceptance was the promotion of collaboration between "Western" (e.g., IHS) and American Indian medicine. Collaboration began with Dr. James R. Shaw, the founding director of the IHS, who considered native healers to be important participants in improving their communities' health. He invited traditional healers to tour IHS clinics and observe demonstrations of techniques such as radiology and laboratory procedures (J. Shaw, pers. comm., 1998). The first formal IHS policy affirming the importance of native healing was issued by the director of the IHS in 1979 (see Chapter 23). IHS participation in and support of the Navajo Medicine Man training program (Bergman 1973) (see also Chapter 23) and incorporation of native healing structures under the control of native healers in IHS facilities were also begun in the 1970s, as was the appointment of a native healer to serve as liaison between the director and other native healers (see Chapter 23).

The Organization of Indian Health Services

The IHS and the tribes now operate 49 hospitals and 492 ambulatory facilities across the nation (Indian Health Service 1997). These activities are carried out in 35 states and provide both curative and preventive services to the approximately five hundred sovereign Indian nations. Emphasis is on decentralized operations integrated through 12 regions identified as Area Offices and in headquarters, located in Rockville, Maryland. In 1988, the IHS was made one of 8 agencies of the PHS. With its approximately fifteen thousand employees, its unique mission, its emphasis on comprehensive community-based care, and the diversity of the sovereign Indian nations, it is one of the most complex organizations of any type. In addition to clinical health-care professionals, it employs sanitarians, engineers, injury-control experts, health educators, and a variety of other professional providers to a far higher degree than that found in any other health-care system in the United States.

The organization of the IHS is shown in Figure 5.1, which also demonstrates some of the complexity of the organization. The chain of command is through the director in headquarters, to the area director, to the service unit director. The dashed lines show organizational changes brought about largely through the Indian Self-Determination and Education Assistance Act and the Indian

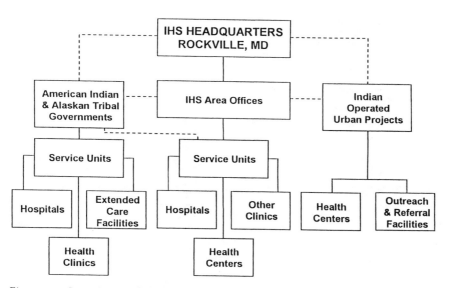

Figure 5.1. Organizational elements in the Indian Health Service (IHS) and tribal health programs. There are three parallel organizations (direct IHS, tribal, and urban), interconnected in various ways. *Source:* Indian Health Service 1997, Chart 1.1

Health Care Improvement Act. By fiscal year 1997, the IHS operated directly 66 Service Units, composed of 37 hospitals and 113 ambulatory clinics of various sizes. The tribes operated 84 Service Units comprising 12 hospitals and 379 ambulatory facilities of various sizes (Indian Health Service 1997).

The basic organizational element in the IHS program is the Service Unit, serving the local community. It is often a hospital-based program with various outlying clinics, but many Service Units are made up of one or more (usually several) ambulatory facilities. Ambulatory facilities usually consist of physician-staffed clinics with a range of primary medical and dental services, with environmental and community services being incorporated into the local program. However, in some of the smaller Service Units, much of the ancillary community and environmental support is provided by the Area Office. Many of the health centers and stations are not staffed by full-time physicians but may be operated on a day-to-day basis by physician's assistants, nurse practitioners, and physicians who visit at regular intervals. Many of the health stations, such as those associated with schools, do not have local physician services available. In Alaska, most of the care provided in villages is by specially trained community members, called Alaska Native community health aides (ANCHAs) to distinguish them from the lay outreach workers called community health representatives (CHRs).

Presently, 34 urban programs, generally operated by local nongovernmental and nontribal organizations, provide various clinical services as well as active outreach programs to assist urban Indians to gain access to other programs. Six of these provide only outreach programs. The urban programs are partially supported through contracts with the IHS.

Headquarters is organized into offices that combine staff functions for the Office of the Director with program guidance and direction to the field. The dual nature of headquarters functions is often a source of confusion as to roles and responsibilities of various staff, understood poorly by both constituents and the Congress. The function of headquarters is to integrate the vast and myriad programs operating in very different circumstances across the nation into a coherent, unified program meeting the various mandates set by Congress. Headquarters staff provide consultation and direction of a national character to the Area Offices and Service Units. Headquarters is also responsible for the formulation and execution of the annual budget. A 1996 reorganization arranged headquarters into three broad divisions. However, activities may be thought of in seven general categories: health programs, planning evaluation and legislation, administration and management, tribal activities, information resources management, development of health personnel, and environmental health and engineering. These different functions tend to correspond to the categories used by the Congress in its annual appropriations. Certain headquarters functions

located in technical support centers in Albuquerque are presently being combined, and some are being moved to headquarters in Rockville, Maryland.

The Field Organization of the Indian Health Service

The field organization of the IHS is shown in Figure 5.2, which displays the
fiscal year 1998 IHS service population by IHS Area. The area with the largest
Indian population is Oklahoma, with more than 303,000 Indians, compared to
the Tucson Area, which is made up of only two tribes with a combined population of just less than 28,000. The Tucson Area was established as a separate
entity largely as a result of the establishment of the Office of Research and
Development and the desirability of having that office also serve the tribes
nearest Tucson. The situation in California is also special in that the service
population in California is a small proportion of the total number of Indians
living there. A large number of Indians, often referred to as *nonaffiliated,* do not
have a specific land base and are not identified with a specific tribe. In addition,
the many Indians living in certain metropolitan areas of California are generally
outside the IHS Service Area.

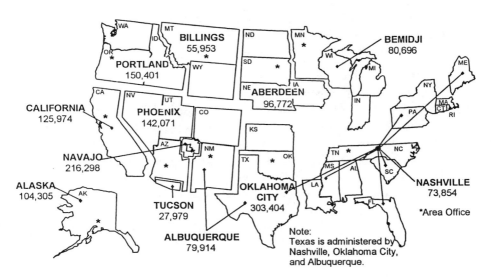

Figure 5.2. The field organization of the Indian Health Service Area Offices with
projected FY 1998 IHS service populations. The approximation to the geocultural
areas noted in Chapter 1 is apparent, as is the considerable variation in numbers of
Indians among various areas. *Source:* Indian Health Service 1997, Chart 2.2

Area Offices headed by top-level Indian managers provide invaluable integrative services on a regional basis. They are responsible for coordinating efforts of the several Service Units within their jurisdiction. Meeting the needs of quite different groups of constituents while responding to headquarters' needs is a continuing challenge to the Area Directors.

Eligibility for Services

As in any program of services, criteria for eligibility for services must be established. The IHS ultimately resolves this into a question of identifying the beneficiaries toward whom congressional appropriations are directed. The Snyder Act merely provided for services for "Indians throughout the United States," giving no further guidance for the establishment of eligibility criteria.

Current criteria for eligibility for IHS services are contained in the *Code of Federal Regulations, Title 42: Public Health* (1958):

In general, (1) Services will be made available as medically indicated, to persons of Indian descent belonging to the Indian community serviced by the local facilities and program, and non-Indian wives of such persons, (2) Generally, an individual may be regarded as within the scope of the Indian health and medical service program if he is regarded as an Indian by the community in which he lives as evidenced by such factors as tribal membership, enrollment, residence on tax-exempt land, ownership of restricted property, active participation in tribal affairs, or other relevant factors in keeping with general Bureau of Indian Affairs practices in the jurisdiction (para 36.12).

The IHS generally applies the following criteria to determine eligibility for services. For directly provided services, a person is eligible to receive health services if he or she is of Indian descent and has close social and economic ties to a federally recognized tribe. One of two criteria is required to establish Indian descent: membership in a federally recognized tribe or a certificate provided by the Bureau of Indian Affairs. In the early 1980s the Congress provided that non-Indian spouses were not eligible except in the case of a non-Indian woman pregnant with an Indian child. Largely for the benefit of the child, she is eligible for prenatal and postpartum care.

With the increasing requirement that the IHS purchase complicated care from the private sector, eligibility criteria had to be reviewed because of the rapid depletion of resources that would result from attempting to pay for care of all Indians "throughout the United States." In addition, the growing need for increasingly complex tertiary care often rapidly depletes funds available for health services purchased from the private sector. It became imperative that the IHS develop a set of criteria to deal with problems arising from the obligation to pay for services rendered in the private sector and for which many thousands of

Indians would be eligible. As a result, a second set of eligibility criteria were developed to deal with "contract care." The more stringent rules of eligibility provided that, in addition to eligibility for direct services, an individual must also reside within a specific contract health services delivery area (CHSDA). This additional criterion for eligibility has greatly increased the complexity of health services delivery. Generally, a CHSDA is made up of the counties on or near reservations that make up the IHS Service Area (discussed in Chapter 6). Indians moving to distant locations lose eligibility for contract health services, and IHS does not pay for private care received in such locations. Upon returning to a CHSDA, it is necessary for an Indian person to re-establish residence and remain there for a period of 180 days before becoming eligible for contract health services. This unsatisfactory arrangement does have the effect of maximizing resources for those residing on or near reservations, a concept that the Congress has been reluctant to modify.

Indian Health Services

Ambulatory Services

Ambulatory services for Indians have increased approximately 800 percent since 1955. In fiscal year 1995, the most recent year for which complete data are available, a total of 6,546,028 outpatient visits were made by the estimated 1,373,408 Indians in the service population (Indian Health Service 1997). This represents an average of 4.8 visits per individual each year, a rate not significantly different from that of the general population. The importance of a hospital as a site for ambulatory care for Indians is reflected in the approximately 2.75 million visits in that setting. This contrasts with the private sector, where the vast majority of ambulatory services are rendered in clinic, rather than hospital, settings. The approximately two million services provided directly by the tribes in 1995 reflects the importance and size of the shift of operation of the IHS program to tribal management, which has approximately doubled since 1990. In 1995, the IHS purchased nearly 150,000 ambulatory services from the private sector, while the tribes purchased more than 264,000. A detailed history, including the site of provision, of ambulatory services is provided in the annual IHS *Trends* (Indian Health Service 1997).

Hospital Services

In fiscal year 1995, the last year for which complete data are available, the IHS and tribes provided for 88,549 direct and contract inpatient admissions, a

TABLE 5.1

Distributions for estimated population, ambulatory medical clinical impressions, and inpatient discharges and days, fiscal year 1995

Age (years)	Estimated user population (%)	Ambulatory medical clinical impressions (%)	Inpatient discharges (%)	Inpatient days (%)
<1	1.5	4.5	5.7	4.7
1–4	9.8	8.9	5.1	3.3
5–14	22.9	12.0	5.5	4.0
15–24	18.2	13.1	16.3	11.4
25–44	28.8	28.2	31.1	28.1
45–54	7.9	12.0	10.9	12.9
55–64	5.2	10.0	10.2	13.5
≥65	5.7	11.2	15.1	22.1

decrease of 18.6 percent from 1985. During this decade, the number of inpatient admissions in tribal and their contract facilities increased from 10,532 to 16,651, an increase of 58 percent. The downward trend in hospital care reflects that occurring in the rest of the country and arises from both a decline in the number of admissions and a 24.4 percent decline in the average daily patient load (ADPL) from 1985 to 1995 (Indian Health Service 1997).

The rate of hospital discharge for Indians of all ages in the IHS system is 64.5/1,000 population, compared to 117.5/1,000 for the United States. Thus, Indians are hospitalized at a rate 45 percent less than that for the general population. Hospitalized Indian people are usually thought to be sicker than those in the general population. The age distribution of hospitalization is also of interest. The only age group in which the hospitalization rate of Indians exceeds that of the general population is the group under one year of age, for which the hospital discharge rate for Indians is 247.3/1,000 population compared to 205.3/1,000 for the general population. In all other age groups, the discharge rates for Indians are considerably less than those for the general population (Indian Health Service 1997).

The average size of IHS hospitals is considerably smaller than that of U.S. short-stay hospitals. Of the 49 hospitals operated by the IHS and tribes (as of September 30, 1996), 38, or 77.6 percent, contained fewer than 50 beds, compared to 23.1 percent for U.S. short-stay hospitals. Only 5.4 percent of U.S. short-stay hospitals have fewer than 25 beds, compared to 38.8 percent of IHS and tribal hospitals. The IHS and tribes operate no hospitals with more than 200 beds.

An analysis of the ambulatory and inpatient load by age group in the IHS is shown in Table 5.1. The age group under one year represents 1.5 percent of the IHS user population, yet is responsible for 4.5 percent of ambulatory visits, 5.7 percent of hospital discharges, and 4.7 percent of inpatient days. On the other hand, the age group 1–4 years constitutes 9.8 percent of the population, 8.9 percent of the ambulatory visits, 5.1 percent of inpatient discharges, and 3.3 percent of inpatient days. Those over the age of 65 years account for 5.7 percent of the population, 11.2 percent of ambulatory visits, 15.1 percent of inpatient discharges, and 22.1 percent of inpatient days.

Contract Health Services

The purchase of medical care and services from non-IHS providers (predominantly the private sector) has become an essential component of IHS programs. The IHS closely monitors medical priorities to expend their limited funds for the most urgent cases. Under present guidelines, funds for contract health services are not to be expended for services that are available and accessible at an IHS facility or when the individual has other available sources such as Medicare/Medicaid, state and local programs, and private insurance. Patients residing within 90 minutes travel time of IHS facilities capable of providing the required services are considered to have reasonable access to direct services. The growth of contract services has emphasized another feature of the IHS: its status as a *residual* provider, expending its funds only for services not available elsewhere.

The load imposed by provision of contract health services is a growing concern. During fiscal year 1991, there were 10,700 services provided by contract health vendors that the IHS did not pay for because the care was not within medical priorities. Also, 48,500 deferred services reported by the Areas, including 23,000 preventive services (e.g., routine Pap smears, routine mammograms, dental hygiene, glasses) and 25,000 acute and chronic secondary and tertiary care cases (e.g., cataract surgery, hernia repair, dermatology evaluations, orthodontics) could not be provided because of a lack of funds (unpublished IHS data).

Discussion

Two major and fundamental achievements characterize the development of the present system of health care for American Indians and Alaska Natives: (1) the development of comprehensive, community-oriented care, with the consolidation of preventive, curative, environmental, and local management within a single national program, and (2) the transition from a directly operated federal program to one under the control and direction of the local Indian community. The latter has been further supported by development and employment of indigenous workers and collaboration with traditional native healers. Taking services

Figure 5.3. Physician injecting the knee of a Havasupai woman outdoors, perhaps the ultimate example of community-oriented care. *Source:* Used with permission of Dr. Elvira Brands. Courtesy of the National Library of Medicine.

into the community has always been a hallmark of IHS programs (Figure 5.3). Subsequent chapters detail how this system has been uniquely successful.

Eligible Indians living within health-care delivery areas receive a comprehensive set of services extending from before birth to old age and death, including many special programs such as mental health services, alcohol and substance abuse services, maternal and child health services, special diabetes programs, health education, public health nursing, nutrition education, environmental services, and many others. This is a vast array of services not generally available within a single system for non-Indian rural or urban residents. The limiting factor is the shortage of resources necessary to accomplish all that's desirable. The limited appropriations of funds to IHS have required that it ration medical care since its founding in 1955. As a result, it has developed a system for making decisions about various priorities for care, thus providing a model that other systems might find useful to study.

No other system of care so completely incorporates and integrates preventive services such as immunizations, environmental services, fluoride dental rinses, community injury-prevention efforts, and many other personal and community services. The magnitude of the accomplishment of melding these into a coherent national program operating in more than five hundred communities, each of which possesses a strong element of sovereignty, is truly unprecedented (Rhoades, D'Angelo, and Hurlburt 1987). Those previously unfamiliar with the scope of the Indian health-care system are often pleasantly surprised upon learning about the IHS (Koop 1991).

Further, fundamental change in Indian health services continues. The recent passage of self-governance legislation and amendments to the Self-Determination and Education Assistance Act has greatly accelerated the rate at which tribes assume full control of their health programs. These changes are occurring at a time of societal questioning of the role and size of the federal government and of continuing budgetary constraints. The result is that the future role of the IHS itself requires consideration and discussion. Its functioning and responsibilities, ultimately under the plenary powers of the Congress, will need to be carefully defined and laid out if possible negative consequences are not to be encountered. Attention to the needs of tribes choosing to continue to receive services directly from the IHS is necessary if they are not to be harmed by resources shifting away from their system of care. In addition, the national integration of the program could be eroded by moving to entirely decentralized tribal enterprises. Such a disruption is not necessary, but its avoidance may require new arrangements. Some national organization is undoubtedly necessary to perform tasks such as providing the Congress with a nationally integrated estimate of overall, as well as individual, tribal needs and the formulation of a national budget and priorities for construction of health and sanitary facilities. Further, it is not clear just which functions can be delegated from the executive branch of the federal government to any other entity. This is the subject of intense discussion by the IHS and the tribes and can be resolved ultimately only by congressional action.

REFERENCES

Bennett EF. 1958. Solicitor, U.S. Department of Interior. *Federal Indian Law,* 281 ff. Washington, D.C.: Government Printing Office.
Bergman RL. 1973. A school for medicine men. *Am J Psychol* 130:663–66.
Code of Federal Regulations. Title 42: Public Health. 1958. U.S. Code, vol 42, para 36.12. Washington, D.C.: Government Printing Office.
Hoover Commission. 1948. Report of the Committee on Indian Affairs of the Commission of the Executive Branch of the Government, 271 ff. Washington, D.C.
Indian Health Service. 1997. *Trends in Indian Health, 1997.* Rockville, Md.: Indian Health Service, Program Statistics Team.
Institute for Government Research. 1928. *The Problem of Indian Administration* [Meriam report]. Baltimore: Johns Hopkins Press.

Johnson EA. 1985. *The Health of American Indians/Alaska Natives.* Report to the Robert Wood Johnson Foundation. February.

Koop CE. 1991. *Koop: The Memoirs of America's Family Doctor,* 154 ff. New York: Random House.

Moorman LJ. 1949. Special article: Health of the Navajo-Hopi Indians — General report of the American Medical Association team. *JAMA* 139:370–75.

Nixon RM. 1970. Special message of the president of the United States to the Congress, July 8. In: *Public Papers of the Presidents,* 564. Washington, D.C.: Government Printing Office.

Office of Technology Assessment, U.S. Congress. 1986. *Indian Health Care.* OTA-H-290. Washington, D.C.: Government Printing Office.

Rhoades ER, D'Angelo AJ, Hurlburt WB. 1987. The Indian Health Service record of achievement. *Public Health Rep* 102:356–60.

Satcher D. 1998. Evolving priorities and challenges in health care. Keynote address presented at the 50th Annual Scientific Assembly, American Academy of Family Physicians, San Francisco, September.

Sorkin AL. 1971. *American Indians and Federal Aid.* Washington, D.C.: Brookings Institution.

U.S. Congress, House. 1953. Concurrent Resolution 108, 83d Cong, 2d sess.

U.S. Department of Health, Education and Welfare. 1957. *Health Services for American Indians.* Report of the Surgeon General. PHS Publication 531. Washington, D.C.: Government Printing Office.

6

Dorothy A. Rhoades, M.D., M.P.H.,
Anthony J. D'Angelo, M.S., and
Everett R. Rhoades, M.D.

Data Sources and Subsets of the Indian Population

The need for statistical information was recognized early by the Indian Health Service (IHS), and a system of gathering and analyzing such information has been useful not only for assuring high quality of health care but also for appropriate planning of health programs and allocation of resources. The need for pertinent data is tempered by the difficulties of collecting highly accurate data and defining the population of Indians that most nearly represents individuals using IHS programs.

Several difficulties and errors are inherent in the acquisition and enumeration of data about Native American populations and must be considered when interpreting reports on Indian health. As noted in Chapter 4, the precise definition of *Indian* remains elusive. Thus, it is not surprising that various subsets of the overall Indian population have from time to time been developed. In addition, certain population groups have evolved depending upon various legislative programs and requirements. Added to these vagaries is the inherent difficulty of enumeration of the members of the many different tribes, bands, and villages across the country. In the case of Indian health programs and systems, the IHS has sought to identify as accurately as possible that proportion of the Indian population for which it has responsibility. This is required not only for the identification of major health issues but also for the design of various programs, as well as to provide information needed by the Congress in its oversight and appropriation functions.

The U.S. Census

By far the dominant sources for estimates of the number of U.S. Indians are the decennial censuses. The census population consists of those who identify themselves as Indian. However, this result is not definitive. As noted in Chapter 3, a substantially greater number of individuals identified themselves as American Indian or Alaska Native in the 1990 Census than in previous census enumerations. In the 1990 Census, although upward of 10 million individuals indicated that they had some Indian heritage, a much smaller number (1,959,234) indicated that this heritage was predominant. Further, minority groups, including Indians, almost always question the accuracy of census enumerations, and the enumeration of Indians is beset by various reporting difficulties. As a result, the Census Bureau refined the age and sex data obtained from the 1990 Census to minimize such errors. The modified census count for U.S. Indians was 5.4 percent greater than the original census count (D'Angelo 1996). The Census Bureau has since also modified the 1980 census count of Indians. These cumulative changes have been reflected in the IHS data since 1994 (Indian Health Service 1997). Because of these changes, data regarding Indian populations collected at different times cannot be readily compared, even if appropriately adjusted for age or sex. In any case, the population number most often referred to and used is that body of persons who have identified themselves as *predominantly* American Indian or Alaska Native in the decennial census enumerations.

Because the national census counts do not provide a sufficiently accurate estimate of the population receiving services from the IHS, the latter has used a subset of the overall Indian population: those (still self-identified) persons living in states having a federal Indian reservation (in contrast to certain state reservations) and in Oklahoma and Alaska. This population has been considered by the IHS to most nearly represent those for whom it has responsibility and therefore provides the most accurate basis for planning and implementation of programs. Before 1972, vital event data for these reservation states were compiled only on a statewide basis. However, beginning in 1973, data became available on a county basis, permitting the IHS further to refine this particular subset of the Indian population to those living in counties in or adjacent to reservations. These counties collectively became known as the IHS Service Area, and the population therein (different from the *statewide* Indian population) became identified as the IHS service population. Thus, vital event data tabulated before 1973 result from a slightly different population base than those collected since (Indian Health Service 1997). In the 1990 Census, 1,103,082 persons identified themselves as *predominantly* American Indian or Alaska Native *in the IHS Service Area,* a 33 percent increase over 1980 (829,695). Most of this increase, as discussed in Chapter 3, seems to be the result of individuals who identified themselves as American Indian or Native American in 1990 who did not do so in 1980.

The IHS estimates annual population numbers through linear regression techniques using the most current 10 years of births and deaths applied to the latest census enumeration (Indian Health Service 1997). Occasionally, increases in population size associated with newly federally recognized tribes must also be added. As of October 1996, the IHS projected that 1,434,529 American Indians resided in the IHS Service Area in fiscal year 1997. A 1987 survey showed that most (82.6%) of the persons in the IHS Service Area who had health-care resources used IHS for some or all of that care and 54.9 percent used IHS exclusively (Cunningham 1993). A comparison of the IHS service population projection for 1990 with the results of the 1990 Census reveals that the IHS projections were remarkably close, with a difference of only 58,547 individuals (5%) out of 1,161,629 (Indian Health Service unpublished data). In the Aberdeen, Billings, and Navajo Areas, the IHS estimates were lower than the 1990 Census estimates, and in the other areas, slightly higher.

Because of the need for even greater specificity and with the development of more sophisticated information systems, the IHS has identified those individuals who actually receive care sponsored by the IHS. This group is known as the IHS user population. In most instances, the differences between the user population and the service population are small, suggesting that the majority of Indians located in IHS Service Areas do use the IHS for care.

The enumeration of Indians is even more complex because the number of counties and reservation states changes as tribes receive federal recognition. Although enrollment in a federally recognized tribe is not required for IHS eligibility, proof of descent from a member of a federally recognized tribe is. As a result of gained federal recognition, between 1980 and 1990 the IHS added 4 states and 58 counties to the IHS Service Area (Rhoades et al. 1992).

The importance of the distinction between the IHS service and user populations is reflected in the fact that the IHS and tribes generally believe the Congress should provide resources to serve all the eligible Indians living in the Service Areas, whereas the Office of Management and Budget has generally supported resources only for those persons actually using IHS and tribal health programs. In fact, the development of the user population designation grew out of assertions that the IHS had not been providing care to as many Indian persons as it had claimed, forcing an actual count. The community orientation of the IHS provides a basis for calculating need based on the service population, rather than on only those who have visited IHS or tribal facilities within the previous three years.

Other Sources of U.S. Indian Population Estimates

No truly representative studies or reports of the U.S. Indian population exist. Whereas the IHS provides statistics that are considered to most accurately reflect its service population, no regular information encompassing the other 39.4 percent of the U.S. Indian population is available. Direct collection of data from the markedly heterogeneous and often geographically remote Indian groups is extremely labor intensive and prohibitively expensive.

Several Area studies have been conducted to help identify the health needs of local Indian communities, but the applicability of such results to other groups is unknown. In addition, the small size of many Indian groups limits the confidence with which investigators may draw statistical inferences. On the other hand, overall reports from large studies or surveillance of Indian communities frequently mask the marked differences between communities. The IHS compiles annual regional as well as national statistics for its service and user populations and averages vital event data for three-year periods, centered on the year under consideration (Indian Health Service 1997).

As noted in Chapter 3, more than one-half of the U.S. Indian population now lives in urban or metropolitan statistical areas. Although the IHS provides modest support for 34 urban programs and the IHS Service Area includes some metropolitan statistical areas, many urban Indians do not have ready access to IHS services. The absence of these groups from IHS data collection is a serious deficiency in estimating the overall health status of Indian people. Additional information about population and data errors is found in other sources (Rhoades et al. 1992; Office of Technology Assessment 1986).

Sources of Vital Event Data

The IHS Program Statistics Team provides the most complete set of data regarding U.S. Indian vital events in its annual publications *Trends* and *Regional Differences*. The IHS does not have a separate system for enumerating births and deaths of Indians, relying on information collected annually by the National Center for Health Statistics (NCHS). The NCHS obtains birth and death certificate data for all U.S. residents from the respective state departments of health. Tribal identities are not included in these records, so the IHS cannot provide tribal-specific statistics. The IHS applies these state-acquired data to its service population to calculate vital event rates.

Several investigators have demonstrated important errors in Indian vital event rates that arise from different racial designations on birth compared to death certificates, especially those relating to infants designated as Indian on the birth certificate but assigned a different race on death certificates (Norris and Shipley 1971; Frost and Shy 1980; Kennedy and Deapen 1991; Centers for Disease Control and Prevention 1993). Hahn (1992), in a national survey of all U.S. infants who died during 1983–85, found that 36.6 percent of infants classified as Indian or Alaska Native on the birth certificate were classified differently on the death certificate.

Similar difficulties have been reported for adult American Indians (Sorlie, Rogot, and Johnson 1992; Hahn, Truman, and Barker 1996). Also, the accuracy of race on death certificates may be influenced by the cause of death. Frost et al. (1994) noted that persons dying from cancer were significantly less likely to be correctly classified as Indian or Alaska Native on the death certificate in Washington State than were persons dying from an alcohol-related condition. Such misclassification is not limited to birth and death registries. Sugarman et al. (1993) noted that injury rates among Indians were substantially underestimated in the Oregon Injury Registry because of misclassification of race.

To determine the degree and scope of such miscoding, IHS conducted a study using the National Death Index (NDI) maintained by the NCHS. The study involved matching IHS patient records of those patients who could have died during 1986–88 with all death records of U.S. residents for 1986–88 as contained on the NDI. The results were published in a document entitled *Adjusting for Miscoding of Indian Race on State Death Certificates* (Indian Health Service 1996). The study revealed that, on 10.9 percent of the matched IHS-NDI records, the race reported for the decedent was other than American Indian or Alaska Native. Misclassification was frequent among the older and the youngest decedents. However, wide regional variations in the percentage of race-inconsistent deaths were noted. The IHS Areas with the greatest percentage of inconsistent classification of Indian race on the death certificates were California (30.4%), Oklahoma City (28%), Bemidji (16.1%), and Nashville (12.1%). The reservation states with more than 25 percent inconsistency included Texas, Michigan, Florida, Kansas, and Oklahoma. These compare to a discrepancy of 1.2 percent in the Navajo Area.

Recognizing that certain assumptions could contain a degree of error, IHS applied reasonable adjustments to the death rates in its publications to provide the most meaningful and comprehensive analysis of health status. These NDI adjustments were used for the first time in the 1997 IHS statistical publications, in which both unadjusted information and adjusted information were shown, as applicable. IHS provides more specific adjustment factors for the data relating to the age group under one year. These are derived from the linked birth/infant death data sets produced by the NCHS. Beginning with 1997 IHS publications, both unadjusted and adjusted infant mortality rates are shown. These adjustments take precedence over the NDI adjustments for the age group under one year, described above.

Another substantial source of error in Indian vital event data is the underreporting of cause of death on death certificates for American Indians. Becker et al. (1990) found that the mortality from "symptoms, signs, and ill-defined conditions" was much higher for Indians in New Mexico than for other ethnic populations in the state. This uncertainty of cause of death may strongly affect cause-specific death rates, particularly for chronic diseases.

Morbidity and Patient Encounter Information

IHS developed a program information system to collect data on the services provided to its user population. The software used by IHS facilities and most tribal facilities is the Resource and Patient Management System (RPMS). Data are collected for each inpatient discharge, ambulatory medical visit, and dental visit (all patient specific) and for community programs, including health education, community health representatives, environmental health, nutrition assessment and education, public health nursing, mental health and social services, and substance abuse. The patient-specific data are collected through the Patient Care Component (PCC) of the RPMS. PCC is an abbreviated computerized medical record designed to give physicians, nurses, and other clinical staff the information needed to make medical treatment decisions. It is used to collect, store, and make accessible patient demographic and health data. PCC data are collected primarily during clinic, hospital, home, and community care visits with physicians or other health-care providers. The data provide health-care professionals with a complete and up-to-date overview of a patient's condition through a health summary report. Managers use data from PCC to allocate staff and other resources, and researchers use the data to analyze and improve the care provided to patients.

The encounter form is used to collect key patient data such as temperature, blood pressure, weight, symptoms, and diagnosis. During each patient visit, the physician completes an encounter form in much the same manner as he or she would have routinely written clinical notes before PCC. In addition to the encounter form, PCC data are obtained from the agency's medical information system via direct links. Data on laboratory tests and results, dental services, and prescriptions are automatically added to PCC via these links. Data collected from the medical information system are integrated with the encounter form data and are available through the PCC health summary. The health summary provides a snapshot of the patient's current health status and a long-term health history that highlights significant events and dates. It includes basic demographic and health information such as address, public and private insurance coverage, weight, blood pressure readings, lists of chronic health problems, laboratory results, medications, and previous or scheduled appointments with other physicians or clinics. Health summaries are printed in advance for patients with scheduled appointments and printed or viewed directly on the computer screen for walk-in or emergency room patients. PCC data are the source of most of IHS's performance measures, since they reflect prevention activities and morbidity and are free of the time lags for mortality data described above. In spite of this extensive system, it is still sometimes necessary to perform local surveys to obtain certain information.

Discussion

In keeping with the overall complexities of Indian life in the United States, data relating to Indian health reflect the usual arbitrary nature of all such data but with special considerations related to definitions of *Indian* and the enumeration of those so identified. Despite a considerable degree of error in various systems, the IHS has made great improvements in the accuracy of health data over the years. The existing data sources and analyses are reasonably satisfactory for most present purposes.

The IHS and tribes are moving into a new information systems environment resulting from (1) tribal takeover of the program and the associated tribal option on whether or not to report the same program data into the IHS central database as IHS providers report, (2) new reporting requirements being prescribed by other federal agencies (e.g., the Health Care Financing Administration, states), and (3) changing information technologies. Therefore, the current IHS information structure and network is likely to change in the next few years.

The IHS program information systems collect data only for persons accessing the IHS-sponsored health-care system. Since these data are not population based, prevalence and incidence rates for the entire population cannot be calculated. However, the data can be used to approximate these rates; in other words, satisfactory prevalence and incidence rates can be calculated from the IHS program databases. IHS would prefer to use the results of national health surveys, such as the National Health Interview Survey conducted annually by NCHS. However, this is not presently feasible because national health surveys are not designed to adequately sample American Indians and Alaska Natives in a way to produce statistically reliable results for Indians. IHS is working with the Department of Health and Human Services and NCHS to develop a long-term strategy that will at least periodically provide reliable information for targeted Indian groups.

REFERENCES

Becker TM, Wiggins CL, Key CR, et al. 1990. Symptoms, signs, and ill-defined conditions: A leading cause of death among minorities. *Am J Epidemiol* 131:664–68.

Centers for Disease Control and Prevention. 1993. Classification of American Indian race on birth and infant death certificates: California and Montana. *MMWR* 42:220–23.

Cunningham PJ. 1993. Access to care in the Indian Health Service. *Health Aff (Millwood)* 12:224–33.

D'Angelo AJ. 1996. American Indians and Alaska Natives: Defining where they reside. *IHS Provider* 21(3):36–42.

Frost F, Shy KK. 1980. Racial differences between linked birth and infant death records in Washington State. *Am J Public Health* 70:974–76.

Frost F, Tollestrup K, Ross A, et al. 1994. Correctness of racial coding of American Indians and Alaska Natives on the Washington State death certificate. *Am J Prev Med* 10:290–94.

Hahn RA. 1992. The state of federal health statistics on racial and ethnic groups. *JAMA* 267:268–71.

Hahn RA, Truman BI, Barker ND. 1996. Identifying ancestry: The reliability of ancestral identification in the United States by self, proxy, interviewer, and funeral director. *Epidemiology* 7(1):75–80.

Indian Health Service. 1996. *Adjusting for Miscoding of Indian Race on State Death Certificates*. Rockville, Md.: Indian Health Service, Program Statistics Team.

———. 1997. *Trends in Indian Health, 1997*. Rockville, Md.: Indian Health Service, Program Statistics Team.

Kennedy RD, Deapen RE. 1991. Differences between Oklahoma Indian infant mortality and other races. *Public Health Rep* 106:97–99.

Norris FD, Shipley PW. 1971. A closer look at race differentials in California's infant mortality, 1965–1967. *HSMHA Health Rep* 86:810–14.

Office of Technology Assessment, U.S. Congress. 1986. *Indian Health Care*. OTA-H-290. Washington, D.C.: Government Printing Office.

Rhoades ER, Brenneman G, Lyle J, et al. 1992. Mortality of American Indian and Alaska Native infants. *Annu Rev Public Health* 13:269–85.

Sorlie PD, Rogot E, Johnson NJ. 1992. Validity of demographic characteristics on the death certificate. *Epidemiology* 3(2):181–84.

Sugarman JR, Soderberg R, Gordon JE, et al. 1993. Racial misclassification of American Indians: Its effect on injury rates in Oregon, 1989 through 1990. *Am J Public Health* 83:681–84.

Part III

Major Diseases and Health Conditions Affecting Indians

7

George R. Brenneman, M.D., FAAP,
Aaron O. Handler, B.A., Stephen F. Kaufman, M.S.,
and Everett R. Rhoades, M.D.

Health Status and Clinical Indicators

During the past 30 to 40 years, the health status of American Indians has in many respects generally improved, sometimes profoundly. However, current data show that Indians still experience an excess burden of illness. Responding to effective prevention and treatment, infectious diseases (e.g., tuberculosis, pneumonia, and influenza) have significantly diminished in importance. Health conditions associated with poverty and harmful lifestyle practices (e.g., heart disease, diabetes, and cirrhosis) now dominate the health-care needs of Indians.

Data in this chapter are primarily from Indian Health Service (IHS) sources and therefore reflect the IHS service population, those most likely to receive direct or contract services through IHS and tribal programs. The data generally do not reflect the status of Indians living outside IHS Service Areas, most of whom are urban residents. Because of their special importance, maternal and child health data are presented in Chapter 9.

Improvements in Indian health (Indian Health Service 1997b) since 1973 include decreases in mortality rates of tuberculosis (78%), gastrointestinal diseases (77%), accidents (56%), pneumonia and influenza (48%), homicide and suicide (45% and 18%, respectively), and alcoholism (33%). These changes have resulted from efforts of concerned Indian communities and families who embraced and promoted effective prevention programs. However, Indian communities still face serious challenges in the development and implementation of community-based programs that give attention to behavioral change and to relief of devastating poverty. Despite these improvements, data from 1992–94 reveal that Indians experience the following excess mortality when compared with the general U.S. population: alcoholism, 579 percent; tuberculosis, 475 percent; injuries, 144 percent; diabetes mellitus, 231 percent; and suicide and homicide, 70 and 41 percent greater, respectively (Indian Health Service 1997b).

Mortality Rates and Leading Causes of Death

The proportion of Indians who die in certain age groups differs considerably from that for the general population, exceeding that of the latter in each age group through 64 years (Indian Health Service 1997b). During 1992–94, 31 percent of Indian deaths occurred in individuals under 45 years of age compared with 11 percent of those among the general U.S. population (U.S. All Races). Conversely, the proportion of the latter who died after age 65 was 73 percent, compared to only 45 percent for Indians (Indian Health Service 1997b) (Figure 7.1).

Variations in death rates of Indians according to gender are striking. The proportion of male to female deaths is equal among Indians under 5 years of age; from 5 to 64 years of age, deaths of males predominate; and after age 65, deaths among females predominate (Figure 7.2).

The overall age-adjusted Indian mortality rate for 1992–94 was 690.4/ 100,000 population, compared to 513.3 for U.S. All Races and 485.1 for Whites for 1993. (The term *U.S. Whites* refers generally to Caucasians. It includes a certain proportion of the Hispanic population.) For all, the leading cause of death was cardiovascular disease, primarily diseases of the heart. Conditions in which the death ratio of Indians to U.S. All Races is higher are striking. Indian

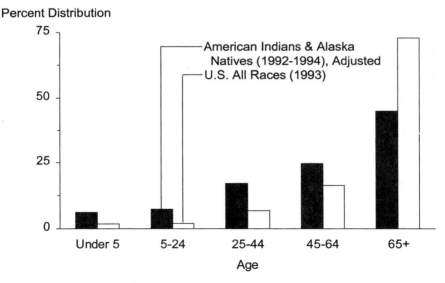

Figure 7.1. Comparison of the proportion of deaths of American Indians and Alaska Natives (1992–94) with U.S. All Races (1993), by age group. The proportions for the American Indians and Alaska Natives have been adjusted for racial miscoding on death reports. *Source:* Indian Health Service 1997b, Chart 4.14

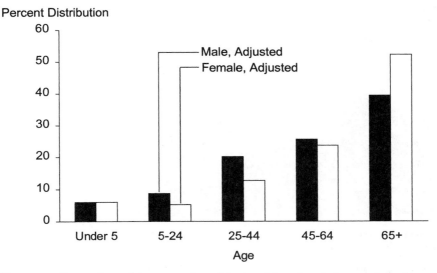

Figure 7.2. Comparison of the proportion of deaths of American Indians and Alaska Natives (1992–94) of either gender, by age group. The numbers of deaths have been adjusted for ethnic miscoding on death reports. *Source:* Indian Health Service 1997b, Chart 4.16

age-adjusted mortality rates were higher than rates due to the same causes among U.S. All Races for the following: unintentional injuries, 3.1 times higher; chronic liver disease and cirrhosis, 4.4; diabetes, 3.3; pneumonia and influenza, 1.6; suicide, 1.7; homicide, 1.4; and tuberculosis, 5.3 times higher (Table 7.1).

The profile of leading causes of Indian deaths also differs from that of the general population. The five leading causes of death, in decreasing order, for Indians in 1992–94 were diseases of the heart, malignancies, unintentional injuries, diabetes mellitus, and chronic liver disease/cirrhosis; for U.S. All Races during 1993, the top five were diseases of the heart, malignancies, cerebrovascular diseases, chronic obstructive pulmonary disease, and unintentional injuries (Indian Health Service 1997b). The fact that diabetes mellitus and chronic liver disease and cirrhosis are among the five leading causes of Indian mortality and not among the top five for U.S. All Races indicates the importance of certain lifestyle behaviors and nutrition in the health status of Indians.

Age-specific Mortality Rates

As mentioned above, maternal and child health are considered of such importance that they are discussed in a separate chapter.

TABLE 7.1

Age-adjusted death rates for American Indians and Alaska Natives, IHS Service Area, 1992–1994, and U.S. All Races and White populations, 1993
(rate per 100,000 population)

Cause of death	American Indian and Alaska Native		U.S. All Races	U.S. White	Ratio[a] of American Indian and Alaska Native to:	
	Actual	Adjusted[a]			U.S. All Races	U.S. White
All causes	601.3	690.4	513.3	485.1	1.3	1.4
Major cardiovascular diseases	167.0	194.6	181.8	173.9	1.1	1.1
Diseases of the heart	133.4	157.6	145.3	139.9	1.1	1.1
Cerebrovascular diseases	25.1	27.8	26.5	24.5	1.0	1.1
Atherosclerosis	2.2	2.3	2.4	2.4	1.0	1.0
Hypertension	1.8	1.8	2.2	1.7	0.8	1.1
Accidents	82.3	94.5	30.3	29.6	3.1	3.2
Motor vehicle	45.5	53.3	16.0	16.1	3.3	3.3
All other	36.9	41.2	14.4	13.5	2.9	3.1
Malignant neoplasms	97.5	112.2	132.6	129.4	0.8	0.9
Chronic liver disease and cirrhosis	30.7	35.0	7.9	7.6	4.4	4.6
Diabetes mellitus	35.1	41.1	12.4	11.0	3.3	3.7
Pneumonia and influenza	20.1	21.7	13.5	12.9	1.6	1.7
Suicide	17.3	19.2	11.3	12.0	1.7	1.6
Homicide	13.4	15.1	10.7	6.9	1.4	2.5
Chronic obstructive pulmonary diseases and allied conditions	15.7	17.4	21.4	21.9	0.8	0.8
Tuberculosis, all forms	2.3	2.3	0.4	0.3	5.3	7.0
Human immunodeficiency virus (HIV) infection	3.3	3.9	13.8	10.5	0.3	0.4

SOURCE: U.S. mortality rates: Monthly vital statistics report. NCHS, DHHS, Advance report of final mortality statistics, 1993, vol. 44, no. 7, supplement, February 29, 1996, Tables 9 and 22.
[a]Adjusted to compensate for miscoding of Indian race on death certificates.

Among Indians aged 15 to 24 years, the distribution of causes of death is similar to that of the general population. Unintentional (accidents) and intentional injuries (suicide and homicide) are by far the commonest causes of death. For accidents and suicide, the death rates among Indian youth are twice the rates experienced by U.S. All Races youth (Figure 7.3). More than 80 percent of deaths among Indian youth are due to injuries (unintentional or intentional). Further, injury death rates of Indian males greatly exceed those of Indian females. Although not among the five leading causes, chronic liver disease and cirrhosis emerge as important causes of death among Indians in this age group (Indian Health Service 1997b).

In 1992–94, the leading cause of death of among Indian adults 25 to 44 years of age continued to be accidents, with a rate 3.7 times that experienced by U.S. All Races of the same age in 1993 (Figure 7.4). Chronic liver disease and cirrhosis were the second leading cause of death, at 6.7 times the rate experienced by U.S. All Races. In contrast, the cancer mortality rate among Indians of this age group was 20 percent less and the human immunodeficiency virus infection

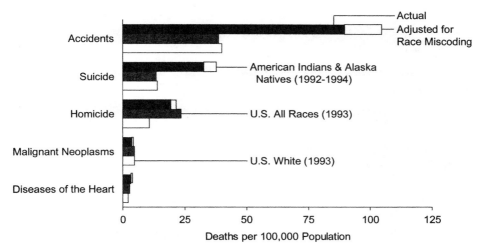

Figure 7.3. Comparison of the leading causes of death of American Indians and Alaska Natives with U.S. All Races and U.S. Whites, aged 15–24. Both reported ("actual") and adjusted figures for American Indians and Alaska Natives are shown. *Source:* Indian Health Service 1997b, Chart 4.3

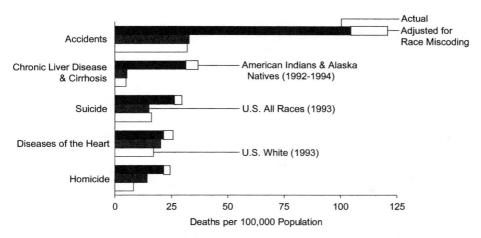

Figure 7.4. Comparison of the leading causes of death of American Indians and Alaska Natives with U.S. All Races and U.S. Whites, aged 25–44. Both reported ("actual") and adjusted figures for American Indians and Alaska Natives are shown. *Source:* Indian Health Service 1997b, Chart 4.4

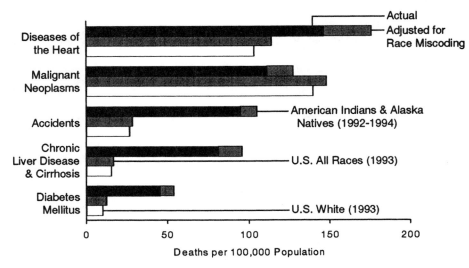

Figure 7.5. Comparison of the leading causes of death of American Indians and Alaska Natives with U.S. All Races and U.S. Whites, aged 45–54. Both reported ("actual") and adjusted figures for American Indians and Alaska Natives are shown. *Source:* Indian Health Service 1997b, Chart 4.5

death rate was 70 percent less than for the general population. Heart disease begins taking a significant toll of both Indians and U.S. All Races in this age group. The mortality rate for pneumonia and influenza among Indians was 2.6 times the rate among U.S. All Races. Indian mortality rates for cerebrovascular diseases and diabetes were 1.4 and 1.5 times those for U.S. All Races (Indian Health Service 1997b).

Among Indians 45 to 54 years of age, the two leading causes of death were diseases of the heart and malignant neoplasms. In this age group, Indian mortality due to malignancies was 86 percent of the rate for U.S. All Races. Cancer mortality rates among Indians have been gradually increasing over the past 20 years, with the primary contributor being lung cancer. Between 1977 and 1992, Indian cancer death rates increased 20 percent, while rates among Whites remained essentially stable. Mortality associated with heart disease is 1.5 times greater for Indians than for U.S. All Races in this age group. Middle-aged Indians continue to experience excess mortality rates due to unintentional injuries, cirrhosis, and diabetes. The mortality rate due to chronic liver disease and cirrhosis is 4.8 times and that due to diabetes is 3.5 times greater than comparable rates among U.S. All Races (Indian Health Service 1997b) (Figure 7.5).

Among both Indians and U.S. All Races aged 55 to 64, the two leading causes of death are diseases of the heart and malignant neoplasms. As with middle-aged Indians, cancer deaths are 82 percent of those for the same age U.S. All

Races group. The diabetes death rate among Indians is 4.5 times that experienced by U.S. All Races (Indian Health Service 1997b) (Figure 7.6).

Indians 65 years and older experience an overall death rate lower than that of the general population. Diseases of the heart, cancer, cerebrovascular diseases, diabetes, pneumonia, and influenza are the leading causes of death (Figure 7.7). Although diminished in relative importance and not among the five leading causes in this age group, unintentional injury death rates of Indians continue to exceed those of U.S. All Races by 67 percent, and liver disease and cirrhosis death rates are 2.4 times those of the general population. The death rate from diabetes is 2.5 times that of the general population. Diseases of the heart, malignancies, and cerebrovascular diseases combined cause a smaller proportion of all deaths among Indians (58.3%) than among the U.S. All Races group (67.9%) (Indian Health Service 1997b).

Table 7.2 shows a composite of the 10 leading causes of Indian deaths (1993–95) by age group. Both intentional and unintentional injuries are prominent in all age groups, illustrating the epidemic nature of these causes of death. Only among those aged 65 years or more is this category not ranked in the top five causes. Homicide steadily rises from eighth place for those under one year of age to the second leading cause of death for those aged one to four years and occupies third place in those 10 to 34 years old. For the years 1993–95, human immunodeficiency virus enters the 10 leading causes of death in youth 15–24

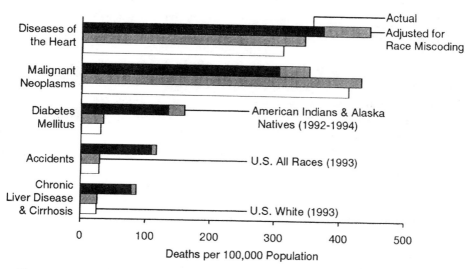

Figure 7.6. Comparison of the leading causes of death of American Indians and Alaska Natives with U.S. All Races and U.S. Whites, aged 55–64. Both reported ("actual") and adjusted figures for American Indians and Alaska Natives are shown. *Source:* Indian Health Service 1997b, Chart 4.6

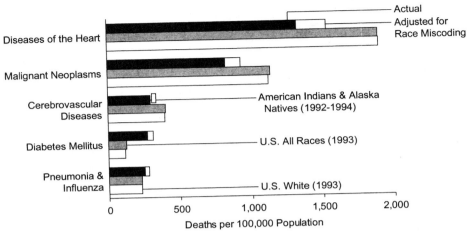

Figure 7.7. Comparison of the leading causes of death of American Indians and Alaska Natives with U.S. All Races and U.S. Whites, aged 65 and older. Both reported ("actual") and adjusted figures for American Indians and Alaska Natives are shown. *Source:* Indian Health Service 1997b, Chart 4.7

years of age; it is the fourth leading cause among those aged 25–34 years and the seventh for those aged 35–44 years. Deaths from alcoholism occupy sixth place for Indians aged 15–24 years and become second after unintentional injuries among those aged 35–44 years. Alcoholism ranks tenth in the leading causes of death of those aged 65 years or more.

The overall rank of deaths is quite revealing. Heart disease and cancer account for approximately the same number of deaths as the other eight leading causes combined, with approximately 49.3 percent of all Indian deaths in 1993–95 due to heart disease and cancer. The data in Table 7.2 are arranged somewhat differently from data customarily presented in the IHS *Trends;* the age intervals are somewhat different and include Indians not served by the IHS.

Certain Trends in Mortality Rates

Various trends in mortality rates during recent decades also provide valuable insight into Indian diseases. The dramatic decreases in maternal and infant mortality are described in Chapter 9. The striking decrease in mortality from infectious diseases is reflected in the death rate from tuberculosis, shown in Figure 7.8, which also illustrates the recent slight rise in tuberculosis deaths. Similar decreases in gastrointestinal deaths have been experienced with the overall increase in sanitation and wide implementation of oral rehydration therapy (Figure 7.9). These salutary trends, as will be noted in subsequent chapters, are not being experienced for cardiovascular diseases, diabetes mellitus, and malignancies. On the contrary, death rates from these latter two conditions are presently increasing.

Regional Differences in Mortality

Differences in death rates for certain conditions between Indians living in different geographical regions provide information that is often useful in further analysis. However, these differences require careful interpretation because of differences in the degree to which Indian births and deaths may be reported throughout the country (Indian Health Service 1996a). As noted in Chapter 6, underreporting seems to be especially common among Indians in the IHS Areas of California (30.4%), Oklahoma (28.0%), Bemidji (16.1%), and Nashville (12.1%). However, differences in the proportion of death rates associated with certain diseases and conditions and between certain Indian groups seem to be significant (Indian Health Service 1996a, 1997a):

— Diseases of the heart are the leading cause of death among Indians on the Northern Plains and in the Great Lakes region, while the leading cause among Alaska Natives and Navajos, respectively, is unintentional injuries.

— The 1992–94 suicide age-adjusted mortality rate among Alaska Natives was 43.6/100,000, while among Navajos it was 16.6/100,000.

— The 1992–94 alcoholism age-adjusted mortality rate among Northern Plains Indians was 112.7/100,000, compared to 15.9/100,000 among Oklahoma Indians.

— The 1992–94 diabetes age-adjusted mortality rate in Alaska Natives was 16.0/100,000, compared to 70.3/100,000 for Indians in the Phoenix Area.

— The 1992–94 cervical cancer age-adjusted mortality rate among Northern Plains women was 11.3/100,000, but it was 0.6/100,000 for Indian women in the Portland Area. These rates compare with a 1993 U.S. All Races rate of 2.5/100,000.

Reasons for these interesting and marked differences are not known and have not been thoroughly studied. Genetic, socioeconomic, environmental, and lifestyle differences all influence these variations. Although these data are derived from IHS databases, others also have confirmed regional differences in health status between Indian populations (Sievers and Fisher 1981). Such variations in causes and rates of death provide a great opportunity for elucidating mechanisms of disease and designing appropriate interventions.

TABLE 7.2

Ten leading causes of death, American Indians and Alaska Natives, 1993–1995

	Cause of death at:				
Rank	<1 yr	1–4 yr	5–9 yr	10–14 yr	15–24 yr
1	SIDS[a] (222)[b]	Unintentional injuries (179)	Unintentional injuries (84)	Unintentional injuries (101)	Unintentional injuries (779)
2	Congenital anomalies (220)	Homicide (28)	Malignant neoplams (16)	Suicide (26)	Suicide (261)
3	Prematurity RDS[a]	Congenital anomalies (19)	Congenital anomalies (6)	Homicide (21)	Homicide (204)
4	Unintentional injuries (48)	Malignant neoplasms (12)	Homicide (5)	Malignant neoplasms (13)	Malignant neoplasms (33)
5	Pneumonia or influenza (44)	Pneumonia or influenza (9)	Heart disease (5)	Congenital anomalies (8)	Heart disease (26)
6	Placenta/cord membranes (35)	Heart disease (8)	Septicemia (5)	Heart disease (3)	Alcoholism (16)
7	Maternal complications (30)	Perinatal period (5)	Benign neoplasms (2)	Nephritis (3)	Congenital anomalies (14)
8	Homicide (18)	Cerebrovascular (4)	Meningitis (2)	Pneumonia or influenza (3)	Alcohol abuse (12)
9	Perinatal infections (17)	Meningitis (4)	Pneumonia or influenza (2)	Tied[c]	Cerebrovascular (9)
10	Intrauterine hypoxia (14)	Bronchitis, emphysema, asthma (3)	Tied[d]		HIV (6)

SOURCE: Data from National Vital Statistics System, National Center for Health Statistics, Centers for Disease Control and Prevention (CDC). Produced by the National Center for Injury Prevention and Control, CDC.

[a] SIDS, sudden infant death syndrome; RDS, respiratory distress syndrome; HIV, human immunodeficiency syndrome.

[b] Numbers in parentheses, numbers of deaths.

[c] HIV (2), meningococcal (2), septicemia (2).

[d] Bronchitis, emphysema, asthma (1); HIV (1); meningococcal (1); suicide (1); viral hepatitis (1).

Cause of death at:					
25–34 yr	35–44 yr	45–54 yr	55–64 yr	65+ yr	Total
Unintentional injuries (868)	Unintentional injuries (650)	Heart disease (698)	Heart disease (1,143)	Heart disease (3,404)	Heart disease (6,572)
Suicide (264)	Alcoholism (458)	Malignant neoplasms (543)	Malignant neoplasms (994)	Malignant neoplasms (2,673)	Malignant neoplasms (4,613)
Homicide (235)	Heart disease (277)	Alcoholism (458)	Diabetes (368)	Cerebrovascular (997)	Unintentional injuries (3,713)
HIV[a] (162)	Malignant neoplasms (224)	Unintentional injuries (372)	Unintentional injuries (264)	Diabetes (854)	Diabetes (1,488)
Alcoholism (140)	Homicide (151)	Diabetes (189)	Alcoholism (243)	Pneumonia or influenza (757)	Alcoholism (1,422)
Malignant neoplasms (99)	Suicide (151)	Cerebrovascular (104)	Cerebrovascular (182)	Bronchitis, emphysema, asthma (631)	Cerebrovascular (1,384)
Heart disease (82)	HIV (141)	Liver disease (85)	Bronchitis, emphysema, asthma (145)	Unintentional injuries (364)	Pneumonia or influenza (1,075)
Pneumonia or influenza (33)	Liver disease (80)	Suicide (67)	Liver disease (98)	Nephritis (238)	Bronchitis, emphysema, asthma (852)
Alcohol abuse (29)	Pneumonia or influenza (68)	Pneumonia or influenza (65)	Pneumonia or influenza (89)	Septicemia (164)	Suicide (821)
Liver disease (27)	Cerebrovascular (63)	Homicide (52)	Nephritis (61)	Alcoholism (159)	Homicide (761)

Per 100,000 Population

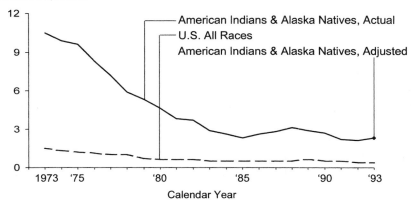

Figure 7.8. Age-adjusted tuberculosis death rates of American Indians and Alaska Natives and of U.S. All Races, since 1973. For 1993, the adjusted rate for American Indians and Alaska Natives is shown by the *diamond point.* Adjustment for racial misclassification in this case is insignificant. *Source:* Indian Health Service 1997b, Chart 4.41

Per 100,000 Population

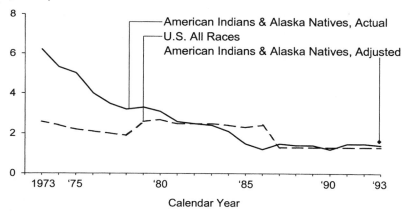

Figure 7.9. Age-adjusted gastrointestinal disease death rates of American Indians and Alaska Natives and of U.S. All Races, since 1973. For 1993, the adjusted rate for American Indians and Alaska Natives is shown by the *diamond point. Source:* Indian Health Service 1997b, Chart 4.48

Morbidity

As important as are mortality rates in providing information about health status, other indices, such as morbidity rates, are equally useful. Such data are often less readily available and subject to greater variation in diagnosis and recording but often provide insights useful for planning programs. Except for the special American Indian and Alaska Native study carried out as part of the National Medical Expenditure Survey (1989), door-to-door health status studies among Indian people are virtually nonexistent.

Until more reliable and consistent sources for morbidity data become available, the preponderance of information about disease conditions will continue to be derived from IHS ambulatory and inpatient data. These provide useful information but have certain limitations. Morbidity data are collected from clinical forms completed by health-care providers and then read and computer-entered by local health records clerical staff. Consistent terminology is not always used among clinicians who must complete the clinical data forms in the press of heavy clinic work. Data error rates in most facilities are not known, and few comparisons have been made with systematically collected community health status data. Further, these clinic-based morbidity data come from Indians who present themselves for health care in a clinic or hospital and do not necessarily reflect the health status of the entire community. Nevertheless, a wealth of morbidity information on Indians served by the IHS is available and, within limitations, is useful for most program planning.

Slightly more than 6.5 million ambulatory visits resulting in more than 8.8 million clinical impressions were made to IHS, tribal, and contract care programs in fiscal year 1995 (Indian Health Service 1997b). The most frequently cited clinical impression for Indian ambulatory visits (13.9%) is "supplemental classifications," which includes well child visits and other preventive care services, such as routine physical examinations, laboratory tests, and radiographic procedures. Respiratory diseases accounted for 11.5 percent of clinical impressions, followed by disorders of the nervous system and sense organs (9.5%) and endocrine and nutritional diseases (5.8%). Circulatory system diseases accounted for less than 5 percent of all outpatient clinical impressions (Indian Health Service 1997b) (Table 7.3).

The most frequent specific clinical impressions in IHS and tribal direct and contract health-care facilities in 1994 were otitis media in males and diabetes in females. Infections continued to be important causes of morbidity, especially among Indian children. Diabetes and hypertension were in the top six clinical impressions for both male and female patients. Considering the relatively young age of Indian people compared to the U.S. general population and the increasing prevalence of obesity and sedentary lifestyles, the importance of these two con-

TABLE 7.3

Number of ambulatory medical clinical impressions for leading major categories, by gender

Male		Female	
Category	No. of clinical impressions	Category	No. of clinical impressions
All categories	3,348,192	All categories	5,740,637
Supplementary classification	465,540	Supplementary classification	760,230
Respiratory system diseases	411,920	Respiratory system diseases	604,621
Nervous system and sense organ diseases	364,953	Nervous system and sense organ diseases	469,367
Injury and poisoning	220,929	Complication of pregnancy, childbirth, and puerperium	428,859
Circulatory system diseases	190,155		
Endocrine, nutritional, and meta-bolic disorders	186,714	Endocrine, nutritional, and meta-bolic disorders	325,964
Skin and subcutaneous tissue diseases	180,799	Musculoskeletal system	276,775
Symptoms, signs, and ill-defined conditions	159,824	Symptoms, signs, and ill-defined conditions	271,190
		Genitourinary system diseases	265,750
Mental disorders	158,578	Skin and subcutaneous tissue diseases	239,823
Musculoskeletal system diseases	153,796		
All other	854,984	Circulatory system diseases	221,146
		All other	1,606,912

SOURCE: Indian Health Service and Tribal Direct and Contract Facilities, FY 95. Direct: Annual Report 1C. Indirect: Annual Report 3A.

ditions is significant indeed. Each will be considered in more detail elsewhere in this volume. A large proportion of ambulatory clinical services to Indians is preventive in nature. Seventeen percent of the 10 leading impressions for males was provision of immunizations and well child care, and 31 percent of the 10 leading impressions for females was prenatal care, family planning, and immunizations (Indian Health Service 1996c) (Table 7.4).

Indian morbidity is also reflected in hospital discharge diagnoses. By far the most frequent reason for hospitalization of Indians is obstetrical care and complications of pregnancy and the puerperium (Table 7.5). The significance of this category is emphasized by the fact that it reflects care provided primarily to Indian women of child-bearing age, approximately 25 percent of the total Indian population. The second leading category is diseases of the respiratory system, followed by diseases of the digestive system and by injuries and poisonings (Indian Health Service 1996d, 1997b).

Although childbirth and its complications lead all causes for hospitalization, this category is responsible for fewer hospital days than other conditions, such as diseases of the respiratory and digestive system. Among admissions for respiratory diseases, all types of pneumonia are prominent. Admissions for asthma have become significant and should be noted, since this condition is one of those formerly thought to be rare among Indians (Rhoades 1990). Diseases of the circulatory system are the fifth leading cause of hospitalization. Malignant neoplasms, while not among the most prominent causes of admission, contribute disproportionately to the hospital load as a result of longer length of stay. Diabetes accounts for relatively few inpatient discharges, although its complications and associated conditions (such as infections and heart disease) are responsible for a significant number of admissions. Burns requiring hospital care, though infrequent, account for a high proportion of hospital days.

TABLE 7.4
American Indian ambulatory care visits, 10 leading clinical impressions, by gender

Male		Female	
Diagnosis	No.	Diagnosis	No.
Otitis media	146,761	Diabetes mellitus	290,905
Diabetes mellitus	133,930	Prenatal care	203,720
URI[a]	127,446	Tests only (lab, x-ray)	192,748
Hypertension	118,735	URI	181,360
Immunizations	108,343	Otitis media	155,664
Test only (lab, x-ray)	88,214	Hypertensive disease	152,284
Medical/surgical follow-up	85,788	Family planning	147,443
Well child care	64,278	Immunizations	127,129
Pharyngitis, tonsillitis, nonstreptococcal	63,113	Refractive error	98,673
Refractive error	62,107	Medical/surgical follow-up	96,760

SOURCE: Indian Health Service 1996c.
[a]URI, upper respiratory infection.

TABLE 7.5
Ten leading causes of hospitalization for general medicine and surgery patients

Diagnostic category	No. of discharges			Percentage distribution		
	Comb.[a]	Direct[b]	Contract[c]	Comb.[a]	Direct[b]	Contract[c]
All categories	80,380	63,015	17,365	100	78.4	21.6
Obstetric deliveries and complications of pregnancy and puerperium	14,170	12,819	1,351	17.6	20.3	7.8
Respiratory system diseases	10,993	9,381	1,612	13.7	14.9	9.3
Digestive system diseases	10,240	7,880	2,360	12.7	12.5	13.6
Injury and poisoning	7,722	4,836	2,886	9.6	7.7	16.6
Circulatory system diseases	6,147	3,604	2,543	7.6	5.7	14.6
Symptoms, signs, and ill-defined conditions	4,983	3,965	1,018	6.2	6.3	5.9
Genitourinary system diseases	4,532	3,692	840	5.6	5.9	4.8
Mental disorders	3,691	2,666	1,025	4.6	4.2	5.9
Endocrine, nutritional, and metabolic disorders	3,528	2,785	743	4.4	4.4	4.3
Skin and subcutaneous tissue diseases	3,155	2,728	427	3.9	4.3	2.5
All other	11,219	8,659	2,560	14	13.7	14.7

SOURCE: Indian Health Service and tribal direct and contract general hospitals, FY 1995.
[a]Comb., combined IHS and tribal direct and contract health services.
[b]Direct, IHS and tribal direct general hospitals.
[c]Contract, contract health services.

Patterns of hospitalization among Indians continue to undergo considerable modification, similar to those in the rest of the population. As noted in Chapter 5, in spite of increasing population size and age, the number of hospitalizations continues to decline, along with a decline in the average length of stay. Similar trends in average daily patient load have been noted (Indian Health Service 1997b).

Life Expectancy and Years of Potential Life Lost

During the past 20 years, the life expectancy of the IHS service population has increased from 63.5 years (1972–74) to 71.4 years (1992–94), or 12 percent, compared to an increase from 71.4 years (1973) to 75.5 years (1993), or 6.2 percent, for the general U.S. population. The gap between the life expectancies of Indians and the general U.S. population of 7.9 years in 1973 fell to 4.4 years by 1993. Should significant advances in preventing deaths, especially among youth, continue to be made, the life expectancy of Indians may reach that of the general population in the not too distant future. This improvement is also re-

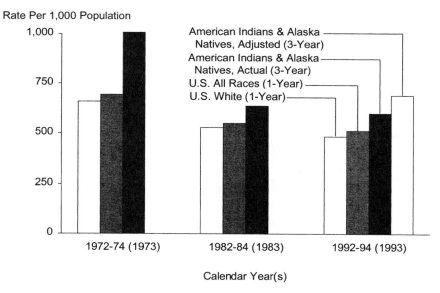

Figure 7.10. Comparison of age-adjusted death rates of American Indians and Alaska Natives with U.S. All Races and U.S. Whites, for several time periods. For 1993, a fourth bar is added to reflect the effect of adjustment for racial misclassification on death reports. *Source:* Indian Health Service 1997b, Chart 4.53.

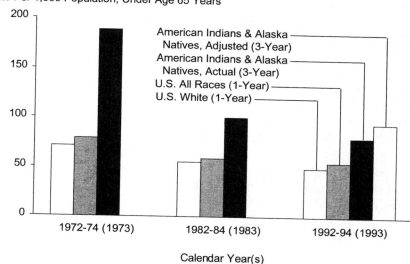

Figure 7.11. Comparison of years of potential life lost of American Indians and Alaska Natives with U.S. All Races and U.S. Whites, for several time periods. *Source:* Indian Health Service 1997b, Chart 4.52.

flected in the decrease of age-adjusted mortality rates of Indians from 1,007/ 100,000 in 1972–74 to 690/100,000 in 1992–94, a decrease of 31 percent (Figure 7.10). During this time the ratio of Indian death rates to those of U.S. All Races fell from 1.45 to 1.35.

Similar substantial decreases have been experienced in years of potential life lost (YPLL), a mortality indicator that measures the burden imposed by premature deaths (Figure 7.11). The rate of YPLL for Indians was 188.3/1,000 population in 1972–74, and it fell to 94.6/1,000 by 1992–94, a decrease of 50 percent. However, the difference in YPLL between Indians and U.S. All Races remains high, reflecting the disproportionately high death rates among young Indian persons.

Discussion

Although much excess Indian morbidity and mortality remains, distinct improvements in each have been realized. Some of these improvements may be associated with lower overall rates among recently federally recognized Indian populations. It is not presently possible to estimate the potential differences in health risk represented by these additional populations, but it is likely that their effects are slight.

The reasons for these morbidity and mortality improvements are not entirely clear but undoubtedly relate to improved socioeconomic conditions, improved sanitation and safe water, and application of comprehensive community-oriented care stressing prevention as well as therapeutic modalities. The successes of the IHS programs have never been systematically analyzed, but it is reasonable to conclude that the attention to prevention, community orientation, and quality health-care services that characterizes the IHS program must have played a prominent role (Rhoades, D'Angelo, and Hurlburt 1987). There is every reason to be optimistic about the long-term health of Indian people, especially if those conditions attributed to lifestyle can be favorably influenced. However, the anomie, isolation, self-destructive lifestyles, and generally depressed socioeconomic conditions that continue in most reservations and Alaska Native villages will also take a tragic toll in Indian lives.

Continued emphasis on prevention is reflected in the targeting of behavioral and lifestyle risk factors in many IHS interventions by an IHS and tribal workgroup (Indian Health Service 1996b). This workgroup developed a menu of performance measures from which IHS and tribes can choose in order to guide interventions and track progress. Although none of these measures is mandatory for tribes, the workgroup selected 10 measures that it classified as "highly recommended." These 10 targets cannot, in most cases, be readily calculated by IHS headquarters; they may require the use of local databases, other data sources (e.g., schools, police departments, state records), or local surveys (e.g., behavioral risk factor surveys). The "highly recommended" targets are

— Age-specific overweight and obesity prevalence rates
— Prevalence of tobacco use
— Prevalence of alcohol and drug dependence of adults, youth, and pregnant women
— Rate of family violence (child, spouse, elder abuse, and neglect)
— Number and percentage of homes (existing and new) with deficiencies in sanitation of drinking water and waste disposal, by community
— Rate of hospital discharges and ambulatory clinic visits for injury
— Proportion of population screened for cancer of the uterine cervix, breast cancer, and colorectal cancer
— Immunization rates of all age groups in accordance with Advisory Committee on Immunization Practice recommendations
— Incidence and prevalence of diabetes mellitus
— Collaboration or incorporation of community values or spiritual healing at each facility, with respect for individual beliefs

REFERENCES

Indian Health Service. 1996a. *Adjusting for Miscoding of Indian Race on State Death Certificates.* Rockville, Md.: Indian Health Service, Program Statistics Team.

——. 1996b. *Baseline Measures Workgroup Report.* Rockville, Md.: Indian Health Service.

——. 1996c. *Summary of Leading Causes for Ambulatory Medical Care Visits, Indian Health Service and Tribal Direct Facilities, Fiscal Year 1994.* Rockville, Md.: Indian Health Service, Program Statistics Team.

——. 1996d. *Utilization of IHS Hospitals, FY 1994.* Rockville, Md.: Indian Health Service, Program Statistics Team.

——. 1997a. *Regional Differences in Indian Health, 1997.* Rockville, Md.: Indian Health Service, Program Statistics Team.

——. 1997b. *Trends in Indian Health, 1997.* Rockville, Md.: Indian Health Service, Program Statistics Team.

National Medical Expenditure Survey. 1989. *Questionnaires and Data Collection Methods for the Household Survey and the Survey of American Indians and Alaska Natives Methods.* PHS Publication No. 89-4350. Rockville, Md.: National Center for Health Services Research.

Rhoades ER. 1990. The major respiratory diseases of American Indians. *Am Rev Respir Dis* 141:595–600.

Rhoades ER, D'Angelo AJ, Hurlburt WB. 1987. The Indian Health Service record of achievement. *Public Health Rep* 102:356–60.

Sievers ML, Fisher JR. 1981. Diseases of North American Indians. In: Rothschild HR, ed. *Biocultural Aspects of Disease.* New York: Academic Press.

8

Jeffrey C. Long, Ph.D., and
Joseph G. Lorenz, Ph.D.

Genetic Polymorphism and American Indian Origins, Affinities, and Health

As noted in Chapter 1, the preponderance of present evidence supports the inference that the Americas were originally settled by Asiatic peoples. Asian origins were recognized by anthropologists early in this century on the basis of body form, dental features, and geographic plausibility. Solid archaeologic evidence demonstrates that both North and South America were completely occupied by about ten thousand years ago, and new findings suggest that both continents were inhabited much earlier. At European contact in the late fifteenth century, American Indian populations were diverse in their cultural and ecological adaptations, as well as in their languages. The conditions accompanying the peopling of the New World and the subsequent cultural and linguistic diversification also favored genetic diversification. To the extent that the American Indian populations have remained intact, the patterns of modern genetic polymorphisms will provide clues regarding their affinities and also provide opportunities to examine the comparative roles of genetic, compared to environmental and sociocultural, factors in disease causation. Even with the distortions of the pre-Columbian genetic signature associated with disease, warfare, and dislocation after European contact, it is likely that studies of genetic affinities and polymorphisms will yield important health benefits.

This chapter summarizes existing information regarding studies of genetic markers and determinants among that heterogeneous group designated Native Americans. Because a comprehensive review of all recent advances is beyond the scope of this chapter, several carefully chosen examples are presented to illustrate this perspective on genetic epidemiology. It will be immediately apparent that the study of genetic markers is not a new phenomenon and that data have been accumulating in various ways for decades. The exquisite precision of present molecular analysis introduced what amounts to a new paradigm. Many Indian people are concerned that such research has unknown consequences, some of which may be adverse. The ultimate judgment of the usefulness of such studies should be made by Indian people themselves.

Patterns of Genetic Polymorphism

Blood Groups and Classical Marker Systems

American Indians are polymorphic for the classic blood groups and erythrocyte and serum protein marker loci. Early genetic studies noted that American Indians and their descendants are generally characterized by the absence of alleles (such as B, A_2, Lu^a, Rh-r, acid phosphatase-p^c, and AK^2) that are frequently found in non-Indians. Indians lack the most common European allele ($Gm^{3;5,13,14}$) in the immunoglobulin system, and they show substantially reduced variation in the major histocompatibility complex (Williams and McAuley 1992a, 1992b; Black 1994). However, some populations are polymorphic for blood protein allozymes ($Al^*Naskapi$, $Al^*Mexico$, $Gc^*Eskimo$, $Gc^*Chippewa$, Tf^*C4), HLA markers ($BN21$, $BW48$, $BN5$, $DRW36$), and the Diego antigen system, which are not seen in non-Indians (Szathmary 1993). These patterns made it possible to trace the introduction of European genes into American Indian gene pools. Thus, European ancestry is often estimated between 5 percent and 15 percent (Szathmary and Reed 1972; Chakraborty 1986; Knowler et al. 1988; Williams et al. 1992). Such admixture estimates must be cautiously interpreted because they assume that the exact ethnic composition of the Europeans who contributed to the American Indian gene pool can be identified. Despite this limitation, they have proven useful for disease study. For example, Knowler et al. (1988) noted a strong negative association between the Gm allele ($Gm^{3;5,13,14}$) and non-insulin-dependent diabetes mellitus (now designated type 2). However, this allele marks Caucasian admixture and it is therefore confounded with disease incidence, making less likely a direct association between Gm and diabetes.

Variations in the DNA of Nuclear and Mitochondrial Genomes

Knowledge of American Indian genetic structure has been augmented by recent observations on genetic variation at the deoxyribonucleic acid (DNA) level. These observations span broad classes of polymorphic loci that differ with respect to function, mutational mechanisms, and modes of inheritance. When DNA techniques are applied to population samples, intricate patterns of variation are observed. These patterns of variation are useful for reconstructing the evolutionary relationships of both DNA sequences and populations.

In American Indians, the most extensively studied genetic element is the small nonrecombining 16.6-kilobase genome found within the mitochondrion. Mitochondrial DNA (mtDNA) has a higher mutation rate than does nuclear DNA (nDNA) and, by contrast to biparental inheritance (which characterizes the vastly larger nuclear genome), the mitochondrial genome is inherited only from the mother. Because of its clonal replication, high mutation rate, and maternal inheritance pattern, mtDNA evolves rapidly and is useful for tracing maternal lineages.

Indian mtDNAs can be linked by mutational history back to four principal lineages, designated A–D (Schurr et al. 1990; Torroni et al. 1992). These lineages, or haplogroups, are identified by the presence or absence of characteristic restriction enzyme cleavage sites (i.e., the presence of a Hae III site at nucleotide pair [np] 663 defines haplogroup A, the absence of a Hinc II site at np 13259 and the presence of an Alu I site at np 13262 define haplogroup C, and the absence of an Alu I site at np 5176 defines haplogroup D) or, in the case of haplogroup B, the presence of a 9-bp deletion in the intergenic region between the cytochrome oxidase II and lysine transfer ribonucleic acid (tRNA) genes (Schurr et al. 1990; Torroni et al. 1992; Torroni et al. 1993a). Recently, a possible fifth mitochondrial haplogroup, X, which is marked by the absence of a Dde I restriction site at np 1715, has been discovered (Forster et al. 1996). Sequence data from the noncoding control region of the mtDNA also identifies the four main haplogroups (Ward et al. 1991; Ginther et al. 1993; Torroni et al. 1993a; Horai et al. 1993), with each haplogroup defined by a set of characteristic point mutations (Forster et al. 1996).

The distribution of the four major haplogroups among North American Indians varies by geography and linguistic affiliation (Merriwether, Rothhammer, and Ferrell 1995; Lorenz and Smith 1996). Generally, haplogroup A is most frequent among populations living in the north. The highest frequencies for haplogroup A have been reported for the Inuit (97%) (Lorenz and Smith 1996), Savonga Eskimo (94%) (Merriwether, Rothhammer, and Ferrell 1995), and Haida (94%) (Torroni et al. 1993a; Ward et al. 1993). The lowest frequencies of haplogroup A are found in populations presently occupying the American Southwest, including the Great Basin. Except in the Apache and Navajo, relative newcomers to the Southwest, haplogroup A is absent or found in low frequencies among the Yuman-speaking groups, the Tanoan-speaking Pueblos, the Pima, Paiute, Shoshone, and Washo (Lorenz and Smith 1996).

The distribution of haplogroup B is almost completely opposite that of A. It is almost completely absent in populations living in the Arctic and reaches its highest frequencies in the Southwest/Great Basin/California area. The frequencies of haplogroups C and D vary from population to population.

Polymorphisms located in the male-specific portion of the Y chromosome are inherited along paternal lineages, and accordingly their distribution provides a natural complement to the distribution of mtDNA variations. However, for several reasons male-specific Y polymorphisms have been difficult to identify and assay: a small effective population size, low mutation rates, and nucleotide sequence organization that is not amenable to convenient genotyping techniques (Underhill et al. 1996). Nevertheless, Indians portray an interesting pattern of variation for a handful of Y polymorphisms that are now routinely surveyed.

A point mutation (C→T) in the *DYS199* locus that is polymorphic in American Indians but generally absent in non-Indians was recently identified (Orita et al. 1989; Underhill et al. 1996). Initially, the *DYS199*-T allele was seen in high prevalence in American Indian subjects representing both continents and all three of the major New World language families, and it was not observed in African, Asian, Oceanic, and European subjects (Underhill et al. 1996). This suggests that the original mutation occurred sometime after New World peoples separated from their Asian ancestors and before they differentiated internally along geographical, cultural, and linguistic lines. Subsequent reports showed the occurrence of *DYS199*-T in more North and South American Indian samples (Bianchi et al. 1997; Karafet et al. 1997; Lell et al. 1997). Moreover, two groups have identified its presence in northern Siberian populations including Evenks, Chukchi, and Siberian Eskimos (Karafet et al. 1997; Lell et al. 1997).

North American Indians have now been typed at highly informative DNA short tandem repeat (STR) loci. These loci are typically located outside of gene coding sequences, and their alleles consist of short nucleotide sequence motifs repeated in tandem. STR loci are ideal genetic markers because they often have many alleles and most genotypes are heterozygous. A recent study of 377 alleles at 33 STR loci shows that Indian samples are approximately 10 percent more homozygous than European samples (Urbanek, Goldman, and Long 1996). Interestingly, homozygosity tended to be increased for the same alleles in all tribes. This suggests that much genetic diversity was lost before tribal groups separated from a common gene pool. It was also seen that the level of genetic differentiation among Indian populations is substantially higher than the level of differentiation among European populations. This reflects both the effects of subdivision into numerous language and culture groups and the effects of post-Columbian population collapse.

A similar pattern is noted at other autosomal marker loci. HLA-DRB1 is a highly polymorphic locus in the major histocompatibility complex whose alleles can be arranged in lineages reflecting descent with mutation from a common ancestral form (Bergström et al. 1997, 1998). Erlich et al. (1997) found that alleles belonging to several lineages commonly observed in non-Indians, such as DR1, DR3, DR5, DR, and DR10, are absent or nearly absent in North and South American Indians. Moreover, the DR2, DR6, DR8, and DR9 lineages are represented by the same few alleles in all Indian populations. This pattern of shared loss of HLA-DRB1 alleles and lineages suggests once again that American Indian populations experienced a severe "bottleneck" before their divergence from a common gene pool.

Indian autosomal gene diversity has also been studied using the distribution of *Alu* insertion polymorphisms. *Alu* elements are short nucleotide sequences (282 base pairs) that occur at approximately 500,000 locations throughout the human genome. *Alu* sequences are a feature of all primate genomes, and all *Alu* sequences are derived from the 7SL RNA gene; however, *Alu* sequences are grouped in families and subfamilies, and members of the HS family appear exclusively in humans. Several HS *Alu* sequences are polymorphic for their presence or absence. They make ideal genetic markers because absence is always their ancestral state and there does not appear to be back mutation. In a study of 5 polymorphic *Alu* loci in 24 Indian populations, Novick et al. (1998) reported a close affinity of North American Indians to Chinese and a general tendency for North, Central, and South American Indian populations to cluster together. While the results varied by *Alu* locus, the Indian samples exhibited generally lower heterozygosity than was observed in non-Indians. Indian populations with high heterozygosity bore the signature of non-Indian admixture. The *APO Alu* sequence was fixed in 14 populations spanning North and South America, thus showing a trend for loss of diversity that was similar to other nDNA polymorphisms.

Origins and Affinities

The Origins of Native Americans

In addition to the evidence of an Asian origin for American Indians noted in Chapter 1, a rapidly accumulating body of information of genetic markers is being applied to origins and ethnic affinities of American Indians. The three-wave migration hypothesis (Greenberg 1987, 1996; Greenberg, Turner, and Zegura 1986) was supported by a tripartite structure of variation in the immunoglobulin heavy chain polymorphism, *Gm*. Williams et al. (1985) demonstrated a consistent pattern of allele frequency differences among the major language groups (Amerind, Na Dene, and Eskimo-Aleut) and the existence of a

Na Dene–associated allele. While these observations are consistent with the introduction of populations by three waves of migration, they are also consistent with isolation after entry into the New World (Szathmary 1993).

Torroni et al. (1992) investigated mtDNA lineage relationships among samples from eight tribes. These included Northern and Southern Na Dene speakers, as well as North, Central, and South American Amerind speakers. mtDNAs belonging to four lineages (A–D) were observed in Amerind speakers. However, only mtDNAs belonging to groups A and B were seen in Na Dene speakers. Torroni et al. (1992) discovered that a *Rsa*I site at np 16,329 was lost from haplogroup A mtDNAs in all Na Dene–speaking populations but was present in all Amerind-speaking populations.

Since the mtDNA haplogroups form lineages related by steps of mutation, the age of a lineage can potentially be revealed by the amount of diversity it has accumulated. The temporal component is potentially a powerful addition to the simple patterns of distribution. Interestingly, Torroni et al. (1994b) found that, in Amerind speakers, mtDNAs belonging to the A, C, and D lineages showed 0.084 percent divergence, which suggests that they began mutating from a common haplotype some 21,000 to 42,000 years before the present (YBP). If most divergence among haplotypes in groups A, C, and D occurred after entry into the New World, then the mtDNA "clock" supports the oldest dates of archaeologic material (up to 35,000 YBP). By contrast, Na Dene mtDNAs in groups A and B show more limited divergence of <0.035 percent, suggesting radiation from a common ancestral haplotype some 5,250–16,000 YBP. In fact, the estimated age range for diversity in the A group haplotypes (5,250–10,500) spans the 9,000 YBP date calculated from linguistic diversity (Greenberg, Turner, and Zegura 1986).

The application of these estimated lineage divergence times to population divergences has, unfortunately, been thwarted by the discovery that all four lineages are more widely distributed among populations than initially realized (Merriwether, Rothhammer, and Ferrell 1995; Lorenz and Smith 1996, 1997). The three-wave model has also been challenged by most other analyses of DNA variations. In studies of mtDNA sequence variation in three tribes of the Pacific Northwest, Ward et al. (1993) found evidence for high effective population size and recent divergence from a common ancestral gene pool. The wide distribution of the (C→T) polymorphism at the *DYS199* locus also suggests that all Native American populations have diverged from a single founding stock. The STRs and HLA-DRB1 autosomal DNA polymorphisms both suggest that all Native American populations have diverged from a common founding stock that experienced a severe population bottleneck. How else could it be that homozygosity was increased for the same alleles in most populations, representing all language groups?

The Affinity to Asian Populations

A recent phylogenetic analysis of worldwide populations employing classical markers such as blood groups, serum proteins, red cell enzymes, HLA, and immunoglobulins demonstrated affinities between Native Americans and Asians (Nei and Roychoudhury 1993). However, too few Asian populations were analyzed to shed light on a specific Asian group with close affinities to the ancestors of Native Americans. The four New World mtDNA haplogroups A, B, C, and D occur in east Asia, where they have been identified among Koreans, Malaysian Chinese, Taiwanese Han (Ballinger et al. 1992), and Tibetans (Torroni et al. 1994a), although at much lower frequencies than in New World populations. In Siberia, haplogroup B is generally absent, but the frequencies of haplogroups A and especially C and D are higher than in east Asia (Torroni et al. 1993a). On mainland Asia, haplogroup B appears at its highest frequencies in Han Chinese and Mongolians (Kolman, Sambuughin, and Bermingham 1996), but other evidence that these populations are closely related to the progenitors of Native Americans is generally lacking.

The Y-chromosome–linked *DYS199*-T allele is generally absent in Asian populations (Underhill et al. 1996; Karafet et al. 1997), but it has recently been identified in several groups of northeast Siberians: Evens, Chukchi, and Siberian Eskimos. The presence of this allele can be accounted for by either of two scenarios. First, the northeast Siberians are closely related to the Native American ancestors within whom the *DYS199*-T mutation arose (Lell et al. 1997). Second, the allele's presence in modern northern Siberians reflects a reflux of genes from the New World (Karafet et al. 1997). Either scenario is plausible; however, the reflux hypothesis is bolstered by the fact that Asian and North American Eskimos have frequently maintained contact by crossing the Bering Strait. Interestingly, these same Siberian populations carry copies of haplogroup B mtDNAs (Forster et al. 1996; Torroni et al. 1993b). Thus, both males and females would need to have traveled back across the Bering Strait if reflux has occurred.

Cautions

Several cautions must be recognized in interpreting these results. First, American Indian populations today are small and semi-isolated. This situation tends to accentuate between-group differences and raises the possibility that the population specificity of the variants will vanish as more representatives within these groups are analyzed. Second, the accumulation of genetic variance is stochastic, and estimates of divergence times are associated with large standard errors that are difficult to evaluate. Thus, an observed pattern of variance can be in accord with more than one population history scenario. Third, certain critical assumptions necessary for divergence time estimates are virtually untestable. We cannot know that most divergence between mtDNAs within the four main haplogroups occurred after the peopling of the Americas or that the population specificity does not arise from the loss of mtDNAs from a common diverse gene pool.

Genetic Polymorphism in Relation to Disease Patterns

The architecture of the American Indian gene pool reflects at least four important historical phases in the accumulation of genetic polymorphism. First, Indians possess many polymorphisms that are ubiquitous in human populations. These polymorphisms are presumably ancient and arose before the geographical expansion of the species and the genetic differentiation of continental and local populations. Second, all (or most) American Indians descended from a common population that experienced a severe population bottleneck at or before the time they migrated to the Americas. Third, the process of cultural and linguistic diversification was accompanied by restricted contact and genetic differentiation. Fourth, European contact caused a nearly total population collapse; entire groups were lost, formerly distinct populations amalgamated, and there has been genetic admixture with non-Indians. Each phase in the generation of diversity superimposed its effect on the signature of the earlier phases. All four phases in this population history will have affected the occurrence of hereditary diseases, and they provide a structure within which to examine genetic, environmental, and sociocultural factors in disease causation (Lander and Schork 1994).

Mendelian Disorders

Mendelian disorders reflect differences in genotype at a single locus. Environment is generally unimportant in their transmission or expression. Since many such genetic disorders involve recessive genes, their prevalence in small populations will randomly fluctuate.

Severe combined immunodeficiency disease (SCID) is a group of heterogeneous diseases characterized by deficient T-cell immunity with or without B-cell immunodeficiency. A severe autosomal recessive form (A-SCID) involving both T cells and B cells has been noted in the Southwestern Athabascan-speaking populations (i.e., Navajos and Apaches). A recent genomewide linkage scan performed in unrelated families has unequivocally localized a gene for this disorder to chromosome 10p in Navajos and Apaches (Li et al. 1998). This distribution is striking because A-SCID is not seen in non-Athabascan-speaking

Southwestern Indians and it is seen in a small Athabascan-speaking tribe of the Northwest Territory, the Diné. Presumably, A-SCID in the Diné is genetically homogeneous with Navajo and Apache A-SCID. If this is so, then the A-SCID disease mutation probably arose sometime after the separation of the Na Dene and Amerindian language families, and the distribution of this disease relates to the third phase of American Indian diversification. Nevertheless, linkage analysis of A-SCID in one Diné family is inconclusive, and the disease may be heterogeneous, even within this language group.

The complexity of origin of recessive disease phenotype distribution is illustrated very well by cystic fibrosis (CF) in Pueblo Indians. CF is the most common recessive lethal disease in Europeans, with a prevalence of approximately four in ten thousand. All known cases of CF are traceable to defects in the CF transmembrane regulator protein, and 70–80 percent of all defective alleles carry the same mutation, a 3-bp deletion of codon 508. CF occurs at Zuni and Jemez Pueblos, both in New Mexico. Both populations number under ten thousand people; thus, these are some of the highest CF prevalences observed.

An analysis of the fine-grained molecular structure of CF-bearing chromosomes revealed two interesting features (Grebe et al. 1992). First, the most frequently occurring European mutation, $\Delta F508$, was absent at both pueblos. Second, different CF mutations were segregating at Zuni and Jemez. A follow-up study showed that four different CF mutations were segregating in Pueblo Indians (Mercier et al. 1994). The most frequent mutation was R1162X, which was first identified in Italians. Using intragenic short tandem repeats, it was determined that Puebloan R1162X genes are identical to those of European origin, that this allele was most likely introduced by European settlers, and that it increased by genetic drift. The next most common CF mutation was the 3849+10kbC→T allele, which is also seen in Europeans. However, this allele was associated with a different haplotype than that generally carried in Europeans, and a multicentric origin of the allele is implicated. Since the Puebloan form of 3849+10kbC→T was seen in CF cases from four different New Mexican pueblos, it can be considered a Native American mutation. Finally, a unique allele, D648V, was observed in one Puebloan patient. CF alleles in Southwestern Indians therefore appear as a consequence of European admixture and the unique histories of local populations.

Complex Diseases

Complex diseases are transmitted in families in a non-Mendelian manner. The genetic basis of complex disease is expressed at the level of risk and susceptibility and reflects the combined action of genes and environment. Because of this, it cannot be determined whether differences between populations are determined by genes, environments, or both. The same complex diseases appear in all human populations: examples include allergies, cancers, diabetes, heart disease, psychiatric disorders, and stroke. Identification of the genes for complex diseases will help to identify the underlying physiologic pathways and to pinpoint environmental mechanisms. Eventually, this research will facilitate the development of better prevention and treatment strategies.

Non-insulin-dependent diabetes mellitus (NIDDM) is a complex disease that afflicts people from all ethnic backgrounds. However, it is now very common in American Indian populations, and the Pima Indians of Arizona experience the world's highest prevalence (Knowler et al. 1978). Interestingly, the Pima were among the first tribes to exhibit high diabetes prevalence, and geneticists tried to explain this observation as a unique Piman phenomenon. Neel (1962) postulated that Piman nutrient uptake was increased by natural selection to better utilize inconsistent resources in their harsh desert environment. The advantage of this adaptation was then reversed upon modernization and a more abundant food supply. However, the Pima tribe also acculturated early, and a sharp increase in diabetes prevalence has recently been observed in many American Indian tribes and Native Alaskans (Gohdes, Schraer, and Rith-Najarian 1996). Thus, the genetic component underlying American Indian diabetes would have originated early in history, perhaps at the time when the Americas were settled. Piman diabetes is now seen as belonging to a phenomenon shared by all or most American Indians and as part of a constellation of metabolic conditions that also includes early-onset obesity, gallstones from lithogenic bile, and cancers of the middle digestive tract (Weiss, Ferrell, and Hanis 1984; Weiss et al. 1984). Although none of these conditions follows a strictly Mendelian mode of inheritance, their genetic underpinnings are confirmed by familial aggregation and the fact that the prevalence of diabetes in genetically admixed Mexican American populations reflects the degree of American Indian admixture.

The dramatic increases in prevalence of these metabolic diseases since World War II indicate that there is an *interaction* between susceptible genotypes and environmental factors, including high-fat, low-fiber, and high-carbohydrate diets coupled with a sedentary lifestyle (Weiss, Ferrell, and Hanis 1984). This *interaction* implies more than a simple combination of genetic and environmental effects. It suggests that neither the specific genes nor the specific environments alone are sufficient for manifestation; high NIDDM prevalence requires that both occur simultaneously. The genetic component of American Indian diabetes seems to have become fixed at an earlier time when these diverse populations shared a common gene pool, perhaps at the time of migration into the Americas.

Alcoholism is another common complex disease that occurs in people of all ethnic backgrounds. Extremely high rates of alcoholism have been observed in some American Indian populations: about 80 percent in men and 50 percent in women (Kinzie et al. 1992; Brown et al. 1993; Robin et al. 1998). Family, twin, and adoption studies have established a genetic component underlying risk for alcoholism in non-Indians (Aston and Hill 1990; Crum and Harris 1996; Kendler et al. 1994; Pickens et al. 1991; Cloninger, Bohman, and Sigvardsson 1981; Sigvardsson, Bohman, and Cloninger 1996). Investigations into the genetics of alcoholism in American Indians have begun only recently. Long et al. (1998) reported that family members are significant predictors of alcoholism risk and that linkage analysis with more than five hundred genetic marker loci indicates that regions on chromosomes 4 and 11 may harbor genes influencing susceptibility.

A region indicating linkage on chromosome 4 contains the alcohol dehydrogenase (ADH) gene cluster. ADH loci are important candidate genes for alcoholism because the ADH enzyme initiates the first step in alcohol metabolism. Many Asians carry alleles for ADH genes with enhanced catalytic activity (Chen et al. 1996; Maezawa et al. 1995; Nakamura et al. 1996). Interestingly, these variants confer *resistance* to alcoholism by increasing sensitivity to alcohol toxicity. However, the most protective ADH allele in Asians, *ADH2−2,* is generally absent in all non-Asians, including American Indians. The chromosome 11 region indicating linkage to alcoholism is similarly interesting. It harbors several genes with neurobiological function, including the DRD4 dopamine receptor gene. Variants at the DRD4 locus have been associated with novelty-seeking personality traits in two European-derived populations (Benjamin et al. 1996; Ebstein et al. 1996). While definitive roles for either ADH or DRD4 remain to be established, it is interesting that linkage and association studies point to the same genes and chromosomes in populations from a variety of ethnic backgrounds.

Interestingly, there are American Indian tribes with a low alcoholism prevalence. One group recently described is a Southeastern tribe that underwent European acculturation in the seventeenth century (Albaugh et al. 1998). Since alcoholism is apparently decreased in this tribe, there is little evidence for the type of gene/environment interaction that characterizes NIDDM. Epidemiologic studies in many non-Indian populations show that the prevalence of alcoholism is increased in several situations: men (relative to women), low education, low income, low occupational status, and marital instability (Bucholz 1992; Helzer, Burnam, and McEvoy 1991). Although American Indians have been studied less, no evidence suggests that alcoholism in American Indians departs from these basic socioeconomic trends (Kinzie et al. 1992; Brown et al. 1993). Unlike the situation in NIDDM, genes and environment apparently contribute to American Indian alcoholism in much the same manner as they contribute to alcoholism in other populations. While many American Indians seem to occupy environments saturated for environmental risk, there is presently no evidence that the prevalence of alcoholism or its transmission in families can be attributed to unique features of the American Indian gene pool.

Other conditions with complex causes and inheritance of considerable interest for both clinicians and investigators were noted by Brenneman (1997). These include familial Navajo arthropathy (Johnsen, Johnson, and Stein 1993; Singleton et al. 1990), congenital adrenal hyperplasia (Hirschfeld and Fleshman 1969), Kuskokwim syndrome (Wright 1970), metachromatic leukodystrophy (Pastor-Soler et al. 1994), and congenital hip dysplasia (Chnell 1989).

Discussion

A large and rapidly accumulating body of information about genetic markers and determinants of disease patterns provides one of the currently most promising avenues of biomedical investigation. In this chapter we have reviewed a historical framework for genetic diversity in American Indians in the hope that it will be useful in understanding the distribution of genetically determined diseases and learning about environmental mechanisms in complex diseases. Although the focus has been on the genetics of disease in American Indians, general knowledge of genetic diversity is relevant to routine medical applications, such as blood transfusion and forensic identification. In addition, the population relationships and history are likely to explain the absence or low incidence of genetic diseases (such as phenylketonuria, Tay-Sachs disease, and erythroblastosis fetalis) that are common in some non-Indian populations.

Finally, it must be recognized that our knowledge of the history of populations deciphered from the study of genes will have some practical applications but must not be treated as a dogma. First, science proceeds by proposing ideas and testing them against new data. Because of this, all scientific interpretations are improved and replaced with yet newer observations over time. Second, scientific investigations relate to material facts, but they cannot reveal the origin of the human spirit or be used to replace spiritual understandings of life. The latter are subjects that can be dealt with, at least presently, only through nonscientific means. Each population will respond according to its own ethos, culture, and understanding of its place in the universe. In presenting this review of observable and readily demonstrable genetic information, the authors remain highly cognizant of and respectful toward these fundamental concerns.

The public's intense interest in genetic testing and research is even more acute in Indian communities. The potential for inadvertent harm to Indian individuals and communities from such studies must be minimized. Making questions of ethical research more complicated is the fact that this is one of the most rapidly unfolding fields of inquiry, creating an urgent need for continual examination of and attention to local concerns.

REFERENCES

Albaugh G, Supple R, Standingwater R, et al. 1998. Alcohol use and dependence among members of a Southeastern American Indian tribe in Oklahoma. *Alcohol Clin Exp Res* 22:115A.

Aston CE, Hill SY. 1990. Segregation analysis of alcoholism in families ascertained through a pair of male alcoholics. *Am J Hum Genet* 46:879–87.

Ballinger SW, Schurr TG, Torroni A, et al. 1992. Southeast Asian mitochondrial DNA analysis reveals genetic continuity of ancient mongoloid migrations. *Genetics* 130: 139–52.

Benjamin J, Li L, Patterson C, et al. 1996. Population association between the D_4 dopamine receptor gene and measures of novelty seeking. *Nat Genet* 12:81–84.

Bergström TF, Josefsson A, Erlich HA, et al. 1997. Analysis of intron sequences at the class II HLA-DRB1 locus: Implications for the age of allelic diversity. *Hereditas* 127:1–5.

———. 1998. Recent origin of HLA-DRB1 alleles and implications for human evolution. *Nat Genet* 18:237–41.

Bianchi NO, Bailliet G, Bravi CM, et al. 1997. Origin of Amerindian Y-chromosomes as inferred by the analysis of six polymorphic markers. *Am J Phys Anthropol* 102:79–89.

Black FL. 1994. An explanation of high death rates among New World peoples when in contact with Old World diseases. *Perspect Biol Med* 37:292–307.

Brenneman G. 1997. Chronic and disabling conditions among American Indian and Alaska Native children and youth. *Fam Syst Health* 15:263–74.

Brown GL, Albaugh BJ, Robin RW, et al. 1993. Alcoholism and substance abuse among selected Southern Cheyenne Indians. *Cult Med Psychiatry* 16:531–42.

Bucholz KK. 1992. Alcohol abuse and dependence from a psychiatric epidemiologic perspective. *Alcohol Health Res World* 16:197–208.

Chakraborty R. 1986. Gene admixture in human populations: Models and predictions. *Yearbook Phys Anthropol* 29:1–43.

Chen WJ, Loh EW, Hsu YP, et al. 1996. Alcohol-metabolizing genes and alcoholism among Taiwanese Han men: Independent effect of ADH2, ADH3, and ALDH2. *Br J Psychiatry* 168:762–67.

Chnell S. 1989. Congenital dislocations of the hip. *IHS Prim Care Provider* 14:38–39.

Cloninger CR, Bohman M, Sigvardsson S. 1981. Inheritance of alcohol abuse: Cross-fostering analysis of adopted men. *Arch Gen Psychiatry* 38:861–68.

Crum RM, Harris EL. 1996. Risk of alcoholism and parental history: Gender differences and a possible reporting bias. *Genet Epidemiol* 13:329–41.

Ebstein RP, Novick O, Umansky R, et al. 1996. Dopamine D4 receptor (D4DR) exon III polymorphism associated with the human personality trait of novelty seeking. *Nat Genet* 12:78–80.

Erlich HA, Mack SJ, Bergström TF, et al. 1997. HLA class II alleles in Amerindian populations: Implications for the evolution of HLA polymorphism and the colonization of the Americas. *Hereditas* 127:19–24.

Forster P, Harding R, Torroni A, et al. 1996. Origin and evolution of Native American mtDNA variation: A reappraisal. *Am J Hum Genet* 59:935–45.

Ginther C, Corach D, Penacino GA, et al. 1993. Genetic variation among the Mapuche Indians from the Patagonian region of Argentina: Mitochondrial DNA sequence variation and allele frequencies of several nuclear genes. In: Pena SDJ, Chakraborty R, Epplen JT, et al., eds. *DNA Fingerprinting: State of the Science*, 211–19. Basel: Birkhauser Verlag.

Gohdes D, Schraer C, Rith-Najarian S. 1996. Diabetes prevention in American Indians and Alaska Natives: Where are we in 1994? *Diabetes Res Clin Pract* 34:S95–S100.

Grebe TA, Doane WW, Richter SF, et al. 1992. Mutation analysis of the cystic fibrosis transmembrance regulator gene in Native American populations of the Southwest. *Am J Hum Genet* 51:736–40.

Greenberg JH. 1987. *Language in the Americas*. Stanford: Stanford University Press.

———. 1996. The "Greenberg hypothesis." *Science* 274:1447 (editorial).

Greenberg JH, Turner CG II, Zegura SL. 1986. The settlement of the Americas: A comparison of the linguistic, dental, and genetic evidence. *Curr Anthropol* 27:477–97.

Helzer JE, Burnam A, McEvoy L. 1991. Alcohol abuse and dependence. In: Robins LN, Regier DA, eds. *Psychiatric Disorders in America: The Epidemiologic Catchment Area Study*, 81–115. New York: Free Press.

Hirschfeld AJ, Fleshman JK. 1969. An unusually high incidence of salt-losing congenital adrenal hyperplasia in the Alaskan Eskimo. *J Pediatr* 75:492–94.

Horai S, Kondo R, Nakagawa-Hattori Y, et al. 1993. Peopling of the Americas founded by four major lineages of mitochondrial DNA. *Mol Biol Evol* 10:23–47.

Johnsen SD, Johnson PC, Stein SR. 1993. Familial sensory autonomic neuropathy with arthropathy in Navajo children. *Neurology* 43:1120–25.

Karafet T, Zegura SL, Vuturo-Brady J, et al. 1997. Y chromosome markers and trans–Bering Strait dispersals. *Am J Phys Anthopol* 102:301–14.

Kendler KS, Neale MC, Heath AC, et al. 1994. A twin-family study of alcoholism in women. *Am J Psychiatry* 151:707–15.

Kinzie JD, Leung PK, Boehnlein J, et al. 1992. Psychiatric epidemiology of an Indian village: A 19-year replication study. *J Nerv Ment Dis* 180:33–39.

Knowler WC, Bennett PH, Hamman RF, et al. 1978. Diabetes incidence and prevalence in Pima Indians: A 19-fold greater incidence than in Rochester, Minnesota. *Am J Epidemiol* 108:497–505.

Knowler WC, Williams RC, Pettitt DJ, et al. 1988. Gm[3;5,13,14] and type 2 diabetes mellitus: An association in American Indians with genetic admixture. *Am J Hum Genet* 43:520–26.

Kolman CJ, Sambuughin N, Bermingham E. 1996. Mitochondrial DNA analysis of Mongolian populations and implications for the origin of New World founders. *Genetics* 142:1321–34.

Lander ES, Schork NJ. 1994. Genetic dissection of complex traits. *Science* 265:2037–48.

Lell JT, Brown MD, Schurr TG, et al. 1997. Y chromosome polymorphisms in Native American and Siberian populations: Identification of Native American Y chromosome haplotypes. *Hum Genet* 100:536–43.

Li L, Drayna D, Hu D, et al. 1998. The gene for severe combined immunodeficiency disease in Athabascan-speaking Native Americans is located on chromosome 10p. *Am J Hum Genet* 62:126–44.

Long JC, Knowler WC, Hanson RL, et al. 1998. Evidence for genetic linkage to alcohol dependence on chromosomes 4 and 11 from an autosome-wide scan in an American Indian population. *Am J Med Genet (Neuropsychiatr Genet)* 81:216–21.

Lorenz JG, Smith DG. 1996. Distribution of four founding mtDNA haplogroups among Native North Americans. *Am J Phys Anthropol* 101:307–23.

———. 1997. Distribution of sequence variation in the mtDNA control region of Native North Americans. *Hum Biol* 69:749–76.

Maezawa Y, Yamauchi M, Toda G, et al. 1995. Alcohol-metabolizing enzyme polymorphisms and alcoholism in Japan. *Alcohol Clin Exp Res* 19:951–54.

Mercier B, Raguénès O, Estivill X, et al. 1994. Complete detection of mutations in cystic fibrosis patients of Native American origin. *Hum Genet* 94:629–32.

Merriwether DA, Rothhammer F, Ferrell RE. 1995. Distribution of the four founding lineage haplotypes in Native Americans suggests a single wave of migration for the New World. *Am J Phys Anthropol* 98:411–30.

Nakamura K, Iwahashi K, Matsuo Y, et al. 1996. Characteristics of Japanese alcoholics with the atypical aldehyde dehydrogenase 2*2. I: A comparison of the genotypes of ALDH2, ADH2, ADH3, and cytochrome P-4502E1 between alcoholics and non-alcoholics. *Alcohol Clin Exp Res* 30:52–55.

Neel JV. 1962. Diabetes mellitus: A "thrifty" genotype rendered detrimental by "progress"? *Am J Hum Genet* 14:353–62.

Nei M, Roychoudhury AK. 1993. Evolutionary relationships of human populations on a global scale. *Mol Biol Evol* 10:927–43.

Novick GE, Novick CC, Yunis J, et al. 1998. Polymorphic *Alu* insertions and the Asian origin of Native American populations. *Hum Biol* 70:23–39.

Orita M, Iwahana H, Kanazawa H, et al. 1989. Detection of polymorphisms of human DNA by gel electrophoresis as single-stranded conformation polymorphisms. *Proc Natl Acad Sci USA* 86:2766–70.

Pastor-Soler NM, Rafi MA, Hoffman JD, et al. 1994. Metachromatic leukodystrophy in the Navajo Indian population: A splice site mutation in intron 4 of the arylsulfatase A gene. *Hum Mutat* 4:199–207.

Pickens RW, Svikis DS, McGue M, et al. 1991. Heterogeneity in the inheritance of alcoholism. *Arch Gen Psychiatry* 48:19–28.

Robin RW, Long JC, Rasmussen J, et al. 1998. Relationship of binge drinking to alcohol dependence, other psychiatric disorders, and behavioral problems in an American Indian tribe. *Alcohol Clin Exp Res* 22:518–23.

Schurr TG, Ballinger SW, Gan YY, et al. 1990. Amerindian mitochondrial DNAs have rare Asian mutations at high frequencies, suggesting they derived from four primary maternal lineages. *Am J Hum Genet* 46:613–23.

Sigvardsson S, Bohman M, Cloninger RC. 1996. Replication of the Stockholm adoption study of alcoholism: Confirmatory cross-fostering analysis. *Arch Gen Psychiatry* 53:681–86.

Singleton R, Helgerson SD, Snyder RD, et al. 1990. Neuropathy in Navajo children: Clinical and epidemiologic features. *Neurology* 40:363–67.

Szathmary EJE. 1993. Genetics of aboriginal North Americans. *Evol Anthropol* 1:202–20.

Szathmary EJE, Reed TE. 1972. Calculation of the maximum amount of gene admixture in a hybrid population. *Am J Phys Anthropol* 48:29–34.

Torroni A, Miller JA, Moore LG, et al. 1994a. Mitochondrial DNA analysis in Tibet: Implications for the origin of the Tibetan population and its adaptation to high altitude. *Am J Phys Anthropol* 93:189–99.

Torroni A, Neel JV, Barrantes R, et al. 1994b. Mitochondrial DNA "clock" for the Amerinds and its implications for timing their entry into North America. *Proc Natl Acad Sci USA* 91:1158–62.

Torroni A, Schurr TG, Cabell MF, et al. 1993a. Asian affinities and continental radiation of the four founding Native American mtDNAs. *Am J Hum Genet* 53:563–90.

Torroni A, Schurr TG, Yang CC, et al. 1992. Native American mitochondrial DNA analysis indicates that the Amerind and the Nadene populations were founded by two independent migrations. *Genetics* 130:153–62.

Torroni A, Sukernik RI, Schurr TG, et al. 1993b. mtDNA variation of aboriginal Siberians reveals distinct genetic affinities with Native Americans. *Am J Hum Genet* 53:591–608.

Underhill PA, Jin L, Zemans R, et al. 1996. A pre-Columbian Y chromosome-specific transition and its implications for human evolutionary history. *Proc Natl Acad Sci USA* 93:196–200.

Urbanek M, Goldman D, Long JC. 1996. The apportionment of dinucleotide repeat diversity in Native Americans and Europeans: A new approach to measuring gene identity reveals asymmetric patterns of divergence. *Mol Biol Evol* 13:943–53.

Ward RH, Frazier BS, Dew-Jager K, et al. 1991. Extensive mitochondrial diversity within a single Amerindian tribe. *Proc Natl Acad Sci USA* 88:8720–24.

Ward RH, Redd A, Valencia D, et al. 1993. Genetic and linguistic differentiation in the Americas. *Proc Natl Acad Sci USA* 90:10663–67.

Weiss KM, Ferrell RE, Hanis CL. 1984. A New World syndrome of metabolic diseases with a genetic and evolutionary basis. *Yearbook Phys Anthropol* 27:153–78.

Weiss KM, Ferrell RE, Hanis CL, et al. 1984. Genetics and epidemiology of gallbladder disease in New World native peoples. *Am J Hum Genet* 36:1259–78.

Williams RC, Knowler WC, Pettitt DJ, et al. 1992. The magnitude and origin of European-American admixture in the Gila River Indian Community of Arizona: A union of genetics and demography. *Am J Hum Genet* 51:101–10.

Williams RC, McAuley JE. 1992a. HLA class I variation controlled for genetic admixture in the Gila River Indian community of Arizona: A model for the Paleo-Indians. *Hum Immunol* 33:39–46.

———. 1992b. HLA class II variation in the Gila River Indian community of Arizona: Alleles, haplotypes, and a high frequency of epitope at the HLA-DR locus. *Hum Immunol* 33:29–38.

Williams RC, Steinberg AG, Gershowitz H, et al. 1985. Gm allotypes in Native Americans: Evidence for three distinct migrations across the Bering Land Bridge. *Am J Phys Anthopol* 66:1–19.

Wright DG. 1970. The unusual skeletal findings of the Kuskokwim syndrome. *Birth Defects* 6:16–24.

9

George R. Brenneman, M.D., FAAP

Maternal, Child, and Youth Health

It is generally believed that maternal and child health status is the single most widely used index of the health systems available for various populations. This principle was emphasized by one of the first actions taken by Dr. Ray Shaw, the new director at the inception of the Indian Health Service (IHS) in 1955, when he appointed a maternal and child health specialist. This chapter will discuss the major changes in maternal and child health (MCH) status in recent decades, current problems, and programs designed to improve these important indices of community health.

Maternal Health Status

Approximately 40,000 Indian births occur each year in the United States, 33,429 of these within the IHS Service Area (Indian Health Service 1997b). The birth rate among Indians decreased from 30 births/1,000 population in 1980–82 to 25.6 in 1992–94. This compares with U.S. White birth rates of 14.8 in 1981 and 14.7 in 1993. Indian birth rates seem to be decreasing while U.S. White rates remain fairly constant (Indian Health Service 1997b).

Maternal Mortality

Year-to-year Indian maternal mortality data require careful interpretation. Relatively small numbers allow wide fluctuations in rates from year to year; one Indian maternal death increases the maternal mortality rate by more than two-fold. Between 1991 and 1994, there was an average of one maternal death per year (Indian Health Service 1997b). From 1982 to 1991, Indian maternal mortality rates varied between 4.0 and 12.0/100,000 live births, 0.9 to 2.1 times the

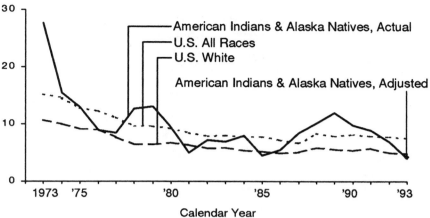

Per 100,000 Live Births

Figure 9.1. Maternal death rates of American Indians and Alaska Natives, U.S. All Races, and U.S. Whites, since 1973. The 1993 rate adjusted for racial misclassification on death records is the same as the actual rate recorded. The fluctuation in the rates for American Indians and Alaska Natives is largely the result of very small numbers. *Source:* Indian Health Service 1997b, Chart 3.7

rates for U.S. White mothers during the same period (Indian Health Service 1995). The sharp decline in maternal mortality rates is shown in Figure 9.1, along with the fluctuations associated with very small numbers. This improvement reflects efforts to provide prenatal care and have deliveries attended by appropriately trained providers in a hospital environment accessible to all Indian women. Approximately 95 percent of all Indian deliveries occur in an accredited facility.

Births

On average, Indian women give birth at younger ages than do women in the general population. Forty-five percent of Indian women are under the age of 20 and 2 percent are older than 34 at the time of the birth of their first child. This compares with 24 percent and 5 percent, respectively, for the general U.S. population of women (U.S. All Races women). Of the Indian births for 1992 to 1994, 20.5 percent were to women under the age of 20 compared to 12.8 percent for U.S. All Races women. Infants born to Indian women under age 20 have a relatively low rate (5.7%) of low birth weight (LBW) (less than 2,500 grams). In contrast, 9.3 percent of births to U.S. All Races mothers less than 20 years of age were LBW births. In general, the LBW rate among Indian births is lower except for Indian mothers older than 30 years of age (Indian Health Service 1997b). Based on this information, newborns of Indian teen mothers may be relatively healthier, which is further supported by the relatively low Indian neonatal infant mortality. Few data are available, but one study showed a much higher rate of low birth weight among urban Indians than among urban Whites and rural Indians (Grossman et al. 1994).

Prenatal Care

Large numbers of Indian women live in isolated and remote rural areas. Prenatal care is not consistently available for nor accepted equally by all Indian women. Generally, 63.6 percent of Indian women who gave birth in 1992 to 1994 started prenatal care in the first trimester. This is considerably lower than the 78.9 percent for U.S. All Races women. However, percentages varied widely among Indians, with only 48.6 percent of Navajo women and as many as 77.6 percent of Alaska Native women entering prenatal care in the first trimester of pregnancy (Indian Health Service 1997a). This relatively high percentage of Alaska Native women receiving early prenatal care undoubtedly reflects the effective village health program in which indigenous workers (community health aides) are trained to provide preventive care services in the villages.

Children

Infant Mortality

The improvement in infant mortality in recent decades is strikingly illustrated in Figure 9.2. The 1992–94 (adjusted for miscoding) Indian infant mortality rate of 10.9 deaths/1,000 live births is an 83 percent decrease since 1954–56, when the unadjusted rate was 62.7/1,000 live births. As noted in Chapter 6, when infant births and deaths were linked, it was learned that a high proportion of Indian infant deaths were not recorded as "Indian." This is especially true for Indians living in California and Oklahoma. When infant deaths and births between 1983 and 1987 in California were linked, Indian infant mortality in California increased 250 percent (Querec 1994). After adjusting for miscoding (Indian Health Service 1996a), the overall Indian infant mortality for 1992–94 was 10.9 deaths/1,000 live births, compared to U.S. White infant mortality of 6.8 in 1993.

Even after correcting for miscoding, important regional differences between Indian groups remain. For 1992–94, the infant mortality rate for Navajos was 10.7, for Aberdeen Area Indians was 15.6, and for Alaska Natives was 11.7

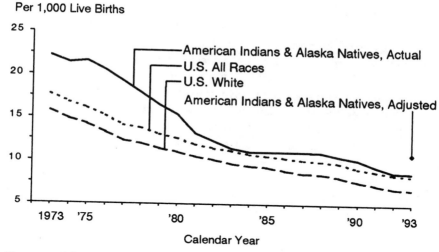

Figure 9.2. Infant mortality rates of American Indians and Alaska Natives, U.S. All Races, and U.S. Whites, since 1973. The American Indian and Alaska Natives rate for 1993 adjusted for racial misclassification on death records is shown by the *diamond point. Source:* Indian Health Service 1997b, Chart 3.8

deaths/1,000 live births. With respect to regional differences in infant mortality rates, two important observations should be noted. First, most (54%) Indian infant mortality occurs in the postneonatal period (28 days to 11 months). For U.S. Whites, neonatal (birth to 27 days) mortality accounts for most (62%) infant deaths. The adjusted Indian neonatal mortality (5.2/1,000 live births) for 1992–94 is slightly more than U.S. White neonatal mortality (4.3/1,000 live births) in 1993. The relatively low neonatal mortality among Indian infants may reflect generally healthy pregnancies and births and is supported by the low proportion of LBW births (Indian Health Service 1997b). Second, the three leading causes of overall, as well as postneonatal, Indian infant mortality are sudden infant death syndrome (SIDS), congenital anomalies, and injuries. For 1992–94, these caused slightly more than half of Indian infant deaths and 65 percent of postneonatal deaths. Among Indians, the rate of SIDS was 2.8 times and that of injuries was 3 times the rate experienced by U.S. Whites. While the adjusted SIDS rate was 1.24/1,000 live births among Navajos, approximately the same rate experienced among U.S. All Races, the SIDS rate among Aberdeen Area Indians was 3.88/1,000 and among Alaska Natives was 3.12/1,000 (Indian Health Service 1997a).

IHS providers gave serious attention to data published from several countries showing an association of SIDS with a prone sleeping position in infants and followed recommendations published by the Task Force on Infant Positioning and SIDS (American Academy of Pediatrics 1992). In collaboration with the National Institutes of Health, a prospective SIDS study has been instituted among Indians of the northern plains. Reports from this study may provide important information leading to other effective interventions that will reduce SIDS in Indian communities. At this time, reasons for these high rates among some Indian populations are not known. It has been noted that reported smoking rates among pregnant women are higher in the same IHS Areas that experience higher rates of SIDS (Indian Health Service 1997a).

From 1990 to 1992, accidents emerged as the third leading cause of infant mortality, but at a low rate, 0.6/1,000 live births. From 1949 to 1953 pneumonia and diarrhea were leading causes of infant death, but from 1990 to 1992 they were not among the five leading causes. Sudden infant death syndrome and congenital anomalies emerged as major causes of Indian infant deaths as acute infectious causes diminished. These are also the major causes of mortality among non-Indian American infants.

Child and Youth Mortality

The death rate from all causes (adjusted for miscoding) for Indian children 1 to 4 years of age in 1992–94 was 96.8/100,000 population, 2.5 times the rate for U.S. Whites. The three leading causes of death among these Indian children were accidents (at three times the rate for U.S. Whites the same age), congenital anomalies, and homicide (at more than four times the rate for U.S. Whites). Although malignant neoplasms were among the 10 leading causes of Indian child deaths, they were only 80 percent of the U.S. White rate (Indian Health Service 1997b).

Not surprisingly, the leading cause of death of Indian children aged 5–14 years in 1992–94 was accidents. The adjusted rate of 20.8/100,000 population was 2.2 times that for U.S. All Races. Motor vehicle-associated injuries accounted for approximately one-half of these deaths. Malignant neoplasms were the second leading cause of death, with an adjusted rate approximately the same as that for U.S. All Races. Homicide was the third leading cause of death, with a rate 2.4 times greater than that for U.S. Whites of the same age. Suicide is the fourth leading cause of death for Indians of this age, with an adjusted rate of 2.5/100,000 population, a rate nearly three times that for U.S. Whites. Trauma associated with intentional and unintentional injury accounted for two-thirds of all deaths of this age group.

For 1990–92, Indian youth 15 to 24 years of age experienced a death rate of 188.3/100,000 population, 2.1 times the rate experienced among U.S. White youth. Leading causes of death were accidents (at twice), suicide (at 2.5 times), and homicide (at almost twice the rates for U.S. Whites). In older children and youth, complications of pregnancy and chronic liver disease emerge among the 10 leading causes of death, at 4.5 and 11.0 times the rates for U.S. Whites, respectively (Indian Health Service 1997b).

Special Conditions

Fetal Alcohol Syndrome

Healthy People 2000: National Health Promotion and Disease Prevention Objectives gives the baseline rate for the incidence of fetal alcohol syndrome (FAS) among the White population as 0.22/1,000 and among Indians as 4/1,000 live births (U.S. Department of Health and Human Services 1991). The Centers for Disease Control and Prevention Birth Defects Monitoring Program reported an FAS rate, based on hospital diagnosis, among Indians that was 33 times the rate among Whites for the years 1981 to 1986 (Chavez, Cordero, and Becerra 1988). Retrospective studies among some Indian groups disclosed FAS rates that ranged from 1.3 to 10.3/1,000 births (May et al. 1983; May 1991). A recent study in a Northwest Indian group found an FAS rate of 9.2/1,000 births (Quaid et al. 1993). High awareness and concern among many Indian communities and better reporting and surveillance on the part of professionals serving Indian communities probably explain at least some of these apparent high rates among Indians. The rate of FAS among Indians in the Southwest seems to be comparable to the rates reported for the United States and European countries (May 1992, 1994). However, many clinicians and community workers involved with Indians, and FAS-prevention programs in the general population as well, cite anecdotal evidence that many infants with FAS are not identified or reported.

Children with FAS represent a relatively small proportion of the total number of those exposed to alcohol in utero, for FAS is the full expression of a larger clinical spectrum (Ernhart 1991; American Academy of Pediatrics 1993). A child with a history of prenatal exposure to alcohol and abnormal findings that do not meet the full definition of FAS is generally referred to as having fetal alcohol effects (FAE). Although the findings of FAE may seem to reflect less alcohol-related damage, the personal and societal effects of FAE may be quite significant (May 1991).

Congenital Anomalies

National surveillance data from 1981 to 1986 collected by the Centers for Disease Control and Prevention (CDC) (which include some non-IHS service population) suggest higher rates of congenital anomalies among Indians than among other ethnic populations. Based on these comparisons, Indians experienced the highest rates of hydrocephalus, atrial septal defect, valve stenosis and atresia, cleft palate without cleft lip, cleft lip without cleft palate, rectal atresia and stenosis, fetal alcohol syndrome, and autosomal abnormalities (excluding Down syndrome) among 18 major congenital defects being monitored (Chavez, Cordero, and Becerra 1988). Previous IHS data suggesting that Indian death rates associated with congenital anomalies were less than for the general U.S. population were undoubtedly skewed because of the misclassification in coding of Indian deaths noted elsewhere in this text. Adjusted mortality rates for Indian congenital defects are, indeed, slightly higher for Indian children under one year of age (Indian Health Service 1997b). Between-Area differences are also noted, and these differences are largely caused by the wide regional differences in proportion of infant deaths due to SIDS.

Genetic Disorders

Some relatively rare genetic disorders that carry life-threatening dangers or significant disability have been reported among certain Indian populations. Some of these are unique conditions, and others demonstrate unusual frequency among specific Indian populations. They include severe combined immune deficiency syndrome (Jones et al. 1991), familial Navajo arthropathy (Johnson, Johnson, and Stein 1993; Singleton et al. 1990), congenital adrenal hyperplasia (Hirschfeld and Fleshman 1969), Kuskokwim syndrome (Wright 1970), metachromatic leukodystrophy (Pastor-Soler et al. 1994), and cystic fibrosis (Mercier et al. 1994; Gerdes and Murphy 1985).

Although prevalence rates of congenital hip dislocation, as seen among children and adults, are influenced by diagnosis and the implementation of early effective treatment, congenital hip dysplasia among some Indian groups may be somewhat more common than in the general population (Chnell 1989). Apparently this condition, once considered to have high prevalence, is now infrequently seen, since IHS clinicians readily diagnose the condition in early infancy and implement effective treatments (D. Hu, pers. comm., 1995). Further discussion of genetic conditions is presented in Chapter 8.

Asthma

Anecdotal information suggests that 30 to 40 years ago asthma among Indian children was very rare (Herxheimer 1964; Slocum, Thompson, and Chavez 1975). Recent studies provide evidence of an increased incidence and the importance of asthma among Indian children. From 1969 to 1977, one Indian death due to asthma was recorded in New Mexico (Samet et al. 1980). Mortality rates of asthma among Indians in 1986 seem to be nearly the same as rates seen among U.S. All Races—1.1 and 1.2/100,000 population, respectively (Coultas et al. 1993). Ambulatory care data for 1991–92 indicate that asthma accounts for 2–3 percent of ambulatory care visits by Indian children under 15 years of age (Indian Health Service 1994). In 1991, asthma was the fourth leading hospital discharge diagnosis for Indian children under 15 years of age. Asthma-related hospitalizations in IHS facilities of Indian children younger than 17 years increased 2.6 percent between 1979 and 1989. The increase among children under 5 years of age was 3.7 percent (Hisnanick, Coddington, and Gergen 1994). In the general population, an increase in hospitalizations for asthma among children has been observed while hospital admissions for other causes seem to be decreasing. Approximately 1 percent of all ambulatory care visits have been attributed to asthma (Murphy and Kelly 1996). In fiscal year 1996, of a total of 18,561 hospital discharges of Indians aged less than 1 year to 19 years (excluding newborn discharges) involving IHS, tribal, and contract hospitals, 951 (5%) were for asthma (Indian Health Service 1996b).

Reasons for this increase are not clear. However, more Indian families and children live in urban environments and may be exposed to increasing levels of pollution; among some Indian populations, smoking rates are high, which may be responsible for secondary smoke exposure of children; infants in some Indian communities experience yearly epidemics of respiratory syncytial virus (RSV), with attack rates exceeding those in the general population. Lower respiratory infection in infants due to RSV is an important risk factor predisposing to childhood asthma (Murphy and Kelly 1996).

Obesity and Diabetes

As recently as 1967, deficient weight for age, kwashiorkor, and marasmus were not uncommon reasons for pediatric admissions to the Tuba City IHS Hospital on the Navajo reservation (Duzen, Carter, and Vanderzwagg 1976). However, overweight and obesity among Indian children have replaced undernutrition. Some populations of Indian children now have rates of obesity 2 to 10 times those found in the general U.S. population (Broussard et al. 1991). Studies of this increase in obesity have focused attention on the profound dietary changes many Indian communities have experienced over the last one hundred years, when traditional foods were replaced by highly processed foods. This dramatic change in diet has been accompanied by a much more sedentary life.

Studies among Pima Indians have shown that intrauterine exposure to the metabolic environment of an obese or diabetic mother may be an important determinant of childhood obesity and diabetes (Pettitt et al. 1987; Byers 1992).

Indian preschool children of mothers who were obese during pregnancy were more than twice as likely to be obese as children whose mothers were not obese (Gallaher et al. 1991). Children born to diabetic mothers had higher glucose concentrations and more diabetes than children who did not experience this intrauterine exposure (Pettitt et al. 1993). These studies provide important considerations for the design of primary prevention programs among Indian populations that experience high rates of obesity and diabetes.

Special Considerations Regarding Indian Youth

Probably the most important health conditions confronting Indian children and youth relate to behavioral risk factors. Injuries, homicides, and suicides account for the highest proportion of deaths among older children and youth. Often these acute conditions are outcomes of underlying emotional, social, and behavioral pathology chronically prevalent among some troubled Indian youth. In addition, alcohol abuse contributes to a vicious cycle, as both cause and result, with increased morbidity and mortality (Beauvias 1992a). Increased understanding of this complex situation and the search for successful interventions are foci of great concern to many health professionals and community leaders. Health status data of Indian youth highlight the effects of behavioral risk factors and reasons for concern. Mortality due to accidents for Indian youth 15 to 24 years of age decreased 63 percent from 1973 to 1991, in contrast to U.S. Whites the same age, who experienced a 53 percent increase in deaths due to accidents. Despite this decline in mortality due to accidents, the Indian mortality rate from accidents for 1992–94 was twice that of U.S. Whites the same age (Indian Health Service 1997b; A. Handler, pers. comm., 1995).

Homicide deaths among Indians 15 to 24 years of age decreased 28 percent, in contrast to a 51 percent increase among U.S. Whites the same age. Even with this gratifying reduction of homicide, Indian youth in 1992–94 experienced a homicide mortality rate twice that for U.S. Whites. Of concern is an apparent 53 percent increase in homicide deaths among Indian infants. Homicide was the fifth leading cause of postneonatal mortality among Indian infants (A. Handler, pers. comm., 1995; Indian Health Service 1997b). It is clear that increased attention to the several aspects of child abuse is required.

Similar to the trends noted in the data on homicides, Indian youth 15 to 24 years of age demonstrate a decrease in suicides, while U.S. Whites the same age show a small increase. Although deaths due to suicide among Indian youth seem to have decreased, the rate in 1992–94 remains almost three times that for U.S. Whites (Indian Health Service 1997b; A. Handler, pers. comm., 1995). Deaths due to accidents, homicide, and suicide among Indian youth in 1990–92 resulted in a yearly average of more than 23,000 person-years of potential life lost among Indian communities.

A school-based adolescent survey of approximately fourteen thousand Indian and Alaska Native 7th- through 12th-grade students during 1988–90 documented many family and community strengths but also provided evidence of significant levels of chronic underlying emotional and behavioral pathology. These undoubtedly contribute to the excess death rates alluded to above (Blum et al. 1992). Fear of loss was a major concern among Indian youth. More than half of all participants had worries about loss of a parent. Loss of a friend was also in the top five worries, especially among girls. Given that 22 percent of youth reported having a family member who attempted or completed suicide, 28 percent reported that at least 1 of their friends had attempted suicide, and 1 in 10 said that he or she had lost a friend from suicide, this concern about loss is not surprising (Blum et al. 1992).

Symptoms of chronic depression and stress among Indian youth seem to be prevalent and may contribute to alcohol and drug abuse and suicide (Sack et al. 1994). In the survey reported by Blum et al. (1992), 17 percent (21.6% of girls and 11.8% of boys) reported ever attempting suicide. Eighteen percent had thought about suicide but would not do it, 3.9 percent would like to kill themselves, and 5.3 percent would commit suicide if they had the chance. Youth at highest risk of suicide used drugs and alcohol more heavily, engaged more often in other risky behaviors, had weaker family support, had a friend who had attempted suicide, and were more likely to have been a victim of abuse. Eighteen percent (9.1% of boys and 26.4% of girls) reported that they had been the victim of sexual abuse, physical abuse, or both (Blum et al. 1992).

Alcohol abuse among Indian youth is the risk factor most often associated with violent behaviors that lead to homicide, suicide, and deaths related to accidents. Abuse of alcohol also may be a symptom of underlying chronic emotional pathology. In response to "Have you ever used alcohol?", Indian youth in 7th to 12th grades in selected schools from 1975 to 1990 showed rates of alcohol use between 74 and 85 percent. The highest prevalence was noted in study schools in the early 1980s and the lowest in the 1988–90 sample. Prevalence among Indian youth consistently exceeded non-Indian rates (Beauvias 1992b). Compared to nonreservation Indian and Anglo youth, reservation Indian youth consistently had higher lifetime alcohol abuse prevalence rates. Further, reservation youth were at greater risk of alcohol use (Beauvias 1992c). In the adolescent survey alluded to above, almost one-half of Indian youth in the 7th to 9th and two-thirds in the 10th to 12th grades reported ever using beer or wine. When the relationship of heavy and problem drinking to the rate of personal problems, depression, risky behaviors, and injuries is examined, it is clear that alcohol is an important associated risk factor (University of Minnesota 1992; Blum et al. 1992).

Discussion

Mother, child, and youth health concerns are central to a discussion of Indian health as well as to successful interventions. Despite the serious nature of the health conditions of Indian children and youth, many improvements have been made in the past 40 years. With these improvements, health issues associated with complex social, economic, behavioral, and lifestyle risk factors have emerged. The outcome of these risk factors is an excess burden of illness, especially among Indian children and youth. Finding community-based programs and services that effectively address these complex risk factors is the present challenge for Indian communities and health professionals.

REFERENCES

American Academy of Pediatrics, Committee on Substance Abuse and Committee on Children with Disabilities. 1993. Fetal alcohol syndrome and fetal alcohol effects. *Pediatrics* 91:1004–6.
American Academy of Pediatrics, AAP Task Force on Infant Positioning and SIDS. 1992. Positioning and SIDS. *Pediatrics* 89:1120–26.
Beauvias F. 1992a. Trends in Indian adolescent drug and alcohol use. *Am Indian Alsk Native Ment Health Res* 5(1):1–12.
———. 1992b. Comparison of drug use rates for reservation Indian, non-reservation Indian and Anglo youth. *Am Indian Alsk Native Ment Health Res* 5(1):13–31.
———. 1992c. The consequences of drug and alcohol use for Indian youth. *Am Indian Alsk Native Ment Health Res* 5(1):32–37.
Blum RW, Harmon B, Harris L, et al. 1992. American Indian–Alaska Native youth health. *JAMA* 267:1637–44.
Broussard BA, Johnson A, Hines JH, et al. 1991. Prevalence of obesity in American Indians and Alaska Natives. *Am J Clin Nutr* 53:1535–42.
Byers T. 1992. Editorial: The epidemic of obesity in American Indians. *Am J Dis Child* 146:285–86.
Chavez GF, Cordero JF, Becerra JE. 1988. Leading major congenital malformations among minority groups in the United States, 1981–1986. *MMWR* 37:17–24.
Chnell S. 1989. Congenital dislocations of the hip. *IHS Primary Care Provider* 14:38–39.
Coultas DB, Gong H Jr, Grad R, et al. 1993. Respiratory diseases in minorities of the United States. *Am J Respir Crit Care Med* 149:S93–S131.
Duzen JV, Carter JP, Vanderzwagg R. 1976. Protein and calorie malnutrition among preschool Navajo Indian children: A follow-up. *Am J Clin Nutr* 29:657–62.

Ernhart CB. 1991. Clinical correlations between ethanol intake and fetal alcohol syndrome. *Recent Dev Alcohol* 9:127–50.

Gallaher MM, Hauck FR, Yang-Oshida M, et al. 1991. Obesity among Mescalero preschool children: Association with maternal obesity and birth weight. *Am J Dis Child* 145:1262–65.

Gerdes JS, Murphy S. 1985. Cystic fibrosis in Pueblo Indian children. *Clin Pediatr (Phila)* 24:104–6.

Grossman DC, Krieger JW, Sugarman JR, et al. 1994. Health status of urban American Indians and Alaska Natives: A population-based study. *JAMA* 271:845–50.

Herxheimer H. 1964. Asthma in American Indians. *N Engl J Med* 270:1128–29.

Hirschfeld AJ, Fleshman JK. 1969. An unusually high incidence of salt-losing congenital adrenal hyperplasia in the Alaskan Eskimo. *J Pediatr* 75:492–94.

Hisnanick JJ, Coddington DA, Gergen PJ. 1994. Trends in asthma-related admissions among American Indian and Alaskan Native children from 1979 to 1989. *Arch Pediatr Adolesc Med* 148:357–63.

Indian Health Service. 1994. *Summary of Leading Causes for Outpatient Visits, Indian Health Service Direct and Contract Facilities, Fiscal Year 1992.* Rockville, Md.: Indian Health Service, Office of Program Statistics.

———. 1995. *Trends in Indian Health, 1995.* Rockville, Md.: Indian Health Service, Division of Program Statistics.

———. 1996a. *Adjusting for Miscoding of Indian Race on State Death Certificates.* Rockville, Md.: Indian Health Service, Division of Program Statistics.

———. 1996b. *Utilization of IHS and Tribal Direct and Contract General Hospitals, Fiscal Year 1996.* Rockville, Md.: Indian Health Service, Program Statistics Team.

———. 1997a. *Regional Differences in Indian Health, 1997.* Rockville, Md.: Indian Health Service, Program Statistics Team.

———. 1997b. *Trends in Indian Health, 1997.* Rockville, Md.: Indian Health Service, Program Statistics Team.

Johnson SD, Johnson PC, Stein SR. 1993. Familial sensory autonomic neuropathy with arthropathy in Navajo children. *Neurology* 43:1120–25.

Jones JF, Ritenbaugh CK, Spence MA, et al. 1991. Severe combined immunodeficiency among the Navajo. *Hum Biol* 63:669–82.

May PA. 1991. Fetal alcohol effects among North American Indians: Evidence and implications for society. *Alcohol Health Res World* 15:239–48.

———. 1992. Fetal alcohol syndrome and American Indians: A positive challenge in public health and prevention. In: Haller EW, Aitken LP, eds. *Mashkiki: Old Medicine Nourishing the New,* chap 4. Lanham, Md.: University Press of America.

———. 1994. The epidemiology of alcohol abuse among American Indians: The mythical and real properties. *Am Indian Culture Res J* 18:121–43.

May PA, Hymbaugh KJ, Aase JM, et al. 1983. Epidemiology of fetal alcohol syndrome among American Indians of the Southwest. *Soc Biol* 30:374–87.

Mercier B, Raguenes O, Estivill X, et al. 1994. Complete detection of mutations in cystic fibrosis patients of Native American origin. *Hum Genet* 94:629–32.

Murphy SJ, Kelly HW. 1996. Advances in the management of acute asthma in children. *Pediatr Rev* 17:227–34.

Pastor-Soler NM, Rafi MA, Hoffman JD, et al. 1994. Metachromatic leukodystrophy in the Navajo Indian population: A splice site mutation in intron 4 of the arylsulfatase A gene. *Hum Mutat* 4:199–207.

Pettitt DJ, Knowler WC, Bennett PH, et al. 1987. Obesity in offspring of diabetic Pima Indian women despite normal birth weight. *Diabetes Care* 10:76–80.

Pettitt DJ, Nelson RG, Saad MF, et al. 1993. Diabetes and obesity in the offspring of Pima Indian women with diabetes during pregnancy. *Diabetes Care* 16:310–14.

Quaid J, Kirkpatrick J, Nakamura R, et al. 1993. Establishing the occurrence of FAS/FAE in a rural community. *IHS Primary Care Provider* 18:71–75.

Querec L. 1994. Measuring underreporting of American Indian infant mortality: Methodology and findings based on linked birth/infant deaths, 1983 to 1987. Rockville, Md.: Indian Health Service, Division of Program Statistics, November.

Sack WH, Beiser M, Baker-Brown G, et al. 1994. Depressive and suicidal symptoms in Indian school children: Findings from the *Flower of Two Soils*. In: *Calling from the Rim: Suicidal Behavior among American Indian and Alaska Native Adolescents*, monograph series from *Journal of the National Center*, University Press of Colorado. *Am Indian Alsk Native Ment Health Res* 4:31–94.

Samet JM, Key CR, Kutvirt DM, et al. 1980. Respiratory disease mortality in New Mexico's American Indians and Hispanics. *Am J Public Health* 70:492–97.

Singleton R, Helgerson SD, Snyder RD, et al. 1990. Neuropathy in Navajo children: Clinical and epidemiologic features. *Neurology* 40:363–67.

Slocum R, Thompson F, Chavez C. 1975. Rarity of asthma among Cheyenne Indians. *Ann Allergy* 34:201–2.

University of Minnesota. 1992. *The State of Native American Youth Health*. Minneapolis: Adolescent Health Program, Division of General Pediatrics and Adolescent Health, University of Minnesota.

U.S. Department of Health and Human Services, Public Health Service. 1991. *Healthy People 2000: National Health Promotion and Disease Prevention Objectives*. DHHS Publication No. (PHS)91-50212. Washington, D.C.: Government Printing Office.

Wright DG. 1970. The unusual skeletal findings of the Kuskokwim syndrome. *Birth Defects* 6:16–24.

10

Dorothy A. Rhoades, M.D., M.P.H.,
Everett R. Rhoades, M.D., and
Thomas Welty, M.D., M.P.H.

The Rise of Cardiovascular Diseases

Cardiovascular disease (CVD) was not considered a major health problem for American Indians and Alaska Natives in the United States until the latter part of the twentieth century. Mortality rates from CVD were substantially lower for Indian populations than for the general population, and the lower rates persisted despite increases in risk factors (Gillum 1988; Welty and Coulehan 1993; Young 1994). However, CVD is the leading cause of death for Indians in the Indian Health Service (IHS) service population and becomes so beginning at age 45, compared to age 65 for the general population (Indian Health Service 1997a). Furthermore, CVD mortality has been substantially underestimated among American Indians, and mortality rates among some now equal or exceed those for the general population (Indian Health Service 1997a; Lee et al. 1998).

Total Cardiovascular Disease

Cardiovascular disease (CVD) is a broad classification of diseases affecting the circulatory system. Currently, the most important CVD among the Indian population is atherosclerotic, or coronary, heart disease (CHD). However, CVD also includes cerebrovascular disease (stroke), hypertension, congestive heart failure, cardiomyopathy, rheumatic heart disease, and others.

Prevalence

In the early part of the twentieth century, most studies reported relatively low prevalence rates of CVD among Indian compared to non-Indian populations (Young 1994; Welty and Coulehan 1993). However, in 1987, the age- and sex-adjusted prevalence of self-reported CVD among a national sample of Indian adults was 9.8 percent, nearly the same as the 10 percent prevalence reported for the U.S. population (Johnson and Taylor 1991). Furthermore, the prevalence among Indian men aged 45–64 years was higher than that among men of the same age group in the U.S. population.

The Strong Heart Study (SHS), a multitribal, prospective cohort study among approximately forty-five hundred Indians aged 45–74 years in three geographically separate regions, which was begun in 1987, applies standardized methods to determine risk factors, prevalence, incidence, and mortality from CVDs (Lee et al. 1990). The participants belong to 13 tribes located in North and South Dakota, central Arizona, and southwestern Oklahoma. The SHS confirms the serious nature of CVD among these separate groups. The prevalence of major electrocardiographic abnormalities suggestive of CVD in the SHS cohort was higher than among older participants in the Cardiovascular Health Study (Oopik et al. 1996).

Mortality

In the past, CVD mortality rates for the IHS service population were falsely low because of miscoding of race on death certificates. For instance, the average age-adjusted CVD mortality rate in the 1992–94 IHS service population was 167/100,000, compared to the 1993 rate of 173.9/100,000 for U.S. Whites. However, after adjustment for miscoding of Indian race, the estimated rate for Indians is substantially higher, at 194.6/100,000 (Indian Health Service 1997a). In recent years, heart disease mortality for Indian persons aged 65 years or older has remained at approximately 70 percent of that for the general U.S. and White populations (Indian Health Service 1997a). However, in 1989–91, heart disease mortality rates for Indians aged 45–64 years exceeded those for same-aged persons in the U.S. All Races population for the first time since such data have been collected (Indian Health Service 1994). Among the SHS cohort the average age-adjusted CVD mortality rates from 1984 to 1988 equaled or exceeded comparable regional rates in each of the three sites (Lee et al. 1998). Except for those aged 65–74 years in Arizona, the Indian rates in each region also exceeded the U.S. All Races rates.

Regional Mortality Studies

The use of overall rates to describe the total CVD mortality experience masks substantial differences between various Indian populations. The results of regional studies reported since 1984 are summarized in Table 10.1. Large differences between heart disease mortality rates for the Northern Plains and Bemidji

Areas and the southwest Areas have been observed for at least two decades (Indian Health Service 1997b). In the SHS, the highest rates of CVD deaths occurred among the Northern Plains tribes (Lee et al. 1998). One risk factor that may be associated with this difference is the much higher prevalence rates of smoking among Indians in the Great Plains states. Variation in the prevalence of CVD risk factors between certain tribal groups is not surprising. An excellent review of studies of CVD risk factors conducted between 1980 and 1991 also describes some of the strengths and limitations of these studies (Ellis and Campos-Outcalt 1994).

Risk Factors for Cardiovascular Diseases

Because of the dominance of coronary artery disease (CHD), hypertension, and cerebrovascular diseases and because major risk factors are shared among them, discussion of risk factors will focus on overall risk factors. Thus, repeating the same set of risk factors for each condition can be largely avoided. However, some repetition is unavoidable.

Diabetes

Diabetes has had a profound effect on CVD in Indian populations (Nelson et al. 1990; Howard et al. 1992; Schraer et al. 1993; Hoy, Light, and Megill 1995), especially among middle-aged women (Howard et al. 1995; Hoy, Light, and Megill 1995). The risk of CVD increases with increasing duration of diabetes (Macaulay, Montour, and Adelson 1988; Nelson et al. 1990). Recently, increased attention has focused on the insulin resistance syndrome and its association with diabetes and CVD. The findings in the SHS suggest that insulin levels were independent predictors of combined possible and definite CHD, although this has yet to be documented among Indians with definite CHD (Howard et al. 1995). However, insulin levels were not independently associated with the incidence of electrocardiographic (ECG) abnormalities among Pima subjects (Liu et al. 1992). Further clarification of the associations between diabetes, insulin levels, and CVD risk is needed.

Smoking

Cigarette smoking has been implicated as a leading risk factor of CHD, particularly in the SHS (Howard et al. 1995). In contrast, Nelson et al. (1990) reported that, among Pima Indians, cigarette smoking was not a significant risk factor for CHD.

TABLE 10.1

Recent regional mortality studies of cardiovascular disease among Native Americans

| | | | | Age-adjusted mortality rate per 100,000 population[a] | | | | |
| | | | | AI rate | | Comparison rate | | |
Study	Dates	AI population	Cause(s) of death	Total	M/F	Total	M/F	Comparison population
			National					
Welty 1993	1981–83	IHS population	CVD	192.3		238.3		All U.S.
Lee 1998	1984–88	Strong Heart Study[b]	Major CVD					
			death certificate data	640	1,140/500			
			study criteria		880/480			
IHS 1997a	1992–94	IHS Service Area	Major CVD	167.0		181.8		All U.S.
		IHS Service Areas[c]	Diseases of heart	194.6		144.3		All U.S.
			Regional					
Gillum 1984	1968–73	Minnesota	Heart disease, stroke	448.7		455.2		All Minn.
Sievers 1990	1975–84	Pima Indians	Diseases of heart	213[de]		336		All U.S.
			death certificate data study criteria	168[e]				
Young 1993	1978–86	NW Territories Indian Inuit	Circulatory disease		195/187 205/149		349/198	All Canada
Davidson 1993	1979–88	Alaska Natives	Diseases of heart		293.8/275.1		370.9/321.5	U.S. White
Middaugh 1990	1980–86	Alaska Natives	Cardiovascular[e]		186.2/125.9		279.3/182.1	Other Alaskans
Grossman 1994	1981–90	Washington State Urban counties	Diseases of heart	141		139		Urban Whites
		Reservation		188				
Lee 1998	1984–88	SHS Site[b] Arizona	Major CVD		1,080/340			
		Oklahoma			880/480			
		N/S Dakota			1,400/660			

IHS 1997[b]	1992–94	IHS Service Area	Diseases of heart	All U.S.
		Aberdeen	232.8	
		Alaska	138.3	
		Albuquerque	81.2	
		Bemidji	230.2 (285.4)[c]	
		Billings	182.9	
		California	83.0 (119.5)[c]	
		Nashville	158.6	
		Navajo	110.0	
		Oklahoma	124.7 (173.9)[c]	
		Phoenix	140.4	
		Portland	127.7 (143.4)[c]	
		Tucson	137.8	145.3

ABBREVIATIONS: AI, American Indian; M/F, male rate/female rate; IHS, Indian Health Service; CVD, cardiovascular disease; NW, Northwest; N/S, North and South; SHS, Strong Heart Study.

[a]Mortality rates are not comparable between studies because of differing methods of adjustment.
[b]SHS included only AI persons aged 45–74 years.
[c]Rate adjusted for underreporting of AI race on death certificates, as well as for age.
[d]Average age- and gender-adjusted rate per 100,000.
[e]Excluding cerebrovascular disease.

Lipid Profiles

Low concentrations of high-density lipoprotein (HDL) cholesterol were more significant predictors of CHD in the SHS (Howard et al. 1995) and Pima cohort studies than were total cholesterol concentrations. HDL levels in the SHS cohort were lower than in the U.S. population as a whole (Welty et al. 1995), and mean HDL concentrations tended to be slightly lower among diabetic participants (Robbins et al. 1996b). HDL cholesterol concentrations were also low among Pimas (Howard et al. 1983), Navajos (Mendlein et al. 1997), and Indian women in Minneapolis (Gillum, Gillum, and Smith 1984). Among Pima Indians, the HDL concentration was significantly and inversely associated with obesity when controlled for age, smoking, alcohol use, and plasma glucose (Howard et al. 1992). HDL concentrations were relatively high among older Canadian Inuit compared to non-Native Canadians but were lower among younger Inuit, suggesting an increased risk factor profile for younger generations (Young, Moffatt, and O'Neil 1993).

Studies in non-Native populations strongly suggest an increasing risk of CHD with increasing concentrations of total cholesterol. Indians have often had lower reported concentrations of total cholesterol than the general population, particularly among Southwestern Indians and Alaska Natives (Clifford, Kelly, and Teal 1963; Savage et al. 1976; Sievers 1968). Indians have been reported to have a lower prevalence of hypercholesterolemia than does the general population (Campos-Outcalt et al. 1995; Robbins et al. 1996b; Young, Moffatt, and O'Neil 1993). However, total cholesterol concentrations among Navajo men were higher than among male participants in the second National Health and Nutrition Examination Survey (NHANES II) (Sugarman et al. 1992). Among participants in the Navajo Health and Nutrition Study, total cholesterol levels in adults were comparable to those in the general U.S. population (Mendlein et al. 1997). Notably, the lowest prevalence rates of hypercholesterolemia occurred among the oldest age groups for men in all three SHS centers, suggesting that young cohorts of subjects are facing higher risks of hyperlipidemia. Relatively high prevalence rates of hypercholesterolemia have been reported among Indians in Oklahoma (Mayberry and Lindeman 1963) and Minneapolis (Gillum, Gillum, and Smith 1984). The prevalence of hypercholesterolemia among participants in the Centers for Disease Control and Prevention (CDC) Intertribal Heart Project (22%) was higher than that reported for participants in NHANES III (17%).

Risk factors for hypercholesterolemia have been inconsistent across studies. Among urban Indians, cholesterol was significantly correlated with age but not weight (Gillum, Gillum, and Smith 1984). Obesity was not significantly associated with total cholesterol or low-density lipoprotein (LDL) cholesterol levels among Pima Indians after adjustment for age, smoking, alcohol, and plasma glucose (Howard et al. 1992). In contrast, body mass index (BMI) and waist-hip ratios were positively associated with cholesterol levels among urban Indian smokers (Folsom et al. 1993). In general, BMI was associated with increased levels of serum lipids among Navajo Indians, with the effect being greater among men (Mendlein et al. 1997). Among women in the SHS, postmenopausal estrogen use was associated with a more favorable lipid profile, but the number of children borne was associated with less favorable levels of HDL cholesterol (Cowan et al. 1997).

Socioeconomic risk factors have been found to be correlated with cholesterol levels. In the Intertribal Heart Project (ITHP), cholesterol levels were highest among those with less formal education and employment (Centers for Disease Control and Prevention 1996). Men with lower incomes had a lower prevalence of hypercholesterolemia, but low-income women had a higher prevalence than did women with higher incomes.

These studies do not account for the effects of medication, renal disease, or other factors that influence lipid concentrations, and other lipid components have rarely been studied in Indian communities. The concentration of apolipo-protein E, which has been implicated as a risk factor for CVD in the general population, was significantly lower among SHS participants than among White Americans (Kataoka et al. 1996). Although increased LDL particle size was associated with lower triglyceride and higher HDL concentrations in the SHS, no association between LDL size and CHD was found (Gray et al. 1997). Triglyceride levels have not been significantly associated with CHD among American Indians in any reported study to date.

Physical Inactivity

The estimated excess risk of CHD attributable to a sedentary lifestyle in the United States is higher than that attributed to obesity, hypertension, or smoking (U.S. Preventive Services Task Force 1996). Among SHS participants, 38.4 percent of the men and 47.5 percent of the women reported no leisure-time physical activity during the past week (Welty et al. 1995). In 1992 one-quarter of Navajo adults reported no exercise during the past month (Mendlein et al. 1997). Ninety-three percent of Yaqui adults aged 35–65 years reported sedentary lifestyles (Molina and Campos-Outcalt 1991). More than 50 percent of most subgroups of two Montana tribes had sedentary lifestyles (Goldberg et al. 1991). However, the unadjusted proportion reporting "no frequent exercise" among Plains Indians in one study was much lower than that reported by non-

Indians in the Behavioral Risk Factor Surveillance Study (BRFSS) (Cheadle et al. 1994). Forty-seven percent of Cree and Ojibwa in a Canadian study were physically inactive (Young 1991). Inactivity was reported by 28 percent of CDC Intertribal Health Project participants and was more common in women, older age groups, and persons with less formal education, less income, and no employment (Centers for Disease Control and Prevention 1996). Only 36 percent of participants aged 25 and older were regularly active, compared to 42 percent for the U.S. population over age 17. Regular activity did not differ by education or income but was slightly higher among males and employed participants. However, men in this study were less likely to engage in regular activity than were Indian men in the BRFSS.

Body Mass Index

Although body mass index was significantly associated with prevalent CHD in the SHS multivariate analysis, the waist-hip ratio was not (Howard et al. 1995). In prior studies, obesity was not associated with prevalent CHD among Navajo or nondiabetic Pima Indians (Liu et al. 1992; Hoy, Light, and Megill 1995), nor with fatal CHD among Pima Indians (Nelson et al. 1990). However, the prevalence of obesity is rapidly increasing among most Indian populations (Byers 1992), and it may take years for the associations with obesity to be fully elucidated.

Alcohol Consumption

The role of alcohol consumption in CVD other than hypertension has rarely been assessed among Indians. Moderate daily alcohol consumption, which decreases the risk of CHD, is thought to be uncommon among Indians. Although the prevalence of alcohol consumption was lower for SHS participants than for the U.S. population, binge drinking was more common among those who did drink (Welty et al. 1995). Welty and Coulehan (1993) suggested that binge drinking may be a risk factor for cardiomyopathy and sudden death among some Indians.

Other Risk Factors

Hypertension and renal disease are strongly associated with CHD (Hoy, Light, and Megill 1994; Nelson et al. 1990; Howard et al. 1995) and will be discussed below. Elevated fibrinogen levels have been associated with CHD in other populations, but the association was not significant in the SHS multivariate analysis (Howard et al. 1995).

Multiple Risk Factors

Among Pascua Yaqui adults studied in 1990, 86 percent of study participants had at least one major risk factor, including diabetes, hypertension, hypercholesterolemia, obesity, or smoking (Campos-Outcalt et al. 1995). Fifty-two percent had two or more of these risk factors. Notably, 85 percent of Onondaga schoolchildren had three or more cardiac risk factors, not including male gender (Botash et al. 1992).

Risk Reduction

Very few studies of the efficacy of various CVD risk-reduction intervention programs among adult Indians have been published (LeMaster and Connell 1994). Although the IHS sponsors and trains many community health representatives to coordinate primary prevention education and activities (Cleaver, Ratcliff, and Rogers 1989), the effectiveness of these programs has not been reported. Efforts to promote physical activity among children and adults are currently under way in a several communities.

Coronary Heart Disease

Prevalence

Early studies among Southwestern tribes and Alaska Natives reported very low prevalence rates of CHD (Gilbert 1955; Fulmer and Roberts 1963; Young 1994). Northern Plains Indian men also had relatively low incidence rates of myocardial infarction (MI) compared to participants in the Framingham study, an extensive study of CVD among people living in Framingham, Massachusetts (Pinkerton and Badke 1974). However, acute myocardial infarction (AMI) incidence rates among Southwestern tribes have nearly tripled in recent decades (Klain et al. 1988). Furthermore, the rates for Indian females were higher than rates for Framingham females (Pinkerton and Badke 1974).

There are a few more recent reports. Among adult Menominee and Ojibwa tribal members, the self-reported prevalence of prior MI was 9 percent (Centers for Disease Control and Prevention 1996). Among persons aged 65 years and older, the prevalence was 25 percent.

Among the SHS cohort (adults aged 45–74), the prevalence of definite CHD was determined based on specific electrocardiographic and clinical criteria during 1989–92. The prevalence ranged from 0.5 percent among nondiabetic women to 5.8 percent among diabetic men. However, the age- and sex-specific prevalence of probable CHD ranged from a low of 15.9 percent among Oklahoma women aged 45–54 to 44.7 percent among Oklahoma men aged 65–74 years (Howard et al. 1995).

Morbidity

Welty and Coulehan (1993), comparing 1982–84 IHS hospital discharge rates with data from the 1983 National Center for Health Statistics Hospital Discharge Survey, noted that the age-adjusted hospitalization rate for AMI was much lower among the IHS user population (11.8/10,000) than among the general population (29.1/10,000). However, wide regional differences were noted, and the discharge rates for the Northern Plains service population were approximately the same as those of the general U.S. population. Hrabovsky, Welty, and Coulehan (1989) reported that hospital discharge rates for AMI among adult Sioux women were twice those for Framingham women, although rates among Sioux and Framingham men were basically the same.

Mortality

Table 10.2 shows the results of recent studies of CHD mortality among Indian populations. Part of the decrease of mortality rates from CHD noted during the 1970s (Gillum 1988) may have been due to changes in the ICD codes for CHD (*International Classification of Diseases* 1998), as well as changes in the population size. However, recent data from the SHS and the IHS Program Statistics Team suggest that mortality is higher and may even be increasing, in contrast to the declining mortality seen among non-Indian populations in the United States (Indian Health Service 1997a; Stern 1998; Lee et al. 1998).

In the past, CHD mortality was relatively low for several tribes and regions (Fulmer and Roberts 1963; Mayberry and Lindeman 1963; Sievers 1967; Becker et al. 1988). However, among a cohort of Pima persons aged 15 years and older, CHD mortality has increased 50 percent in recent years (Sievers, Nelson, and Bennett 1996). During the 1980s, Alaska Natives had lower average age-adjusted CHD mortality than the general population (Davidson, Bulkow, and Gellin 1993), but mortality from AMI was comparable (Middaugh 1990). Also, the mortality rate from CHD was much higher among Aleut than among Inuit persons (Davidson, Bulkow, and Gellin 1993). Reasons for the wide differences in regional mortality rates have yet to be elucidated but may be related to differences in the prevalence of certain risk factors, such as smoking (Centers for Disease Control 1992).

Hypertension

Similar to CHD, hypertension was previously thought to be less common among Indians than among the general population (Sievers 1977; DeStefano, Coulehan, and Wiant 1979; Broussard et al. 1993; Acton, Preston, and Rith-Najarian 1996). However, in 1987 the prevalence of self-reported hypertension among Indians was nearly identical to that of the general U.S. population (Johnson and Taylor 1991). Studies among Aleuts (Torrey, Reiff, and Noble 1979), urban Indians (Gillum, Gillum, and Smith 1984), and Penobscots (Deprez, Miller, and Hart 1985) also disclosed prevalence rates as high or higher than those for the general population. Furthermore, the prevalence of hypertension may be rising rapidly (Sievers 1977; Sugarman 1990; Klain et al. 1988; Mendlein et al. 1997). Most recent studies, summarized in Table 10.3, report rates that are similar to or higher than those for the general U.S. population (Centers for Disease Control and Prevention 1996; Campos-Outcalt et al. 1995; Howard et al. 1996). Earlier studies were well summarized by Young (1994).

Striking regional variations in hypertension prevalence have been demonstrated among Indians. Among Dakota SHS participants, the prevalence of hypertension was significantly lower than that for participants from Oklahoma and Arizona (Howard et al. 1996). However, after four years of follow-up, the prevalence of hypertension among Dakota participants increased nearly 10 percent (Welty et al., unpublished data). A possible explanation may be that Indians in the Dakotas have a higher prevalence of cigarette smoking, which was inversely associated with hypertension in the SHS (Howard et al. 1996). Several studies have documented relatively high rates of elevated blood pressure (BP) among young Indians, including Mohawk and Onondaga children (Botash et al. 1992) and Navajo adolescents (Coulehan et al. 1990; Gilbert et al. 1992). These studies are of concern because children with increased BP have a greater risk of developing hypertension as adults (U.S. Preventive Services Task Force 1996).

The self-reported occurrence of being screened for hypertension was lower among American Indians and Alaska Natives than among the general population in 1987 (Lefkowitz and Underwood 1991). However, levels of awareness and treatment of hypertension among male SHS participants were as good as or better than those among White men in the third National Health and Nutrition Examination Survey, and the rate of controlled hypertension was higher for Indians (Welty et al. 1995). Indian women were slightly less likely to be aware of their disease or to be treated. Awareness of hypertension increased with increasing education for both men and women (Lee and Go 1996), but higher education was associated with better control only for women. However, in a study of a Plains tribe, only 50 percent of persons with elevated BP were aware of their

TABLE 10.2

Recent studies of coronary heart disease mortality among Native Americans

| | | | | Age-adjusted mortality rate per 100,000 population[a] | | | | |
| | | | | AI rate | | Comparison rate | | |
Study	Dates	AI population	Cause(s) of death	Total	M/F	Total	M/F	Comparison population
National								
Gillum 1988	1969–71	IHS states[b]	CHD	132				
	1979–81	IHS states	CHD	94				
Welty 1993	1981–83	IHS population	IHD	98.2		139.3		All U.S.
Lee 1998	1984–88	SHS[c]	CHD					
			death certificate data		640/240			
			definite MI	120	160/80			
			definite sudden death	140	220/80			
			other definite CHD	140	180/100			
Regional								
Nelson 1990	1975–84	Pima, ages 50–79	CHD, study criteria[d]					
			no diabetes	0				
			diabetes	640		430		Framingham Study
Sievers 1996	1975–82[e]	Pima, ages 15+	IHD, study criteria[d]					
			no diabetes	7				
			diabetes	190				
	1982–89[e]	Pima, ages 15+	no diabetes	38				
			diabetes	290		1,160		
Davidson 1993	1979–88	Alaska Natives	CHD	151.8	178.3/114.1		280.8/227.5	U.S. White
Middaugh 1990	1980–86	Alaska Natives	Acute MI	50.2	54.3/43.4	49.5	60.6/32.8	Other Alaskans

Lee 1998	1984–88	SHS site[f]	CHD/death certificate data	
		Arizona		600/180
		Oklahoma		480/220
		N/S Dakota		800/320
		Arizona	Study criteria/definite fatal MI	140/80
		Oklahoma		60/80
		N/S Dakota		260/100
		Arizona	Definite sudden death	220/80
		Oklahoma		200/100
		N/S Dakota		240/60
		Arizona	Other definite CHD	160/20
		Oklahoma		120/140
		N/S Dakota		240/140

ABBREVIATIONS: AI, American Indian; M/F, male rate/female rate; IHS, Indian Health Service; CHD, coronary heart disease; IHD, ischemic heart disease; SHS, Strong Heart Study; MI, myocardial infarction; N/S, North and South.

[a]Mortality rates are not comparable between studies because of differing methods of adjustment.
[b]The 1969–71 IHS state population included AIs living in 25 states; the 1979–81 population included AIs from 28 states.
[c]SHS subjects include AI persons aged 45–74 years only.
[d]Age- and gender-adjusted mortality rate per 100,000 person-years.
[e]Time periods were (1) from January 1975 through June 1982 and (2) from July 1982 through December 1989.
[f]SHS included only AI persons aged 45–74 years.

TABLE 10.3

Recent studies of hypertension prevalence among Native Americans (excluding cerebrovascular disease)

Study	Dates	AI population	Ages (yr)	AI rate Total	AI rate M/F	Comparison rate Total	Comparison rate M/F	Comparison population
			National					
Johnson 1991	1987	SAIAN[a]	19+	22.7	23.2/22.2	22.8	22.2/23.4	1987 NMES II
			19–44	11.6		12.6		
			45–64	37.8		36.1		
			65 or older	36.7		49.3		
Broussard 1993	1987	IHS service population[b]	15+	10.9		21.0		NHANES II, Whites, ages 18–74
						17.0		NHIS, Whites, ages 18+
			15–44	3.3				
			45–64	19.2				
			65+	27.9				
Welty 1995	1989–92	SHS[c]	45–74		37.7/39.1		43/38	NHANES III, ages 45–74
Howard 1996	1989–92	SHS	45–54		34.7/27.6			
			55–64		40.9/41.5			
			65–74		49.2/56.2			
Acton 1996	FY 1992	IHS service population[d]	15+	10.4				
			15–44	3.1				
			45–64	17.5				
			65+	25.6				
			Regional					
Sharlin 1993	1986	SD reservations	18 or older	13.9	14.8/13.7	12–21	43/38	BRFS, 26 U.S. states
Welty 1995	1989–92	SHS site[c]						NHANES III, ages 45–74
		Arizona			44.2/42.5			
		Oklahoma			46.7/42.3			
		S/N Dakota			27.2/27.6			

Reference	Year	Population	Age	M/F	Prevalence	Comparison M/F	Comparison population
Campos-Outcalt 1995	1990	Pascua Yaqui	25–65	25.6/25.4	24		NHANES III, ages 20+
			25–34	25.8/9.8			
			35–44	23.1/22.7			
			45–54	42.9/47.1			
			55–64	13.3/46.7			
CDC 1996	1992–94	Menominee, Ojibwa (MN)	25 or older	38/27	31		
Schraer 1996	1992	Yupik, Alaska	39 or older		27		
Mendlein 1997	1992	Navajo	20 or older	23/14			
			20–39	15/5			
			40–59	22/18			
			60 or older	44/28			
Youth							
Coulehan 1990	1981	Navajo boarding school residents	13–18	11.1/1.6			NHANES I
Gilbert 1996	1988–92	Navajo adolescents[e]	14–18	8.7/9.1		8.5/4.2	1987 U.S. adolescents
Botash 1992	1989	Onondaga and Mohawk (NY)[f]	5–16	22	5	5/5	1980 U.S. pediatric population

ABBREVIATIONS: AI, American Indian; M/F, male rate/female rate; SAIAN, Survey of American Indians and Alaska Natives; NMES II, National Medical Expenditure Survey II, 1987; IHS, Indian Health Service; NHANES, National Health and Nutrition Evaluation Survey: I (1971–75), II (1976–80), III (1988–91); NHIS, National Health Insurance Survey, 1985–94; SHS, Strong Heart Study; BRFS, Behavioral Risk Factor Survey; S/N, South and North.

[a] Self-reported hypertension prevalence, age- and gender-adjusted to the 1987 U.S. population.

[b] Prevalence rates among the IHS service population were based on clinical diagnoses as noted on computerized ambulatory patient care forms. Prevalence rates among the comparison populations were obtained by actual standardized measurements. Rates were age-adjusted to the 1980 U.S. population.

[c] SHS included only AI persons aged 45–74 years.

[d] Prevalence rates were based on clinical diagnoses as noted on computerized ambulatory patient care forms. Adjusted for differences in sampling fractions, population sizes, and response rates among the participating communities.

[e] Prevalence of high-normal systolic and/or diastolic blood pressure, defined as between the 90th and 95th percentiles for similarly aged U.S. children.

[f] Hypertension was defined as systolic or diastolic blood pressure above the 95th percentile for height for 5–18-year-olds in the United States.

hypertension (Sharlin et al. 1993). In a study among Great Lakes tribes, only 28 percent of persons receiving antihypertensive medication were considered adequately controlled (Centers for Disease Control and Prevention 1996).

The association between age and hypertension frequently noted for the general population has been inconsistently demonstrated among Indians. Earlier studies of the prevalence of hypertension among Indians showed little or no increase after middle age (DeStefano, Coulehan, and Wiant 1979; Johnson and Taylor 1991; Hoy, Light, and Megill 1995). However, as shown in Table 10.3, several recent studies show increasing prevalence of hypertension with increasing age.

Hypertension and diabetes mellitus are closely linked in many studies of Indians (Sugarman 1990; Broussard et al. 1993; Hoy, Light, and Megill 1994, 1995; Welty et al. 1995; Will et al. 1997). This association persists after adjustment for age, sex, BMI, percentage of body fat, and other factors (Saad et al. 1990; Howard et al. 1996). However, the association between hypertension and diabetes among Pima Indians was not statistically significant in one study (Nelson et al. 1990). Unlike CHD, hypertension among diabetic Navajo persons was not associated with increasing duration of diabetes (Sugarman 1990; Hoy, Light, and Megill 1995).

Obesity, increasing BMI, and percentage of body fat have been significantly associated with elevated systolic (SBP) or diastolic blood pressure (DBP) among Indian adults (DeStefano, Coulehan, and Wiant 1979; Gillum, Gillum, and Smith 1984; Saad et al. 1990; Hoy, Light, and Megill 1994; Mendlein et al. 1997). The independence of this association has been confirmed in multivariate analyses (Young 1991), except for SBP among men in the SHS (Howard et al. 1996). BMI was significantly associated with mean BP for Navajo female, but not male, adolescents (Coulehan et al. 1990). Both SBP and DBP were associated with increasing BMI among Navajo girls, and SBP was associated with increasing BMI among Navajo boys and Indian children in Minneapolis (Gilbert et al. 1992; Gillum et al. 1980). In the SHS cohort, smoking was associated with lower SBP and DBP among both males and females, independent of percentage of body fat (Howard et al. 1996).

An association between hyperinsulinemia and hypertension, noted in the general U.S. population, has not been consistently demonstrated among Native Americans (Saad et al. 1990). Fasting insulin was related to DBP but not SBP among Yupik Eskimos (Schraer et al. 1996). Fasting insulin levels were not associated with either SBP or DBP in the SHS after adjustment for several other factors (Howard et al. 1996).

Albuminuria was significantly and independently associated with hypertension among SHS participants (Welty et al. 1995; Howard et al. 1996) and Navajo patients (Hoy, Light, and Megill 1994), as well as among diabetic Chippewa Indians (Hirata-Dulas et al. 1996). The association was especially pronounced among Arizona SHS participants (Robbins et al. 1996a). Interestingly, albuminuria was also increased among nonhypertensive, nondiabetic participants in Arizona. Follow-up studies will help clarify whether albuminuria is a sensitive marker for persons at risk of CVD or diabetes.

Alcohol use has been associated with elevated BP among Indians (DeStefano, Coulehan, and Wiant 1979; Kunitz and Levy 1986), and the association persists after adjustment for other factors (Howard et al. 1996). In particular, binge drinking, the more common pattern of drinking among American Indians (Welty et al. 1995), has been associated with increased BP.

Although physical inactivity was associated with increasing BP among Canadian Natives (Young 1991), in the SHS physical activity was inconsistently associated with BP after adjustment for other factors (Howard et al. 1996). Some Indian persons with hypertension were less likely to exercise to control their BP than was the general population (Centers for Disease Control and Prevention 1996). An association between sodium intake and hypertension among Indians has not been consistently demonstrated (Helgeson, Berg, and Juhl 1993; Welty et al. 1986). Also, calorie-adjusted sodium intake among subarctic Indians was not associated with elevated BP (Young 1991). Other factors associated with hypertension among Indians include family history, single marital status, and higher cholesterol levels (Young 1991). Helgeson, Berg, and Juhl (1993) noted an interaction of age, sex, coffee, alcohol, and cigarette use with BP levels. Postmenopausal estrogen users in the SHS were more likely to be hypertensive than were nonusers (Cowan et al. 1997). Lower income, less formal education, and unemployment have been associated with increased BP in Indian populations (Centers for Disease Control and Prevention 1996; Lee and Go 1996; Young 1991). Less education, however, was not consistently significant in multivariate analyses in the SHS (Howard et al. 1996). An association between a history of hypertension and selected cultural factors, including social isolation, off-reservation education, and fluency in English, was found for Navajo women but not men (Kunitz and Levy 1986). However, the study did not control for potential confounding by dietary or lifestyle changes. Acculturation was not associated with hypertension among Navajo adults (DeStefano, Coulehan, and Wiant 1979) or adolescent boys attending boarding school (Coulehan et al. 1990), although female adolescents with higher BPs tended to exhibit poorer life adjustment.

Cerebrovascular Disease

Cerebrovascular disease was the third leading cause of death for the general U.S. population but only the sixth leading cause of death among Indians in 1992–94.

However, mortality rates from cerebrovascular disease among Indians are very similar to those of the general U.S. population and of U.S. Whites. Neither the prevalence nor the incidence of cerebrovascular disease is known for most Indian populations. Among adult Chippewa and Menominee Indians of Minnesota and Wisconsin, the self-reported prevalence of prior stroke was 4 percent from 1992 to 1994 (Centers for Disease Control and Prevention 1996). From 1982 to 1984 the age-adjusted hospital discharge rate for the IHS user population was much less than the 1983 U.S. rate (17.7/10,000 vs. 32.5/10,000) (Welty and Coulehan 1993). However, survival rates from stroke are unknown for Indians, and hospitalization patterns may differ from those of the general population. Mortality rates from cerebrovascular disease among Indians have fallen in recent years. As shown in Table 10.4, cerebrovascular mortality rates among Indians have been comparable to those for the general population (Welty and Coulehan 1993; Grossman et al. 1994; Gillum 1995).

Like CHD mortality, CVD mortality rates among Indians vary by regions (Table 10.4). Higher relative rates have been found for Alaska Natives (Middaugh 1990) and rural versus urban Indians in Washington State (Grossman et al. 1994). For many years the Aberdeen Area has consistently had the highest rates of all IHS Areas (Welty and Coulehan 1993; Indian Health Service 1997b). Cerebrovascular deaths for Indians 45 years or older were more likely to be due to subarachnoid hemorrhage than cerebral thrombosis (Gillum 1995). A slight excess in cerebrovascular mortality among Alaska Natives was attributed to higher rates of intracerebral hemorrhage (Middaugh 1990). Reasons for this are not clear. Risk factors for stroke have not been specifically studied among Indians. However, diabetes was found to be a strong predictor of cerebrovascular disease among Navajo and Mohawk Indians (Macaulay, Montour, and Adelson 1988; Hoy, Light, and Megill 1994).

Peripheral Arterial Disease

Although peripheral arterial disease (PAD) is a major source of disability, it has rarely been studied formally among Native Americans. The prevalence rates of PAD among SHS participants were 4.8 percent for men and 5.6 percent for women, similar to those reported for non-Indians (Fabsitz et al. 1999). However, the sequelae of PAD may be more severe for Indians, particularly the Arizona participants, who had very high rates of lower extremity amputation. Significant independent risk factors for PAD included age, SBP, cigarette smoking, albuminuria, LDL cholesterol, and fibrinogen levels. Although diabetes was also a significant predictor of PAD, the association was not independent of albuminuria. Albuminuria may thus be a marker for macrovascular as well as microvascular disease. In earlier studies diabetes was associated with a greatly increased risk of PAD among Mohawk (Macaulay, Montour, and Adelson 1988) and Navajo (Hoy, Light, and Megill 1995) Indians. In the 1980s, lower extremity amputation was more common among Alaska Natives with diabetes than among the general U.S. and Navajo diabetic populations (Schraer et al. 1993).

Rheumatic Heart Disease

Rheumatic heart disease (RHD), the major sequela of acute rheumatic fever, was once the major cause of cardiac morbidity and mortality among Indians (Coulehan et al. 1980). Although mortality rates have substantially decreased, chronic RHD may still be a greater problem for some Indians than for the general population (Alpert et al. 1991). From 1958 to 1982, RHD mortality among New Mexico Indians was usually higher than that for non-Indians, and peak rates occurred between 1968 and 1972 (14.9/100,000 for males, 10.6/100,000 for females) (Becker et al. 1989). During the 1980s the Alaska Native RHD mortality was twice the all-Alaska and U.S. White rates (Davidson, Bulkow, and Gellin 1993). A genetic link between RHD and the HLA system may exist in some Native populations. Alaskan Inupiats and Yupiks have a high gene frequency of HLA-DR4 (Hansen et al. 1986), a cell marker that cross-reacts with streptococcal antibodies in patients with RHD (Rajapakse et al. 1990). Continued vigilance for re-emergence of pathogenic strains and prompt treatment of pharyngeal infections will probably keep rheumatic fever and chronic RHD under control in the future.

Congenital Heart Disease

Congenital heart disease among Indians has not been extensively studied. In a study of radiographs at the Phoenix Indian Medical Center from 1955 to 1970, Goldman et al. (1972) reported relatively fewer diagnoses of tetralogy of Fallot and more occurrences of total anomalous venous return and transposition of great vessels among Indians compared to the general population. High rates of isolated total anomalous pulmonary venous drainage among Native Canadian newborns have also been reported (McCrindle et al. 1996). Ojibwa and Sioux children with congenital heart disease had more frequent occurrences of isolated atrial septal defects than expected, but aortic valvular stenosis and coarctation of the aorta occurred less often (Anderson 1977). Chavez, Cordero, and Becerra (1988) also noted high rates of atrial septal defects and valve stenosis and atresia in data obtained from the Centers for Disease Control and Preven-

TABLE 10.4

Recent cerebrovascular mortality rates among Native Americans

Study	Dates	AI population	Age-adjusted mortality rate per 100,000 population[a]				Comparison population
			AI rate		Comparison rate		
			Total	M/F	Total	M/F	
		National					
Gillum 1988	1969–81	IHS states[b]					
		1969–71		42/40			
		1979–81		23/23			
Welty 1993	1981–83	IHS service population	32.3		35.8		All U.S.
Lee 1998	1984–88	Strong Heart Study[c] death certificate data study criteria		100/100 100/80			
IHS 1997b	1992–94	All IHS Areas[d]	27.8		26.5		All U.S.
		Regional					
Kattapong 1993	1958–87	New Mexico					U.S. White
		1958–62		52.2/36.5		121.6/108.7	
		1963–67		54.2/32.8		108.7/95.7	
		1968–72		70.1/55.7		105.5/80.8	
		1973–77		58.8/43.9		90.4/78.1	
		1978–82		39.8/34.6		66.6/60.8	
		1983–87		31.3/19.3		52.5/78.1	
Sievers 1990	1975–84	Pima Indians[e] death certificate data study criteria	99 130		75		All U.S.
Middaugh 1990	1980–86	Alaska Natives		43.7/60.0		38.7/58.0	Other Alaskans
Grossman 1994	1981–90	WA State counties					Urban WA Whites
		urban	26		28		
		reservation	56				
Welty 1993	1981–83	IHS Service Area			35.8		All U.S.
		Aberdeen	52.2				
		Alaska	44.2				
		Albuquerque	25.5				
		Bemidji	45.9				
		Billings	40.6				
		Nashville	50.9				

Study	Years	Area	Location	Rate	M/F
			Oklahoma	29.9	
			Phoenix	33.0	
			Portland	41.3	
			Tucson	25.1	
Lee 1998	1984–88	Strong Heart Study[a]			
		death certificate data			
			Arizona		80/100
			Oklahoma		60/120
			Dakotas		160/100
		study criteria			
			Arizona		80/100
			Oklahoma		80/80
			Dakotas		120/60
IHS 1997b	1992–94	IHS Service Area[d]			
			Aberdeen	36.6	
			Alaska	40.4	
			Albuquerque	19.7	
			Bemidji	36.8	
			Billings	37.9	
			California	22.4	
			Nashville	29.4	
			Navajo	21.6	
			Oklahoma	24.2	
			Phoenix	28.2	
			Portland	39.1	
			Tucson	23.7	
		All U.S.			

ABBREVIATIONS: AI, American Indian; M/F, male rate/female rate; IHS, Indian Health Service.

[a]Mortality rates are not comparable between studies because of differing methods of adjustments.

[b]During 1969–71 the IHS state population included AIs living in 25 states. During 1979–81, the population included AIs from 28 states. Rates in this study are unadjusted.

[c]Strong Heart Study subjects include AI persons aged 45–74 years only.

[d]Rate adjusted for underreporting of AI race on death certificates, as well as for age.

[e]Rates are average, age- and gender-adjusted per 100,000.

tion birth defects monitoring program. Reasons for these findings are not clear; a possible link between lead exposure and congenital heart disease has been suggested and deserves further study.

Studies in Canada have noted high prevalence rates of congenital heart and circulatory defects among Indian patients (Lowry, Thunem, and Silver 1986). A series of eight Native Canadian children with multiple congenital anomalies was recently reported (Marles et al. 1995). These cases were thought to be due to the Ritscher-Schinzel syndrome, which is characterized by cranial, cerebellar, and several cardiac defects. Several malformations associated with fetal alcohol syndrome (FAS) have been described, including atrial and ventricular septal defects (Sandor, Smith, and MacLeod 1981), but rates of FAS-associated heart defects have not been reported for Indians.

Discussion

The incidence rate for CVD has increased greatly among Native American populations, and an epidemic of CVD is now threatening. Strategies for stemming the effects of CVD are urgently needed. The relative protection noted in the past has disappeared from many communities and is rapidly disappearing from many others. The prevalence of major CVD risk factors is increasing, and little is known regarding risk-reduction strategies in Indian communities. The interplay of lifestyle, environment, and genetics with the risk of major cardiovascular disease is not well understood. However, marked changes in behavioral and dietary patterns have occurred almost universally among Native American populations in recent decades. These changes have already resulted in increased rates of CVD and, without aggressive prevention and control programs, further increases in CVD morbidity and mortality are expected.

Many issues affecting CHD morbidity and mortality among Indians have not been explored. For instance, survival rates of AMI are unknown for most Indian populations. Among Navajo patients diagnosed with AMI from 1984 to 1986, 18.5 percent died within one month (Klain et al. 1988), a lower rate than that noted in a previous study by Coulehan et al. (1986). Mortality rates of patients hospitalized with AMI in the general population range from 5 to 15 percent, and the mortality in the first year after discharge is 6–8 percent (Massie and Amidon 1997).

Many Indians may be at risk for higher out-of-hospital mortality because of limited access to emergency cardiac care and delays in seeking or receiving treatment. Further, diabetes may mask the symptoms typically associated with AMI and is disproportionately represented in Indian populations. The frequency of silent MI among Indians is unknown, but 25 percent of MIs in the general population occur without symptoms (Massie and Amidon 1997). Patterns of treatment have not been well described for Indians. Neither the effect of depression on survival after MI nor the efficacy and availability of cardiac rehabilitation programs have been assessed in Indian populations. The effect of postmenopausal estrogen therapy on CHD prevalence is being examined in the SHS cohort (Cowan et al. 1997). Recently, C-reactive protein and homocysteine levels have been linked to CHD, but these associations have not yet been systematically studied among Indian populations.

Until effective interventions are implemented, an unprecedented surge in CVD morbidity and mortality may be expected as the Indian population enters a new millennium. Studies such as the SHS suggest that important inter-Indian variations in the prevalence and manifestations of CVD may exist. Further comparisons of CVD and its many associated manifestations between Indian groups may prove to be quite enlightening.

REFERENCES

Acton KJ, Preston S, Rith-Najarian S. 1996. Clinical hypertension in Native Americans: A comparison of 1987 and 1992 rates from ambulatory care data. *Public Health Rep* 111 (suppl 2):33–36.

Alpert JS, Goldberg R, Ockene IS, et al. 1991. Heart disease in Native Americans. *Cardiology* 78:3–12.

Anderson RC. 1977. Congenital heart malformations in North American Indian children. *Pediatrics* 59:121–23.

Becker TM, Wiggins CL, Key CR, et al. 1988. Ischemic heart disease mortality in Hispanics, American Indians, and non-Hispanic Whites in New Mexico, 1958–1982. *Circulation* 78:302–9.

———. 1989. Ethnic differences in mortality from acute rheumatic fever and chronic rheumatic heart disease in New Mexico, 1958–1982. *West J Med* 150:46–50.

Botash AS, Kavey RW, Emm N, et al. 1992. Cardiovascular risk factors in Native American children. *NY State J Med* 92:378–81.

Broussard BA, Valway SE, Kaufman S, et al. 1993. Clinical hypertension and its interaction with diabetes among American Indians and Alaska Natives: Estimated rates from ambulatory care data. *Diabetes Care* 16 (suppl 1):292–96.

Byers T. 1992. The epidemic of obesity in American Indians. *Am J Dis Child* 146:285–86.

Campos-Outcalt D, Ellis J, Aickin M, et al. 1995. Prevalence of cardiovascular disease risk factors in a Southwestern Native American tribe. *Public Health Rep* 110:742–48.

Centers for Disease Control. 1992. Cigarette smoking among American Indians and Alaska Natives: Behavioral risk factor surveillance system, 1987–1991. *MMWR* 41:861–63.

Centers for Disease Control and Prevention. 1996. *Inter-tribal Heart Project: Results from the Cardiovascular Health Survey.* Atlanta: Centers for Disease Control and Prevention.

Chavez GF, Cordero JF, Becerra JE. 1988. Leading major congenital malformations among minority groups in the United States, 1981–1986. *MMWR* 37:17–24.

Cheadle A, Pearson D, Wagner E, et al. 1994. Relationship between socioeconomic status, health status, and lifestyle practices of American Indians: Evidence from a Plains reservation population. *Public Health Rep* 109:405–13.

Cleaver VL, Ratcliff R, Rogers B. 1989. Community health representatives: A valuable resource for providing coronary heart disease health education activities for Native Americans. *Health Educ* 20(6):16–20.

Clifford N, Kelly JJ, Teal L. 1963. Coronary heart disease and hypertension in the White Mountain Apache tribe. *Circulation* 28:926–31.

Coulehan J, Grant S, Reisinger K, et al. 1980. Acute rheumatic fever and rheumatic heart disease on the Navajo reservation, 1962–77. *Public Health Rep* 95:62–68.

Coulehan JL, Lerner G, Helzlsouer K, et al. 1986. Acute myocardial infarction among Navajo Indians, 1976–83. *Am J Public Health* 76:412–14.

Coulehan JL, Topper MD, Arena VC, et al. 1990. Determinants of blood pressure in Navajo adolescents. *Am Indian Alsk Native Ment Health Res* 3(3):27–36.

Cowan LD, Go OT, Howard BV, et al. 1997. Parity, postmenopausal estrogen use, and cardiovascular disease risk factors in American Indian women: The Strong Heart Study. *J Women's Health* 6:441–49.

Davidson M, Bulkow LR, Gellin BG. 1993. Cardiac mortality in Alaska's indigenous and non-Native residents. *Int J Epidemiol* 22:62–71.

Deprez RD, Miller E, Hart SK. 1985. Hypertension prevalence among Penobscot Indians of Indian Island, Maine. *Am J Public Health* 75:653–54.

DeStefano F, Coulehan JL, Wiant MK. 1979. Blood pressure survey on the Navajo Indian reservation. *Am J Epidemiol* 109:335–45.

Ellis JL, Campos-Outcalt D. 1994. Cardiovascular disease risk factors in Native Americans: A literature review. *Am J Prev Med* 10(5):295–307.

Fabsitz RR, Sidawy AN, Go OT, et al. 1999. Prevalence of peripheral arterial disease and associated risk factors in American Indians: The Strong Heart Study. *Am J Epidemiol* 149:330–38.

Folsom AR, Johnson KM, Lando HA, et al. 1993. Plasma fibrinogen and other cardiovascular risk factors in urban American Indian smokers. *Ethn Dis* 3:344–50.

Fulmer HS, Roberts RW. 1963. Coronary heart disease among the Navajo Indians. *Ann Intern Med* 59:740–64.

Gilbert J. 1955. Absence of coronary thrombosis in Navajo Indians. *Calif Med* 82:114–15.

Gilbert TJ, Percy CA, Sugarman JR, et al. 1992. Obesity among Navajo adolescents: Relationship to dietary intake and blood pressure. *Am J Dis Child* 146:289–95.

Gilbert TJ, Percy CA, White LL, et al. 1996. Blood pressure and body measurements among Navajo adolescents. *Public Health Rep* 111 (suppl 2):44–48.

Gillum RF. 1988. Ischemic heart disease mortality in American Indians, United States, 1969–1971 and 1979–1981. *Am Heart J* 115:1141–44.

——. 1995. The epidemiology of stroke in Native Americans. *Stroke* 26:514–21.

Gillum RF, Gillum BS, Smith N. 1984. Cardiovascular risk factors among urban American Indians: Blood pressure, serum lipids, smoking, diabetes, health knowledge, and behavior. *Am Heart J* 107:765–76.

Gillum RF, Prineas R, Palta M, et al. 1980. Blood pressure of urban Native American school children. *Hypertension* 2:744–49.

Goldberg HI, Warren CW, Oge LL, et al. 1991. Prevalence of behavioral risk factors in two American Indian populations in Montana. *Am J Prev Med* 7(3):155–60.

Goldman SM, Sievers ML, Carlile WK, et al. 1972. Roentgen manifestations of diseases in Southwestern Indians. *Radiology* 103:303–6.

Gray RS, Robbins DC, Wang W, et al. 1997. Relation of LDL size to the insulin resistance syndrome and coronary heart disease in American Indians: The Strong Heart Study. *Arterioscler Thromb Vasc Biol* 17:2713–20.

Grossman D, Krieger J, Sugarman J, et al. 1994. Health status of urban American Indians and Alaska Natives: A population-based study. *JAMA* 271:845–50.

Hansen J, Lanier A, Nisperos B, et al. 1986. The HLA system in Inupiat and central Yupik Alaskan Eskimos. *Hum Immunol* 16:315–28.

Helgeson DM, Berg CL, Juhl N. 1993. Blood pressure comparison in a selected Native American and White population. *Public Health Nurs* 10:36–41.

Hirata-Dulas CA, Rith-Najarian SJ, McIntyre MC, et al. 1996. Risk factors for nephropathy and cardiovascular disease in diabetic Northern Minnesota American Indians. *Clin Nephrol* 46:92–98.

Howard BV, Davis MP, Pettitt DJ, et al. 1983. Plasma and lipoprotein cholesterol and triglyceride concentrations in the Pima Indians: Distributions differing from those of Caucasians. *Circulation* 68:714–24.

Howard BV, Lee ET, Cowan LD, et al. 1995. Coronary heart disease prevalence and its relation to risk factors in American Indians: The Strong Heart Study. *Am J Epidemiol* 142:254–68.

Howard BV, Lee ET, Yeh JL, et al. 1996. Hypertension in adult American Indians: The Strong Heart Study. *Hypertension* 28:256–64.

Howard BV, Welty TK, Fabsitz RR, et al. 1992. Risk factors for coronary heart disease in diabetic and nondiabetic Native Americans: The Strong Heart Study. *Diabetes* 41 (suppl 2):4–11.

Hoy W, Light A, Megill D. 1994. Blood pressure in Navajo Indians and its association with type 2 diabetes and renal and cardiovascular disease. *Am J Hypertens* 7, pt 1:321–28.

———. 1995. Cardiovascular disease in Navajo Indians with type 2 diabetes. *Public Health Rep* 110:87–94.

Hrabovsky S, Welty T, Coulehan J. 1989. Acute myocardial infarction and sudden death in Sioux Indians. *West J Med* 150:240–42.

Indian Health Service. 1994. *Trends in Indian Health, 1994*. Rockville, Md.: Indian Health Service, Division of Program Statistics.

———. 1997a. *Trends in Indian Health, 1997*. Rockville, Md.: Indian Health Service, Program Statistics Team.

———. 1997b. *Regional Differences in Indian Health, 1997*. Rockville, Md.: Indian Health Service, Program Statistics Team.

International Classification of Diseases. 1998. 9th rev., 5th ed. Los Angeles: Practice Management Information Corp.

Johnson AJ, Taylor A. 1991. Prevalence of chronic diseases: A summary of data from the Survey of American Indians and Alaska Natives. Agency for Health Care Policy Research. *National Medical Expenditure Survey* Data Summary 3. Rockville, Md.: Public Health Service.

Kataoka S, Robbins DC, Cowan LD, et al. 1996. Apolipoprotein E polymorphism in American Indians and its relation to plasma lipoproteins and diabetes: The Strong Heart Study. *Arterioscler Thromb Vasc Biol* 16:918–25.

Kattapong VJ, Becker TM. 1993. Ethnic differences in mortality from cerebrovascular disease among New Mexico's Hispanics, Native Americans, and non-Hispanic Whites, 1958 through 1987. *Ethn Dis* 3:75–82.

Klain M, Coulehan JL, Arena VC, et al. 1988. More frequent diagnosis of acute myocardial infarction among Navajo Indians. *Am J Public Health* 78:1351–52.

Kunitz SJ, Levy JE. 1986. The prevalence of hypertension among elderly Navajos: A test of the acculturative stress hypothesis. *Cult Med Psychiatry* 10:97–121.

Lee ET, Cowan L, Welty T, et al. 1998. All-cause mortality and cardiovascular disease mortality in three American Indian populations, aged 45–74 years, 1984–88: The Strong Heart Study. *Am J Epidemiol* 147:995–1008.

Lee ET, Go OT. 1996. Socioeconomic status and cardiovascular health and disease in American Indians: The Strong Heart Study. In: *Report of the Conference on Socioeconomic Status and Cardiovascular Health and Disease, National Heart, Lung and Blood Institute, November 6–7, 1995,* 93–99. Bethesda, Md.: National Institutes of Health.

Lee ET, Welty TK, Fabsitz R, et al. 1990. The Strong Heart Study: A study of cardiovascular disease in American Indians. Design and methods. *Am J Epidemiol* 132:1141–55.

Lefkowitz D, Underwood C. 1991. Personal health practices: Findings from the survey of American Indians and Alaska Natives. AHCPR Pub. No. 91-003. *National Medical Expenditure Survey* Research Findings 10, Agency for Health Care Policy and Research. Rockville, Md.: Public Health Service.

LeMaster PL, Connell CM. 1994. Health education interventions among Native Americans: A review and analysis. *Health Educ Q* 21:521–38.

Liu QZ, Knowler WC, Nelson RG, et al. 1992. Insulin treatment, endogenous insulin concentration, and ECG abnormalities in diabetic Pima Indians: Cross-sectional and prospective analyses. *Diabetes* 41:1141–50.

Lowry RB, Thunem NY, Silver M. 1986. Congenital anomalies in American Indians of British Columbia. *Genet Epidemiol* 3:455–67.

Macaulay AC, Montour LT, Adelson N. 1988. Prevalence of diabetic and atherosclerotic complications among Mohawk Indians of Kahnawake, PQ. *Can Med Assoc J* 139:221–24.

Marles SL, Chodirker BN, Greenberg CR, et al. 1995. Evidence for Ritscher-Schinzel syndrome in Canadian Native Indians. *Am J Med Genet* 56:343–50.

Massie BM, Amidon TA. 1997. Chap 10: Heart. In: Tierney LM, McPhee SJ, Papadakis MA, eds. *Current Medical Diagnosis and Treatment.* 36th ed. Stamford, Conn.: Appleton & Lange.

Mayberry R, Lindeman R. 1963. A survey of chronic disease and diet in Seminole Indians in Oklahoma. *Am J Clin Nutr* 13:127–34.

McCrindle BW, Wood MM, Collins GF, et al. 1996. An increased incidence of total anomalous pulmonary venous drainage among aboriginal Canadians. *Can J Cardiol* 12:81–85.

Mendlein JM, Freedman DS, Peter DG, et al. 1997. Risk factors for coronary heart disease among Navajo Indians: Findings from the Navajo Health and Nutrition Survey. *J Nutr* 127 (10, suppl):2099S–2105S.

Middaugh JP. 1990. Cardiovascular deaths among Alaskan Natives, 1980–86. *Am J Public Health* 80:282–85.

Molina J, Campos-Outcalt D. 1991. Coronary artery disease risk factors in Yaqui Indians and Mexican Americans. *J Natl Med Assoc* 83:1075–80.

Nelson RG, Sievers ML, Knowler WC, et al. 1990. Low incidence of fatal coronary heart disease in Pima Indians despite high prevalence of non-insulin-dependent diabetes. *Circulation* 81:987–95.

Oopik AJ, Dorogy M, Devereux RB, et al. 1996. Major electrocardiographic abnormalities among American Indians aged 45–64 years (the Strong Heart Study). *Am J Cardiol* 78:1400–1405.

Pinkerton RE, Badke FR. 1974. Coronary heart disease: An epidemiologic study of Crow and Northern Cheyenne Indians. *Rocky Mountain Med J* 71:577–83.

Rajapakse C, Al-Balla S, Al-Dallan A, et al. 1990. Streptococcal antibody cross-reactivity with HLA-DR4 + VE B-lymphocytes: Basis of the DR4 associated genetic predisposition to rheumatic fever and rheumatic heart disease? *Br J Rheumatol* 29:468–70.

Robbins DC, Knowler WC, Lee ET, et al. 1996a. Regional differences in albuminuria among American Indians: An epidemic of renal disease. *Kidney Int* 49:557–63.

Robbins DC, Welty TK, Wang WY, et al. 1996b. Plasma lipids and lipoprotein concentrations among American Indians: Comparison with the U.S. population. *Curr Opin Lipidol* 7:188–95.

Saad MF, Knowler WC, Pettitt DJ, et al. 1990. Insulin and hypertension: Relationship to obesity and glucose intolerance in Pima Indians. *Diabetes* 39:1430–35.

Sandor GG, Smith DF, MacLeod PM. 1981. Cardiac malformations in the fetal alcohol syndrome. *J Pediatr* 98:771–73.

Savage PJ, Hamman RF, Bartha G, et al. 1976. Serum cholesterol levels in American Pima Indian children and adolescents. *Pediatrics* 58:274–82.

Schraer CD, Bulkow LR, Murphy NJ, et al. 1993. Diabetes prevalence, incidence, and complications among Alaska Natives, 1987. *Diabetes Care* 16:257–59.

Schraer C, Ebbesson S, Boyko E, et al. 1996. Hypertension and diabetes among Siberian Yupik Eskimos of St. Lawrence Island, Alaska. *Public Health Rep* 111 (suppl 2):51–52.

Sharlin KS, Heath GW, Ford ES, et al. 1993. Hypertension and blood pressure awareness among American Indians of the Northern Plains. *Ethn Dis* 3:337–43.

Sievers ML. 1967. Myocardial infarction among southwestern American Indians. *Ann Intern Med* 67: 801–7.

——. 1968. Serum cholesterol levels in Southwestern American Indians. *J Chronic Dis* 21:107–15.

——. 1977. Historical overview of hypertension among American Indians and Alaskan Natives. *Ariz Med* 34:607–10.

Sievers ML, Nelson RG, Bennett PH. 1996. Sequential trends in overall and cause-specific mortality in diabetic and nondiabetic Pima Indians. *Diabetes Care* 19:107–11.

Stern MP. 1998. Invited commentary: Cardiovascular mortality in American Indians. Paradox explained? *Am J Epidemiol* 147:1009–10.

Sugarman JR. 1990. Prevalence of diagnosed hypertension among diabetic Navajo Indians. *Arch Intern Med* 150:359–62.

Sugarman JR, Gilbert TJ, Percy CA, et al. 1992. Serum cholesterol concentrations among Navajo Indians. *Public Health Rep* 107:92–99.

Torrey E, Reiff F, Noble G. 1979. Hypertension among Aleuts. *Am J Epidemiol* 110:7–14.

U.S. Preventive Services Task Force. 1996. *Guide to Clinical Preventive Services.* 2d ed. Baltimore: Williams & Wilkins.

Welty TK, Coulehan JL. 1993. Cardiovascular disease among American Indians and Alaska Natives. *Diabetes Care* 16:277–83.

Welty TK, Freni-Titulaer L, Zack MM, et al. 1986. Effects of exposure to salty drinking water in an Arizona community: Cardiovascular mortality, hypertension prevalence, and relationships between blood pressure and sodium intake. *JAMA* 255:622–26.

Welty TK, Lee ET, Yeh J, et al. 1995. Cardiovascular disease risk factors among American Indians: The Strong Heart Study. *Am J Epidemiol* 142:269–87.

Welty TK, Rhoades DA, Lee ET, et al. Unpublished data: Changes in cardiovascular disease risk factors among American Indians. The Strong Heart Study.

Will JC, Strauss KF, Mendlein JM, et al. 1997. Diabetes mellitus among Navajo Indians: Findings from the Navajo Health and Nutrition Survey. *J Nutr* 127 (10, suppl): 2106S–13S.

Young TK. 1991. Prevalence and correlates of hypertension in a subarctic Indian population. *Prev Med* 20:474–85.

———. 1994. *The Health of Native Americans: Toward a Biocultural Epidemiology.* New York: Oxford University Press.

Young TK, Moffatt ME, O'Neil JD. 1993. Cardiovascular diseases in a Canadian Arctic population. *Am J Public Health* 83:881–87.

11

James W. Hampton, M.D., James F. Maher, Ph.D., M.D.,
Charles R. Key, M.D., Ph.D.,
and Everett R. Rhoades, M.D.

Cancer among American Indians and Alaska Natives

At the beginning of the twentieth century, cancer was reported to be rare among American Indians (Currier 1891; Hrdlicka 1905; Levin 1910; Stefansson 1960) and, as epidemiologic data from different regions and tribes were obtained, cancer was indeed noted to be less common in Indians than in other ethnic groups in the United States (Sievers and Fisher 1983; Mahoney et al. 1989; Baquet 1996). However, during the past three decades, cancer incidence and mortality rates have been observed to be increasing in this population (Valway et al. 1992; Burhansstipanov and Dresser 1993). Further, Native Americans with cancer are the least likely to survive when compared to other ethnic groups (Baquet 1996; Miller et al. 1996). Cancer is now the second leading cause of death of Indians (Indian Health Service 1997). The observed regional differences in cancer among Indians (Sievers and Fisher 1983; Valway et al. 1992; Miller et al. 1996) have in the past been attributed to differences in lifestyle (Hampton 1984; Welty 1992; Cobb 1996), but they may be due to genetic differences as well (Sievers 1966; Fraumeni 1975; Cobb 1996).

Although complete and accurate information is often lacking, several facts seem to characterize cancer among Indians:

1. Overall cancer mortality rates for Indians are reported to be lower than rates for the general U.S. population (U.S. All Races) and U.S. Whites, but for certain specific cancer sites and types and for certain regions the rates are higher.
2. Cancer incidence data are relatively sparse, but where available they are consistent with the mortality patterns and trends.
3. Survival rates for Indian patients with cancer are less favorable than rates for other groups, perhaps because the cancers of Indian patients are fre-

quently diagnosed late, at more advanced stages, or because Indians may develop more aggressive cancers with less effective therapies.

Whether the rising cancer incidence and mortality rates of the past several decades reflect better recognition and documentation or exposure to increased risk factors may never be totally resolved, but as surveillance statistics are improved the answer may yet be found (Sievers 1966).

Cancer Statistics: Methods of Assembly

The known difficulties of assembling accurate statistics for diseases such as cancer include inaccurate counts of confirmed cases or deaths ("numerator data") within the appropriate "population at risk," which often is based on decennial U.S. census data. As has been noted in other chapters, these difficulties are often compounded by problems with "denominator data" in studies of diseases of American Indians (see Chapter 6).

Building on existing cancer registry models in New Mexico and Alaska, the Surveillance, Epidemiology and End Results (SEER) program of the National Cancer Institute (NCI) has gathered cancer incidence, extent of disease at diagnosis, treatment, and outcome data for about 25 years from the southwestern United States (New Mexico and Arizona) and more recently from Alaska, where the Indian and Alaska Native populations are somewhat easier to define. Publications from these registries form a considerable portion of the available information about cancer in Indian people. However, because of the heterogeneity of Native American populations and their markedly different genetic heritage, environments, "lifestyles," and cancer mortality patterns, the findings from the Alaska and New Mexico registries and from the SEER program cannot be uniformly extrapolated to all American Indians. Since many states now have population-based cancer registries supported by funding from the Centers for Disease Control and Prevention, prospects are somewhat improved for more accurate data in the future (Sugarman et al. 1996).

Techniques to improve analysis of cancer rates among Indians include using inpatient discharge data (Nutting et al. 1993) and linking Indian Health Service (IHS) service population or user population rosters with state cancer registries (Sugarman et al. 1996; Bleed et al. 1992). Calculations of complete cancer statistics for population subsets, as by region or tribe, are often limited by small numbers of cases. In a SEER publication (Miller et al. 1996), cancer incidence and mortality rates for Indians (New Mexico) and for Alaska Natives were not presented in the tables and graphs for some specific cancer sites because fewer than 25 cases were recorded during the five-year period. (Actual case counts for each major cancer site were tabulated in appendices.)

A frequent observation is that the median age for Indian patients with cancer is young in comparison to other groups, and this has been interpreted as early onset of the disease. However, it really is a reflection of the relatively smaller number of persons in the older age groups where the risk of developing cancer is most common. Further, agencies and authors may use different age standards as weighting factors when adjusting populations for age. For example, the IHS and the National Center for Health Statistics (NCHS) typically use the 1940 U.S. Population Standard. The National Cancer Institute and the American Cancer Society tend to use the 1970 U.S. Population Standard. The World Health Organization and many countries use the World Population Standard for international comparisons.

Cancer Incidence and Mortality

The age-adjusted (and 1992–94 rates adjusted for racial misclassification) Indian death rate for cancer in 1992–94 was 112.2/100,000 population, compared to 132.6/100,000 among U.S. All Races and 129.4/100,000 for U.S. Whites. The ratio of Indian deaths to U.S. All Races and U.S. Whites is 0.8 to 0.9, respectively (Table 11.1). The 19 percent increase in mortality rates among Indians since about 1975 is shown in Figure 11.1.

The five leading causes of cancer mortality are shown in Figure 11.2. The dominance of lung as a primary site is striking, followed by colon, breast, prostate, and stomach. The mortality due to stomach cancer differs from that for U.S. All Races. Prostate cancer is the second leading cause of cancer deaths in Indian men, and cancer of the breast is second among Indian women. In both sexes, the colon is the third most frequent site.

In a 23-year (1929–51) review of 34,500 admissions of Navajos to Sage Memorial Hospital in Ganado, Arizona, Smith, Salsbury, and Gilliam (1956) reported 66 cases of cancer. No women with breast cancer were seen. Except for the pancreas in males and hepatocellular cancer in females, cancer of the digestive tract was recorded less commonly than expected. Cancer of the lung was uncommon, in contrast to Indians elsewhere, as was genitourinary cancer, especially of the prostate. In females, only one death from cancer was noted during this period, far fewer than expected. Cancer of the cervix occurred at approximately the same incidence rates experienced by White women. The authors estimated that cancer mortality among Indian males was approximately 25 percent and among Indian females 33 percent less than expected.

TABLE 11.1

Malignant neoplasm deaths and death rates for American Indians and Alaska Natives (IHS Service Area), U.S. All Races, and U.S. White populations, 1955–1993 (age-adjusted rate per 100,000 population)

| Calendar year(s)[a] | American Indian and Alaska Native | | Rate | | Ratio of American Indian and Alaska Native to: | |
	No.	Rate	U.S. All Races	U.S. Whites	U.S. All Races	U.S. Whites
(1994)	1,046 (1,201)[b]					
1992–94 (1993)	1,025 (1,169)	97.5 (112.2)[b]	132.6	129.4	0.7 (0.8)[b]	0.8 (0.9)[b]
1991–93 (1992)	1,026 (1,174)	98.8	133.1	129.9	0.7	0.8
1990–92 (1991)	1,021	96.2	134.5	131.3	0.7	0.7
1989–91 (1990)	859	94.6	135.0	131.5	0.7	0.7
1988–90 (1989)	913	91.1	133.0	130.2	0.7	0.7
1987–89 (1988)	831	90.0	132.7	130.0	0.7	0.7
1986–88 (1987)	768	87.6	132.9	130.1	0.7	0.7
1985–87 (1986)	756	85.8	133.2	130.4	0.6	0.7
1984–86 (1985)	714	88.1	133.6	130.7	0.7	0.7
1983–85 (1984)	712	88.8	133.5	130.2	0.7	0.7
1982–84 (1983)	662	89.6	132.6	129.4	0.7	0.7
1981–83 (1982)	617	87.5	132.5	129.4	0.7	0.7
1980–82 (1981)	578	86.3	131.6	128.5	0.7	0.7
1979–81 (1980)	567	82.7	132.8	129.6	0.6	0.6
1978–80 (1979)	480	81.7	130.8	130.2	0.6	0.6
1977–79 (1978)	503	80.2	133.8	130.8	0.6	0.6
1976–78 (1977)	456	82.4	133.0	130.0	0.6	0.6
1975–77 (1976)	441	80.3	132.3	129.5	0.6	0.6
1974–76 (1975)	395	81.4	129.4	128.1	0.6	0.6
1973–75 (1974)	403	82.2	131.8	129.0	0.6	0.6
1972–74 (1973)	385	85.6	130.7	127.7	0.7	0.7
(1972)	354					
1954–56 (1955)	296	95.0	125.8	125.8	0.8	0.8

NOTE: Data are presented for the year in which the IHS was established (1955). For this year, reservation state data are shown. Starting in 1972, data are first available, and are shown above, for the specific counties in the IHS Service Area. Data for these two geographical boundary systems are not directly comparable.

[a]American Indian and Alaska Native rates are for the three-year periods specified. Numbers of deaths and rates for U.S. populations are for the single-year period.

[b]Numbers in parentheses are numbers, rates, or ratios of rates adjusted to compensate for miscoding of Indian race on death certificates.

Smith (1957) reported that average annual mortality rates for cancers among all Indians, except for cancer of the liver, pancreas, and cervix among women, were lower than expected, when compared to non-Indians. Sievers and Fisher (1981) reported that the age-adjusted cancer mortality rate among Southwestern Indians was 39 percent lower than that of the general population and was also lower than that of other U.S. population groups. Sometimes striking differences in the proportion of certain cancers by site of origin, such as stomach and kidney, were also noted when comparing Southwestern Indians and non-Indians.

Creagan and Fraumeni (1972), analyzing 5,897 cancer deaths among Indians during 1950–67, found that overall Indian cancer mortality was significantly lower than expected, particularly from cancers of the colorectal area, lung, prostate, breast, ovary, bladder, and brain and from Hodgkin's lymphoma. The only cancer site associated with a mortality rate of both Indian males and females that was significantly greater than that of the general U.S. population was the gallbladder. Indian females had significantly increased mortality from cancers of the thyroid, nasopharynx, and paranasal sinuses. Creagan and Fraumeni suggested that the relatively favorable cancer mortality of Indians may be related in some way to their high rates of diabetes, an observation previously made in other populations.

Nutting et al. (1993), using IHS inpatient discharge data for 1980–87 for 21 cancer sites among women and 18 among men, standardized according to the SEER program, found that, in many Indian communities, incidence rates for cancers of the gallbladder, kidney, stomach, and cervix were relatively high, with strikingly high rates of cancer of the liver and nasopharynx among Alaska Natives. On the other hand, Indians experienced lower cancer rates than Whites for breast, uterus, ovary, prostate, lung, colorectal area, urinary bladder, leukemia, and melanoma.

Bleed et al. (1992) estimated the cancer incidence and survival of Indians in Montana through linking IHS databases with the Montana Cancer Tumor Registry (MCTR) for the years 1982–87. Using SEER criteria, the authors identi-

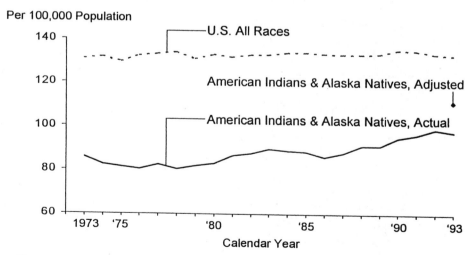

Figure 11.1. The trend in age-adjusted cancer mortality of American Indians and of U.S. All Races, since 1973. The 1993 rate adjusted for racial misclassification on death records is shown by the *diamond point*. *Source:* Indian Health Service 1997, Chart 4.33.

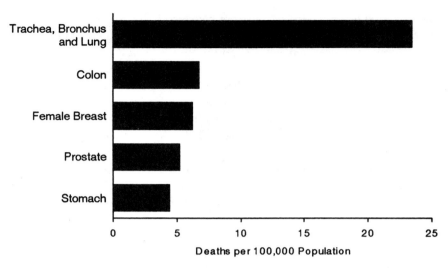

Figure 11.2. Death rates for leading cancer sites, American Indians and Alaska Natives (1992–94). *Source:* Indian Health Service 1997, Chart 4.35.

fied 344 cases of cancer. Of these, 249 (72%) were listed in both the MCTR and the IHS databases; 56 (16%) and 39 (11%) were listed in only the MCTR or the IHS database, respectively. The overall cancer incidence of Montana Indian males was lower than that for U.S. White men, as was the incidence of colorectal and bladder cancers and non-Hodgkin lymphoma. Montana Indian women had higher incidence rates for cancer of the cervix but lower rates for cancer of the colorectal area, breast, and uterus. The overall cancer survival rates of Montana Indians, as with the SEER data, were considerably lower than those of U.S. Whites.

Sugarman, Dennis, and White (1994) compared cancer survival rates among 551 Indians to those among 110,899 Whites included in the Seattle–Puget Sound Cancer Registry for the years 1974–89. For the five sites studied, except the prostate, the stage at diagnosis for Indians was not significantly different from that for Whites, and the proportion of treatment of Indians was similar to that for Whites. After adjustment for age differences, Indians experienced poorer survival from prostate, breast, cervical, and colorectal cancer than did Whites, and these differences persisted after adjustment for differences in cancer stage at diagnosis, lack of cancer treatment, and residence in a nonurban county. Survival among Indians recorded as non-Indians in the cancer registry but listed as Indians in IHS records was more favorable than among those persons initially coded as Indians in the cancer registry. Thus, cancer survival among Indians in western Washington is poorer than that among Whites in the same region, and factors other than age, differences in stage at diagnosis, lack of cancer treatment, and residence in nonurban counties seem to be responsible.

Sorem (1985) reported that the age-adjusted incidence of cancer in Zuni Indians was significantly lower than that of New Mexico Anglo populations during 1969–82. This was especially true of cancers of the colon, rectum and anus, lung, breast, endometrium, and pancreas and of melanoma of the skin and leukemia. On the other hand, Zunis had higher rates of stomach and gall-bladder cancer compared to New Mexico Anglos. Further, they had lower rates of lung, colon, and pancreas cancer than found among other New Mexico tribes. Mahoney et al. (1989) reported a lower mortality ratio between Seneca Indians and the general population of New York State, excluding New York City. Lanier et al. (1976) found that Alaska Natives had lower overall incidence rates of cancer, but certain cancers were present in higher numbers than expected. The latter included cancers of the nasopharynx, liver, salivary glands, gallbladder, kidney, and thyroid. Lanier and Key (1993) noted that certain changes in cancer incidence among Alaska Natives had occurred over the past two decades, with declines in esophageal and invasive cervical cancers and increases in cancers of the lung and colorectal area.

An analysis of cancer mortality among Indians in the IHS Service Area (counties with a substantial number of Indian residents in the 35 reservation states) during 1968–87 confirmed the relatively lower incidence and mortality rates of cancer in Arizona and New Mexico Indians and the high mortality rates for cancer in Northern Plains Indians (Valway et al. 1992). The different incidence rates of various cancers between Alaska Natives and New Mexico Indians, where the data are considered to be the most accurate, contrast two different regional populations of Native Americans, as shown in Figure 11.3. Not only is the distribution of cancer types different between the two different regions, but also the rates for each are generally quite different. For example, cancer of the lung is prominent for both Alaska Native men and women, but among New Mexico Indians it is in the top five cancers of only the men. Prostate cancer is the most common cancer among New Mexico Indian men compared to lung and bronchus among Alaska Native men. While cancer of the breast is the most common cancer of both Alaska Native and New Mexico Indian women, the incidence rate for Alaska Native women is more than twice that of New Mexico Indian women. The unusually high rate of kidney cancer in Alaska Native men and women and New Mexico men invites further study as to etiology. The high incidence of colorectal cancer in Alaska Native women (67.4/100,000 versus 39.2/100,000 in non-Hispanic Whites) deserves investigation. The information in Figure 11.3 graphically illustrates the widely different incidence rates

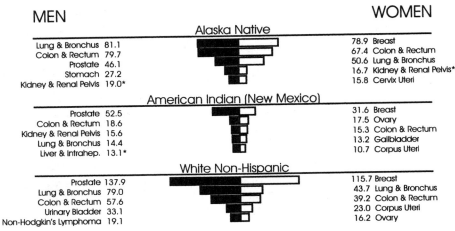

MEN   WOMEN

Alaska Native

MEN			WOMEN
Lung & Bronchus	81.1	78.9	Breast
Colon & Rectum	79.7	67.4	Colon & Rectum
Prostate	46.1	50.6	Lung & Bronchus
Stomach	27.2	16.7	Kidney & Renal Pelvis*
Kidney & Renal Pelvis	19.0*	15.8	Cervix Uteri

American Indian (New Mexico)

MEN			WOMEN
Prostate	52.5	31.6	Breast
Colon & Rectum	18.6	17.5	Ovary
Kidney & Renal Pelvis	15.6	15.3	Colon & Rectum
Lung & Bronchus	14.4	13.2	Gallbladder
Liver & Intrahep.	13.1*	10.7	Corpus Uteri

White Non-Hispanic

MEN			WOMEN
Prostate	137.9	115.7	Breast
Lung & Bronchus	79.0	43.7	Lung & Bronchus
Colon & Rectum	57.6	39.2	Colon & Rectum
Urinary Bladder	33.1	23.0	Corpus Uteri
Non-Hodgkin's Lymphoma	19.1	16.2	Ovary

Figure 11.3. Comparison of SEER incidence rates of the five most common cancers of Alaska Natives, New Mexico Indians, and New Mexico non-Hispanic whites, 1988–92. The rates are "average annual" per 100,000 population, age adjusted to 1970 U.S. Standard. The *asterisks* indicate rates based on fewer than 25 cases, which may be subject to greater variability than the other rates based on larger numbers. *Source:* Miller et al. 1996.

of cancer in these different regions for Native Americans and illustrates that the heterogeneous population precludes random sampling for meaningful data (Hampton 1989).

Cancer Survival Rates

Survival rates after the diagnosis of cancer are approximately 13 percent lower for Indian men and 17 percent lower for Indian women than for U.S. All Races (Baquet 1996). Between 1969 and 1982, one- and five-year survival rates were lower for New Mexico Indians and Hispanics compared to non-Hispanic Whites (Samet et al. 1987). Although not the case for all cancer sites, Indian patients tended to have more advanced disease at the time of diagnosis, and for many primary cancer sites, Indian patients were less likely to receive treatment than were non-Hispanic Whites. However, even after adjustment for stage and treatment, Indians still had poorer survival rates, suggesting that additional, as yet unidentified, factors may be present (Sugarman et al. 1996). The lower survival rate of Indians could be due to several factors but may be the result of three major influences: a difference in the biological aggressiveness of the specific cancers, the availability of optimal treatment, and, more importantly, late diagnosis with inadequate early detection measures for a population unaware of those available.

Cancer among New Mexico Indians

Implementation of a comprehensive statewide tumor registry in New Mexico has permitted a series of important observations about New Mexico Indians. Black and Key (1980) reported that the incidence rates for most of the common cancers among New Mexico Anglos resembled those for U.S. Whites. Except for higher rates for cancer of the gallbladder, stomach, and uterine cervix, Hispanic males and females were found to have fewer cancers than either New Mexico Anglos or U.S. Whites. Indians experienced lower total cancer incidence rates, but their rates for gallbladder, stomach, and cervix were higher even than for Hispanics. Lung cancer was found in only one-fourth as many Indian men and women as U.S. Whites or New Mexico Anglos. Carcinoma of the stomach was found to be more common among both Hispanic and Indian populations, while colorectal carcinoma was quite uncommon among Indians.

Incidence rates of carcinoma of the cervix during the reproductive years were slightly higher among Hispanic women than among Indians, but among women older than 60 years the rate for Indians was considerably higher than that for either Hispanic or Anglo women of the same age. It was estimated that only about 25 percent of Indian women 60 years of age or older have ever undergone cervical cytologic examination. Older Indian patients with carcinoma of the cervix frequently presented with advanced disease. Among an estimated 43,500 Navajo women at risk (including those living in Arizona), about half were screened each year between 1976 and 1978. Indian women had proportionally fewer carcinomas of the endometrium than either Anglo or Hispanic women. Carcinoma of the breast appeared to be less common among Indian women, although as a group they tended to present with more advanced disease than did Hispanic or Anglo patients, and the disease tended to appear at a somewhat younger age among Indians.

Wiggins et al. (1989) found higher rates of stomach cancer among New Mexico Indians than among New Mexico non-Hispanic Whites. While the incidence rates of stomach cancer declined for both Hispanic and non-Hispanic Whites before 1968, the rate remained constant for Indians. However, during 1969–82, incidence rates of stomach cancer remained constant for Hispanic Whites, non-Hispanic Whites, and Indian males but more than doubled among Indian females.

Wiggins et al. (1993) examined differences in gender- and age-adjusted and age-specific cancer mortality rates among New Mexico Hispanics, Indians, and non-Hispanic Whites during the 30-year span 1958–87. They found higher cancer rates among males compared to females, with an overall increase in cancer mortality for each group during the period of study. Cancer mortality rates for New Mexico non-Hispanic Whites tended to be comparable with those reported for U.S. Whites. For most cancer sites, the mortality rates of Indians were the lowest, with Hispanics intermediate between the other two groups. Both Hispanics and Indians had higher mortality rates for cancers of the gallbladder, cervix, and stomach compared to non-Hispanic Whites.

Cancer among Alaska Natives

As in New Mexico, a special emphasis on an accurate tumor registry has permitted more thorough analysis of cancer among Alaska Natives. Blot et al. (1975) reported 321 deaths from cancer among Alaska Natives during 1960–69, resulting in a rate not significantly different from that reported for U.S. Whites but significantly higher than that of New Mexico Indians, especially for cancers of the nasopharynx, esophagus, kidneys, and salivary glands (Lanier 1986). A survey of cancer incidence rates among Alaska Natives for the years 1969–73 revealed fewer cancer cases overall than expected in relation to U.S. All Races rates but a significantly increased number of cases for certain cancer sites: the nasopharynx in both sexes (Lanier et al. 1980), the liver in males (Lanier et al. 1976), and the salivary glands, gallbladder, kidney, and thyroid in females (Lanier et al. 1976).

Subsequent studies by Lanier, Bulkow, and Ireland (1989), Lanier (1993), and Lanier et al. (1994) confirmed the earlier observations but noted certain changes in the proportion of all cancers produced by certain anatomical sites. Cancer of the lung had become the most frequently diagnosed cancer among all Alaska Natives, while breast cancer was most common among women. Cancers of the lung, colorectal area, and breast accounted for one-half of all cancers. The most striking increases in cancer incidence rates occurred with cancer of the lung in women, but significant increases were also seen for cancer of kidney in both genders and for breast and colorectal cancer among women. Differences in the distribution of cancers by ethnicity among the Alaska Native population were often distinct. For example, among males, cancer of the lung was the leading cancer for all three major ethnic groups of Alaska Natives, followed by cancer of the colorectal area. Among Aleuts, the third leading cause of cancer among males was cancer of the oral/pharyngeal cavities, while among the Indian population prostate was third, and among Eskimo males the third-ranking cancer site was the stomach. Cancer of the liver was much more frequent among the Eskimo than among the other two groups. Leukemia/lymphomas occurred more frequently among Indians than among the other two groups. Among women, breast cancer ranked first only among the Indian population, while among both Aleut and Eskimo women the leading site was the colorectal area. The authors noted tobacco use in approximately 50 percent of Alaska Native adults.

Among Alaska Natives, Eskimos have the highest risk for cancer of the esophagus and liver and the lowest risk for cancer of the breast and prostate. The risk for multiple myeloma in Indian men in Alaska exceeds not only that of other Native groups in Alaska but also that of U.S. Whites. In addition, increases in incidence rates were found for lung cancer in Eskimo men and women and for cervical cancer in Indian women during the period of study (Lanier et al. 1989).

Lanier et al. (1987) found that, among 19 Alaska Natives (15 men, 4 women) with primary hepatocellular carcinoma (PHC) diagnosed during 1980–85, 16 were seropositive for hepatitis B surface antigen (HBsAg). Alpha-fetoprotein (AFP) was elevated in 15 patients, all of whom were HBsAg positive. The patients ranged in age from 8 to 80 years. Sixteen were Eskimo, 13 of whom were Yupik. Among 7 patients undergoing resection, 6 showed no recurrence one to four years after surgery. In 16 specimens in which nontumorous liver could be studied, only 6 had evidence of cirrhosis; 10 others showed variants of chronic persistent hepatitis. Alberts et al. (1991) found that, during 1969–88, 15 of 45 cases of hepatocellular carcinoma in Alaska Natives occurred in five families. Hepatitis B virus infection was an important factor in four of the five families. Heyward et al. (1981) reported a bimodal age distribution among PHC patients, with peaks at 15–25 and 40–65 years. A high prevalence of HBsAg in serum of patients in the younger age group further supports the view that hepatitis B virus infection is associated with the development of PHC in young Eskimos (Hayward et al. 1985). PHC in Alaska Natives is apparently not related to alcoholic cirrhosis.

Lanier, Kilkenny, and Wilson (1985) identified 42 patients with esophageal cancer among Alaska Natives from 1955 through 1981. Estimated incidence rates were 1.3 and 3.8 times greater than those reported for U.S. Whites for men and women, respectively. Forty (95%) of the patients were Eskimo or Aleut. Among this group, an incidence rate of 10.9/100,000 for males and 8.3/100,000 for females was calculated. Marked regional clustering, similar to that reported in other parts of the world, was observed. The importance of smoking as a risk factor in Alaska has been noted (Hampton 1992; Lanier et al. 1994).

Cancer of Specific Sites

Cancer of the Lung

Lung cancer is the most common cause of cancer deaths for all Indians (Miller et al. 1996; Welty 1992). Higher overall cancer mortality rates for Northern Plains Indians (Aberdeen, Bemidji, and Billings Areas) were largely attributable to lung cancer, according to Welty (1992), and this in turn was linked to the prevalence of cigarette smoking. The latter association was also reported by Sievers (1966). Cancer of the lung seems to be a relatively recent phenomenon among certain Southwest Indians. Smith, Salsbury, and Gilliam (1956), in the study of the Navajo discussed above under "Cancer Incidence and Mortality," found only two recorded deaths due to lung cancer in men and none in women, nearly tenfold fewer than expected. Cancer of the lung is unevenly distributed among various Indian groups (Samet et al. 1988; Sievers and Cohen 1961). For example, the mortality rate of bronchogenic carcinoma among Indians of the Southwest tends to be about 3–6/100,000 population, in contrast to the Northern Plains Indians, where the rates are 35–45/100,000. These differences are undoubtedly associated with the much higher rates of smoking in the northern regions compared to the Southwest (Sievers 1966; Welty 1992). In the northern regions, where the rate of cigarette smoking of Indians exceeds that of the general population, mortality rates for lung cancer among Indians equaled or exceeded those among the general population (Welty 1992). A genetic factor must also be considered.

The striking association of uranium mining with lung cancer in Navajo men was described by Archer, Gillam, and Wagoner (1976) and confirmed by Gottlieb and Husen (1982). Samet et al. (1984) also confirmed the association of uranium mining with lung cancer among Southwest Indian men who had very low rates of cigarette smoking.

Cancer of the Cervix

Baquet (1996) noted that carcinoma of the uterine cervix occurs more than twice as frequently among Indian women compared to U.S. All Races women (20.5 compared to 8.6/100,000 population). Miller et al. (1996), utilizing 1988–92 SEER data, reported a rate of 9.9/100,000 for New Mexico Indian women and 15.8/100,000 for Alaska Native women. The death rate of Oklahoma Indian women for the period 1955–74 was higher than that for the general U.S. population (Skye and Hampton 1976). Jordan, Munsick, and Stone (1969) observed a lower rate of cervical carcinoma for southwestern Indian women compared to Caucasian controls matched as closely as possible for age and social and economic factors. They explained the difference between their observation and that of Sheehan, Basque, and Barrett (1965), who reported a higher rate in northwestern Indian women (18.6/100,000), by differences in referral rates for gynecological complaints.

Jordan et al. (1972), in a study of predominantly Navajo Indian women, reported that, for women younger than 60 years, newly diagnosed cervical carcinoma was more frequent among non-Indians, but at 60 years or older the

Indian women's rate surpassed that of non-Indians. A cytologic detection program in New Mexico during 1966–75 (Jordan and Key 1981) indicated that cervical carcinoma occurred more frequently in Indian and Hispanic women younger than 35 years than among Caucasian women of the same ages. The incidence rates of invasive cervical cancer were particularly high among the older group. None of the older Indian women gave a history of previous cytologic screening. Eighty percent of the deaths were among women older than 44 years, suggesting that increased screening in older Indian women might be a successful intervention. The extent of routine Papanicolaou testing among Indian women is not well documented but is considered to be low. Cultural barriers and lack of education about cancer detection may contribute to the failure of many Indian women to be screened.

Several public health programs in New Mexico directed toward screening Indian women have been associated with an apparent decrease in the age-adjusted incidence rate of cervical carcinoma from 30.3 to 10.3/100,000 (Chao et al. 1996). A shift to earlier stages was observed during the study period, with a substantially higher proportion of in situ carcinoma in the most recent period of observation when compared to the most remote time period. Throughout the study, a greater proportion of cervical cancer cases were diagnosed at a more advanced stage in Southwestern Indian women compared to non-Hispanic Whites and a smaller proportion of these women received treatment (Chao et al. 1996).

Although extensive data are lacking, suggested risk factors for cervical cancer among Indians include human papilloma virus (HPV) infection, micronutrient deficiencies, vaginal deliveries, and cigarette smoking (Becker et al. 1992, 1993). The risk of cervical cancer is strongly influenced by sexual behavior, suggesting a causal role for an infectious agent. Certain types of HPVs may be related to the genesis of the disease. Herpes simplex viruses may also be implicated. However, HPV infection rates in asymptomatic women do not seem to be related to sexual behavior, and sexual behavior and HPV infection seem to be independent predictors of the risk of acquiring cervical cancer (Becker et al. 1993).

Jordan and Key (1981), in an extensive study of a Southwestern detection program, reported that, among those younger than 35 years, cervical carcinoma was found more frequently among Indians and Spanish-American Caucasians than among other Caucasian women. At ages 60 and older, the Indian cervical cancer rate was much higher than that of non-Indians. The detection rate for invasive cervical carcinoma among Indian patients was inversely related to the proportion screened at 30 years of age or older. Although at least 60 percent of Indian women 20 years and older in the geographical area served by the detection program were screened for cervical cancer during a nine-year period, only

27 percent of those 50 years or older were screened. The age-related variation in screening percentage, in conjunction with the disproportionately large numbers of younger low-risk women, serves to explain the finding of significant invasive cervical carcinoma in an extensively screened population.

In an Alaska study, Davidson et al. (1994) found interval cancer (no prior dysplasia and a negative screening report within three years of diagnosis) in 23 of 44 women with invasive cervical cancer. The sensitivity of the Papanicolaou smear to demonstrate dysplasia in the year before diagnosis was 51 percent. The authors concluded that annual cytologic screening, with current methods, of all Alaska Native women would provide earlier diagnoses for only an additional 15 percent of cervical cancer cases. Possible explanations included rapid progression to neoplasia or errors in random screening. Davidson and Schnitzer (1994) suggested that improved or additional screening methods are necessary to assure early diagnosis and intervention.

Buckley et al. (1992) found that Indian women in the Southwest who reported a low intake of vitamin C, folic acid, vitamin E, carotenoids, and retinol were at slightly increased risk of cervical cytologic abnormalities. They suggested that the possible relationship between dietary micronutrients and cervical dysplasia among Indian women warranted further investigation using more refined measures of dietary micronutrient intake, together with consideration of other risk factors for cervical disease.

Cancer of the Breast

Although the incidence of breast cancer among Indian women seems to be lower than that for the non-Indian population (Baquet 1996), it also seems to be increasing (Nutting et al. 1994). As with cancers generally, survival rates for breast cancer are lower among Indian women than among the general population (Frost et al. 1996). According to the SEER data from New Mexico, at the time of diagnosis, remote metastases were present in 25 percent of Indian women, 12.5 percent of Hispanic women, and 10.2 percent of Anglo women. Breast cancer incidence in Oklahoma Indian women may be increasing in frequency (Hampton and Maher 1998), and breast cancer accounted for the largest number of cancer deaths in all U.S. Indian women from 1984 to 1988 (Valway et al. 1992).

According to Frost and co-workers (1996), Indian women living in the Southwest experienced poorer survival than did non-Hispanic Whites during the time periods 1973–82 and 1983–92. The five-year survival rate among Southwestern Indian women is 56 percent, compared to 73 percent for non-Hispanic White women. The 1982 mortality rate from breast cancer in Indian women was 11.4/100,000 population, compared to 22.0/100,000 for U.S. All

Races women. However, in the Bemidji area, the mortality rate from breast cancer exceeds the U.S. All Races rate, being 24.5/100,000 among Indians, compared to 22.0/100,000 among the general U.S. population. Eidson et al. (1994) reported that incidence rates during the years 1969–87 and mortality rates during 1958–87 for New Mexico's non-Hispanic White women were comparable to those for White women nationwide. However, the incidence and mortality rates of breast cancer among Indian women were substantially lower.

Gastric Cancer

Although mortality rates for gastric cancer have decreased markedly for the general population, the same is not true for Indians, and the latter appear to have lower survival rates compared to other groups (Baquet 1996). Gastric cancer is the second leading cause of death due to cancer in the Indian population of the Southwest (Wiggins et al. 1989). The incidence rate for Indians is 16.6/100,000, compared to 8.9/100,000 for Whites (Baquet 1996). Among Alaska Natives, the mortality rate is 11.9/100,000, compared to 5.2/100,000 in Whites.

Colorectal Cancer

The variations in cancer mortality rates among Indians are also seen in colorectal carcinoma (Valway et al. 1992): 26.3/100,000 in the Alaska Area, 13.3/100,000 in the Aberdeen Area, 16.9/100,000 in the Bemidji Area, and 12.6/100,000 in the Billings Area, compared to a 1982 U.S. overall rate of 20.0/100,000. These rates compare to 8.6/100,000 in the Albuquerque Area, 8.4/100,000 in the Phoenix Area, and 4.6/100,000 in the Navajo Area. Thus, among Alaska Natives, the incidence rate is more than six times greater than that found in Southwest Indians.

Cancer of the Prostate

Cancer of the prostate is the most commonly diagnosed cancer in New Mexico Indian men and ranks first as a cause of cancer death in that population. The mortality rate from cancer of the prostate in Southwest Indian men (1988–92) is 16.2/100,000, compared to 24.1/100,000 in Whites (Miller et al. 1996). The mortality rate in Indian men in the Aberdeen, Albuquerque, and Billings Areas is also higher than the U.S. rate (Valway et al. 1992). Indians have lower survival rates compared to the general population (Baquet 1996; Sugarman et al. 1996).

Gilliland et al. (1994), in a New Mexico study, found that Indians had the lowest incidence of prostate cancer of the four major ethnic groups studied in that region. During the period of study, local-stage cancer rates increased by 93 percent and 81 percent among non-Hispanic Whites and Hispanics, respectively, but were stable for Indians and Blacks, whereas rates for regional-stage cancers in the latter two groups increased sharply. After 1983, age-adjusted mortality rates of prostate cancer decreased among all groups except Hispanics. The authors concluded that differential access to medical care and screening for prostate cancer may account for these trends.

Cancer of the Gallbladder and Biliary Tree

Black et al. (1977) found that, in New Mexico, cancer of the gallbladder was primarily a disease of women, with very high rates in Indians compared to Anglos and intermediate rates among the Hispanic population. Except for certain in situ carcinomas and skin cancers, carcinoma of the gallbladder was the third most common malignant neoplasm in New Mexico Indian women, exceeded only by carcinoma of the uterine cervix and breast. Further, at laparotomy, most cases were unresectable. Histologic type may also be somewhat different for Indian women. Black and Key (1980) described more squamous cell carcinoma and anaplasia than has generally been reported.

Indians in the southwestern United States have been reported to have higher than expected rates of carcinoma of the gallbladder and biliary tree (Sievers 1966; Fraumeni 1975; Black et al. 1977; Lowenfels 1992). Similar findings have been reported for Alaska Natives (Boss et al. 1982). According to Baquet (1996) the incidence rate for Indians is 10.9, compared to 1.3/100,000 among Whites. The association of cholelithiasis and carcinoma of the gallbladder in Indians has been reported by several investigators (Black et al. 1977; Boss et al. 1982). In a recent SEER report on Southwest Indian women, gallbladder cancer ranked fourth in incidence (13.2/100,000 population) and was associated with the highest cancer mortality rate (8.9/100,000 population) (Miller et al. 1996).

Current Cancer Interventions

Among many Indian groups, tobacco abuse has emerged as a major risk factor for cancer, especially of the lung. Efforts to curtail the extent of tobacco abuse should be greatly expanded.

In 1990, the Breast and Cervical Cancer Mortality Prevention Act established the National Breast and Cervical Cancer Early Detection Program (NBC-CEDP) for increasing access to breast and cervical cancer screening services for underserved women (Centers for Disease Control and Prevention 1993). From

1990 to 1995 the NBCCEDP was implemented in 35 state health agencies and 9 Indian/Alaska Native programs. It provides for screening, referral, and follow-up services; public and professional education; quality assurance; surveillance; and coalition partnership development. Outreach efforts were initiated for women in high-priority groups, including racial/ethnic minority groups.

The 1992 National Health Interview Survey indicated that only 35 percent of women aged 50 and older reported having had a screening mammogram during the previous year. Only 63 percent of women aged 50–64 years reported having had a Papanicolaou test during the previous three years. Use of mammograms and Papanicolaou tests is lower among women who have less than a high school education and/or a low income. Although cervical cancer death rates are higher among older women, older women are also less likely to receive Papanicolaou tests on a regular basis (Anderson and May 1995). In 1996, the NBCCEDP was expanded to 13 Indian tribes and to all 50 states (Centers for Disease Control and Prevention 1996).

The Network for Cancer Control Research among American Indians was established by the NCI in collaboration with the IHS (Hampton 1993). Two strategic plans for cancer control were developed by this network: one designed for federal and private funding from national organizations and one for state agencies, specifically state health departments (Burhansstipanov and Dresser 1993). National conferences allowed for the exchange of information and planning of additional strategies (Hampton, Keala, and Luce 1996). Several surveys conducted by members of the network have provided important information on the knowledge, attitudes, and behavior of Native Americans about cancer, as well as the agencies responsible for their cancer control activities.

In 1990, the IHS implemented a Cancer Prevention and Control program that included surveillance and implementation of smoking-prevention programs where rates of smoking are known to be high. Patient education programs, especially concerning breast and cervical cancers, have been increased throughout the IHS. Mammography programs, often using mobile units in remote areas, have been increased in most areas. These early detection efforts may improve Indian women's survival statistics.

Gordon et al. (1994) reported that only 31–36 percent of a sample of Pascua-Yaqui women in and near Tucson, Arizona, had received an annual Papanicolaou smear during the years 1986–90, while 65 percent had received at least one test during the five-year period. Only 41–43 percent of women aged 50–65 years had received a mammogram in the years studied, and 51–58 percent of women ages 40–49 had been screened. A total of 67 percent had received at least one mammogram during the 1988–90 period. Although these screening rates are comparable to those for the general U.S. population, they occur in a population in which financial access is often a barrier to screening. Nutting et al.

(1994) pointed out that factors such as cost, interpretation of results, stage at diagnosis, and certain survival factors vary considerably among Indians and need to be taken into account in devising screening strategies.

Using a Seneca legend, Schinke, Moncher, and Singer (1994) developed computer software designed to improve dietary choices and prevent tobacco abuse among Native American adolescents. Initial testing suggested that interactive computer software aimed at modifying dietary habits and preventing tobacco abuse among Native American youth might be useful in cancer risk reduction. Among Luiseno Indians of San Diego County, California, cancer is considered to be any tumor or growth that is possibly life threatening (Weiner 1993). Current and former Luiseno cancer patients shared illness causation theories distinct from those of their kin. The cancer patients believed that their bouts with cancer resulted from genetic predilection and/or God's will. In contrast, Luiseno band members without cancer asserted that almost all cancer is caused by either (1) chemical pollutants in the air, water, and food or (2) prior biomedical treatments that have gone awry.

Among inhabitants of an Alaska village, Sprott (1988) reported that, in 74 percent of the households queried, at least one person believed that smoking causes cancer, but an equal number believed that drinking water was a possible cause. These various beliefs are important and must be taken into account in planning strategies for prevention.

Michalek and Mahoney (1994) found that, while 32 percent of the states have cancer detection and intervention programs specifically directed toward Indians, few had culturally relevant cancer education materials for Indians. In addition, many state respondents were unfamiliar with cancer and general health problems among Indians.

REFERENCES

Alberts SR, Lanier AP, McMahon BJ, et al. 1991. Clustering of hepatocellular carcinoma in Alaska Native families. *Genet Epidemiol* 8:127–39.

Anderson LM, May DS. 1995. Has the use of cervical, breast and colorectal cancer screening increased in the United States? *Am J Public Health* 85:840–42.

Archer VE, Gillam JD, Wagoner JK. 1976. Respiratory disease mortality among uranium miners. *Ann NY Acad Sci* 271:280–93.

Baquet CR. 1996. Native Americans' cancer rates in comparison with other peoples of color. *Cancer* 78:1538–44.

Becker TM, Wheeler CM, Key CR, et al. 1992. Cervical cancer incidence and mortality in New Mexico's Hispanics, American Indians, and non-Hispanic Whites. *West J Med* 156:376–79.

Becker TM, Wheeler CM, McPherson RS, et al. 1993. Risk factors for cervical dysplasia in southwestern American Indian women: A pilot study. *Alaska Med* 35:255–63.

Black WC, Key CR. 1980. Epidemiologic pathology of cancer in New Mexico's tri-ethnic population. *Pathol Annu* 15:181–94.

Black WC, Key CR, Carmany TB, et al. 1977. Carcinoma of the gallbladder in a population of Southwestern American Indians. *Cancer* 39:1267–79.

Bleed DM, Risser DR, Sperry S, et al. 1992. Cancer incidence and survival among American Indians registered for Indian Health Service care in Montana, 1982–1987. *J Natl Cancer Inst* 84:1500–1505.

Boss LP, Lanier AP, Dohan PH, et al. 1982. Cancers of the gallbladder and biliary tract in Alaska Natives. *J Natl Cancer Inst* 69:1005–7.

Buckley DI, McPherson RS, North CQ, et al. 1992. Dietary micronutrients and cervical dysplasia in Southwestern American Indian women. *Nutr Cancer* 17:179–85.

Burhansstipanov L, Dresser C. 1993. Documentation of the cancer research needs of American Indians and Alaska Natives. *Native American Monogr* no. 1 (August).

Centers for Disease Control and Prevention. 1993. Implementation of the breast and cervical mortality prevention act. *1992 Progress Report to Congress.* Atlanta: Centers for Disease Control and Prevention.

———. 1996. Division of Cancer Prevention and Control, National Center for Chronic Disease Prevention and Health Promotion. *MMWR* 45 (June 14).

Chao A, Becker TM, Jordan SW, et al. 1996. Decreasing rates of cervical cancer among American Indians and Hispanics in New Mexico (United States). *Cancer Causes Control* 7:205–13.

Cobb N. 1996. Environmental causes of cancer among Native Americans. *Cancer* 78 (7, suppl):1603–6.

Creagan ET, Fraumeni JF Jr. 1972. Cancer mortality among American Indians, 1950–67. *J Natl Cancer Inst* 49:959–67.

Currier AF. 1891. A study relative to the functions of the reproductive apparatus in American Indian women. *Trans Am Gynecol Soc (Phila)* 16:264–94.

Davidson M, Bulkow LR, Lanier AP, et al. 1994. Incidence of invasive cervical cancer preceded by negative screening in high-risk Alaska Native women. *Int J Epidemiol* 23:238–45.

Davidson M, Schnitzer PG. 1994. The prevalence of cervical infection with human papilloma viruses and cervical dysplasia in Alaska Native women. *J Infect Dis* 169:1–9.

Eidson M, Becker TM, Wiggins CL, et al. 1994. Breast cancer among Hispanics, American Indians and non-Hispanic Whites in New Mexico. *Int J Epidemiol* 23:231–37.

Fraumeni JF. 1975. Cancers of the pancreas and biliary tract: Epidemiological considerations. *Cancer Res* 35:3437–46.

Frost F, Tollestrup K, Hunt WC, et al. 1996. Breast cancer survival among New Mexico Hispanic, American Indians and non-Hispanic White women (1973–1992). *Cancer Epidemiol Biomarkers Prev* 5:861–66.

Gilliland FD, Becker TM, Key CR, et al. 1994. Contrasting trends of prostate cancer incidence and mortality in New Mexico's Hispanics, non-Hispanic Whites, American Indians, and Blacks. *Cancer* 73:2192–99.

Gordon PR, Campos-Outcalt D, Steele L, et al. 1994. Mammography and Pap smear screening of Yaqui Indian women. *Public Health Rep* 109:99–103.

Gottlieb LS, Husen LA. 1982. Lung cancer among Navajo uranium miners. *Chest* 81:449–52.

Hampton JW. 1984. Conquering cancer among Indians requires education, lifestyle changes. *Natl Indian Health Board Health Rep* 3:10–11.

——. 1989. The heterogeneity of cancer in Native American populations. In: Jones LA, ed. *Minorities and Cancer,* 45–53. New York: Springer Verlag.

——. 1992. Cancer prevention and control in American Indian/Alaska Native. *Am Indian Culture Res J* 16:41–50.

——. 1993. Cancer in Indian country: Keynote address. *Alaska Med* 35:243–44.

Hampton JW, Keala J, Luce P. 1996. Overview of National Cancer Institute Network for Cancer Control research in Native American populations. *Cancer* 78:1545–52.

Hampton JW, Maher JF. 1998. Pedigree analysis of breast cancer in Oklahoma Indian women. *Cancer* 83:1796–98.

Heyward WL, Lanier AP, Bender TR, et al. 1981. Primary hepatocellular carcinoma in Alaska Natives, 1969–1979. *Int J Cancer* 28:47–50.

Heyward WL, Lanier AP, McMahon BJ. 1985. Early detection of primary hepatocellular carcinoma. *JAMA* 254:3052–54.

Hrdlicka A. 1905. Diseases of the Indians, more especially of the Southwest United States and Northern Mexico. *Washington Med Ann* 6:372–94.

Indian Health Service. 1997. *Trends in Indian Health, 1997.* Rockville, Md.: Indian Health Service, Program Statistics Team.

Jordan SW, Key CR. 1981. Carcinoma of the cervix in Southwestern American Indians: Results of a cytologic detection program. *Cancer* 47:2523–32.

Jordan SW, Munsick RA, Stone RS. 1969. Carcinoma of the cervix in Indian women. *Cancer* 23:1227–32.

Jordan SW, Sopher RL, Key CR, et al. 1972. Carcinoma of the cervix in Southwestern American Indian women. *Cancer* 29:1235–41.

Lanier AP. 1986. Death from cancer in Alaska. *Alaska Med* 28(3):57–60.

——. 1993. Epidemiology of cancer in Alaska Natives. *Alaska Med* 35:245–47.

Lanier AP, Bender TR, Blot WJ, et al. 1976. Cancer incidence in Alaska Natives. *Int J Cancer* 18:409–12.

Lanier A, Bender T, Talbot M. 1980. Nasopharyngeal carcinoma in Alaskan Eskimos, Indians, and Aleuts: A review of cases and study of Epstein-Barr virus, HLA, and environmental risk factors. *Cancer* 46:2100–2106.

Lanier AP, Blot WJ, Bender TR, et al. 1980. Cancer in Alaskan Indians, Eskimos and Aleuts. *J Natl Cancer Inst* 65:1157–59.

Lanier AP, Bulkow LR, Ireland B. 1989. Cancer in Alaskan Indians, Eskimos, and Aleuts, 1969–83: Implications for etiology and control. *Public Health Rep* 104:658–64.

Lanier A, Kelly JJ, Smith B, et al. 1994. Cancer in the Alaska Native population: Eskimo, Aleut, and Indian incidence and trends, 1969–1988. *Alaska Med* 36:7–92.

Lanier AP, Key CP. 1993. *Cancer in the Alaska Native Population: Eskimo, Aleut, and Indian Incidence Area Trends, 1969–1988.* Rockville, Md.: Indian Health Service.

Lanier AP, Kilkenny SJ, Wilson JF. 1985. Oesophageal cancer among Alaskan Natives, 1955–1981. *Int J Epidemiol* 14:75–78.

Lanier AP, McMahon BJ, Alberts SR, et al. 1987. Primary liver cancer in Alaskan Natives, 1980–1985. *Cancer* 60:1915–20.

Levin I. 1910. Cancer among the American Indians and its bearing upon the ethnological distribution of the disease. *Z Krebsforsch* 9:423–25.

Lowenfels AB. 1992. Gallstones and gallbladder cancer in Southwestern Native America. *Am Indian Culture Res J* 16:77–86.

Mahoney MC, Michalek AM, Cummings MK, et al. 1989. Cancer mortality in a Northeastern Native American population. *Cancer* 64:187–90.

Michalek AM, Mahoney MC. 1994. Provision of cancer control services to Native Americans by state health departments. *J Cancer Educ* 9:145–47.

Miller BA, Kolonel LN, Bernstein L, et al., eds. 1996. *Racial/Ethnic Patterns of Cancer in the United States, 1988–1992.* NIH Pub. No. 96-4104. Bethesda, Md.: National Cancer Institute.

Nutting PA, Calonge BN, Iverson DC, et al. 1994. The danger of applying uniform clinical policies across populations: The case of breast cancer in American Indians. *Am J Public Health* 84:1631–36.

Nutting PA, Freeman WL, Risser DR, et al. 1993. Cancer incidence among American Indians and Alaska Natives, 1980 through 1987. *Am J Public Health* 83:1589–98.

Samet JM, Key CR, Hunt WC, et al. 1987. Survival of American Indian and Hispanic cancer patients in New Mexico and Arizona, 1969–82. *J Natl Cancer Inst* 79:457–63.

Samet JM, Kutvirt BA, Waxweiler RJ, et al. 1984. Uranium mining and lung cancer in Navajo men. *N Engl J Med* 310:1481–84.

Samet JM, Wiggins CL, Key CR, et al. 1988. Mortality from lung cancer and chronic obstructive pulmonary disease in New Mexico, 1958–82. *Am J Public Health* 78:1182–86.

Schinke SP, Moncher MS, Singer BR. 1994. Native American youths and cancer risk reduction: Effects of software intervention. *J Adolesc Health* 15:105–10.

Sheehan JF, Basque GJ, Barrett HV. 1965. Carcinoma of the cervix in Indian women. *Nebr Med J* 50:553–58.

Sievers ML. 1966. Disease patterns among Southwestern Indians. *Public Health Rep* 12:1075–83.

Sievers ML, Cohen SL. 1961. Lung cancer among Indians of the Southwestern United States. *Ann Intern Med* 54:912–15.

Sievers ML, Fisher JR. 1981. Diseases of North American Indians. In: Rothschild H, ed. *Biocultural Aspects of Disease,* 191–253. New York: Academic Press.

———. 1983. Cancer in North American Indians: Environment versus heredity. *Am J Public Health* 73:485–87.

Skye GE, Hampton JW. 1976. A survey of neoplastic disease in Oklahoma North American aborigines. In: Nieburg HE, ed. *Proceedings of the Third International Symposium on Detection and Prevention of Cancer,* 291–96. New York: Marcel Dekker.

Smith RL. 1957. Recorded and expected mortality among Indians of the United States, with special reference to cancer. *J Natl Cancer Inst* 18:385–96.

Smith RL, Salsbury CG, Gilliam AG. 1956. Recorded and expected mortality among the Navajo, with special reference to cancer. *J Natl Cancer Inst* 17:77–89.

Sorem KA. 1985. Cancer incidence in the Zuni Indians of New Mexico. *Yale J Biol Med* 58:489–96.

Sprott JE. 1988. Cancer causation beliefs in an Alaskan village. *Alaska Med* 30(1):155–58.

Stefansson V. 1960. *Cancer: Disease of Civilization? An Anthropological and Historical Study,* 72–92. New York: Hill & Wang.

Sugarman JR, Dennis LK, White E. 1994. Cancer survival among American Indians in western Washington State (United States). *Cancer Causes Control* 5:440–48.

Sugarman JR, Holliday M, Ross A, et al. 1996. Improving American Indian cancer data in the Washington State Cancer Registry using linkages with the Indian Health Service and tribal records. *Cancer* 78:1564–68.

Valway S, Kileen M, Paisano R, et al. 1992. *Cancer Mortality among Native Americans in the United States: Regional Differences in Indian Health, 1984–1988, and Trends over Time, 1968–1987*, 1–113. Rockville, Md.: Indian Health Service, Cancer Prevention and Control Program.

Weiner D. 1993. Health beliefs about cancer among the Luiseno Indians of California. *Alaska Med* 35:285–96.

Welty TK. 1992. Cancer and cancer prevention and control programs in the Aberdeen Area Indian Health Service. *Am Indian Culture Res J* 16:117–37.

Wiggins CL, Becker TM, Key CR, et al. 1989. Stomach cancer among New Mexico's American Indians, Hispanic Whites, and non-Hispanic Whites. *Cancer Res* 49:1595–99.

———. 1993. Cancer mortality among New Mexico's Hispanics, American Indians, and non-Hispanic Whites, 1958–1987. *J Natl Cancer Inst* 85:1670–78.

12

Mary Story, Ph.D., R.D., Karen F. Strauss, M.S., R.D.,
Tim J. Gilbert, M.P.H., R.D., and
Brenda A. Broussard, R.D., M.P.H., M.B.A., CDE

Nutritional Health and Diet-Related Conditions

Nutrition is essential for sustenance, health, and well-being. But dietary factors also contribute substantially to the burden of preventable illness and premature death in the United States. Of the six leading causes of death among American Indian adults (heart disease, malignant neoplasms, accidents, diabetes mellitus, chronic liver disease and cirrhosis, and cerebrovascular disease), five are diet-related (Indian Health Service 1997). Patterns of both diet and physical activity have changed markedly in American Indian communities over recent decades. Traditional lifestyles have been replaced with sedentary physical activity patterns and the adoption of a contemporary Western diet, high in fat. These changes are believed to be related to the high rates of diabetes and obesity in American Indian populations (Welty 1991; Gohdes 1995).

As with adult health, child health and nutritional status have also changed markedly over the past 30 years. Before the 1970s, low weight-for-height and nutrient deficiency diseases were frequently observed in American Indian infants and children (Institute for Government Research 1928; Owen et al. 1981; Carlile et al. 1970). Among Navajo children protein-calorie malnutrition was also observed (Van Duzen et al. 1969). A 1969 review of all cases of severe malnutrition admitted to the Public Health Service Indian Hospital in Tuba City, Arizona, during a five-year period revealed that a total of 616 children were admitted and diagnosed as having malnutrition, 15 had kwashiorkor, and 29 had marasmus (Van Duzen et al. 1969). Among children enrolled in the Head Start program on the reservation, nearly one-third were below the third percentile for weight (Van Duzen et al. 1969). A 1969 survey of White Mountain Apache preschool children indicated that a substantial proportion of the children were at high nutritional risk (Owen et al. 1981). Low intakes of calories and key nutrients were common, and about 20 percent of the children were anemic. By 1976, the proportion of children with low nutrient intakes and anemia was about half that in 1969 (Owen et al. 1981). Changes in nutritional status were attributed to improved health care delivery, housing, sanitation, and food availability. Childhood undernutrition has now been replaced with obesity, which is currently a major health problem among American Indian children (Broussard et al. 1991; Story et al. 1998).

Although there are similarities among tribes regarding nutrition-related behaviors and health concerns, subgroup differences exist and should be considered. There are only limited nutrition survey data on American Indians. Studies are usually of specific tribes, often with small sample sizes. When we discuss the nutrition status of American Indians and Alaska Natives, we must be aware of the heterogeneity of the tribes and our limited data and not overgeneralize about their health and nutrition needs.

Adults

Obesity

Although American Indians are not a homogeneous group, all tribes have suffered adverse effects from the high prevalence of obesity. Many of the health problems of American Indians are related to obesity (Welty 1991). Among the general U.S. population (and probably among American Indians), the health risks of obesity increase with severity and reach significance at a body mass index (BMI) greater than 27 (Pi-Sunyer 1991). Known obesity-related health risks for adults include non-insulin-dependent diabetes mellitus (type 2 diabetes), hypertension, cardiovascular disease, hypertriglyceridemia, and low high-density lipoprotein cholesterol (National Research Council 1989). Mortality from gallbladder cancer, endometrial cancer in women, and colorectal cancer in men is also increased (National Research Council 1989).

Diabetes is epidemic among American Indian populations, strongly associated with the increasing prevalence of obesity (Lee et al. 1995; Welty 1991). Obesity is also more common among children of diabetic parents (Knowler et al. 1993). Obesity and parental diabetes increase diabetes incidence rates synergistically, with the highest rates in obese subjects with at least one parent with diabetes of early onset. It is estimated that half of all type 2 diabetes is preventable by obesity control (McGinnis and Foege 1993). Interestingly, the association of obesity with increased risk for certain chronic diseases seems to be higher for centralized fat than for peripheral fat distribution (Knowler et al. 1991; Howard et al. 1995).

The causes of obesity are complex and incompletely understood, but it seems that determinants are rooted in multiple factors associated with genetics and the environment (Bouchard 1992; National Research Council 1989). Studies of energy expenditure among the Pima Indians suggested that a low metabolic rate contributes to the familial aggregation of obesity (Bogardus et al. 1986; Ravussin et al. 1988). In addition, there may be multiple metabolic differences between Indians and non-Indians that may predispose the former to become obese when food is abundant. Neel's thrifty-gene hypothesis suggested that obesity results from the introduction of a continuous and ample food supply to people who have evolved an ability to store energy efficiently, permitting survival through millennia of feast-famine cycles (Neel 1962). Since obesity may have multiple possible determinants, it is unclear whether the primary defect is genetic, environmental, or an interaction between the two (Howard et al. 1991).

Recent research has identified genetic and metabolic factors that may contribute to obesity. For example, an inherited mutation in mice seems to cause a propensity for obesity and type 2 diabetes and is suspected to have a human counterpart (Pelleymounter et al. 1995). The obesity gene is expressed only in adipose tissue, and its encoded hormone product, leptin, is secreted into the circulation in proportion to body adiposity (Considine et al. 1996). In addition, the ß-3 adrenergic-receptor gene has been identified in Pima Indians (Walston et al. 1995). Pima subjects homozygous for the ß-3-adrenergic-receptor mutation had an earlier onset of type 2 diabetes and had a lower resting metabolic rate. This mutation may accelerate the onset of type 2 diabetes by altering the balance of energy metabolism in visceral adipose tissue (Walston et al. 1995).

Although genetic factors invariably influence a propensity toward obesity, behavioral and lifestyle conditions related to diet and physical activity play a critical role in the development and extent of obesity (Bouchard 1992). Most American Indian populations developed obesity only in the past few generations, and this change is believed to be related to the relative abundance of high-fat foods accompanied by rapid changes from an active to a sedentary lifestyle (Welty 1991; Broussard et al. 1991). Despite widespread obesity in American Indians, there is a paucity of data on dietary and exercise patterns among Indians and the relationships among physical activity, dietary patterns, and obesity (Broussard et al. 1995). Several dietary practices may contribute to obesity, including the wide use of butter, lard, whole milk, fry bread, and fried meats and vegetables, as well as the generous use of fats in the preparation of beans. Sweets and snacks may account for high calorie intakes in some groups (Gilbert et al. 1992).

A recent study by Ravussin et al. (1994) assessed the probable effect of the environment on the prevalence of obesity and type 2 diabetes. The Pima Indians of Arizona, who have the highest reported prevalence of obesity and type 2 diabetes, were compared to members of a population of Pima ancestry (separation 700–1,000 years ago) living in a remote mountainous location in north-western Mexico, whose lifestyle contrasts markedly with that of Arizona Pimas. The authors found that both obesity and possibly type 2 diabetes were less prevalent among people of Pima heritage living a "traditional" lifestyle than among Pimas living in an "affluent" environment. These findings suggest that, despite a similar potential genetic predisposition to these conditions, a more traditional lifestyle, characterized by a diet including less fat and more complex carbohydrates and by greater energy expenditure, may protect against the development of obesity, type 2 diabetes, and cardiovascular disease.

Cancer

It is estimated that approximately 35 percent of cancer deaths may be related to diet (National Research Council 1989). A high intake of fat has been associated with cancers of the breast, colon, rectum, and prostate and possibly with those of the pancreas, uterus, and ovary. Populations consuming diets rich in vegetables, fruits, and grain products have significantly lower rates of cancer of the colon, breast, lung, oral cavity, larynx, esophagus, stomach, bladder, uterine cervix, and pancreas. High alcohol consumption has been associated with cancers of the buccal cavity, pharynx, larynx, esophagus, liver, large bowel, breast, head, and neck (National Research Council 1989).

Children

Growth Retardation

Retardation in linear growth in preschool children serves as an indicator of overall health and development but may especially reflect the adequacy of a child's diet (U.S. Department of Health and Human Services 1990). Growth retardation can result from poor nutrition, an increased number of infections, or both (Wilcox and Marks 1995). Therefore, the prevalence of growth retardation or stunting (defined as height-for-age below the fifth percentile of children in the National Center for Health Statistics [NCHS] reference population) is used as a measure of chronic undernutrition. The Pediatric Nutrition Surveillance System (PedNSS) of the Centers for Disease Control and Prevention (CDC) is designed to monitor the nutritional status of low-income children served by various publicly funded health and nutrition programs. The PedNSS uses anthropometric and hematologic measurements to assess the three most common nutrition-related problems among U.S. children (linear growth retardation, overweight, and iron deficiency anemia), as well as birth weight and breast-feeding practices (Wilcox and Marks 1995). The 1994 PedNSS included data from 39 states and 6 American Indian reservations. Data were processed from more than 8 million PedNSS records, of which 112,586 were those of American Indians.

In the 1994 PedNSS, the overall prevalence of growth retardation for all low-income children younger than 24 months was 9.6 percent. The highest prevalence was among Black children (13.1%), compared to Indian children (9.5%) and White children (9.6%) (Centers for Disease Control and Prevention 1996). For children two to four years of age, the overall prevalence for U.S. All Races was 6.2 percent. The prevalence for Indian children was 5.1 percent, compared to 6.9 percent for White, non-Hispanic children. These data undoubtedly reflect general improvements made in child nutritional health over the past 30 years.

Underweight

Low weight-for-height (less than the fifth NCHS percentile), also referred to as *underweight* or *thinness,* is often associated with recent severe disease (Wilcox and Marks 1995). In developing countries, underweight indicates acute malnutrition, which is commonly the result of insufficient food supply, infectious diseases, or both. In the 1994 PedNSS, among children younger than two years and those two to four years of age, the overall prevalence of underweight was 3.2 percent and 2.2 percent, respectively. Across ethnic groups, the prevalence of underweight was lowest among American Indian children and highest among Black and Asian children. The prevalence of underweight was 2.1 percent for American children younger than two years and 1.0 percent for Indian children two to four years of age (Centers for Disease Control and Prevention 1996). This indicates that underweight is not a major public health issue in the American Indian populations monitored by the PedNSS.

Overweight

As in adults, overweight has emerged as the major nutrition-related health issue affecting American Indian children (Jackson 1993; Broussard et al. 1991; Sugarman, White, and Gilbert 1990). Since obesity in childhood persists into adulthood and is associated with significant morbidity, this has major implications for the health of American Indian adults.

Preschool Children

A high weight-for-height (greater than the 95th NCHS percentile) is indicative of being overweight. American Indian children have consistently exhibited the highest prevalence of overweight of all ethnic groups in the PedNSS. In the

1994 PedNSS, 11.9 percent of American Indian children two to four years old were overweight. This rate is similar to that for same-age Hispanic children (11.7%) but considerably higher than that for White children (6.2%) (Centers for Disease Control and Prevention 1996). Other studies have also indicated a high prevalence of overweight among young Indian children (Goran et al. 1995; Broussard et al. 1991; Hauck et al. 1992). Overall, these studies demonstrate that obesity seems to begin early for Indian children.

School-aged Children and Adolescents

In 1990, a national survey of the height and weight status of 9,464 American Indian schoolchildren (ages 5–18) living on or near American Indian reservations was conducted by Indian Health Service (IHS), CDC, and tribal nutrition programs in nine IHS Areas (Jackson 1993). Data for height, weight, and BMI of the schoolchildren were compared with two national reference data sets, the second National Health and Nutrition Examination Survey (NHANES II) and the Mexican-American population of the Hispanic Health and Nutrition Examination Survey (HHANES-MA). Although the three populations were similar in height, the Indian children had significantly higher BMIs for nearly every age and sex group compared to the reference populations. The overall prevalence of overweight in the Indian children (exceeding the 85th percentile of the reference population) was 39.3 percent compared with the NHANES II population and 28.6 percent compared with the HHANES-MA population. These data indicate that overweight is much more prevalent among Indian children than among other children in the United States at all ages and in both sexes.

Increasing Trend of Obesity

Data suggest that there has been a secular change in height, weight, and obesity among Indian children (Broussard et al. 1991). Over the past 35 years, obesity has increased in Navajo schoolchildren; compared with data from 1955, mean weights increased 29 percent among boys and 19 percent among girls across all age groups (Sugarman, White, and Gilbert 1990). Pima children are also significantly heavier than children measured at the turn of the century. In 1905, Pima boys who were 165 cm in height weighed an average of 58 kg. During the period 1981–88, Pima boys of the same height weighed an average of 69 kg, an increase of approximately 11 kg (Knowler et al. 1991).

Relationships between Weight and Chronic Disease Risk Factors

A few studies have examined risk factors for type 2 diabetes and cardiovascular disease in American Indian children and adolescents. Gilbert et al. (1992) reported high normal (greater than the 90th percentile) blood pressures in 10 percent of adolescent Navajo boys and 6 percent of girls. There was a positive relationship between body weight and blood pressure. Of those with high normal blood pressure, 36 percent of the boys and 64 percent of the girls were overweight. Blackett and colleagues (1996) explored the interrelationships between weight, BMI, lipids, apolipoproteins, insulin, and glucose in 103 Oklahoma Indian children between the ages of 4 and 19 years. BMI increased with age in boys and girls and tended to be higher than in Caucasian children. Children 10 to 14 years old in the highest quartile for BMI had higher triglyceride levels and lower high-density lipoprotein cholesterol when compared with those in the lower quartiles. In contrast, 15–19-year-olds in the highest quartile for BMI had higher cholesterol and apolipoprotein B levels. The mean fasting insulin levels were not related to BMI. These data suggest that obesity associated with elevated lipid levels begins at an early age in Indian children.

Centrally distributed body fat is associated with several chronic diseases, including hypertension, heart disease, gallstones, diabetes, and some types of cancer. Two studies have shown that Indian children have increased central body fat (Gilbert et al. 1992; Goran et al. 1995). Whether the pattern of central distribution of body fat continues from childhood to adulthood is not well established, but it is reasonable to expect that it does.

Determinants of Childhood Obesity

Both maternal obesity and high birth weight have been shown to be strong predictors of obesity in early childhood (Gallaher et al. 1991). It has also been speculated that the metabolic milieu of the intrauterine environment may play a role in the etiology of obesity. Infants born to Pima mothers who were diabetic during pregnancy were much more likely to later become obese than were their siblings born before the full manifestation of their mother's diabetes (Pettitt et al. 1983).

It also seems that environmental factors such as diet and physical activity have contributed substantially to the epidemic of childhood obesity. Gilbert et al. (1992) documented that Navajo adolescents consumed sugared carbonated beverages at more than twice the national average. Fontvieille, Kriska, and Ravussin (1993) assessed physical activity in Pima and Caucasian children and found that Pima children spent more time watching television and were less involved in sports than Caucasian children.

Iron Deficiency

Iron deficiency anemia is associated with impaired learning and increased susceptibility to lead poisoning (U.S. Department of Health and Human Services 1990). It can be prevented and treated through consumption of adequate dietary iron and/or supplementation. The CDC criteria for anemia are based on NHANES II data. For children younger than 24 months, the cut-off point is a hemoglobin measure of 11.0 g/dL or a hematocrit of 33 percent. For children two to five years of age, the cut-off point is a hemoglobin measurement of 11.2 g/dL or a hematocrit measurement of 34 percent (Wilcox and Marks 1995). In the 1994 PedNSS, the prevalence of anemia for all children younger than 24 months and aged two to four years was 20.2 percent and 18.3 percent, respectively. The prevalence of anemia for Indian children younger than 24 months was 20.6 percent, and that for two- to four-year-olds was 14.9 percent. The rates for same-age White children were 17.2 percent and 13.7 percent, respectively (Centers for Disease Control and Prevention 1996). Thus, the prevalence of iron deficiency among low-income Indian children is similar to the U.S. All Races rate for those younger than two years and less than the U.S. All Races rate for those two to four years of age. This is still above the Healthy People 2000 goal of reducing iron deficiency to less than 3 percent among children aged one through four (U.S. Department of Health and Human Services 1990).

Breast-feeding

Breast-feeding is the optimal method of nurturing full-term infants. Advantages of breast-feeding include biochemical, immunologic, enzymatic, and endocrinologic to psychosocial, developmental, hygienic, and economic benefits. The Pima Infant Feeding Study showed a beneficial effect of breast- versus bottle-feeding on the risk of gastroenteritis and upper respiratory infections for Pima infants exclusively breast-fed for the first four months of life (Forman et al. 1984). Breast-feeding is also associated with a lower prevalence of type 2 diabetes in breast-fed Indians; both nonpregnant and pregnant breast-fed Pima Indians had lower plasma glucose concentrations at ages 20 to 24 years (Pettitt et al. 1995). Thus, breast-feeding should be viewed as a preventive strategy for type 2 diabetes.

Data from the 1994 PedNSS indicate that 36 percent of low-income children were breast-fed on hospital discharge, whereas 18 percent were consuming some breast milk at six months of age. Across the ethnic groups, American Indian and Asian mothers had the highest prevalence of breast-feeding initiation and duration, with 44 percent of American Indian mothers breast-feeding at hospital discharge and 24 percent breast-feeding at six months postpartum (Centers for Disease Control and Prevention 1996). This is still below the goals set in Healthy People 2000 (U.S. Department of Health and Human Services

1990): at least 75 percent of mothers breast-feed their babies in the early post-partum period, and at least 50 percent breast-feed through 5–6 months of age. Greater effort is needed to promote breast milk as the preferred source of nutrition for young infants.

Studies of Dietary Intake

The authors conducted an extensive review of the 1980–98 literature and found 13 studies reporting nutrient intakes (Ballew et al. 1997; Bell, Shaw, and Dignan 1995; Betts and Crase 1986; Brown and Brenton 1994; Buckley et al. 1992; Gilbert et al. 1992; Harland et al. 1992; Nobmann et al. 1992; Smith et al. 1996; Story et al. 1986; Teufel and Dufour 1990; Wolfe and Sanjur 1988; Zephier et al. 1997). No study involved children under the age of 10 years. The studies included 20 tribal groups throughout the United States. Sample sizes ranged from 21 to 946, with ages from 10 through 91 years. Nine of the studies included both males and females, and four included females only. The largest studies were the Strong Heart Dietary Study (Zephier et al. 1997), with 892 men and women aged 45–74 years from 10 tribes in Arizona, Oklahoma, and the Dakotas, and the Navajo Health and Nutrition Survey (Ballew et al. 1997), with 946 Navajo males and females aged 12–91 years. Although there are variations in methods of data collection and analysis, dietary intake information was collected using 24-hour dietary recalls, multiple-day food records, and food frequency questionnaires. All of the studies used visual guides such as pictures, cardboard shapes, or measuring utensils to quantify serving sizes. Nutrient values for traditional native foods, when available, were used in the analysis.

Table 12.1 shows selected nutrient intake data from the 13 studies. Because age groups vary among the studies and are not always consistent with age ranges used in the Recommended Dietary Allowances (RDA), a study population was determined not to have met the RDA if the group's mean nutrient intake was less than the RDA for any age group. This approach would tend to overestimate inadequate intakes. In all of the studies, mean protein intake met the RDA. Vitamin C was adequate in all groups except adolescent Cherokee (North Carolina) boys. Mean intakes of vitamin A were below the RDAs for all age groups and both genders in the Navajo Health and Nutrition Survey. The RDA for iron was not met for most of the groups of females. Calcium intake was below the RDA for most of the groups. Low intakes of iron and calcium are of concern for the general U.S. population. National data indicate that calcium intakes are consistently below the RDA for adolescent and adult females and for

TABLE 12.1
Daily energy and nutrient intakes (mean ± standard deviation) of American Indians:
Results of selected studies, 1981–1997

Tribe/population (state)	Study	No.	Age	Gender	Energy (kcal)	Protein (g)
			Children			
Cherokee (NC)	Story et al. 1986	139	13–17	M	2,288±1,181	79±45
		138	13–17	F	1,809±690	64±27
Navajo (NM)	Gilbert et al. 1992	168	14–18	M	2,512±794	92±34
		205	14–18	F	1,960±832	66±27
Hopi (AZ)	Brown and Brenton 1994	96	10–13	M/F	2,123±721	89±31
Navajo (AZ, NM, UT)	Ballew et al. 1997	89	12–19	M	2,262±119	86±5
		73	12–19	F	2,031±191	75±7
			Adults			
Omaha/Sioux (NE)	Betts and Crase 1986	20	50+	M/F	1,695±330	69±18
Navajo (NM, UT, AZ)	Wolfe and Sanjur 1988	107	20–90	F	1,632±610	65±30
Hualapai (AZ)	Teufel and Dufour 1990	28	18–35	F	2,602±766	77±21
Siouan (NC)	Harland et al. 1992	35	18–87	M	2,722±976	85±29
		21	18–87	F	1,643±614	56±22
Alaska Native	Nobmann et al. 1992	165	21–60	M	2,754±84	127±6
		186	21–60	F	1,945±55	90±3
Pueblo/Navajo (NM)	Buckley et al. 1992	56	18–65	F	2,247	
Lumbee (NC)	Bell et al. 1995	107	21–60	F	1,538±46	57±1.8
Pima (AZ)	Smith et al. 1996	273	18–74	M	2,234±70	84.2±3
		302	18–74	F	1,813±44	70±2
Strong Heart Survey	Zephier et al. 1997					
AZ		137	45–74	M	1,958±987	73±34
OK		143	45–74	M	1,831±1,015	68±36
ND/SD		118	45–74	M	1,873±1,183	74±47
AZ		160	45–74	F	1,574±564	62±26
OK		173	45–74	F	1,431±718	55±26
ND/SD		161	45–74	F	1,651±881	62±33
Navajo (AZ, NM, UT)	Ballew et al. 1997	157	20–39	M	2,127±65	83±3
		77	40–59	M	2,066±105	90±4
		67	60+	M	1,650±135	70±7
		225	20–39	F	1,958±60	78±3
		163	40–59	F	1,708±90	73±4
		95	60+	F	1,618±74	70±3

[a]Value less than the Recommended Dietary Allowance.

males of most age and racial/ethnic groups (Federation of American Societies for Experimental Biology 1995). Iron intakes are below the RDA for female adolescents and women 20–59 years of age.

In all of the studies, dietary fat intake was above the recommended level of 30 percent of total calories, ranging from 31 percent to 47 percent. In the 11 studies in which dietary fat was reported, half of the study groups had fat

Carbohydrate (g)	Fat (g)	Fat (% kcal)	Calcium (mg)	Iron (mg)	Vitamin A (RE)	Vitamin C (mg)
N/A	N/A	N/A	990±631[a]	16.7±7	1,019±1,114	57±89[a]
N/A	N/A	N/A	707±395[a]	9.8±4[a]	1,233±2,589	66±73
333±116	93±34	33	1,018±555[a]	15.6±8	2,065±2,236	174±132
269±120	71±35	33	720±354[a]	11.6±5[a]	1,369±1,265	140±112
261±96	84±33	35	874±288[a]	21±18	1,867±1,853	122±75
296±12	84±7	33	876±157[a]	15±1	650±80[a]	174±33
274±28	73±7	31	637±71[a]	13±1[a]	751±87[a]	166±38
199±52	70±17	37	506±248[a]	13±3	1,219±657	122±75
200±88	56±27	31	574±359[a]	11.5±5.1[a]	917±989	82±70
333±95	101±25	35	N/A	N/A	N/A	N/A
296±127	122±61	44	708±436[a]	15±5	3,498±2,563	134±102
154±58	89±41	47	476±230[a]	10±4[a]	2,255±1,276	77±44
282±10	117±5	38	689±33[a]	20.2±0.8	2,570±190	131±10
214±8	81±3	38	516±23[a]	14.1±0.6[a]	2,411±195	128±9
		36	N/A	N/A	N/A	91.8
190±6	62±3	36	466±22[a]	9.3±0.3[a]	1,225±175	56±3.8
276±8	88±3	34	905±38	19.1±0.6	221±26	111±9
216±5	75±2	36	802±28[a]	20.6±3	250±29	97±6
235±123	74±45	34	—	—	—	102±126
210±111	76±54	37	—	—	—	109±102
209±127	78±57	37	—	—	—	84±70
192±77	63±29	35	—	—	—	108±124
175±96	59±37	36	—	—	—	112±143
202±103	66±41	36	—	—	—	100±79
267±10	81±3	34	560±33[a]	16±1	763±84[a]	113±14
242±13	82±6	35	447±37[a]	16±1	707±243[a]	98±18
205±16	62±6	33	402±33[a]	14±1	525±81[a]	67±11
236±8	79±3	35	483±19[a]	14±1[a]	661±64[a]	95±10
206±9	67±5	34	378±22[a]	14±1[a]	686±102[a]	85±8
196±9	62±4	33	386±37[a]	14±1	437±60[a]	65±8

intakes of 30–35 percent of calories from fat and half had intakes greater than 35 percent. In only one study did the percentage of calories from fat exceed 40 percent. An intake of total fat above the recommended level is a public health concern for a large proportion of Americans. In 1988–91, mean total fat intake as a percentage of calories was about 34 percent for American adults (Federation of American Societies for Experimental Biology 1995).

Traditional and Contemporary Foods

During the past century, dietary patterns among the various Indian tribes have changed drastically. Diets historically high in complex carbohydrate/high fiber foods have been replaced by high-fat modern foods (Boyce and Swinburn 1993). Concomitant with these dietary changes have been dramatic increases in obesity and diabetes. A striking example is seen with the Pima Indians, who have the highest rates of type 2 diabetes of any geographically defined population, with a prevalence of about 50 percent in adults older than 35 years (Knowler et al. 1993). Before the turn of the twentieth century, however, the disease was virtually nonexistent. For at least 500–1,000 years, the Pima lived in the Sonoran Desert, cultivating crops irrigated by an intricate canal system, hunting, fishing, and gathering foods from the desert. As the area became more settled in the 1880s, the upstream waters of the Gila River were diverted and farming in the desert was no longer possible. Eventually, food from subsistence farming, hunting, and gathering was replaced with food from trading posts and government food programs. It has been estimated that the traditional Pima diet of one hundred years ago was 70–80 percent carbohydrate, 8–12 percent fat, and 12–18 percent protein. By the 1950s the Pima diet comprised about 61 percent carbohydrate, 24 percent fat, and 15 percent protein. The current diet of the Pima is about 47 percent carbohydrate, 35 percent fat, 15 percent protein, and 3 percent alcohol (Boyce and Swinburn 1993).

During the past fifty years, the amount of wild and home-grown foods in the American Indian diet has greatly diminished, and a significantly greater proportion of food is processed and commercially prepared, a trend also seen among the general U.S. population. However, many Indian families are still involved in some aspect of home food production. In a 1990 U.S. Department of Agriculture (USDA) study of program participants in the Food Distribution Program on Indian Reservations (FDPIR), about half of all households reported producing some of their food themselves, including growing fruits and vegetables, maintaining livestock for dairy and meat, raising poultry for eggs, and hunting and fishing (U.S. Department of Agriculture 1990).

In general, the diets of American Indians today are high in refined carbohydrates (especially refined sugars), fat, and sodium and low in milk products, fruits, and vegetables (Porter 1987; Pearce 1990). Traditional preparation over direct heat has been replaced with pan frying or deep-fat frying. The recent proliferation of fast-food restaurants and convenience food stores on and near reservations also encourages the consumption of high-fat, high-sugar foods (Broussard et al. 1995). It is generally conceded that poverty in Indian communities further limits access to a healthy food supply.

Several reports have examined both traditional and contemporary food use among tribal groups (Pearce 1990; Aspenland and Pelican 1992; Boyce and Swinburn 1993; Wolfe, Weber, and Arviso 1985; Terry and Bass 1984). Although all report use of traditional foods, most of these foods seem to be consumed only occasionally. The declining use of traditional foods among the Hopi was noted by Brown and Brenton (1994), who found that less than 25 percent of dietary recalls from 420 children and female homemakers included at least one traditional food in the daily diet. The most popular Hopi-grown traditional foods continue to be corn and beans, which are ancient dietary staples (Brown and Brenton 1994). Nobmann and colleagues (1992) found that native foods such as salmon and other fish were used frequently by Alaska Natives. Traditional fermented foods, including seasonally consumed heads and eggs of salmon and other fish, seal, beaver, caribou, and whales were reported by 23 percent of those surveyed.

For many American Indians, foods regarded as traditional often have particular spiritual and social value and represent purity, healthfulness, and strength — symbols of a prereservation (and pre-European contact) life and culture. These foods are held in high regard and are seen as having healthful properties, in contrast to the modern-day diet (Lang 1989). Traditional foods are an integral part of numerous celebrations, feast days, powwows, and religious ceremonies. Most traditional foods are low in fat and sugar, with relatively high nutritive value. Today, Indian populations are being encouraged to incorporate more of their traditional foods into their diet (Figure 12.1). Many traditional belief systems include the concepts of harmony and balance respecting food, and these can be useful concepts in motivating individuals and communities to increase their use of traditional foods and adopt healthier lifestyles. It is possible to reproduce the composition of the native diet reasonably well with traditional foods and certain commercially available foods (Boyce and Swinburn 1993). When traditional foods are not available, healthy substitutes may be suggested, such as carrots for wild roots, spinach for wild greens, and fresh fruit for wild berries.

Food Assistance Programs

Since the 1960s, several federal supplemental food programs administered by the U.S. Department of Agriculture have been implemented for low-income households on Indian reservations. These programs include the School Lunch and Breakfast Programs, the Supplemental Food Program for Women, Infants, and Children (WIC), the Food Distribution Program on American Indian Reservations, and the Food Stamp Program. Federal nutrition services are also provided to American Indian and Alaska Native elders through both Title III and Title VI of the Older Americans Act. These include both congregate and home-

Figure 12.1. Man gathering wild greens in Cherokee, North Carolina

delivered meals. Collectively, these programs contribute significantly to American Indian diets.

A 1990 report evaluating the FDPIR noted that approximately 65–70 percent of American Indians living on reservations received either food commodities or food stamps (U.S. Department of Agriculture 1990). (The FDPIR is not available in Alaska.) In 1996, 119,969 individuals participated in the FDPIR and another 124,902 households participated in the Food Stamp program. The first federal food distribution program for American Indians living on reservations was the Needy Family Program established in 1936 through USDA. Families received packages of rice, cornmeal, flour, dry beans, and nonfat dry milk. In 1977, the Food Stamp Act created the FDPIR to replace the Needy Family Program. The original 5-food-item packages were expanded to include 60 types of foods, including canned and frozen meats; evaporated and dry milk; cheese; fruit juices; fruit canned in water, juice, or light syrup; canned vegetables; grain products; dried egg mix; peanut butter; and fats and sweeteners. Participants can tailor their food package by making selections within a food group and electing not to receive the fats and sweeteners. It is estimated that the package meets or exceeds the RDA for food energy and many key nutrients (U.S. General Accounting Office 1989). Unfortunately, the food package also provides several high-fat foods. In 1994, USDA established the Commodity Improvement Council to improve the nutritional profile of USDA commodity offerings in their food assistance programs. Currently, a fresh fruit and vegetable pilot project is being implemented through the FDPIR on selected reservations, with the Department of Defense purchasing and delivering fresh produce on a weekly basis.

Discussion

Health education interventions are vital to public health efforts to prevent disease and promote healthy behaviors (Figure 12.2). Since many of the major health problems of American Indians have diet/nutrition-related components and are preventable, interventions are particularly important, yet relatively few health education interventions directed at health behaviors among Indians have been reported in the literature (LeMaster and Connell 1994). Little research has been done in the area of obesity intervention. Community-based nutrition education programs have been conducted by IHS and tribal nutritionists; however, evaluative research is not usually done. Some of these activities include adult diabetes camps, cooking classes, community fun walks, youth health camps, nutrition education via the supermarket, community aerobic classes, and 100-

Figure 12.2. First-grade students at Zuni Pueblo learning about nutrition through the local Women, Infants, and Children (WIC) program. *Source:* Courtesy of the Zuni Diabetes Prevention Program

mile walking clubs (Burhansstipanov and Dresser 1993). While these activities tend to be culturally appropriate, their effectiveness has not been established.

Comprehensive obesity-prevention programs beginning early in childhood are necessary if the epidemics of obesity and diabetes among American Indians are to be reversed. School- and community-based interventions are needed to encourage lifelong healthy eating and regular physical activity. While the number of published nutrition-related intervention studies with Indians is limited, promising studies have been done or are in progress.

The Zuni Pueblo, a southwest Indian community with high rates of obesity and diabetes, has succeeded in developing community-based wellness programs to promote physical activity and facilitate weight loss through weight loss competitions in adults (Heath et al. 1991). The results showed improved metabolic control in individuals with type 2 diabetes and modest weight loss. The Southwestern Cardiovascular Curriculum Project in New Mexico was a comprehensive, culturally oriented curriculum designed to increase knowledge and promote healthy behavior changes in fifth-grade Navajo and Pueblo Indian children. Preliminary results show a significant increase in overall knowledge and self-reported physical activity (Davis et al. 1993, 1995). Pathways, a school-based primary prevention study of obesity in American Indian schoolchildren, was recently funded by the National Heart, Lung and Blood Institute (NHLBI). This five-year multisite study involves seven American Indian Nations/tribes and five universities (Caballero et al. 1998). The intervention that will take place in 20 schools involves (1) a classroom curriculum focused on healthy lower-fat eating patterns and increased physical activity, (2) modification of school meals, (3) a physical education program in school, and (4) family involvement. Although intervention studies such as these are promising, more effort is needed to develop and evaluate other culturally appropriate health education interventions. The active involvement of the American Indian community is critical when planning, conducting, and evaluating interventions.

ACKNOWLEDGMENTS

We acknowledge the contributions of Suzanne Pelican, M.S., R.D., and Jean Charles-Azure, M.P.H., R.D. The writing of this chapter was supported in part by the following grants to Mary Story: MCHB, HRSA (MCJ 273A03-03-0) and NIH-HL50885-0351.

REFERENCES

Aspenland S, Pelican S. 1992. Traditional food practices of contemporary Taos Pueblo. *Nutr Today* 27:6–12.

Ballew C, White LL, Strauss KF, et al. 1997. Intake of nutrients and food sources of nutrients among the Navajo: Findings from the Navajo Health and Nutrition Survey. *J Nutr* 127:2085S–93S.

Bell RA, Shaw HA, Dignan MB. 1995. Dietary intake of Lumbee Indian women in Robeson County, North Carolina. *J Am Diet Assoc* 95:1426–28.

Betts NM, Crase C. 1986. Nutrient intake of urban elderly American Indians. *J Nutr Elderly* 5:11–19.

Blackett PR, Taylor T, Russell D, et al. 1996. Lipoprotein changes in relation to body mass index in Native American adolescents. *Pediatr Res* 40:77–81.

Bogardus C, Lillioja S, Ravussin E, et al. 1986. Familial dependence of the resting metabolic rate. *N Engl J Med* 315:96–100.

Bouchard C. 1992. Current understanding of the etiology of obesity: Genetic and non-genetic factors. *Am J Clin Nutr* 53:1561S–65S.

Boyce VL, Swinburn BA. 1993. The traditional Pima Indian diet. *Diabetes Care* 16:369–71.

Broussard BA, Johnson A, Himes JH, et al. 1991. Prevalence of obesity in American Indians and Alaska Natives. *Am J Clin Nutr* 53(suppl):1535S–42S.

Broussard BA, Sugarman JR, Bachman-Carter K, et al. 1995. Toward comprehensive obesity prevention programs in Native American communities. *Obes Res* 3:289S–97S.

Brown AC, Brenton B. 1994. Dietary survey of Hopi Native American elementary students. *J Am Diet Assoc* 94:517–22.

Buckley DI, McPherson RS, North CQ, et al. 1992. Dietary micronutrients and cervical dysplasia in Southwestern American Indian women. *Nutr Cancer* 17:179–85.

Burhansstipanov L, Dresser C. 1993. *Documentation of the Cancer Research Needs of American Indians and Alaska Natives.* Bethesda, Md.: National Institutes of Health.

Caballero B, Davis S, Davis CE, et al. 1998. Pathways: A school-based program for the primary prevention of obesity in American Indian children. *J Nutr Biochem* 9:535–43.

Carlile WK, Olson GH, Gorman J, et al. 1970. Contemporary nutritional status of North American Indian children. In: Moore WM, Silverberg MM, Read MS, eds. *Nutrition, Growth, and Development of North American Children.* DHEW Publication No. (NIH)72-26. Washington, D.C.: Government Printing Office.

Centers for Disease Control and Prevention. 1996. Data from the 1994 Pediatric Nutrition Surveillance System. Pers. comm.

Considine RV, Sinha MK, Heiman ML, et al. 1996. Serum immunoreactive-leptin concentrations in normal-weight and obese humans. *N Engl J Med* 334:292–95.

Davis S, Gomez Y, Lambert L, et al. 1993. Primary prevention of obesity in American Indian children. *Ann NY Acad Sci* 699:167–80.

Davis SM, Lambert LC, Gomez Y, et al. 1995. Southwest cardiovascular curriculum project: Study findings for American Indian elementary students. *J Health Educ* 26(2):S72–S81.

Federation of American Societies for Experimental Biology, Life Sciences Research Office. 1995. *Third Report on Nutrition Monitoring in the U.S.* Executive Summary. Washington, D.C.: Government Printing Office.

Fontvieille AM, Kriska A, Ravussin E. 1993. Decreased physical activity in Pima Indians compared with Caucasian children. *Int J Obes* 17:445–52.

Forman MR, Graubard BI, Hoffman HJ, et al. 1984. The Pima infant feeding study: Breastfeeding and respiratory infections during the first year of life. *Int J Epidemiol* 13:447–53.

Gallaher MM, Hauck FR, Yang-Oshida M, et al. 1991. Obesity among Mescalero pre-school children: Association with maternal obesity and birth weight. *Am J Dis Child* 145:1252–65.

Gilbert TJ, Percy CA, Sugarman JR, et al. 1992. Obesity among Navajo adolescents: Relationship to dietary intake and blood pressure. *Am J Dis Child* 146:289–95.

Gohdes D. 1995. Diabetes in North American Indians and Alaska Natives. In: *Diabetes in America*, 2d ed, 683–702. NIH Publication No. 95-1468. Bethesda, Md.: National Institutes of Health.

Goran MI, Kaskoun M, Johnson R, et al. 1995. Energy expenditure and body fat distribution in Mohawk children. *Pediatrics* 95:89–95.

Harland BF, Smith SA, Ellis R, et al. 1992. Comparison of the nutrient intakes of Blacks, Siouan Indians, and Whites in Columbus County, North Carolina. *J Am Diet Assoc* 92:348–50.

Hauck FR, Gallaher MM, Yang-Oshida M, et al. 1992. Trends in anthropometric measurements among Mescalero Apache Indian preschool children. *Am J Dis Child* 146:1194–98.

Heath GH, Wilson RH, Smith J, et al. 1991. Community-based exercise and weight control: Diabetes risk reduction and glycemic control in Zuni Indians. *Am J Clin Nutr* 53:1642S–46S.

Howard BV, Bogardus C, Ravussin E, et al. 1991. Studies of the etiology of obesity in Pima Indians. *Am J Clin Nutr* 53:1577S–85S.

Howard BV, Lee ET, Cowan LD, et al. 1995. Coronary heart disease prevalence and its relation to risk factors in American Indians: The Strong Heart Study. *Am J Epidemiol* 142:254–68.

Indian Health Service. 1997. *Trends in Indian Health, 1997*. Rockville, Md.: Indian Health Service, Program Statistics Team.

Institute for Government Research. 1928. *The Problem of Indian Administration* [Meriam report]. Baltimore: Johns Hopkins Press.

Jackson MY. 1993. Height, weight, and body mass index of American Indian school-children, 1990–91. *J Am Diet Assoc* 93:1136–40.

Knowler WC, Pettitt DJ, Saad MF, et al. 1991. Obesity in the Pima Indians: Its magnitude and relationship with diabetes. *Am J Clin Nutr* 53:1543S–51S.

Knowler WC, Saad MF, Pettitt DJ, et al. 1993. Determinants of diabetes mellitus in the Pima Indians. *Diabetes Care* 16(suppl):216S–75.

Lang GC. 1989. "Making sense" about diabetes: Dakota narratives of illness. *Med Anthropol* 11:305–27.

Lee ET, Howard BV, Savage PJ, et al. 1995. Diabetes and impaired glucose tolerance in three American Indian populations aged 45–74 years: The Strong Heart Study. *Diabetes Care* 18:599–610.

LeMaster PL, Connell CM. 1994. Health education interventions among Native Americans: A review and analysis. *Health Educ Q* 21:521–38.

McGinnis JM, Foege WH. 1993. Actual causes of death in the United States. *JAMA* 270:2207–12.

National Research Council, Committee on Diet and Health. 1989. *Diet and Health: Implications for Reducing Chronic Disease*. Washington, D.C.: National Academy Press.

Neel JV. 1962. Diabetes mellitus: A "thrifty" gene genotype rendered detrimental by "progress?" *Am J Hum Genet* 14:353–62.

Nobmann ED, Byers T, Lanier AP, et al. 1992. The diet of Alaska Native adults, 1897–1988. *Am J Clin Nutr* 55:1024–32.

Owen GM, Garry PJ, Seymoure RD, et al. 1981. Nutrition studies with White Mountain Apache preschool children in 1976 and 1969. *Am J Clin Nutr* 34:266–77.

Pearce J. 1990. Dietary changes in a northern Minnesota Indian community in the last fifty years. *IHS Prim Care Provider* 15(September):127–31.

Pelleymounter MA, Cullen MJ, Baker MB, et al. 1995. Effects of the obese gene product on body weight regulation in ob/ob mice. *Science* 260:540–43.

Pettitt DJ, Baird HR, Aleck KA, et al. 1983. Excessive obesity in offspring of Pima Indian women with diabetes during pregnancy. *N Engl J Med* 308:242–45.

Pettitt DJ, Roumain J, Hanson R, et al. 1995. Lower glucose in pregnant and nonpregnant Pima Indians who were breast fed as infants. *Diabetologia* 38 (suppl 1):A61.

Pi-Sunyer FX. 1991. Health implications of obesity. *Am J Clin Nutr* 53:1595S–1603S.

Porter J. 1987. *Native Americans: Nutrition and Diet-Related Diseases.* Congressional Research Service Report for Congress, July.

Ravussin E, Lillioja S, Knowler WC, et al. 1988. Reduced rate of energy expenditure as a risk factor for body-weight gain. *N Engl J Med* 318:467–72.

Ravussin E, Valencia ME, Esparza J, et al. 1994. Effects of a traditional lifestyle on obesity in Pima Indians. *Diabetes Care* 17:1067–74.

Smith CJ, Nelson RG, Hardy SA, et al. 1996. Survey of the diet of Pima Indians using quantitative food frequency assessment and 24-hour recall. *J Am Diet Assoc* 96:778–84.

Story M, Strauss KF, Zephier E, et al. 1998. Nutritional concerns in American Indian and Alaska Native children: Transitions and future directions. *J Am Diet Assoc* 98:170–76.

Story M, Tompkins PS, Bass MA, et al. 1986. Anthropometric measurements and dietary intakes of North Carolina Cherokee Indian teenagers. *J Am Diet Assoc* 86:1555–60.

Sugarman JR, White LL, Gilbert TJ. 1990. Evidence for a secular change in obesity, height, and weight among Navajo schoolchildren. *Am J Clin Nutr* 52:960–66.

Terry RD, Bass MA. 1984. Food practices of families in an eastern Cherokee township. *Ecol Food Nutr* 14:63–70.

Teufel NI, Dufour DL. 1990. Patterns of food use and nutrient intake of obese and nonobese Hualapai Indian women of Arizona. *J Am Diet Assoc* 90:1229–35.

U.S. Department of Agriculture, Food and Nutrition Service. 1990. *Evaluation of the Food Distribution Program on Indian Reservations.* Vol 1, *Final Report.* Washington, D.C.: USDA, Food and Nutrition Service, Office of Analysis and Evaluation.

U.S. Department of Health and Human Services. 1990. *Healthy People 2000: National Health Promotion and Disease Prevention Objectives.* Washington, D.C.: USDHHS.

U.S. General Accounting Office, Food Assistance Programs. 1989. *Report to Congress: Food Assistance Programs. Nutritional Adequacy of Primary Food Programs on Four Indian Reservations.* Washington, D.C.: General Accounting Office.

Van Duzen J, Carter JP, Secondi J, et al. 1969. Protein and calorie malnutrition among preschool Navajo Indian children. *Am J Clin Nutr* 22:1362–69.

Walston J, Silver K, Bogardus C, et al. 1995. Time of onset of non-insulin-dependent diabetes mellitus and genetic variation in the ß$_3$-adrenergic-receptor gene. *N Engl J Med* 333:343–47.

Welty T. 1991. Health implications of obesity in American Indians and Alaska Natives. *Am J Clin Nutr* 53:1616S–20S.

Wilcox L, Marks JS, eds. 1995. *From Data to Action: CDC's Public Health Surveillance for Women, Infants, and Children.* Atlanta: CDC.

Wolfe WS, Sanjur D. 1988. Contemporary diet and body weight of Navajo women receiving food assistance: An ethnographic and nutritional investigation. *J Am Diet Assoc* 88:822–27.

Wolfe WS, Weber CW, Arviso KD. 1985. Use and nutrient composition of traditional Navajo foods. *Ecol Food Nutr* 17:323–44.

Zephier EM, Ballew C, Mokdad A, et al. 1997. Intake of nutrients related to cardiovascular disease risk among three groups of American Indians: The Strong Heart Dietary Study. *Prev Med* 26:508–15.

13

Dorothy M. Gohdes, M.D., FACP, and
Kelly Acton, M.D., M.P.H., FACP

Diabetes Mellitus and Its Complications

Diabetes is one of the most common serious diseases of certain ethnic groups in the United States, including many American Indian tribes. Over the past 50 years, the incidence of diabetes in some American Indian communities has grown to epidemic proportions (Gohdes 1986). Diabetes mellitus is a complex, chronic disorder characterized by abnormalities in the metabolism of all the body fuels. Over time, it is often accompanied by microvascular (renal and retinal), macrovascular (cardiac, cerebrovascular, and peripheral vascular), and neuropathic complications. Although diabetes mellitus encompasses a group of clinically and genetically heterogeneous disorders, the actual diagnosis depends on recognition of abnormalities in plasma glucose levels (American Diabetes Association 1997).

The recently revised classification of diabetes mellitus includes several clinical subclasses, each with its own distinguishing characteristics: type 1 diabetes (formerly known as insulin-dependent diabetes mellitus, or IDDM), type 2 diabetes (formerly known as non-insulin-dependent diabetes mellitus, or NIDDM), and other specific types associated with specific genetic defects or other medical conditions. Gestational diabetes mellitus (GDM) is defined as the onset of diabetes during pregnancy. *Impaired glucose tolerance* and *impaired fasting glucose* are terms used to describe plasma glucose levels that are higher than normal but lower than those used to diagnose diabetes (American Diabetes Association 1997).

Type 2 diabetes accounts for about 90 percent of the U.S. population with diabetes, and almost all American Indians with diabetes have type 2 (Gohdes 1995). The etiology of type 2 diabetes is unknown, although it seems to be a heterogeneous disorder in which both genetic and environmental factors are important. Two defects occur in the pathogenesis of type 2 diabetes: (1) secretion of insulin from the beta cells of the pancreas is impaired, and (2) although measured insulin levels may be high, normal, or low, the plasma insulin response to glucose is inappropriately low relative to the prevailing plasma glucose concentration. In addition to abnormal insulin secretion, diminished tissue sensitivity to insulin, known as *insulin resistance,* occurs at the hepatic and peripheral (i.e., skeletal muscle) tissues. Impaired muscle glucose uptake is accompanied by impaired glycogen formation and decreased glucose oxidation, contributing to the rise in plasma glucose concentration after ingestion of glucose. And, despite the presence of fasting hyperinsulinemia, basal hepatic production of glucose is not correspondingly suppressed. The recently published classification of diabetes emphasizes the continuum from normoglycemia to diabetes (American Diabetes Association 1997).

Type 2 diabetes can occur at any age but is diagnosed most often after the age of 30. Most individuals diagnosed with type 2 diabetes are obese or have a history of obesity, yet it can occur in nonobese individuals, especially the elderly. Type 2 diabetes may or may not present with classic symptoms of polydipsia (increased thirst), polyphagia (excess hunger), polyuria (increased urination), fatigue, and weight loss. Individuals with type 2 diabetes are not prone to develop the acute problem of ketoacidosis except under conditions of extreme stress, such as trauma, surgery, or infection. Although patients with type 2 diabetes may not always depend on exogenous insulin for their survival, many patients require insulin for adequate blood sugar control. Insulin may also be needed temporarily for glucose control in stress-induced hyperglycemia.

The two major management goals of type 2 diabetes are to achieve normal metabolic (glucose and lipids) control and to prevent complications. Diet and exercise are considered the cornerstones of therapy for type 2 diabetes. Although many individuals with diabetes require oral medications or insulin injections to control blood sugar, diabetes remains largely a lifestyle disease, and medications serve only as an adjunct to, not a substitute for, dietary modifications and exercise. The longstanding clinical impression that control of the blood sugar can prevent the development of microvascular complications has been confirmed by the Diabetes Control and Complications Trial Research Group (1993).

Determinants of Diabetes

In the broadest sense, the emergence of diabetes in American Indian communities has resulted from an interaction between genetics and environment (Gohdes 1986). It is unlikely that any new gene has emerged within the later half of this century, and the 50 years of the diabetes epidemic's rise has hardly been long enough for any major genetic shift to have occurred in the many populations now suffering from diabetes and cardiovascular disease. The environment, however, has very clearly changed during those years, with what can be broadly called "Westernization" (Zimmet 1991). More specifically, increased obesity and decreased physical activity are linked to diabetes in Indian communities; the documented changes in obesity rates among Pima Indians since World War II are striking (Hall, Hickey, and Young 1992; Price et al. 1993). However, the search for the underlying genes, the role of specific environmental contributing factors, and the biochemical or physiologic mechanisms linking changes in environment to the genetic determinants of diabetes has been intense in recent years.

Neel (1962) suggested that many Native people survived periods of feast and famine because of a "thrifty gene." Although segregation analysis in Pima Indians showed evidence for a major gene effect, the "thrifty gene" has thus far been elusive (Hanson et al. 1995a). Examinations of multiple candidate genes for diabetes, obesity, and aspects of insulin metabolism have not identified a major diabetes gene in the Pima Indians. Studies have described a mutation of Trp64argB3-adrenergic-receptor gene that is associated with an earlier onset of diabetes among Pima Indians homozygous for the mutation (Walston 1995).

Because insulin resistance, obesity, and diabetes are linked, the search for genetic antecedents of glucose intolerance is complicated (Hanson et al. 1995b). Insulin resistance is a major risk factor and occurs before insulin secretory defects are obvious (Lillioja et al. 1993). Although variations in insulin resistance are related to differences in obesity, insulin resistance also aggregates in families (Hanson et al. 1995c). Features of the insulin resistance syndrome and obesity have been examined in the Pima Indians, but loci of potential significance reported in other populations have not been confirmed. An amino acid substitution in the human intestinal fatty acid binding protein associated with insulin resistance has been described (Baier, Bogardus, and Sacchettini 1996).

The "protective" effects of a traditional lifestyle have been documented in an interesting comparison between Pima Indians living in an isolated region of Mexico and the Pima Indians from the Gila River reservation in Arizona (Ravussin et al. 1994). The traditional lifestyle of Mexican Pimas included diets lower in animal fat and much greater energy expenditure from physical labor compared to today's Arizona lifestyle. Studies from Alaska have described a negative association between rates of diabetes and traditional physical activity and seal oil consumption (Adler et al. 1994, 1996). Physical activity is undoubtedly very important, as lower levels of physical activity have been associated with increased obesity, changes in body fat distribution, and glucose intolerance (Kriska et al. 1993). In a simple mechanistic overview, high levels of physical activity and low-fat diets decrease insulin resistance and the demand for insulin secretion in contrast with the low levels of activity and high-fat diets of the current U.S. lifestyle. Changing these two aspects of the contemporary lifestyle

224 Major Diseases and Health Conditions Affecting Indians

presently holds the most promise for preventing type 2 diabetes (Knowler and Narayan 1994; Bogardus 1995).

The complex physiology of insulin secretion, insulin action, obesity, and glucose intolerance can be recognized in several related manifestations. Acanthosis nigricans, a skin lesion associated with insulin resistance and hyperinsulinemia, has been described in several Indian communities and may be helpful in identifying individuals at high risk for diabetes (Stuart et al. 1994). Hyperinsulinemia has also been described in association with menstrual irregularities in young women in a syndrome similar to the polycystic ovary syndrome (Weiss et al. 1994). It is postulated that these irregularities may be responsible for the decreased fertility in young women at highest risk for diabetes (Charles et al. 1994b). Insulin resistance may also be responsible for the selective survival of low-birth-weight babies, accounting for the U-shaped relationship between birth weight and risk for diabetes in later life (McCance et al. 1996).

Prevalence

The most accurate estimates of diabetes prevalence have come from the longitudinal epidemiologic study of diabetes in the Pima Indians of Arizona, where community members are invited for screening every two years. In this community, diabetes rates have increased dramatically, and in 1981 approximately 50 percent of adults age 35 and older had diabetes (Knowler et al. 1993).

Rates of diabetes among Indians are derived from registries maintained in local communities; in some locations, as in Alaska, these registries are verified by chart review (Schraer et al. 1988). In other communities the registries represent efforts by individual investigators to gather information about diabetes from electronic medical records maintained at particular facilities. These estimates cannot include individuals who may have undetected diabetes. Table 13.1 presents a compilation of the rates of diabetes ascertained from local data sources by several methods in recent years. Estimates of diabetes rates are also available from the reported outpatient diagnoses of individual patient encounters at facilities included in Indian Health Service (IHS) data systems (Gohdes, Kaufman, and Valway 1993). Table 13.2 shows these rates by IHS Area for fiscal year 1995. Most prevalence studies in Indians reveal that females have higher rates of diabetes than males (Lee et al. 1995). In addition, rates of diabetes increase with increasing Indian heritage (Lee et al. 1995; Knowler et al. 1988).

Changes in the rates of diabetes have been dramatic. Among the Pimas, there was a 42 percent increase between 1967 and 1977 (Bennett and Knowler 1979). Increases, sometimes dramatic, have also been reported for Navajo Indians

(Glass 1996), Cree and Ojibway Indians in Canada (Young and Harris 1994), and Alaska Natives (Schraer et al. 1997).

Diabetes in Children

In recent years a growing caseload of Indian children with diabetes has prompted concern about both proper identification and treatment of these children and has highlighted the urgency of preventing or delaying the onset of diabetes and the subsequent complications of long-term metabolic abnormalities. As young mothers have developed GDM, many more children have been exposed to the risk of obesity and diabetes at a young age. In 1979, a high prevalence of diabetes was reported in young Pima Indians (Savage et al. 1979). The investigators proposed that both children with asymptomatic hyperglycemia and those with aggressively presenting diabetes represented part of the clinical spectrum of the same form of diabetes, which has subsequently been classified as type 2 diabetes.

As more cases of type 2 diabetes have occurred in Indian children, the widespread problem of obesity in children has also become an issue of major concern (Jackson 1993). Studies comparing Indian and Caucasian children found that body fat tended to be more centrally distributed in the Indian children, but no differences in metabolic rates at rest could be measured (Goran et al. 1995; Fontvielle and Ravussin 1993). However, the Indian children studied were heavier than the Caucasian children, so the question of differences in metabolic rates at comparable body weights could not be explored completely (Fontvielle and Ravussin 1993). In a study of fasting insulin levels, a comparison of Pima children ages 6–19 with Caucasian children showed that Indian children of each gender had higher fasting insulin levels after controlling for age, glucose, and relative weight (Pettitt et al. 1993). Fasting insulin and obesity, which are major risk factors for diabetes in Indian children and adolescents, also predicted higher systolic blood pressure in children (McCance et al. 1994; Charles et al. 1994a). Today's Indian children grow into adulthood with a significant burden of interrelated cardiovascular risk factors, including not only obesity and diabetes but also lipid abnormalities and increased blood pressure (Blackett et al. 1996).

Pregnancy

Early reports from the Pima studies documented that type 2 diabetes in pregnancy was accompanied by the same pattern of obstetrical complications and congenital anomalies originally described in type 1 diabetes (Pettitt et al. 1980; Comess et al. 1969). Because of the relatively young age of onset of type 2, or

TABLE 13.1
Rates of diabetes from selected studies

Reservation/location	Tribe	Age	Date	Rate/1,000	Adjustment	Method	Reference
Southwest							
Tohono O'odham, AZ	Tohono O'odham	≥18	1985–86	183	Crude	Case registry with record review	Wirth et al. 1993
Gila River, AZ	Pima	30–64	1982–87	500	Age World pop.	Biennial community screening	King et al. 1993
Arizona	Pima/Maricopa/Papago	45–74	1989–92	700	Age Standardized	Screening	Lee et al. 1995
New Mexico	Pueblo (Rio Grande)	35+	1985	213	Crude	Case registry with record review	Carter et al. 1989
Zuni, NM	Zuni	35+	1985	282	Crude	Case registry with record review	Carter et al. 1989
Jicarilla Apache, NM	Apache	35+	1985	98	Crude	Case registry with record review	Carter et al. 1989
Mescalero Apache, NM	Apache	35+	1985	164	Crude	Case registry with record review	Carter et al. 1989
Navajo, NM	Navajo	35+	1985	165	Crude	Case registry with record review	Carter et al. 1989
Arizona and New Mexico reservations	Apache	≥15	1987	101	Age US 1980	Outpatient records not verified	Gohdes et al. 1993
Navajo, AZ and NM	Navajo	≥15	1987	72	Age US 1980	Outpatient records not verified	Gohdes et al. 1993
Navajo, AZ	Navajo	20–74	1989	165	Age/sex US 1980	Case registry, community screening	Sugarman et al. 1992
Navajo, AZ	Navajo	20+	1988	124	Age US 1980	Community sample with screening	Hall et al. 1992
Rocky Mountain West							
Fort Hall, ID	Shoshone/Bannock	All	1987	95	Age/sex US 1980	Case registry with chart review	Freeman et al. 1989
Nez Perce, ID	Nez Perce	All	1987	105	Age/sex US 1980	Case registry with chart review	Freeman et al. 1989
Blackfeet, MT	Blackfeet	≥15	1986	168	Age ≥15 US 1980	Case registry with chart review	Acton et al. 1993a

Location	Tribe	Age	Year	Number	Standard	Method	Reference
Crow, MT	Crow	≥15	1986	85	Age ≥15 US 1980	Case registry with chart review	Acton et al. 1993a
Fort Belknap, MT	Assiniboine/Gros Ventre	≥15	1986	118	Age ≥15 US 1980	Case registry with chart review	Acton et al. 1993a
Fort Peck, MT	Assiniboine/Sioux	≥15	1986	173	Age ≥15 US 1980	Case registry with chart review	Acton et al. 1993a
Northern Cheyenne, MT	Northern Cheyenne	≥15	1986	59	Age ≥15 US 1980	Case registry with chart review	Acton et al. 1993a
Wind River, WY	Shoshone/Arapaho	≥15	1986	125	Age ≥15 US 1980	Case registry with chart review	Acton et al. 1993a
Utah and Colorado	Ute	≥15	1987	124	Age US 1980	Outpatient records not verified	Gohdes et al. 1993
Plains							
Cheyenne River, SD	Sioux	All	1987	106	Age US 1980	Outpatient records not verified	Stahn et al. 1993
Crow Creek, Lower Brule, SD	Sioux	All	1987	83	Age US 1980	Outpatient records not verified	Stahn et al. 1993
Devil's Lake, ND	Sioux	All	1987	111	Age US 1980	Outpatient records not verified	Stahn et al. 1993
North and South Dakota	Sioux	45–74	1989–92	400	Age Standardized	Screening	Lee et al. 1995
Oklahoma	Multiple	45–74	1989–92	400	Age Standardized	Screening	Lee et al. 1995
Pine Ridge, SD	Sioux	All	1987	70	Age US 1980	Outpatient records not verified	Stahn et al. 1993
Rosebud, SD	Sioux	All	1987	82	Age US 1980	Outpatient records not verified	Stahn et al. 1993
Sisseton/Wahpeton, SD	Sioux	All	1987	64	Age US 1980	Outpatient records not verified	Stahn et al. 1993
Turtle Mountain, ND	Chippewa	All	1987	105	Age US 1980	Outpatient records not verified	Stahn et al. 1993
Standing Rock, ND/SD	Sioux	All	1987	125	Age US 1980	Outpatient records not verified	Stahn et al. 1993
Yankton/Santee, SD	Sioux	All	1987	196	Age US 1980	Outpatient records not verified	Stahn et al. 1993
Winnebago/Omaha, NE	Winnebago/Omaha	All	1987	218	Age US 1980	Outpatient records not verified	Stahn et al. 1993

table continues

TABLE 13.1
continued

Reservation/location	Tribe	Age	Date	Rate/1,000	Adjustment	Method	Reference
North and South Dakota	Sioux	≥15	1987	117	Age US 1980	Outpatient records not verified	Gohdes et al. 1993
Upper Midwest							
Red Lake, MN	Chippewa	All	1987	148	Age/sex US 1980	Case registry Verified/screening	Rith-Najarian et al. 1993
Chippewa reservations combined, MN and ND	Chippewa	≥15	1987	144	Age US 1980	Outpatient visits not verified	Gohdes et al. 1993
Ontario and Manitoba, Canada	Cree/Ojibwa	≥10	1994	172	Crude	Screening	Harris et al. 1997
SW Ontario, Canada	Oneida/Chippewa	≥5	1985	147	Age Canada 1985	Case registry with chart review	Evers et al. 1987
Oneida, WI	Oneida	All	1993	87	Age/sex US 1990	Chart records with review	Schulz et al. 1997
Northeast							
St. Regis, NY	Mohawk	All	1989	49	Age US 1980	Case registry with chart review	Martinez, Strauss 1993
River Desert, Quebec	Algonquin	≥15	1995	M, 163 F, 239	Age/world	Screening	Delisle et al. 1995
Lac Simon, Quebec	Algonquin	≥15	1995	M, 239 F, 486	Age/world	Screening	Delisle et al. 1995
Nova Scotia	Micmac	All	1989	53	Crude	Case registry	Locke et al. 1993
James Bay, Canada	Cree	20+	1989	52	Crude	Chart review	Brassard et al. 1993
South							
Choctaw, MS	Choctaw	All	1989	163	Age US 1980	Case registry with chart review	Johnson, Strauss 1993
Cherokee, NC	Cherokee	All	1988	106	Age US 1980	Case registry with chart review	Farrell et al. 1993
Pacific Northwest							
Lummi, WA	Lummi	All	1987	40	Age/sex US 1980	Case registry with chart review	Freeman et al. 1989
Tahola, WA	Quinault	All	1987	50	Age/sex US 1980	Case registry with chart review	Freeman et al. 1989

Makah, WA	Makah	All	1987	53	Age/sex US 1980	Case registry with chart review	Freeman et al. 1989
Colville, WA	Colville	All	1987	52	Age/sex US 1980	Case registry with chart review	Freeman et al. 1989
Spokane, WA	Spokane	All	1987	56	Age/sex US 1980	Case registry with chart review	Freeman et al. 1989
Yakima, WA	Yakima	All	1987	75	Age/sex US 1980	Case registry with chart review	Freeman et al. 1989
Umatilla, OR	Umatilla	All	1987	65	Age/sex US 1980	Case registry with chart review	Freeman et al. 1989
Warm Springs, OR	Warm Springs	All	1987	75	Age/sex US 1980	Case registry with chart review	Freeman et al. 1989
British Columbia, Canada	Multiple	35+	1987	M, 41 F, 50	Crude	Case reports	Martin 1991
Far North							
Alaska	All Native	All	1993	19	Age US 1980	Case registry with chart review	Schraer et al. 1993
Alaska	Eskimo	All	1993	12	Age US 1980	Registry-verified chart audit	Schraer et al. 1993
Alaska	Indian	All	1993	24	Age US 1980	Case registry with chart review	Schraer et al. 1993
Alaska	Aleut	All	1993	33	Age US 1980	Case registry with chart review	Schraer et al. 1993
Yukon Indian	Indian	All	1987	9	Age World pop.	Case registry not verified	Young et al. 1992
NW Territories	Indian	All	1987	7	Age World pop.	Case registry not verified	Young et al. 1992
NW Territories	Inuit	All	1987	4	Age World pop.	Case registry not verified	Young et al. 1992

SOURCE: Adapted from National Diabetes Data Group 1995, 683–95.

TABLE 13.2
Age-adjusted rates of diagnosed diabetes in
Indian Health Service Areas, fiscal year 1995

Area	Rate per 1,000 population
Tucson	115
Aberdeen	110
Billings	108
Albuquerque	102
Phoenix	100
Bemidji	98
Nashville	84
Navajo	81
Oklahoma	69
Portland	57
California	41
Alaska	26
All IHS Areas	76

NOTE: U.S. 1990 reference population, FY1995 data exclude Pasqua Yaqui, Northern Ponca, Grand Portage, Minnesota River, Ysleta del Sur, Norton Sound, Flathead, Shawnee, Miccosukee, Narragansett, Pequot, Oneida, Micmac, Modoc, Sycuan, Warner Mountain, Puget Sound, Western Oregon, Klamath, Puyallup, and Coeur d'Alene.

maturity-onset, diabetes in Indian communities, diabetes that antedates pregnancy has been observed in many Indian communities. One to 3 percent of Indian deliveries seem to be associated with pre-existing diabetes (Benjamin et al. 1993; Livingston et al. 1993).

Criteria for establishing a diagnosis of GDM in the United States, unfortunately, differ from those of other areas in the world. Thus, comparisons of reports on the prevalence and outcomes of GDM in Indian communities depend in part on the criteria used (World Health Organization [WHO] 1985; National Diabetes Data Group 1979). Reported percentages of deliveries complicated by GDM, diagnosed according to the criteria of the National Diabetes Data Group (NDDG), were 14.5 percent in the Zuni, 3.4 percent in the Navajo, and 5.8 percent in Yupik Eskimos (Benjamin et al. 1993; Sugarman 1989; Murphy et al. 1993). The longitudinal studies of the Pima Indians used the WHO criteria and documented that 27.5 percent of Pima women with abnormal glucose tolerance in pregnancy developed diabetes within 4–8 years after delivery (Pettitt et al. 1988). Thirty percent of Zuni women with GDM (NDDG criteria) developed diabetes during a follow-up period of 0.5–9 years (Benjamin et al. 1993). Steinhart, Sugarman, and Connell (1997) estimated that the risk of subsequent diabetes among Navajo women with GDM is 50–70 percent.

The effects of GDM are not limited to the mother, however. The longitudinal studies of diabetes in the Pima community have revealed strikingly increased risks for obesity and diabetes in the offspring of mothers with abnormal glucose tolerance (Pettitt et al. 1983). In addition, fasting hyperinsulinemia, obesity, and abnormal glucose tolerance in pregnancy occurred more frequently in the offspring of a diabetic pregnancy compared with offspring exposed to normal glucose tolerance in utero (Pettitt et al. 1988, 1991). Thus, the effects of diabetes during pregnancy continued to be measurable in subsequent generations. It is likely that significant abnormalities of glucose tolerance occur more commonly in American Indian communities than are detected using the present U.S. criteria (Pettitt et al. 1994).

Mortality and Cardiovascular Disease

It is difficult to measure with certainty the mortality from diabetes in Indian communities because most of the published rates are underestimates. Death certificates frequently fail to list diabetes as a contributing cause of death and also fail to report Native American ancestry. Table 13.3 lists the published rates of age-adjusted mortality for diabetes by IHS Area and notes those Areas where the data must be interpreted cautiously.

In a detailed study of sequential trends in overall mortality among Pima Indians for 1975–89, Sievers, Nelson, and Bennett (1996) noted that all-cause mortality rates did not change among diabetic and nondiabetic Pima Indians

TABLE 13.3
*Age-adjusted diabetes mellitus mortality rates,
calendar years 1991–1993*

Geographic Area	No. deaths	Rate[a]
U.S. All Races (1992)	50,067	11.9
All IHS Areas	953	31.7
Nine Areas[b]	668	41.4
Aberdeen	93	54.7
Alaska	34	16.6
Albuquerque	65	41.4
Bemidji	67	45.8
Billings	50	50.5
California*	39	14.7
Nashville	50	33.9
Navajo	126	31.0
Oklahoma*	177	21.5
Phoenix	151	63.1
Portland*	69	24.2
Tucson	32	55.6

[a]Age-adjusted rate per 100,000 population. Rates based on a small number of deaths should be interpreted with caution.
[b]The IHS Areas with asterisks (California, Oklahoma, and Portland) have a particular problem with underreporting of Indian race on death certificates. Therefore, a separate IHS rate was calculated excluding these three Areas.

from the first half of the study period to the second half. The death rate for diabetic nephropathy decreased, but the death rate for ischemic heart disease increased during the second half of the time period.

Increases in the rates of death from coronary heart disease have occurred in Pimas and Navajos as the rates of diabetes have increased (Hoy, Light, and Megill 1995). Similar increases have been noted for participants in the Strong Heart Study (SHS), particularly diabetic women (Howard et al. 1995). Thus, although it is difficult to measure mortality from diabetes, increasing mortality from cardiovascular disease in Indian communities is closely related to increasing rates of glucose intolerance and must be considered in assessments of diabetes-associated mortality (Lee et al. 1993a).

Hypertension

Findings from the SHS indicate that, despite the high frequency of diabetes and obesity, the prevalence rates of hypertension in Indians in Arizona and Oklahoma were similar to those reported in the U.S. population, whereas rates in North/South Dakota Indians were significantly lower. According to the study, the degree of hypertension seemed to be mild, and the proportion of Indians who were treated and controlled was higher than that of the U.S. population (Howard et al. 1996a).

The SHS also found diabetes to be associated with significantly higher blood pressures among Indians, with prevalence rates of hypertension approximately twofold higher in people with diabetes than in those with normal glucose tolerance (Howard et al. 1996b). Similar associations with diabetes were noted by others (Sugarman 1990; Farrell et al. 1993; deCourtan, Pettitt, and Knowler 1996). This suggests that hypertension and diabetes are closely related; however, no significant correlation was found between insulin resistance and blood pressure among Pima Indians (Saad et al. 1991). The features of the insulin resistance syndrome in American Indians may differ from the relationships between insulin resistance and hypertension described in other populations.

Diabetic Nephropathy

The incidence of end-stage renal disease (ESRD) in Pima Indians, nearly all cases of which are attributable to type 2 diabetes, was more than 20 times that in the general population (Nelson and Bennett 1995). Progression to ESRD in Pima Indians with proteinuria was 40 percent after 10 years and 61 percent after 15 years, which parallels the course of renal disease seen in type 1 diabetes

(Nelson et al. 1996). The incidence of ESRD in this population was significantly related to the duration of diabetes, duration of proteinuria, two-hour postprandial glucose level, type of diabetes treatment, and presence of retinopathy (Nelson et al. 1993).

Clustering of diabetic renal disease has been reported in Pima Indian families (Pettitt et al. 1990). Diabetic nephropathy in parents conferred a 2.5 greater risk of diabetes on offspring than if the parent had diabetes without nephropathy (McCance 1995). Many Indian people have become fatalistic about the high rates of ESRD, and renal dialysis has become a major endeavor across the country.

Proteinuria is a common, important, but rather nonspecific risk factor associated with increased morbidity and mortality in Pima Indians with diabetes (Stephenson et al. 1995). Another study showed that nearly all of the excess mortality associated with diabetes in Pima Indians occurred in people with proteinuria (Nelson et al. 1988). Elevated urinary albumin excretion was found to be an early clinical marker of diabetic renal disease, and the incidence of proteinuria rose with increasing duration of diabetes (Nelson and Bennett 1995). Renal disease progressed among individuals with elevated urinary albumin excretion, occurring in 15 percent of diabetes patients after 20 years duration. A high prevalence of albuminuria, which was strongly associated with diabetes and systolic hypertension, was noted among Indians in the SHS (Robbins et al. 1996). Both micro- and macroalbuminuria were significantly more common in people with a high degree of Indian heritage (Robbins et al. 1996). The presence of albuminuria (both micro- and macro-) was significantly associated with coronary heart disease in each of the three SHS sites (Howard et al. 1996b).

Diabetic Eye Disease

Data on the incidence of blindness among American Indians are lacking, but risk factors for diabetic eye disease and its progression have been described in detail in Oklahoma, Pima, and Sioux Indians (Newell et al. 1989; Dorf et al. 1976; Lee et al. 1992). Hyperglycemia, hypertension, therapy with insulin, and long duration of diabetes have been associated with the increased prevalence of retinopathy and its progression to the proliferative phase. Hypercholesterolemia also was associated with the incidence of proliferative retinopathy (Nelson et al. 1989; Lee et al. 1992). Elevated levels of hemoglobin A_{1c} (HbA_{1c}) were slightly more strongly associated with the prevalence and incidence of retinopathy in Pimas than was a single elevated blood glucose level (Liu 1993). Among Sioux participants in the SHS, the prevalence of diabetic retinopathy was 45 percent. The severity of retinopathy increased with poor metabolic control, higher systolic blood pressure, elevated urine albumin excretion, renal dialysis, and duration of diabetes (Berinstein et al. 1997). Retinopathy has been reported in many tribes, and the risk factors for retinopathy are widespread in tribal communities in the United States and Canada (Ross and Fick 1990; Acton 1993a). Efforts to prevent the progression of diabetic retinopathy to blindness must continue as a priority.

Cataracts have also been associated with diabetes, and diabetic Pima Indians experienced more than twice the rate of cataract surgery than comparable non-diabetic individuals (Schwab et al. 1985). Rates of surgery for cataract increased with longer duration of diabetes and insulin treatment. Diabetic retinopathy and cataracts associated with diabetes represent a major threat to vision in Indian communities.

Amputations

Lower extremity amputation (LEA) is one of the most common complications of diabetes among American Indians. The combination of peripheral vascular disease and neuropathy can lead to infections and ulcerations from repetitive stress or minor trauma (Mayfield et al. 1996). Males have higher amputation rates than females (Valway, Linkins, and Gohdes 1993). Duration of diabetes and other end-organ complications were associated with higher amputation rates in several studies (Mayfield et al. 1996; Lee et al. 1993b). In Pimas, arterial medial calcification in the lower extremities correlated not only with LEA but also with mortality and appeared to be familial (Everhart et al. 1988; Narayan et al. 1996). Simple screening for neuropathy with Semmes Weinstein monofilaments identified a group of diabetic Chippewa Indians at highest risk for lower extremity problems (Rith-Najarian et al. 1992).

Remarkable decreases in LEA rates have been reported with the introduction of comprehensive programs in Indian communities (Gohdes, Schraer, and Rith-Najarian 1996; Rith-Najarian et al. 1998). Successful programs rely on identifying individuals at highest risk and providing them with education, follow-up, and proper footwear. Specific protocols to guide ulcer care and the recruitment of well-trained foot care specialists have introduced skills and defined appropriate referral patterns to optimize the care of acute foot problems (Rith-Najarian et al. 1997).

Risk factors for LEA have been described in detail in several epidemiologic studies, including studies in Oklahoma and in the Pima. Efforts to identify individuals at highest risk and target foot care programs to those at high risk are part of the strategy to prevent amputation that is emerging in several Indian communities. Nonetheless, these programs have not yet become uniformly available in all Indian communities.

Periodontal Disease

The association of periodontal disease and diabetes has been described in the Pima Indian studies. Seventy-five percent of Pimas with diabetes were edentulous after 20 years of diabetes (Löe 1993). Periodontal disease among diabetic patients was 2.6 times higher than the rate in nondiabetic individuals (Nelson and Schlossman 1990). Destructive periodontal disease was more severe among the diabetic patients, and severe periodontal disease at baseline was associated with an increased risk of poor glycemic control at follow-up (Emrich et al. 1991; Taylor et al. 1996). In a study comparing treatment regimens for diabetic patients with periodontal disease, significant reductions in $HbA1_c$ at three months were documented in patients receiving antibiotic therapy (Grossi et al. 1997). Although all published studies have come from Gila River, dental professionals in many American Indian communities are encountering this clinical entity, and sometimes the severe periodontal disease is the initial presenting symptom of diabetes. Oral health is discussed in Chapter 21.

Infections

Infections are commonly associated with diabetes and hyperglycemia, yet literature describing the frequency of particular infections in diabetic American Indians is limited. All cases of the rare but severe soft tissue infection, necrotizing fasciitis, described at the Phoenix Indian Medical Center occurred in diabetic patients (Fisher et al. 1979). However, the association of tuberculosis and diabetes quantified in a recent case-control study among the Sioux is a much more common concern (Mori, Leonard, and Welty 1992). Diabetic patients were more than four times as likely to develop tuberculosis than were nondiabetic patients. Anecdotal reports of tuberculosis among diabetic dialysis patients from American Indian communities are not uncommon. Older, debilitated diabetic patients may harbor a significant reservoir of potentially infectious tuberculosis in many American Indian communities.

Discussion

Many Indian communities have approached diabetes prevention and control in a stepwise fashion (Gohdes, Schraer, and Rith-Najarian 1996). As the number of diagnosed diabetic patients began to increase rapidly, it became imperative to provide quality care that actually improved metabolic outcomes and reduced complication rates. In many instances this care had to be incorporated into the already overburdened primary care system in small rural sites. In 1986, the IHS defined the first standards of care incorporating research data from Indian studies with clinical recommendations from authoritative sources. Aimed at preventing morbidity from complications (tertiary prevention), implementation of these simple standards was measured and the rates of implementation improved (Acton et al. 1993b). Surveillance of the quality of care became ongoing, using a simple, unique annual audit of a random sample of charts (Mayfield et al. 1994). As the standards of care have evolved, so has the surveillance system, which now provides data about important intermediate clinical outcomes and has shown that improvements have continued (Gohdes et al. 1996). In 1996, 29 percent of patients included in the overall audit ($n = 9,985$) achieved glycemic control equivalent to a HbA1$_c$ level of less than 7.5 percent. Twenty-three percent had documented proteinuria, a group needing focused efforts to prevent progression to end-stage renal disease. These data, now derived in part from computer-based medical records, provide a unique combination of clinical and public health outcome measures to guide progress and quality improvement.

To help patients prevent the progression of diabetes, educators have adapted diabetes education programs for many specific Indian cultures (Hosey and Gohdes 1991). Community programs giving dietary advice and food preparation techniques have been successfully piloted (Stegmayer et al. 1988; Broussard 1991). Education materials for Indian communities are now widely available and include material with a special focus on gestational diabetes. Screening for GDM and intensive therapy with self-monitoring are now standard practice. A unique curriculum adapted for American Indians has been implemented in Pueblo communities (Carter et al. 1997).

Increasingly, health-care facilities are adopting consensus-based treatment guidelines, customized to the community, using staged diabetes management, a systems approach to diabetes treatment (Mazze et al. 1994). The introduction of comprehensive treatment guidelines has resulted in decreased amputation rates in northern Minnesota (Rith-Najarian et al. 1998). In addition, hypertension control and metabolic control have improved in communities that have adopted and continue to use consistent guidelines for care (Gohdes et al. 1996). Preliminary reports from Alaska show that decreases in amputation and ESRD rates are associated with defined diabetes care carried out by a multidisciplinary team working in conjunction with primary care providers to supplement education and monitoring and to provide consistent care (Schraer et al. 1997). As these reports show, the scientific base to guide secondary and tertiary prevention is well developed, and strategies to decrease morbidity from complications have been demonstrated to be successful in several communities (Gohdes, Schraer, and Rith-Najarian 1996).

Primary prevention of type 2 diabetes remains a challenge, which many communities have accepted by developing fitness programs (Wilson et al. 1994; Broussard et al. 1995; Benjamin 1995). Theoretically, this form of diabetes should be preventable, but the best of the realistic strategies are still under investigation. The Zuni Wellness Center has successfully encouraged individuals of the community to increase their physical activity to prevent diabetes (Heath et al. 1994; Benjamin 1995). Many other communities have modeled similar programs, in which they have revived traditional activities such as canoe racing and running. School-based prevention efforts have been directed at children, and these have resulted in reduced rates of weight gain in children (Broussard et al. 1995). Southwestern American Indians are currently participating in the national multicenter study of diabetes prevention. There has been progress in implementing both community-wide approaches and programs targeted to high-risk individuals in many communities, and these programs should serve as guides for other communities as researchers seek the scientific basis for primary prevention of type 2 diabetes.

REFERENCES

Acton K, Rogers B, Campbell G, et al. 1993a. Prevalence of diagnosed diabetes and selected related conditions of six reservations in Wyoming and Montana. *Diabetes Care* 16 (suppl 1):263–65.

Acton K, Valway S, Helgerson S, et al. 1993b. Improving diabetes care for American Indians. *Diabetes Care* 16 (suppl 1):372–75.

Adler A, Boyko EJ, Schraer CD, et al. 1994. Lower prevalence of impaired glucose tolerance and diabetes associated with daily seal oil or salmon consumption among Alaska Natives. *Diabetes Care* 17:1498–1501.

———. 1996. The negative association between traditional physical activities and the prevalence of glucose intolerance in Alaska Natives. *Diabet Med* 13:555–60.

American Diabetes Association, Expert Committee on the Diagnosis and Classification of Diabetes Mellitus. 1997. Report of the Expert Committee on the Diagnosis and Classification of Diabetes Mellitus, American Diabetes Association. *Diabetes Care* 20:1183–97.

Baier LJ, Bogardus C, Sacchettini JC. 1996. A polymorphism in the human intestinal fatty acid binding protein alters fatty acid transport across Caco-2 cells. *J Biol Chem* 271:10892–96.

Benjamin EM. 1995. Community-based exercise programs. In: Ruderman N, Devlin JT, eds. *The Health Care Professional's Guide to Diabetes and Exercise*, 259–64. Alexandria, Va.: American Diabetes Association Clinical Education Series.

Benjamin E, Winters D, Mayfield J, et al. 1993. Diabetes in pregnancy in Zuni Indian women: Prevalence and subsequent development of clinical diabetes after gestational diabetes. *Diabetes Care* 16:1231–36.

Bennett PH, Knowler WC. 1979. Increasing prevalence of diabetes in the Pima (American) Indians over a ten year period. In: Waldhausl WK, ed. *Proceedings of the 10th Congress of the International Diabetes Federation,* 507–11. Amsterdam: Excerpta Medica.

Berinstein DM, Stahn RM, Welty TK, et al. 1997. The prevalence of diabetic retinopathy and associated risk factors among Sioux Indians. *Diabetes Care* 20:757–59.

Blackett PR, Taylor T, Russell D, et al. 1996. Lipoprotein changes in relation to body mass index in Native American adolescents. *Pediatr Res* 40:77–81.

Bogardus C. 1995. Antagonist: The case for insulin resistance as a necessary and sufficient cause of type II diabetes mellitus. *J Lab Clin Med* 125:556–58.

Brassard P, Robinson E, Lavallee C. 1993. Prevalence of diabetes mellitus among the James Bay Cree of northern Quebec. *Can Med Assoc J* 149:303–7.

Broussard BA. 1991. Innovative diabetes nutrition education in American Indians and Alaska Natives. In: Rifkin H, Colwell JA, Taylor SI, eds. *Diabetes 1991: Proceedings of the 14th International Diabetes Federation Congress,* 793–96. Washington, D.C.: Elsevier Science Publishers BV.

Broussard BA, Sugarman JR, Bachman-Carter K, et al. 1995. Toward comprehensive obesity prevention programs in Native American communities. *Obes Res* 3 (suppl 2):289–97.

Carter JS, Gilliland SS, Perez GE, et al. 1997. Native American diabetes project: Designing culturally relevant materials. *Diabetes Educ* 1997:133–39.

Carter J, Horowitz R, Wilson R, et al. 1989. Tribal differences in diabetes: Prevalence among American Indians in New Mexico. *Public Health Rep* 104:665–69.

Charles MA, Pettitt DJ, Hanson RL, et al. 1994a. Familial and metabolic factors related to blood pressure in Pima Indian children. *Am J Epidemiol* 140:123–31.

Charles MA, Pettitt DJ, McCance DR, et al. 1994b. Gravidity, obesity, and non-insulin-dependent diabetes among Pima Indian women. *Am J Med* 97:250–55.

Comess LJ, Bennett PH, Burch TA, et al. 1969. Congenital anomalies and diabetes in the Pima Indians of Arizona. *Diabetes* 18:471–77.

deCourtan MP, Pettitt DJ, Knowler WC. 1996. Hypertension in Pima Indians: Prevalence and predictors. *Public Health Rep* 3 (suppl 2):40–43.

Delisle HF, Rivard M, Ekoe JM. 1995. Prevalence estimates of diabetes and of other cardiovascular risk factors in the two largest Algonquin communities of Quebec. *Diabetes Care* 18:1255–59.

Diabetes Control and Complications Trial Research Group. 1993. The effect of intensive treatment of diabetes on the development and progression of long term complications in insulin-dependent diabetes mellitus. *N Engl J Med* 329:977–86.

Dorf A, Ballintine EJ, Bennett PH, et al. 1976. Retinopathy in Pima Indians: Relationships to glucose level, duration of diabetes, age at diagnosis of diabetes, and age at examination in a population with a high prevalence of diabetes mellitus. *Diabetes* 25:554–60.

Emrich L, Schlossman M, Knowler WC, et al. 1991. Periodontal disease in non-insulin-dependent diabetes mellitus. *J Periodontol* 62:123–31.

Everhart JE, Pettitt DJ, Knowler WC, et al. 1988. Medial arterial calcification and its association with mortality and complication of diabetes. *Diabetologia* 31:16–23.

Evers S, McCracken E, Antone I, et al. 1987. The prevalence of diabetes in Indians and Caucasians living in southwestern Ontario. *Can J Public Health* 78:240–43.

Farrell MA, Quiggins PA, Eller JD, et al. 1993. Prevalence of diabetes and its complications in the eastern band of Cherokee Indians. *Diabetes Care* 16 (suppl 1):253–56.

Fisher JR, Conway MJ, Takeshita RT, et al. 1979. Necrotizing fasciitis: Importance of roentgenographic studies for soft tissue gas. *JAMA* 241:803–6.

Fontvielle AM, Ravussin E. 1993. Metabolic rate and body composition of Pima Indians and Caucasian children. *Crit Rev Food Sci Nutr* 33:363–68.

Freeman WL, Hosey GM, Diehr P, et al. 1989. Diabetes in American Indians of Washington, Oregon, Idaho. *Diabetes Care* 12:282–88.

Glass M. 1996. Diabetes in Navajo Indians. *Federal Practitioner* 13:41–48.

Gohdes DM. 1986. Diabetes in American Indians: A growing problem. *Diabetes Care* 9:609–13.

———. 1995. Diabetes in North American Indians and Alaska Natives. In: National Diabetes Data Group. *Diabetes in America*, 2d ed, 683–701. NIH Publication No. 95-1468. Bethesda, Md.: National Institutes of Health.

Gohdes DM, Kaufman S, Valway S. 1993. Diabetes in American Indians: An overview. *Diabetes Care* 16 (suppl 1):239–43.

Gohdes DM, Rith-Najarian S, Acton K, et al. 1996. Improving diabetes care in the primary health setting: The Indian Health Experience. *Ann Intern Med* 124 (1, pt 2):149–52.

Gohdes DM, Schraer C, Rith-Najarian S. 1996. Diabetes prevention in American Indians and Alaska Natives: Where are we in 1994? *Diabetes Res Clin Pract* 34(suppl): S95–100.

Goran MI, Kaskoun M, Johnson R, et al. 1995. Energy expenditure and body fat distribution in Mohawk children. *Pediatrics* 95:89–95.

Grossi S, Skrepcinski F, DeCaro T, et al. 1997. Treatment of periodontal disease in diabetics reduces glycated hemoglobin. *J Periodontol* 68:713–19.

Hall T, Hickey M, Young T. 1992. Evidence for recent increases in obesity and non-insulin-dependent diabetes mellitus in a Navajo community. *Am J Hum Biol* 4:547–53.

Hanson RL, Elston RC, Pettitt DJ, et al. 1995a. Segregation analysis of non-insulin-dependent diabetes mellitus in Pima Indians: Evidence for a major-gene effect. *Am J Hum Genet* 57:160–70.

Hanson RL, Narayan KMV, McCance DR, et al. 1995b. Rate of weight gain, weight fluctuation and incidence of NIDDM. *Diabetes* 44:261–66.

Hanson RL, Pettitt DJ, Bennett PH, et al. 1995c. Familial relationships between obesity and NIDDM. *Diabetes* 44:418–22.

Harris SB, Gittelsohn J, Hanley A, et al. 1997. The prevalence of NIDDM and associated risk factors in Native Canadians. *Diabetes Care* 20:185–87.

Heath GW, Leonard B, Wilson RW, et al. 1994. Community-based exercise intervention: Zuni diabetes project. *Diabetes Care* 10:579–83.

Hosey GM, Gohdes DM. 1991. Designing and evaluating diabetes education material for special populations. In: Rifkin H, Colwell JA, Taylor SI, eds. *Diabetes 1991: Proceedings of the 14th International Diabetes Federation Congress*, 1127–29. Washington, D.C.: Elsevier Science Publishers BV.

Howard BV, Lee ET, Cowan LD, et al. 1995. Coronary heart disease prevalence and its relation to risk factors in American Indians: The Strong Heart Study. *Am J Epidemiol* 142:254–68.

Howard BV, Lee ET, Yeh J, et al. 1996a. Hypertension in adult American Indians: The Strong Heart Study. *Hypertension* 28:256–64.

Howard BV, for the Strong Heart Study Investigators. 1996b. Risk factors for cardiovascular disease in individuals with diabetes: The Strong Heart Study. *Acta Diabetol* 33:180–84.

Hoy W, Light A, Megill D. 1995. Cardiovascular disease in Navajo Indians with type 2 diabetes. *Public Health Rep* 110:87–94.

Jackson MY. 1993. Height, weight and body mass index of American Indian school children, 1990–1991. *J Am Diet Assoc* 93:1136–40.

Johnson LG, Strauss K. 1993. Diabetes in Mississippi Choctaw Indians. *Diabetes Care* 16 (suppl 1):250–52.

King H, Rewers M, WHO Ad Hoc Diabetes Reporting Group. 1993. Global estimates for prevalence of diabetes mellitus and impaired glucose tolerance in adults. *Diabetes Care* 16:157–77.

Knowler WC, Narayan VKM. 1994. Prevention of non-insulin-dependent diabetes mellitus. *Prev Med* 23:701–3.

Knowler WC, Saad MF, Pettitt DJ, et al. 1993. Determinants of diabetes mellitus in the Pima Indians. *Diabetes Care* 16 (suppl 1):216–27.

Knowler WC, Williams RC, Pettitt DJ, et al. 1988. Gm 3;5,13,14 and type II diabetes mellitus: An association in American Indians with genetic admixture. *Am J Hum Genet* 43:520–26.

Kriska AM, LaPorte RE, Pettitt DJ, et al. 1993. The association of physical activity with obesity, fat distribution and glucose intolerance in Pima Indians. *Diabetologia* 36:863–69.

Lee ET, Howard B, Savage P, et al. 1995. Diabetes and impaired glucose tolerance in three American Indian populations ages 45–74 years: The Strong Heart Study. *Diabetes Care* 18:599–610.

Lee ET, Lee VS, Lu M, Russell D. 1992. Development of proliferative retinopathy in NIDDM: A follow-up study of American Indians in Oklahoma. *Diabetes* 41:359–67.

Lee ET, Russell D, Jorge N, et al. 1993a. A follow-up study of diabetic Oklahoma Indians: Mortality and causes of death. *Diabetes Care* 16 (suppl 1):300–305.

Lee JS, Lu M, Lee VS, et al. 1993b. Lower extremity amputation: Incidence, risk factors, and mortality in the Oklahoma Indian diabetes study. *Diabetes* 42:876–82.

Lillioja S, Mott DM, Spraul M, et al. 1993. Insulin resistance and insulin secretory dysfunction as precursors of non-insulin-dependent diabetes mellitus. *N Engl J Med* 329:1988–92.

Liu QZ, Pettitt DJ, Hanson RL, et al. 1993. Glycated haemoglobin, plasma glucose and diabetic retinopathy: Cross sectional and prospective analysis. *Diabetologia* 36:428–32.

Livingston RC, Bachman-Carter K, Frank C, et al. 1993. Diabetes mellitus in Tokono O'odham pregnancies. *Diabetes Care* 16 (suppl 1):318–21.

Locke K, Noseworthy R, Davies A. 1993. Management of diabetes mellitus in Nova Scotia Micmac communities. *J Can Dietetic Assoc* 54:92–96.

Löe H. 1993. Periodontal disease: The sixth complication of diabetes mellitus. *Diabetes Care* 16 (suppl 1):329–34.

Martin JD, Bell P. 1991. Diabetes mellitus in the Native population of British Columbia, Canada. *Arctic Med Res* (suppl):433–35.

Martinez CB, Strauss K. 1993. Diabetes in St. Regis Mohawk Indians. *Diabetes Care* 16 (suppl 1):260–62.

Mayfield JA, Reiber GE, Nelson RG, et al. 1996. A foot risk classification system to predict diabetic amputation in Pima Indians. *Diabetes Care* 19:704–9.

Mayfield JA, Rith-Najarian SJ, Acton KA, et al. 1994. Assessment of diabetes care by medical record review: The Indian Health Service model. *Diabetes Care* 17:918–23.

Mazze RM, Etzwiler D, Strock E, et al. 1994. Staged diabetes management: Toward an integrated model of diabetes care. *Diabetes Care* 17(suppl):56–66.

McCance DR, Hanson RL, Pettitt DJ, et al. 1995. Diabetic nephropathy: A risk factor for diabetes mellitus in offspring. *Diabetologia* 38:221–26.

McCance DR, Pettitt DJ, Hanson RL, et al. 1994. Glucose insulin concentrations and obesity in childhood and adolescence as predictors of NIDDM. *Diabetologia* 37:617–23.

———. 1996. Birth weight and non-insulin-dependent diabetes: Thrifty phenotype or surviving small baby genotype? *BMJ* 308:942–45.

Mori MH, Leonard G, Welty TK. 1992. The benefits of isoniazid chemo-prophylaxis and risk factors for tuberculosis among Oglala Sioux Indians. *Arch Intern Med* 152:547–50.

Murphy NJ, Bulkow LR, Schraer CD, et al. 1993. Prevalence of diabetes mellitus in pregnancy among Yupic Eskimos, 1987–1988. *Diabetes Care* 16 (suppl 1):315–17.

Narayan KMV, Pettitt DJ, Hanson RL, et al. 1996. Familial aggregation of medial arterial calcification in Pima Indians with and without diabetes. *Diabetes Care* 19:968–71.

National Diabetes Data Group. 1979. Classification and diagnosis of diabetes mellitus and other categories of glucose intolerance. *Diabetes* 28:1039–57.

Neel JV. 1962. Diabetes mellitus: A thrifty genotype rendered detrimental by "progress"? *Am J Hum Genet* 14:353–63.

Nelson RG, Bennett PH. 1995. The development and course of renal disease among Pima Indians with non-insulin-dependent diabetes mellitus. *Diab Nutr Metab* 8:149–58.

Nelson RG, Knowler WC, McCance DR, et al. 1993. Determinants of end-stage renal disease in Pima Indians with type 2 (non-insulin-dependent) diabetes mellitus and proteinuria. *Diabetologia* 36:1087–93.

Nelson RG, Pettitt DJ, Carraher MA, et al. 1988. Effect of proteinuria on mortality in NIDDM. *Diabetes* 37:1499–1504.

Nelson RG, Pettitt DJ, deCourten MP, et al. 1996. Parental hypertension and proteinuria in Pima Indians with NIDDM. *Diabetologia* 39:433–38.

Nelson RG, Schlossman M. 1990. Periodontal disease and NIDDM in Pima Indians. *Diabetes Care* 13:836–40.

Nelson RG, Wolfe JA, Horton MB, et al. 1989. Proliferative retinopathy in NIDDM: Incidence and risk factors in Pima Indians. *Diabetes* 38:435–40.

Newell SW, Tolbert B, Bennett J, et al. 1989. The prevalence and risk of diabetic retinopathy among Indians of southwest Oklahoma. *J Okla State Med Assoc* 82:414–24.

Pettitt DJ, Aleck KA, Baird R, et al. 1988. Congenital susceptibility to NIDDM: Role of intrauterine environment. *Diabetes* 37:622–28.

Pettitt DJ, Aleck KA, Bennett PH, et al. 1983. Excessive obesity in offspring of Pima Indian women with diabetes during pregnancy. *N Engl J Med* 308:242–45.

Pettitt DJ, Bennett PH, Hanson RL, et al. 1994. Comparison of World Health Organization and National Diabetes Data Group procedures to detect abnormalities of glucose tolerance during pregnancy. *Diabetes Care* 17:1264–68.

Pettitt DJ, Bennett PH, Saad MF, et al. 1991. Abnormal glucose tolerance during pregnancy in Pima Indian women: Long term effects on offspring. *Diabetes Care* 40 (suppl 2):126–30.

Pettitt DJ, Knowler WC, Baird R, et al. 1980. Gestational diabetes: Infant and maternal complications of pregnancy in relation to third-trimester glucose tolerance in the Pima Indians. *Diabetes Care* 3:458–69.

Pettitt DJ, Moll PP, Knowler WC, et al. 1993. Insulinemia in children at low and high risk of NIDDM. *Diabetes Care* 16:608–15.

Pettitt DJ, Saad MF, Bennett PH, et al. 1990. Familial predisposition to renal disease in two generations of Pima Indians with type 2 (non-insulin-dependent) diabetes mellitus. *Diabetologia* 33:438–43.

Price RA, Charles MA, Pettitt DJ, et al. 1993. Obesity in Pima Indians: Large increases among post World War II birth cohorts. *Am J Phys Anthropol* 92:473–79.

Ravussin E, Valencia ME, Esparanza J, et al. 1994. Effects of a traditional lifestyle on obesity in Pima Indians. *Diabetes Care* 17:1067–74.

Rith-Najarian SJ, Braunchard C, Beaulieu O, et al. 1998. Reducing lower extremity amputation due to diabetes: Application of the staged diabetes management approach in the primary care setting. *J Fam Pract* 47:127–32.

Rith-Najarian SJ, Stolusky T, Gohdes DM. 1992. Identifying diabetic patients at high risk for lower extremity amputations in a primary health care setting. *Diabetes Care* 15:1386–89.

Rith-Najarian SJ, Valway SE, Gohdes DM. 1993. Diabetes in a northern Minnesota Chippewa tribe: Prevalence and incidence of diabetes and incidence of major complications, 1986–1988. *Diabetes Care* 16 (suppl 1):266–70.

Robbins DC, Knowler WC, Lee ET, et al. 1996. Regional differences in albuminuria among American Indians: An epidemic of renal disease. *Kidney Int* 49:557–63.

Ross SA, Fick GH. 1990. Vascular complications in diabetic native Canadians (abstract 500). *Diabetes* 39 (suppl 1):125A.

Saad MF, Lillioja S, Nyomba BL, et al. 1991. Racial differences in the relation between blood pressure and insulin resistance. *N Engl J Med* 324:733–39.

Savage PJ, Bennett PH, Senter RG, et al. 1979. High prevalence of diabetes in young Pima Indians: Evidence of phenotypic variation in a genetically isolated population. *Diabetes* 28:937–42.

Schraer CD, Adler AI, Mayer AM, et al. 1997. Diabetes complications and mortality among Alaska Natives: Eight years of observation. *Diabetes Care* 20:314–21.

Schraer CD, Bulkow LR, Murphy NJ, et al. 1993. Diabetes prevalence, incidence and complications among Alaska Natives, 1987. *Diabetes Care* 16 (suppl 1):257–59.

Schraer CD, Lanier AP, Boyko EJ, et al. 1988. Prevalence of diabetes mellitus in Alaskan Eskimos, Indians, and Aleuts. *Diabetes Care* 11:693–700.

Schulz LO, Lalicata M, Carnes D, et al. 1997. Prevalence of diabetes and factors associated with diabetic complications in Oneida Indians. *Life Sci* 60:299–306.

Schwab IR, Dawson CR, Hoshiwara I, et al. 1985. Incidence of cataract extraction in Pima Indians. *Arch Ophthalmol* 103:208–12.

Sievers ML, Nelson RG, Bennett PH. 1996. Sequential trends in overall and cause-specific mortality in diabetic and non-diabetic Pima Indians. *Diabetes Care* 19:107–11.

Stahn RM, Gohdes D, Valway SE. 1993. Diabetes and its complications among selected tribes in North Dakota, South Dakota, and Nebraska. *Diabetes Care* 16 (suppl 1):244–47.

Stegmayer P, Lovrien FC, Smith M, et al. 1988. Designing a diabetes nutrition program for a Native American Indian community. *Diabetes Educator* 14:64–66.

Steinhart JR, Sugarman JR, Connell FA. 1997. Gestational diabetes is a herald of NIDDM in Navajo women: High rate of abnormal glucose tolerance after GDM. *Diabetes Care* 20:943–47.

Stephenson JM, Kenny S, Stevens LK, et al. 1995. Proteinuria and mortality in diabetes: The WHO multinational study of vascular disease in diabetes. *Diabet Med* 12:149–55.

Stuart C, Smith M, Gilkison C, et al. 1994. Acanthosis nigricans among Native Americans: An indicator of high diabetes risk. *Am J Public Health* 84:1839–42.

Sugarman JR. 1989. Prevalence of gestational diabetes in a Navajo Indian community. *West J Med* 150:548–51.

———. 1990. Prevalence of diagnosed hypertension among diabetic Navajo Indians. *Arch Intern Med* 150:359–62.

Sugarman JR, Gilbert TJ, Weiss NS. 1992. Prevalence of diabetes and impaired glucose tolerance among Navajo Indians. *Diabetes Care* 15:114–20.

Taylor GW, Burt BA, Becker MP, et al. 1996. Severe periodontitis and the risk for poor glycemic control in patients with non-insulin-dependent diabetes mellitus. *J Periodontol* 67:1085–93.

Valway SE, Linkins RW, Gohdes DM. 1993. Epidemiology of lower extremity amputations in the Indian Health Service, 1982–1987. *Diabetes Care* 16 (suppl 1):349–53.

Walston J, Silver K, Bogardus C, et al. 1995. Time of onset of non-insulin-dependent diabetes mellitus and genetic variation in the B$_3$-adrenergic-receptor gene. *N Engl J Med* 333:343–47.

Weiss DJ, Charles MA, Dunaif A, et al. 1994. Hyperinsulinemia is associated with menstrual irregularity and altered serum androgens in Pima Indian women. *Metabolism* 43:803–7.

Wilson R, Graham C, Booth KG, et al. 1994. Community approaches to diabetes prevention. In: Joe JR, Young RS, eds. *Diabetes as a Disease of Civilization: The Impact of Cultural Change on Indigenous Peoples*, 495–503. New York: Mouton DeGruyter.

Wirth RB, Marfin AA, Grau DW, et al. 1993. Prevalence and risk factors for diabetes and diabetes-related amputations in American Indians in southern Arizona. *Diabetes Care* 16 (suppl 1):354–56.

World Health Organization. 1985. *Diabetes Mellitus: Report of a WHO Study Group.* Technical Report Series No. 727. Geneva: WHO.

Young TK, Harris SB. 1994. Risk of clinical diabetes in a northern Native Canadian cohort. *Arctic Med Res* 53:64–70.

Young TK, Schraer CD, Shubnikoff EV, et al. 1992. Prevalence of diagnosed diabetes in circumpolar indigenous populations. *Int J Epidemiol* 21:730–35.

Zimmet PZ. 1991. Kelly West Lecture, 1991: Changes in diabetes epidemiology from west to the rest. *Diabetes Care* 15:232–52.

14

Richard J. Smith III, M.S., and
Leon S. Robertson, Ph.D.

Unintentional Injuries and Trauma

Injuries may be classified into one of two categories, intentional or unintentional. Intentional injuries are those deliberately carried out either by the individual (as in suicide) or by another person (as in homicide). Unintentional injuries, as the term implies, occur without the intent of harm. They are often thought of as untoward acts of nature and are usually described with the unsatisfactory term *accidents*. This term is deeply embedded in lay and professional use and, as it is considered synonymous with *unintentional injury*, it will undoubtedly continue to be used for some time. Injuries are a major public health problem, particularly in low-income areas (Baker et al. 1992; Berger and Mohan 1996). Therefore, it is not surprising that injury is a major cause of premature death and disability among American Indians and Alaska Natives (Sewell et al. 1989). In recent years, these populations have experienced approximately 1,500 fatal injuries, 8,000 hospital admissions (46,000 days in hospital), and 400,000 medical contacts for injuries each year. Approximately two-thirds of injury deaths are considered to be unintentional. The medical care costs for injuries in 1998 were estimated to be $154 million, based on Medicare/Medicaid reimbursement rates multiplied by hospital inpatient days and outpatient visits (Table 14.1). While the total outpatient costs are greater than those for hospitalizations, the more severe injuries obviously have higher priority. Not included in these cost estimates are the costs of emergency medical systems, including costly air transport from remote areas; long-term care for disability; various equipment and appliances; home modifications; rehabilitation; and other indirect costs of injuries.

Because suicide is discussed in Chapter 15, this chapter will focus on unintentional injury in American Indians. As noted in Chapter 7, the importance of unintentional injury as a cause of death among Indian people is reflected in the fact that it is the leading cause of death of Indians aged 1 to 44 and is not less

TABLE 14.1
*Hospital days, outpatient visits, and approximate cost of these services
for injury, American Indians and Alaska Natives, 1998*

Service	Number	Cost	Total cost
Hospital days			
Alaska	8,743	$1,380/day	$12,065,340
Lower 48	22,486	1,105/day	24,847,030
Outpatient visits			
Alaska	30,597	241/visit	7,373,877
Lower 48	369,223	168/visit	62,029,464
SUBTOTAL			$106,315,711
Contract health services			48,044,300
TOTAL			$154,360,011

than the fourth leading cause in any preretirement age group. Almost 60 percent of deaths of Indian persons 1 to 24 years of age are due to unintentional injury. While the rank of injury as a cause of death in each age group is similar to that of the total U.S. population, the injury mortality rates among Indians are substantially higher than those of the general population. In the mid-1980s, injury mortality among Indians occurred at more than twice the rate for the total U.S. population. That difference narrowed in the late 1980s and early 1990s, mainly because of reductions in the Indian rate (Figure 14.1). Nevertheless, the rate continues to substantially exceed the general U.S. rate. Indians in some areas, such as Arizona, Montana, and North Dakota, have injury mortality rates four to five times the U.S. All Races rate. The misclassification of Indians in medical records shown for many conditions has also been identified for injuries in the Portland Area (Sugarman et al. 1993). Thus, the rate of fatal injuries of Indians is undoubtedly significantly underestimated.

There is also considerable variation in the distribution of kinds of injuries between various Indian Health Service (IHS) Areas. For example, as expected, the rate of drowning is considerably higher in Alaska than in Oklahoma. The distribution of causes of intentional and unintentional injuries among Indians for calendar year 1994 is shown in Table 14.2. The overwhelming contribution made by motor vehicle deaths is apparent and exceeds all other causes combined. An analysis of all injury deaths among various age groups of American Indians for the years 1993–95 is provided in Table 14.3. These data are compiled and made available by the Centers for Disease Control and Prevention in Atlanta, Georgia. The numbers and categories are likely to vary somewhat from data collected by the IHS. Nevertheless, this table provides a cross section of injury deaths across all age groups of Indians. The importance of deaths associated with being a pedestrian for those under the age of 10 years is impressive. Homicide is the second leading cause of injury deaths of Indians under 1 year of age and is the fourth leading cause of injury deaths among those aged 1–4 years.

Per 100,000 Population

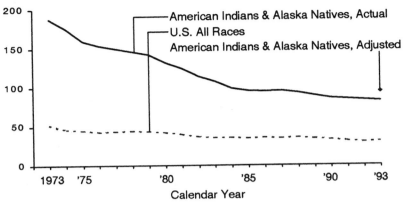

Figure 14.1. Comparison of overall injury death rates of American Indians and Alaska Natives with U.S. All Races, 1973–93. *Source:* Indian Health Service 1997, Chart 4.19

TABLE 14.2

Distribution of injury deaths among American Indians and Alaska Natives, 1994

Type of injury	No. deaths	
	Unadjusted	Adjusted[a]
All injuries	1,464	1,665
Unintentional	1,022	1,173
Motor vehicle related	552	642
All others	470	531
Intentional	418	464
Suicide	242	263
Homicide	176	201
Undetermined	24	28

SOURCE: IHS 1997, Tables 4.17, 4.19, 4.21, 4.23, and 4.25.
[a]Adjusted for miscoding of ethnicity on death certificates.

Once again, the overwhelming importance of motor vehicle injury as a cause of death for all age groups is stark.

One statistic that gives perspective on the importance of injury is the "years of potential life lost" (YPLL, i.e., years of life remaining to age 65 at time of death). Assuming an average retirement age of 65, subtracting age at death from 65 for each cause of death, and adding the results, unintentional injuries account for approximately four times the preretirement years lost each to heart disease, homicide, suicide, and cancer (Figure 14.2). The high rate of fatal injuries among the very young (Olson et al. 1990) is obviously a major contributor to YPLL.

Because of the paucity of reports relating to injuries among Indian people, particularly prior to 1980, this chapter focuses on efforts of tribes and the IHS, often in collaboration with state and other federal agencies, to reduce the personal suffering and loss, as well as the private and public costs, of injury. While not all of the many activities undertaken can be discussed, several illustrate the effectiveness of targeted interventions, often at modest cost, in reducing the rate of unintentional injuries.

The Association of Injuries with Alcohol Abuse

Several reports document high rates of alcohol-associated injury among Indians. Gallaher et al. (1992) examined the death certificates of all New Mexicans who died from an unintentional injury in the period 1980–89. Indians' age-adjusted mortality rate from unintentional injury was three times that of non-Indians. Deaths due to hypothermia or involving pedestrians struck by cars were far more common among Indians than non-Indians. Deaths attributed to drowning, falls, poisoning, and burns were also more prevalent among Indians.

Examination of all job-related deaths in New Mexico in 1980–91 revealed that, although Indians had the lowest death rate (i.e., 6.4/100,000 employed workers), alcohol was detected in a significantly larger proportion of deaths of Indians (41.7%) than of Hispanic people (15.0%) or Whites (5.0%). Nearly 80 percent of Indian decedents were working in construction or farming jobs, a proportion much higher than the comparable rate for non-Hispanic Whites and Hispanics. These high-risk occupations accounted for nearly 40 percent of the 613 occupational deaths in New Mexico during this period.

Gilliland et al. (1995) evaluated trends in alcohol-related injury mortality between 1958 and 1991 among Indians, Hispanics, and non-Hispanic Whites living in New Mexico. Indian men and women generally had the highest mortality rates. Between 1958 and the early 1980s, alcohol-related injury mortality rates increased 50 percent, 120 percent, and 600 percent in Caucasian, Hispanic, and Indian men, respectively. Alcohol-associated Indian deaths occurred primarily among men aged 30–49; most alcohol-associated Hispanic and Caucasian deaths occurred in older persons.

One noteworthy study found that urban (King County, Wash.) Indians were significantly more likely to be homeless and to have blood alcohol concentrations exceeding 0.10 g/dL than were Caucasians or African Americans who had been treated for injury in the same trauma unit (Sugarman and Grossman 1996). Unadjusted traumatic injury incidence rates for Caucasians, African Americans, and Indians (per 100,000 county residents) were 110.7, 524.9, and 489.5, respectively. Indian patients had higher rates of injuries due to falls, blunt

TABLE 14.3

Ten leading causes of injury death, American Indians and Alaska Natives,
1993–1995

Rank	<1 yr	1–4 yr	5–9 yr	10–14 yr	15–24 yr	25–34 yr
				Cause of death at:		
1	Suffocation (22)[a]	Fire/burn (44)	Drowning (18)	MV[b] occu- pant (32)	MV occupant (353)	MV occupant (273)
2	Homicide (18)	Pedestrian (40)	Pedestrian (12)	Suicide (26)	Suicide (261)	Suicide (264)
3	MV occupant (12)	Drowning (29)	Fire/burn (11)	Homicide (21)	Homicide (204)	Homicide (235)
4	All other causes (5)	Homicide (22)	MV occupant (9)	Pedestrian (16)	MV other (155)	MV other (137)
5	Adverse effects (3)	MV occupant (25)	Unintentional firearm (7)	Drowning (9)	Pedestrian (93)	Pedestrian (122)
6	Drowning (3)	Suffocation (14)	MV other (7)	MV other (8)	Drowning (44)	Poisoning (82)
7	Fire/burn (3)	MV other (9)	Suffocation (6)	Fire/burn (6)	Unintentional firearm (32)	Drowning (73)
8	Natural/envi- ronmental (2)	Fall (4)	Homicide (5)	Unintentional firearm (6)	All other causes (25)	Fall (35)
9	Tied[c]	Poisoning (3)	Pedal cyclist (5)	Fall (4)	Fire/burn (19)	Natural/envi- ronmental (28)
10		Unspecified (3)	Tied[e]	Tied[f]	Poisoning (15)	All other causes (25)

SOURCE: Data from National Vital Statistics System, National Center for Health Statistics, Centers for Disease Control and Prevention (CDC). Produced by the National Center for Injury Prevention and Control, CDC.
[a]Numbers in parentheses, numbers of deaths.
[b]MV, motor vehicle.

trauma, stabbing, shootings, bites, burns, and pedestrian-vehicle accidents than did Caucasian patients. Intentional injury rates were much higher among Indians and African Americans than Caucasians. In the same county, Ballard et al. (1992) estimated that Indian residents had fire-injury rates five times higher than Caucasians and twice those of African Americans.

Initial Prevention Programs

As the prominent role of injury in the health status of Native Americans became evident, planning for increased injury-prevention efforts by the IHS began in 1981. The Environmental Health Services Branch, traditionally responsible for such things as monitoring sanitation in hospitals, restaurants, and homes and

35–44 yr	45–54 yr	55–64 yr	65+ yr	Total
MV occupant (175)	MV occupant (83)	MV occupant (49)	Fall (68)	MV occupant (1,067)
Homicide (151)	Suicide (67)	Pedestrian (44)	MV occupant (56)	Suicide (821)
Suicide (151)	Pedestrian (62)	Natural/environmental (33)	Unspecified (45)	Homicide (761)
Poisoning (107)	Homicide (52)	Homicide (31)	Fire/burn (37)	Pedestrian (513)
Pedestrian (97)	MV other (44)	Fall (29)	Natural/environmental (36)	MV other (479)
MV other (75)	Poisoning (35)	Suicide (27)	Suffocation (26)	Poisoning (273)
Drowning (52)	Fall (26)	MV other (24)	Adverse effects (25)	Drowning (267)
Fall (34)	Natural/environmental (26)	Poisoning (15)	Pedestrian (24)	Fall (214)
All other causes (29)	Drowning (20)	Tied[d]	Suicide (23)	Fire/burn (196)
Natural/environmental (25)	Fire/burn (19)	Nephritis (54)	MV other (20)	Natural/environmental (168)

[c]Fall, pedestrian, unspecified (one each).
[d]Drowning, fire/burn, unspecified (12 each).
[e]Fall, natural/environmental, poisoning, struck by or against (two each).
[f]Pedal cyclist, poisoning, suffocation, other transport (three each).

inoculating animals against rabies, was given primary responsibility for the program. The environmental health officer in each Service Unit was asked to form a Community Injury Control (CIC) Committee. These committees included both clinical personnel and community members. Committee tasks were to establish priorities and develop programs to prevent injuries and reduce their severity. Implementation remained the responsibility of the environmental health officer.

A 1984 survey assessed the types and frequency of activities initiated by the CIC committees or environmental health personnel. The survey, patterned after the activity reports required of local environmental health officers, permitted an estimate of specific activities among various Indian populations. Among the 54 Service Units responding, the major focus was on training individuals to take precautions to avoid injury to themselves or family members; the training used

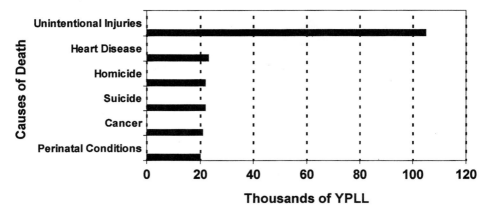

Figure 14.2. Leading causes of years of potential life lost (YPLL) of American Indians and Alaska Natives before age 65, 1990–92. *Source:* National Center for Health Statistics underlying-cause-of-death files

curricula, films, and demonstration materials from traditional safety organizations such as the National Safety Council and the American Red Cross. Although these programs covered an array of potential injuries, it was evident that reaching the entire population would not be accomplished at such a pace, even in the unlikely event that everyone in the population would be willing to participate in each program. Only one program, gun safety training, reached 10 percent of the population in a three-year period. More than two-thirds of the programs reached fewer than 2 percent of the population in that period. Given the variety of responsibilities of the environmental health officers and other CIC committee members and considering budget limits, the likelihood of an increase in these programs was problematic. Also, an evaluation of the effectiveness of many programs had not been carried out.

Preliminary Evaluation

The initial evaluation revealed deficiencies in the program but identified areas where some successes had been achieved and suggested areas of further emphasis. Although the IHS medical records are generally more complete than those of many health-care providers, the detail necessary to identify the type of injuries potentially changeable by the specific programs was often missing from outpatient records. During 1981–84, little change in the average number of outpatient visits per capita for injuries related to motor vehicles, falls, or assaults was noted. However, there was a dramatic reduction in the "other" category, suggesting that the increased interest in injuries had resulted in more accurate recording. Nevertheless, it was concluded that the use of routine out-patient records failed to provide the specificity necessary. On the other hand, inpatient records proved to be accurate in identifying the broad categories of injuries, falls, and motor vehicle collisions.

During 1982–84, trends in hospitalization from falls, motor vehicle accidents, and assaults per capita declined noticeably, with slight declines in suicide attempts, poisonings, fire/smoke injuries, and cutting and piercing. Regression models (Robertson 1986) disclosed large variations in injury trends among Service Units, and changes attributable to the injury-control activities were small.

However, significant reductions in the rates of hospitalization for falls were related to the percentage of the population that received general safety, recreational safety, first aid, and CPR training. Changes in other types of injuries were not significantly related to the percentage of the population receiving training for those specific activities. Since the severity of motor vehicle injuries was declining nationally, primarily due to motor vehicle safety standards (Robertson 1996), the decline in IHS hospitalizations for motor vehicle–related injuries was not necessarily due to local injury-control activities.

A New Approach

While the initial CIC efforts seemed to have some beneficial effect in decreasing injury from falls, the small proportion of the population reached, uncertainty that the programs addressed the highest-priority injuries, and the questionable effectiveness of the training approach for several types of injuries led to recommendations for modification of the program (Robertson 1988). Specific emphasis was placed on three principles: (1) specification of to whom, when, where, and how injuries occurred; (2) implementation of technical countermeasures known to be effective; and (3) follow-up to be sure that the technology is applied appropriately and is having the anticipated effect (Robertson 1992).

It was quickly learned that clinical data did not provide information on the multiplicity of factors involved in most injuries. The circumstances of injury often vary substantially among communities, requiring specification of the various elements contributing to a given injury. For example, in the case of motor vehicle occupants, injury-prevention options vary depending on the type of vehicle (car, truck, motorcycle), the angle of a crash, the objects struck, whether rollover occurs, and the location of the incident (e.g., at an intersection). Do the most severe injuries occur from running into objects placed too close to roadsides, from lack of guardrails on curves, or from ill-defined curve markings? If pedestrians or bicyclists are being struck, are they darting into roads or walking or riding beside the road or off-road? What proportion of each of these occurs on unlighted roads at night? Are people taking precautions, such as using seat belts, child restraints, or motorcycle and bicycle helmets?

Similar analyses may be applied to other types of injuries. For example, are falls mainly among the elderly or children slipping on level surfaces in their homes or from elevated points? Or are they mainly concentrated among workers or persons engaged in recreation or other activities? What are the specific surfaces or heights involved? Are drownings mainly among children in ponds and streams or adult hunters and fishers from capsized boats? Are house fires caused more often by dropped cigarettes (as in the population generally) or by cooking, space heating, or other activities? Do deaths from fires occur more frequently among persons while asleep? If so, where are these persons sleeping relative to potential exits?

Thus, without data on who, when, where, and how people are injured, injury-prevention activities can be substantially misdirected. When the answers to these questions are known, options for injury control are often obvious or deducible from systematic reviews of technical options. For example, Haddon (1970) identified 10 general options for the control of injury-producing hazards, including biological and other hazards: (1) prevent the creation of the hazard, (2) reduce the concentration of amounts of the hazard, (3) prevent the release of concentrations of the hazard, (4) modify the rate or spatial distribution of the hazard, (5) separate those to be protected by time or space, (6) use physical barriers, (7) modify basic qualities of the hazard, (8) make people more resistant, (9) begin to counter damage in the emergency phase, and (10) stabilize, repair, and rehabilitate.

To obtain data on the various specific elements of injury needed to target programs more efficiently, supplemental data forms were developed for each of the major types of injury: motor vehicle collisions, falls, drownings, fire-smoke injuries, assaults, and suicides. Since the most costly and debilitating injuries may not occur to the same populations or in the same circumstances as less serious injuries, collection of data was recommended only for fatal and hospitalized cases or if the individual experienced a fracture or loss of consciousness. Analysis of data collected in this way provided information that permitted more appropriate and targeted interventions. The CIC Committees were also encouraged to develop pin maps of the locations of subsets of related types of injuries to identify sections of roads, types of housing, the proximity to taverns, and similar locational factors that might increase the efficiency of programs by concentrating efforts at specific locations.

Based on the clear need for training in data interpretation and choice of countermeasures, the IHS, in 1987, initiated an injury-control specialist fellowship program that allows tribal and IHS personnel to receive training in injury control intermittently over a year while attending to their usual duties (Smith 1988). Ten to 20 applicants have been selected each year to attend four courses and complete an analysis of injury data or of an implementation problem. At the end of the year, a presentation at IHS headquarters and the submission of a written report result in certification as an injury prevention specialist. The value of this training has been repeatedly demonstrated, both during the fellowship year and in subsequent projects.

This is not to say that all of the successes in reducing injury among Indians were initiated by persons who had such formal training. Before the supplemental data collection or fellowship program began, an x-ray technician in Cherokee, North Carolina, noticed that pedestrians were being struck on a curve with no sidewalk and poor visibility. She persuaded the local government and state highway department to widen the road and install sidewalks. Later she took part in the injury prevention specialist fellowship and became a leader in the field.

Successful Interventions

Alaska Drownings

Noting that drowning was the leading cause of injury deaths in Alaska and that personal flotation devices were seldom used, the Injury Prevention Program of the Yukon Kuskokwin Health Corporation initiated a "float coat" program. Float coats have the appearance of regular coats but have built-in buoyancy so that the wearer will not sink in water. It was reasoned that, since people generally wear coats in cold climates, the substitution of float coats for ordinary coats should result in fewer drownings. There are social-psychological barriers to self-protection, such as fatalism or the fear of appearing to be weak, but wearing the coats conveys no sign of concern, or lack of concern, for safety. A disadvantage, however, is that they are more expensive. To promote the use of float coats, a coalition of local leaders, health professionals, and merchants offered and promoted the coats at discounted prices in sizes, color schemes, and styles that would appeal to the population. Local media cooperated with promotions.

Since the initiation of the program, drownings have declined about 30 percent in the targeted area. This success has persuaded other Native corporations in Alaska to adopt the program. Challenged by such local efforts, the state legislature enacted legislation to require that all children under 13 years of age must use flotation devices when in boats in Alaska.

Injuries to Motor Vehicle Occupants

Aware that injuries to motor vehicle occupants were by far the leading cause of severe injury and death in the Navajo Nation, injury-control specialists undertook surveys of seat belt use (Centers for Disease Control 1992). The use rate was about 10 percent. In 1988, the Navajo Council revamped the Motor Vehicle Safety Code. New tribal laws required that seat belts and motorcycle helmets be used. Noting the high proportion of Indians reporting that they had ridden with a driver who was drinking alcohol (Oken et al. 1995), the illegal level of blood alcohol while operating a motor vehicle was reduced to 0.08 g/dL. After a two-year phase-in period, during which the new requirements were widely publicized, the Navajo Nation's Police Department began issuing citations for nonuse of seat belts. The local government, the police, and the Bureau of Indian Affairs worked closely with the IHS in this effort. A health promotion grant by the Robert Wood Johnson Foundation helped cover the costs of the public information and education phase of the effort. During the 1990s, with active enforcement, belt use increased markedly, reaching 70 percent by 1996, and hospitalizations for motor vehicle-related injuries declined more than 28 percent.

Pedestrian Injuries

A study of the first 150 cases of injury surveyed by the CIC Committee of the White Mountain Apache Indian Reservation identified two frequent injury problems — pedestrians struck at night in a certain 1.1-mile stretch of road in Whiteriver, one of the population centers, and collisions of motor vehicles with large animals on reservation roads (Rothfus and Akin 1985). The committee decided first to attempt reduction of pedestrian injuries. The injury-prevention specialist reviewed the literature on motor vehicle injuries and concluded that illumination of roads in problem areas at night was among the most cost-effective countermeasures. When the findings were presented to the tribal council, other tribal committees, and key agencies, a coalition was formed to obtain overhead lighting in the location of the cluster of pedestrian injuries. Approximately twenty-seven thousand dollars was raised, and the lighting was installed. The numbers of pedestrians struck at night declined from about 30 during the five years before the lighting to 2 during the same period afterward. The news of this success resulted in lighting projects on four other reservations, again with similarly impressive results.

In Browning, Montana, a center of the Blackfeet Tribe, a cluster of 59 severe motor vehicle injuries, including 13 fatalities, occurred over a seven-year period on a short stretch of road between two taverns. The injuries were mostly to pedestrians crossing the road, but some pedestrians and vehicle occupants were injured in collisions when vehicles were leaving the parking areas along the road. When presented the data, local citizens, the local electrical utility, the State of Montana Highway Department, and the IHS collaborated to remedy the problem. At a cost of only sixty-five hundred dollars, overhead lights were installed along the highway between the taverns and concrete barriers were installed along the parking areas to channel the traffic to controlled entry and exit points. There were only two severe injuries at the site in the two years following completion of the project. A significant related cause of pedestrian mortality is that associated with alcohol-related hypothermia (Gallaher et al. 1992), occasioned by individuals beginning a long walk home from off-reservation taverns.

Collisions with Domestic Animals

Indians are also at relatively greater risk of farm injuries (Crandall et al. 1997), especially those related to tractor rollover, alcohol use, and electrocution. Domestic animal collisions are also prominent and are especially susceptible to correction. A health educator in the White Mountain Apache health program, without training in injury control, suspected that large domestic animals wandering on public roads were a hazard. He investigated and learned that injury-control specialists had documented injuries from collisions of motor vehicles and domestic animals. He also learned that the tribal council had previously been concerned about the problem and had adopted a 1976 ordinance prohibiting owners from letting their animals stray onto the road. The issue had been before the council several times since, the educator was told by his father, a respected former member of the council, but a means of strong enforcement had not been adopted. At least part of the problem was the lack of indication of concern from the community.

The health educator decided to do a survey of community opinion of the issue. He recruited several friends to distribute a survey form in major population districts of the reservation, soliciting opinions of the presence of livestock on the roads. The results were overwhelmingly in favor of active and strong enforcement of the ordinance. Armed with this evidence, he briefed members of the council. A special session of the council was convened, and an ordinance directing the police to enforce the prohibition of livestock on the roads was adopted. Further, $10,000 was appropriated to pay a wrangler to capture stray animals and take them to a stockade, where owners were required to pay a fine to retrieve their animals. The health educator went on to participate in the injury-prevention specialist fellowship and, as part of his project, documented a

60 percent decline in the number of collisions between motor vehicles and domestic animals after implementation of enforcement in 1994.

Other Programs

Numerous other projects have been undertaken regarding such important issues as smoke detector installations and their readiness, hot water scalds, falls among elderly persons, use of child restraints in motor vehicles, and channeling traffic at high-crash intersections. Anecdotes abound about action on matters as simple as a misplaced stop sign or a bush obstructing sight at intersections where one or more people have been injured. In many instances, the populations affected or numbers of injury cases are too small to establish statistical significance of efforts in the relatively short time since implementation.

In other cases, the implementation of countermeasures has stalled because of a lack of funds or other problems. For example, one fellowship project found large differences in dimensions and levelness of porch steps and absence of handrails and lighting in households in which an older person had a fall injury on the steps compared to other randomly selected households in the community. Attempts to implement a porch step repair program have been delayed by a variety of questions: Is step repair appropriate when the remainder of the house is severely dilapidated? Who is going to pay for the repairs? What standards should be applied to contractors when each porch and its steps have unique qualities? How can the work be monitored to assure that the standards are met?

Recent Developments in Injury-Prevention Programs

The IHS Injury Prevention initiative has undergone several significant changes since the 1970s. In the early years (1950s–60s), efforts of the Division of Indian Health to address injuries were largely health education programs attempting to change human behavior. This was exemplified by extensive film libraries, safety pamphlets, and assorted paraphernalia. Robertson's evaluation recommended de-emphasis on public information/education activities and a corresponding increased emphasis on developing community-based injury surveillance systems (Robertson 1986). Interventions should emphasize changes in the physical environment whenever feasible. Many IHS field environmental health programs began gathering community-specific data on factors contributing to injury causation and/or severity.

Since that time, measures have been taken to broaden the quality of the injury-prevention program. Some of the advances include:

Before 1985	Primary emphasis on public information and education
1985	Adoption of community-based surveillance systems
1988	Adoption of the concept of coalition building
1990	Development of complete injury-prevention models
1993	Increased emphasis on tribal capacity building
1997	First grants for tribal injury-prevention infrastructure projects

In addition, in the 1990s, a five-year injury-prevention plan was developed. This plan outlined a comprehensive framework for future program enhancement integrated at local, regional, and national levels. The IHS Injury Prevention Program has developed a simple model for community-based interventions, comprising seven general components. Prevention efforts are often initiated because of a particular issue or concern (e.g., an elderly patient may be seen in an emergency room as a result of a fall from the steps of the patient's home). This might prompt a review of background data through review of medical records for similar events during the previous few years. This survey leads to a case definition, and all cases meeting the criteria are investigated further. Data analysis then examines the presence or absence of trends. If a determination is made that an intervention should be implemented, persons who have a potential role in prevention efforts are recruited to be part of a team or coalition to address the problem. An action plan with specific objectives is then developed. Finally, the intervention phase is monitored on a regular basis, and an annual evaluation is conducted to determine results.

Discussion

A gratifying trend is the increased participation of tribal members in the fellowship and other training courses devoted to injury control. As a result of these programs, several tribes have full-time injury-prevention coordinators who develop and implement projects, sometimes in collaboration with their IHS counterparts but often without additional assistance. Unfortunately, a full-time injury coordinator cannot be supported by the majority of tribes who live in communities too small for such resources. Those who understand the importance of using data to set priorities, choose technically effective countermeasures, and involve community members or state and federal agencies in a position to implement the countermeasures are likely to make a contribution, no matter what their vocational duties.

One important lesson that IHS injury-prevention trainees learn is that resources outside the tribe or the IHS can often be tapped to implement countermeasures, as illustrated by the cases cited. Monies are generally available in state and federal highway budgets for road modifications. To have them allocated to a road on or near a reservation, however, one must present complete and accurate data to convince the highway department that the site in question has priority. Tribes that do not send crash reports to state governments, whether based on sovereignty grounds or concern for expenses, may have difficulty convincing highway departments that they have a problem and may lose their shares of such outside funds.

A major justification for increased injury prevention is its potential for cost savings. The rising costs of medical care are driving health maintenance organizations and managed care organizations to devote greater attention to effective prevention strategies. Although many Service Units do not have broad-ranging injury-prevention programs, such programs should appeal to those concerned with costs. Injury prevention has immediate benefits in cost reduction, often at very modest outlays, as noted in the brief case reports. While the reduction of diseases such as cancer and heart disease is important, the benefits of preventive efforts are usually not realized until years after preventive measures are implemented. The initial response of a community may be that it cannot afford injury control. After understanding the economic and other costs, the response may be that the community cannot afford to be without it.

Gradually, especially after 1980, state-of-the-art emergency medical services (EMS) programs began to be implemented in many, but unfortunately not all, Indian communities (Rousseau, Jensen, and Decker 1993). There are currently approximately 70 EMS programs, essentially all operated by tribes, in the "lower 48" states, providing the only prehospital EMS care for more than 500,000 Native Americans in approximately 20 states (P. Decker, pers. comm., 1999). A 1993 assessment by the National Highway Transportation Administration, while lauding local and individual efforts, was critical of the overall level of IHS support for the program (National Highway Transportation Administration 1993), pointing out the need for increased personnel and training and the need for Congress and the IHS to recognize EMS as an integral part of the overall Indian program.

REFERENCES

Baker SP, O'Neill B, Ginsburg MJ, et al. 1992. *The Injury Fact Book*. 2d ed. New York: Oxford University Press.
Ballard JE, Koepsell TD, Rivara FP, et al. 1992. Descriptive epidemiology of unintentional residential fire injuries in King County, WA, 1984 and 1985. *Public Health Rep* 107:402–8.
Berger LR, Mohan D. 1996. *Injury Control: A Global View*. Delhi: Oxford University Press.

Centers for Disease Control. 1992. Safety-belt use and motor-vehicle-related injuries, Navajo Nation. *MMWR* 41:705–8.

Crandall CS, Fullerton L, Olson L, et al. 1997. Farm-related injury mortality in New Mexico, 1980–91. *Accid Anal Prev* 29:257–61.

Gallaher MM, Fleming DW, Berger LR, et al. 1992. Pedestrian and hypothermia deaths among Native Americans in New Mexico between bar and home. *JAMA* 267:1345–48.

Gilliland FD, Becker TM, Samet JM, et al. 1995. Trends in alcohol-related mortality among New Mexico's American Indians, Hispanics, and non-Hispanic Whites. *Alcohol Clin Exp Res* 19:1572–77.

Haddon W Jr. 1970. On the escape of tigers: An ecologic note. *Technol Rev* 72:44–48.

Indian Health Service. 1997. *Trends in Indian Health, 1997.* Rockville, Md.: Indian Health Service, Program Statistics Team.

National Highway Transportation Administration. 1993. *Indian Health Service: An Assessment of Emergency Medical Services.* Report of the Technical Assistance Team, National Highway Transportation Administration. Rockville, Md.: Indian Health Service, Emergency Medical Services Program.

Oken E, Lightdale JR, Welty TK. 1995. Along for the ride: The prevalence of motor vehicle passengers riding with drivers who have been drinking in an American Indian population. *Am J Prev Med* 11(6):375–80.

Olson LM, Becker TM, Wiggins CL, et al. 1990. Injury mortality in American Indian, Hispanic, and non-Hispanic White children in New Mexico, 1958–1982. *Soc Sci Med* 30:479–86.

Robertson LS. 1986. Community injury control programs of the Indian Health Service: An early assessment. *Public Health Rep* 101:632–37.

———. 1988. Epidemiological assessment of the contributing factors of injury mortality and morbidity among Native Americans. Springfield, Va.: National Technical Information Service.

———. 1992. *Injury Epidemiology.* New York: Oxford University Press.

———. 1996. Reducing death on the road: The effects of minimum safety standards, publicized crash tests, seat belts, and alcohol. *Am J Public Health* 86:31–34.

Rothfus G, Akin D. 1985. Motor vehicle collisions on White Mountain Apache Indian Reservation. Unpublished document. Rockville, Md.: Indian Health Service, Injury Prevention Program.

Rousseau CJ, Jensen G, Decker P. 1993. National EMS Program Staff's Perspective on Emergency Medical Services in the Indian Health Service. Unpublished document. Rockville, Md.: Indian Health Service.

Sewell CM, Becker TM, Wiggins CL, et al. 1989. Injury mortality in New Mexico's American Indians, Hispanics, and non-Hispanic Whites, 1958 to 1982. *West J Med* 150:708–13.

Smith RJ. 1988. IHS Fellows Program aimed at lowering injuries, deaths of Indians, Alaska Natives. *Public Health Rep* 103:204.

Sugarman JR, Grossman DC. 1996. Trauma among American Indians in an urban county. *Public Health Rep* 111:321–27.

Sugarman JR, Soderberg R, Gordon JE, et al. 1993. Racial misclassification of American Indians: Its effect on injury rates in Oregon, 1989 through 1990. *Am J Public Health* 83:681–84.

15

Lawrence S. Wissow, M.D., M.P.H.

Suicide among American Indians and Alaska Natives

Suicide is a problem that spans the world's cultures, causing an estimated 1.4 million deaths a year (Desjarlais et al. 1995). Suicides take place in both industrialized and developing societies and in rural and urban areas. However, suicide is a particularly important public health issue for American Indian communities. Indian Health Service (IHS) compilations for 1992–94 put the rate of completed suicides among American Indians and Alaska Natives at 19.2/ 100,000/year (age-adjusted to the U.S. population and adjusted for ethnic misclassification), about one and a half times the rate for the U.S. population as a whole. This overall ratio, however, hides an even more disturbing figure, the excess of suicide deaths among Indian youth. Suicide is second only to nonintentional injuries as a cause of death among Indians aged 15–24 (Indian Health Service 1997b). The adjusted rates of suicide death in that age group (37.1/ 100,000 for 1992–94) are 2.7 times those in the general population.

Among concerns that arise when discussing Indian morbidity, suicide is one of the most sensitive and difficult. The student approaching the subject must be aware of ongoing debates that color decisions about what constitutes valid data and how the data should be interpreted. One debate centers on the extent to which "indigenous knowledge," or culturally specific explanations of feelings and behavior, should be explored to understand the causes and treatment of Indian suicide, or whether paradigms arising from European scientific traditions of sociology or psychology should be applied (Purcell 1998). Medical anthropologists tend to argue that culturally specific explanatory models play a determining role in how individuals respond to symptoms, the kind of help sought, and ultimately the course of an illness (Angel and Thoits 1987; Kirmayer, Young, and Robbins 1994). In contrast, proponents of "universal" theories from European traditions suggest that an emphasis on local culture, in fact, detracts from understanding. May and Van Winkle (1994b, 297–98), applying

Durkheim's conceptualization of suicide to American Indian data, state that "the focus on the uniqueness of each tribal culture can only go so far in promoting the type of understanding of social behavior which is most useful for proposing practical and transferable solutions in such areas as . . . the prevention of behavioral health problems."

A third group, largely based on their work as Western-trained clinicians in Indian communities, suggests that explanations from both local cultural and Western medical perspectives are simultaneously important in the development of health programs (Jecker, Carrese, and Pearlman 1995). This third view parallels that of Devereux (1985), an anthropologist who studied the Mojave during first half of the twentieth century. For Devereux, it was not only possible but also "obligatory" to be able to explain any human behavior from at least two independent systems of reference. Behind this requirement was Devereaux's belief that explanations from any one point of view inevitably are colored by the methods of observation themselves. Thus, at least two "complementary" explanations are needed — and more are better — if one truly seeks understanding.

This debate has more than theoretical significance. First, as noted in Chapter 1, within the United States, American Indian peoples can be divided into several geographical and cultural groups, a number of major language stocks, and about 550 individual tribes, including Alaska Native villages (Thomas et al. 1993; U.S. Bureau of the Census 1994; *Federal Register* 1996). Although many native languages are threatened with extinction, many remain in active use and play a central role in cultural identity. In the 1990 Census, 23 percent of those who identified themselves as American Indian reported that they spoke a language other than English. Seventy-four percent of Navajo and 61 percent of Pueblo Indians reported speaking a language other than English (U.S. Bureau of the Census 1994). Especially across major language and cultural groups, tribes have distinct knowledge and beliefs about well-being, illness, and social organization. Thus, if one subscribes to a need to work within a cultural framework, each community must be approached separately.

Second, the debate has personal meaning for tribal members who are invested in revitalizing their cultures and re-enforcing their distinctiveness against the influence of European American culture (Medicine 1998). Tribal members repeatedly make the case that it is difficult even to express in English — as opposed to their own languages — their distinct way of experiencing life (Lyons 1995). To overemphasize European universalist explanations for suicide and other health problems implicitly risks derogating this rebirth and risks appearing to be one more example of social and medical constructs imposed upon Indian populations, often with untoward results.

This chapter presents theories and data from both within-culture and universalist (sociologic and psychiatric) frameworks. Discussion of prevention and treatment will be based on the third perspective cited above — that complementary observations from inside and outside Indian cultures have been suggested to be most promising, and that individual tribes have much to offer each other as they in turn address the problem of suicide.

The Extent of the Problem

Suicide is among the 10 leading causes of death of Indians 10–54 years old. Among those aged 10–14, it is in third place; among those aged 15–24, it is in second place; and among those aged 25–34, it is in third place. Only after age 35, when heart diseases and cancer become more common, does suicide begin to occupy a lower place among the 10 leading causes of death (see Table 7.2). For all Indians, it is the seventh leading cause of death (Indian Health Service 1997b). As noted above, the rate (adjusted for ethnic misclassification) of completed suicides among American Indians for 1992–94 was 19.2/100,000 (age-adjusted to the U.S. population). Suicide rates for Canadian Natives are reported to be even higher (about 30/100,000), but figures age-adjusted to the general U.S. population are not available (Kirmayer 1994). In both countries these rates are about one and a half to three times those of the general population.

The true extent of suicide attempts is not known in either Indian or non-Indian communities, but one survey of students attending Native community middle and high schools found that 17 percent of respondents had made at least one attempt in their lifetime; 11 percent said they had made an attempt in the past year (Blum et al. 1992). These figures, while high, are nearly identical to the findings of another survey of the general U.S. population, in which 10 percent of high school girls and 6 percent of boys reported making one or more attempts in the past year (Centers for Disease Control 1991).

Trends over Time

Few accurate data are available regarding Indian suicide in precolonization times or even in the early part of the twentieth century. Most historians indicate that, before the arrival of Europeans, suicide was probably rare and seen as a tragedy or improper among most tribes (Lester 1997). Some accounts report a tradition among subarctic tribes of altruistic suicide by the seriously ill, the disabled, and those in mourning or as a response to insoluble marital problems, but other scholars doubt that this was ever prevalent (Kirmayer 1994). Everett (1975), reviewing Western Apache records dating back to the beginning of the twentieth century, suggested that suicide among that tribal group was probably rare until about the 1930s, when it began to increase. Levy and Kunitz (1987),

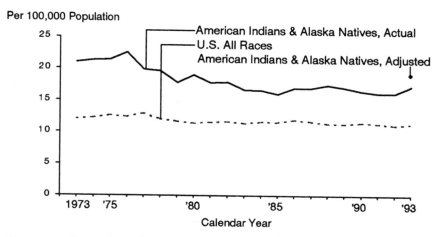

Figure 15.1. Comparison of the trend in age-adjusted suicide death rates of American Indians with U.S. All Races, since 1973. For 1993, a rate adjusted for racial misclassification is shown by the *diamond point. Source:* Indian Health Service 1997b, Chart 4.21

in their study of Hopi records, came to a similar conclusion, believing that present rates of suicide did not evolve until the middle of the twentieth century.

The trend in suicide death rates since 1973 is shown in Figure 15.1. Overall, the rate of suicide among the IHS service population gradually declined between 1972 and about 1985, with the (unadjusted for ethnic misclassification) rate declining from 21/100,000 in 1972–74 to 17.2/100,000 in 1992–94 (Indian Health Service 1997b). However, for the past several years the rate of suicide deaths has been fairly constant. A decrease in firearm-related deaths among young people (ages 15–24) may be the main factor behind the overall trend, but, as noted above, this may be partially offset by a rise in deaths among the elderly. Other possible explanations include changes in the population served by the IHS: more tribes have been recognized by the federal government and qualify for IHS services, and an increasing proportion of U.S. Natives live outside tribal reservations or in urban areas (see Chapter 3). Given the apparent relationship of suicide to poverty (see below), the decreases observed are even more significant. According to U.S. census figures, the proportion of American Indians living below the poverty level increased from 28.2 percent in 1980 to 31.6 percent in 1989 (Indian Health Service 1990, 1997b).

The same IHS data, analyzed by the Centers for Disease Control, suggest that trends over time have not been uniform among regions of the country (Wallace et al. 1996). Alaska and, to a lesser extent, the Navajo reservation have experienced moderate increases, while other IHS Service Areas have experienced grad-

ual decreases. Van Winkle and May (1993), analyzing New Mexico death certificates from 1957 to 1987, found marked differences among tribal groups.
Suicide rates for Navajos in New Mexico began to rise in the 1970s, peaked in
1976, and, with some variation, declined and then stabilized in the 1980s. In
contrast, Apache rates fluctuated widely in five- to six-year cycles, with gradually decreasing peaks in 1968, 1975, 1980, and 1985. Pueblo rates fluctuated on
a less marked and longer cycle: their peaks gradually increased from 1968
through 1983 and then declined.

Trends by Age

One of the factors that has most distinguished Indian suicide deaths from patterns in the general population is the predominance of deaths among the young
(Figure 15.2). From 1979 through 1992, males aged 15–34 accounted for 64
percent of all Indian suicides (Wallace et al. 1996). Both male and female rates
peak in the 15–24 age group (males at about 62/100,000 and females at about
11/100,000) (Wallace et al. 1996) and then decline with increasing age. In contrast, in the general population suicides occur predominantly among the elderly.
The suicide rate among Indians aged 45–54 is basically the same as that for U.S.
Whites, at 15.6 and 15.7/100,000, respectively (Indian Health Service 1997b).

A recurring question in the epidemiology of Indian suicide is how to distinguish enduring patterns from more recent trends that may be the result of

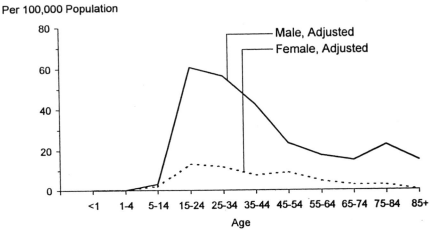

Figure 15.2. Distribution of suicide death rates of American Indians, by age and gender,
1992–94. *Source:* Indian Health Service 1997b, Chart 4.22

changing social conditions and the influence of outside cultures. In Alaska, the emergence of suicide as a problem among younger Natives seems to be relatively recent; before the 1960s, suicide deaths among Alaska Natives were more prevalent in the elderly (Kraus and Buffler 1979). Among the Hopi, the young-predominant pattern appears to have been present at least since the 1950s (Levy and Kunitz 1987). However, for Indians and Alaska Natives as a whole, these patterns may be shifting. From 1979 through 1992, suicide rates in the 15–24-year age group decreased, while rates among those aged 65 and over increased by almost 200 percent. The increase in the comparable overall U.S. elderly population was about 15 percent (Wallace et al. 1996). Suicide rates among the Indian elderly, however, are still less than half those among the overall U.S. elderly population (about 8 versus 20/100,000) (Indian Health Service 1997b).

Geographical Variations

As reflected in Figure 15.3, considerable variation in rates of suicide among Indians of various IHS Areas is observed. Rates are relatively low in the California, Oklahoma, Nashville, Bemidji, and Navajo Areas compared to those experienced in the Phoenix, Albuquerque, Aberdeen, and Alaska Areas. Even correcting for ethnic misclassification on death certificates, some of the differences are quite large. However, among Indians in all the Areas except California and Oklahoma, suicide rates exceed that for the general U.S. population.

Recent (1992–94) data place Alaska Natives as having the highest rate of completed suicides among those within the IHS service population (43.6/100,000). Excluding Oklahoma and California, where ethnic misclassification is especially common, the Nashville Area (which includes the southeast United States as well as some tribes in Texas, the mid-Atlantic states, and New England) has the lowest rate: 14.2/100,000 (about the same as the U.S. average) (Indian Health Service 1997a). During this three-year period, 18 percent of the 639 recorded suicide deaths among the IHS service population occurred in Alaska. Alaska is the only IHS Area in which suicide ranked among the top five causes of death. These rankings, however, vary from year to year. At times the rate of suicide deaths in the Billings Area (Montana and Wyoming) has exceeded that in Alaska.

Interpreting geographical variation is complicated, however, because many reservation-based Indian populations live in parts of the United States where other residents also have relatively high rates of suicide. Detailed comparisons of suicide rates in Arizona and New Mexico, for example, disclose that Indian rates are similar to or only marginally higher than those for non-Hispanic White residents (Becker et al. 1990; Phoenix Area Indian Health Service n.d.). In the

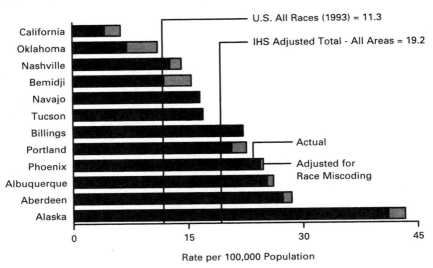

Figure 15.3. Comparison of age-adjusted suicide death rates of American Indians in the IHS Service Areas and with U.S. All Races, 1992–94. In certain states, adjustments for racial miscoding on death certificates are shown. *Source:* Indian Health Service 1997a, Chart 4.19

general population, suicide rates in the Mountain West (Montana, Idaho, Wyoming, Colorado, New Mexico, Arizona, Utah, and Nevada) are 35–40 percent higher than the U.S. average and have been rising at a faster than average rate (May and Van Winkle 1994a). For the period 1990–94, the age-adjusted rate of suicide in the western United States (14.1/100,000) was 70 percent higher than the rate of suicide in the Northeast (8.6/100,000) (Centers for Disease Control and Prevention 1997). It is not known what factors are responsible for this trend, which is also reflected in higher than average death rates from nonintentional injuries (Baker, O'Neill, and Karpf 1984).

Gender Differences

Among the IHS service population, suicide is the fifth leading cause of death among Indian males but is not in the top 10 leading causes of death among Indian women (Indian Health Service 1997b). In both Indian and other U.S. populations, the rate of completed suicides among males far exceeds that among females (see Figure 15.2), but suicide attempts are more frequent among females. In some parts of the United States, however, the relative excess of suicide deaths among Indian males (compared to females) is even further increased. In the general U.S. population, about four men die by suicide for each female victim. Across the IHS Service Areas, the male:female ratios for 1979–92 ranged from a low of 3.7 (in the Bemidji Area) to a high of 17 (54.0 vs. 3.2/100,000) in the Albuquerque Area (which includes Colorado, New Mexico, and parts of Texas) (Wallace et al. 1996). The Navajo Area had the next highest ratio, 9.8:1 (31.2 vs. 3.2/100,000). Levy and Kunitz (1987) found that the male:female ratio for suicides among the Hopi tribe in Arizona was about 13:1, and this pattern seemed to have been stable over many years.

The reasons for this even greater excess of suicide deaths among males are not known. In the general population, the excess of male deaths is thought to be related, at least in part, to the fact that men chose more dangerous means of suicide (firearms or hanging) more often than the somewhat less lethal means used predominantly by women (ingestion). This pattern is also seen among Indians. Some of the difference could also be attributable to variation in the availability of medical care after an attempt or the ease with which persons in rural areas can commit suicide without being discovered (thus increasing the lethality of rapidly fatal mechanisms of death). Support for this hypothesis comes from the observation that the male:female ratio among suicides in the general population is also higher in the western United States (May and Van Winkle 1994a).

Possible Causes of Native American Suicide

The Loss of Traditional Culture

A widely held hypothesis about Indian suicide is that its increase in the post-colonization era relates to a loss of the support and structure inherent in traditional culture. As noted above, suicides seem to have been rare before colonization by Europeans. Many traditional religious, social, and curative practices became rare or were lost in postcolonization times. These losses often came as a result of policies instituted by Western religious denominations and the federal government and in the course of forced relocations, which often scattered families and separated tribes from their traditional homelands. Simultaneously, tribal cultures were directly challenged by the beliefs and practices of Western culture. Indians were encouraged or prodded to look down on their traditional beliefs and embrace Western social and economic thinking (Brown 1970; Hall 1994). Durkheim's construct of "anomie"—demoralization resulting from the breakdown of social order and a subsequent lack of social regulation—predicts that suicide should increase under these circumstances (Roy 1989).

Exposure to Western Culture

Berry et al. (1992) separate "acculturation" into two processes. First, the culture within which one lives changes, forcing individuals to confront new situations with different rules. Second, individuals in these situations have to decide personally how to respond, including decisions to abandon or maintain former ways of doing things. Individuals from minority cultures are often pressured to abandon their own ways entirely. For example, in some American Indian communities, traditional values hold that it is wrong for individuals openly to compete with each other or cause others shame by appearing to be more successful. This creates dilemmas for young Indians in Western-run schools that encourage competition by grading and ranking students and then publicly honoring those who do best (Berlin 1987).

A similar example related to mental health treatment involves differing Western and Indian views about the causes of emotional distress. Although Western theory includes mental distress among medical conditions and promotes treatment as something that should be sought in a quasi-public manner without stigma (though stigma certainly remains), many Indian communities view emotional problems as outside the medical realm and often as resulting from relatively stigmatizing causes, such as witching or improper conduct (Everett 1971). Western-driven attempts to identify at-risk individuals or bring them to easily visible, clinic-based services might actually increase risk rather than reduce it (Levy and Kunitz 1987).

Exposure to a new and dominant culture can cause emotional distress among members of a dominated minority. Sami (a contemporary Scandinavian Native population) adolescents reported increased levels of emotional distress regardless of where they lived, but distress levels were higher in communities where Sami were in a minority (and where there were conflicts over what language should be spoken, among other issues) compared to communities with a Sami majority, where Sami language and family structure were more intact (Kvernmo and Heyerdahl 1998).

Contemporary analyses of U.S. tribes suggest that successful ongoing cultural adaptation may be more protective against suicide than either strict adherence to traditional practices or abandonment of tradition. For example, Levy and Kunitz (1987) argued that, among the Hopi, individuals labeled as deviant were at highest risk for suicide. This labeling often came about because the individuals were products of marriages that made sense in contemporary economic terms but violated traditional patterns. Levy and Kunitz suggested that adhering rigidly to traditional culture would foreclose the tribe's ability to adapt and could be just as harmful as completely abandoning traditional values. Zitzow and Desjarlait (1994), in an analysis of suicide attempts within four Ojibway communities, found that communities at opposite ends of the traditional-acculturated spectrum had the highest rates of attempts. Adult attempts were associated with the most traditional community, while adolescent attempts were associated with the most cross-culturally influenced. Not all analyses have found similar trends, however. Van Winkle and May (1986), examining suicide rates in New Mexico, noted that tribes they labeled as acculturated or transitional had higher rates of suicide than did those labeled as traditional.

Social Integration

May and Van Winkle (1994b) proposed that, at a tribal level, Native American suicide rates can best be explained by an interaction of these cultural stresses with the tribe's underlying level of social integration, which Durkeim also proposed would be related to the prevalence of suicide. May and Van Winkle defined social integration as a set of processes that form groups of individuals into yet larger groups. In low-integration communities, individuals belong to few permanent groups — usually only their immediate family or band — and overall come under few expectations for their behavior to adhere to any particular set of rules. In high-integration communities, individuals belong to multiple groups and feel strong pressure to adhere to behavioral norms. May and Van Winkle postulated that suicide rates would vary inversely with social integration and directly with the level of disorganization related to exposure to outside influences. They were able to show that published suicide rates for a selected group of tribes fit this pattern.

Associations with Alcoholism and Psychiatric Conditions

From the viewpoint of contemporary psychiatric research, suicide is largely explicable as a complication of mental illness, personality, and substance abuse. Posthumous psychiatric diagnoses of suicide victims in developed countries (based on reviewing medical records and talking to friends and family members) consistently find that the overwhelming majority of victims had a major mood disorder (depression or bipolar illness), a problem with conduct that caused harm to others, alcohol or drug problems, or some combination of these (Hirschfeld and Russell 1997). A widely accepted model for youth suicide involves children developing problems with conduct early in life, gradually associating with more deviant members of their peer group, adopting the use of alcohol and drugs, and ultimately succumbing to stresses that result in suicide (Shaffer et al. 1988).

Support for the applicability of this theory to American Indians is derived from data suggesting that both suicide and medical problems associated with alcohol are more common among Native populations than in the general population (Indian Health Service 1997b). Van Winkle and May (1993), in their analysis of completed suicides in New Mexico, found that the prevalence of positive tests for alcohol among Native American suicide victims (about 60–70%) exceeded that of non-Native victims (45%). Jarvis and Boldt (1982), in a systematic study of Native deaths in Alberta, found measurable blood alcohol levels in 72 percent of suicide victims; about 60 percent were said by significant others to have been problem drinkers.

One line of reasoning suggests that the association between alcohol and suicide among Indians is fallacious — both occur at elevated rates, but they have no causal connection. Evidence supporting this argument includes the observation that the prevalence of drinking among Native American youth (at least those attending school) may not be any greater than that in same-age non-Native populations (Office of Technology Assessment 1990). Particular patterns of drinking, rather than the simple prevalence of alcohol use, may be a better indicator of suicide risk. Grossman, Milligan, and Deyo (1991), examining data from Navajo youth, found that self-reports of suicide attempts were increased among those who drank hard liquor on a weekly basis, but risk was not elevated among those who drank only beer or wine.

On the other hand, there is a theoretical basis for proposing a causal link between alcohol and suicide. Most psychoactive substances decrease inhibitions and thus contribute to impulsive acts; withdrawal from alcohol and other intoxicants can be associated with depression and disordered thought processes, which might lead to misperceptions of social interactions and poor judgment about the consequences of potentially harmful acts. Everett (1971), in his study of the White Mountain Apache, proposed that group drinking (which had existed before contact with Western society but involved lower potency Native alcoholic beverages) created opportunities in which, because of lowered inhibitions, unintended slights and minor disagreements were difficult to resolve under Apache codes of interpersonal conduct. In that context, suicide or a suicide attempt could occur as a way of eliciting remorse or an apology from a perceived aggressor. Levy and Kunitz (1987), in their study of the Hopi, noted that alcohol use might act in another way — as a stigmatized behavior that could isolate an individual or family from the rest of the community. They found that suicide victims were more likely than other Hopi individuals to come from socially "deviant" families — families that had a history of traditionally disapproved behaviors such as public drunkenness or marriage across forbidden family, clan, or social lines. The risk of suicide seemed particularly strong for the children of these families. Shameful behavior on the part of parents seemed to result in shameful feelings among their children, which were then reinforced by the community's ongoing negative judgment of the parents' behavior.

There are similar difficulties marshaling data to support the relationship between mood disorders (such as depression) and elevated rates of suicide among Indians. There have been relatively few studies of the prevalence of mood disorders among Indian populations, and they have yielded conflicting results with regard to whether the prevalence of mood problems is greater or less than in the general population (Office of Technology Assessment 1990). Exploring this hypothesis is made more difficult by observations that classifications of mood disorders derived from Western populations may not be applicable in some Indian cultures. For example, O'Nell (1996), in her study of the Flathead reservation, found several depressive syndromes that overlapped with the Western psychiatric diagnosis of major depression, but only one of them — feeling "worthless" — was associated with suicidality.

Poverty

In both the United States and Canada, suicide rates among Native peoples are positively correlated with the proportion of individuals living below accepted poverty levels (Kirmayer 1994; Lester 1995; Bachman 1992). Suicide is also a problem among Native peoples in other parts of the world, including Australia (Swan and Raphael 1995) and Latin America (Pan American Health Organization/Division of Health Systems and Services Development 1993), where Native peoples also generally contend with poverty and discrimination. Poverty creates underlying stresses that might increase vulnerability to triggers for impulsive self-destructive acts (Shaffer et al. 1988) and creates competition for scarce resources, which can promote conflict and lack of support within a community. Native Americans in both the United States and Canada are more likely than the general population to live in poverty. In 1987, 47 percent of American Indians and Alaska Natives over age 17 were not employed, compared to 35 percent of the total U.S. population. Of those working, 38 percent made less than five dollars an hour, compared to 26 percent of working Americans overall (Beauregard, Cunningham, and Cornelius 1991).

Emotional Trauma

For American Indians, poverty has been maintained, and its effects exacerbated, by longstanding patterns of discrimination and disenfranchisement. Most, if not all, Indian communities have lived through periods when there were large-scale dislocations of their population and a rapid destruction of their culture (Brown 1970). For example, in the late 1800s, American reformers under the banner of the Indian Rights Association championed the idea that Indians would be better off if they were completely assimilated into European

American life. This philosophy resulted in policies that encouraged Christian proselytizing, the suppression of tribal identity, and the separation of young children from their families so they could obtain a Western education. The Indian boarding school movement promoted the education of Native children at the cost of long separations from their families and culture (O'Neil 1995). Elders from many tribes look back on this period as one of great tragedy and a time of both personal and group loss (O'Nell 1996). Some scholars believe that the trauma of colonization may be transmitted from one generation to another through pessimism about the future and a heightened sense of anxiety and distrust. In addition, generations of parents lost the opportunity to experience normal childhood and absorb the teachings of their own tradition, making it more difficult for them to foster healthy coping skills in their own children.

Another way in which past traumas may influence current suicidality is through their influence on current levels of intrafamilial violence. The hypothesized link includes internalization of self-hatred and helplessness (imposed by longstanding political and economic powerlessness combined with ongoing discrimination), which is then acted out within the family in both victim and aggressor roles (Duran, Guillory, and Tingley 1993). Domestic or "intimate partner" disputes have historically been implicated in suicides in some tribes (Levy 1965), in the context of both the murder of a woman followed by her partner's suicide and the suicide of a battered woman. However, tradition in Indian communities has generally been seen as historically protective against partner violence because of both an emphasis on harmony and mutual respect and the specific, high-status roles often assumed by women (Wolk 1982). Some researchers believe that domestic violence is more prevalent among Native communities than in the general population, although only limited systematically collected data are available (Bachman 1992). Child abuse (both sexual and physical) is reported among Native youth at rates that are somewhat higher than in the general population and is associated with an increased prevalence of suicidal thought (Blum et al. 1992; Grossman, Milligan, and Deyo 1991).

Suicide Clusters

Another hypothesis to explain elevated rates of suicide among Indians relates to the observation that some suicides seem to happen in clusters defined by both time and community. Two proposed mechanisms of clustering are that (1) groups of unrelated individuals respond more or less simultaneously to a common stimulus for suicide or (2) suicidality can be transmitted from individual to individual among friends or acquaintances, often after some triggering event, such as the suicide of or the expression of suicidal thought by a key member of the group.

Suicide clusters have been observed in both Indian and non-Indian communities (Bechtold 1988). In the general population they are thought to account for only a small proportion of suicide deaths (Gould, Wallenstein, and Kleinman 1990). However, many Indian communities have characteristics thought to facilitate clusters, such as tightly knit social networks that facilitate rapid communications. The number of suicides involved in Indian clusters is often two or three times what would be expected from long-term average rates and, thus, within some periods of observation, can account for a substantial minority of all suicide deaths. Clustering is difficult to prove statistically, however, because most of the communities involved are very small (10,000 total population or less). Even relatively high rates of suicide actually involve only a few deaths each year, making it hard to separate by purely statistical means random year-to-year variation from a situation where a group of suicides have some true connection to each other. Many investigations of the apparent Native community clusters have identified the predominant victims as young males with long-standing patterns of angry, antisocial behavior, and noted violent means of death, such as hanging (Kirmayer 1994). Few of the victims had prior mental health contact. Prevention of clustering thus may prove to be an important way to reduce Indian suicides.

Efforts at Prevention

Efforts at preventing suicide in Indian communities have taken a combination of three main approaches. Broad, public health–based interventions examine underlying risk factors and try to improve opportunities for young people to engage in meaningful activities, gain self-esteem, and avoid the use of illegal drugs or alcohol. Targeted prevention strategies attempt to identify "at risk" individuals (sometimes by screening large groups, sometimes by identifying groups among established social networks), including those who have friends or family members who have committed suicide, those who voice significant depression, and those who have had recurrent thoughts of suicide. Prevention at the individual level often targets those who have already expressed suicidality or have made prior attempts.

Broad, public health–based measures have appeal in that they reflect positive steps to empower community members. In particular, they avoid singling out particular individuals or families, often a very sensitive issue in close-knit Indian communities where emotional distress or talk about death may be stigmatizing subjects. By emphasizing collective concern and action, these measures are congruent with many tribal philosophies about communal responsibility. Programs have included cultural enrichment, parenting education, job and housing assistance, and recreation (Lester 1997). Critics argue, however, that these efforts are inefficient and often do not attract the participation of those most at risk.

Screening programs are attractive in that they offer wide coverage of a community and have the potential to identify groups of people at increased risk. They are hampered, however, by lack of locally specific knowledge about which individuals are really at highest risk. As noted above, O'Nell (1996) and others have questioned the applicability to Indian populations of risk profiles developed in Western cultures. Screening programs can be stigmatizing in any community and may be resisted in Indian communities that place a premium on family autonomy and privacy. Identifying at-risk groups by involving experts from the community to track specific social networks may be more acceptable and accurate. Individual treatment is the most targeted intervention but relies on a community's ability to identify those who are distressed and to offer acceptable and effective treatment.

All prevention and treatment programs depend on knowledge of locally specific expressions of distress or problematic behavior and of locally acceptable means of offering help to troubled individuals (Desjarlais et al. 1995). Successful programs must develop from alliances between community members and professionals (with both traditional and Western training) from a wide variety of disciplines, including medicine, mental health, and law enforcement.

One prevention program that attempted to combine all of these elements was based in a tribe of about three thousand individuals in New Mexico. The program received "seed" funding from the IHS as a national demonstration project (Centers for Disease Control and Prevention 1998). Based on a "community mobilization model," the program was started by convening 40 focus groups aimed at identifying problems and solutions related to suicidal behavior. One of the earliest lessons from the focus groups was the need to address suicide as a component of broader changes in the mental health and social service systems. The IHS grant was used to leverage funds from other agencies, including the Centers for Disease Control and Prevention, the Department of Justice, and the Bureau of Indian Affairs. Key parts of the program included (1) training young people to be "natural helpers" who could respond to crises and link distressed youth to mental health services, (2) reaching out to families affected by suicide or other traumatic losses, (3) screening for suicidality within mental health and social services, and (4) placing greater emphasis on the prevention of substance use and family violence. Since the program was initiated in January 1990, the rates of suicidal acts (attempts and completions) among young people have fallen dramatically and remained low.

The program's organizers felt that the peer helper component was the most powerful preventive aspect. The helpers first took part in a three-day retreat where they learned additional skills; they had weekly contact with the program organizers for help and feedback. They were encouraged to work on their own intervention programs in addition to responding to crises. Ten to 25 individuals were trained each year. Another important component was a change in how mental health follow-up was scheduled. Much greater emphasis was placed on outreach by mental health workers, including visits at worksites or homes and during hours outside normal clinic schedules. Such programs are not inexpensive. The National Demonstration Project had a total 1994 budget of about $300,000; the IHS has estimated that the real cost of comprehensive suicide treatment and prevention programs is about $400,000 annually per community, not counting the cost of psychiatric hospitalizations outside the community that may be required (U.S. Department of Health and Human Services 1996).

Several other tribes have developed prevention programs, some assisted by the IHS Special Initiatives Team (now called the Family Violence Prevention Team), formed in response to a suicide outbreak in 1985 (DeBruyn, Hymbaugh, and Valdez 1988). A variety of methods have been used to engage at-risk individuals without having to enroll them in an individual treatment plan. The health authority of the Confederated Salish and Kootenai tribes started an Indian studies group that combined cultural awareness activities (including learning traditional crafts and skills) with crisis and family counseling and group psychoeducation (Fleming 1994). One school-based program among the Zuni yielded mixed results (LaFromboise and Howard-Pitney 1994). The curriculum involved studies of Zuni culture and rights as well as general material on problem solving. It also included explicit material about suicide that some students found depressing; there was concern that some who might have been at risk may have had inappropriate responses, indicating increased rather than decreased risk.

Discussion

Native American communities, like most communities, are heterogeneous. While they may be populated by many individuals who function within traditional belief systems of illness causation and cure, they are also inhabited by other individuals who are fluent in Western culture and seek out and prefer Western treatment. However, these Western services must still be provided by clinicians with a firm grounding in local culture. Ideally, members of the community will have had the opportunity to seek clinical training; in their stead, providers from outside the community need to be thoroughly educated about the local culture and to work alongside those with more local knowledge.

Some Western concepts, such as the need for appropriate medical management of acute alcohol intoxication and detoxification, remain valid across cultural lines. In many rural Indian communities, jails function as emergency response centers and holding facilities for suicidal, intoxicated, or homeless individuals, often with the consequence that subsequent attempts or completions occur in the jail or individuals suffer ill effects from medically unattended detoxification (Duclos, LeBeau, and Elias 1994). Tribal police are, in many communities, appropriate first responders to mental health emergencies, but they need to work closely with medical emergency facilities, collaborations that are often difficult to develop and maintain. Tribes have increasingly been trying to develop emergency mental health beds in their hospitals, or "holding facilities" with trained staff, as an alternative to the use of jails.

Despite these needs for Western-based services, many Indian individuals function largely within the concepts and belief system of their own language and culture or, despite acculturation, have more confidence in traditional methods of healing. Especially when distressed, they may have difficulty expressing themselves in a non-Indian language or being helped through modalities — such as psychodynamically oriented psychotherapy — whose basic beliefs and vocabulary are not embedded in their culture. In most Indian communities, traditional healers have not been included in organized systems for delivering and paying for medical care, and thus they sometimes, paradoxically, are harder to access than in Western care (Donovan 1997).

Some components, in addition to appropriate funding support, that have been suggested to be important in effective suicide prevention and treatment programs (U.S. Department of Health and Human Services 1996) include the following:

— Availability of both traditional and Western treatments and practitioners. Although some experts question the applicability of Western psychiatric services to many Indian communities, access to both Western and traditional services needs to be improved.

— Integration of a variety of mental health and social services, including mental health and substance abuse/alcohol abuse treatment, treatment and prevention of domestic violence and child abuse, and legal assistance (with divorce, educational entitlements, financial and housing assistance, etc.).

— Outreach components that avoid the logistic and behavioral barriers to using clinic-based services; outreach works best when it is discreet and carried out by culturally acceptable messengers, often respected elders familiar with the community in question; peer (student and adult) outreach workers may also be effective. Outreach should be available both for crises and for those who are chronically distressed or at risk.

— Availability of attractive youth-oriented activities (athletics, outdoors challenge/adventure courses, cultural skills building) that are therapeutic in themselves and offer venues for prevention and for identifying those at risk.

Other components mentioned include an effective and consistent system for tracking suicidal behavior (registry or surveillance system); programs in parenting education built around locally acceptable positive models and social realities; the provision of safe emergency evaluation, shelter, or hospitalization for suicidal individuals; and broad-based support within the community (Centers for Disease Control and Prevention 1998). Because suicide is a painful and stigmatizing issue, for both individuals and the community as a whole, organizers and community leaders have to consider carefully how to present the program to the community and how to attract needed resources without simultaneously attracting unwanted or negative attention.

Reports of suicide in Native American communities are often notable for a paucity of specific information about victims' strengths, vulnerabilities, prior sources of care, and relationships. May and McCloskey (1997), in their third edition of an annotated bibliography on suicide among American Indians and Alaska Natives, identified only one detailed "psychological autopsy" of an Indian suicide victim (Blanchard, Blanchard, and Roll 1976). More studies that include descriptions of victims' motivations, interrelationships, and histories of help-seeking are needed. Such studies would allow tribal leaders to design interventions appropriate to their own communities.

Finally, programs aimed at treating and preventing suicide must recognize that, because suicide is so strongly linked to interpersonal conflict and communication, efforts will inevitably need to be linked to those of other programs that treat child abuse, domestic violence, and substance abuse, as well as efforts to reform divorce proceedings and civil commitment laws; even such issues as tribal policies regarding housing and land allocations are interconnected. Suicide is an issue that can only be addressed by respecting how closely it exposes a community's core values, strengths, and weaknesses.

ACKNOWLEDGMENTS

Ms. Anita Sinha provided invaluable assistance in locating and collating materials. Dr. Lemyra DeBruyn provided thoughtful suggestions for improvements to early drafts of the chapter.

REFERENCES

Angel R, Thoits P. 1987. The impact of culture on the cognitive structure of illness. *Cult Med Psychiatry* 11:465–94.

Bachman R. 1992. *Death and Violence on the Reservation: Homicide, Family Violence, and Suicide in American Indian Populations.* New York: Auburn House.

Baker SP, O'Neill B, Karpf RS. 1984. *The Injury Fact Book.* Lexington, Mass.: Lexington Books.

Beauregard K, Cunningham P, Cornelius L. 1991. Access to health care: Findings from the survey of American Indians and Alaska Natives. *National Medical Expenditure Survey* Research Findings 9. AHCPR Publication No. 91-0028. Rockville, Md.: Agency for Health Care Policy and Research.

Bechtold DW. 1988. Cluster suicide in American Indian adolescents. *Am Indian Alsk Native Ment Health Res* 1(3):26–35.

Becker TM, Samet JM, Wiggins CL, et al. 1990. Violent death in the West: Suicide and homicide in New Mexico, 1958–1987. *Suicide Life Threat Behav* 20:324–34.

Berlin IN. 1987. Suicide among American Indian adolescents: An overview. *Suicide Life Threat Behav* 17:218–32.

Berry JW, Poortinga YH, Segall MH, et al. 1992. *Cross-cultural Psychology: Research and Applications.* Cambridge: Cambridge University Press.

Blanchard JD, Blanchard EL, Roll S. 1976. A psychological autopsy study of an Indian adolescent suicide with implications for community services. *Suicide Life Threat Behav* 6:3–10.

Blum RW, Harmon B, Harris L, et al. 1992. American Indian–Alaska Native youth health. *JAMA* 267:1637–44.

Brown D. 1970. *Bury My Heart at Wounded Knee: An Indian History of the American West.* New York: Holt, Rinehart & Winston.

Centers for Disease Control. 1991. Attempted suicide among high school students— United States, 1990. *MMWR* 40:633–35.

Centers for Disease Control and Prevention. 1997. Regional variation in suicide rates— United States, 1990–1994. *MMWR* 46:789–93.

———. 1998. Suicide prevention evaluation in a Western Athabaskan American Indian Tribe—New Mexico, 1988–1997. *MMWR* 47:257–61.

DeBruyn LM, Hymbaugh K, Valdez N. 1988. Helping communities address suicide and violence: The special initiatives team of the Indian Health Service. *Am Indian Alsk Native Ment Health Res* 1(3):56–65.

Desjarlais R, Eisenberg L, Good B, et al. 1995. *World Mental Health: Problems and Priorities in Low-Income Countries.* New York: Oxford University Press.

Devereux G. 1985. *Ethnopsychanalyse complémentariste.* 2d ed. Paris: Flammarion.

Donovan B. 1997. Navajos face charlatans in medicine. *Ariz Republic* (July 14): B1–B2.

Duclos CW, LeBeau W, Elias GL. 1994. American Indian adolescent suicidal behavior in detention environments: Cause for continued basic and applied research. *Am Indian Alsk Native Ment Health Res* 4(monograph):189–221.

Duran E, Guillory B, Tingley P. 1993. Domestic violence in Native American communities: The effects of intergenerational post traumatic stress. Unpublished manuscript.

Everett MW. 1971. White Mountain Apache health and illness: An ethnographic study of medical decision-making. Ph.D. diss., University of Arizona (available in Human Relations Area Files archive).

———. 1975. American Indian "social pathology": A re-examination. In: Williams TR, ed. *Psychological Anthropology,* 249–85. The Hague: Mouton Publishers.

Federal Register. 1996. Indian entities recognized and eligible to receive services from the United States Bureau of Indian Affairs. *Federal Register* 61:58211–16.

Fleming CM. 1994. The Blue Bay Healing Center: Community development and healing as prevention. *Am Indian Alsk Native Ment Health Res* 4(monograph):134–65.

Gould MS, Wallenstein S, Kleinman M. 1990. Time-space clustering of teenage suicide. *Am J Epidemiol* 131:71–78.

Grossman DC, Milligan BC, Deyo RA. 1991. Risk factors for suicide attempts among Navajo adolescents. *Am J Public Health* 81:870–74.

Hall ET. 1994. *West of the Thirties.* New York: Doubleday.

Hirschfeld RMA, Russell JM. 1997. Assessment and treatment of suicidal patients. *N Engl J Med* 337:910–15.

Indian Health Service. 1990. *Trends in Indian Health.* Rockville, Md.: Indian Health Service, Program Statistics Team.

———. 1997a. *Regional Differences in Indian Health, 1997.* Rockville, Md.: Indian Health Service, Program Statistics Team.

———. 1997b. *Trends in Indian Health, 1997.* Rockville, Md.: Indian Health Service, Program Statistics Team.

Jarvis GK, Boldt M. 1982. Death styles among Canada's Indians. *Soc Sci Med* 16:1345–52.

Jecker NS, Carrese JA, Pearlman RA. 1995. Caring for patients in cross-cultural settings. *Hastings Cent Rep* 25(1):6–14.

Kirmayer LJ. 1994. Suicide among Canadian aboriginal peoples. *Transcultural Psychiatr Res Rev* 31:3–56.

Kirmayer LJ, Young A, Robbins JM. 1994. Symptom attribution in cultural perspective. *Can J Psychiatry* 39:584–95.

Kraus RF, Buffler PA. 1979. Sociocultural stress and the American Native in Alaska: An analysis of changing patterns of psychiatric illness and alcohol abuse among Alaskan Natives. *Cult Med Psychiatry* 3:111–51.

Kvernmo S, Heyerdahl S. 1998. Influence of ethnic minority factors on behavior problems in indigenous Sami and majority Norwegian adolescents. *J Am Acad Child Adolesc Psychiatry* 37:743–51.

LaFromboise TD, Howard-Pitney B. 1994. The Zuni life skills development curriculum: A collaborative approach to curriculum development. *Am Indian Alsk Native Ment Health Res* 4(monograph):98–121.

Lester D. 1995. Social correlates of American Indian suicide and homicide rates. *Am Indian Alsk Native Ment Health Res* 6(3):46–55.

———. 1997. *Suicide in American Indians.* Commack, N.Y.: Nova Science Publishers.

Levy JE. 1965. Navajo suicide. *Hum Organization* 24:308–18.

Levy JE, Kunitz SJ. 1987. A suicide prevention program for Hopi youth. *Soc Sci Med* 25:931–40.

Lyons O, Beavert V, McKinley F, et al. 1995. Traditionalism and the reassertion of Indianness. In: Philip K, ed. *Indian Self-rule,* 243–50. Logan: Utah State University Press.

May PA, McCloskey J. 1997. *Suicide and Suicide Attempts among American Indians and Alaska Natives: An Annotated Bibliography.* Albuquerque: Center on Alcoholism, Substance Use, and Addictions, University of New Mexico.

May PA, Van Winkle NW. 1994a. Indian adolescent suicide: The epidemiologic picture in New Mexico. *Am Indian Alsk Native Ment Health Res* 4(monograph):2–34.

———. 1994b. Durkeim's suicide theory and its applicability to contemporary American Indians and Alaska Natives. In: Lester D, ed. *Emile Durkeim: Le Suicide 100 Years Later*, 296–318. Philadelphia: Charles Press.

Medicine B. 1998. American Indians and anthropologists: Issues of history, empowerment, and application. *Hum Organization* 57:253–57.

Office of Technology Assessment, Adolescent Mental Health, U.S. Congress. 1990. *Indian Adolescent Mental Health*. GPO stock no. 052-003-02275-1, Publication OTA H-446. Washington, D.C.: Government Printing Office.

O'Neil FA. 1995. The Indian New Deal: An overview. In: Philip K, ed. *Indian Self-rule*, 30–46. Logan: Utah State University Press.

O'Nell TD. 1996. *Disciplined Hearts: History, Identity, and Depression in an American Indian Community*. Berkeley and Los Angeles: University of California Press.

Pan American Health Organization/Division of Health Systems and Services Development. 1993. *Health of Indigenous Peoples in the Region of the Americas*. Working Document. Washington, D.C.: Pan American Health Organization.

Phoenix Area IHS. n.d. *Suicidal Acts Report, 1987 to 1995*. Phoenix, Ariz.: Phoenix Area Indian Health Service, Mental Health Program.

Purcell TW. 1998. Indigenous knowledge and applied anthropology: Questions of definition and direction. *Hum Organization* 57:258–72.

Roy B. 1989. Suicide. In: Kaplan HT, Sadock BJ, eds. *Comprehensive Textbook of Psychiatry*, 1414–27. Baltimore: Williams & Wilkins.

Shaffer D, Garland A, Gould M, et al. 1988. Preventing teenage suicide: A critical review. *J Am Acad Child Adolesc Psychiatry* 27:675–87.

Swan P, Raphael B. 1995. *Ways Forward: National Consultancy Report on Aboriginal and Torres Strait Islander Mental Health*. Canberra: Australian Government Printing Service.

Thomas DH, Miller J, White R, et al. 1993. *The Native Americans*. Atlanta: Turner Publishing.

U.S. Bureau of the Census. 1994. Characteristics of American Indians by tribe and language. In: *1990 Census of Population*, CP-3-7, SSTF 13. Washington, D.C.: Government Printing Office.

U.S. Department of Health and Human Services. 1996. Report to Congress on the need for and cost of suicide intervention in Indian Country, Assistant Secretary for Management and Budget, typescript.

Van Winkle NW, May PA. 1986. Native American suicide in New Mexico, 1959–1979. *Hum Organization* 45:296–309.

———. 1993. An update on American Indian suicide in New Mexico, 1980–1987. *Hum Organization* 52:304–15.

Wallace LJD, Calhoun AD, Powell KE, et al. 1996. Homicide and suicide among Native Americans, 1979–1992. *Violence Surveillance Summary* Series, no. 2. Atlanta: Centers for Disease Control and Prevention, National Center for Injury Prevention and Control.

Wolk LE. 1982. *Minnesota's American Indian Battered Women: The Cycle of Oppression*. St. Paul: St. Paul American Indian Center.

Zitzow D, Desjarlait F. 1994. A study of suicide attempts comparing adolescents to adults on a northern plains American Indian reservation. *Am Indian Alsk Native Ment Health Res* 4(monograph):35–69.

16

Matthew O. Howard, Ph.D.,
R. Dale Walker, M.D., Patricia S. Walker, Ph.D.,
and Everett R. Rhoades, M.D.

Alcoholism and Substance Abuse

Alcohol consumption among American Indians and Alaska Natives, except for intermittent ceremonial use of mildly fermented potions, is a condition in which the European influence was perhaps greater and more intractable than in almost any other medical condition, not excluding the devastations of communicable microbial diseases. Significant quantities of alcohol were introduced into Indian communities with the arrival of British colonists. The latter tended to be heavy drinkers by modern standards, and taverns were central to colonial social life (Mankill 1995). Indians obtained alcohol from traders in exchange for pelts and other goods, an arrangement ultimately outlawed in most colonies but never eradicated.

Excessive alcohol use among Indians was recognized as a problem soon after European colonization. Little Turtle, a leader of the Miami tribe, pleaded for prohibition of the sale of alcohol to Indian people (Mankill 1995). In 1802, Congress authorized the president to take any measures necessary to prevent or restrain the traffic of liquor to Indians. A stronger provision was enacted in 1832, with prohibition of the selling of alcoholic beverages to Indians throughout the United States and its territories. This provision was always controversial, and in 1953 the sale of liquor to Indians was permitted, with control of the sale or use of alcohol on reservations remaining with the respective tribal governments. By the mid-1970s, only slightly more than 30 percent of the tribes had made the sale of alcohol legal within their borders (May 1977). Today, many reservations remain technically "dry," although the enforcement of prohibition seems little more effective than it was nationally, and it is generally recognized that alcohol can be readily obtained on most reservations.

Adverse physical and social consequences of excessive alcohol consumption are endemic among many Indian communities. May (1996) estimated that 17.3 percent of all Indian deaths in Indian Health Service (IHS) Areas between 1987 and 1989 were alcohol-related. Deaths directly attributable to alcohol, including those caused by alcoholic liver disease, alcoholic cardiomyopathy, alcohol dependence, alcohol overdose, and other conditions, were 3.3 to 13.0 times more common among Indian men and 4.6 to 31.0 times more common among Indian women than among age- and gender-matched members of the general U.S. population. IHS figures for 1992–94 indicate that the age-adjusted rate (also adjusted for ethnic misclassification) of deaths attributable to alcohol abuse or alcoholism among Indians was 6.8 times that of the U.S. general population and 7.5 times that of U.S. Whites. Drugs other than alcohol, especially inhalants (Howard et al. 1999), also adversely affect Indian communities, including students (Loretto, Beauvais, and Oetting 1988).

Although stereotypical misconceptions and unsubstantiated claims about Indian alcoholism date to colonial times (Leland 1976), Whittaker (1982) found no published research pertaining to Indian alcoholism before 1950. The present authors identified 329 articles examining Indian alcohol or drug abuse between 1966 and 1992 in journals included in *Index Medicus*. (Average annual citation rates were: 1966–75: 6.7; 1976–79: 8.8; 1980–85: 10.7; 1986–91: 15.2; 1992–96: 17.4). However, many, if not most, of these articles were not empirical. Although research interest in Indian substance use has increased during the past 30 years, the available scientific literature is limited, particularly given the questionable generalizability of study findings across diverse Indian groups. The extant literature does, however, provide an adequate foundation for a review of the epidemiology, adverse consequences, etiology, and prevention of alcohol and drug abuse among Indians.

The Prevalence of Substance Abuse

Adolescents

Bachman et al. (1991) examined ethnic differences in rates of substance use by studying large, nationally representative samples of high school seniors surveyed annually between 1985 and 1989. Indian men and women had higher annual rates of using marijuana, hallucinogens, lysergic acid diethylamide, heroin, stimulants, sedatives, barbiturates, and tranquilizers than did other groups of the same age. Indians also had the highest current rate of marijuana, hallucinogens, heroin, stimulants, sedatives, and cigarette use. Daily alcohol, marijuana, and cigarette use was substantially more prevalent among Indians than among other ethnic groups. Nearly one-half of Indian males and one-third of Indian females had consumed five or more drinks consecutively during the two weeks preceding the survey. Annual marijuana, cocaine, stimulant, and tranquilizer use of Indian females exceeded that of Indian males.

Bachman et al.'s (1991) findings indicate that rates of "hard" drug use among Indian youth may be higher than previously acknowledged. The investigators considered their Indian sample to be representative of the U.S. Indian population, while previous studies often have assessed youth living in rural or reservation settings, where the supply of illicit drugs may be limited.

Between 1975 and 1987, Beauvais et al. (1989) annually surveyed substance use among 7th- to 12th-grade students from five to six tribes. Males and females had similar substance use rates, except that lifetime rates of smokeless tobacco and cocaine use were higher among males and lifetime cigarette use was more prevalent among females. By the 7th grade, 44 percent of Indian youth in this sample had smoked marijuana, 22 percent had used inhalants, 72 percent had smoked cigarettes, and 28 percent had gotten drunk. Indian seniors had higher lifetime rates of marijuana, stimulant, sedative, heroin, psychedelic, phencyclidine (PCP), and cigarette use than U.S. high school seniors nationally (Johnston, O'Malley, and Bachman 1987).

Approximately 7 percent of the 10th- to 12th-grade Indian girls studied by Story et al. (1994) had used diet pills at least monthly. Approximately one-half of 11th- and 12th-grade Navajos assessed by Cole et al. (1992) reported having consumed beer at least monthly. A strong relationship between frequency of self-reported alcohol use and drunkenness was noted, suggesting that most drinking episodes culminated in drunkenness.

Adults

Indian alcohol use patterns vary widely across tribes. Whittaker (1962, 1982) found moderately high abstinence rates among the Standing Rock Sioux but also reported that 40 percent of male and 16 percent of female drinkers considered themselves alcoholic. Among abstainers, 50 percent of the men and 20 percent of the women were recovered alcoholics. Significant proportions of male (64%) and female (43%) Sioux drinkers typically drank seven or more bottles of beer or glasses of wine or five or more drinks of distilled beverages at a sitting.

Leung et al. (1993) surveyed a northwest Pacific coastal village in 1969 and 1988. Rates of current alcohol abuse or dependence for Indian men and women were 52 percent and 26 percent in 1969 and 36.4 percent and 7 percent in 1988, respectively. The lifetime prevalence of alcohol use disorders in 1988 was 56.9 percent. A majority of alcoholics experienced remission of the disorder in midlife.

In a review of eight studies of drinking among Indian tribes, May (1996) noted that the percentage of adult tribal members who were drinkers ranged from 30 percent for Navajos surveyed in 1969 to 84 percent for Ojibwa surveyed in 1978. He concluded that (1) a larger proportion of Indian men than women drink; (2) many reservations are characterized by high abstention rates, particularly among women; (3) many previously heavy-drinking Indian men moderate their alcohol use or quit drinking in midlife; (4) abstinence rates tend to be higher among reservation-based than urban Indians; and (5) in some tribes, problem drinking is limited to a small percentage of Indians.

Barker and Kramer (1996) interviewed 282 Indian elders living in Los Angeles County; 73 percent were abstainers, and an additional 10 percent drank less than once a month. Older Indians living alone, living in single-generation households, or who were depressed were more likely to drink than were their counterparts who lived with other people, in multigenerational homes, or were not depressed.

Adverse Substance-Related Consequences

A comparison of age-adjusted alcoholism death rates of American Indians with the general U.S. population (U.S. All Races) is shown in Figure 16.1. There was a fairly constant mortality rate of about 8/100,000 for U.S. All Races since 1980, but this was not true for Indians during this period. After a steady decline

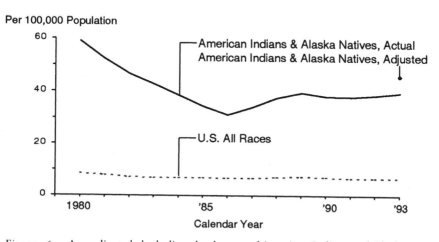

Figure 16.1. Age-adjusted alcoholism death rates of American Indians and Alaska Natives and of U.S. All Races, since 1980. For 1993, a rate adjusted for racial misclassification is shown by the *diamond point. Source:* Indian Health Service 1997, Chart 4.29

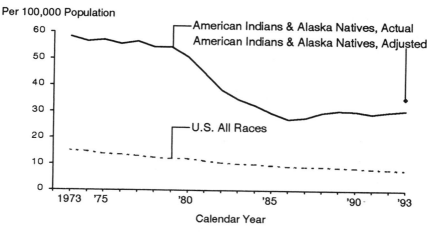

Figure 16.2. Age-adjusted cirrhosis death rates of American Indians and Alaska Natives and of U.S. All Races, since 1973. For 1993, a rate adjusted for racial misclassification is shown by the *diamond point. Source:* Indian Health Service 1997, Chart 4.31

from approximately 60/100,000 in 1980 to a low of 31/100,000 in 1986, the mortality rate for Indians gradually increased to approximately 40/100,000 in 1993. While the latter is still considerably lower than the 1980 level and part of the increase may be related to changes in diagnostic criteria, the failure to continue the downward trend suggests that improvements have not continued to be experienced. That the trend in Indian mortality rates for cirrhosis of the liver during the same time period (Figure 16.2) parallels that of Indian alcohol mortality rates suggests that the increased rate of deaths from alcoholism for Indians shown in Figure 16.1 is valid. Alcohol-specific deaths are 10 times more prevalent among Indian men aged 25–34 and 24 times more prevalent among Indian women aged 25–34 than among U.S. residents of comparable age (Indian Health Service 1997). The distribution of Indian alcoholism mortality rates by age and gender is shown in Figure 16.3. Alcohol deaths of both genders begin to occur in the age group 15–24 years, following which there is a sharp increase, particularly among men aged 45–54. After this age, there is a rather rapid drop in alcohol mortality rates for both genders, which for men, however, does not reach zero even by age 85.

Other important consequences also accompany alcoholism. High rates of substance-related problems among 12th-grade reservation Indians (RIs) compared to nonreservation Indian (NRI) and Anglo youth of the same age were noted by Beauvais (1992). More than one-half of the RI youth also reported having passed out (54%) or experienced blackouts (58%) while drinking; 50 percent had used alcohol and marijuana concomitantly. More than one-third of

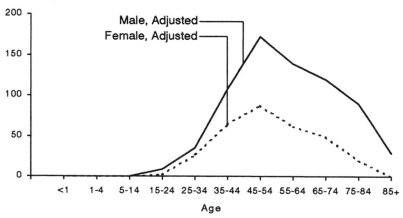

Figure 16.3. Alcoholism mortality rates of American Indians and Alaska Natives, by age and gender, fiscal years 1992–94. *Source:* Indian Health Service 1997, Chart 4.30

RI youth reported a history of alcohol-related peer (42%) and parental (35%) conflict; 24 percent and 27 percent had alcohol-related legal and school problems. Rates of adverse alcohol-related events were lower among NRI than RI youth but were substantial nonetheless and exceeded those of Anglo youth. Approximately 18 percent and 28 percent of RIs reported money problems caused by their drug and alcohol use, respectively.

One investigation disclosed that approximately 19 percent of males and 9 percent of females 14 years of age or older who were hospitalized in IHS facilities between 1980 and 1988 were diagnosed with alcohol-related disorders (Hisnanick and Erickson 1993). Patients discharged from IHS hospitals had alcohol-related disorder rates two to four times higher than individuals discharged from general hospitals participating in the National Hospital Discharge Survey. More than one-third (34.5%) of men and 11.7 percent of women hospitalized in IHS facilities on one day in 1992 were receiving treatment for alcohol-related conditions (Sugarman 1992).

The association of alcohol and injuries has been well documented (Gilliland et al. 1995; Sugarman and Grossman 1996). Alcohol-associated injuries include automobile injuries, hypothermia, drowning, falls, poisoning, burns, and job-related deaths, especially in construction or farming jobs. Among Indians, deaths associated with alcohol occurred primarily among men aged 30–49; most alcohol-associated Hispanic and Caucasian deaths occurred in older persons (Gilliland et al. 1995).

Additional studies indicate that alcohol has highly detrimental effects on Indian health. Mendenhall et al. (1989) observed that Indian veterans with alcoholic liver disease were younger, had more severe liver disease, and had higher mortality rates than similarly afflicted non-Indian veterans. A national study of decedents found daily consumption of seven or more alcoholic drinks in more than 40 percent of Indians with cirrhosis and in approximately 10 percent of Indian decedents without cirrhosis (Parrish et al. 1993). Alcohol abuse among Indians is implicated in other adverse medical and social outcomes, such as mesangial glomerulonephritis (Hoy, Smith, and Megill 1989), abdominal tuberculosis (Jakubowski, Elwood, and Enarson 1988), driving while intoxicated (James et al. 1993), gambling (Elia and Jacobs 1993), violent crime (Wolf 1984; Mills 1989), autistic behavior in offspring (Harris, MacKay, and Osborn 1995), and suicide (Spaulding 1985, 1986).

Etiology

Despite the lack of a comprehensive account or empirical findings, speculation regarding the causes of Indian alcoholism continues, usually in stereotypical caricature. The most popular of these is the "firewater" myth, the view that "Indians are constitutionally prone to develop an inordinate craving for liquor and to lose control over their behavior when they drink" (Leland 1976, 1). One unfortunate consequence of this view is that it seems to influence the beliefs of Indians themselves.

Male Indian high school and junior high school students were more likely to attribute their drinking to heredity and fate and less likely to attribute their drinking to environmental factors than were either Indian female or Euroamerican male and female students (Sage and Burns 1993). Sigelman et al. (1992) found that Indian sixth-graders were significantly more in agreement with a disease theory of a hypothetical teenager's problem drinking and significantly less likely to view the teenager as responsible for his drinking than were Hispanic or Anglo sixth-graders. A majority (63%) of Navajos surveyed by May and Smith (1988) agreed that Indians were physiologically more susceptible to alcoholism than were non-Indians. Acceptance of the view that they suffer from a hereditary vulnerability to alcoholism may diminish Indians' self-efficacy in moderating alcohol use and may create a self-fulfilling prophecy leading to higher rates of alcohol abuse by adolescents and adults.

Lamarine (1988) discussed two additional theories of substance abuse among Indians. The historical theory emphasizes the relatively recent introduction of alcohol into Indian communities and the aberrant drinking practices of the early frontiersmen who provided alcohol to Indians and "role-modeled" inappropriate alcohol use. This perspective stresses the limited time Indians have had to develop norms promoting healthful drinking practices.

Sociologic theories highlight the role of poverty, unemployment, and other social problems of Indians as determinants of substance abuse (Ferguson 1976). Life stress theories suggest that threats to self-esteem, anomie, and other forms of acculturation distress lead to drinking as a coping response. Few studies of Indians who drink without problems have been conducted (Mail and Wright 1989). Some authors have actively discouraged the search for "exotic" causative factors among Indians (Oetting, Beauvais, and Edwards 1988; Young 1988).

Psychosocial Factors

Recent investigations suggest that alcohol-related expectancies play a role in Indian alcohol use. Conner and Conner (1992) assessed the alcohol use and alcohol expectancies of 41 adolescents attending a week-long celebration. Approximately one-quarter of the youth got drunk during the festivities, and 68 percent agreed with at least one statement suggesting that alcohol use increases sexual pleasure. Level of alcohol use during the celebration and agreement with the view that alcohol use enhances sexual enjoyment were positively correlated.

Two studies examined the association of perceived locus of control with drinking among Indians. Thurman, Jones-Saumty, and Parsons (1990) found that alcoholic men from an Oklahoma tribe had significantly less internal orientation (i.e., the belief that they had control over the life events they experienced) than did nonalcoholic men from the same tribe; alcoholic and nonalcoholic men from another Oklahoma tribe did not differ significantly in this regard. Mariano et al. (1989) reported that Indian problem drinkers were significantly more external in orientation than were Indians who were recovered alcoholics or nonproblem drinkers.

King et al. (1992) and King and Thayer (1987) tested two models of substance use among Indian students. Analysis of a life stress model revealed significant, though weak, positive associations between measures of stressful life events and depression. Support from family and friends did not mediate the relationship between life stress and outcomes, except for a significant negative association between family support and alcohol use. A peer cluster model indicated that parental expectations were significantly positively related to friend and family support and significantly negatively related to school adjustment. School adjustment and perceived support of friends were moderately associated with choosing same-age drinking partners. As is the case in the general population, drinking with friends of the same age and drinking with older friends were significantly positively associated with students' alcohol use (Oetting et al. 1989; Swaim et al. 1993). On the other hand, King and Thayer (1987) concluded that neither life stress nor peer cluster models were highly predictive of students' alcohol use.

Dick, Manson, and Beals (1993) assessed rates of depression, stressful life events, and alcohol use in 9th- to 12th-grade boarding school students. More than one-half (53%) of the students met criteria for depression; 51 percent were moderate to heavy drinkers. Stressful events were prevalent in the lives of these youth. Associations between family and peer support, stressful life events, depression, and alcohol use were weak. Only the degree of family support significantly predicted alcohol use, and the relationship was weak.

Binion et al. (1988) reported that Indian eighth-grade students were significantly more likely to endorse 11 of 13 rationales for alcohol use (e.g., boredom) than were non-Indians of the same age. Non-Indians were significantly more likely than Indians to report using alcohol and marijuana in association with parties or to obtain or enhance sex.

Biological Factors

Efforts to identify differences between Indians and other groups vis-à-vis metabolism of alcohol have yielded mixed findings. An early study found a significantly lower rate of ethanol metabolism among Eskimos and Amerinds compared to Caucasians (Fenna et al. 1971). However, intravenous rather than oral administration of ethanol and selection of Indian and Caucasian samples from different populations (i.e., hospital inpatients and staff, respectively) cloud the interpretation of these findings. Farris and Jones (1978a, 1978b) identified significantly faster rates of ethanol metabolism in Indian men and women compared to matched Caucasian controls. Indian men had a significantly higher peak blood alcohol concentration and faster alcohol absorption rate than did Caucasian men. Indian and Caucasian women did not differ significantly with regard to peak blood alcohol concentration or absorption rate. Bennion and Li (1976) found no significant differences between Indians and Caucasians with respect to alcohol metabolism rate, liver alcohol dehydrogenase (ADH) activity, or liver isoenzyme distribution patterns. At this juncture, it is difficult to reconcile the disparate findings of Fenna et al. (1971), Farris and Jones (1978a), and Bennion and Li (1976). Differences among studies with regard to methods and the population of Indians studied may account, in part or whole, for the conflicting findings.

Several investigations have examined ADH and aldehyde dehydrogenase (ALDH) phenotypes in Indians and other ethnic groups. Rex et al. (1985) concluded that the pattern of ADH and ALDH distribution in the livers of 50 autopsied New Mexico Indians was similar to that of Caucasians but quite different from the liver isoenzyme patterns of Japanese and African American subjects. None of the American Indians had the deficient ALDH isoenzyme associated with flushing and other unpleasant reactions to alcohol; 50 percent of the Japanese subjects evidenced the deficient ALDH isoenzyme. Bosron et al. (1988) examined liver specimens of 33 Lakota Sioux and reported that none had the deficient ALDH phenotype. None of the adult Sioux assessed had the $ALDH_2{}^2$ and $ALDH_2{}^3$ alleles, a finding similar to that reported for Caucasians.

Zeiner et al. (1984) found that 16 percent of the 63 Oklahoma Indians they examined had the deficient ALDH isoenzyme, compared to none of 10 Caucasian controls. Overall, the Indians they examined drank more than did the Caucasians. However, Indians with the ALDH isoenzyme deficiency drank significantly less than did the Indians without the deficiency (but more than the Caucasian controls). Dyck (1993) found no evidence of the deficient ALDH isoenzyme in 35 Caucasians or 28 Cree Amerindians; 58 percent of the Asians examined possessed the atypical ALDH isoenzyme. Goldman et al. (1993) found no significant differences between alcohol- or drug-abusing and nonabusing Cheyenne Indians vis-à-vis the proportion with the dopamine D2 receptor DRD2/Taq1 A1 allele and concluded that "the high A1 allele frequencies in these populations may be unrelated to vulnerability to alcoholism" (202).

There is presently little firm evidence indicating that Indians are biologically predisposed to alcohol dependence. However, the physiologic bases of many alcohol-related effects have not been adequately evaluated (Reed 1985). Further investigation of potential differences between Indians and other ethnic groups with regard to the psychophysiological effects of ethanol is needed.

Treatment

Adolescents

Treatment outcomes of substance-abusing Indian adolescents have rarely been evaluated. A recent retrospective review of youth treated in a tribally operated inpatient adolescent substance abuse treatment program found high rates of depression, antisocial behavior, previous suicide attempts, polysubstance abuse, and psychiatric symptoms (Novins et al. 1996). Only one-fifth of the adolescents received mental health services, despite the notable prevalence of psychiatric disorders in this sample. A majority (56%) of youth failed to complete the program successfully. Other investigators also identified high rates of polysubstance abuse, psychiatric comorbidity, and treatment dropout among the Indian boys and girls they studied (Hustead, Johnson, and Redwing 1995; Johnson and Stewart 1990).

Adults

Two-thirds of the 42 Indian alcoholics Westermeyer and Neider (1984) studied 10 years after inpatient treatment were either in worse condition or deceased. The typical posttreatment course for men was a progressive deterioration in health and social functioning. Greater Indian cultural affiliation, more Indian friends, having been married, and complying with treatment recommendations were favorable prognostic factors.

Kivlahan et al. (1985) followed 50 Indians admitted to a metropolitan alcohol detoxification center and found high rates of detoxification and inpatient treatment during the two years after the index admission. These authors also noted that "rather than slowing down the 'revolving door' and facilitating the rehabilitation process, the existing system tended to perpetuate a 'patient career'" (1470).

Comorbid psychiatric and medical conditions are prevalent among Indian alcoholics. These include organic brain disorders (Westermeyer and Neider 1994), probable pathologic gambling (Elia and Jacobs 1993), depression and panic disorder (Neligh et al. 1990), and other psychiatric conditions (Brown et al. 1993; Maser and Dingus 1993; Walker et al. 1993; Westermeyer, Neider, and Westermeyer 1993). Cultural factors play an important role in diagnosis and treatment of substance use and psychiatric disorders (Terrell 1993; Thompson 1996). Westermeyer (1996) and Manson, Walker, and Kivlahan (1987) offered helpful recommendations for diagnosing and treating Indians with substance use and other psychiatric disorders. It has been argued that culturally sensitive treatment should address stresses related to acculturation experiences (Schinke et al. 1988) and cultural beliefs promoting substance abuse (Santiesteban and Szapoczik 1982).

Although the contours of culturally appropriate interventions have not been fully outlined and studies of the efficacy of different therapeutic approaches are needed, several innovative treatment approaches deserve mention. The Saint Cloud Veterans Administration Medical Center in Minnesota recently integrated sweat lodge and other indigenous healing ceremonies into their alcoholism treatment program (Walker et al. 1993). Community mobile treatment, an intervention bringing alcoholism treatment to isolated groups of Indians, has been applied with promising results (Wiebe and Huebert 1996). It represents a systematic application of the community change efforts instituted at Alkali Lake, which virtually eliminated alcohol abuse from a small Indian community (Willie 1989).

Prevention

Although efforts to prevent or ameliorate harmful drinking practices among Indians emerged more than a quarter-century ago (May 1986), empirical evaluations of prevention programs are relatively rare (May and Moran 1995). Even when prevention interventions are evaluated, the methods used frequently do not allow for clear-cut conclusions. For example, Cheadle et al. (1995) were unable to find a suitable reservation control group for their five-year community-based adolescent substance abuse prevention program. Results reflected substantial reductions in alcohol and marijuana use among youth living on the reservation receiving the intervention. However, similar, though less substantial, reductions were also observed among control groups in another state.

The most numerous and rigorously evaluated prevention efforts are those targeting high-risk youth. Exemplary investigations were conducted by Schinke et al. (1988) and Gilchrist et al. (1987), who evaluated the effects of a 10-session skills training program on the substance-related knowledge and attitudes and substance use of Indian youth residing in the Pacific Northwest. In both studies, subjects in the prevention group had more knowledge about, more negative attitudes toward, and less use of alcohol and drugs at the six-month follow-up than did subjects assigned to the control group. Promising findings using fitness training and peer-based interventions have been reported (Carpenter, Lyons, and Miller 1985; Scott and Meyers 1988). Community-wide substance abuse prevention programs have been less well studied than have secondary prevention efforts.

Public Policy and Program Development

The establishment of treatment programs for Indian people was authorized by the 1970 Comprehensive Alcohol Abuse Treatment, Prevention, and Rehabilitation Act, administered by the National Institute on Alcohol Abuse and Alcoholism (NIAAA). The transfer of programs from NIAAA to IHS oversight commenced in 1978; by 1983, some 158 well-developed programs had been successfully transferred. Early IHS efforts focused on (1) defining the scope of alcohol treatment and prevention at all levels, (2) improving the quality of care provided to persons in alcohol treatment programs, and (3) seeking ways to expand the services available to Indian people (Rhoades et al. 1988).

Several working groups convened at the request of the IHS director offered more than one hundred recommendations to reduce the toll taken by alcohol on Indian health. These recommendations provided the framework for IHS's strategic plan addressing Indian alcoholism, which included 50 action steps, many of them concerned with the prevention of alcoholism. In the late 1980s, community- and school-based prevention efforts proliferated across many Indian communities, and other developments suggested a tidal shift in the way Indians themselves viewed alcohol. In 1987, the Cheyenne River Sioux formally resolved to be drug and alcohol free by the year 2000 (Tribal Resolution No. 313-87-CR).

The 1986 Anti-Drug Abuse Act provided for the establishment of 11 regional IHS substance abuse treatment centers for adolescents and for community-based treatment, aftercare, and health promotion/disease prevention programs. Intensified efforts by the IHS to address Indian alcoholism over the past two decades and a growing awareness on the part of Indians themselves have contributed to the noteworthy decline in age-adjusted alcoholism mortality rates between 1979–81 (59/100,000) and 1990–92 (37.2/100,000).

Recently, IHS and tribal efforts have specifically targeted alcohol- and drug-affected Indian women and children. An evaluation indicated that Indian women in treatment had experienced high rates of childhood and adult physical and sexual abuse and were principally motivated to seek treatment because of their desire to be better parents. The fiscal year 1999 IHS Budget Justification included a proposal to "1) assess and measure the treatment outcomes achieved by the women receiving treatment in IHS-sponsored projects, 2) attempt to relate treatment outcomes to the IHS-supported treatment services provided, and 3) describe the organization and provision of IHS-sponsored substance abuse treatment and aftercare services available for adult American Indian and Alaska Native women, identifying common strengths, problems, and recommendations." A newly funded IHS contract will support an evaluation of the effectiveness of IHS aftercare services for substance-dependent women.

IHS, in conjunction with the Bureau of Indian Affairs, developed alcohol and other drug assessment and treatment units in juvenile detention centers in six locations (Ft. Peck, Mont.; Eagle Butte and Pine Ridge, S.D.; Tuba City and Chinle, Ariz.; and Stroud, Okla.). The Regional Treatment Center Outcomes Tracking Protocol was initiated in 1998 to improve methods of monitoring adolescent clients' clinical outcomes and other program outputs.

One controversial issue concerns the prohibition of alcohol on the majority of reservations. May (1977, 1992) contended that prohibition exacerbates alcohol problems by discouraging the development of norms proscribing alcohol abuse and contributing to the binge-drinking pattern that is associated with many alcohol-related problems.

Discussion

Additional investigation of psychosocial and biological factors as they relate to the pathogenesis of substance abuse among Indians is needed. A particular concern is the high rate of substance use among adolescent Indian girls. The comparatively disadvantaged socioeconomic status of many Indians may explain the findings of some studies, which document the early onset of substance use and abuse and associated problems among Indians.

IHS prevention and treatment efforts over the past two decades, in association with the efforts of individuals and tribes to combat alcohol abuse, seem to have reduced the level of alcohol-related harm. These programs provide a basis for optimism about the future of Indian health in this important area.

Mail and Wright (1989) contended that much of relevance to the etiology, treatment, and prevention of Indian substance abuse could be learned from the study of Indian social drinkers and women, a perspective that seems to have considerable merit. Systematic studies of Indian abstainers and of adults who have "matured" out of substance dependence are also needed.

Prevention and public policy measures targeting substance use among Indians should be implemented more widely and evaluated more rigorously. A vigorous program of research addressing substance use disorders among Indian people is needed. Particularly pressing is the need to examine the apparent increases in alcoholism mortality at a time when greater attention than ever has been paid to interventions.

REFERENCES

Bachman JG, Wallace JM, O'Malley PM, et al. 1991. Racial/ethnic differences in smoking, drinking, and illicit drug use among American high school seniors, 1976–89. *Am J Public Health* 81:372–77.

Barker JC, Kramer BJ. 1996. Alcohol consumption among older urban American Indians. *J Stud Alcohol* 57:119–24.

Beauvais F. 1992. The consequences of drug and alcohol use for Indian youth. *Am Indian Alsk Native Ment Health Res* 5(1):32–37.

Beauvais F, Oetting ER, Wolf W, et al. 1989. American Indian youth and drugs, 1976–87: A continuing problem. *Am J Public Health* 79:634–36.

Bennion LJ, Li TK. 1976. Alcohol metabolism in American Indians and Whites: Lack of racial differences in metabolic rate and liver alcohol dehydrogenase. *N Engl J Med* 294:9–13.

Binion A, Miller CD, Beauvais F, et al. 1988. Rationales for the use of alcohol, marijuana, and other drugs by eighth-grade Native American and Anglo youth. *Int J Addict* 23:47–64.

Bosron F, Rex DK, Harden CK, et al. 1988. Alcohol and aldehyde dehydrogenase in Sioux North American Indians. *Alcohol Clin Exp Res* 12:454–55.

Brown GL, Albaugh BJ, Robin RW, et al. 1993. Alcoholism and substance abuse among selected Southern Cheyenne Indians. *Cult Med Psychiatry* 16:1531–42.

Carpenter R, Lyons C, Miller W. 1985. Peer-managed self-control program prevention of alcohol abuse in American Indian high school students: A pilot evaluation. *Int J Addict* 20:299–310.

Cheadle A, Pearson D, Wagner E, et al. 1995. A community-based approach to preventing alcohol use among adolescents on an American Indian reservation. *Public Health Rep* 110:439–47.

Cole G, Timmreck TC, Page R, et al. 1992. Patterns and prevalence of substance abuse among Navajo youth. *Health Values J Health Behav Educ Promotion* 16(3):50–57.

Conner JL, Conner CN. 1992. Expected benefits of alcohol use on sexual behavior: Native American adolescents. *Psychol Rep* 70:91–98.

Dick RW, Manson SM, Beals J. 1993. Alcohol use among male and female Native American adolescents: Patterns and correlates of student drinking in a boarding school. *J Stud Alcohol* 54:172–77.

Dyck LE. 1993. Absence of the atypical mitochondrial aldehyde dehydrogenase (ALDH2) isoenzyme in Saskatchewan Cree Indians. *Hum Hered* 43:116–20.

Elia C, Jacobs DF. 1993. The incidence of pathological gambling among Native Americans treated for alcohol dependence. *Int J Addict* 28:659–66.

Farris JJ, Jones BM. 1978a. Ethanol metabolism in male American Indians and Whites. *Alcohol Clin Exp Res* 2:77–81.

———. 1978b. Ethanol metabolism and memory impairment in American Indian and White women social drinkers. *J Stud Alcohol* 39:1975–79.

Fenna D, Mix L, Schaefer O, et al. 1971. Ethanol metabolism in various racial groups. *Can Med Assoc J* 105:472–75.

Ferguson FM. 1976. Stake theory as an explanatory device in Navajo alcoholism treatment response. *Hum Organization* 35:65–78.

Gilchrist LD, Schinke SP, Trimble JE, et al. 1987. Skills enhancement to prevent substance abuse among American Indian adolescents. *Int J Addict* 22:869–79.

Gilliland FD, Becker TM, Samet JM, et al. 1995. Trends in alcohol-related mortality among New Mexico's American Indians, Hispanics, and non-Hispanic Whites. *Alcohol Clin Exp Res* 19:1572–77.

Goldman D, Brown GL, Albaugh B, et al. 1993. DRD2 dopamine receptor genotype, linkage disequilibrium, and alcoholism in American Indians and other populations. *Alcohol Clin Exp Res* 17:199–204.

Harris SR, MacKay LLJ, Osborn JA. 1995. Autistic behaviors in offspring of mothers abusing alcohol and other drugs: A series of case reports. *Alcohol Clin Exp Res* 19:660–65.

Hisnanick JJ, Erickson PM. 1993. Hospital resource utilization by American Indians/Alaska Natives for alcoholism and alcohol abuse. *Am J Drug Alcohol Abuse* 19:387–96.

Howard MO, Walker RD, Walker PS, et al. 1999. Inhalant use among urban American Indian adolescents. *Addiction* 94:83–95.

Hoy WE, Smith SM, Megill DM. 1989. Mesangial proliferative glomerulonephritis in southwestern American Indians. *Transplant Proc* 21:3909–12.

Hustead J, Johnson T, Redwing L. 1995. Multi-dimensional adolescent treatment with American Indians. *Am Indian Alsk Native Ment Health Res* 6:23–30.

Indian Health Service. 1997. *Trends in Indian Health, 1997.* Rockville, Md.: Indian Health Service, Program Statistics Team.

Jakubowski A, Elwood RK, Enarson DA. 1988. Clinical features of abdominal tuberculosis. *J Infect Dis* 158:687–92.

James WH, Hutchinson B, Moore DD, et al. 1993. Predictors of driving while intoxicated (DWI) among American Indians in the Northwest. *J Drug Educ* 23:317–24.

Johnson RH, Stewart CG. 1991. Outcome of substance abuse treatment in American Indian youth. Paper presented at the Fourth Annual Research Conference of the Indian Health Service, Tucson, 22–24 April 1991.

Johnston LD, O'Malley RM, Bachman JG. 1987. National trends in drug use and related factors among American high school students and young adults, 1975–86. Rockville, Md.: National Institute on Drug Abuse.

King J, Beals J, Manson SM, et al. 1992. A structural equation model of factors related to substance use among American Indian adolescents. *Drugs Soc* 6(3–4):253–68.

King J, Thayer JF. 1987. Examining conceptual models for understanding drug use behavior among American Indian youth. In: Trimble JE, Padilla A, Bell CS, eds. *Drug Abuse among Ethnic Minorities*. Rockville, Md.: Department of Health and Human Services.

Kivlahan DR, Walker RD, Donovan DM, et al. 1985. Detoxification recidivism among urban American Indian alcoholics. *Am J Psychiatry* 142:1467–70.

Lamarine RJ. 1988. Alcohol abuse among American Indians. *J Community Health* 1(3):143–55.

Leland J. 1976. *Firewater Myths*. New Brunswick, N.J.: Rutgers Center of Alcohol Studies.

Leung PK, Kinzie JD, Boehnlein JK, et al. 1993. A prospective study of the natural course of alcoholism in a Native village. *J Stud Alcohol* 54:733–38.

Loretto G, Beauvais F, Oetting ER. 1988. The primary cost of drug abuse: What Indian youth pay for drugs. *Am Indian Alsk Native Ment Health Res* 2(1):21–32.

Mail PD, Wright LJ. 1989. Indian sobriety must come from Indian solutions. *Health Educ* 20(5):19–22.

Mankill PC. 1995. *Deadly Medicine: Indians and Alcohol in Early America*. Ithaca: Cornell University Press.

Manson SM, Walker RD, Kivlahan DR. 1987. Psychiatric assessment and treatment of American Indians and Alaska Natives. *Hosp Community Psychiatry* 38(2):165–73.

Mariano AJ, Donovan DM, Walker PS, et al. 1989. Drinking-related locus of control and the drinking status of urban Native Americans. *J Stud Alcohol* 50:331–38.

Maser JD, Dinges N. 1993. Comorbidity: Meaning and issues in cross-cultural clinical research. *Cult Med Psychiatry* 16:409–25.

May PA. 1977. Alcohol beverage control: A survey of tribal alcohol statutes. *Am Indian Law Rev* 5:217–28.

———. 1986. Alcohol and drug misuse prevention programs for American Indians: Needs and opportunities. *J Stud Alcohol* 47:187–95.

———. 1992. Alcohol policy considerations for Indian reservations and bordertown communities. *Am Indian Alsk Native Ment Health Res* 4(3):5–59.

———. 1996. Overview of alcohol use epidemiology for American Indian populations. In: Sandefur GD, Rundfuss RR, Cohen B, eds. *Changing Numbers, Changing Needs: American Indian Demography and Public Health*. Washington, D.C.: National Academy Press.

May PA, Moran JR. 1995. Prevention of alcohol misuse: A review of health promotion efforts among American Indians. *Am J Health Promotion* 9(4):288–99.

May PA, Smith MB. 1988. Some Navajo opinions about alcohol abuse and prohibition: A survey and recommendations for policy. *J Stud Alcohol* 49:324–34.

Mendenhall CL, Gartside PS, Roselle GA, et al. 1989. *Alcohol Alcohol* 24(1):11–19.

Mills DK. 1989. Alcohol and crime on the reservation: A ten-year perspective. *Federal Probation* 53(4):12–15.

Neligh G, Baron AE, Braun P, et al. 1990. Panic disorder among American Indians: A descriptive study. *Am Indian Alsk Native Ment Health Res* 4(2):43–54.

Novins DK, Beals J, Shore JH, et al. 1996. Substance abuse treatment of American Indian adolescents: Comorbid symptomatology, gender differences, and treatment patterns. *J Acad Child Adolesc Psychiatry* 35:1593–1601.

Oetting ER, Beauvais F, Edwards RW. 1988. Alcohol and Indian youth: Social and psychological correlates and prevention. *J Drug Issues* 18:87–101.

Oetting ER, Swaim RC, Edwards RW, et al. 1989. Indian and Anglo adolescent alcohol use and emotional distress: Path models. *Am J Drug Alcohol Abuse* 15:153–72.

Parrish KM, Dufour MC, Stinson FS, et al. 1993. Average daily alcohol consumption during adult life among decedents with and without cirrhosis: The 1986 National Mortality Followback Survey. *J Stud Alcohol* 54:450–56.

Reed TE. 1985. Ethnic differences in alcohol use, abuse, and sensitivity: A review with genetic interpretation. *Soc Biol* 32:195–209.

Rex DK, Bosron WF, Smialek JE, et al. 1985. Alcohol and aldehyde dehydrogenase isoenzymes in North American Indians. *Alcohol Clin Exp Res* 9:147–52.

Rhoades ER, Mason RD, Eddy P, et al. 1988. The Indian Health Service approach to alcoholism among American Indians and Alaska Natives. *Public Health Rep* 103:621–27.

Sage D, Burns GL. 1993. Attributional antecedents of alcohol use in American Indian and Euroamerican adolescents. *Am Indian Alsk Native Ment Health Res* 5(2):46–56.

Santisteban D, Szapocznik J. 1982. Substance abuse disorders among Hispanics: A focus on prevention. In: *The Hispanic Substance Abuser: The Search for Prevention Strategies*, 83–100. New York: Grune & Stratton.

Schinke SP, Orlandi MA, Botvin GJ, et al. 1988. Preventing substance abuse among American-Indian adolescents: A bicultural competence skills approach. *J Counseling Psychol* 35(1):87–90.

Scott K, Meyers A. 1988. Impact of fitness training on Native adolescent's self-evaluation and substance use. *Can J Public Health* 79:424–48.

Sigelman C, Didjurgis T, Marshall B, et al. 1992. Views of problem drinking among Native American, Hispanic, and Anglo children. *Child Psychiatry Hum Dev* 22(4): 265–76.

Spaulding JM. 1985–86. Recent suicide rates among ten Ojibwa Indian bands in northwestern Ontario. *Omega J Death Dying* 16:347–54.

Story M, Hauck FR, Broussard BA, et al. 1994. Weight perceptions and weight control practices in American Indian and Alaska Native adolescents. *Arch Pediatr Adolesc Med* 148:567–71.

Sugarman JR. 1992. Alcohol-related hospitalizations: Indian Health Service and tribal hospitals, United States, May. *MMWR* 41(4):757–60.

Sugarman JR, Grossman DC. 1996. Trauma among American Indians in an urban county. *Public Health Rep* 111:321–27.

Swaim R, Oetting ER, Thurman PJ, et al. 1993. American Indian adolescent drug use and socialization characteristics: A cross-cultural comparison. *J Cross-Cultural Psychol* 24(1):53–70.

Terrell MD. 1993. Ethnocultural factors and substance abuse: Toward culturally sensitive treatment models. *Psychol Addict Behav* 1(3):162–67.

Thompson JW. 1996. Native American perspectives. In: Mezzich JE, Kleinman A, Fabrega H, et al., eds. *Culture and Psychiatric Diagnosis: A DSM-IV Perspective*, 31–33. Washington, D.C.: American Psychiatric Press.

Thurman PJ, Jones-Saumty D, Parsons OA. 1990. Locus of control and drinking behavior in American Indian alcoholics and non-alcoholics. *Am Indian Alsk Native Ment Health Res* 4(1):31–39.

Walker RD, Lambert MD, Walker PS, et al. 1993. Treatment implications of comorbid psychopathology in American Indians and Alaska Natives. *Cult Med Psychiatry* 16:555–72.

Westermeyer J. 1996. Culture and the diagnostic classification of substance-related disorders. In Mezzich JE, Kleinman A, Fabrega H, et al., eds. *Culture and Psychiatric Diagnosis: A DSM-IV Perspective*, 81–89. Washington, D.C.: American Psychiatric Press.

Westermeyer J, Neider J. 1984. Predicting treatment outcome after ten years among American Indian alcoholics. *Alcohol Clin Exp Res* 8:179–84.

———. 1994. Substance disorders among 100 American Indians versus 200 other patients. *Alcohol Clin Exp Res* 18:692–94.

Westermeyer J, Neider J, Westermeyer M. 1993. Substance use and other psychiatric disorders among 100 American Indian patients. *Cult Med Psychiatry* 16:519–29.

Whittaker JO. 1962. Alcohol and the Standing Rock Sioux tribe: I. The pattern of drinking. *Q J Stud Alcohol* 23:468–79.

———. 1982. Alcohol and the Standing Rock Sioux tribe: A twenty-year follow-up study. *J Stud Alcohol* 43:191–200.

Wiebe J, Huebert KM. 1996. Community mobile treatment: What it is and how it works. *J Subst Abuse Treat* 13(1):23–31.

Willie E. 1989. The story of Alkali Lake: Anomaly of community recovery or national trend in Indian country? *Alcohol Treat Q* 6(3/4):167–74.

Wolf A. 1984. Alcohol and violence in the Alaskan Native: A follow-up and theoretical considerations. *Alcohol Treat Q* 1(1):133–38.

Young TJ. 1988. Substance use and abuse among American Indians. *Clin Psychol Rev* 8:125–38.

Zeiner AR, Girardot JM, Nichols N, et al. 1984. ALDH I isoenzyme deficiency among North American Indians. *Alcohol Clin Exp Res* 8:129.

17

Dorothy A. Rhoades, M.D., M.P.H.,
Everett R. Rhoades, M.D.,
Candace M. Jones, R.D.H., M.P.H., and
Robert J. Collins, D.M.D., M.P.H.

Tobacco Use

American Indians have had a long and complex relationship with tobacco, apparently beginning in South America (Wilbert 1991) and spreading throughout the Western Hemisphere over the course of eight thousand years (Goodman 1993). The use of both smoking and smokeless tobacco dates to prehistoric times (de Smet 1985), and by the time of European contact, tobacco had become an important item of cultivation and trade. Before about A.D. 1700, tobacco use seemed to be largely confined to religious and therapeutic practices (La Barre 1964; Wilbert 1991).

Today, tobacco may be smoked during a healing procedure, sprinkled around a house for protection, or included in burial offerings. Some Indians keep tobacco in their homes, often hanging a pouch in a certain location, and tobacco is often presented as a gift to others. In the past decade, with the development of "smokeshops," tobacco sales have become an important economic force in some Indian communities.

In contrast to what has been thought to be the largely ceremonial and therapeutic use by ancient Indians, the casual, habitual use of tobacco by smoking, snuffing, chewing, or "dipping" (the application of tobacco into the buccal cavity) is now highly prevalent among many Indian groups and is increasing among others. Of particular concern is the increasing use among young Indians of both sexes. In many, if not most, Indian communities, tobacco use is clearly an important public health concern, and its habitual use is a leading risk factor for many diseases among Indians. Welty et al. (1995) confirmed the association between cardiovascular disease, the leading cause of death for Indians, and cigarette smoking among Indians aged 45–74 participating in the Strong Heart Study (SHS). In particular, SHS participants from North and South Dakota had a high prevalence of cardiovascular disease and smoking despite lower rates of diabetes, obesity, and hypertension when compared to Arizona or Oklahoma Indians (Howard et al. 1995).

TABLE 17.1

Nutritional estimates of the prevalence of tobacco use among American Indians in the United States

Reference	Study	Date	NA population	Age	Tobacco usage	NA prevalence (%)		Comparison prevalence (%)		Comparison population
						Total	Male/female	Total	Male/female	
Lefkowitz 1991	SAIAN	1987	U.S.	18+	Smoking					All U.S.
					Current	32.8	37.7/28.3	27.1	29.5/25.0	
					Former	16.9	18.8/15.1	22.2	27.3/17.7	
					Never	47.3	40.0/54.1	44.5	36.4/51.7	
CDC 1992	BRFSS	1987–91			Smoking		33.4/26.6		25.7/23.0	U.S. White
Welty 1995	SHS	1989–92	AZ, OK, ND/SD	45–74	Smoking					
					Current		40.5/29.3			
					Former		41.3/28.7			
					Never		18.2/42.0			
					Smokeless		3.2/0.1			
CDC 1994	NHIS	1993	U.S.	18+	Smoking	38.7		25.4		U.S. White

NOTE: All prevalence estimates are unadjusted. NA, Native American.

The high rate of sudden infant death syndrome (SIDS) among Indians in Washington State was significantly associated with smoking during pregnancy (Irwin, Mannino, and Daling 1992). Differences in SIDS rates between certain Indian Health Service (IHS) Areas seemed to relate more to maternal smoking during pregnancy than to birth weight, socioeconomic status, maternal age, or prenatal care (Bulterys 1990). Bulterys et al. (1990) estimated that the proportion of infant deaths attributable to maternal smoking may range from 5.2 percent in the Navajo Area to 16.6 percent in the Aberdeen Area. Smoking was significantly associated with lower birth weight among infants born to Native women smokers in Alaska (Murphy et al. 1996) and lower birth weight and length in the Northwest Territories of Canada (Godel et al. 1992).

A high rate of lung cancer was explained by the high rates of smoking among Sioux aged 45–74 (Welty et al. 1993). Cervical dysplasia was associated with current cigarette smoking in a pilot study of southwestern Indian women (Becker et al. 1993). Human papilloma virus infection, a risk factor for cervical dysplasia, was associated with cigarette smoking among Alaska Native women (Davidson et al. 1994). Nasopharyngeal carcinoma tended to occur more frequently among Alaska Native smokers than nonsmokers (Lanier et al. 1980). Both the duration and frequency of use of smokeless tobacco were associated with oral leukoplakia among Navajo Indian adolescents (Wolfe and Carlos 1987).

Mortality and hospitalization rates for respiratory diseases among IHS users were greatest in those areas with the highest rates of cigarette smoking (Rhoades 1990). Acute respiratory infections were more frequent among Native smokers in Canada (Fraser-Lee and Hessel 1994). Dental studies in Indian communities confirm the association of smoking with tooth loss and periodontal disease (Alpagot et al. 1996; Genco 1994). Smoking has also been associated with alcoholic pancreatitis among male Indians (Lowenfels et al. 1987).

Smoking Rates among Indian Adults

Indians currently have the highest rates of smoking in the United States (Table 17.1); about one-third of adult Indians are current smokers compared to about one-fourth of the general U.S. or U.S. White populations. In the 1987 Survey of American Indians and Alaska Natives (SAIAN), adult Indians were more likely to be current smokers than were adults in the U.S. population (Lefkowitz and Underwood 1991). However, Indian adults were also more likely to have never smoked. The national studies of smoking prevalence have not been adjusted for age. Despite the generally higher rates of tobacco use among many Indian groups, the intensity of its use among Indians is lower than among other groups in the United States (Centers for Disease Control 1992; Centers for Disease Control and Prevention 1994; Welty et al. 1995). This was true across all age and education levels in one study (Centers for Disease Control 1992).

High rates of smoking among adult Indians have been well documented in many local and regional studies: Pascua Yaqui (Campos-Outcalt et al. 1995), Alaska Natives (Hensel et al. 1995), Ojibwa and Menominee (Centers for Disease Control and Prevention 1996), Chippewa in Wisconsin (Peterson et al. 1994), Indians in Northern California (Hodge et al. 1995) and Washington State (Kimball, Goldberg, and Oberle 1996), and the Eastern Band of Cherokee (Spangler, Dignan, and Michielutte 1997). Rates among some of these communities frequently exceeded 50 percent, especially among Indians of the Northern Plains and Minnesota.

However, variation in rates of smoking between certain Indian groups is also notable. In one of the earliest studies of tobacco use among Indians, Sievers (1968) found that 20.9 percent of patients aged 15 years and older at the Phoenix Indian Medical Center in 1961–65 reported regular use of cigarettes, compared to 50 percent for nonsouthwestern Indians and 47.7 percent for the U.S. general population. The intensity of smoking was also much lower among southwestern smokers than among nonsouthwestern smokers. Arizona participants in the SHS had a much lower prevalence of smoking than did Dakota participants, and Oklahoma participants had intermediate rates (Welty et al. 1995). Similar findings were reported for Indians participating in a Behavioral Risk Factor Surveillance Study (BRFSS) (Sugarman et al. 1992). Low rates of smoking have been reported for several southwestern tribes (Sievers 1968; DeStefano, Coulehan, and Wiant 1979; Nelson et al. 1990).

Urban and nonreservation Indians have been reported to have high rates of smoking. In Minneapolis, 70 percent of adults reported a history of smoking (Gillum, Gillum, and Smith 1984). Among Indians on the Blackfoot reservation, Goldberg et al. (1991) reported that 50 percent of women smoked compared to 62 percent of Indian women living in Great Falls, Montana. Only 34 percent of on-reservation men smoked, compared to 63 percent of off-reservation men.

Smoking during Pregnancy

After adjustment for maternal age and marital status in Washington State, Native American women were more likely to smoke during pregnancy (prevalence rate, 39.8%) than were White women in Washington State (RR = 1.3) (Davis, Helgerson, and Waller 1992). Bulterys et al. (1990) estimated that 50 percent of pregnant women in the Alaska and Aberdeen IHS Areas smoked and that 13 percent of Navajo women smoked during pregnancy.

Smoking among Youth

The studies cited above clearly indicate that, among many Indian adults, tobacco use is a serious problem. Of even graver concern are the high rates of tobacco use among both male and female Indian youth. Indian youth tend to smoke more often and to have more lenient attitudes toward smoking than non-Indian youth (Bachman et al. 1991; Davis et al. 1995). Both male and female Indian smokers were more likely to begin smoking at earlier ages than were Caucasians (Hodge, Fredericks, and Kipnis 1996; Centers for Disease Control 1992).

In the 1989 Indian Adolescent Health Survey, Blum et al. (1992) found that the prevalence of daily cigarette smoking among Indian youth attending reservation or Bureau of Indian Affairs schools was slightly higher among girls than boys for both junior high (8.9% vs. 8.1%) and high school (17.8% vs. 15.0%) students. In a several-year study of various Indian junior and senior high school students living on or near reservations, Beauvais (1996) noted a rate of ever use of cigarettes of 79 percent in 1984–86, with a modest decrease to 71 percent in 1992–94. In a predominantly Indian group of younger children (mean age, 10.3 years) from the Plains, Idaho, and Colorado, 34.1 percent of girls and 33.2 percent of boys reported ever use of cigarettes (Moncher et al. 1989). The prevalence of cigarette use in the previous week was 9.2 percent for both boys and girls. Okwumabua and Duryea (1987) reported that 81 percent of Native American students in grades 7 through 12 had ever tried cigarettes and that smoking began as early as 10 years of age. In a study of Navajo and Pueblo students, both cigarette use and intention to use increased between the fifth and seventh grades (Davis et al. 1995). Boys in this study were more likely than girls to use and intend to use cigarettes.

Passive Smoking and Risk Factors

Persons exposed to cigarette smoke during childhood may be more likely to become smokers as youth or adults (Schieken 1989). Passive smoking has been linked to cardiovascular changes in children (American Heart Association 1994) and up to a 300 percent increase in the risk of death from heart disease among adults (Glantz and Parmley 1996; Steenland 1992). Ninety percent of Onondaga and Mohawk schoolchildren in New York State reported at least some passive exposure to smoking in the home (Botash et al. 1992). No study of the effects of passive smoking on Indian adults or children is available. This topic deserves further attention, especially given the already increased risk of lower respiratory tract infections for many Indian children.

Risk Factors Favoring Tobacco Use

Unlike adult Caucasians, Indians with higher levels of formal education had higher rates of smoking than those with less education (Centers for Disease Control 1992; Centers for Disease Control and Prevention 1996; Hodge, Fredericks, and Kipnis 1996). However, younger generations of Indians generally have higher levels of formal education compared with older generations, and more recent generations are more likely to smoke than are previous generations. Correlates of smoking among Eastern Band Cherokee women included younger age, alcohol use, no yearly physical examination, separated or divorced marital status, and lack of friends or church participation (Spangler, Dignan, and Michielutte 1997). A predictor of regular tobacco use among Indian and White youth in Appalachia was use of alcohol (Federman et al. 1997). As noted in the previous section, although adult Indian women are generally less likely to be current smokers than are Indian men, younger women and girls are often more likely to smoke than are males.

The best predictor of the use of smokeless tobacco among Native American adolescents in Washington State was having friends who were users (Hall and Dexter 1988). High school dropouts were at highest risk of tobacco use among Indian students on or near reservations (Beauvais 1996).

The association of higher smoking rates among Indians living in the Northern Plains, compared to the Southwest, and higher disease rates is very striking. According to IHS data (Indian Health Service 1997a, 1997b), Indians in northern regions such as Montana, North and South Dakota, and Minnesota have higher than expected mortality rates. Although well-carried-out comparative studies are lacking, it is difficult to disregard the association, as pointed out elsewhere in this chapter, between this excess mortality and tobacco use.

Smokeless Tobacco

Recent experience suggests a considerable shift toward addictive use of smokeless tobacco, especially among younger Indians. As with smoking, there are large regional differences in patterns of use between certain Indian tribes. Among adult Indian participants in the BRFSS from 1985–88, the lowest rate of smokeless tobacco use was among men in the West, with a prevalence of 1.9 percent (Sugarman et al. 1992), compared to a reported prevalence of 14.5 percent among men in the Northern Plains. Indians had higher prevalence rates than Whites in the Southwest, Plains, and other regions, but not the West. Indian women had much lower rates of smokeless tobacco use than Indian men in each region, but White women had lower rates than Indian women in all regions except the Southwest. In the SHS, of those aged 45–74, the rate of smokeless tobacco use was only 3.2 percent in men and 0.1 percent in women (Welty et al. 1995). Thirty-three percent of a sample of Montana reservation men used smokeless tobacco (Goldberg et al. 1991).

Smokeless tobacco is very popular among Indian children and youth. Surveys of smokeless tobacco use among Native American schoolchildren from South Dakota, Montana, Nebraska, Washington, Arizona, New Mexico, and Alaska reflect a prevalence of regular smokeless tobacco use of 18 percent in kindergartners through 6th-graders to 55.9 percent among 9th- and 10th-graders. Significant findings are (1) a young age of onset of smokeless tobacco use, (2) similar prevalence of use among adolescent boys and girls, and (3) a higher overall prevalence of smokeless tobacco use when compared to non–Native American populations. Acceptance of the habit, peer pressure, and addiction seem to be contributing to the high smokeless tobacco use in Native American communities (Bruerd 1990).

The use of smokeless tobacco was 58 percent among Indian students on or near reservations (Beauvais 1996). High prevalence rates have also been reported in several regional studies, including rural Alaska school-age children (Centers for Disease Control 1987) and Indian sixth-grade students at IHS sites (Backinger et al. 1993). In the latter study, the prevalence among boys in the 5–9-year age group was extremely high, at 21 percent, and the prevalence among girls was 8 percent. High prevalence rates have also been reported for children on reservations in South Dakota and Montana (47% of boys and 45% of girls) (Batliner, Keltenbach, and Bothwell 1987), as well as Indian youth in Washington State (20–34% among boys and girls) (Hall and Dexter 1988; Schinke et al. 1989). Among youth on Washington State reservations who used smokeless tobacco weekly, 72 percent were under 12 years of age (Schinke et al. 1989). In contrast to the low prevalence of smokeless tobacco use among adult Indians in the Southwest, the prevalence of such use reported in a study of Navajo youth aged 14–19 years was much higher, at 75.4 percent for males and 49 percent for females (Wolfe and Carlos 1987). Of these, more than 95 percent used snuff alone or in combination with chewing tobacco. A high prevalence of leukoplakia, 25.5 percent, was noted among the users, compared to 3.7 percent among nonusers.

Knowledge, Attitudes, and Beliefs Concerning Habitual Tobacco Use

Present evidence suggests that the desire to quit or abstain from tobacco use may be less among Indians compared to other populations. Bashshur and Quick (1991) surveyed western Alaska villagers and reported that 50 percent of smokers did not believe that smoking cessation was important for health and 36 percent had never tried to stop smoking. In the BRFSS, Indian smokers were less likely than most other ethnic populations to be interested in quitting (Centers for Disease Control and Prevention 1994). Indians who had ever smoked were also less likely than other ethnic populations to have ever stopped. However, more than 70 percent of current Indian smokers in urban areas had tried to quit (Lando et al. 1992). The percentage of respondents who successfully quit smoking was 29.7, considerably lower than the 45 percent reported for the general U.S. population.

The majority of Indian 6th-grade students had experimented with smokeless tobacco despite awareness of the health risks (Backinger et al. 1993). However, Beauvais (1996) showed a trend toward less use of smokeless tobacco among 7th- to 12th-grade Indian youth, as well as a slight trend toward less habitual use of cigarettes. Rates of use remain very high in this group.

Discussion

Great attention to developing successful prevention and cessation programs and policies for Native Americans is needed. Schinke, Moncher, and Singer (1994) and Schinke et al. (1996) reported significantly less tobacco use as well as increases in knowledge of tobacco facts, awareness of the motives of tobacco advertising, ability to resist peer pressure, and ability to refuse offers of tobacco among Native American youth in a controlled intervention program. Among adult Alaska Native participants in a tobacco cessation program, the one-year success rate was comparable to those reported in studies of non-Native populations (Hensel et al. 1995). A few other intervention trials are under way (Hodge et al. 1995; Burhansstipanov 1993).

Most tribal council chambers, once heavily smoke filled, are now generally smoke free. Smoking is discouraged at most, if not all, Indian meetings. The IHS was perhaps the first federal governmental agency to adopt a smoke-free policy throughout its facilities (Rhoades and Fairbanks 1985; Welty et al. 1987). Glasgow et al. (1995) reported that tribal leaders in the northwest United States generally support more stringent policies on tobacco use and concluded that prospects for policy change depend on tribal initiatives. Lichtenstein et al. (1995)

suggested that certain policy changes are feasible. This is especially true given the traditional and economic roles played by tobacco in many Native communities. Regulatory measures now under consideration by the general population, such as limiting access to tobacco products for youth and raising their cost, may be effective. The importance of tobacco shops as economic enterprises throughout Indian country adds a confounding factor. One must remember that the problem is with *abuse* of tobacco, not with its medical-religious-sacramental use.

REFERENCES

Alpagot T, Wolff LF, Smith QT, et al. 1996. Risk indicators for periodontal disease in a racially diverse urban population. *J Clin Periodontol* 23:982–88.

American Heart Association. 1994. Active and passive tobacco exposure: A serious pediatric health problem. *Circulation* 90:2581–90.

Bachman J, Wallace JM, O'Malley P, et al. 1991. Racial/ethnic differences in smoking, drinking, and illicit drug use among American high school seniors, 1976–89. *Am J Public Health* 81:372–77.

Backinger CL, Bruerd B, Kinney MB, et al. 1993. Knowledge, intent to use, and use of smokeless tobacco among sixth grade schoolchildren in six selected U.S. sites. *Public Health Rep* 108:637–42.

Bashshur R, Quick R. 1991. Health attitudes and behaviors of Native Alaskans. *Arctic Med Res* (suppl):313–19.

Batliner T, Keltenbach R, Bothwell E. 1987. Smokeless tobacco use by rural and reservation children. Unpublished data. Rockville, Md.: Indian Health Service.

Beauvais P. 1996. Trends in drug use among American Indian students and dropouts, 1975–1994. *Am J Public Health* 86:1594–98.

Becker TM, Wheeler CM, McPherson RS, et al. 1993. Risk factors for cervical dysplasia in southwestern American Indian women: A pilot study. *Alaska Med* 35:255–63.

Blum RW, Harmon B, Harris L, et al. 1992. American Indian–Alaska Native youth health. *JAMA* 267:1637–44.

Botash AS, Kavey RW, Emm N, et al. 1992. Cardiovascular risk factors in Native American children. *NY State J Med* 92(9):378–81.

Bruerd B. 1990. Smokeless tobacco use among Native American schoolchildren. *Public Health Rep* 105:196–201.

Bulterys M. 1990. High incidence of sudden infant death syndrome among northern Indians and Alaska Natives compared with southwestern Indians: Possible role of smoking. *J Community Health* 15(3):185–94.

Bulterys M, Morgenstern H, Welty TK, et al. 1990. The expected impact of a smoking cessation program for pregnant women on infant mortality among Native Americans. *Am J Prev Med* 6(5):267–73.

Burhansstipanov L. 1993. National Cancer Institute's Native American cancer research projects. *Alaska Med* 35:248–54.

Campos-Outcalt D, Ellis J, Aickin M, et al. 1995. Prevalence of cardiovascular disease risk factors in a southwestern Native American tribe. *Public Health Rep* 110:742–48.

Centers for Disease Control. 1987. Smokeless tobacco use in rural Alaska. *MMWR* 36:140–43.

———. 1992. Cigarette smoking among American Indians and Alaska Natives: Behavioral Risk Factor Surveillance System, 1987–1991. *MMWR* 41:861–63.

Centers for Disease Control and Prevention. 1994. Cigarette smoking among adults, United States, 1993. *MMWR* 43:925–30.

———. 1996. *Inter-tribal Heart Project: Results from the Cardiovascular Health Survey.* Atlanta: Centers for Disease Control and Prevention.

Davidson M, Schnitzer PG, Bulkow LR, et al. 1994. The prevalence of cervical infection with human papillomaviruses and cervical dysplasia in Alaska Native women. *J Infect Dis* 169:792–800.

Davis RL, Helgerson SD, Waller P. 1992. Smoking during pregnancy among northwest Native Americans. *Public Health Rep* 107:66–69.

Davis SM, Lambert LC, Cunningham-Sabo L, et al. 1995. Tobacco use: Baseline results from Pathways to Health, a school-based project for southwestern American Indian youth. *Prev Med* 24:454–60.

de Smet PA. 1985. A multidisciplinary overview of intoxicating snuff rituals in the Western Hemisphere. *J Ethnopharmacol* 13(1):3–49.

DeStefano F, Coulehan JL, Wiant MK. 1979. Blood pressure survey on the Navajo Indian reservation. *Am J Epidemiol* 109:335–45.

Federman EB, Costello EJ, Angold A, et al. 1997. Development of substance use and psychiatric comorbidity in an epidemiologic study of White and American Indian young adolescents: The Great Smoky Mountains Study. *Drug Alcohol Depend* 44(2–3):69–78.

Fraser-Lee NJ, Hessel PA. 1994. Acute respiratory infections in the Canadian Native Indian population: A review. *Can J Public Health* 85:197–200.

Genco RJ. 1994. Assessment of risk of periodontal disease. *Compendium Suppl* 18: S678–83.

Gillum RF, Gillum BS, Smith N. 1984. Cardiovascular risk factors among urban American Indians: Blood pressure, serum lipids, smoking, diabetes, health knowledge, and behavior. *Am Heart J* 107:765–76.

Glantz SA, Parmley WW. 1996. Passive and active smoking: A problem for adults. *Circulation* 94:596–98.

Glasgow R, Lichtenstein E, Wilder D, et al. 1995. The tribal tobacco policy project: Working with Northwest Indian tribes on smoking policies. *Prev Med* 24:434–40.

Goldberg HI, Warren CW, Oge LL, et al. 1991. Prevalence of behavioral risk factors in two American Indian populations in Montana. *Am J Prev Med* 7(3):155–60.

Goodman J. 1993. *Tobacco in History: The Cultures of Dependence.* London: Routledge.

Hall RL, Dexter D. 1988. Smokeless tobacco use and attitudes toward smokeless tobacco among Native Americans and other adolescents in the northwest. *Am J Public Health* 78:1586–88.

Hensel M, Cavanagh T, Lanier A, et al. 1995. Quit rates at one year follow-up of Alaska Native Medical Center Tobacco Cessation Program. *Alaska Med* 37(2):43–47.

Hodge F, Cummings S, Fredericks L, et al. 1995. Prevalence of smoking among adult American Indian clinic users in northern California. *Prev Med* 24:441–46.

Hodge F, Fredericks L, Kipnis P. 1996. Patient and smoking patterns in northern California American Indian clinics: Urban and rural contrasts. *Cancer* 78 (7 suppl):1623–28.

Howard BV, Lee ET, Cowan LD, et al. 1995. Coronary heart disease prevalence and its relation to risk factors in American Indians: The Strong Heart Study. *Am J Epidemiol* 142:254–68.

Indian Health Service. 1997a. *Regional Differences in Indian Health, 1997.* Rockville, Md.: Indian Health Service, Program Statistics Team.

———. 1997b. *Trends in Indian Health, 1997.* Rockville, Md.: Indian Health Service, Program Statistics Team.

Irwin KL, Mannino S, Daling J. 1992. Sudden infant death syndrome in Washington State: Why are Native American infants at greater risk than White infants? *J Pediatr* 121:242–47.

Kimball E, Goldberg H, Oberle M. 1996. The prevalence of selected risk factors for chronic disease among American Indians in Washington State. *Public Health Rep* 111:264–71.

La Barre W. 1964. The narcotic complex of the New World. *Diogenes* 48 (winter):125–38.

Lando H, Johnson K, Graham-Tomasi R, et al. 1992. Urban Indians' smoking patterns and interest in quitting. *Public Health Rep* 107:340–44.

Lanier A, Bender T, Talbot M, et al. 1980. Nasopharyngeal carcinoma in Alaskan Eskimo Indians and Aleuts: A review of cases and study of Epstein-Barr virus, HLA, and environmental risk factors. *Cancer* 46:2100–2106.

Lefkowitz D, Underwood C. 1991. Personal Health Practices: Findings from the Survey of American Indians and Alaska Natives. AHCPR Pub. No. 91-003. *National Medical Expenditure Survey* Research Findings 10. Rockville, Md.: Agency for Health Care Policy and Research.

Lowenfels AB, Zwemer Fl, Jhangiani S, et al. 1987. Pancreatitis in a Native American Indian population. *Pancreas* 2:694–97.

Moncher MS, Schinke SP, Holden GW, et al. 1989. Tobacco use by American Indian youth. *JAMA* 262:1469–70.

Murphy NJ, Butler SW, Petersen KM, et al. 1996. Tobacco erases 30 years of progress: Preliminary analysis of the effect of tobacco smoking on Alaska Native birth weight. *Alaska Med* 38(1):31–33.

Nelson RG, Sievers ML, Knowler WC, et al. 1990. Low incidence of fatal coronary heart disease in Pima Indians despite high prevalence of non-insulin-dependent diabetes. *Circulation* 81:987–95.

Niendorff W. 1994. *The Oral Health of Native Americans: A Summary of Recent Findings, Trends, and Regional Differences.* Rockville, Md.: Indian Health Service, Division of Clinical and Preventive Services.

Okwumabua JO, Duryea EF. 1987. Age of onset, periods of risk, and patterns of progression in drug use among American Indian high school students. *Int J Addict* 22:1269–76.

Peterson D, Remington P, Kuykendall M, et al. 1994. Behavioral risk factors of Chippewa Indians living on Wisconsin reservations. *Public Health Rep* 109:820–23.

Rhoades ER. 1990. The major respiratory diseases of American Indians. *Am Rev Respir Dis* 141:595–600.

Rhoades ER, Fairbanks LL. 1985. Smoke-free facilities in the Indian Health Service (letter). *N Engl J Med* 313:1548.

Schieken RM. 1989. The management of the family at high risk for coronary heart disease. *Cardiol Clin* 7(2):467–77.

Schinke SP, Moncher M, Singer B. 1994. Native American youths and cancer risk reduction: Effects of software intervention. *J Adolesc Health* 15:105–10.

Schinke SP, Schilling RF II, Gilchrist LD, et al. 1989. Native youth and smokeless tobacco: Prevalence rates, gender differences, and descriptive characteristics. *NCI Monogr* 8:39–42.

Sievers ML. 1968. Cigarette and alcohol usage by southwestern American Indians. *Am J Public Health* 58:71–82.

Spangler JG, Dignan MB, Michielutte R. 1997. Correlates of tobacco use among Native American women in western North Carolina. *Am J Public Health* 87:108–11.

Steenland K. 1992. Passive smoking and the risk of heart disease. *JAMA* 267:94–99.

Sugarman JR, Warren CW, Oge L, et al. 1992. Using the Behavioral Risk Factor Surveillance System to monitor Year 2000 objectives among American Indians. *Public Health Rep* 107:449–56.

Welty TK, Lee ET, Yeh J, et al. 1995. Cardiovascular disease risk factors among American Indians: The Strong Heart Study. *Am J Epidemiol* 142:269–87.

Welty TK, Tanaka ES, Leonard B, et al. 1987. Indian Health Service facilities become smoke-free. *MMWR* 36:348–50.

Welty TK, Zephier N, Schweigman K, et al. 1993. Cancer risk factors in three Sioux tribes: Use of the Indian-specific health risk appraisal for data collection and analysis. *Alaska Med* 35:265–72.

Wilbert J. 1991. Does pharmacology corroborate the nicotine therapy and practices of South American Shamanism? *J Ethnopharmacol* 32:179–86.

Wolfe MD, Carlos JP. 1987. Oral health effects of smokeless tobacco use in Navajo Indian adolescents. *Community Dent Oral Epidemiol* 15(4):230–35.

18

Scott H. Nelson, M.D., M.P.H., and
Spero M. Manson, Ph.D.

Mental Health and Mental Disorders

Native Americans seem to be at higher risk for mental disorders and suicide than other ethnic minority groups and the general population in the United States. Many Indians face difficult life circumstances, which include poverty, poor educational and employment opportunities, and increasing separation from traditional Indian activities. In addition, Indians and their communities are confronted with racial discrimination, geographical isolation, and cultural identity conflicts that result from the encroachment of a dominant technological society. Their significant behavioral health risks are also related to well-known historical events, including forced relocation of entire communities from traditional lands to distant, often harsh terrain, attempted extinction of tribal language and culture through boarding schools and similar assimilationist mechanisms, and the plunder of Native lands and other resources (Nelson et al. 1992).

Definitions

Mental health in the dominant society is often generally considered to be the ability to love and to work or the ability to relate positively to oneself and others. In Indian communities, however, mental health may be conceptualized in quite different ways (Trimble et al. 1984). As Thompson (1996) pointed out, from a traditional Indian perspective, the term *mental health* is a misnomer, implying by virtue of a deeply held Cartesian dualism that the mental aspect of a person can be separated from the rest of the person. Thus, according to many Indian definitions, which do not derive from a similar philosophical legacy, one's mental state exists in balance with the other aspects of the self. It is not necessarily distinct from the social, emotional, and spiritual components comprising the whole individual.

Similarly, Native concepts of mental disorder often differ from that of the larger U.S. population and from current psychiatric nosology. The current *Diagnostic and Statistical Manual IV (DSM-IV)* (American Psychiatric Association 1994) defines mental disorders as "clinically significant behavioral or psychological syndromes or patterns that occur in an individual that are associated with present distress (e.g., a painful symptom) or disability (e.g., impairment in one or more important areas of functioning) or with a significantly increased risk of suffering death, pain, disability, or an important loss of freedom. In addition, this syndrome or pattern must not be merely an expectable and culturally sanctioned response to a particular event, for example, the death of a loved one" (xxi). *DSM-IV* mental disorders include schizophrenia and other psychotic disorders, such as mood disorders (including depression and bipolar disorder), and anxiety disorders, such as phobias, panic disorder, posttraumatic stress disorder, and generalized anxiety disorder.

Another way of defining mental disorders is to relate them to the causes of a given problem. For example, the origins of serious mental disorders are increasingly known to be biological (i.e., associated with biochemical imbalances in the brain). The focus of much research into these mental disorders is on genetic and other potential causes that relate to physiologic dysfunctions of the brain. However, the causes of many *DSM-IV* diagnostic categories are not clearly delineated in terms of biological and nonbiological factors, and family, social, and community factors play a role in their expression.

As one might anticipate, traditional Indian persons frequently view mental disorder as a lack of balance of forces within the individual, which require the harmonious restoration of mental processes. The largely Plains symbol of the Medicine Wheel with four spokes in a circle is frequently used to conceptualize this balance of forces within the individual, as well as the forces outside him or her (i.e., family, community, nature, and the spiritual world). Traditional Indians often resent Western diagnostic labels, which they typically experience as stigmatizing. Mental illness may also be viewed as being caused by external rather than internal forces (e.g., by spirits or being "witched"). The degree to which mental disorder is viewed from an indigenous or Western orientation often is related to the person's traditionality and the degree to which an individual has assumed the beliefs, values, and knowledge base of the larger society. This frequently is characterized as the degree to which an Indian person has been assimilated into the larger, dominant society.

Childhood and Adolescence

Developmental Disorders

Neurosensory disorders and certain developmental disabilities occur from 4 to 13 times more frequently in Indians than in the population at large (Native American Rehabilitation and Training Center 1979). High rates of mental retardation and learning, emotional, and sensory disabilities, often occurring together, have been identified among Navajo youth (Joe 1980). For the United States as a whole, Indians have the highest rates of learning disabilities and the second highest rate of mental retardation, and Indians exceed national averages for speech impairment and multiple handicaps (O'Connell 1987).

Mood Disorders

High rates of affective illness have been reported among Indian youth (Manson et al. 1990). One study indicated that depression was the most common specific diagnosis assigned teenage girls examined in the Mental Health Branch of the Indian Health Service (IHS) (Beiser and Attneave 1982). Depression was diagnosed in approximately 3 percent of all youth aged 10 to 19 years seen as outpatients in the Albuquerque Area of the IHS (May 1983). A 20-item scale was used to identify depressive symptoms among students in a boarding school operated by a tribe, one operated by the Bureau of Indian Affairs, and a cohort including Indian students from five universities. The scores for three cohorts were 19.28, 19.53, and 17.75, respectively, suggesting high risk for major depression (Office of Technology Assessment 1990). Beals et al. (1997), in a reinterview of a cohort of Northern Plains youth first assessed approximately six years earlier by Sack et al. (1987), found a six-month prevalence of major depressive disorder or dysthymia of 6.4 percent. Though significant and deserving attention, this rate is significantly lower than the lifetime occurrence of mood disorders of groups reported by Lewinsohn et al. (1993) in the Oregon Adolescent Study. These preliminary efforts support the assertion that Indian youth are at substantial risk for depressive disorders.

Anxiety Disorders

Beiser and Attneave (1982) observed rates of anxiety disorders among Indian youth approximately equal to those of depressive disorders. May (1983) identified anxiety disorders in up to 13 percent of Indian outpatients aged 10–19 years.

At least three separate dimensions of anxiety among Indian youth have been suggested: physiologic, phobic, and performance anxiety reactions (Beals et al. 1997). Conditions such as panic disorder, overanxious disorder, generalized anxiety disorder, school avoidance, and separation anxiety disorder remain relatively unexamined. Slightly more than 17 percent of the teenagers who were reinterviewed by Beals et al. (1997) met criteria for an anxiety disorder: specifically, simple phobias, 8.7 percent; social phobias, 3.9 percent; separation anxiety, 3.9 percent; overanxious disorder, 2.8 percent; and obsessive compulsive disorder, 9.3 percent. The six-month prevalence of any anxiety disorder was double the lifetime rate observed in the Oregon Adolescent Study. The simple phobias and obsessive compulsive disorder were largely responsible for this difference. Beals et al. (1997) noted, however, significant cultural influences affecting interpretation of the diagnostic criteria for obsessive compulsive disorder that temper the magnitude of this finding and serve as an important reminder about uncritical application of *DSM-IV* across populations from different cultural backgrounds. Posttraumatic stress disorder has been reported among these youth as well (Manson et al. 1996; Jones et al. 1997).

Psychoactive Substance Use Disorders

Numerous studies indicate that young Indians manifest higher rates of use and abuse for most drugs, including alcohol (Beauvais and Laboueff 1985; Beauvais et al. 1989; Oetting, Beauvais, and Edwards 1988; Beauvais, Oetting, and Edwards 1985b). Differences in rates are particularly dramatic for stimulants, marijuana, inhalants, and alcohol (Beauvais, Oetting, and Edwards 1985a; Beauvais et al. 1989). Rates of inhalant use by Indians have been reported to be almost twice the national average in the 12–17-year age group (Oetting and Goldstein 1979). Inhalant use, however, tends to decrease as substances such as marijuana and alcohol become more available.

The data also suggest that Indian youth begin abusing various substances at a younger age than do their non-Indian counterparts and that alcohol consumption and problem drinking are extending to progressively younger youth (Young 1988). Likewise, Indian youth have been reported to escalate to serious substance abuse more rapidly and to tend more strongly toward polysubstance use and abuse (Weibel-Orlando 1984). Of the youth in the study by Beals et al. (1997), 18.3 percent reported current (six-month) substance abuse: 11.0 percent alcohol dependence/abuse, 8.6 percent marijuana dependence/abuse, and 2.6 percent dependence abuse of other substances. Once more, the point prevalence of alcohol dependence/abuse among these young Indian people significantly exceeded the lifetime rate of their counterparts in the Oregon study (Lewisohn et al. 1993). Likewise, the former's six-month rates of comorbidity between substance use disorders and both anxiety and disruptive behavior disorders were significantly greater than the lifetime rates of the same comorbid conditions among Oregon youth. There is little doubt that substance use and abuse pose one of the greatest threats to the well-being of young Indians and Alaska Natives.

Suicide

Elevated rates of suicide during adolescence and young adulthood are well documented among Indian youth. In 1987, suicide rates for Indian youth aged 10–14, 15–19, and 20–24 years were reported to be 2.8, 2.4, and 2.3 times greater, respectively, than averages for the general U.S. population of corresponding ages (May 1987). In fact, the peak incidence of suicide among Indian people occurs among young persons, as opposed to among elderly persons, as is the case for the population at large (McIntosh and Santos 1981). The preponderance of completed suicides among young Indian males exceeds that for the population at large (Blum et al. 1992). Substance abuse, use of highly lethal means such as guns or hanging, and an absence of strongly held traditional values are associated with suicide among Indians (Shore 1974). Indian youth have been reported to be at increased risk for suicide because of interpersonal conflict, unresolved grief over past losses, familial instability, depression, unemployment, and family history of psychiatric disorder, especially alcoholism, depression, and suicide (Ross and Davis 1986; Jilek-Aall 1974; Dizmang et al. 1974; National Task Force on Suicide in Canada 1987; Spaulding 1985; Shore et al. 1972). Sociocultural variables such as multiple home placements, social disintegration, and acculturation pressures have also been cited as risk factors for suicide among Indian youth (Berlin 1986; Levy and Kunitz 1971; Hochkirchen and Jilek 1985).

As these findings suggest, the etiologic pathways to suicide are many. Nonetheless, the inescapable conclusion is that many young Indian people are at substantially increased risk for death by suicide (Duclos and Manson 1994). Suicide is discussed further in Chapter 15.

Behavior Disorders

Behavior disorders in children and adolescents—notably conduct disorder and attention deficit/hyperactivity disorder—presently receive an enormous amount of attention. The work by Beals and associates (1997) suggests that formal epidemiologic inquiry along these lines will confirm the need for concern. Their study of Northern Plains youth revealed that 22 percent of the sample met criteria for a current disruptive disorder: 18.1 percent attention deficit/hyperactivity disorder, 3.8 percent oppositional defiant disorder, and 9.5

percent conduct disorder. The prevalence rates of the first and last of these problems proved to be significantly greater than those ever reported for Oregon adolescents (Lewinsohn et al. 1993).

Though not formal psychiatric syndromes, some other clinical issues are of interest. Indian youth seem to drop out of school at rates two to three times greater than those of the general population (Developmental Associates 1983; Grant 1975; U.S. Department of the Interior 1976). High rates of delinquency, characterized by a preponderance of petty offenses and misdemeanors, have been documented among Indian youth, especially among boys (Forslund and Cranston 1975; May 1983). In addition, running away from home and delinquency are strongly related among Indian youth. The typical Indian runaway has been described as having a history of academic dysfunction, socioeconomic disadvantage, and an absence of strong traditional values (Indian Center 1986). Family problems, legal problems, substance abuse, and peer pressures are commonly reported as well. Runaway youth typically support themselves through illegal means, such as theft and prostitution, and have extensive arrest records.

Child Abuse and Neglect

The nature and extent of child abuse and neglect vary widely across Indian communities, yet high rates have been consistently documented. Interpersonal conflict, marital disruption, parental substance abuse, attachment problems, parental unemployment, and violent death are common among many abused and neglected Indian children (Fischler 1985; Ishisaka 1978; White and Cornely 1981). Indian youth also are at risk for abuse and neglect because of sociocultural shifts, such as the transition away from traditional values, changes in gender roles and expectations, and the changing nature of the extended family in Indian culture (Grayburn 1987; Hauswald 1987). Abuse and neglect seem to render young Indian people more vulnerable to a variety of psychiatric disorders. Significantly higher rates of depressive disorders, sleep disorders, anxiety disorders, conduct disorders, drug use disorders, schizotypal disorders, and developmental disorders have been reported among abused and neglected Indian youth (Piasecki et al. 1989).

Adulthood

Mood and Anxiety Disorders

Among an increasing number of studies of the general U.S. population (U.S. All Races) and Indian adults, depressive disorders are of particular interest as a focus for intervention. They are common and have serious consequences, such as loss of social contacts, decreased work productivity, and the risk of suicide, and highly effective treatments are available.

Earlier studies provide insight into depression among adult Indians. Shore, Kinzie, and Pattison (1973), in a study of a Northwest Coast Indian village, found that the overall prevalence of psychiatric impairment was 69 percent — compared with rates of 23 percent, 40 percent, 45 percent, and 57 percent from studies using similar methods in South Africa, two sites in Nigeria, and Nova Scotia, respectively. Sampath (1974) found a rate of *DSM-II* neuroses of 116/1,000 in Alaska Eskimos (depression being most common), compared to rates of 2/1,000 to 52/1,000 in other U.S. populations. However, Murphy and Hughes (1965), in a different Eskimo community, found rates of psychopathology consistent with those of the general Canadian population. These results, together with considerable anecdotal information, suggest that depression is at least as prevalent, and may be much more so, among Indians as among other populations. Suicide as a complication of depression is of particular concern. As noted earlier, suicide rates are extremely high in some Indian communities, as are mortality rates from accidental injury, which may represent disguised suicide. The latter are often referred to as *parasuicide* or *quasi-suicidal behavior*. In view of the common co-occurrence of severe depressive symptoms with high alcohol abuse, the disinhibiting effects of alcohol, and the potential for suicide, attention to this particular dual diagnosis (e.g., depression and alcoholism) seems to be of paramount importance.

Foulks and Katz (1973) reported that the treated prevalence of anxiety neurosis in five Alaska Native culture groups was nearly as high as the prevalence of depression, and for some groups was much higher, consistent with more recent findings in a Northwest Coast village, where a wide range of psychoses, neuroses, and personality disorders was reported by Kinzie et al. (1992). The latter investigators found that the prevalence of alcohol use generally and of affective disorders in particular among women in a Northwest Indian community was significantly higher than in a national study.

Recent studies have focused on the mental health sequelae of high rates of social and personal trauma in Indian Vietnam veterans. Manson et al. (1996) noted that ethnic minorities such as Indians seem to be at higher risk for trauma and posttraumatic stress disorder because of their higher exposure to stressful situations generally, rather than because of their cultural attributes or milieu. Cultural traditions and healing ceremonies have been found to be effective in recovery from trauma (Manson 1996a, 1996b).

Manson (1990) reported that 32 percent of Indian elders visiting one urban Indian health outpatient facility reported depressive symptoms, a rate dramatically greater than those published in regard to elderly Whites. In another investigation, 19 percent of primary care patients had symptoms suggesting significant psychiatric morbidity (Goldwasser and Badger 1989), with higher rates among older adults. Last, in a survey of older urban Indians, depression and sadness/grieving were reported by 11 percent and 22 percent, respectively (Kramer 1991). Taken together, these limited data suggest that the prevalence of psychiatric illness probably is significant among Indian elders, especially among those seen in primary care clinics and perhaps in urban settings.

Other risk factors for depression in the elderly population include being female, social isolation (particularly after a spouse's death), lack of social support, and stressful life events. Factors specific to Indian elders, such as incomes well below federal poverty levels and residing in substandard living conditions, are common (John 1994). For two reasons, older Indians may also be more apt, compared to older non-Indians, to experience loss due to the death of family members. First, the death rate of Indians is higher than that among most other segments of the U.S. population (Minton and Soule 1990). Second, the concept of family in some tribes is a psychosocial concept derived from a sharing of kindred spirit and extends beyond mere blood relationships. In addition, depression among Indians is believed to be an outcome of a long history of discrimination, exclusion, and acts sometimes regarded as genocidal. Because of acculturation, older Indians may also feel less valued as important contributors to their culture—a culture that historically equated old age with wisdom and teaching. The inability of elders to fulfill long-held expectations of instructing the young and advising tribal leaders by relating tribal philosophies, myths, traditions, and stories may negatively affect their mental health and predispose them to depression. This was noted among the Coastal Salish Indians of the Pacific Northwest (Jilek-Aall 1974).

Elder Abuse and Neglect

Little is known about victimization in general, and elder abuse in particular, among Indians. In regard to the former, Norton and Manson (1995) found that domestic violence was associated with not being married, low socioeconomic status, and substance abuse. In a recent survey of approximately 350 Indian women, adult verbal, physical, or sexual domestic violence was reported by 53 percent of respondents (Fairchild and Fairchild 1996). Abuse was associated with lower income and younger age (<40 years). Minton and Soule (1990) noted that 11 percent of Eskimos 55 years and older reported that being victimized made them feel sad. However, "victimization" was not further defined.

Many emotional problems of Indian individuals, families, and communities, particularly problems that do not seem to have biological roots, can be traced to intergenerational patterns of alcoholism, depression, violence, and anxiety. The frustrations and loss of self-esteem experienced in forced culture, language, and land loss, discrimination, and other forms of oppression have accentuated these emotional and social difficulties and problems, which are not consistent with traditional Indian values. Without intervention, these dysfunctional behaviors are passed down from generation to generation through role modeling and group reinforcement. These behaviors are difficult to reverse but are helped with mental health and substance abuse treatment and with cultural activities and restoration of language, which restore pride in Indian identity.

The incidence of more serious forms of mental illness, such as schizophrenia and bipolar disorder, as well as Alzheimer disease, seems to be lower in the Indian population than in the larger society. These illnesses are considered to have biological causes. A major epidemiologic study of the incidence and prevalence of mental disorders and the use of mental health services is currently being conducted by Manson and his colleagues at the National Center on American Indian and Alaska Native Mental Health Research at the University of Colorado Health Sciences Center in Denver. This study will be important in clarifying the nature and frequency of mental health problems among Indian people and comparing them with those of the general population.

Mental Health Programs: Structure and Funding

As it was for many Indian health programs, enactment of the Indian Health Care Improvement Act (P.L. 94-437) in 1976 was profoundly important for the IHS mental health program. In the October 1990 amendments, Congress authorized a comprehensive mental health program for Indians that included increased staffing, staff training, and community mental health planning and education, among other initiatives. However, funds for these initiatives have not yet been provided (Nelson et al. 1992).

Within severely limited resources, all of the slightly more than 140 Service Units have implemented some form of mental health service program. The most common model is a crisis-oriented outpatient service staffed by one or more mental health professionals, often with the assistance of a local tribal mental health technician who provides interpreter, outreach, and other services. Mental health professionals provide consultation to medical staff and, within staffing constraints, to other programs operated by Service Units or tribes. Relatively few specialized mental health services for populations such as children and elders are available because of limited resources and difficulty in recruiting trained specialists.

Inpatient services are provided under contract with psychiatric units in local general hospitals or with private psychiatric hospitals. Emergency hospitalizations and hospitalization of longer duration are sometimes provided by state mental hospitals. Very few partial hospitalization, transitional living, or child residential mental health programs exist in IHS or tribal programs; therefore, these services usually must be purchased from local or state resources, if available.

The IHS line-item mental health budget has increased from less than $500,000 in 1965 to $33 million in 1997. Many tribes and Service Units also use other sources of funds to purchase mental health services. Some states and localities provide substantial services to Indians through local community mental health programs. Indians usually are considered fully eligible to receive mental health services from state or public mental health systems. However, state or local services may not be used by Indian people because of their distant location, fee requirements, or lack of sensitivity and receptiveness to indigenous people and their traditions. Currently, states are pursuing strategies for shifting their Medicaid programs to managed care operation. How to involve Indian communities in this process poses significant challenges for both tribes and state Medicaid programs.

An important component, as noted in Chapters 5 and 23, was the policy of cooperation and collaboration with traditional Indian healers. Perhaps it is not surprising that psychiatrists have often been more receptive to collaboration with the latter. The support of the Navajo Medicine Man training program was managed through the IHS mental health program (Bergman 1973).

The Diagnosis, Treatment, and Prevention of Mental Disorders

Cultural Formulation in Diagnosis

DSM-IV, published in 1994, includes an outline for cultural formulation, and a glossary of culture-bound syndromes is included in its Appendix I. The outline for cultural formulation is meant to supplement the multi-axial diagnostic assessment process and to address difficulties that may be encountered in applying *DSM-IV* criteria in a multi- or bicultural environment. It provides for a systematic review of the individual's cultural background, the role of the cultural context in the expression and evaluation of symptoms and dysfunction, and the effect that cultural differences may have on the relationship between the individual and the clinician. The cultural formulation provides an opportunity to describe systematically the individual's cultural and social reference group and the ways in which cultural context is relevant to clinical care.

This sensitivity of *DSM-IV* to mental disorders of the Indian patient is unprecedented and extremely valuable. It allows the clinician to incorporate cultural factors as modified by varying traditional practices and degrees of assimilation in the diagnostic and treatment process. The section on culture also incorporates descriptions of several culture-specific syndromes, many of which apply to Indian populations. Novins et al. (1997) made additional suggestions for improved cultural formulations related to mental health disorders in Indian children.

Therapeutic Intervention

As previously noted, relatively little is known about the effectiveness of different approaches to treating mental disorders in Indian populations or even about the factors that affect the use of available services. Several authors have emphasized the effectiveness of traditional healing and cultural ceremonies for Indian persons with mental disorder, especially those who do not suffer from psychotic illness (Thomason 1991; Nelson, O'Neal, and Plummer 1996).

The treatment of specific mental disorders in Indian patients frequently combines Western methods with traditional healing, depending on the degree of acculturation of the patient. Some Indian persons who seek help for emotional problems, particularly elders, may speak only their native language. Effective treatment of these persons often requires knowledgeable and sensitive interpreters as well as traditional healers. Indian persons who are assimilated into the larger society often will be effectively treated through medication, psychotherapy, and other forms of Western intervention. In tightly knit Indian communities, group and family therapy may not be well accepted because of concerns about confidentiality. In addition, given the significant stigma that still surrounds mental illness in this population, persons in need of treatment may not readily seek treatment or may do so outside their home communities to minimize visibility. Few family or patient support groups exist in reservation communities; only recently have advocacy efforts begun to make some improvements in these situations.

Local, culturally based systems of healing in many traditional Indian communities seem to be highly effective both as first-line treatment and in complementing Western treatment methods. Tribes differ in the number and types of such traditional practitioners, who range from herbalists and diagnosticians to medicine men and traditional healers. The Navajo Nation, for example, has an elaborate system of diagnostic and ceremonial healing practices and ceremonies, which is often sought out to restore balance when a person suffers from an emotional disturbance (Nelson, O'Neal, and Plummer 1996). Western clinicians should be aware of their patients' beliefs about traditional healing, familiarize themselves with local options, and refer patients to qualified traditional healers as appropriate (Thomason 1991; Thompson 1996).

Involuntary Commitment

Because of tribal sovereignty, Indian persons who reside on reservation land are not subject to state or local jurisdiction (unless agreed to by their respective tribe). Since no Indian tribe or organization operates an inpatient hospital for the mentally ill, a significant issue for the Indian mental health system has been to find ways to involuntarily hospitalize and treat Indian persons who are dangerous to themselves or others by virtue of mental illness.

The issue of involuntary commitment of mentally ill Indians came to national prominence in a famous 1978 case in South Dakota, *White v. Califano*, also known as the "Red Dog case." Georgia White was the guardian of Florence Red Dog, who was a mentally ill member of the Oglala Sioux tribe and lived on the Pine Ridge reservation. In April 1976, a psychiatrist at Pine Ridge determined that Ms. Red Dog was mentally ill and needed involuntary commitment to a mental hospital. However, the state of South Dakota refused to accept the psychiatrist's commitment or a tribal court order; the state claimed that it had no jurisdiction over Ms. Red Dog because she lived on the Pine Ridge reservation. Ms. White then took the case to federal court, claiming that South Dakota had denied Ms. Red Dog equal protection for care of her mental illness. The judge upheld the state's position and, in addition, found that the IHS, which is charged with providing health care for Indians, was responsible both for assuring that the involuntary hospital care was provided and for paying for the care. Both payment and jurisdictional issues were a major concern to the state.

Bloom, Manson, and Neligh (1980) and Manson et al. (1987) identified several factors that contribute to lack of care for Indian persons who require involuntarily hospitalization. These include lack of relationships between state officials and reservation-based mental health staff, lack of psychiatric beds on or near reservations, limited IHS funds to pay for care pursuant to involuntary commitments, the unwillingness of IHS mental health programs to detain or transport patients, and the lack of a federal commitment process and/or tribal commitment codes. At the time of the 1987 study by Manson et al., at least five different processes for commitment of reservation Indians were identified.

To help alleviate the payment issue, in 1989 the Congress appropriated $1.8 million to pay for committed mentally ill or chemically dependent Indian patients in North and South Dakota. This relieved the IHS of much of its financial concerns in the Aberdeen Area, which covers most of the jurisdiction of the eighth circuit. Current policy is that IHS follow the *White v. Califano* court order only in the eighth circuit (the Dakotas, Montana, and Nebraska). Otherwise, the IHS position continues to be that it is a "residual provider" and that states cannot refuse to pay for the care of a mentally ill Indian person committed to inpatient care through the state court system. A 1992 "round table" discus-

sion resulted in a recommendation that tribes, states, and the IHS initiate negotiations to address these problems (Indian Health Service 1992, 4–5).

State or federal legislation has been recommended as a more efficient resolution of the issues, with legislation passed by the Arizona legislature in 1992 as
an example. This provides for acceptance of tribal court orders and has improved involuntary commitment of Indians in Arizona but has not entirely
resolved the payment issue. For most tribes in the lower 48 states, mentally ill
tribal members residing on the reservation must still be transported off the
reservation to a state court, and disagreements often continue over who (IHS,
the tribe, or the state) is responsible for payment. The state of Minnesota set an
excellent precedent for other states in accepting tribal courts as a court of competent jurisdiction for involuntary commitment in Minnesota mental hospitals.

Prevention

Manson and colleagues presented several strategies for and approaches to
the prevention of various mental disorders in Indians (Manson 1982; Beiser and
Manson 1987; Manson et al. 1989a). An IHS Family Violence Prevention Team
was established in 1986 in response to a suicide epidemic in a Plains tribal
community. The team expanded its mission over the subsequent 10 years to
provide technical assistance to tribes in preventing a wide range of family violence, including child abuse, domestic violence, and homicide.

Discussion

Although many Indians are at high risk for mental disorders, Indian communities also possess significant strengths, both currently and historically, that can
be used to reduce family and community risk factors. These strengths include
the discrete political and geographical unity of reservation communities; respect
for the individual, especially elders and children; and cultural traditions and
language. Tribes thus have enormous assets to bring to bear upon reduction of
mental disorders, especially those stemming largely from family and community social pathologies, and overcoming the stigma of emotional and social
problems. Indeed, several Indian communities have organized to combat serious social and psychological problems that cause mental disorders among their
tribal members. These include issues related to family violence, child abuse, and
substance abuse, as well as suicide prevention. Methods used by tribes have
included peer counseling, grass-roots advocacy organizations, advocacy by traditional healers and religious leaders, and passage of tribal resolutions or laws.
In addition to tribal officials and councils, religious leaders, traditional healers,

and concerned family members, particularly women, are often key factors in the acknowledgment of these problems and the implementation of effective action strategies. The future of Indian communities probably rests on the success of their own efforts to combat these serious psychosocial issues and problems; just as the roots of many of these problems may be found in their communities, so too are the solutions.

REFERENCES

American Psychiatric Association. 1994. *Diagnostic and Statistical Manual for Mental Disorders, Version Four.* Washington, D.C.: American Psychiatric Press.

Beals J, Piasecki J, Nelson S, et al. 1997. Psychiatric disorder in a sample of American Indian adolescents. *J Am Acad Child Adolesc Psychiatry* 36:1252–59.

Beauvais F, Laboueff S. 1985. Drug and alcohol abuse intervention in American Indian communities. *Int J Addict* 20:139–71.

Beauvais F, Oetting ER, Edwards RW. 1985a. Trends in drug use of Indian adolescents living on reservations, 1975–1983. *Am J Drug Alcohol Abuse* 11:209–29.

———. 1985b. Trends in the use of inhalants among American Indian adolescents. *White Cloud J* 3(4):3–11.

Beauvais F, Oetting ER, Wolf W, et al. 1989. American Indian youth and drugs, 1976–87: A continuing problem. *Am J Public Health* 79:634–36.

Beiser M, Attneave CL. 1982. Mental disorders among Native American children: Rate and risk periods for entering treatment. *Am J Psychiatry* 139:193–98.

Beiser M, Manson SM. 1987. Prevention of emotional disorders in Native North American children. *J Prev Psychiatry* 3(3):225–40.

Bergman RL. 1973. A school for medicine men. *Am J Psychiatry* 130:663–66.

Berlin IN. 1986. Psychopathology and its antecedents among American Indian adolescents. *Adv Clin Child Psychology* 9:125–52.

Bloom JD, Manson SM, Neligh G. 1980. Civil commitment of American Indians. *Bull Am Acad Psychiatry Law* 8(1):13–22.

Blum RW, Hamon B, Harris L, et al. 1992. American Indian Alaska Native youth health. *JAMA* 267:1637–44.

Developmental Associates. 1983. *Final Report: The Evaluation of the Impact of the Part A Entitlement Program Funded under Title IV of the Indian Education Act.* Arlington, Va.: Developmental Associates.

Dizmang LH, Watson J, May PA, et al. 1974. Suicide in the American Indian. *Psychiatr Ann* 4(9):22–28.

Duclos CW, Manson SM, eds. 1994. *Calling from the Rim: Suicidal Behavior among American Indian and Alaska Native Adolescents.* Niwot, Colo.: University Press of Colorado.

Fairchild DG, Fairchild MW. 1995. Adult domestic violence in a Native American community. *J Gen Intern Med* 11 (April suppl):46.

Fischler R. 1985. Child abuse and neglect in American Indian communities. *Child Abuse Negl* 9:95–106.

Forslund MA, Cranston VA. 1975. A self-report comparison of Indian and Anglo delinquency in Wyoming. *Criminology* 13(2):193–97.

Foulks EF, Katz S. 1973. The mental health of Alaska Natives. *Acta Psychiatr Scand* 49:91–96.

Goldwasser HD, Badger LW. 1989. Utility of a psychiatric screen among the Navajo of Chinle: A fourth-year clerkship experience. *Am Indian Alsk Native Ment Health Res* 3(1):6–15.

Grant WV. 1975. Estimates of school dropouts. *Am Educ* 11(4):42.

Grayburn N. 1987. Severe child abuse among the Canadian Inuit. In: Scheper-Hughes N, ed. *Child Survival*, 211–26. Norwell, Mass.: Kluwer Academic Publications.

Hauswald L. 1987. External pressure/internal change: Child neglect on the Navajo reservation. In: Scheper-Hughes N, ed. *Child Survival*, 145–64. Norwell, Mass.: Kluwer Academic Publications.

Hochkirchen B, Jilek W. 1985. Psychosocial dimensions of suicide and parasuicide in American Indians of the Pacific Northwest. *J Operational Psychiatry* 16(2):24–28.

Indian Center, Lincoln, NE, and University of Nebraska Lincoln, Department of Sociology, Bureau of Sociological Research. 1986. The Native American adolescent health project: Report on interview surveys of runaways, parents, community leaders and human service workers. Lincoln, Neb.: authors.

Indian Health Service. 1992. *Involuntary Commitment of Dangerously Mentally Ill Indian Patients*. An IHS Roundtable Conference, Final Report. Rockville, Md.: Indian Health Service.

Ishisaka H. 1978. American Indians in foster care: Cultural factors and separation. *Child Welfare* 57(5):299–308.

Jilek-Aall L. 1974. Psychosocial aspects of drinking among Coast Salish Indians. *Can Psychiatr Assoc J* 19:357–61.

———. 1976. The Western psychiatrist and his non-Western clientele. *Can Psychiatr Assoc J* 21:353–59.

Joe JR. 1980. Disabled children in Navajo society. Ph.D. diss., University of California, Berkeley.

John R. 1994. The state of research on American Indian elders health, income security, and social support networks. In: *Minority Elders: Five Goals toward Building a Public Policy Base*, 46–58. Washington, D.C.: Gerontological Society of America.

Jones M, Dauphinais P, Sack W, et al. 1997. Trauma-related symptomology among American Indian adolescents. *J Trauma Stress* 10(2):163–73.

Kinzie DJ, Leung PK, Boehnlein J, et al. 1992. Psychiatric epidemiology of an Indian village: A nineteen-year replication study. *J Nerv Ment Dis* 180:33–39.

Kramer BJ. 1991. Urban American Indian aging. *J Cross-Cultural Gerontol* 6(2):205–17.

Levy J, Kunitz S. 1971. Indian reservations, anomie, and social pathologies. *Southwestern J Anthropol* 27(2):97–128.

Lewinsohn PM, Hops H, Roberts RE, et al. 1993. Adolescent psychopathology I: Prevalence and incidence of depression and other DSM-III-R disorders in high school students. *J Abnorm Psychol* 102:133–44.

Manson SM. 1990. Older American Indians: Status and issues in income, housing, and health. In: Stanford P, ed. *Toward Empowering the Minority Elderly: Alternatives and Solutions*. Washington, D.C.: American Association of Retired Persons.

———. 1996a. Cross-cultural and multi-ethnic assessment of trauma. In: Wilson JP, Keane TM, eds. *Assessing Psychological Trauma and PTSD: A Handbook for Practitioners*, 239–66. New York: Guilford Press.

———. 1996b. The wounded spirit: A cultural formulation of post-traumatic stress disorder. *Cult Med Psychiatry* 20:489–98.

———, ed. 1982. *New Directions in Prevention among American Indian and Alaska Native Communities*. Portland: Oregon Health Sciences University.

Manson SM, Ackerson LM, Dick RW, et al. 1990. Depressive symptoms among American Indian adolescents: Psychometric characteristics of the CES-D. *J Consult Clin Psychol* 2:231–37.

Manson SM, Beals J, Dick R, et al. 1989a. Risk factors for suicide among Indian adolescents at a boarding school. *Public Health Rep* 104:609–14.

Manson SM, Beals J, O'Nell T, et al. 1996. Wounded spirits, ailing hearts: The nature and extent of PTSD among American Indians. In: Marsella AJ, Friedman M, Gerrity ET, Scurfield RM, eds. *Ethnocultural Aspects of Post-traumatic Stress and Related Disorders*, 255–83. Washington, D.C.: American Psychiatric Association Press.

Manson SM, Bloom J, Rogers J, et al. 1987. Emerging tribal models for the civil commitment of American Indians. *Am Indian Alsk Native Ment Health Res* 1(1):9–26.

Manson SM, Shore JH, Bloom JD, et al. 1989b. Alcohol abuse and major affective disorders: Advances in epidemiologic research among American Indians. In: Spiegler DL, Tate DA, Aitken SS, et al., eds. *Alcohol Use and Abuse among U.S. Ethnic Minorities*, 291–300. National Institute on Alcohol Abuse and Alcoholism Monograph Series, No. 18 (ADM 89-1435). Washington, D.C.: Government Printing Office.

May PA. 1983. A survey of the existing data on mental health in Albuquerque Area. Unpublished report prepared under Contract 3-200423, Indian Health Service.

———. 1987. Suicide and self-destruction among American Indian youths. *Am Indian Alsk Native Ment Health Res* 1(1):52–69.

McIntosh JL, Santos JF. 1981. Suicide among minority elderly: A preliminary investigation. *Suicide Life Threat Behav* 11(3):151–66.

Minton BA, Soule S. 1990. Two Eskimo villages assess mental health strengths and needs. *Am Indian Alsk Native Ment Health Res* 4(2):7–24.

Murphy JM, Hughes CC. 1965. The use of psychophysiological symptoms as indicators of disorder among Eskimos. In: Murphy JM, Leighton AH, eds. *Approaches to Cross-cultural Psychiatry*. Ithaca: Cornell University Press.

National Task Force on Suicide in Canada. 1987. *Suicide in Canada*. Ottawa: Health and Welfare Canada.

Native American Rehabilitation and Training Center. 1979. Unpublished program report. Tucson: University of Arizona.

Nelson SH, McCoy GF, Stetter M, et al. 1992. An overview of mental health services for American Indians and Alaska Natives in the 1990s. *Hosp Community Psychiatry* 4(3):257–61.

Nelson SH, O'Neal MA, Plummer A. 1996. Native healing. *Harvard Med Alumni Bull*, Summer, 46–49.

Norton IM, Manson SM. 1995. The silent minority: Battered American Indian women. *J Fam Violence* 10:307–18.

Novins DK, Bechtold DW, Sack WH, et al. 1997. The *DSM-IV* Outline for Cultural Formulation: A critical demonstration with American Indian children. *J Am Acad Child Adolesc Psychiatry* 36:1244–51.

O'Connell JC, ed. 1987. *A Study of the Special Problems and Needs of American Indians with Handicaps Both on and off the Reservation*. Report submitted to the U.S. Department of Education, Office of Special Education and Rehabilitative Services.

Oetting E, Beauvais F, Edwards RW. 1988. Alcohol and Indian youth: Social and psychological correlates and prevention. *J Drug Issues* 18:87–101.

Oetting ER, Goldstein GS. 1979. Drug use among Native American adolescents. In:
Beschner G, Friedman A, eds. *Youth Drug Abuse.* Lexington, Mass.: Lexington
Books.

Office of Technology Assessment, U.S. Congress. 1990. *Indian Adolescent Mental
Health.* OTA-H-446. Washington, D.C.: Government Printing Office.

Piasecki JM, Manson SM, Biernoff MP, et al. 1989. Abuse and neglect of American
Indian children: Findings from a survey of federal providers. *Am Indian Alsk Native
Ment Health Res* 3(2):43–62.

Ross CA, Davis B. 1986. Suicide and parasuicide in a Northern Canada Native community. *Can J Psychiatry* 3:331–34.

Sack WH, Beiser M, Clarke G, et al. 1987. The high achieving Sioux Indian child: Some
preliminary findings from the Flower of Two Soils project. *Am Indian Alsk Native
Ment Health Res* 1(1):37–51.

Sampath HM. 1974. Prevalence of psychiatric disorders in a Southern Baffin Island
Eskimo settlement. *Can Psychiatr Assoc J* 19:363–67.

Shore JH. 1974. Psychiatric epidemiology among American Indians. *Psychiatr Ann*
4(11):56–66.

Shore JH, Bopp JE, Walter TR, et al. 1972. A suicide prevention center on an Indian
reservation. *Am J Psychiatry* 128:1086–91.

Shore JH, Kinzie JD, Pattison EM. 1973. Psychiatric epidemiology of an Indian village.
Psychiatry 36(1):70–81.

Spaulding JM. 1985. Recent suicide rates among ten Ojibwa Indian bands in northwestern Ontario. *Omega J Death Dying* 16:347–54.

Thomason TC. 1991. Counseling Native Americans: An introduction for non-Native
American counselors. *J Counseling Dev* 69:321–27.

Thompson JW. 1996. A curriculum for learning about American Indians and Alaska
Natives in psychiatric residency training. *Acad Psychiatry* 20(1):5–12.

Trimble JE, Manson SM, Dinges NG, et al. 1984. A conceptual framework for under-
standing American Indians and mental health: Challenging cultural presumptions.
American Indian concepts of mental health: Reflections and directions. In: Pedersen
PB, Marsella AJ, eds. *Cultural Conceptions of Mental Health and Therapy,* 199–220.
Beverly Hills, Calif.: Sage Publications.

U.S. Department of the Interior, Bureau of Indian Affairs. 1976. *Research and Evaluation Report Series,* No. 42.00, reprinted. Washington, D.C.: Government Printing
Office.

Weibel-Orlando J. 1984. Substance abuse among American Indian youth: A continuing
crisis. *J Drug Issues* 14:313–35.

White R, Cornely D. 1981. Navajo child abuse and neglect study: A comparison group
examination of abuse and neglect of Navajo children. *Child Abuse Negl* 5:9–17.

Young TJ. 1988. Substance use and abuse among Native Americans. *Clin Psychol Rev*
8:125–38.

19

R. Hal Scofield, M.D.

Diseases of the Immune and Collagen Vascular Systems

The so-called connective tissue diseases are a group of related but clinically diverse illnesses that in general can be characterized as inflammatory and rheumatic. While the clinical manifestations vary greatly, inflammatory arthritis is a common (but not universal) feature. Among these diseases are rheumatoid arthritis, systemic lupus erythematosus, dermato- and polymyositis, scleroderma, Sjögren syndrome, and the spondyloarthropathies. While there is no simple pattern of inheritance, there is a tendency for each of these diseases to be familial.

In addition to their predilection to involve the musculoskeletal system, another common theme among the autoimmune rheumatic diseases is evidence of an immune pathogenesis, many times in the form of autoimmunity, with autoantibodies found in the sera of patients. For instance, more than 95 percent of individuals with systemic lupus erythematosus have antinuclear antibodies (ANAs). Most patients with rheumatoid arthritis have rheumatoid factor, which is immunoglobulin that binds the Fc portion of immunoglobulin G, in their sera. The autoimmunity in rheumatic disease is systemic; that is, autoantibodies are directed against self-components found in all cell types. In contrast, organ-specific autoimmune disease, such as Graves hyperthyroidism, produces autoimmunity largely directed toward the injured organ only.

Data showing that connective tissue diseases are associated with specific alleles of the major histocompatibility complex are further evidence of an immune mechanism of disease. The major histocompatibility complex is located on chromosome 6 in humans and contains genes encoding for the class I and class II human lymphocyte antigens (HLA). The proteins of the HLA system are critical molecules within the immune system. HLA class I molecules are present on all nucleated cells and bind short peptides, which are presented to cytotoxic T cells. If such peptides are recognized as foreign by the cytotoxic T cells, a cascade of events leads to the destruction of the cell presenting the foreign antigen. HLA class II alleles are found on antigen-presenting cells, where they also present peptides to T cells, designated CD4-positive T helper cells. If the peptide presented is recognized as foreign, helper T cells are stimulated and an immune response to the foreign antigen is initiated. The genes encoding HLA class I and II are the most polymorphic in the human genome. Several genes and haplotypes are unique to the peoples native to the Americas.

Rheumatoid Arthritis

Rheumatoid arthritis is a chronic, inflammatory arthritis that is usually symmetrical and erosive. The disease can lead to severe joint destruction and deformity, with resultant disability. Any joint can be affected, but involvement of the small joints of the hand, especially the metacarpophalangeal and proximal interphalangeal, is typical. There are several extra-articular manifestations, including rheumatoid nodules and rheumatoid vasculitis. Most studies indicate that rheumatoid arthritis affects about 1 percent of the population, and the prevalence is remarkably similar in the many ethnically and racially divergent populations that have been studied (Lawrence et al. 1989; reviewed in Beasley et al. 1973a and Harvey et al. 1981b).

Rheumatoid factor is usually immunoglobulin M (IgM) but can also be IgG, which binds the Fc portion of IgG, and is characteristically found in the sera of patients with rheumatoid arthritis. Patients with rheumatoid arthritis occasionally are found to have a positive ANA test. In most studies of Caucasians, about 10 percent of those with the disease are positive for ANA. Rheumatoid arthritis is associated with certain alleles of HLA-DR that contain a particular short amino acid sequence. That this sequence is critical to the pathogenesis of the disease has been termed the "shared epitope hypothesis" (Winchester, Dwyer, and Rose 1992).

Rheumatoid arthritis has been studied in American Indians and Alaska Natives more frequently and more thoroughly than any other connective tissue disease. Nonetheless, the most interesting aspect of the disease and the native population of the Americas may not be its relation to the modern population, but its relation to ancient Native Americans, because there are now data to suggest that rheumatoid arthritis had its origin in the Western Hemisphere.

The Origin of Rheumatoid Arthritis

Evidence for a host of rheumatic diseases, from osteoarthritis to bone infection to spondyloarthropathy, is found in skeletal remains from prehistorical or historical times (Karsh 1960). There is, however, as yet no convincing evidence of rheumatoid arthritis in the Old World before about 1800. In addition, there is no clinical description of a disease consistent with rheumatoid arthritis until about this same time. Thus, in the Old World, rheumatoid arthritis seems to be a disease of recent origin (Short 1974).

In the New World, rheumatoid arthritis may be a disease of ancient times. In 1988, Rothschild and co-workers presented evidence that an erosive, symmetrical arthritis existed in people living in what is now Alabama from 450 to 6,500 years before the present (Rothschild, Turner, and DeLuca 1988). In subsequent work (Rothschild, Woods, and Ortel 1990; Woods and Rothschild 1988; Rothschild and Woods 1990), these investigators proposed that this arthritis, which is consistent with a diagnosis of rheumatoid arthritis, was isolated to a small area in what is now Tennessee until approximately one thousand years ago (Rothschild et al. 1992). The disease then expanded in geographical area. European contact with the expanded area in which the arthritis existed began around 1750 (Rothschild et al. 1992). The timing of the European appearance of rheumatoid arthritis and contact fits well with the disease being caused by a transmittable agent, although no such agent has been yet identified.

A criticism of the data from Rothschild has been that the bony findings may be only artifact. This has been addressed in part by examination of defleshed modern skeletons from persons with and without the diagnosis of rheumatoid arthritis (Rothschild, Woods, and Ortel 1990). Although agreement has not been reached that rheumatoid arthritis began in the Americas (Appelboom 1981; Leden, Persson, and Persson 1988; Kilgore 1989; Dequeker and Rico 1992), the data presented thus far are provocative. Clearly, a disease existed in the ancient people of what is now the southern United States that is consistent with rheumatoid arthritis. Such a disease was distinctly uncommon in the Old World before the nineteenth century.

Rheumatoid Arthritis in Modern Populations

Several tribes have been intensely studied as to the prevalence and genetics of rheumatoid arthritis (Table 19.1). These include Alaska Natives, both Eskimos and Indians, as well as a wide range of other North American Indians. Some tribes have a strikingly high prevalence of rheumatoid arthritis; other groups have little disease, but the HLA genes associated with disease are commonly found. In addition, the sera of rheumatoid arthritis patients and controls have been studied for the presence of rheumatoid factor and antinuclear antibodies.

The Mille Lac Band of Chippewa (or Ojibway) in Minnesota have been studied by the rheumatology group at the Johns Hopkins University (Harvey, Lotze, and Stevens 1981). Like many studies of rheumatic illness, this one began after the clinical observation that joint disease was common among members of the Chippewa tribe. The Mille Lac Band, consisting of 209 persons over age 18,

TABLE 19.1
Studies of rheumatoid arthritis in American Indians or Alaska Natives

Tribe	Population[a]	Rheumatoid arthritis		
		Prevalence (%)	Incidence	Features
Chippewa	209	6.8	ND[b]	75% +ANA/DR4
Yakima	465	3.4 F	ND	60% +ANA/Dw16
Pima	1,800	2.3 M	42.2/10[6]	↓ incidence
		6.95 F		
Blackfeet	1,100	1.1	ND	
Tlingit	8,000	3.5	ND	70% +ANA/DRB11402
Inuit	4,000	1.0	ND	None in males
Yupik	13,230	0.7	ND	
Inupiat	4,600	1.0	ND	
Kiowa	12[a]	ND	ND	75% +ANA
				33% +anti-Ro

[a]The total number of individuals in the studied population is given, except for the Kiowa study, where the number of patients with rheumatoid arthritis is given.
[b]ND, not done.

was studied, with 205 (98%) persons examined. Fourteen (6.8%) of the band had rheumatoid arthritis, with rheumatoid factor found in 75 percent of the 14. Rheumatoid arthritis was found in 8.2 percent of women. Twelve of the 14 patients with rheumatoid arthritis had a positive ANA, defined as a titer greater than 1:80. Studies of the genetics at HLA-D were reported in two subsequent papers (Harvey et al. 1981, 1983). HLA-DR4, as determined serologically, was common in the population, with 68 percent of persons bearing this marker, but serologic HLA-DR4 was found in 100 percent of rheumatoid arthritis patients (Harvey et al. 1983). More extensive analysis of HLA in the Mille Lac Band showed that only 57 extended HLA-A, -B, -C, -D haplotypes were found; there were several variants of HLA-DR4 in the population as a whole and within the group of patients with rheumatoid arthritis (Harvey et al. 1981; Harvey, Lotze, and Stevens 1981; Bias et al. 1981). Sequencing of the specific HLA-DR genes from the Mille Lac Band is not available, however.

The Yakima of the Pacific Northwest also have a high prevalence of rheumatoid arthritis (Beasley, Willkins, and Bennett 1973). A random, age-stratified survey was carried out on 465 women of the 5,665-member Yakima tribe. The survey consisted of a preliminary screening history and physical examination, followed by confirmatory evaluation and hand radiographs. Seventeen women were identified with rheumatoid arthritis, for a prevalence of 3.4 percent (Beasley, Willkins, and Bennett 1973). As in the Chippewa, antinuclear antibodies were frequently positive (19 of 33) in Yakima Indians with rheumatoid arthritis, but titers were not shown (Willkins et al. 1976).

Other follow-up studies have concerned genetics of rheumatoid arthritis within the tribe. In a study of 28 Yakima with rheumatoid arthritis, no increase in HLA-DR4 or HLA-Dw4 was found (Willkins et al. 1982). However, HLA-Dw16 is found frequently in patients (83%), as well as within the tribe (60%). This rare allele carries the specific sequence in the third hypervariable region that is associated with rheumatoid arthritis (the "shared epitope"). This HLA gene is rare (<1%) in Caucasians (Willkins et al. 1991).

Rheumatoid arthritis among the Pima has been extensively studied. Among this tribe, rheumatoid arthritis has been found to have both a high prevalence and a high incidence. Over a 20-year period, annual examinations were performed on members of the Gila River Indian community. Radiographs of the hands were taken every four years. Among approximately eighteen hundred participants, rheumatoid arthritis had a prevalence rate of 3.23 percent among men and 6.95 percent among women (del Puente et al. 1989). The incidence rate (42.2 cases per 10,000 person years) during the study period was also higher than that of two non-Indian populations. A previous study found an aggregation of rheumatoid arthritis in large sibships among the Pima but not in Blackfeet, suggesting an environmental influence (Bennett and Burch 1968). No increased prevalence of rheumatoid arthritis, however, has been found in the Blackfeet (Bennett and Burch 1968; O'Brien et al. 1967).

Long-term follow-up data are available for rheumatoid arthritis in Pima Indians. Jacobsson et al. (1994), again studying the Gila River Pima Indians, found that both incidence and prevalence rates of rheumatoid arthritis fell from 1965 until 1990. The incidence and prevalence rates in both men and women fell by more than 50 percent over these 25 years. The results were similar when full-blood subjects were evaluated separately. Even when controlled for use of oral contraception, the prevalence rate in women fell 40 percent and that in men dropped by 29 percent.

Confounding variables, such as changing diagnostic criteria and ascertainment bias, do not account for these changes, as similar criteria were applied to the diagnosis in the population-based study (Jacobsson et al. 1994). Genetic admixture, emigration, and use of estrogens (Spector and Hochberg 1990) were also controlled for in this study, making these unlikely confounding variables. What, then, can account for the changed prevalence of rheumatoid arthritis among the Pima? A change in some environmental exposure has been proposed (Jacobsson et al. 1994). The changes among these people have been profound in the last few generations. Among other things, there is an increased standard of living, decreased rates of tuberculosis and a host of other serious infections, but an increase in diabetes mellitus. Thus, discovering the change(s) that have altered the incidence and prevalence rates of rheumatoid arthritis in this population will be difficult.

Rheumatoid arthritis has been studied in Alaska Natives. The Tlingit have classical, severe disease with a high rate of ANA positivity with 70 percent of patients having a >1:80 titer (Templin et al. 1994). A high rate of positive ANA tests among control members of the tribe without rheumatoid arthritis was also reported (Templin et al. 1994). In addition, rheumatoid arthritis among the Tlingit was associated with the presence of the HLA-DR shared epitope in the form of HLA-DRB1*1402 (Templin et al. 1994; Nelson et al. 1992). In a study of Southeast Coast of Alaska Indians that included the approximately eight thousand Tlingit, a prevalence rate of 3.5 percent was found for rheumatoid arthritis. The Tlingit constituted 80 percent of the population studied (Boyer, Templin, and Lanier 1991).

Several studies have examined rheumatoid arthritis in Eskimos. In Inuits of the Northwest Territory, no evidence of an increased incidence of rheumatoid arthritis was found (Oen et al. 1986). In fact, in this population-based study of about four thousand individuals, not a single case of rheumatoid arthritis in a man was confirmed (Oen et al. 1986). In Yupik Eskimos a prevalence of 0.7 percent was found for rheumatoid arthritis, a rate not different from that in Caucasian populations studied (Boyer et al. 1990). Likewise, a 1 percent prevalence rate was found in Inupiat Eskimos (Boyer, Lanier, and Templin 1988). The above three studies confirmed older work that rheumatoid arthritis is not found frequently in Eskimos (Beasley, Retailliau, and Healey 1973; Blumberg et al. 1961; Hill and Robinson 1969).

Although prevalence and incidence studies have not been performed, Kiowa with rheumatoid arthritis have been found to have not only a high rate of ANA positivity (75%) but also an usually high rate (33%) of positive anti-Ro/SSA (Scofield et al. 1996). Members of other tribes using the same Indian Health Service (IHS) facility had ANAs and anti-Ro/SSA at a rate not different from those expected in Caucasians (Scofield et al. 1996).

In summary, rheumatoid arthritis is found in excess among members of some but not all tribes (Table 19.1). In particular, there is no evidence of an increased prevalence or incidence among Alaska Natives. An HLA-DR allele containing the "shared epitope" associated with rheumatoid arthritis is found in most of the tribes with increased rheumatoid arthritis. The serologic findings in rheumatoid arthritis among American Indians may be different from the findings in other racial and ethnic groups. Some American Indians, including the Chippewa, Tlingit, and Kiowa, have higher rates of positive ANA than expected. ANA is also found in tribal members without rheumatoid arthritis.

Spondyloarthropathy

Ankylosing spondylitis, Reiter syndrome (reactive arthritis), psoriatic arthritis, and arthritis associated with inflammatory bowel disease are collectively known as the seronegative spondyloarthropathies. The prototypic manifestation of these diseases is enthesopathy — inflammation at the site of ligamentous attachment to bone. The clinical features of ankylosing spondylitis include sacroiliitis and spinal disease that results in inflammatory back pain and spinal fusion. Reiter syndrome and reactive arthritis occur after gastrointestinal infection with several organisms including salmonella, shigella, and yersinia. In addition, reactive arthritis may occur after sexually transmitted infection with chlamydia. The triad of clinical features seen in Reiter and reactive arthritis is peripheral arthritis, urethritis, and inflammatory eye disease. Patients may have a chronic, relapsing illness, which may include all or only some of the features during a single episode.

There is a powerful population association of the spondyloarthropathies and the major histocompatibility complex gene HLA-B27 (Brewerton 1973). HLA-B27 is found in approximately 8 percent of persons of European descent, but in more than 90 percent of those with ankylosing spondylitis. The prevalence of HLA-B27 in patients with Reiter syndrome and other spondyloarthropathies is lower than that in ankylosing spondylitis, but this HLA-B allele is found in these diseases far more frequently than in the general population (Morris et al. 1974). An estimated 20 percent of persons with HLA-B27 are at risk for spondyloarthropathy, but a primary relative with disease increases the chance of disease to about 50 percent (Moller and Berg 1983; Rubin et al. 1994).

Neither population association nor genetic linkage proves involvement in pathogenesis. However, other evidence, including that from studies of HLA-B27-transgenic rats (Hammer et al. 1990) or mice (Khare, Luthra, and David 1995), indicates that, in fact, HLA-B27 is directly involved in the pathogenesis of the spondyloarthropathies. The mechanism by which involvement occurs is not known, although altered infectivity of enteric bacteria in cells with HLA-B27 (Kapasi and Inman 1992) and mimicry of HLA-B27 by bacteria (Scofield et al. 1993, 1995) have both been suggested.

Spondyloarthropathy has been studied extensively in Eskimos (Table 19.2), perhaps because HLA-B27 is carried by up to 40 percent of some Eskimo populations (Oen et al. 1986; Hansen et al. 1986) and because of the clinical observation that arthritis seems unusually common in Eskimos (Beasley, Retailliau, and Healey 1973). In addition, the Eskimos continue to live in an isolated manner, and virtually the entire population uses the Alaska Area Native Health Service, where birth-to-death single-file medical records are available.

Boyer and colleagues reported their findings concerning spondyloarthropathies over several years (Boyer, Lanier, and Templin 1988; Boyer et al. 1994; Boyer et al. 1990). A study of forty-six hundred Inupiat Eskimos found that 1.7 percent of men had spondyloarthropathies (Boyer, Lanier, and Templin 1988). A second study of Yupik Eskimos found 67 patients with spondyloarthropa-

TABLE 19.2
Spondyloarthropathy in American Indians and Alaska Natives

Tribe	Population[a]	Spondyloarthropathy		
		Prevalence (%)	Incidence	Features
Yupik	13,230	0.5	ND[b]	Overlap/undifferentiated ↑ childhood
Inupiat	4,600	1.5 M	ND	Overlap/undifferentiated ↑ childhood
Yupik	3,690	2.5	ND	Undifferentiated
Inupiat	3,059	2.5		Undifferentiated
SECAI[c]	10,000	1.1	ND	
Haida[d]	209	6.7[e]	ND	All with AS[f]
Navajo	18,000	ND	1/1,000/yr	Reiter syndrome

[a]The total number of individuals in the population studied.
[b]ND, not done.
[c]Southeast Coast of Alaska Indians.
[d]Canadian Haida.
[e]For men over age 25, in whom the prevalence of radiographic sacroiliitis was 14%.
[f]AS, ankylosing spondylitis.

thies in a population of 13,230 (Boyer et al. 1990). In both of these studies, a high incidence of spondyloarthropathy was undifferentiated or presented as an overlap between recognized specific spondyloarthropathy categories. The Inuit Eskimos in the Northwest Territory have about the same prevalence of spondyloarthropathy as the closely related Inupiat Eskimos of Alaska (Oen et al. 1986). In the Inuits (Oen et al. 1986) and the Inupiats (Boyer, Lanier, and Templin 1988), there is a marked increase in childhood spondyloarthropathy, with most patients having chronic disease later in adult life (Boyer, Lanier, and Templin 1988; Oen et al. 1986). In all of these Eskimo groups, the prevalence of HLA-B27 in the population is high, such that the relative risk of disease if one has HLA-B27 is low; that is, there are large numbers of HLA-B27-positive individuals without disease (Oen et al. 1986).

Boyer et al. (1994) also studied smaller groups of Inupiats ($n = 3,059$) and Yupiks ($n = 3,690$) in more detail. These studies included special clinics and interviews with health care providers to identify as many afflicted individuals as possible. The overall prevalence of spondyloarthropathy was 2.5 percent. Again, many patients did not fall into the usual diagnostic categories and were classified as having overlap or undifferentiated disease.

The Indians of the Southeast Alaska coast (the Athabascan, Tlingit, Haida, and Tsimshian) were studied with regard to spondyloarthropathies (Boyer, Templin, and Lanier 1991). Fifty-eight patients were found, for a prevalence rate of 1.1 percent. This is a figure not different from that reported in North American Caucasian populations and was the same for all four tribes. However, this report differs from that of Gofton et al. (1972), who found that 4.7 percent of Canadian Haida (6.7% of males older than 25) had ankylosing spondylitis and 14 percent of men over 25 years of age had radiographic sacroiliitis (Gofton et al. 1972). Almost 50 percent of the Canadian Haida have HLA-B27, but HLA-B27 has not been studied in Alaska Haida. Perhaps the difference in disease between the Alaska and Canadian Haida is a difference in the rate of HLA-B27 in the two populations, possibly due to a founder effect.

Related to these studies of Southeast Alaska coast Indians are the studies of the Navajo and Hopi carried out at the Keams Canyon Indian Hospital on the Hopi reservation in northern Arizona. About half of the patients at this facility are Hopi and half are Navajo from the surrounding Navajo reservation. Before the description of the association of HLA-B27 with spondyloarthropathy, clinicians at this hospital had reported a "Navajo arthritis" that was common in the Navajo but not seen in the Hopi living in the same geographical area. Initially, "Navajo arthritis" was thought to be a unique illness distinct from other known arthritides, including spondyloarthropathy. The majority of adults diagnosed with arthritis within the Navajo population had this entity in 1969 (Muggia, Bennahum, and Williams 1971).

Later studies of HLA-B27 and arthritis in the Navajo confirmed that "Navajo arthritis" was best classified as a variant of Reiter syndrome or ankylosing spondylitis and was associated with HLA-B27 (Rate et al. 1980). Among 92 patients over age 15 with acute arthritis seen over a three-year period, there were 16 cases of complete Reiter syndrome, 6 cases of incomplete Reiter syndrome, and 7 cases of ankylosing spondylitis. In total, 85 percent of these 29 patients had HLA-B27 (Rate et al. 1980). These authors concluded that "Navajo arthritis" is in fact acute reactive arthritis (Rate et al. 1980; Morse et al. 1981).

Another study found that the Navajo have high incidence and prevalence rates of Reiter syndrome, with 18 cases diagnosed over a one-year period among eighteen thousand Navajo (Morse et al. 1980). Again, Hopi living in the same area of Northern Arizona had neither high incidence nor prevalence rates of Reiter syndrome. This was despite the fact that in both the Hopi and Navajo shigellosis is endemic. *Shigella flexneri* was the most common isolate, an organism known to be associated with reactive arthritis (Morse et al. 1980).

The difference in the prevalence and incidence between the Navajo and Hopi is surely related to the frequency of HLA-B27 in the populations. Up to 36 percent of Navajo carry this allele (Morse et al. 1980; Kuberski et al. 1981), while among Hopi HLA-B27 is found in only 9 percent of the population (Kuberski 1981). The difference in the frequency of HLA-B27 is likely related to the disparate ethnic origin of these two tribes. The Hopi have inhabited what is now the southwestern United States for centuries and are thought to have originated from more ancient people in Central America. In contrast, the Navajo are an Athabascan tribe and migrated to the southwestern United States only about five hundred years ago. The Navajo are related to the southeast Alaska coast tribes such as the Haida, in whom there is a high frequency of HLA-B27 as well as in some groups (Canadian Haida) a high prevalence rate of spondyloarthropathy (Gofton et al. 1972, 1975).

Scleroderma

Systemic sclerosis, or scleroderma, is a multisystem disease that is characterized by fibrosis of both viscera and skin. The striking cutaneous involvement consists of thickened, hide-bound skin. Virtually any organ can be involved, but pulmonary fibrosis and renal failure are the most common serious manifestations. Scleroderma is uncommon, with an incidence rate of approximately 2/100,000 per year and a prevalence rate of 1 in 10,000 (Lawrence et al. 1989). The disease does not have a strong familial tendency. The reported concordance rate in monozygotic twins is low.

Several disease-specific autoantibodies are markers for disease subsets and prognosis. Anticentromere is found in the sera of patients with the CREST variant of scleroderma, which consists of calcinosis, Raynaud phenomenon, esophageal dysmotility, and telangiectasia. On the other hand, antibodies against topoisomerase (anti-Scl70) are found in patients with diffuse skin involvement and progressive pulmonary fibrosis.

There has been a single, but interesting and provocative, study of scleroderma among American Indians. This study sprang from the clinical observation by an IHS rheumatologist that scleroderma seemed unusually common in Choctaw of southeastern Oklahoma. Arnett et al. (1996) found that, in fact, scleroderma is extremely common in Oklahoma Choctaw, compared to other Oklahoma Indians or Caucasian controls (Table 19.3). Of the more than twenty-one thousand Choctaw in southeastern Oklahoma in the Talihina Service Unit of the IHS, 1,704 are full-blooded. The prevalence of scleroderma was almost 1 in 200 full-blooded Choctaw. Within the population less than full-blooded, the disease was found in 1 in 3,259, for an overall prevalence rate in the tribe of 1 in 1,518. The

TABLE 19.3
Scleroderma (systemic sclerosis) in Native Americans

| Tribe | No. | Scleroderma | |
		Prevalence	Features
Choctaw	20[a]	1/213 full[b] 1/3,259 <full[b]	anti-topo I; pulmonary fibrosis common

SOURCE: Data from Arnett et al. 1996.
[a]Twenty patients were found among approximately 20,000 Choctaw in Eastern Oklahoma.
[b]Full-heritage Choctaw vs. less than full heritage.

prevalence of scleroderma in non-Choctaw Indians residing in Oklahoma and receiving their medical care within the IHS was 1 in 10,000, the rate previously reported among North American Caucasians (Lawrence et al. 1989).

The Choctaw came to Oklahoma in 1837 on the "Trail of Tears" from their ancestral home in what is now the southeastern United States. Some Choctaw, however, remained in Mississippi. The study also examined the forty-five hundred Mississippi Choctaw and found no scleroderma (Arnett et al. 1996). This difference in prevalence between the geographically separate Choctaw populations suggested an environmental exposure common to the Oklahoma group. However, an extensive questionnaire administered to patients and controls failed to uncover any factor related to scleroderma. Of course, if an environmental trigger exists, it may be ubiquitous in southeastern Oklahoma, such that all persons are unknowingly exposed. Data on the prevalence of scleroderma among the Caucasian population in southeastern Oklahoma are not available.

In addition to the strikingly high prevalence rate of disease, the Oklahoma Choctaw with scleroderma had a markedly consistent disease expression. The patients tended to have diffuse skin involvement, Raynaud phenomenon, and pulmonary fibrosis with autoantibodies binding topoisomerase I. In addition, all patients had a particular extended HLA haplotype containing the alleles HLA-B35, Cw4, DRB1*1602 (DR2), DQA1*0501, and DQB1*0301 (DQ7). This haplotype is unique to Amerindians and was found in 54 percent of a control group of Choctaw without scleroderma. In addition, this haplotype was found commonly among Mississippi Choctaw who had no scleroderma.

The increased scleroderma in Oklahoma Choctaw and the lack of disease in Eastern Choctaw also suggest a genetic determinant involved in the disease. This possibility has recently been explored by exploiting the genetics of mouse models of scleroderma (Tan et al. 1998). The tight skin 1 and tight skin 2 mice have phenotypes similar to that of human scleroderma. The tight skin 1 mouse has an autosomal dominant mutation that maps to mouse chromosome 2, which is homologous to human chromosome 15q. This mutation is known to involve the fibrillin 1 gene. Mutations of this gene cause Marfan syndrome. In the tight skin 2 mouse, the gene responsible for the disease has been mapped to mouse chromosome 1, which is homologous to human chromosome 2q. Thus, Tan and his co-workers examined microsatellite markers on human chromosomes 15 and 2 in regions that are homologous to murine chromosomal regions responsible for the two mouse models of scleroderma. The Choctaw with scleroderma were found to share a series of microsatellite markers on chromosome 15q and to have this haplotype much more commonly than Choctaw without scleroderma. These genetic markers are close to, or even within, the gene for fibrillin. Therefore, this region of human chromosome 15q may contain a gene that predisposes Oklahoma Choctaw to scleroderma, and fibrillin 1 is a candidate for this gene. No linkage was found on chromosome 2.

These workers also investigated the genealogy of the Oklahoma Choctaw. This work shows that the Choctaw with scleroderma are descended from five founding families from the middle of the eighteenth century. These common founders, some of whom were European, may have introduced disease genes into the population about 10 generations ago. The chance that the patients shared the identified microsatellite haplotype simply because of familial aggregation was very low (Tan et al. 1998). As noted in an accompanying editorial (Harley and Neas 1998), there is much work to be done in both the Choctaw and non-Choctaw populations to determine the contribution of specific genes. However, the genetic study of an isolated population with an increased burden of a collagen vascular disease has been highly informative thus far. More recently, this group of investigators has found autoantibodies binding fibrillin in the sera of Choctaw and non-Choctaw with scleroderma (Tan et al. 1999).

Thus, the Oklahoma Choctaw are the only population of any ethnicity in which an increased prevalence of scleroderma has been found. The difference in scleroderma between the Mississippi and Oklahoma Choctaw suggests an environmental or genetic difference; however, any such environmental or genetic factor related to the pathogenesis of the disease may be so common in the population that isolating it will be difficult. There are no other data relating to scleroderma in other tribal groups. Thus, further study of scleroderma in the Choctaw as well as other Native Americans is warranted.

Systemic Lupus Erythematosus

Systemic lupus erythematosus (SLE) is a chronic, systemic connective tissue disease that can affect virtually any organ system. Disease manifestations can vary widely. Diagnostic classification (Tan et al. 1982) is such that two individuals might share no feature except the diagnosis. SLE is much more common in women than men, in a ratio of 10:1, and is more common in American Blacks than Caucasians, in a ratio of about 4:1. As many as 1 in 250 Black women in the United States has SLE (Fessel 1988). The epidemiology of SLE, including differences and similarities among racial and ethnic groups, has been reviewed (Fessel 1988). There is no simple pattern of inheritance, but the disease has a strong family tendency. Excellent population data from twins are available (Järvinen and Aho 1994).

Despite the protean clinical manifestations, patients with SLE are united by their autoimmune, serologic manifestations. Several autoantibodies are found exclusively, or almost exclusively, in the sera of individuals with SLE. These include anti–double stranded (native) deoxyribonucleic acid (DNA), anti-Sm, and anti-ribosomal P. While the presence of some autoantibodies is associated with particular clinical manifestations (e.g., antinative DNA is associated with renal disease), the antigens themselves are usually found in all cells and perform important, essential cellular functions. The finding of autoantibodies in the sera of patients with SLE is the major evidence by which the illness is considered autoimmune.

SLE has been studied on a limited basis in Indians and Alaska Natives. In 1971 Morton and colleagues reviewed the recorded discharge diagnoses from IHS hospitals during the period 1971–75. These data included 72 Indian and Alaska tribes. The annual incidence rate of SLE was similar to that found in other ethnic and racial groups in 69 of the 72 tribes, ranging from 0 to 6.9/ 100,000 (Morton 1976). However, in 3 tribes, the Crow, Arapaho, and Sioux, there was a possible increased annual incidence of SLE. Medical records review confirmed or refuted the diagnosis for each patient who was a member of one of these three tribes. Because of their large population (30,120), the Sioux were chosen for further study. There were a total of 20 Sioux SLE patients, of whom 18 were women. The annual incidence rate of SLE among full-blooded Sioux was 31.3/100,000, and that among less than full-blooded members was 20.8/ 100,000 (Morton 1971). There was no apparent increase in SLE among the non-Sioux population living in the same geographical area, and the risk of SLE was increased at all facilities participating in the medical care of the Sioux (Morton 1976).

Boyer, Templin, and Lanier (1991) studied the prevalence of SLE in Alaska Southeast Coast Indians. As noted above, this population is about 80 percent Tlingit and, while sharing a common geographical area, these four tribes are thought to have distinct origins (Boas 1989). In total, 13 patients with SLE were identified in this study. When adjusted for age, the prevalence rate was significantly higher than that reported for Caucasian populations but below that reported for American Black populations (Boyer, Templin, and Lanier 1991).

Thus, SLE has not been studied extensively in North American Indian or Alaska Native populations. As with rheumatoid arthritis, the prevalence and incidence in some tribes are increased above those found in other ethnic groups. In both previous reports (Boyer, Templin, and Lanier 1991; Morton 1971), the manifestations of SLE were said to be similar to those found in other groups. Scofield and colleagues found that Oklahoma Indians with anti-Ro/SSA in their serum tend to have a uniform clinical illness (unpublished data). This consists of mild SLE and a rheumatoid-like arthritis that is nonerosive. Whether in fact SLE manifests differently in American Indians compared to other ethnic populations has otherwise not been determined.

Juvenile Arthritis

Inflammatory arthritis can have its onset in childhood. Such disease is heterogeneous and can be categorized according to its onset. Systemic-onset juvenile rheumatoid arthritis (JRA) presents with characteristic spiking fevers, a maculopapular salmon-pink rash located over joints as well as the soles and palms, and occasionally pruritus. Many patients have hepatosplenomegaly or lymphadenopathy. Arthritis is usually polyarticular and associated with the same HLA antigens as is rheumatoid arthritis. Other patients have a polyarticular presentation of JRA with an insidious onset, few constitutional symptoms, and negative rheumatoid factor. When onset is polyarticular and rheumatoid factor is positive, the disease is indistinguishable from adult rheumatoid arthritis. The pauciarticular group (fewer than four joints involved at onset) makes up about 50 percent of juvenile rheumatoid arthritis and usually affects girls under 4 years of age. Juvenile spondyloarthropathy is considered a separate category of juvenile arthritis. This usually affects boys over age nine and is associated with HLA-B27. Older literature, however, usually classifies juvenile spondyloarthropathies as pauciarticular JRA.

As early as 1969, chronic arthritis was thought to be more common among Canadian Indians than Caucasians (Hill and Robinson 1969). A compilation of children attending a single arthritis clinic in British Columbia showed that 18.6 percent were of Indian origin, while the population was only 3.6 percent Indian (Hill and Walters 1969). A second report from multiple arthritis clinics in western Canada found an increased ratio of juvenile rheumatoid arthritis to juvenile spondyloarthropathy in Indian children compared to Caucasian children attending the same clinics (Rosenberg et al. 1982). Among those with JRA, Indian children were significantly more likely to have rheumatoid factor than were Caucasian children. The patients in this study were members of the Cree, Assiniboine, Sioux, Haida, Cowichan, or Salish tribe.

Among Alaska Eskimos, onset of inflammatory arthritis in childhood is more common than in other ethnic groups. In both the Inupiat (Boyer, Lanier, and Templin 1988) and Yupik (Boyer et al. 1990), this increase in juvenile arthritis is due to a high prevalence of juvenile-onset spondyloarthropathy. As discussed above, both of these populations have a high rate of HLA-B27. The annual incidence rate among Yupik Eskimos was 42.5/100,000, with 24 cases diagnosed over a 12-year period. Twenty-one had spondyloarthropathy and, over the study period, 15 of the 17 with follow-up developed chronic disease (Boyer et al. 1990).

To the author's knowledge, there have been no systematic studies of juvenile arthritis in Indian children residing in the lower 48 states of the United States. In Eskimos and Canadian Indians, the excess in juvenile arthritis is accounted for by childhood-onset spondyloarthropathy in populations with a high prevalence of HLA-B27.

Discussion

Rheumatoid arthritis may have had its origin in ancient Native Americans and then spread to the Old World after European contact. If true, this is the most powerful evidence available that an environmental trigger, such as an infectious agent or an allergen, initiates rheumatoid arthritis. The prevalence of rheumatoid arthritis in some American Indian groups is higher than that in any other ethnic or racial group. In some tribes the disease is associated with a high prevalence of HLA-DR alleles carrying the shared epitope associated with rheumatoid arthritis. However, these alleles are just as common in some tribes that have no increase in rheumatoid arthritis. Rheumatoid arthritis in American Indians is associated with an increase in ANA and anti-Ro/SSA positivity.

Spondyloarthropathy has been studied in American Indians and Alaska Natives who carry HLA-B27 in high numbers. The relative risk of disease if one has HLA-B27 is lower in some other populations, but overall there are high prevalence and incidence rates of spondyloarthropathy. However, HLA-B27-associated disease in American Indians does not easily fall into the usual categories of Reiter syndrome or ankylosing spondylitis. Many patients have an undifferentiated or overlap syndrome.

Other rheumatic diseases have also been evaluated in American Indians. Systemic lupus erythematosus has increased prevalence in a few tribes but has not been extensively studied. Preliminary data suggest that patients with certain immunologic features may have a similar clinical picture. Systemic sclerosis has a high prevalence in Oklahoma Choctaw. The clinical and serologic profile is remarkably uniform among these patients. Choctaw residing elsewhere do not have this disease.

From the available data one can draw several conclusions. Rheumatic diseases are more common in American Indians and Alaska Natives by virtue of their genetic heritage (e.g., increased HLA-B27 or "shared epitope" HLA-DR) and also by virtue of their environment (e.g., endemic shigella among Navajo). Native Americans with these diseases (1) have a uniform clinical illness, such as the Choctaw with scleroderma, or (2) have disease not easily classified under the present nomenclature, such as spondyloarthropathies, or (3) have unusual features of disease, such as rheumatoid arthritis with antinuclear antibodies. Thus, the usual rheumatic diagnoses may be difficult to apply to a Native American population. For example, the European Spondyloarthropathy Study Group Preliminary Classification Criteria (Dougados et al. 1991) performed well in an Eskimo population (Boyer, Templin, and Goring 1993), but assignment of a precise diagnosis of ankylosing spondylitis or Reiter syndrome is difficult in this group.

REFERENCES

Appelboom T, de Boelpaepe C, Ehrlich GE, et al. 1981. Rubens and the question of antiquity of rheumatoid arthritis. *JAMA* 45:483–86.
Arnett FC, Howard RF, Tan F, et al. 1996. Increased prevalence of systemic sclerosis in a Native American tribe in Oklahoma: Association with an Amerindian HLA haplotype. *Arthritis Rheum* 39:1362–70.
Beasley RP, Retailliau H, Healey LA. 1973a. Prevalence of rheumatoid arthritis in Alaskan Eskimos. *Arthritis Rheum* 16:737–42.
Beasley RP, Willkins RF, Bennett PH. 1973b. High prevalence of rheumatoid arthritis in Yakima Indians. *Arthritis Rheum* 16:743–47.
Bennett PH, Burch TA. 1968. The distribution of rheumatoid factor and rheumatoid arthritis in families of Blackfeet and Pima Indians. *Arthritis Rheum* 11:546–53.
Bias WB, Hsu SH, Pollard MK, et al. 1981. HLA-DR characterization of a Chippewa Indian subpopulation with high prevalence of rheumatoid arthritis. *Hum Immunol* 2:155–63.
Blumberg BS, Bloch KJ, Black RL, et al. 1961. A study of the prevalence of arthritis in Alaskan Eskimos. *Arthritis Rheum* 4:325–41.
Boas F. 1989. The Indian tribes of the North Pacific Coast. In: McFeat T, ed. *Indians of the North Pacific Coast,* 1–7. Seattle: University of Washington Press.
Boyer GS, Lanier AP, Templin DW. 1988. Prevalence rates of spondyloarthropathies, rheumatoid arthritis, and other rheumatic disorders in an Alaskan Inupiat Eskimo population. *J Rheumatol* 15:678–83.
Boyer GS, Lanier AP, Templin DW, et al. 1990. Spondyloarthropathy and rheumatoid arthritis in Alaskan Yupik Eskimos. *J Rheumatol* 17:489–96.
Boyer GS, Templin DW, Cornoni-Huntley JC, et al. 1994. Prevalence of spondyloarthropathies in Alaskan Eskimos. *J Rheumatol* 21:229a–97.
Boyer GS, Templin DW, Goring WP. 1993. Evaluation of the European spondyloarthropathy study group preliminary classification criteria in Alaskan Eskimo populations. *Arthritis Rheum* 36:534–38.
Boyer GS, Templin DW, Lanier AP. 1991. Rheumatic diseases in Alaskan Indians of the Southeast Coast: High prevalence of rheumatoid arthritis and systemic lupus erythematosus. *J Rheumatol* 18:1477–84.
Brewerton DA, Hart FD, Nicholls A, et al. 1973. Ankylosing spondylitis and HL-A B27. *Lancet* 1:904–7.
del Puente A, Knowler WC, Pettitt DJ, et al. 1989. High prevalence of rheumatoid arthritis in Pima Indians. *Am J Epidemiol* 129:1170–78.
Dequeker J, Rico H. 1992. Rheumatoid arthritis-like deformities in an early 16th-century painting of the Flemish-Dutch school. *JAMA* 268:249–51.
Dougados M, van der Linden S, Juhlin R, et al. 1991. The European spondyloarthropathy study group preliminary criteria for the classification of spondyloarthropathy. *Arthritis Rheum* 34:1218–27.
Fessel WJ. 1988. Epidemiology of systemic lupus erythematosus. *Rheum Dis Clin North Am* 14:15–23.

Gofton JP, Bennett PH, Smythe HA, et al. 1972. Sacroiliitis and ankylosing spondylitis in North American Indians. *Ann Rheum Dis* 31:474–81.

Gofton JP, Chalmers A, Price GE, et al. 1975. HL-A27 and ankylosing spondylitis in B.C. Indians. *J Rheumatol* 2:314–18.

Hammer RE, Maika SD, Simmons WA, et al. 1990. Spontaneous inflammatory arthritis in transgenic rats expressing HLA-B27 and human beta 2-microglobulin: An animal model of HLA-B27 associated disorders. *Cell* 63:1099–1112.

Hansen JA, Lanier AP, Nisperos B, et al. 1986. The HLA system in Inupiat and Central Yupik Alaskan Eskimos. *Hum Immunol* 16:315–28.

Harley JB, Neas BR. 1998. Oklahoma Choctaw and systemic sclerosis: The founder effect and genetic susceptibility. *Arthritis Rheum* 41:1725–28.

Harvey J, Arnett FC, Bias WB, et al. 1981a. Heterogeneity of HLA-DR4 in the rheumatoid arthritis of a Chippewa band. *J Rheumatol* 8:797–803.

Harvey J, Lotze M, Arnett FC, et al. 1983. Rheumatoid arthritis in a Chippewa band: II. Field study with clinical, serologic and HLA-D correlations. *J Rheumatol* 10:28–32.

Harvey J, Lotze M, Stevens MB, et al. 1981b. Rheumatoid arthritis in a Chippewa band: I. Pilot screening study of disease prevalence. *Arthritis Rheum* 24:717–20.

Hill RH, Robinson HS. 1969. Rheumatoid arthritis and ankylosing spondylitis in British Columbia Indians: Their prevalence and the challenge of management. *Can Med Assoc J* 100:509–11.

Hill RH, Walters K. 1969. Juvenile rheumatoid arthritis: A medical and social profile of non-Indian and Indian children. *Can Med Assoc J* 100:458–64.

Jacobsson LT, Hansen RL, Knowler WC, et al. 1994. Decreasing incidence and prevalence of rheumatoid arthritis in Pima Indians over a twenty-five-year period. *Arthritis Rheum* 37:1158–65.

Järvinen P, Aho K. 1994. Twin studies in rheumatic diseases. *Semin Arthritis Rheum* 24:19–28.

Kapasi K, Inman RD. 1992. HLA-B27 expression modulates invasion by gram-negative bacteria into transfected L-cells. *J Immunol* 148:3554–59.

Karsh RS, McCarthy JD. 1960. Archeology and arthritis. *Arch Intern Med* 105:640–44.

Khare SD, Luthra HS, David CS. 1995. Spontaneous inflammatory arthritis in HLA-B27 transgenic mice lacking beta 2 microglobulin: A model of human spondyloarthropathies. *J Exp Med* 182:1153–58.

Kilgore L. 1989. Possible case of rheumatoid arthritis from Sudanese Nubia. *Am J Phys Anthropol* 79:177–83.

Kuberski TT, Morse HG, Rate RG, et al. 1981. A hospital-based survey of radiological sacroiliitis and HLA-B27 and Cw2 in Navajo and Hopi Indians. *Hum Immunol* 3:77–83.

Lawrence RC, Hochberg MC, Kelsey JL, et al. 1989. Estimates of the prevalence of selected arthritic and musculoskeletal diseases in the United States. *J Rheumatol* 16:427–41.

Leden I, Persson E, Persson O. 1988. Aspects of the history of rheumatoid arthritis in the light of recent osteo-archeological finds. *Scand J Rheumatol* 17:341–52.

Moller P, Berg K. 1983. Family studies in Berchterew's syndrome (ankylosing spondylitis): III. Genetics. *Clin Genet* 24:73–89.

Morris R, Metzger AL, Bluestone R, et al. 1974. HL-A B27 — a clue to the diagnosis and pathogenesis of Reiter's syndrome. *N Engl J Med* 290:554–56.

Morse HG, Rate RG, Bonnell MD, et al. 1980. High frequency of HLA-B27 and Reiter's syndrome in Navajo Indians. *J Rheumatol* 7:900–902.

———. 1981. HLA-B27 related arthropathies in Hopi and Navajo Indians. *Ariz Med* 38:510–13.

Morton RO, Gershwin ME, Brady C, et al. 1976. The incidence of systemic lupus erythematosus in North American Indians. *J Rheumatol* 3:186–90.

Muggia AL, Bennahum DA, Williams RC. 1971. Navajo arthritis — an unusual, acute, self-limited disease. *Arthritis Rheum* 14:348–55.

Nelson JL, Boyer G, Templin D, et al. 1992. HLA antigens in Tlingit Indians with rheumatoid arthritis. *Tissue Antigens* 40:57–63.

O'Brien WM, Bennett PH, Burch TA, et al. 1967. A genetic study of rheumatoid arthritis and rheumatoid factor in Blackfeet and Pima Indians. *Arthritis Rheum* 10:163–79.

Oen K, Postl B, Chalmers IM, et al. 1986. Rheumatic diseases in an Inuit population. *Arthritis Rheum* 29:65–74.

Rate RG, Morse HG, Donnell MD, et al. 1980. "Navajo arthritis" reconsidered: Relationship to HLA-B27. *Arthritis Rheum* 23:1299–1302.

Rosenberg AM, Petty RE, Oen KG, et al. 1982. Rheumatic diseases in western Canadian Indian children. *J Rheumatol* 9:589–92.

Rothschild BM, Turner KR, DeLuca MA. 1988. Symmetrical erosive polyarthritis in the late Archaic Period of Alabama. *Science* 241:1498–1501.

Rothschild BM, Woods RJ. 1990. Symmetrical erosive disease in archaic Indians: The origin of rheumatoid arthritis in the New World? *Semin Arthritis Rheum* 19:278–84.

Rothschild BM, Woods RJ, Ortel W. 1990. Rheumatoid arthritis "in the buff": Arthritis in defleshed bones. *Am J Phys Anthropol* 82:441–49.

Rothschild BM, Woods RJ, Rothschild C, et al. 1992. Geographic distribution of rheumatoid arthritis in ancient North America: Implications for pathogenesis. *Semin Arthritis Rheum* 22:181–87.

Rubin LA, Amos CI, Wade JA, et al. 1994. Investigating the genetic basis for ankylosing spondylitis linkage studies with the major histocompatibility complex region. *Arthritis Rheum* 37:1212–20.

Scofield RH, Fogel M, Rhoades ER, et al. 1996. Rheumatoid arthritis in a United States Public Health Service Hospital in Oklahoma: The serologic manifestations of rheumatoid arthritis vary among tribal groups. *Arthritis Rheum* 39:283–86.

Scofield RH, Kurien BT, Warren WL, et al. 1995. HLA-B27 binds a peptide from its own sequence as well as selected similar bacterially-derived peptides: Implications for the pathogenesis of spondyloarthropathies. *Lancet* 345:1542–44.

Scofield RH, Warren WL, Koelsch G, et al. 1993. An hypothesis for the HLA-B27 immune dysregulation in spondyloarthropathies: Contribution of enteric organisms, HLA-B27 structure, peptides bound by HLA-B27 and convergent evolution. *Proc Natl Acad Sci USA* 90:9330–34.

Short CL. 1974. The antiquity of rheumatoid arthritis. *Arthritis Rheum* 17:193–204.

Spector TD, Hochberg MC. 1990. The protective effect of the oral contraceptive pill on rheumatoid arthritis: An overview of the analytic epidemiological studies using meta-analysis. *J Clin Epidemiol* 43:1221–23.

Tan EM, Cohen AS, Fries JF, et al. 1982. The 1982 revised criteria for the classification of systemic lupus erythematosus. *Arthritis Rheum* 25:1271–77.

Tan FK, Arnett FC, Antochi S, et al. 1999. Autoantibodies to the extracellular matrix microfibrillar protein, fibrillin-1, in patients with scleroderma and other connective tissue diseases. *J Immunol* 163:1066–72.

Tan FK, Stivers DN, Foster MW, et al. 1998. Association of microsatellite markers near the fibrillin 1 gene on human chromosome 15q with scleroderma in a Native American population. *Arthritis Rheum* 41:1729–37.

Templin DW, Boyer GS, Lanier AP, et al. 1994. Rheumatoid arthritis in Tlingit Indians: Clinical characterization and HLA associations. *J Rheumatol* 21:1238–44.

Williams R, Harrison HR, Tempest B, et al. 1989. Chlamydia infection and arthritis. *J Rheumatol* 16:846 (letter).

Willkins RF, Blandau RL, Aoyama DT, et al. 1976. Studies of rheumatoid arthritis among a tribe of Northwest Indians. *J Rheumatol* 3:9–14.

Willkins RF, Hansen JA, Malmgren JA, et al. 1982. HLA antigens in Yakima Indians with rheumatoid arthritis: Lack of association with HLA-Dw4 and HLA-DR4. *Arthritis Rheum* 25:1435–39.

Willkins RF, Nepom GT, Marks CR, et al. 1991. Association of HLA-Dw16 with rheumatoid arthritis in Yakima Indians. *Arthritis Rheum* 34:43–47.

Winchester R, Dwyer E, Rose S. 1992. The genetic basis of rheumatoid arthritis: The shared epitope hypothesis. *Rheum Dis Clin North Am* 18:761–83.

Woods RJ, Rothschild BM. 1988. Population analysis of symmetrical erosive arthritis in Ohio Woodland Indians (1200 years ago). *J Rheumatol* 15:1258–63.

20

Edwin Asturias, M.D.,
George R. Brenneman, M.D., FAAP,
Kenneth M. Petersen, M.D.,
Mohamed Hashem, M.D., and
Mathuram Santosham, M.D., M.P.H., FAAP

Infectious Diseases

There can be little doubt but that, at the time of European contact, the aboriginal peoples of America represented a population with virginal susceptibility to a number of pathogens, especially those transmitted via the respiratory and oral-fecal routes. This general susceptibility persists to the present and is largely unexplained. An interesting hypothesis suggested that the extensive cold enveloping northern latitudes during the long periods of aboriginal migration served as a "germ filter," eliminating common human pathogens in the small, scattered, and isolated bands (Stewart 1973). It is likely that basic studies of the immune system of Indian people, especially of its phagocytic and antigen-processing properties, now readily accessible to study, would yield important information.

It is not possible to cover the entire field of infectious diseases in this chapter. Therefore, we present information on a selected group of infectious diseases that have a special relevance for and that have been extensively studied in Indian populations.

Diarrheal Diseases

Epidemics of diarrheal diseases with high mortality have plagued Indian people since at least European contact. Epidemics of cholera were particularly devastating (Dobyns 1983). As recently as the 1960s, diarrhea was a leading cause of infant mortality among Indian populations (Hirshhorn and Spivey 1972). Two developments have played major roles in the drastic reductions in the incidence and mortality rates associated with diarrheal diseases: sanitation projects and oral rehydration therapy (Hirschhorn et al. 1972; Santosham et al. 1982, 1985).

With these largely successful efforts to control bacterial diarrhea, viral causes

came to be recognized as equally important. The most severe viral gastroenteritis seems presently to be associated with rotavirus, estimated to be responsible for over 800,000 deaths annually in developing countries (De Zoysa and
Feachmen 1985). A promising vaccine against rotavirus (Santosham et al. 1997;
Rennels et al. 1996) has been withdrawn from the market because of concerns
about a possible relationship between vaccine administration and intussusception (American Academy of Pediatrics Committee on Infectious Diseases 1999).

Haemophilus infuenzae *Infections*

Before licensure of *Haemophilus influenzae* type b (Hib) vaccines, Hib was the
leading cause of invasive bacterial disease among children under five years of
age in the United States, accounting for an estimated twelve thousand cases of
meningitis per year and an additional eight thousand cases of other invasive
disease, such as epiglottitis, cellulitis, and primary bacteremia (Cochi, Broome,
and Hightower 1985). Some of the highest attack rates have been observed in
Indian populations (Ward et al. 1986; Santosham et al. 1992). Although representing only 16 percent of the population, Alaska Native children experienced
half of all invasive Hib disease in Alaska. In Alaska Natives, 25 percent of all
invasive Hib diseases and 35 percent of the meningitis cases presented before six
months of age. In the Navajo and Apache populations, 27–40 percent of cases
occurred before six months of age and 80–90 percent of cases occurred before
one year of age (Santosham et al. 1992). Indian children seem to experience
greater neurological morbidity compared to other children (Letson et al. 1992).

    In addition to young age, large crowded households and extended family
groups are associated risk factors for Hib disease. Other factors that increase
the risk for Hib colonization and diseases include day care attendance, viral
respiratory infections (odds ratio 2.0), and parental smoking (odds ratio 5.7)
(Takala et al. 1993; Petersen et al. 1991).

    A vaccine prepared from Hib capsular polysaccharide (polyribosylribitol
phosphate [PRP]) was effective among children older than two years but not
younger than two (Peltola et al. 1984). Because almost all cases of Hib in Indian
populations occurred before the patient was two years of age and because
Indian children seemed to have diminished antibody response, the pure PRP
was not an effective means of preventing this disease in Native American populations (Siber et al. 1990).

    In the 1980s, Hib conjugate vaccines prepared by linking the Hib-PRP to
diphtheria toxoid protein carrier proved to be more immunogenic and effective
among Finnish infants (Eskola et al. 1987) than among Alaska Native infants

(Ward et al. 1990). On the other hand, a vaccine linking the Hib-PRP to the meningococcal type b outer membrane protein (PRP-OMP) was demonstrated to be both immunogenic (Santosham et al. 1991a; Bulkow et al. 1993) and protective (Santosham et al. 1991b; Harrison et al. 1994) in Navajo infants. Since the introduction of the Hib conjugate vaccines, childhood invasive Hib disease has been virtually eliminated from the general and Indian populations. In addition, Hib conjugate vaccines seemed to be associated with reduction of oropharyngeal carriage in older Navajo, Apache, and Alaska Native children (Takala et al. 1993).

Respiratory Syncytial Virus

Respiratory syncytial virus (RSV), the most important cause of acute lower respiratory infections in infants in the United States, occurs in annual outbreaks that usually peak in February. RSV is responsible for one-fourth to one-third of all pediatric hospitalizations for pneumonia (LaVia, Marks, and Stutman 1992) and for one-half of the hospitalizations for bronchiolitis (Heilman 1990).

Hospitalization rates for RSV disease from 1986 through 1992 were 10 times higher for Alaska Native children than for other U.S. populations (Petersen 1993). Among Alaska Native infants residing in Anchorage, the peak age of hospitalization was 4.5 months (Singleton et al. 1995), similar to that of the U.S. population (Hall 1979), compared to a peak of 2 months for Yukon-Kuskokwim (Y-K) Delta infants. Sixteen percent of hospitalized children from the Y-K Delta were <1 month of age, compared to less than 5 percent for Anchorage Alaska Native and U.S. infants (LaVia, Marks, and Stutman 1992). The hospitalization rate among Alaska Native infants was 33/1,000, among the highest reported in the world (Singleton et al. 1995). The hospitalization rate was even higher in the Y-K Delta, with 1 in 10 infants requiring hospitalization.

Risk factors for serious RSV disease include young age, prematurity, cardiac disease, chronic pulmonary disease, and immunodeficiency (Law and De Carvalho 1993). Since the disease itself provides limited protective immunity, repeated infections occur. Environmental smoke, such as that from wood-burning stoves in the home, also place young infants at increased risk (Morris et al. 1990). Household crowding, common in the Y-K Delta, where three or four children often share the same bed (Singleton et al. 1995), is also a significant risk factor. Although studies show a limited link between RSV bronchiolitis in infancy and childhood asthma (Morgan and Martinez 1992), clinicians have wondered for some time if the high rates of RSV experienced among Indian infants may be associated with the rising rates of asthma among Indian children.

Streptococcus pneumoniae

Some of the highest rates of pneumococcal diseases have been reported among Alaska Natives (Davidson et al. 1989) and the White Mountain Apache (Cortese et al. 1992), especially among children under the age of two years (Davidson et al. 1989). The attack rate in Y-K Delta children ≤ 2 years is two times higher than that among Alaska Native children living elsewhere and 20 times the rate for Alaska non-Natives of the same age. The incidence and mortality rates of invasive pneumococcal disease among all age groups of Alaska Natives are fivefold higher than among Alaska non-Natives (Davidson et al. 1994). The attack rate of invasive pneumococcal disease (associated with positive cultures of blood, cerebrospinal fluid, pleural fluid, or other normally sterile body fluids) in different populations is shown in Table 20.1.

Pneumococcal pneumonia, meningitis, and endocarditis occur at a higher rate in Indian populations compared to the general population. The seriousness of pneumococcal disease was noted by Finley et al. (1992), who reported that, in a group of Alaska Natives with infective endocarditis, none had known pre-existing heart disease and the mortality rate was 33 percent. Alcoholism was a common underlying condition (56%) in these patients. From 1980 to 1993, 70 percent of all cases of bacterial empyema in Alaska Native children were due to *S. pneumoniae* (Petersen 1993), compared to only 18 percent in the general U.S. population (Brook 1990).

Capsular serotype 6B was responsible for 22 percent of the invasive pneumococcal disease in infants under 24 months of age in the Y-K Delta from 1982 to 1991. Seventy-seven percent of isolates had intermediate levels of penicillin resistance, compared to an expected 4.7 percent in the U.S. population. Also, all multiple-drug-resistant organisms were type 6B (Ussery et al. 1996). This finding is of importance in vaccine development, since serotype 6b is one of the least immunogenic serotypes contained in pneumococcal vaccines.

A 1992 survey of nasopharyngeal colonization among healthy Y-K Delta children disclosed that 29 percent of pneumococcal isolates from the nasopharynx of asymptomatic children ≤ 5 years old exhibited intermediate (minimum inhibitory concentration, 0.12–1.0 μg/mL) or high (minimum inhibitory concentration, ≥ 2 μg/mL) resistance to penicillin (Ussery et al. 1996), compared to 6.6 percent among hospitalized patients elsewhere during the same time period (Brieman et al. 1994).

The case-fatality rate for invasive pneumococcal disease among Alaska Natives is relatively low (8%), the same as for Alaska non-Natives, and compares favorably with rates of 5–33 percent elsewhere in the United States (Davidson et al. 1994). This is noteworthy, since the proportion of pneumococcal cases with pneumonia and meningitis is high in Alaska Natives and a substantial

TABLE 20.1
Annual incidence rates of invasive pneumococcal disease (per 100,000 population) in various populations

Population	Incidence at age (yr):		
	0–2	>65	All ages
White Mountain Apache (1983–90)	1,820	172[a]	207
Alaska Native (1980–86)	1,235	145[a]	108
Alaska Native (1986–90)	624	186	84
Alaska non-Native (1986–90)	130	90	90
Kaiser Permanente Southern California (1992–95)	143	31	13
Charleston County, S.C. (1986–87)	162	53	19
Hawaii (1986–87)	103	22[a]	9
Sweden (1970–80)	26	14[a]	7
Finland (1985–89)	33		
Finland (1983–92)		27	
Denmark (1995)		55[a]	

[a]Sixty years old or more.

proportion of the population live in remote areas under harsh environmental and difficult travel conditions. The reason for the high rates of pneumococcal diseases among Indian populations is not known, but several factors may contribute to increased risk of these diseases, including crowded living conditions, poor ventilation, and exposure to smoke, common conditions in rural Alaska.

The currently licensed pure polysaccharide pneumococcal vaccine contains 23 serotypes of *S. pneumoniae*. This vaccine is effective among adults and children older than two years. Recently, a new generation of conjugate vaccines, developed with technology similar to that used in the production of Hib conjugate vaccines and containing seven serotypes, seem to be immunogenic in infants younger than two years. Trials are currently in progress to evaluate the efficacy of at least one of the conjugate vaccines. Other conjugate vaccines are also expected to be evaluated for efficacy in the next few years.

Tuberculosis

Tuberculosis had for many decades a devastating effect in essentially all Native American communities. The origin of tuberculosis in North America is still a matter of controversy (Paulsen 1987). Whether or not tuberculosis was present during the pre-Columbian era, it is clear that the disease spread in epidemic nature across all tribes and by 1900 had become one of the most serious health problems among North American Indians (Rieder 1989). Since the implementation of tuberculosis control strategies and the introduction of effective chemotherapy in the early 1950s, the prevalence rate of tuberculosis has declined dramatically (Becker et al. 1990). However, the ratio of age-adjusted tuberculosis mortality of Indians compared to the general U.S. population (U.S. All Races) in 1992–94 remains high, six times the rate for U.S. All Races (Indian Health Service 1997). In 1997, the incidence of tuberculosis among American Indians remained at 13.4/100,000 population, a rate fivefold higher than the national average (Centers for Disease Control and Prevention 1998). Significant risk factors for the development of active tuberculosis include diabetes, chronic renal failure, and alcohol abuse (Mori, Leonardson, and Welty 1992).

From 1935 to 1953, Aronson and colleagues conducted one of the first controlled studies of BCG vaccination for tuberculosis (Aronson, Aronson, and Taylor 1958). Of the 1,547 vaccinated individuals, 0.84 percent died of tuberculosis, compared to 4.7 percent of the unvaccinated controls. Among the vaccinated, tuberculosis was responsible for 12.5 percent of all deaths, in contrast to 45.3 percent of deaths attributed to tuberculosis among the controls. Recent studies have confirmed the value of BCG vaccination (Houston et al. 1990). Adequate control continues to involve the treatment of cases with active disease and the active identification of and provision of preventive therapy for those at risk of developing the disease.

Otitis Media

Otitis media has been a major health problem for Native American children. In the 1960s in an Apache community, evidence of present or past ear infection was found in 23 percent of 500 residents (draining ears, 5.6%; perforation, 2.8%; healed perforation or tympanosclerosis or both, 13.1%) (Zonis 1968). In the 1960s otorrhea occurred in 38 percent of Alaska Eskimos by one year of age and in 62 percent by four years of age (Reed, Struve, and Maynard 1967); in point prevalence it occurred in 31 percent of Canadian Eskimo children under 11 years (Ling, McCoy, and Levinson 1969). In the 1970s the incidence of acute otitis media among American Indians was 40 times that of the White population (Berg, Larsen, and Yarington 1971), and its sequelae (draining ears, perforations) are about 15 times more common among Indians than among Whites (Wiet 1979).

Otitis media remains the third most prevalent specific condition noted on Indian Health Service (IHS) ambulatory records, behind only diabetes and upper respiratory infections (Indian Health Service 1994). Differences in the eustachian tube position (Doyle 1977) and function (Beery 1980; Todd and Bowman 1985) in Native Americans have been postulated as risk factors. Young age at the time of the first episode is a known risk factor for more frequent infections, and surveillance among Arizona Indians indicated that 70 percent of the initial attacks of acute otitis media occurred during the first year of life (Todd 1990).

Iron deficiency anemia, which is still prevalent among some Alaska Native children (Petersen et al. 1996), has been associated with higher rates of acute otitis media (Brown, Brown, and Bonehill 1967). In some Native American populations, higher prevalence rates during the transitional period to urbanization were reported, but with lower rates once urbanization was established (Baxter 1991; Johonnott 1973). Improved socioeconomic conditions, sanitation, and housing and the greater availability of health care are all considered important in the reduction of otitis media attack rates among Native American children (Baxter 1991; Johonnott 1973). In a Canadian Inuit population, breast-feeding offered a fivefold protection against ear disease when compared to bottle-feeding (Schaefer 1971).

Hearing loss associated with chronic otitis media is a major concern. The prevalence of chronic otitis media in children in the United States and England has been 3–5 percent, compared to 15–30 percent among Indian children (Pedersen and Zachau-Christiansen 1986).

Hantavirus Pulmonary Syndrome

In May 1993, a cluster of unexplained deaths from cardiopulmonary illness in young adults was noted in the Four Corners area (N.M., Ariz., Colo., and Utah) (Centers for Disease Control and Prevention 1993). One month later, confirmation of the causative agent, hantavirus, was made using polymerase chain reaction assays, revealing matching viral genetic sequences in case-patients and host-rodents from the area. This new syndrome was called hantavirus pulmonary syndrome (HPS). Hantavirus is a single-stranded ribonucleic acid virus of the Bunyaviridae family. Other hantaviruses have been recognized around the world and have been associated with hemorrhagic fever and renal syndrome, especially in Asia. Rodents are the natural host for hantavirus, and shedding from urine, saliva, and feces provide mechanisms of transmission to humans.

After its initial identification, 131 cases in the United States were confirmed by the Centers for Disease Control and Prevention (CDC) as of March 1996 (Centers for Disease Control and Prevention 1996a). Most cases continue to occur in New Mexico (21%), Arizona (16%), and California (10%). The organism associated with HPS has been named sin nombre virus (SNV). The most important rodent reservoir is the deer mouse, but other rodents carrying the virus include the cotton rat and the white-footed mouse. The mean age of the patients with HPS was 35 years. Illness commonly begins with fever, malaise, and minor respiratory symptoms. Within a week, progression to respiratory distress and capillary leak syndrome (hemoconcentration, hypoalbuminemia, pulmonary edema) ensues, in addition to acidosis, leukocytosis, and thrombocytopenia. The overall case-fatality rate approaches 50 percent (Centers for Disease Control and Prevention 1996a; Simonsen et al. 1995).

There is no proven antiviral therapy for HPS. Intravenous ribavirin is under investigation. Some evidence suggests that early intensive monitoring and respiratory support may improve patient survival. Primary prevention through avoidance of contact with rodents and decrease in peridomestic rodent populations is recommended in endemic areas.

Hepatitis A

Hepatitis A is an acute infection of the liver caused by an enterically transmitted nonenveloped ribonucleic acid virus. It is distributed worldwide, and humans are the only reservoir. Hepatitis A virus (HAV) is acquired primarily by the fecal-oral route by either person-to-person contact or ingestion of contaminated food or water. In developing countries the infection affects 30–40 percent of young children and 70–95 percent of adults. In the United States, HAV is also endemic, with periodic outbreaks occurring in certain high-risk populations, such as Native Americans, Hispanic communities, certain religious groups, and intravenous drug users (Shaw et al. 1990). Rates of HAV infection in the Indian population average 10–12-fold greater than among the total U.S. population (121.2/100,000 and 10.3/100,000, respectively). Estimates among the Navajo have been as high as 417/100,000 in children 5–14 years of age, a rate 18–24-fold higher than national incidence rates (Newcomer et al. 1994).

Cyclic outbreaks of 6 to 24 months occur every 7–10 years in South Dakota (Shaw et al. 1990; Gildon, Malantubee, and Istre 1992). The highest rates of infection were observed among children 5–9 years of age. By age 15–30 years more than 90 percent of the population had acquired antibodies. Thirty-seven percent of Navajo kindergarten children were found to have anti-HAV antibodies, increasing to 87 percent among those in the eighth grade (Williams 1986).

When administered within two weeks of exposure, immune serum globulin is more than 85 percent effective in preventing hepatitis A (Newcomer et al. 1994; McMahon et al. 1996). In 1993, a program to control outbreaks of hepatitis in several Alaska villages demonstrated that the use of hepatitis A vaccine could provide short- and long-term protection and help control outbreaks (McMahon et al. 1996). Routine vaccination with hepatitis A vaccine is now recommended for children ≥2 years of age living in communities with high endemicity of HAV infection. Hepatitis A vaccine in addition to immune globulin is recommended in the control of outbreaks in communities with a high incidence of HAV infection or during common-source exposure (Centers for Disease Control and Prevention 1996b).

Hepatitis B

Hepatitis B virus infection is a serious health problem in many parts of the world. It is spread by close personal contact with body fluids. In some areas more than 10 percent of the population is positive for hepatitis B surface antigen (HBsAg). Annually, ten thousand cases of hepatitis B are reported in the United States (Centers for Disease Control and Prevention 1995b), and approximately 5 percent of the population has been infected. However, only 1–2 percent of Sioux and Navajo populations studied have markers for past or present infection (Ahtone and Kuberski 1982; Shaw et al. 1990). On the other hand, the prevalence of hepatitis B has been very high among certain Alaska Natives (McMahon et al. 1981). A serologic prevalence study in two Alaska Native villages disclosed that 14 percent were HBsAg positive and 41 percent had antibody to hepatitis B (anti-HBs) (Barrett et al. 1977). The highest seroprevalence rates were found in Yupik Eskimo communities of Bristol Bay and the Y-K Delta. Subsequent studies in Alaska demonstrated a 14–24 percent seropositive (HbsAg and anti-HBs) rate (Schreeder et al. 1983), and 17–19 percent of children in the Bristol Bay area and Y-K Delta were seropositive by 10 years of age (McMahon et al. 1993).

A plasma-derived hepatitis vaccine became available in 1981 and was shown to be immunogenic in Eskimos (Heyward et al. 1985a). After widespread immunization, the annual incidence of hepatitis B infection in this group declined from 50/1,000 population to less than 1/1,000 (Wainwright et al. 1997). Only 1 percent became core antibody (anti-HBc) positive, and none of these individuals were symptomatic or remained HBsAg positive.

In the hyperendemic villages, the hepatitis B virus spread rapidly from child to child, especially among those younger than two years. Hepatitis Be antigen (HBeAg), associated with infectivity and high levels of viral replication, was found in >95 percent of HBsAg-positive children under five years of age (Alward 1985), and the percentage tended to decrease with age (McMahon et al. 1993).

Transmission of hepatitis B virus occurs most commonly and efficiently through percutaneous, sexual, and perinatal exposures. However, in Alaska, compared to other parts of the world, the perinatal route plays a less important role. Among Alaska Natives who become HBsAg carriers, the majority are infected after birth but before the fifth birthday (McMahon et al. 1985; Estroff et al. 1985). Child-to-child transmission is the dominant mechanism of spread. HbsAg has been found in impetiginous lesions and in gingival washings of carriers, as well as on the walls of homes and on school lunchroom tables (McMahon and Wainwright 1990).

Infected Alaska Native children under 4 years of age had a 28.8 percent risk of becoming chronic carriers, compared to 7.7 percent of those older than 30 years (McMahon et al. 1985). An inverse relationship between age at infection and the development of the chronic carrier state was found, but with increased age at the time of infection there was increased likelihood of clinically apparent acute hepatitis B (McMahon et al. 1985). Only 10 percent of persons infected when younger than 5 years developed clinical hepatitis, compared to 33 percent of those over 30 years of age (McMahon et al. 1985). The children younger than 5 years were not only the primary reservoir for infection, but also more likely to suffer long-term sequelae of the infection. Sequelae include necrotizing vasculitis, hepatocellular carcinoma, chronic active hepatitis, and cirrhosis of the liver. The annual incidence of hepatitis B–associated necrotizing arteritis was 15/100,000 population, the highest reported in the world (McMahon et al. 1989). The incidence of chronic active hepatitis and secondary cirrhosis in hepatitis B carriers was 193 and 107/100,000, respectively, in Alaska Native men and 158 and 95/100,000, respectively, in women (McMahon et al. 1990).

Among Alaska Natives, the majority of cases of primary hepatocellular carcinoma are associated with hepatitis B virus infection. Although the carcinoma develops many years after the acquisition of chronic HBsAg carriage, Alaska Native carriers under the age of 20 years had a high incidence of primary hepatocellular carcinoma (McMahon et al. 1990). In the 1970s, the case fatality rate of primary hepatocellular carcinoma in Alaska Natives was 100 percent, with a mean survival of less than three months after diagnosis (Heyward et al. 1981). Serum alpha-fetoprotein (AFP), an embryonic protein, could be elevated up to two years before the clinical presentation of hepatocellular carcinoma (Heyward et al. 1982, 1985b). After the implementation of twice-yearly AFP screening, the one-year survival rate for hepatocellular carcinoma in Alaska Natives has increased from zero to 80–90 percent, with a five-year survival rate of 70–80 percent (B. J. McMahon, unpublished data).

Following the implementation of immunization of serosusceptible Alaska Natives and all newborn Alaska Natives and the administration of hepatitis B immune globulin to those born of HBsAg-positive mothers (McMahon and Wainwright 1990), the incidence of acute symptomatic hepatitis B cases decreased from 215/100,000 to 6/100,000 population in the Y-K Delta within five years. The proportion of infants born to HBsAg carrier mothers who became chronically infected fell from 40 percent to 1 percent (McMahon and Wainwright 1990).

Sexually Transmitted Diseases

American Indians historically have experienced high rates of sexually transmitted diseases, with gonorrhea being the most frequently reported communicable disease among Indians (Cheek and Johanes 1994). In 1980, the rates of gonorrhea among Alaska Indians were five times higher than those of non-Native Alaskans (Blackwood 1981). In 1985, a study conducted in eight states revealed that gonorrhea rates among Indians were twice that of the general population and rates of syphilis were almost four times higher than national rates. Recent data disclose a dramatic decrease in reported cases of gonorrhea from an average of 5,100 cases/year in 1984–88 to 1,375 cases reported in 1995 (Toomey, Oberschelp, and Greenspan 1989; Centers for Disease Control and Prevention 1995b).

In 1992, the rate of gonorrhea among the Indian populations was 84/100,000, compared to 201/100,000 nationwide. However, several Native American communities continue to report rates of gonorrhea of 200–1,000/100,000 population. Rates of gonorrhea are significantly higher in Alaska, Arizona, and South Dakota (Toomey, Oberschelp, and Greenspan 1989) and among those aged 20–24. Because of the increasing resistance of *Neisseria gonorrhoeae* to penicillin, recommended regimens include ceftriaxone, cefixime, or ciprofloxacin (Cheek and Johanes 1994). Coinfection with *Chlamydia trachomatis* is common, and persons treated for gonorrhea should be presumptively treated with a regimen effective against *C. trachomatis*. Individuals with gonococcal infection should also be screened for syphilis and human immunodeficiency virus (HIV).

From 1984 to 1988, the rates of primary and secondary syphilis among Indians were 12.9/100,000, compared to 5.4/100,000 among non-Native Americans. Among Indians, Arizona and New Mexico reported 74 percent of the total cases, and the rates of disease were seven and four times higher, respectively, compared to the rates for non-Indians in the area (Toomey, Oberschelp, and Greenspan 1989). The incidence of syphilis among Indians has decreased from an average of 136.4 cases per year in 1984–88 to 42.3 cases per year in 1993–95 (Toomey, Oberschelp, and Greenspan 1989; Centers for Disease Control and Prevention 1995b).

Infections with *Chlamydia trachomatis* are prevalent in Indian communities. Case rates ranging from 200 to 1,200/100,000 population have been reported. In one IHS Area, the rate of *C. trachomatis* infection among women aged 15–44 years was 3,800/100,000 population (Harrison et al. 1983). In the Alaska Eskimo population, 39 percent of teenage women and 30 percent of prenatal patients had direct fluorescent antibody stain positive for *C. trachomatis* (Toomey, Rafferty, and Stamm 1987). In this study, only 15 percent of women with chlamydial infection, mostly teenagers, had evidence of gonococcal infection, but 57 percent of patients with gonorrhea had concurrent infection with *C. trachomatis*. Young age, urban residence, and low average income are all associated with increased risk of chlamydial and gonococcal infection (Jolly et al. 1995).

Chlamydial infection may be transmitted to offspring during pregnancy and delivery and may be manifested in these infants as conjunctivitis and interstitial pneumonitis. Navajo infants exposed to maternal chlamydial infection had twice the rate of pneumonitis and recurrent otitis media in the first six months of life, compared to nonexposed infants (Schaefer et al. 1985). *C. trachomatis* is also the most common cause of blindness around the world. Ocular trachoma was formerly very common among Indians in the Southwest (Lawler et al. 1970; Portney and Hoshiwara 1970). The disease was most common in the young, with 54–74 percent of schoolchildren screened being positive for the disease (Portney and Hoshiwara 1970). Treatment with sulfonamide and doxycycline has resulted in virtual eradication of most forms of trachoma (Portney and Hoshiwara 1970; Hoshiwara et al. 1973). For most *C. trachomatis* genital infections, treatment with azithromycin in a single dose is as effective as a seven-day course of doxycycline. Alternatives include erythromycin and ofloxacin.

Human Immunodeficiency Virus and Acquired Immune Deficiency Syndrome

Infection with HIV has become one of the most serious world epidemics. In 1995, a total of 71,500 cases of AIDS were reported, mostly in young adults 25–44 years of age (Centers for Disease Control and Prevention 1995a). The proportion of American Indians affected by the epidemic of acquired immune deficiency syndrome (AIDS) has been relatively low, although rising steadily. The underrepresentation of AIDS cases among Indians has been attributed to racial misclassification in the surveillance registry (Lieb et al. 1992). As of the end of 1996, 475 cases of HIV infection and 1,569 cases of AIDS among Indians had been reported since 1982. The annual AIDS case rate among Indians has increased from 4.0 to 10.7/100,000 population since 1990. AIDS is now the seventh leading cause of death among Indians aged 25–44 years (Rowell and Bouey 1997). The exposure distribution of AIDS cases among Indians has differed somewhat from that of other groups. The most common exposure among Indians is homosexual/bisexual contact (48%), a figure lower than that reported for Whites in the United States. Other sources of transmission include intravenous drug use (33%), heterosexual contact (5%), and perinatal transmission (4%) (Rowell and Bouey 1997; Metler, Conway, and Stehr-Green 1991).

From 1990 to 1995, the incidence rates of opportunistic illnesses among Indians with AIDS increased 45 percent. The most common opportunistic infection is *Pneumocystis carinii* pneumonia (PCP), followed by cytomegalovirus and *Mycobacterium avium*-complex disease. Other infections include *Mycobacterium tuberculosis,* toxoplasmosis, and fungal infections. Presently, management of AIDS among Indians seems to follow that recommended for non-Indians.

Helicobacter pylori *Infections*

Helicobacter pylori, one of the most common causes of human infections, is a cause of chronic active gastritis and duodenal and gastric ulcers (Tytgat and Rauws 1990). Chronic infection is associated with gastric carcinomas and gastric B-cell lymphomas (Nomura et al. 1991; Wotherspoon et al. 1991). In the general population the prevalence of immunoglobulin G antibodies to *H. pylori* is 30 to 40 percent, with a seroconversion rate estimated at 0.5 percent per year. Antibodies in adults seem to reflect acquisition of disease earlier in life (Dubois 1995). In developing countries and in lower socioeconomic groups, seroprevalence rates often approach 100 percent, with most persons becoming infected before 10 years of age (Sitas et al. 1991; Graham et al. 1991). Increased transmission of infection occurs in disadvantaged socioeconomic groups because of crowding or poor hygiene (Dubois 1995). Although the actual route of transmission is unknown, oral-oral or fecal-oral transmission is suspected. Contamination of drinking water may also play a role (Hulten et al. 1996). Humans are the only known reservoir (Thomas et al. 1992).

Attention became focused on *H. pylori* among Alaska Natives when it was discovered that anemia due to intestinal blood loss seemed to be associated with *H. pylori.* High rates of iron deficiency anemia have been observed among Alaska Natives since at least the 1950s despite adequate intake of iron-containing nutrients (Petersen et al. 1996). Further investigation revealed that 99 percent of those with increased intestinal blood loss had chronic active gastritis due to *H. pylori* (Yip et al. 1997).

Overall, 75 percent of more than two thousand serum samples collected in Alaska Native villages in the 1980s were positive for *H. pylori,* with rates increasing from 32 percent among children 0–4 years of age to 86 percent in individuals at least 20 years old. Marked regional variation was most pronounced among the youngest children (0–4 years), where rates ranged from 5 percent in south central (Anchorage vicinity) to 65 percent in interior Alaska. Ferritin determinations on the same samples supported an association between *H. pylori* infection and iron deficiency, especially in those under 20 years of age (Parkinson et al. 1997).

The high rates of anemia, gastritis, and gastric cancer in Alaska Natives are probably related to the high rates of infection with *H. pylori*. The overall impact in terms of the potential health and economic costs resulting from chronic *H. pylori* infection in this population is still unknown but could be substantial.

Botulism

Since the 1920s, outbreaks of botulism have been described among Alaska Eskimos and the Native people of Canada (Dolman 1974; Hauschild and Gauvreau 1985). The disease is caused by the toxin of *Clostridium botulinum*. The toxin binds irreversibly at the presynaptic level of the neuromuscular junction, blocking the release of acetylcholine and causing paralysis.

The majority of cases of botulism among Indians have been attributed to ingestion of contaminated food (Hauschild and Gauvreau 1985), especially among the Native people of Canada, Eskimos, and Pacific Coast Indians. Although foodborne botulism is commonly traced to improperly home-canned fruits and vegetables, in the Native American population most outbreaks have been attributed to the ingestion of raw, parboiled, or preserved meats from marine mammals and fermented fish or salmon eggs (Hauschild and Gauvreau 1985).

In contrast to the "lower 48" states, where most cases are associated with type A or B toxin, most Alaska and Canada cases are type E and exclusively related to the ingestion of fish or meats (Ferrari and Weisse 1995). Since 1947, more than 70 confirmed outbreaks of botulism in Alaska have been reported. All were food borne and all involved Alaska Native foods, primarily fish and sea mammals (Beller et al. 1998). No Alaska outbreaks have been associated with home-canned vegetables or meats (Wainwright et al. 1988). The clinical presentation of type E botulism is similar to that of types A and B (Ferrari and Weisse 1995). The diagnosis is based on clinical symptoms, serum levels of toxin, and isolation of *C. botulinum* in the suspected food. Treatment is directed at support of vital functions and administration of specific antitoxin (Ferrari and Weisse 1995). Public education has emphasized careful cleaning of foods, cooking of fermented foods, and avoidance of plastic bags or sealed containers for fermentation (Wainwright et al. 1988).

Plague

Plague is a worldwide zoonotic disease caused by infection with *Yersinia pestis*. This infection is endemic in native wild rodents (squirrels), prairie dogs, and fleas of the western United States and along the Pacific coast (Barnes et al. 1988). Humans become accidental hosts and usually acquire the disease when bitten by infected rodent fleas. In the United States, most cases occur during the summer months. The majority of plague cases are confined to New Mexico (56%), Arizona (14%), Colorado (10%), and California (10%).

Almost one-half of the U.S. plague cases have occurred among Indians (Barnes et al. 1988). The attack rate among American Indians living in endemic areas is 10 times higher than that among non-Indians living in the same states (Kaufmann, Boyce, and Martone 1980). Explanations for this high proportion of Indian cases include involvement in pastoral activities (sheep-herding), hunting of prairie dogs, and ownership of free-roaming dogs and cats. The majority of Indians affected belong to the Navajo (81.3%) tribe, among whom the attack rate in 1983 was 12.1/100,000 population. Fifty-five percent of cases occur in children. The case fatality rate among Indians was 16.5 percent, similar to that for the general U.S. population. Two-thirds of the cases were acquired from infective flea bites, and 22 percent resulted from direct contact with infected animals (rodents, rabbits, domestic cats, etc.).

A formalin-killed vaccine (plague vaccine U.S.P.) is available for travelers to epidemic or hyperendemic areas or individuals working in close contact with rodents or in the laboratory. The IHS has implemented measures to control plague among Indians: surveillance of rodent populations and serosurveys in dogs; dissemination of educational material to the public and the medical and veterinary community, describing how to recognize and avoid risks; and control of fleas and rodent reservoirs.

Echinococcosis

Echinococcosis is a tapeworm infection with worldwide distribution and is indigenous to Alaska. *Echinococcus granulosus* is a natural parasite of the wolf population. Dogs may become parasitized when they feed on infected viscera of moose or caribou. The human becomes an accidental intermediate host in environments contaminated with echinococcal eggs excreted from dog feces. Disease in humans manifests as a liver or lung cyst, usually benign unless there is pressure on adjacent structures. The treatment is surgical.

In Northwest Alaska, alveolar hydatid disease due to *Echinococcus multilocularis* is endemic. This is one of the most lethal helminthic infections in humans. The primary hosts are foxes and dogs, and intermediate hosts are voles or lemmings. Humans become parasitized by ingesting eggs from environmental sources. In contrast to echinococcosis due to *Echinococcus granulosus,* alveolar hydatid disease is an invasive, cancerlike lesion in the liver, which invades and metastasizes. In Alaska, during the early years after the discovery of this infection in 1947 (Rausch and Schiller 1951), all patients died an average of five years after diagnosis due to massive hepatomegaly, ascites, anasarca, and fatal metastases (Wilson and Rausch 1980). However, in the 1970s clinical trials in Alaska showed mebendazole and albendazole to be effective in the eradication of echinococcus infestation and resulted in improved survival (Wilson et al. 1992). Screening with an ELISA test, with ultrasound follow-up examinations of those found to be positive, was introduced in the mid-1980s, affording earlier diagnosis and treatment. A dog control program plus improvements in diagnosis and treatment have improved the outlook for this serious disease in Alaska Natives.

Discussion

The continuing importance of infectious diseases among American Indians cannot be overstated. Very soon after contact with European explorers in the early 1500s, tidal waves of infectious diseases began to decimate aboriginal inhabitants in the Western Hemisphere. Presumably, their immune systems were not prepared for the infecting microorganisms that landed with the Europeans. Allusion to just a few epidemics that raged among Indian communities gives support to estimates by some demographers that the Indian population in North America was reduced by as much as 75 percent from infectious diseases from 1520 to the late 1800s. Forty-one separate smallpox epidemics from 1520 to 1899, 17 measles epidemics between 1531 and 1892, and others including influenza, plague, and cholera have been documented (Stiffarm and Lane 1992). Although we recognize the continued uncertainty regarding the presence of tuberculosis in pre-Columbian times, it certainly did cause subsequent epidemics, the range and extent of which will probably never be known completely.

Although the reduction of infectious causes of death among American Indians has been remarkable, allowing the emergence of leading causes of death associated with lifestyle and behavioral risks, infectious diseases remain important. Infectious diseases continue to be causes of relatively higher morbidity and mortality among Indians. Current observations on rates of infectious diseases and the historical legacy of the devastating outcomes after exposure to unfamiliar infectious agents should raise awareness and alertness among healthcare providers and planners and among communities as new viruses (e.g., HIV, sin nombre) emerge and pose potential threats for American Indians.

REFERENCES

Ahtone J, Kuberski TT. 1982. Hepatitis B and its ancestors. *Lancet* 1:447.
Alward WLM, McMahon BJ, Hall DB, et al. 1985. The serologic course of hepatitis B

surface antigen and e antigen and the development of primary hepatocellular carcinoma in asymptomatic carriers of hepatitis B virus. *J Infect Dis* 151:604–9.

American Academy of Pediatrics Committee on Infectious Diseases. 1999. Possible association of intussusception with rotavirus vaccination (RE9938). *Pediatrics* 104:575.

Aronson JD, Aronson CF, Taylor HC. 1958. A twenty-year appraisal of BCG vaccination
in the control of tuberculosis. *Arch Intern Med* 101:881–93.

Barnes AM, Quan TJ, Beard ML, et al. 1988. Plague in American Indians, 1956–1987.
MMWR CDC Surveill Summ 37(3):11–16.

Barrett DB, Burks J, McMahon BJ, et al. 1977. Epidemiology of hepatitis B in two
Alaskan communities. *Am J Epidemiol* 105:118–22.

Baxter JD. 1991. An overview of twenty years of observation concerning etiology, prevalence, and evolution of otitis media and hearing among the Inuit in the Eastern
Canadian Arctic. In: Postl BD, Gilbert P, Goodwill J, et al., eds. *Circumpolar Health
90*, 616–19. Winnipeg: University of Manitoba Press.

Becker TM, Wiggins C, Peek C, et al. 1990. Mortality from infectious diseases among
New Mexico's American Indians, Hispanic Whites and other Whites, 1958–87. *Am J
Public Health* 80:320–23.

Beery QC, Doyle WJ, Cantekin EI, et al. 1980. Eustachian tube function in an American
Indian population. *Ann Otol Rhinol Laryngol* 89(3 pt. 2):28–33.

Beller M, Gessner B, Wainwright R, et al. 1998. *Botulism in Alaska: A Guide for Physicians and Health Care Providers.* Anchorage: Section of Epidemiology, State of
Alaska Department of Health and Social Sciences.

Berg DE, Larsen AE, Yarington CT. 1971. Association between serum and secretory
immunoglobulins and chronic otitis media in Indian children. *Ann Otol* 80:766–72.

Blackwood L. 1981. Epidemiology of gonorrhea in Native Alaskans. *Br J Vener Dis*
57:372–75.

Brieman RF, Butler JC, Tenover FC, et al. 1994. Emergence of drug-resistant pneumococcal infections in the United States. *JAMA* 271:1831–35.

Brook I. 1990. Microbiology of empyema in children and adolescents. *Pediatrics* 85:722–
26.

Brown CV, Brown GW, Bonehill B. 1967. Relationship of anaemia to infectious illnesses
on Kodiak Island. *Alaska Med* 9:93–95.

Bulkow LR, Wainwright RB, Letson GW, et al. 1993. Comparative immunogenicity of
four *Haemophilus influenzae* type b conjugate vaccines in Alaska Native infants.
Pediatr Infect Dis J 12:484–92.

Centers for Disease Control and Prevention. 1993. Update: Outbreak of hantavirus
infection, Southwestern United States, 1993. *MMWR* 42:441–43.

——. 1995a. First 500,000 AIDS cases, United States. *MMWR* 44:849–53.

——. 1995b. Summary of notifiable diseases, United States, 1995. *MMWR* 44:1–86.

——. 1996a. Hantavirus pulmonary syndrome, United States, 1995 and 1996. *MMWR*
45:291–95.

——. 1996b. Prevention of hepatitis A through active and passive immunization: Recommendations of the ACIP. *MMWR* 45(RR-15):1–26.

——. 1998. Reported tuberculosis in United States, 1997. From CDC Surveillance Web
Site, July 1998.

Cheek JE, Johanes P. 1994. Introduction to STD treatment guidelines. *IHS Prim Care
Provider* 19(2):17–40.

Cochi SL, Broome CV, Hightower AW. 1985. Immunization of U.S. children with *Haemo-*

philus influenzae type b polysaccharide vaccine: A cost effective model of strategy assessment. *JAMA* 253:521–29.

Cortese MM, Wolff M, Almeido-Hill J, et al. 1992. High incidence rates of invasive pneumococcal disease in the White Mountain Apache Population. *Arch Intern Med* 152:2277–82.

Davidson M, Parkinson AJ, Bulkow LR, et al. 1994. The epidemiology of invasive pneumococcal disease in Alaska, 1986–1990: Ethnic differences and opportunities for prevention. *J Infect Dis* 170:368–76.

Davidson M, Schraer CD, Parkinson AJ, et al. 1989. Invasive pneumococcal disease in an Alaska Native population, 1980 through 1986. *JAMA* 261:715–18.

De Zoysa I, Feachem RG. 1985. Interventions for the control of diarrhoeal diseases among young children: Rotavirus and cholera immunization. *Bull World Health Organ* 63:569–83.

Dobyns HF. 1983. *Their Numbers Become Thinned: Native American Population Dynamics in Eastern North America*. Knoxville: University of Tennessee Press.

Dolman CE. 1974. Human botulism in Canada (1919–1973). *Can Med Assoc J* 110:191–200.

Doyle MG, Morrow AL, Van R, et al. 1992. Intermediate resistance of *Streptococcus pneumoniae* to penicillin in children in day-care centers. *Pediatr Infect Dis J* 11:831–35.

Doyle WJ. 1977. A functiono-anatomic description of eustachian tube vector relations in four ethnic populations: An osteologic study. Ph.D. diss., University of Pittsburgh.

Dubois A. 1995. Spiral bacteria in the human stomach: The gastric helicobacters. *Emerging Infect Dis* 1:79–85.

Eskola J, Peltola H, Takala AK, et al. 1987. Efficacy of *Haemophilus influenzae* type b polysaccharide-diphtheria vaccine in infancy. *N Engl J Med* 317:717–22.

Estroff DT, Greenman JA, Heyward WL, et al. 1985. Increased prevalence of hepatitis B surface antigen in pregnant Alaskan Eskimos. In: Fortuine RF, ed. *Circumpolar Health 84*, 206–8. Seattle: University of Washington Press.

Ferrari ND, Weisse ME. 1995. Botulism. *Adv Pediatr Infect Dis* 10:81–91.

Finley JC, Davidson M, Parkinson AJ, et al. 1992. Pneumococcal endocarditis in Alaska: A population based experience, 1978–90. *Arch Intern Med* 152:1641–45.

Gildon B, Malantubee S, Istre GR. 1992. Community-wide outbreak of hepatitis A among an Indian population in Oklahoma. *South Med J* 85(1):9–13.

Graham DY, Malaty HM, Evans DG, et al. 1991. Epidemiology of *Helicobacter pylori* in an asymptomatic population in the United States. *Gastroenterology* 100:1494–1501.

Hall CB. 1979. Respiratory syncytial virus. In: Benner J, Mandell G, Douglas RJ Jr, eds. *Principles and Practices of Infectious Diseases*. New York: Wiley.

Harrison HR, Boyce WT, Haffner WH, et al. 1983. The prevalence of genital *Chlamydia trachomatis* and mycoplasmal infections during pregnancy in an American Indian population. *Sex Transm Dis* 10:18–20.

Harrison LH, Tajkowski C, Croll J, et al. 1994. Postlicensure effectiveness of the *Haemophilus influenzae* type b polysaccharide—*Neisseria meningitidis* outer-membrane protein complex conjugate vaccine among Navajo children. *J Pediatr* 125:571–76.

Hauschild AHW, Gauvreau L. 1985. Food-borne botulism in Canada, 1971–84. *Can Med Assoc J* 133:1141–46.

Heilman CA. 1990. Respiratory syncytial and parainfluenza viruses. *J Infect Dis* 161:402–6.

Heyward WL, Bender TR, Lanier AP, et al. 1982. Serological markers of hepatitis B virus and alpha-fetoprotein levels preceding primary hepatocellular carcinoma in Alaskan Eskimos. *Lancet* 2:889–91.

Heyward WL, Bender TR, McMahon BJ, et al. 1985a. The control of hepatitis B virus infection with vaccine in Yupik Eskimos: Demonstration of safety, immunogenicity and efficacy under field conditions. *Am J Epidemiol* 121:914–23.

Heyward WL, Lanier AP, Bender TR, et al. 1981. Primary hepatocellular carcinoma in Alaskan Natives, 1969–1979. *Int J Cancer* 28:47–50.

Heyward WL, Lanier AP, McMahon BJ, et al. 1985b. Early detection of primary hepatocellular carcinoma by screening for alpha-fetoprotein among persons infected with hepatitis B virus. *JAMA* 254:3052–54.

Hirschhorn N, Cash R, Woodward W, et al. 1972. Oral therapy of Apache children with acute infectious diarrhea. *Lancet* 1:15–18.

Hirschhorn N, Spivey GH. 1972. Health and the White Mountain Apache. *J Infect Dis* 126:348–50.

Hoshiwara I, Ostler HB, Hanna L, et al. 1973. Doxycycline treatment of chronic trachoma. *JAMA* 224:220–23.

Houston S, Fanning A, Soskolne CL, et al. 1990. The effectiveness of bacillus Calmette-Guerin (BCG) vaccination against tuberculosis. *Am J Epidemiol* 131:340–48.

Hulten K, Enroth H, Nystrom T, et al. 1996. *Helicobacter pylori* detected by PCR and hybridization in water from Sweden. *Gut* 39:52A87.

Indian Health Service. 1994. *Summary of Clinical Impressions for Respiratory System Diseases, Indian Health Service and Tribal Direct and Contract Facilities, Fiscal Year 1994*. Rockville, Md.: Indian Health Service.

———. 1997. *Trends in Indian Health, 1997*. Rockville, Md.: Indian Health Service, Program Statistics Team.

Johonnott SC. 1973. Differences in chronic otitis media between rural and urban Eskimo children: A comparative study. *Clin Pediatr (Phila)* 12:318–33.

Jolly AM, Orr PH, Hammond G, et al. 1995. Risk factors for infection in women undergoing testing for *Chlamydia trachomatis* and *Neisseria gonorrhoeae* in Manitoba, Canada. *Sex Transm Dis* 22(5):289–95.

Kaufmann AF, Boyce JM, Martone WJ. 1980. Trends in human plague in the United States. *J Infect Dis* 141:522–24.

LaVia WV, Marks MI, Stutman HR. 1992. Respiratory syncytial virus puzzle: Clinical features, pathophysiology, treatment, and prevention. *J Pediatr* 121:503–10.

Law BJ, De Carvalho V. 1993. Respiratory syncyctial virus in hospitalized Canadian children: Regional differenecs in patient populations and management practices. *Pediatr Infect Dis J* 12:659–63.

Lawler DJ, Biswell R, Sharvelle DJ, et al. 1970. Trachoma among the Navajo Indians. *Arch Ophthalmol* 83:187–89.

Letson GW, Gellin BG, Bulkow LR, et al. 1992. Severity and frequency of sequelae of bacterial meningitis in Alaska Native infants. *Am J Dis Child* 146:560–66.

Lieb LE, Conway GA, Hedderman M, et al. 1992. Racial misclassification of American Indians with AIDS in Los Angeles County. *J Acquir Immune Defic Syndr* 5:1137–41.

Ling D, McCoy RH, Levinson ED. 1969. The incidence of middle ear disease and its educational implication among Baffin Island Eskimo children. *Can J Public Health* 60:385–90.

McMahon BJ, Alberts SR, Wainwright RB, et al. 1990. Hepatitis B-related sequelae:

Prospective study in 1400 hepatitis B surface antigen-positive Alaska Native carriers. *Arch Intern Med* 150:1051–54.

McMahon BJ, Alward WLM, Hall DB, et al. 1985. Acute hepatitis B infection: Relationship of age to the clinical expression of disease and the subsequent development of the carrier state. *J Infect Dis* 151:599–603.

McMahon BJ, Beller M, Williams J, et al. 1996. A program to control an outbreak of hepatitis A in Alaska by using an inactivated hepatitis A vaccine. *Arch Pediatr Adolesc Med* 150:733–39.

McMahon BJ, Bender TR, Berquist KR, et al. 1981. Delayed development of antibody to hepatitis B surface antigen after symptomatic infection with hepatitis B virus. *J Clin Microbiol* 14:130–34.

McMahon BJ, Heyward WL, Templin DW, et al. 1989. Hepatitis B-associated polyarteritis nodosa in Alaskan Eskimos: Clinical and epidemiologic features and long-term followup. *Hepatology* 9:97–101.

McMahon BJ, Schoenberg S, Bulkow L, et al. 1993. Seroprevalence of hepatitis B viral markers in 52,000 Alaska Natives. *Am J Epidemiol* 138:544–49.

McMahon BJ, Wainwright RB. 1990. Hepatitis B virus infection: A program to reduce the incidence of infection and sequelae in Alaska Natives. In: Coursaget P, Tong MJ, eds. *Progress in Hepatitis B immunization,* 194:491–500. London: Colloque INSERM/John Libbey Eurotest.

Metler R, Conway GA, Stehr-Green J. 1991. AIDS surveillance among American Indians and Alaska Natives. *Am J Public Health* 81:1469–71.

Morgan WJ, Martinez FD. 1992. Risk factors for developing wheezing and asthma in childhood. *Pediatr Clin North Am* 39:1185–1203.

Mori MA, Leonardson G, Welty TK. 1992. The benefits of isoniazid chemoprophylaxis and risk factors for tuberculosis among Oglala Sioux Indians. *Arch Intern Med* 152:547–50.

Morris K, Morganlander M, Coulehan JL, et al. 1990. Wood-burning stoves and lower respiratory tract infection in American Indian children. *Am J Dis Child* 144:105–8.

Newcomer W, Rivin B, Reid R, et al. 1994. Immunogenicity, safety and tolerability of varying doses and regimens of inactivated hepatitis A virus vaccine in Navajo children. *Pediatr Infect Dis J* 13:640–42.

Nomura A, Stemmermann GN, Chou PH, et al. 1991. *Helicobacter pylori* infection and gastric carcinoma among Japanese Americans in Hawaii. *N Engl J Med* 325:1132–36.

Parkinson AJ, Bulkow L, Wainwright RB, et al. 1997. High prevalence of *Helicobacter pylori* and an association with low serum ferritin in the Alaska Native population. Anchorage: Centers for Disease Control and Prevention, Arctic Investigations Program. Manuscript in preparation.

Paulsen HJ. 1987. Tuberculosis in the Native American: Indigenous or introduced. *Rev Infect Dis* 9:1180–86.

Pedersen CB, Zachau-Christiansen B. 1986. Otitis media in Greenland children: Acute, chronic and secretory otitis media with effusion. *J Otolaryngol* 15:332–35.

Peltola H, Kayhty H, Virtanen M, et al. 1984. Prevention of *Haemophilus influenzae* type b bacteremic infections with the capsular polysaccharide vaccine. *N Engl J Med* 310:1561–66.

Petersen GM, Silimperi DR, Chiu C-Y, et al. 1991. Effects of age, breastfeeding, and household structure on *Haemophilus influenzae* type b disease risk and antibody acquisition in Alaskan Eskimos. *Am J Epidemiol* 134:1212.

Petersen KM. 1993. Empyema in Alaska Native children, 1980–1992. Anchorage: Centers for Disease Control and Prevention, Arctic Investigations Program. Unpublished report.

Petersen KM, Parkinson AJ, Nobmann ED, et al. 1996. Iron deficiency anemia among Alaska Natives may be due to fecal loss rather than inadequate intake. *J Nutr* 126: 2774–83.

Portney GL, Hoshiwara I. 1970. Prevalence of trachoma among southwestern American Indian tribe. *Am J Ophthalmol* 70:843–46.

Rausch RL, Schiller EL. 1951. Hydatid disease (echinococcosis) in Alaska and the importance of rodent intermediate hosts. *Science* 118:57–58.

Reed D, Struve S, Maynard JE. 1967. Otitis media and hearing deficiency among Eskimo children: A cohort study. *Am J Public Health* 57:1657–62.

Rennels M, Glass RI, Dennehy P, et al. 1996. For the US Rotavirus Vaccine Efficacy Group: Safety and efficacy of high dose rhesus-human reassortant rotavirus vaccines. Report of the National Multicenter Trial. *Pediatrics* 97:7–13.

Rieder HL. 1989. Tuberculosis among American Indians in the contiguous United States. *Public Health Rep* 104:653–57.

Rowell RM, Bouey PD. 1997. Update on HIV/AIDS among American Indians and Alaska Natives. *IHS Prim Care Provider* 22(4):49–53.

Santosham M, Burns B, Nadkarni V, et al. 1985. Oral rehydration therapy for acute diarrhea in ambulatory children in the United States: A double blind comparison of four different solutions. *Pediatrics* 76:159–66.

Santosham M, Daum RS, Dillman L, et al. 1982. Oral rehydration therapy of infantile diarrhea: A controlled study of well-nourished children hospitalized in the United States and Panama. *N Engl J Med* 306:1070–76.

Santosham M, Hill J, Wolff M, et al. 1991a. Safety and immunogenicity of *Haemophilus influenzae* type b conjugate vaccine in a high risk American Indian population. *Pediatr Infect Dis J* 10:113–17.

Santosham M, Rivin B, Wolff M, et al. 1992. Prevention of *Haemophilus influenzae* type b infections in Apache and Navajo children. *J Infect Dis* 165 (suppl 1):S144–51.

Santosham M, Wolff M, Reid R, et al. 1991b. The efficacy in Navajo infants of a conjugate vaccine consisting of *Haemophilus influenzae* type b polysaccharide and *Neisseria meningitidis* outer-membrane protein complex. *N Engl J Med* 324:1767–72.

Santosham M, Lawrence MH, Reid R, et al. 1997. Efficacy and safety of high-dose rhesus-human reassortant rotavirus vaccine in Native American populations. *J Pediatr* 131:632–38.

Schaefer C, Harrison R, Boyce T, et al. 1985. Illnesses in infants born to women with *Chlamydia trachomatis* infection. *Am J Dis Child* 139:127–33.

Schaefer O. 1971. Otitis media and bottle-feeding: An epidemiological study of infant feeding habits and incidence of recurrent and chronic middle ear disease in Canadian Eskimos. *Can J Public Health* 62:478–89.

Schreeder MT, Bender TR, McMahon BJ, et al. 1983. Prevalence of hepatitis B in selected Alaskan Eskimo villages. *Am J Epidemiol* 118:543–49.

Shaw FE, Shapiro CN, Welty TK, et al. 1990. Hepatitis transmission among the Sioux Indians of South Dakota. *Am J Public Health* 80:1091–94.

Siber GR, Santosham M, Reid R, et al. 1990. Impaired antibody response to *Haemophilus influenzae* type b polysaccharide and low IgG2 and IgG4 concentrations in Apache children. *N Engl J Med* 323:1387–92.

Simonsen L, Dalton MJ, Breiman RF, et al. 1995. Evaluation of the magnitude of the

1993 hantavirus outbreak in the Southwestern United States. *J Infect Dis* 172:729–33.

Singleton RJ, Petersen KM, Berner JE, et al. 1995. Hospitalizations for respiratory syncytial virus infection in Alaska Native children. *Pediatr Infect Dis J* 14:26–30.

Sitas F, Forman D, Yarnell JW, et al. 1991. *Helicobacter pylori* infection rates in relation to age and social class in a population of Welsh men. *Gut* 32:25–28.

Stewart TD. 1973. *The People of America*. New York: Scribner.

Stiffarm LA, Lane P. 1992. The state of Native America genocide, colonization, and resistance. In: Jaimes MA, ed. *The Demography of Native North America: A Question of American Indian Survival*, 23–53. Boston: South End Press.

Takala AK, Santosham M, Almeido-Hill J, et al. 1993. Vaccination with *Haemophilus influenzae* type b meningococcal protein conjugate vaccine reduces oropharyngeal carriage of *Haemophilus influenzae* type b among American Indian children. *Pediatr Infect Dis J* 12:593–99.

Thomas JE, Gibson GR, Darboe MK, et al. 1992. Isolation of *Helicobacter pylori* from human faeces. *Lancet* 340:1194–95.

Todd NW. 1990. Otitis media in four populations of Arizona Indian children. *Ann Otol Rhinol Laryngol* 99 (suppl 149):22–23.

Todd NW, Bowman CA. 1985. Otitis media at Canyon Day, Arizona: A 16-year follow-up in Apache Indians. *Arch Otolaryngol* 111:606–8.

Toomey KE, Oberschelp AG, Greenspan JR. 1989. Sexually transmitted diseases and Native Americans: Trends in reported gonorrhea and syphilis morbidity, 1984–88. *Public Health Rep* 104:566–72.

Toomey KE, Rafferty MP, Stamm WE. 1987. Unrecognized high prevalence of *Chlamydia trachomatis* infection in an isolated Alaskan Eskimo population. *JAMA* 258:53–56.

Tytgat GNJ, Rauws EAJ. 1990. *Campylobacter pylori* and its role in peptic ulcer disease. *Gastroenterol Clin North Am* 19:183–96.

Ussery XT, Gessner BD, Lipman H, et al. 1996. Risk factors for nasopharyngeal carriage of resistant *Streptococcus pneumoniae* and detection of a multiply resistant clone among children living in the Yukon-Kuskokwim Delta region of Alaska. *Pediatr Infect Dis J* 15:986–92.

Wainwright RB, Bulkow LR, Parkinson AJ, et al. 1997. Protection provided by hepatitis B vaccine in a Yupik Eskimo population — results of a 10-year study. *J Infect Dis* 175:674–77.

Wainwright RB, Heyward WL, Middaugh JP, et al. 1988. Food-borne botulism in Alaska, 1947–1985: Epidemiology and clinical findings. *J Infect Dis* 157:1158–62.

Ward JI, Brenneman G, Letson GW, et al. 1990. Limited efficacy of a *Haemophilus influenzae* type B conjugate vaccine in Alaska Native infants. *N Engl J Med* 323:1393–1401.

Ward JI, Lum MK, Hall DB, et al. 1986. Invasive *Haemophilus influenzae* type b disease in Alaska: Background epidemiology for a vaccine efficacy trial. *J Infect Dis* 153:17–26.

Wiet RJ. 1979. Pattern of ear disease in the southwestern American Indian. *Arch Otolaryngol* 105:381–85.

Williams R. 1986. Prevalence of hepatitis A virus antibody among Navajo school children. *Am J Public Health* 76:282–83.

Wilson JF, Rausch RL. 1980. Alveolar hydatid disease: A review of clinical features of 33 indigenous cases of *Echinococcus multilocularis* infection in Alaskan Eskimos. *Am J Trop Med Hyg* 29:1340–55.

Wilson JF, Rausch RL, McMahon BJ, et al. 1992. Parasiticidal effect of chemotherapy in alveolar hydatid disease: A review of experience with mebendazole and albendazole in Alaska Eskimos. *Rev Infect Dis* 15:234–49.

Wotherspoon AC, Ortiz-Hildago C, Falzon MF, et al. 1991. *Helicobacter pylori*-associated gastritis and primary B-cell gastric lymphoma. *Lancet* 338:1175–76.

Yip R, Limburg PJ, Ahlquist DA, et al. 1997. Pervasive occult gastrointestinal bleeding in an Alaska Native population with prevalent iron deficiency: Role of *Helicobacter pylori* gastritis. *JAMA* 277:1135–59.

Zonis RD. 1968. Chronic otitis media in the southwestern American Indian. *Arch Otolaryngol Head Neck Surg* 88:360–65.

21

Robert J. Collins, D.M.D., M.P.H.,
Candace M. Jones, R.D.H., M.P.H., and
Robert F. Martin, D.D.S., M.P.H.

Oral Health

The term *oral health* generally applies to the condition of the hard and soft tissues of the mouth and jaws. Oral diseases are generally not life threatening, but often have a significant effect on overall health and quality of life (Gift and Atchison 1995). Traditional views of oral health have focused on the teeth and their supporting structures, the gums and the alveolar (jaw) bone, known collectively as the periodontium. Although recent surveys have attempted to go beyond the condition of the teeth and their supporting structures, most descriptions of the oral health of American Indians emphasize the epidemiology and treatment needs associated with dental caries (tooth decay) and the periodontal diseases (chronic or acute infections of the periodontium).

In general, oral health has improved in the United States over the past two decades for both adults (National Institutes of Health [NIH] 1987) and children (NIH 1989). The findings of Indian Health Service (IHS) patient-based surveys indicate a generally higher prevalence of traditional oral diseases for American Indians.

Most oral disease results from limited access to community and personal preventive measures, such as fluoridated water and fluoride toothpaste, as well as a lack of personal oral hygiene. The higher prevalence of oral disease in the Indian population has been attributed to these factors, combined with less access to professional care. Although resources for the dental program serving Indians have grown since 1955, they have not kept pace with the rapid growth of the Indian population (Niendorff 1994). As a result, only about one-third of the Indian population has a dental visit each year, compared with nearly 70 percent for the U.S. population (Indian Health Service 1992a, 1992b). Thus, both access to dental care and the oral health of Indian people lag behind those of the U.S. population overall.

Oral Health 371

Oral Health Service Delivery Systems for Native Americans

Attention to oral health care for Indians began in 1913, when five itinerant dentists were employed by the Bureau of Indian Affairs (BIA) to provide services to various Indian reservations (Figure 21.1). These services were aimed at eliminating pain and infection, and little attention was paid to assessing the overall need or to otherwise organizing a service delivery system. In 1932, the Public Health Service assigned a dental officer to the BIA to organize a more effective delivery care program. Schools were identified as major sites of dental care delivery for children (Indian Health Service 1970, 1992a, 1992b).

From 1956 to 1979, the newly created IHS included modern dental clinics within its newly constructed hospitals and clinics, beginning a shift of dental service delivery from the school to the health facility. The IHS also surveyed all patients seen in its clinics and used these data to estimate the oral health and treatment resources required to address the need for care (Abramowitz 1970, 1971). Although emphasis remained on services for schoolchildren, changes in the dental program were initiated: dental assistant training programs (Nixon 1980), automated data collection (Collins, Broderick, and Herman 1993), dental internship and residency training programs (Collins 1983), quality of care

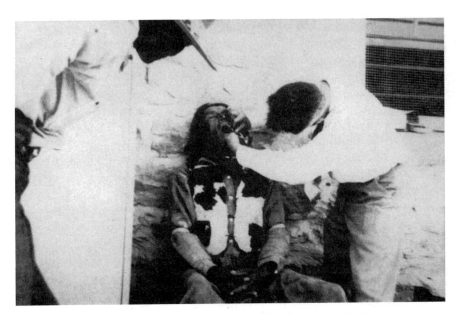

Figure 21.1. Early field dentists were able to provide only the most basic care.

evaluation (Indian Health Service 1992a, 1992b), and the introduction of water fluoridation and supplemental fluorides. In the late 1970s, as the demand for adult care increased, the focus on comprehensive care for children and only emergency care for adults shifted to treatment for the family unit. As with other health programs, tribes assumed successful operation of dental programs (Indian Health Service 1992b).

Since 1980, there has been increased operation of programs by tribes and an increased emphasis on prevention, a shift to a program offering a wider variety of services to those of all ages, and establishment of national oral health objectives patterned after the 1990 Objectives for the Nation (U.S. Department of Health and Human Services 1980). The IHS objectives were based on the findings of a survey indicating that Native Americans had a much higher prevalence of tooth decay, periodontal disease, and tooth loss (Niendorff 1985) than did the general U.S. population. As the result of an audit revealing that many water fluoridation programs operated in substandard conditions and that few children were receiving dental sealants, efforts were renewed to fluoridate water supplies effectively and to ensure that a majority of children received dental sealants. A community-oriented primary care (COPC) model was adopted (Indian Health Service 1992b; Maas 1987), and dental services were organized into levels of care (Indian Health Service 1992b), with special emphasis on community prevention programs.

A special program was instituted to address the relationship between diabetes and periodontal disease and to seek possible intervention strategies (Shlossman et al. 1990). An Oral Health Status Survey conducted in 1991–92 reflected significant progress in reducing oral disease — particularly among children and youth. However, the Second International Collaborative Study of Oral Health (ICS-II) organized by the World Health Organization (WHO), while confirming progress in oral health, also disclosed continuing oral health discrepancies of Indians relative to other U.S. populations (Anderson, Davidson, and Nakazono 1997; Reifel et al. 1997).

Dental Caries

Dental caries, or "tooth decay," is a dissolution of tooth enamel resulting from a complex interaction involving teeth, fermentable carbohydrates, and oral bacteria, primarily *Streptococcus mutans* (U.S. Department of Health and Human Services, National Institute of Dental Research 1990). The caries process seems to be multifactorial; diet, bacteria, and tooth susceptibility all play critical roles in its development (Bratthall 1996; Bratthall, Hansell-Petersson, and Sundberg 1996). Tooth decay rates are usually expressed as either a percentage of the population with the condition or as the average amount of disease in the population. The number of decayed (D), missing (M), and filled (F) teeth (T) (DMFT) or surfaces (S) (DMFS) is a reflection of the accumulation or prevalence of disease. Decayed teeth are those that have active decay, whereas those filled or missing reflect teeth that have had carious lesions that have been treated by restoration (filled) or extraction (missing). DMFT and DMFS are indices that reflect the cumulative decay experience and, therefore, increase with age.

Permanent Teeth

Although early surveys of American Indian children indicated a relatively low rate of dental caries (Cady 1934; Arnim, Aberle, and Pitney 1937; Klein and Palmer 1937), the prevalence of caries in the permanent teeth of American Indian children began to increase in the 1960s (Abramowitz 1970; Fasano and Zwemer 1969; Curzon and Curzon 1970). The mean DMFT per child increased from 4.0 in 1957 to 5.91 in 1970. Although the mean number of filled teeth increased, the decayed and missing components decreased only slightly. In five of eight IHS Areas, both the mean decayed and DMFT rose (Indian Health Service 1970). Overall caries prevalence, as indicated by the DMFT, increased from about 4 in 1957 to 6.5 in 1984, before declining to 3.6 in 1991 (Figure 21.2). The rise in the DMFT from 1957 to 1984 resulted almost entirely from an in-

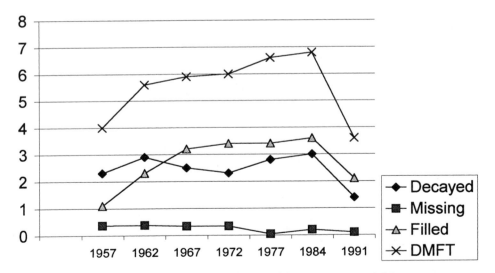

Figure 21.2. Trends in decay in permanent teeth of Native American children, 1957–91. *Source:* Niendorff 1994

crease in the filled component — probably due largely to the intense clinical focus on restoring rather than extracting decayed teeth during most of this period. The recent significant decrease is very likely attributable to the widespread use of dental sealants beginning in 1984 and to incremental improvements in the water fluoridation program throughout the 1980s (Niendorff 1994).

Despite this dramatic improvement, the Indian population continued to experience decay rates higher than those for the general population or other minority populations in either urban or rural locations (NIH 1989). The DMFS for 5–17-year-old Native Americans was 5.0, compared to 3.2 for U.S. rural children and 3.4 for minority children. Nonetheless, the decayed and missing components are similar for all populations, so that the higher mean prevalence for Indian children is due entirely to a higher rate of filled surfaces.

Two cautions are in order when using the IHS patient survey data. First, since the national survey data for Native Americans are obtained through convenience sampling of patients, it cannot be assumed that the results are necessarily representative of all Native Americans. Data from the ICS-II study, however, which used standardized examiners and a random sample of the Navajo and Sioux Indian populations, indicate that the national IHS data probably are reasonably representative of all Native Americans (Niendorff 1994). A 1989 survey of Indian and Caucasian children in Oklahoma indicated that the mean dmfs for 5–6-year-old Caucasians was 5.06, compared to 10.35 for Indian children. (Note: The designation for decayed, missing, and filled teeth or surfaces for the *primary* dentition is expressed in *lowercase* letters.) For 15–17-year-old Caucasian children, the mean DMFS was 5.99, compared to 10.12 for the Indian group (Grim et al. 1994).

Second, the IHS program in the 1960s and 1970s emphasized treatment of decay as early as possible to prevent the need for larger fillings or extractions. To the extent that preventive fillings were placed to treat the early signs of decay, the DMFS may be higher than it would have been if dental sealants had been used in lieu of restorations.

In summary, the overall decay prevalence for Native American school-age children seems to be declining after many years; however, the mean prevalence of decay and rate of untreated caries are still much higher than those for U.S. schoolchildren. Given the current widespread use of sealants by programs serving Native Americans, it is possible that the mean DMF for Indian children could approach that of other U.S. children within the next decade.

Tooth decay in adults also seems to be declining slowly, with the average number of DMFT for young adults 25–34 years of age falling from 17 in 1970 to 13.4 in 1991. Of teeth experiencing decay, a much higher proportion was filled in 1991 than in 1970, reflecting improved access to dental care and fluoridated water (Niendorff 1994). The overall prevalence of tooth decay in Indians 35–44 years of age was approximately the same in 1991 as in 1984; however, decayed teeth were a smaller proportion, indicating both improved access to treatment services and the need for more emphasis on prevention for those of all ages.

There are a paucity of data on the oral health of elderly Indians. Elderly persons represent a relatively small proportion of the overall Indian population and, until recently, treatment programs of the IHS gave priority to children. As a result, only a very small proportion of the elderly have been represented in the IHS dental patient database. A special survey of the oral health of 204 Sioux, 65–74 years old, from the Pine Ridge and Rosebud reservations in South Dakota noted that only 85 (42%) of the participants were dentate and, of these, 58 percent had active decay, with an average number of 10 teeth remaining and a mean DFT of 4.35 (Phipps, Reifel, and Bothwell 1991). On average, those with teeth required either restoration or extraction for 59 percent of their teeth.

Primary Dentition

Decay in the primary dentition, or "baby teeth," of Indian children has also declined over the past two decades, from a mean of 6.2 dmft for patients 0–9 years of age in 1974 to 5.9 in 1984 and 4.5 in 1991. Most of the decline occurred in the prevalence of decayed teeth. Nevertheless, the mean dfs for 5–9-year-olds in 1991 was two to three times as high at every age than for U.S. children surveyed in 1987 (Niendorff 1994).

A particularly severe form of primary tooth decay, often referred to as "baby bottle tooth decay" (BBTD) to denote its most common etiology, is a major problem among American Indian infants and children (O'Sullivan et al. 1994; Milnes 1996). This form of caries is also described by the broader term *nursing caries* to reflect the fact that this pattern of decay also appears in children who have been breast-fed on demand. Johnsen (1982) found that 95 percent of children with lesions characteristic of nursing caries had been given a nursing bottle at bedtime. He also reported that the parents of these children were less likely to have attended college, were more pessimistic about their own dentition, and were reluctant to say "no" to the child. Figure 21.3 illustrates a typical pattern of BBTD, with the upper maxillary incisors characteristically involved first, followed by a pattern of decay that mimics the pooling of the cariogenic fluid in the oral cavity (Johnsen 1984).

The IHS 1984 Oral Health Status Survey revealed that, depending on the index used, 24–50 percent of Indian infants and children had BBTD. A study of Navajo and Oklahoma Indian children in Head Start programs found that 70 percent had BBTD and that, of those with the condition, 87 percent displayed extensive destruction (Broderick et al. 1989). Among 544 Head Start children studied in 1989, the mean dmft and dmfs scores were 3.91 and 8.73, respec-

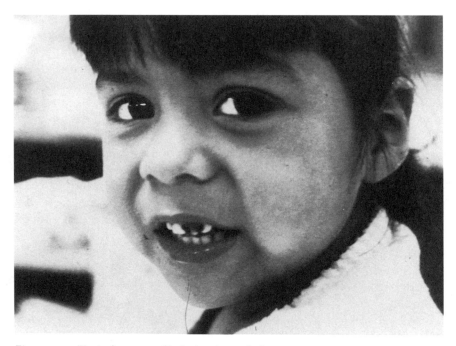

Figure 21.3. Typical pattern of baby bottle tooth decay

tively. Alaska Native children had significantly higher rates than those of non-Native children. Those children living in rural communities had significantly higher caries scores than did urban children (Jones, Schlife, and Phipps 1992). In addition to pain and suffering, BBTD seems to predispose to the development of further carious lesions in the primary dentition (Johnsen et al. 1986; O'Sullivan and Tinanoff 1996). Those with BBTD have much higher caries rates and require much more extensive restorative treatment — often under general anesthesia — than do those without BBTD. Thus, this preventable condition has an enormous impact on the limited time and financial resources of the IHS care system (Broderick et al. 1989; Bruerd and Jones 1996).

In an attempt to reduce the prevalence of BBTD, the IHS, in conjunction with the Head Start program, supported an intervention trial from 1986 to 1989. A combination of strategies, including counseling, group presentations, a media campaign, and educational materials, were successful in reducing the overall prevalence from 57 percent to 43 percent — a 25 percent overall reduction in BBTD over the three-year period (Bruerd, Kinney, and Bothwell 1989). In those sites that continued the intervention over the next several years, the reduction was sustained (Bruerd and Jones 1996). These strategies, however, require intense community involvement and have been difficult to transfer to, and sustain, in other Native American communities. As a result, the national prevalence of BBTD for Native American children changed little between 1984 and 1991 (Niendorff 1994). Berkowitz (1996) suggested that, in the absence of significant and widespread sociobehavioral changes, chemotherapeutic clinical interventions to limit *S. mutans* activity should be considered. An expanded IHS initiative launched in 1996 incorporates lessons learned from the earlier research efforts as well as risk factor identification, pharmacologic protocols, and preventive recall visits (Bruerd, Jones, and Krise 1997).

Periodontal Diseases

There are two broad classes of periodontal diseases: gingivitis and periodontitis. Gingivitis is an inflammation of the soft tissue surrounding teeth, which is often characterized by spontaneous or pressure-induced bleeding. Periodontitis is a condition in which the soft-tissue attachment is eroded and the alveolar bone supporting the tooth is lost. Left unattended, periodontitis often leads to loss of teeth. Periodontal disease is often reflected in clinical attachment loss. Carlos et al. (1988) found that clinical attachment loss in a group of Navajo aged 14–19 was best explained by a combination of calculus, gingival bleeding, and the presence of *Prevotella intermedia*.

Tobacco has been linked to a higher prevalence of periodontal disease, with a risk of periodontitis two to six times higher for smokers than for nonsmokers (American Academy of Periodontology 1996a, 1996b). In addition, there is increasing evidence that smoking also affects the host's response to periodontal therapy, suggesting that smoking interferes with the periodontal healing process (Grossi et al. 1996). Niendorff (1994) found that tobacco use by Native American youth and adolescents was relatively low but cautioned that the self-reported data probably underestimated actual prevalence. The high use of smokeless tobacco among Native American youth identified in other studies (Glover and Glover 1992) should be cause for concern about localized periodontal destruction and the potential for the development of oral cancer (Christen 1980).

Diabetes, a condition common in many Native American tribes, is related to periodontal destruction (Cianciola et al. 1982). Shlossman et al. (1990) found the prevalence of periodontal disease to be much higher in Native Americans with diabetes. In addition, periodontitis has a negative effect on the metabolic control of diabetes (Grossi et al. 1996).

About 30–38 percent of dental patients 35–44 years of age examined in IHS surveys over the last three decades, as well as a random sample of Sioux and

Navajo in the 1990 WHO study, experienced gingivitis. The prevalence of periodontitis ranged from 47 percent in 1984 to 61 percent in the 1990 WHO study. The IHS Dental Program uses the Community Periodontal Index of Treatment Needs to assess periodontal health and determine the type of treatment needed for patients (WHO 1987). The higher level of periodontitis in more recent years has been attributed to the increased retention of teeth by adults, although variations in methodology may account for some of the differences (Niendorff 1994). A survey of employed U.S. adults by the National Institute of Dental Research disclosed that approximately 17 percent of 35–44-year-olds had advanced disease (NIH 1987), compared to 21 percent in the ICS-II community-based sample of Indians examined in 1990 (Niendorff 1994). In the 1991 IHS patient survey, 19 percent of the nondiabetic patients had advanced disease and 34 percent of the diabetic patients had advanced disease. The narrowing of this difference after age 60 is explained by the high rates of tooth loss for persons with diabetes.

Recent advances in the understanding of periodontal diseases are offering new approaches for prevention and treatment in a public health setting (Hunt 1988). Treatment is directed toward removing all soft and hard debris from the root surfaces (Drisko and Lewis 1996). Future treatment will probably use subgingival ultrasonic debridement combined with anti-infective irrigation, followed by the placement of resorbable, locally delivered antibiotics. These new technologies may lengthen the time between recall intervals for even high-risk individuals (Grossi et al. 1994) and allow treatment of a greater proportion of the Native American population.

Occlusion

Several studies validate the clinical impressions of the IHS dentists that Native American youth have a higher rate of malocclusion than the general U.S. population (Jenny et al. 1991; Kellam 1982; Moorrees 1957). Anthropologists have long thought there might be a genetic basis for dental traits (Turner 1996). The 1991 IHS Patient Survey indicated that only 3–10 percent of Native American children had received orthodontic treatment, compared to over 24 percent of the general U.S. population of children in 1980.

Edentulism

American Indians exhibit higher rates of tooth loss earlier in life than do other U.S. populations. In 1991, for example, 42 percent of Indians 65 years and older were fully edentulous (Niendorff 1994), compared to 44 percent for the general U.S. population 75 years and older and only 31 percent for U.S. individuals aged 65–69 years (Marcus et al. 1996). The level of edentulism is often underestimated in patient-based surveys; however, the 1991 IHS national data seem to be a reasonable estimate. In this survey, 42 percent of Indians 65 years and older were edentulous, compared to the same percentage for a random sample of adults aged 65–74 years in the 1990 WHO survey of the Navajo and Sioux.

Among IHS Areas, there is considerable variation in the prevalence of total tooth loss. The Aberdeen Area, for example, has a rate two to three times that of tribes in the Southwest (Niendorff 1994; Marcus, Reifel, and Nakazono 1997). Although no definitive explanation can be offered for this wide variation, the rate of edentulism does seem to be lowest in those areas that have experienced the lowest rates of dental caries in the permanent teeth. Tooth loss is a particular problem for those with diabetes. American Indian diabetics at every age exhibit a much higher rate of edentulism than do nondiabetic persons (Niendorff 1994).

Oral Cancer

The average annual incidence rate (estimate based upon 1980–87 hospital discharge data) for oral and pharyngeal cancers among female Indians in all IHS Areas was 3.0 cases per 100,000 population, compared to 6.5/100,000 for White females. Only the Alaska (13.1/100,000) and Billings (4.6/100,000) Areas had higher rates than that for White females in the general population. For males in all IHS Areas, the incidence rate for oral and pharyngeal cancer was 5.7/100,000, compared to 16.8/100,000 for Whites. Only the Alaska Area was close to the rate for Whites, with a rate of 16.5/100,000. In general, except for nasopharyngeal cancer, the incidence rates for oral cancer among Indians are less than those among the general population (Nutting et al. 1993). A general discussion of cancer among Native Americans is provided in Chapter 11.

The Use of Tobacco

Chapter 17 discusses the various uses of tobacco among Indian people. The adverse effects of smokeless tobacco on oral health and its increasing use among the young are cause for growing concern. According to a 1991 survey of IHS dental patients (Niendorff 1994), 9 percent of children and adolescents 5–19 years old used tobacco. Approximately 39 percent of 20–34-year-old adults, 35 percent of those aged 35–44, 33 percent of those aged 45–54, and 23 percent of those aged 55–64 used tobacco. The Aberdeen, Billings, Bemidji, and Nashville Areas generally reported that 50 percent or more of dental patients aged 20 to 54 years were using tobacco. Of major concern is the finding of increased leukoplakia in one survey among Navajo youth (Wolfe and Carlos 1987).

Community-Oriented Primary Care

Representative of the overall IHS, the IHS Dental Program utilizes a community-oriented primary care approach to elevating the oral health status of Indians. This approach is based on epidemiologic methods, universal coverage of basic services, and involvement of the community served in health policy decisions (Institute of Medicine 1984). IHS Service Unit and tribal dental staff are expected to use available data to define the nature and extent of oral health problems unique to the *community as a whole* and to develop, implement, and evaluate appropriate strategies, as described by Maas (1987).

A pilot project to reduce the prevalence of BBTD in several reservations across the country, described earlier in this chapter, exemplifies the COPC process. The problem of BBTD was documented through screening of children in Head Start programs, and the results were discussed with local tribal health boards to gain their involvement. Local community members were trained, and interventions were developed by community members. Educational materials were also developed by local dental staff; Women, Infants, and Children (WIC) staff; community health representatives (CHRs), and community volunteers. As mentioned above, in those sites where community-based efforts are ongoing, the prevalence of BBTD continues to decline (Bruerd and Jones 1996).

Dental Care Priorities

A key structural element in the COPC process is the IHS Schedule of Dental Services, developed by the IHS in 1980 to guide the delivery of oral health services. The Schedule of Dental Services provides a means of rationing care to ensure that individual patients receive those services that prevent further deterioration of their oral health while assuring access to dental care for as many members of the community as possible, given resource limitations. A general description of the hierarchy of services is given in Table 21.1. The minimum services for individual patients are those in levels I–III, and these levels accounted for 94 percent of all services provided in fiscal year 1995. Services included in levels IV–VI, however, are needs that should be addressed by a comprehensive health-care program, and, by limiting their availability, a large portion of the dental care needed by IHS patients remains not provided. The

TABLE 21.1
IHS levels of dental care

Level	Service	Description
I	Emergency dental care	Those services necessary for the relief of acute conditions and defined by the patient to be of an emergent nature
II	Preventive dental care	Those activities that prevent the onset of dental disease (e.g., topical fluorides, sealants, and oral prophylaxis)
III	Secondary dental care	Those procedures that intervene early in the dental disease process (e.g., basic fillings)
IV	Limited rehabilitation	Those services that restore the oral structures to improved form and function (e.g., single crowns)
V	Rehabilitation	Rehabilitative services requiring more provider time, skill, or expense than those in level IV (e.g., dentures and bridgework)
VI	Complex rehabilitation	Those services that are considered most complex and that often require delivery by a specialist (e.g., implants and comprehensive orthodontics)

schedule also provides a matrix through which the delivery of additional services may be provided as additional resources become available.

The Benefits of Community Strategies

Comparing the findings of the 1991 programwide survey with a similar evaluation conducted in 1984, the results show a

— 42 percent increase in the number of youth aged 5–19 years with no decay;

— 35 percent decrease in the number of children aged 5–9 years with high decay rates (seven or more cavities); and

— 17 percent increase in the number of adults aged 35–44 years with 20 or more teeth remaining, a 29 percent increase for those 45–54 years, and a 40 percent increase for those 55 years and older.

Undoubtedly one of the most cost-effective preventive measures contributing to the observed reduction of dental decay in less than a decade is community water fluoridation (Ripa 1993). Relatively few tribally managed fluoridated water systems were operative in early years. The number has risen to nearly four hundred today. Many of these systems, however, are quite small, with 80 percent serving fewer than five hundred people. Today, approximately 42 percent of the Native American population receives the benefits of community water fluoridation, compared to 5 percent in 1980 (Indian Health Service 1995). These tribally managed systems are operated and maintained by the communities with support through IHS training and technical assistance upon request.

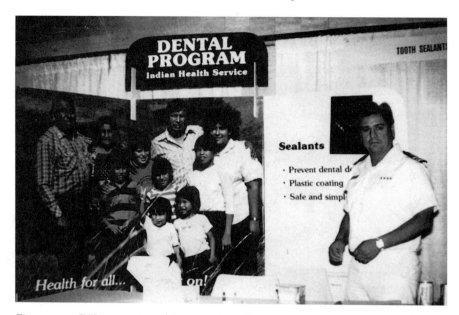

Figure 21.4. IHS promotion of dental sealants illustrates progress made in providing oral health services.

Another preventive strategy is the use of dental sealants — plastic coatings placed on the biting surfaces of teeth to prevent tooth decay. The IHS began promoting dental sealants in 1984 (Figure 21.4), and there has been a significant improvement in the oral health of Native American children since that time. Changes in oral health practices, such as the use of fluoridated toothpaste, and a general increase in exposure to fluoride may also have contributed to this encouraging health trend. A change in the socioeconomic status of many Native Americans and better access to dental care may have contributed to these improvements in oral health status as well.

Discussion

This chapter has summarized the oral health status of American Indians during the twentieth century. Although the levels of caries increased during the 1950s and 1960s and then plateaued at high levels during the 1970s and 1980s, this trend seems to have been reversed. Nonetheless, oral disease rates remain much higher than those for the U.S. population as a whole. Eliminating this disparity in an era of both rapid population growth and shrinking federal resources will require a continued emphasis on disease prevention.

Although not widely accepted as standard practice in the United States, the Atraumatic Restorative Treatment (ART) program is undergoing extensive testing under the auspices of the World Health Organization and may provide a means of early intervention that will greatly reduce operating time and the need for costly restorative or rehabilitative services in the future. The ART technique is a procedure based on removing carious tooth structure using only hand instruments and restoring the cavity with adhesive filling materials. It requires no electricity or running water, and its simplicity and minimal resource requirements may make it ideal for many isolated, rural Indian communities. Community trials have concluded that ART can make dental caries control a reality for many communities (Phantumvanit et al. 1996; Frencken et al. 1996). A research agenda for ART has been developed (Holmgren 1996), and participation by Indian communities may yield valuable information that could further promote the oral health of Native Americans.

Studies of the effectiveness of expanded function dental auxiliaries allowed the IHS to greatly increase the quantity of dental care provided to Indian people with no loss of quality (Nixon 1980). A programmatic commitment to use dental sealants allowed the national objective for sealants to be met for Native Americans — a still distant goal for the remainder of the United States (Palmer 1992). Ongoing collaboration with other government agencies and with university-based researchers holds genuine promise for reducing the prevalence of periodontitis, a condition once thought not to be amenable to public health intervention.

Additional research efforts directed toward combating the microorganisms that cause dental caries and increasing tooth resistance are under way. Among these are genetically engineered vaccines, which hold promise of both safety and effectiveness; the blocking of plaque buildup; protective foods; and salivary protective molecules (Mandel 1996). The identification of groups at high risk for periodontal diseases (American Academy of Periodontology 1996a), dental caries, and oral cancer offers avenues to reduce the prevalence of these conditions without the need for enormous increases in clinical staffing.

Increased funding from alternative sources has made it possible for some tribal programs to offer a more comprehensive array of health services than is currently offered by the IHS. The considerable flexibility offered by Public Law 93-638 and its amendments can aid or deter the attainment of improved oral health for all Native Americans (Jorgensen 1996; Kunitz 1996). However, tribal programs operated under Public Law 93-638 tend to be more expensive than those of the IHS, and federal appropriations have not been increased to meet these additional costs (Kunitz 1996). As a result, some tribes are likely to fare poorly in the current, competitive environment for scarce federal resources (Jorgensen 1996). The challenge for both the near and long term will be to balance resource allocations, ensuring the continuation of preventive measures, such as water fluoridation and sealants, for a broad segment of the population while addressing the pent-up demand for restorative and rehabilitative services for adults. Giving greater priority to the latter will delay gains in oral health for years. Essential to the public health perspective is monitoring of disease patterns, selecting scientifically sound interventions, evaluating and adjusting strategies as necessary, and, especially, committing resources for monitoring and training activities. If the basis for community-oriented oral health care built so carefully over the years by the IHS can be maintained, the overall health of Indian people should be materially improved.

REFERENCES

Abramowitz J. 1970. A children's dental program for American Indians. *J Am Dent Assoc* 28:395–405.
———. 1971. Planning for the Indian Health Service. *J Public Health Dent* 31(2):77–78.
American Academy of Periodontology. 1996a. Epidemiology of periodontal diseases. *J Periodontol* 67:935–45.
———. 1996b. Tobacco use and the periodontal patient. *J Periodontol* 67:51–56.
Anderson R, Davidson P, Nakazono T. 1997. Oral health policy and programmatic implications: Lessons from ICS-II. *Adv Dent Res* 11:291–303.
Arnim SS, Aberle SD, Pitney EH. 1937. A study of the dental changes in a group of Pueblo Indian children. *J Am Dent Assoc* 24:478–80.
Berkowitz R. 1996. Etiology of nursing caries: A microbiologic perspective. *J Public Health Dent* 56(1):51–54.
Bratthall D. 1996. Dental caries: Intervened-interrupted-interpreted. Concluding remarks and cariography. *Eur J Oral Sci* 104:486–91.
Bratthall D, Hansell-Petersson G, Sundberg H. 1996. Reasons for the caries decline: What do the experts believe? *Eur J Oral Sci* 104:416–22.
Broderick E, Mabry J, Robertson D, et al. 1989. Baby bottle tooth decay in Native American children in Head Start centers. *Public Health Rep* 104:50–54.
Bruerd B, Jones C. 1996. Preventing baby bottle tooth decay: Eight-year results. *Public Health Rep* 111:63–65.
Bruerd B, Jones C, Krise D. 1997. Preventing baby bottle tooth decay and early childhood caries among AI/AN infants and children. *IHS Prim Care Provider* 22(3):37–39.
Bruerd B, Kinney MB, Bothwell E. 1989. Preventing baby bottle tooth decay in American Indians and Alaska Native communities: A model for planning. *Public Health Rep* 104:631–40.
Cady FC. 1934. Indian dental service. *J Am Dent Assoc* 21:1099–1104.
Carlos JP, Wolfe MD, Zambon JJ, et al. 1988. Periodontal disease in adolescents: Some clinical and microbiological correlates of attachment loss. *J Dent Res* 67:1510–14.
Christen AG. 1980. The case against smokeless tobacco: Five facts for the health professional to consider. *J Am Dent Assoc* 101:464–69.
Cianciola LJ, Park BH, Bruck E, et al. 1982. Prevalence of periodontal disease in insulin-dependent diabetes mellitus (juvenile diabetes). *J Am Dent Assoc* 104:653.

Collins RJ. 1983. General practice residency training and subsequent clinical production. *J Dent Educ* 47:609–14.

Collins RJ, Broderick EB, Herman DJ. 1993. Dental manpower planning in the Indian Health Service. *J Public Health Dent* 53(2):109–14.

Curzon ME, Curzon JA. 1970. Dental caries prevalence in the Baffin Island Eskimo. *Pediatr Dent* 1 (September):169–74.

Drisko CH, Lewis LH. 1996. Ultrasonic instruments and antimicrobial agents in supportive periodontal treatment and retreatment of recurrent or refractory periodontitis. *Periodontology 2000* 12:90–115.

Fasano RJ, Zwemer TJ. 1969. Incidence of dental disease among the Navajo Indians of Monument Valley, Utah. *J Dent Res* 48:328.

Frencken JE, Pilot T, Songpaisan Y, et al. 1996. Atraumatic restorative treatment (ART): Rationale, technique, and development. *J Public Health Dent* 56(3):135–40.

Gift HC, Atchison KA. 1995. Oral health, health, and health-related quality of life. *Med Care* 33(11):NS57–77.

Glover ED, Glover PN. 1992. The smokeless tobacco problem: Risk groups in North America. In: *Smokeless Tobacco or Health: An International Perspective*, 3–10. NIH Publication No. 92-3461. Bethesda, Md.: National Cancer Institute.

Grim CW, Broderick EB, Jasper B, et al. 1994. A comparison of dental caries experience in Native American and Caucasian children in Oklahoma. *J Public Health Dent* 54(4):220–27.

Grossi SG, Skrepcinski FB, DeCaro T, et al. 1996. Response to periodontal therapy in diabetics and smokers. *J Periodontol* 67:1094–1102.

Grossi SG, Zambon JJ, Ho AW, et al. 1994. Assessment of risk for periodontal disease: Risk indicators for attachment loss. *J Periodontol* 65:260–67.

Holmgren CJ. 1996. Preliminary research agenda for minimal intervention techniques for caries. *J Public Health Dent* 56(3):164–65.

Hunt RJ. 1988. Is it time to reassess the public health implications of periodontal diseases? A review of current concepts. *J Public Health Dent* 48(4):241–44.

Indian Health Service. 1970. *Dental Services for American Indians and Alaska Natives, FY 1970*, viii. PHS Pub. No. 1870. Washington, D.C.: Government Printing Office.

———. 1992a. *Dental Services for American Indians and Alaska Natives, 1980–90*. Rockville, Md.: Indian Health Service.

———. 1992b. *Indian Health Service Manual*, pt 3, chap 2. Rockville, Md.: Indian Health Service.

———. 1995. Unpublished data from the Dental Data System, fiscal year 1995. Rockville, Md.: Indian Health Service.

Institute of Medicine. 1984. *Community Oriented Primary Care: A Practical Assessment*. Vol 1. Washington, D.C.: National Academy Press.

Jenny J, Cons NC, Kohout FJ, et al. 1991. Differences in need for orthodontic treatment between Native Americans and the general population based on DAI scores. *J Public Health Dent* 51(4):234–38.

Johnsen DC. 1982. Characteristics and background of children with nursing caries. *Pediatr Dent* 4:218–24.

———. 1984. Dental caries patterns in preschool children. *Dent Clin North Am* 28(1):3–10.

Johnsen DC, Gerstenmaier JH, DiSantis TA, et al. 1986. Susceptibility of nursing caries children to future approximal molar decay. *Pediatr Dent* 8:168–70.

Jones DB, Schlife CM, Phipps KR. 1992. An oral health survey of Head Start children in Alaska: Oral health status, treatment needs, and cost of treatment. *J Public Health Dent* 52(2):86–93.

Jorgensen JG. 1996. Comment: Recent twists and turns in American Indian health care. *Am J Public Health* 86:1362–64.

Kellam GA. 1982. Tooth size and arch perimeter—their relation to crowding of the dentition: A comparison between Navajo Indians and American Caucasians. Ph.D. diss., University of Iowa.

Klein H, Palmer CE. 1937. Dental caries in American Indian children. *Public Health Bulletin* No. 239. Washington, D.C.: Government Printing Office.

Kunitz SJ. 1996. The history and politics of U.S. health care policy for American Indians and Alaskan Natives. *Am J Public Health* 86:1464–73.

Maas W. 1987. Oral health in the community. In: Nutting PA, ed. *Community-Oriented Primary Care: From Principle to Practice,* 201–11. HRSA Publ. No. HRS-A-PE 86-1.

Mandel ID. 1996. Caries prevention: Current strategies, new directions. *J Am Dent Assoc* 127:1477–88.

Marcus M, Reifel N, Nakazono T. 1997. Clinical measures and treatment needs. *Adv Dent Res* 11:263–71.

Marcus SE, Drury TF, Brown LJ, et al. 1996. Tooth retention and tooth loss in the permanent dentition of adults: United States, 1988–1991. *J Dent Res* 75(spec. issue February):684–95.

Milnes AR. 1996. Description and epidemiology of nursing caries. *J Public Health Dent* 56(1):38–50.

Moorrees CFA. 1957. *The Aleut Dentition: A Correlative Study of Dental Characteristics in an Eskimoid People.* Cambridge: Harvard University Press.

National Institutes of Health. 1987. *Oral Health of United States Adults: The National Survey of Oral Health in U.S. Employed Adults and Seniors, 1985–86.* NIH Publ. No. 87-2868. Bethesda, Md.: Department of Health and Human Services.

———. 1989. *Oral Health of United States Children: The National Survey of Dental Caries in U.S. School Children, 1986–87. National and Regional Findings.* PHS:NIH Publ. No. 89-2247. Bethesda, Md.: Department of Health and Human Services.

Niendorff W. 1994. *The Oral Health of Native Americans: A Chart Book of Recent Findings, Trends and Regional Differences.* Dental Field Support and Program Development Section, Headquarters West Dental Program, Indian Health Service.

Niendorff WJ. 1985. Unpublished data from the 1983–84 Indian Health Service Oral Health Status Survey. *IHS Dent Newsletter* 24:47–51.

Nixon J. 1980. The Indian Health Service study of the expanded-duty dental auxiliary II. *J Public Health Dent* 40(2):99–117.

Nutting PA, Freeman WL, Risser DR, et al. 1993. Cancer incidence among American Indians and Alaska Natives, 1980 through 1987. *Am J Public Health* 83:1589–98.

O'Sullivan DM, Douglass JM, Champany R, et al. 1994. Dental caries prevalence and treatment among Navajo preschool children. *J Public Health Dent* 54(3):139–44.

O'Sullivan DM, Tinanoff N. 1996. The association of early dental caries patterns with caries incidence in preschool children. *J Public Health Dent* 56(2):81–83.

Palmer C. 1992. Sealant use for Indians nears 75%. *ADA News,* March 23.

Phantumvanit P, Songpaisan Y, Pilot T, et al. 1996. Atraumatic restorative treatment (ART): A three-year community field trial in Thailand. Survival of one-surface restorations in the permanent dentition. *J Public Health Dent* 56(3):141–45.

Phipps KR, Reifel N, Bothwell E. 1991. The oral health status, treatment needs, and dental utilization patterns of Native American elders. *J Public Health Dent* 51(4):228–33.

Reifel N, Davidson P, Rana H, et al. 1997. ICS-II USA locations: Environmental, dental care delivery system, and population sociodemographic characteristics. *Adv Dent Res* 11:210–16.

Ripa LW. 1993. A half century of community water fluoridation in the United States: Review and commentary. *J Public Health Dent* 53:17–44.

Shlossman M, Knowler WC, Pettitt DJ, et al. 1990. Type 2 diabetes mellitus and periodontal disease. *J Am Dent Assoc* 121:532–36.

Turner C. 1996. Telltale teeth. *Nat History* 96:6–10.

U.S. Department of Health and Human Services. 1980. *Promoting Health/Preventing Disease: Objectives for the Nation. Fluoridation and Dental Health.* Washington, D.C.: Government Printing Office.

U.S. Department of Health and Human Services, National Institute of Dental Research. 1990. *Broadening the Scope: Long Range Research Plan for the Nineties.* NIH Publ. No. 90-1188. Bethesda, Md.: DHHS.

Wolfe MD, Carlos JP. 1987. Oral health effects of smokeless tobacco use in Navajo Indian adolescents. *Community Dent Oral Epidemiol* 15:230–35.

World Health Organization. 1987. *Oral Health Surveys: Basic Methods.* 3d ed. Geneva: World Health Organization.

22

Gary J. Hartz, M.S., P.E.,
John G. Todd, M.S., M.P.H., Dr.P.H., RS,
and Everett R. Rhoades, M.D.

Environmental Health and Construction Programs

The development of environmental programs for Indian people generally followed their gradual introduction into the general population during the nineteenth century. Although the need for environmental health programs for Indians was noted in the early 1800s, little was done until later in the century. An 1889 notice to those applying for appointment as Bureau of Indian Affairs (BIA) physicians stated: "The Agency physician is required not only to attend Indians who may call upon him at his office, but also to visit the Indians at their homes and, in addition to prescribing and administering needed medications, to do his utmost to educate and instruct them in proper methods of living and caring for health. He should exercise special care in regard for sanitary conditions of the agency and the schools and promptly report to the agent, any condition, either of buildings or grounds, liable to cause sickness, in order that proper steps may be taken to remedy the evil" (Indian Health Service 1985).

However, before the late 1920s, sanitation efforts did not extend beyond occasional "clean-up" campaigns and physicians' inspections of homes, schools, and agency compounds. A 1912 report to Congress called attention to the need for improved sanitary conditions in schools and homes (U.S. Congress, Senate 1913). The comprehensive report of conditions in "Indian country" by the Institute for Government Research (1928), calling attention to inadequate and crowded dwellings with insufficient light and ventilation, received wide public attention. It noted that, with only a few exceptions, potable water supplies and adequate waste facilities were nonexistent. In 1927, the BIA, with the assistance of the Public Health Service Sanitary Engineering Corps, surveyed water and sewer systems, following which several water systems were constructed for New Mexico Pueblo tribes and California rancherias (U.S. Public Health Service 1957).

Another survey in the 1930s noted that the Indians' adverse economic situation forced them to live at a bare existence level amid environmental conditions highly conducive to certain diseases (Mountain and Townsend 1936). While describing the deplorable conditions in Indian communities, the surveyors, however, also noted that BIA health programs included preventive health services and that these often exceeded those available to much of the general population. They also noted that "the entire service should be thought of as preventive in character and the Indian must be made an active participant." The common theme throughout the various surveys and field experience was lack of safe and sufficient water supplies and unsanitary waste disposal facilities.

The Evolution of the Environmental Health Program

At the time of the 1954 Transfer Act (P.L. 83-568), only 13 sanitation engineers and sanitarians and 31 sanitarian aides were employed by the program (Indian Health Service 1985). In the first year after the transfer, the number of sanitary engineers and sanitarians increased to 23 and sanitarian aides to 53. Immediately following the transfer in 1955, the surgeon general initiated legislative proposals designed to improve the environmental program. This eventually led to one of the important milestones in Indian health, passage of Public Law 86-121, the Indian Sanitation Facilities Construction Act (USC 42, para. 2004a). Enactment of Public Law 86-121 provided the basis for the development of comprehensive improvements to Indian environmental health. This endeavor provided safe water supplies, adequate means of waste disposal, and a diversified array of environmental services. Of equal importance, the multifaceted environmental health program became an integral part of the total Indian Health Service (IHS) health delivery system.

   With the authorities of the Transfer Act of 1954 and the 86-121 legislation of 1959, additional Indian sanitation aides were trained and employed. Surveys of sanitation facilities and individual Indian homes were conducted to identify environmental deficiencies that most urgently needed correction. The sanitarian aides became educators, teaching Indian families how to construct and repair outdoor privies; how to construct and protect individual water supplies; how to safely store water in the home; how to store, prepare, and serve food; and how to spray surfaces safely to control or kill insects. Selected aides were trained to handle other special environmental health activities, including refuse collection and disposal; insect control; spraying techniques and demonstrations; and public gatherings such as Indian fairs, festivals, and rodeos. Public events received advance planning and preparation from the environmental health staff regarding the provision of safe drinking water, sanitary food handling and preparation, adequate waste disposal, and insect control.

A major and pioneering innovation, later extended throughout other IHS programs, was the idea of cooperative problem solving with Indian participation, not only with the individual Indian family but also with tribal governing bodies. The Environmental Health Program and the tribes became true partners, and the professional expertise of IHS staff was made available to tribal authorities to assist in planning, decision making, and implementation of efforts to address environmental health needs. Such an effort laid the groundwork for additional cooperation and collaboration with state and local agencies.

The many innovations that followed the 1955 transfer received even greater impetus with passage of the 1976 Indian Health Care Improvement Act (P.L. 94-437), which provided the basis for the present comprehensive and highly successful program. In the years after enactment of Public Law 94-437, the environmental health and construction program developed a specific set of objectives: (1) to provide optimum availability of functional, well-maintained health-care facilities and adequate staff housing at health-care delivery locations and (2) to reduce the incidence of environmentally related illness and injury by (a) determining and addressing factors contributing to injuries, (b) advocating for improvement of environmental conditions, and (c) constructing sanitation facilities and ensuring the availability of a safe water supply and adequate waste disposal facilities in homes and communities.

The Construction of Sanitation Facilities

The construction of sanitary facilities, responsible for the provision of safe water and an adequate means of waste disposal, is in many respects the core of the environmental health program. Although tremendous improvements have been made, many Indian communities have not achieved the high levels of basic infrastructure and sanitation enjoyed by the general population. The proportion of Indian homes provided with safe water and adequate waste disposal systems has increased from 20 to 90 percent since 1960. However, availability of such facilities among all U.S. populations is approximately 98 percent.

Deficiencies in sanitation facilities are estimated and reported to the Congress each year. At the end of fiscal year 1999, the estimated cost necessary to correct priority sanitation deficiencies was $770,000,000. This estimate was limited to those projects considered feasible from an economic and engineering standpoint. In many remote Alaskan villages, especially above the Arctic Circle, given the small numbers of inhabitants and permafrost conditions, infrastructure development is often prohibitively costly. As of October 1, 1999, the estimated cost of correcting all sanitation deficiencies throughout Indian

Figure 22.1. An integral, and often challenging, part of the IHS clinical program is the installation of sewage disposal lines, such as this project on the Hopi reservation. *Source:* Environmental Health Program of the IHS.

country totaled approximately $1.7 billion. In addition, operation and maintenance costs for such facilities often greatly exceed the available funds of local residents.

The sanitation facilities legislation requires that Indian communities operate and maintain the facilities, which they generally do through user fees collected from residents. However, in some Indian communities, as throughout rural America, payment of fees is insufficient to maintain the program, and supplemental revenue is not available. The operation of systems under these conditions is not likely to be optimal. Technical assistance and guidance to families and communities regarding the operation and maintenance of water supply and waste disposal facilities are provided by environmental health personnel, who often assist in the creation and operation of maintenance organizations and the establishment of appropriate sanitation ordinances and user fee schedules.

Since the implementation of Public Law 86-121, the IHS has constructed community and individual water supply and waste disposal systems serving more than 230,400 Indian homes (Figure 22.1). The $89,328,000 for sanitation facilities construction appropriated in fiscal year 1999 provided first-service to an estimated 4,600 Indian homes and upgrading of existing service to

Figure 22.2. This illustration is so representative of the mission of the IHS that it was selected by the director to represent the IHS in a mural depicting the history of the Public Health Service.

7,230 more. Many tribes, along with other federal and state entities, contribute funds to address the backlog of sanitation deficiencies. Recent contributions have ranged from $20 million to more than $40 million annually. As a result of the cooperative nature of this program, 60–70 percent of the sanitation facilities construction work is performed by Indian tribes and firms. An example of a successful tribal enterprise is the Navajo Engineering and Construction Authority, which constructs virtually all sanitation facilities on the Navajo reservation and employs approximately 350 Navajos. Such programs as the construction of sewage disposal facilities should be thought of as the delivery of health services.

The sanitation facilities construction program exemplifies the numerous tangible and intangible benefits of IHS and the tribes working together throughout all aspects of a project. Tribal involvement has been the cornerstone of sanitation facilities activity since its inception. Projects are initiated only after receipt of a tribal request expressing willingness to participate in carrying out the project and willingness to execute a tribal agreement to assume ownership, including operation and maintenance responsibilities, for completed facilities.

It is widely acknowledged that the provision of safe water and sanitation has resulted in greater improvements in the health of Indians than any other activity.

The provision of safe and potable water, sometimes through only a community hydrant, is a profound achievement for many Indian and Alaska Native communities. The significance of this program is so great that a depiction of a water pump in a remote location was chosen to represent the IHS in a montage of the history of the Public Health Service (Figure 22.2). That this emblem was chosen to represent its health program is a commentary on the philosophy of the IHS. Such integration of environmental programs into a health-care system is perhaps unprecedented.

The Construction of Health-Care Facilities

The IHS, the largest direct health-care program within the Department of Health and Human Services, operates and maintains more than 10 million square feet of space in hospitals, clinics, staff quarters, and other facilities in 2,820 buildings and structures. In addition, the IHS operates health-care delivery and administrative program elements in an additional 625,000 square feet of leased space and 900,000 square feet of space assigned from other entities. Continued maintenance and improvements of these structures and other occupied space is thus a major activity.

The objectives of the Health Care Facilities Construction (HCFC) Program are enhancement of health-care delivery by providing for functional, well-maintained facilities and adequate staff housing. The capital improvement program, funded through HCFC budget activity, constructs health-care facilities and staff quarters, renovates and constructs regional substance abuse treatment centers, and replaces modular dental units. To determine the locations where new and replacement facilities are most critically needed, the IHS uses a comprehensive priority system methodology, the Health Facilities Construction Priority System. This system objectively ranks proposals using factors reflecting the total amount of space needed; age and condition of the existing facility, if any; degree of isolation of the proposed facility; and availability of alternate health-care resources, as shown in IHS Area Facilities Master Plans. The application of the HCFC program to tribes operating their own programs has grown somewhat more complicated, and several tribes have provided for their own construction without waiting to emerge at the top of the priority list through the IHS system.

In 1993, the Congress extended the scope of use of Medicare/Medicaid collections to fund limited construction of temporary or permanent space needs to correct accreditation deficiencies, without advance approval by congressional appropriations committees. This provision expanded the IHS ability to upgrade urgently needed space and facilities that would be unlikely to achieve a place on the priority system for the limited construction appropriations available. Because the IHS health-care facilities are very old by industry standards (32 years vs. 9 years for the U.S. average), the need for renovation or replacement is rapidly escalating. Currently, many efforts are under way to identify alternative methods of financing necessary construction.

The Maintenance and Improvement of Facilities

The IHS has a formal program for establishing maintenance and improvement of the buildings and occupied space for which it is responsible. The condition of all IHS and tribal facilities and grounds is evaluated through annual surveys conducted by local facility personnel and engineers. In addition, "Deep Look" surveys are conducted every five years by a team of engineers drawn from various backgrounds. These surveys, together with routine observations by facilities personnel, identify tasks to be added to the list of needed improvements in buildings and equipment. The current identified backlog of essential maintenance and repair in IHS and tribal facilities exceeds $446,000,000.

Maintenance and improvement (M&I) program objectives include (1) routine maintenance of IHS and tribally owned and operated buildings and space; (2) compliance with appropriate accreditation standards; (3) provision of improved facilities for inpatient and outpatient care; (4) compliance with existing building codes and standards; and (5) compliance with requirements of various laws, such as utilization of alternate energy sources, energy conservation, accessibility for those who are disabled, and seismic safety. The principal tool used for identifying and planning M&I activities is the IHS Facilities Engineering Program Plan. This document is prepared by IHS Area and Service Unit personnel to delineate facilities-related activities and projects to be accomplished during each fiscal year. The Facilities Engineering Program Plan establishes annual M&I workload targets and provides guidance for determination of the most prudent use of available resources.

Many IHS facilities predate current environmental laws and regulations; consequently, there is continuing concern that some IHS and tribal buildings may contain environmental hazards. An examination of the extent of such problems is now being completed. Compliance with federal, state, and local environmental regulations has been mandated by the Congress. The IHS, through an environmental audit program, develops plans and projects to address facility compliance with these regulations and to correct environmental deficiencies, as well as audit and monitor all facilities for environmental hazards.

Environmental Health Services

In addition to the extensive programs having to do with construction and maintenance of a variety of buildings and facilities, an extensive program of environmental services is also incorporated into the IHS program. Comprehensive environmental health inspections, surveys, and consultations became an early major focus of the expanded environmental health programs. The early evolution of this institutional environmental health component involved the development of protocols for periodic inspection and training of food service personnel at hospitals, schools, jails, and other institutions located throughout the reservations. Food service inspection activities have contributed greatly toward the prevention of food-borne diseases throughout the country. During these early food service inspections, environmental health staff noted instances of unsafe equipment and situations that could be sources of contagious diseases, injury, and other problems for patients, staff, and visitors. These early inspections and food service surveys developed into comprehensive environmental health institutional surveys with an ongoing need for trained specialists. This led to the establishment of an institutional environmental health residency program. The training of these specialists is now conducted in cooperation with the Uniformed Services University of the Health Sciences in Bethesda, Maryland. Thus, the IHS and tribal environmental team, through its comprehensive approach to environmental health, plays a major role in minimizing hazards and the inherent risks associated with operations of various types on the reservations.

Area- and district-based experts visit health facilities and Indian communities to make institutional (hospital, school, restaurant, water supply) inspections, complete sanitation facilities construction survey work, train water/wastewater treatment plant operators and hospital maintenance personnel, survey real property and staff quarters, perform epidemiologic studies of injury occurrences, provide on-site construction inspection services, and identify and correct mechanical and electrical problems in facilities. A majority of these personnel are located in the 140 Service Units, where federal and tribal staffing levels vary with workload and the season. This work force includes engineers, sanitarians, facilities managers, environmental health technicians, biomedical technicians, boiler plant operators, maintenance mechanics, real property and safety specialists, and security personnel.

Generally, Service Unit personnel are "hands-on" operators and service providers. For example, a biomedical technician calibrates, maintains, and repairs medical equipment (defibrillator, sterilizers, etc.), as well as pumps and other types of mechanical and electrical equipment that support the operation of medical equipment in a hospital or health center. Mechanics operate and maintain the heating, ventilation, and air conditioning systems; the lighting systems; and the water, sewer, gas, oil, and electrical utility systems. IHS engineers and sanitarians provide environmental health services to Indian homes, communities, and tribes and to IHS and tribal hospitals and health centers. They also participate directly in planning, design, construction, and operator training for water/waste disposal systems. Often, non-IHS programs that also require environmental services are developed. One example is the establishment of Head Start programs on many reservations. IHS assists in the development of standards, provides inspections, and assists in assuring conformance with accepted standards.

Environmental Compliance

In building and operating facilities, one must comply with an extraordinary number of federal, tribal, state, and local laws, acts, and regulations. These include the Historic Preservation Act, Historic Properties Act, Coastal Zone Management Act, Floodplain Management Act, Endangered Species Act, Fish and Wildlife Act, Wild Rivers and Scenic Rivers Act, Federal Water Pollution Control Act, Clean Water Act, Clean Air Act, Marine Sanctuary Act, and others, all of which must be considered and which profoundly influence the operation of the IHS and tribal environmental health programs.

Public Law 103-399, the Indian Lands Open Dump Cleanup Act of 1994, identified congressional concerns that solid waste open dump sites located on Indian lands often threaten the health and safety of residents of those lands and contiguous areas. The act assigns responsibility to the director of the IHS for implementation of actions related to these open dump sites. However, as is often the case, the resources made available to carry out the provisions of the act are limited. The IHS completed an initial inventory of known solid waste sites, including observations about each site and estimates concerning potential health threats of each site. At the end of fiscal year 1999, the IHS had identified a need for approximately $126 million to provide solid waste collection, disposal facilities, and equipment for an estimated 120,000 Indian homes.

Certain Zoonoses

The danger of rabies, human injury from animal bites, and the economic effects when livestock are killed require attention to animal control throughout many reservations. Early efforts to address the most serious of these hazards involved the organization of rabies immunization clinics where dog bite reports indicated a high level of potential danger. Environmental health staff enlisted the assistance of federal and local veterinarians along with tribal governments to conduct routine and periodic immunization clinics. These efforts to assist tribes have been effective in the establishment and implementation of rabies control programs.

In the United States, most cases of plague occur in the Southwest, coincident with many reservations and Indian communities. The presence of enzootic plague requires constant surveillance and an education program to prevent spread to humans. Such surveillance is among the many activities carried out by members of the environmental health team. The IHS and tribal staff coordinate their activities with personnel from the Public Health Service, Centers for Disease Control and Prevention, and state health agencies.

Community Public Health

A constant requirement is attention to a variety of environmental hazards. Recent concerns have included abandoned uranium mines, with their accompanying tailings; the use of radioactive tailings in construction, as in road bed repairs; and natural radiation in water supplies. Remediation has included the placement of an earth cover to stabilize the tailings pile of a closed uranium mill site in Arizona. A major function is the fluoridation of water supplies. The first system to receive a fluoridation unit in a Public Law 86-121 sanitation facilities project was the Alaska Native community of Metlakatla, Alaska (Indian Health Service 1985). By the end of 1966, the number of such systems had grown to 24; currently, there are nearly five hundred operating systems that provide for fluoridation.

Discussion

The IHS Environmental Health Program is an integral component of the IHS comprehensive health-care and services delivery system. It complements other curative, preventive, and rehabilitative efforts on behalf of the Indians and Alaska Natives living on reservations or in small communities and villages throughout the United States. A wide range of environmental health services are provided, including those that might be traditionally categorized within public works, urban and regional planning, natural resources conservation, and public safety. The IHS Environmental Health Program is unlike state and county programs; it is not an enforcement arm for tribal organizations but rather an advisory service designed to assist Indians and Alaska Natives in the resolution of environmental/public health problems.

Together, the IHS and the tribal environmental health programs have achieved some impressive results: (1) The age-adjusted gastrointestinal disease death rate for American Indians and Alaska Natives has declined steadily in concert with the provision of sanitation facilities. This rate, which was 2.7 times the rate for the general U.S. population (U.S. All Races) in 1973, was reduced to 1.2 times the U.S. All Races rate by 1980 and has remained at that level since. (2) Life expectancy has increased significantly, largely because a decrease in infant mortality rates has been achieved; the latter was significantly influenced by improved environmental conditions. The real challenge is in the future — in how well IHS can assist Native Americans as they become more involved in controlling and managing their environment as the products and technology of contemporary life are increasingly becoming more available within their environs.

REFERENCES

Indian Health Service. 1985. *The American Indian and Alaska Native: Their Environmental Health and the Environmental Health Program — A Historical Perspective, 1955–1985.* Rockville, Md.: Indian Health Service.
Institute for Government Research. 1928. *The Problem of Indian Administration* [Meriam report]. Baltimore: Johns Hopkins Press.
Mountain JW, Townsend JG. 1936. *Observations on Indian Health Problems and Facilities.* Public Health Service Bulletin No. 223. Washington, D.C.: Government Printing Office.
U.S. Congress, Senate. 1913. *Contagious and Infectious Diseases among the Indian,* U.S. Public Health Service. Senate Document No. 1038. 62nd Cong, 3d sess. Washington, D.C.: Government Printing Office.
U.S. Public Health Service. 1957. *Health Services for American Indians.* Public Health Service Publication No. 531. Washington, D.C.: Government Printing Office.

Part IV

Special Cultural and Ethical Considerations

23

Everett R. Rhoades, M.D., and
Dorothy A. Rhoades, M.D., M.P.H.

Traditional Indian and
Modern Western Medicine

The historical prominence of "traditional medicine" in Indian life; the role that spiritism, spiritualism, and magic play in much Indian nosology; differences between traditional and "scientific" or "Western" medicine; and the use of Indian medicine to illuminate Indian culture all combine to create a subject of intense interest. This interest has accelerated with the increasing popularity of New Age, holistic, and alternative medicine. Despite much study, questions continue to be asked about traditional medicine: What is it? Is traditional medicine destined to disappear by attrition along with so many other cultural aspects of Indians? Can traditional medicine and modern medicine complement each other?

The literature on Indian healing is extensive and includes descriptions of many common practices (Grinnell 1874; Toner 1877; Hrdlicka 1932; Brooks 1933; Corlett 1935; Hultkrantz 1989), tribally specific practices (Haile 1938; Leighton and Leighton 1941; Kluckhohn and Leighton 1962; Adair 1963; Hallowell 1963; Kluckhohn 1967; Bourke 1971; Mooney 1982; Kunitz and Levy 1997), and commonly used herbs and botanicals (Brooks 1933; Vogel 1970; Densmore 1974). Vogel (1970) provided the standard single reference relating to Indian medicine. In this chapter we outline some overall aspects of Indian medicine but focus on the role of Indian medicine in a rapidly changing world, the advent of "alternative" medicine, and questions about blending traditional and Western systems.

As has been remarked elsewhere in this text, the language currently available to define and describe much of Indian phenomena is not satisfactory. This is true of Indian healing as well. Terms such as *traditional, shaman, medicine person, Western,* and even *medicine* itself are imprecise and may often be applied to describe both Indian and "scientific" systems. *Western medicine* generally refers to the application of scientific principles initially promulgated by Euro-American cultures, centered on *disease* as a concept. The term *traditional medicine* is generally used to describe the healing practices and beliefs of the Indian population. Although much of Indian medicine is based on empiric observation, the application of the principles of scientific inquiry utilizing blinded and carefully controlled observations is absent from traditional healing. In daily discourse, Indian people often refer to Indian healers simply as *Indian doctors*, applying a term that is actually less descriptive than *medicine man*. The term *biomedicine*, recommended by Kleinman (1993) to replace the term *Western medicine*, seems to be an improvement. As he pointed out, biomedicine stands alone "by its insistence on materialism as the grounds of knowledge, and by its discomfort with dialectical modes of thought. . . . And particularly because of its peculiarly powerful commitment to an idea of Nature that excludes the teleological" (17).

Some Characteristics of Traditional Indian Medicine

The understanding of traditional Indian medicine by many scientists, lay persons, and the rapidly increasing number of New Age healers remains meager, fragmented, and often distorted. True traditional medicine is a profound system that is far more deeply rooted and complex than is commonly understood (Hrdlicka 1932; Brooks 1933; Task Force on Indian Health 1976; Adair, Deuschle, and Barnett 1988). Both Western and traditional medicine are vast systems of health maintenance and treatment that operate at several levels: personal care of most common maladies not requiring special expertise, "folk" healing by "lay" individuals with special skills, and an elaborate system of practitioners who dedicate a substantial portion of their lives to the "healing arts" (Kleinman, Eisenberg, and Good 1978).

Pre-eminent among characteristics of Indian medicine is the degree to which it includes religion and a realm of spirits capable of doing either good or harm, characterized as a complex "theologicophysical" dualism (Stone 1932). The term *shaman*, originating in a specific Siberian region, has come to be applied to traditional (or indigenous) healers who possess special power to communicate with the spirits, heal the sick, and foretell future events (Eliade 1972; Hultkrantz 1979; La Barre 1980). Such power is often transcendentally obtained through a trancelike state, which is facilitated by fasting, meditation, and a certain degree of sensory deprivation, often through the popularly noted vision quest or by mind-altering drugs. At other times, power may be obtained through a simple dream. This power is generally not a personal attribute of the individual but a higher power invoked by the practitioner, more often described than defined (Basso 1967).

The term *shaman,* properly reserved for its specific identification of the special Siberian mystics, has taken on an almost generic meaning. Shamanistic medicine generally recognizes four major causes of disease: soul loss, spirit possession, breach of taboo, or witchcraft (Kunitz and Levy 1997). These conditions were, and in many instances still are, treated by religious practitioners who controlled supernatural power (e.g., shamans). In contrast to these four causes, symptoms (e.g., pain, loss of function) are treated by more naturalistic methods, including herbs, physiatry, heat, cupping, and so forth.

In the reception of supernatural power, the shaman's soul is understood to leave the body and proceed to the spirit world, where it comes into contact with its future "spirit helper." The trance is the sign that the individual has the "gift" of healing and could become a shaman after an appropriate period of training (Levy, pers. comm., 1998). Boyer and colleagues (1964) proposed the following definition of shaman: "A native medicine man who is considered to possess supernatural powers which support and are supported by the common values of his culture" and who is capable of living "both in the worlds of spirits and men" (173). Levy distinguished between shamans, who control supernatural power, and priests, who may act as intermediaries between humans and the supernatural. Priests usually receive their powers through inheritance or appointment, using various rituals as part of their armamentarium (Levy, pers. comm., 1998). Levy added that both forms of healing rely on the principles of sympathetic magic as described by Frazer (1956, 12–14). He also pointed out that shamanistic and priestly healing are based on a formal and logical system of nosology and treatment and on the use of modalities according to immutable laws of cause and effect. An apparently invariable accompaniment of shamanic healing is an altered state of consciousness. Ackerknecht (1943) pointed out that descriptions of Siberian shamanism suggested that the individuals involved were suffering from, or recovered from, what now would often be termed a psychosis. Regardless of the source of power, the traditional healer usually benefits from years of study, an apprenticeship, and strictures guiding personal conduct.

It is widely recognized that shamanic power can be used for good or evil and that, if used for the latter, serious consequences invariably redound to the practitioner, either personally or to a loved one. Landes (1963), in an account of the Potawatomi of Kansas, described features of a tribe undergoing profound changes, including the loss of many folkways without obvious unifying replacements. She described shamanism and sorcery that was far more perniciously practiced than has been generally recorded. It is fair to say that in most, if not in all, Indian communities, utilization of ancient and powerful shamanic power is continuing to give way to practices that many might consider superficial or even improper.

Differences between Indian and Western Medicine

The critical, and often profound, differences between Indian and Western medicine obviously derive from the underlying cultural precepts of each. A generally accepted Indian concept of *health* is that it is a tangible reality, not simply the state of being free of disease. This health, or wellness, is often described as the ability to exist in a harmonious relationship with all other living things, but also with a number of spirits, including a great and all-powerful spirit. The emphasis on the spirit world, supernatural forces, and religion stand in sharp contrast to the secular emphasis on disturbed physiology and purely physical explanations of Western medicine.

One interesting (and neglected) example of the difference between the two systems is the degree to which music is used. Densmore (1954) explained that, in traditional healing, music has two components. The words of a song themselves convey significant meaning, asserting the powers of the healer and invoking the powers of a higher spirit or a totemic animal. This obviously supports the patient, increases confidence in the ability of the medicine person to succeed, and helps create a positive atmosphere of expected cure. However, equally important is the rhythm of the healing songs, usually produced by a rattle or small drum. This rhythm is thought to contribute to establishing the proper mental state in both the healer and the ill person.

As Ackerknecht (1972) noted, "primitive" medicine is *not* an embryonic modern medicine, or forerunner of more "advanced" modern medicine, but is an entirely different entity. Clearly, a certain degree of Indian medicine depends upon phenomena that can best be described as mystical, even magical. Further, traditional medicine has a greater societal, rather than biological, basis, and plays a greater role in the maintenance of community integrity than does Western medicine. Ackerknecht further noted that "primitive" healers made no distinction between natural and supernatural and that perceptions of real and nonreal, natural and supernatural, are simply ways of dealing with the world that are mediated by the culture under consideration. Further, Fejos (1963) emphasized that the anthropologic use of the term *magic* "does not denote trickery, prestidigitation or pulling a white rabbit out of a hat" (13), but rather "means all the formulas for doing things which are beyond one's personal powers" (14). Further, magic exists throughout the world, including industrialized societies, and is certainly not limited to "primitive" peoples.

A prominent, if not dominant, theme in much Western literature is that the traditional healer is practicing some form of shrewd "folk" psychiatry. However, relegation of Indian healing simply to the area of mental health is a much too narrow view. In one sense, Indian medicine may perhaps be thought of as metapsychiatric.

An essential characteristic of the shamanistic aspects of "true" Indian healing seems to be its ineffable nature. Perhaps it can never be satisfactorily defined; perhaps all one can do is to experience it or describe its elements. Further, it is entirely possible that the acts of describing, analyzing, testing, or perhaps even discussing traditional medicine under the wrong circumstances may injure or debase it. As a young Apache woman remarked, because of its special "sacred" nature, traditional medicine should not be casually discussed, nor should attempts to include traditional medicine in "non-Indian" training programs be made (Task Force on Indian Health 1976).

In contrast, scientific medicine is very heavily based upon skeptical reasoning, careful and reproducible observations, and the formulation of hypotheses designed to explain observable phenomena. Science rests largely upon probability theory and the comparison of one set of phenomena against another in a way to eliminate incorrect explanations. Testing the "fit" of one set of observations against another permits inferences about the likelihood that a given event is causally related to something else or whether the observed phenomenon may have simply occurred randomly. Science, resting as it so heavily does on probability theory, cannot make firm statements about isolated events or even events that are few in number. Despite its extraordinary efficiency in elucidating mechanisms and quantifying nature, science may not be capable of elucidating ultimate causality. Although controversial, an important element of scientific methodology is that a given hypothesis can be proved wrong (Popper 1959). Truth extends only to the hypothesis that best explains observable phenomena. Hypotheses, by their very nature, are tentative and thus contrast sharply with the certainty with which Indian medicine is practiced. In addition, the concept of randomness seems to be largely absent from traditional Indian thought, and it remains to be seen whether Indian medicine can be "tested" scientifically.

Narrow adherence to scientific principles not infrequently results in individuals who deny the reality of any phenomenon that cannot be measured in some way. This conviction is perhaps as important as any in the elimination of spiritual content from American life and Western medicine. The predominance of this attitude has undoubtedly deprived "allopathic" medicine of an essential component of healing and has led to a great deal of dissatisfaction with and distrust of the medical profession by much of the general U.S. and, especially, Indian populations. As pointed out by Kleinman (1993), "This radically reductionistic and positivistic value orientation (e.g., biomedicine) is ultimately dehumanizing" (18). Further, it is characteristic of both the narrowness and the shallowness of many scientists. The eminent essayist Lewis Thomas once remarked that the shaman simply exorcized hostile spirits, as part of the many passing fads that have been experienced by humans (Thomas 1978). Such attitudes not only are remarkably narrow, but also exhibit the arrogance typical of

European American scientific medicine that is so abhorrent to Indian people generally.

Kleinman, Eisenberg, and Good (1978) pointed out that biomedical research is often irrelevant to solutions for common problems experienced by individuals. Further, modern physicians diagnose and treat *diseases* (abnormalities in the structure and function of body organs and systems), whereas patients suffer *illnesses* (the human experience of sickness, including disvalued changes in states of being and social functions). If scientific medicine were to investigate illness as well as disease and direct clinical care more toward both (Kleinman, Eisenberg, and Good 1978), it would probably greatly narrow the distance between it and traditional Indian medicine. An important limitation of modern medicine is its deficiency in teaching about *caring* (Eisenberg 1977). Those who are interested in understanding the tremendous growth in interest in "alternative medicine" would be well advised to study Eisenberg's discussion.

Gould (1957) emphasized the important role played by folk healers in most communities. He suggested that a division of labor exists in which folk therapists care for chronic, incapacitating conditions and scientific medicine deals with acute and critical incapacitating dysfunction, thus implying that traditional Indian medicine serves as the Native folk medicine and that more severe and threatening illnesses are cared for by the "scientific" practitioner. Although this may have some validity in comparing Indian with Western medicine, it is equally applicable to a differentiation of labor within Indian communities in which a family member (often the grandmother) treats common maladies as a folk healer and specialists (e.g., medicine men and women) treat the more disabling conditions. Gould went on to suggest that the limitations of scientific medicine result in a permanent situation characterized by chronic, nonincapacitating dysfunctions in which "primitive" healing systems may thrive. The events of recent decades, with the tremendous interest in alternative or complementary systems, would seem to verify Gould's suggestion. The prevalence of such "pseudoscientific" medical practices suggests that folk remedies, or their equivalent, will never disappear.

Certain Similarities between Traditional and Scientific Medicine

Although there may be irreconcilable differences, certain similarities between the two systems of traditional and scientific medicine are of some interest.

Cultures seem to share certain characteristics that include: Categories by which illness is diagnosed; narrative structures that synthesize complaints into culturally meaningful syndromes; master metaphors, idioms, and other core symbolic forms that conduce to the construction of aetiological interpretations of pathology so as to legitimate practical therapeutic actions; healing roles and careers; rhetorical strategies that healers deploy to move patients and families to engage in therapeutic activities; and an immense variety and number of therapies, combining almost seamlessly, symbolic and practical operations whose intention is to control symptoms or their putative sources (Kleinman 1993).

This succinct description well describes the bases common to both forms of healing. Further, both depend upon extensive and serious training, and generally, both callings are regarded as important by their respective publics. Each offers support or cure to those who are seeking relief and who are prepared to put substantial faith in the ability of the healer to provide benefit (Fejos 1959). In each instance, a diagnosis is essential to a successful outcome. Each has specific paraphernalia. After diagnosis, a course of treatment is undertaken, sometimes by a generalist, sometimes by a specialist. Just as society tends to hold both in high regard, society tends to penalize those healers who violate the strictures of their office.

Notwithstanding the importance of shamanistic and spiritual aspects of Indian healing, empiricism, as in mainstream medicine, is also an important component of care. Historical accounts of Indian medicine reveal many specific interventions that could only have arisen from an empirical process. Personal hygiene practices, for example, were extensive and included the use of soap from the root of the yucca plant, hairbrushes of grass stems, and evergreen resins as dentifrices (Rhoades 1996). Sutures obtained from the fiber of tamarack or the inner bark of basswood have been described, as have been syringes made of a bladder to which a quill or other tube was attached (Toner 1877). Such instruments require specific skills and training as well as ingenuity in their creation.

Formal Support for Traditional Medicine

The issue of the routine use of medicine people as employees of the Indian Health Service (IHS) or as consultants paid for by third parties is a difficult one. In the case of the IHS, some practical considerations have not been resolved. The IHS remains an official governmental agency subject to the bureaucratic necessities therein. Given the special and even sacred nature of traditional medicine and the ease with which it may be disturbed or debased, the IHS may not be the most appropriate system for its operation. An essential part of Indian healing, payment for the services by the patient, could inevitably be disrupted by a third party making the payment.

As noted in Chapters 5 and 18, the IHS has long fostered close relationships with traditional healers and has in the past employed a traditional healer to as-

Figure 23.1. Mr. A. Paul Ortega, a prominent Mescalero traditional healer and musician, for many years educated Indian Health Service and other personnel about the sensitivities of traditional medicine. *Source:* A. Paul Ortega

sist with decisions and to educate IHS practitioners about means of supporting the services of Indian healers. Mr. A. Paul Ortega, traditional healer, musician, and former president of the Mescalero Tribe, for years provided this service. Ortega exemplifies the successful compartmentalization required of traditionalists living in present-day America. His 1960s recording, "Two Worlds" (duplicated and distributed by Canyon Records, 4143 N. 16th St., Phoenix, Ariz.), may well be considered the cardinal event in the modern evolution of Indian music (Figure 23.1). In 1979, a policy circular established a formal basis for cooperation with and support of traditional medicine. When requested by the local community, special construction, such as the healing room in the Chinle hospital, is built specifically for traditional healing. At the recently constructed hospital at Shiprock, New Mexico, the Navajo tribe preferred that a separate building be constructed on site.

Because of the obvious difficulties in payment from a governmental source, to say nothing of difficult credentialing questions, the IHS has avoided direct hiring or financial support of traditional healers, leaving decisions relating to local traditional policies to the respective tribes. In 1993, the IHS sponsored a roundtable discussion on the question of formal support for traditional medicine (Indian Health Service 1993). An inquiry preparatory to the roundtable discussion disclosed considerable variation in official policy throughout the IHS Areas. The most complete and formal policy specifically addressing traditional healing was in the Navajo Area. In other Areas, local Service Units were in various stages of formalizing unwritten policies. The California Rural Indian Health Board (CRIHB) Traditional Indian Health Committee addresses the question as follows: "Tribes/tribal organizations/tribal health programs in efforts to provide access to traditional healers by clients and patients may make referrals and cover the costs of the traditional healers' expenses (i.e., mileage, gas, lodging, meals, supplies). Compensation for the traditional healer's services rests with the patient and his/her family" (CRIHB 1997).

The question of formal training programs for traditional healers, like their employment by the government, is difficult to resolve. The establishment of the Navajo School for Medicine Men (Bergman 1973) received wide attention. It was conceived by the tribe during operation of the Rough Rock demonstration school, which began in 1965. A modified apprentice system was utilized, with each medicine person having two apprentices. The medicine people received a modest salary, and the students a small subsistence allowance. This program received support from the IHS but was ultimately discontinued. There seems to be general consensus that it was a worthwhile effort.

As the financial stability of many Indian communities is further threatened and as society in general moves into further technological development, it is difficult to predict the future of much of traditional medicine as it is now known. The long period of apprenticeship, the privation, the requirement that no one be turned down who asks for help, and the encroachments by other societies all threaten the long-term viability of traditional healing as it is now practiced. However, the growing self-governance movement should permit employment of traditional healers by tribes who choose to do so.

The literature relating to traditional medicine continues to grow and, with the present impetus for alternative approaches to allopathic medicine, is likely to increase even more. Many thoughtful discussions of the two approaches are found in the anthropologic, not medical, literature.

Comparisons of different healing modalities have led to what may now be regarded as three groups of medical professions (Last 1990, 354):

1. The conventional professions "privileged by almost every state and the World Health Organization as the scientifically efficacious system for a nation's health services"
2. Alternative medicine, which includes "homeopathy, Ayurveda, acupuncture and osteopathy" and "which may be recognized by government and public alike as a formal system of therapy, with a set curriculum taught in special colleges or as a special subject"
3. Traditional medicine, "where there is an attempt to create a new professional grouping — amalgamating ordinary, individual healers of varying kinds and specialties into a single body as the basis for obtaining government recognition and for improving public acceptance of its members"

This author makes clear that, in much of the "Third World," indigenous healers will continue to form an important component of care, especially where government support for psychiatric programs is likely to remain meager.

Cooperation between Traditional and Western Healers

A frequent concern is the degree of cooperation and collaboration between Indian healers and physicians. The fundamental differences in backgrounds constitute a natural and powerful barrier to well-integrated programs. The private nature of true Indian healing makes it less accessible to Western physicians. The extreme skepticism of the pure scientist may from time to time make dialogue virtually impossible. On the other hand, many physicians, on a personal basis, work closely with traditional healers (Driver 1969). Leighton and Leighton (1944) pointed out that cooperation is possible and should be encouraged. This important question was specifically examined by the Cornell University–Navajo demonstration project at Many Farms (McDermott et al. 1960). It is important to recognize that benefits accrue to the physician. "What I have seen . . . is the blending of traditional medicine with modern ways, which lends beauty and balance to a medical career" (Porvaznik 1988).

However, some tribes have expressed considerable ambivalence toward integrating traditional and Western medicine. As in virtually all Indian matters, local customs, beliefs, and practices vary considerably, and different communities within a tribe may differ on the subject. Not all Indian communities seem to feel as strongly as many that integration of the two systems would be desirable. Certainly, continued serious and respectful examination of the ways in which two fundamentally dissimilar systems may work together for the benefit of patients is needed. Future investigation might discover that the two approaches to health are not so diametrically opposed after all (Rhoades 1996). It is quite likely that even more refined evaluations of physiologic processes may demonstrate hitherto undefined neural or other pathways that result in specific and measurable changes associated with traditional Indian healing.

Inherent in any such evaluation is the appropriateness of examining instances in which the application of traditional medicine might be associated with potential harm. Coulehan (1976) noted that, on occasion, medicine men would refuse to permit a baby with meningitis to be taken to the hospital before traditional treatment but pointed out that such situations were rare. McDermott et al. (1960) reported that such occurrences were rare during the Many Farms demonstration but that attention should be given to such a possibility.

Alternative Medicine and the Exploitation of Indian Healing

Recently, the coopting of Indian spirituality and healing, largely by those caught up in the New Age movement, has dramatically accelerated (Melmer 1996a, 1996b, 1996c; Porterfield 1997a, 1997b). This movement seems to have provided a fruitful venue for both Indian and non-Indian persons to assume the mantle of traditional healing with little or none of the required intense preparation and apprenticeship and with an eye to the great possibilities for financial gain. In addition, much alternative medicine is caught up in a kind of pop mysticism, self-fulfillment, "indigenous" fad of the "Wannabe" Indian. This explosion of interest in alternative medicine naturally finds Indian healing very attractive. Indeed, Martin (1981) drew on Indian medicine as a way of explaining the current search for alternative methods of healing, which he termed *posttraditional,* a term arising in response to popular dissatisfaction with the dichotomy between traditional and modern societies.

On the other hand, a particularly pernicious development in recent decades is the synergism between much alternative medicine and an antiscience attitude that pervades much of society. In spite of the limitations and sterility of science, it is still by far the most useful technique for determining relationships, eliminating spurious explanations for phenomena, and providing knowledge that can be used by large numbers of persons. Ultimately, to be widely useful for the public, all practices must be tested in the cold atmosphere of skeptical inquiry. Even if techniques are not susceptible to analysis and if blinded, controlled studies are not possible, outcomes of such practices can often be rigorously compared. Absolute identification of the illness under investigation is also required (e.g., biopsy or other documentation of disturbed physiology). There is no question but that the health of the general public would be harmed by diminishing the advances that continue in science, especially in this time of continuing extraordinary advances.

Certain tribes and organizations are formally adopting positions in regard to spirituality and traditional medicine. A number of California tribes, in collaboration with the California Rural Indian Health Board, not only conduct seminars and conferences on traditional healing but also have developed policies and guidelines relating to healing practices (CRIHB 1997). It is the position of the CRIHB Committee for Traditional Indian Health that "non-Indians do not perform Indian ceremonies." The committee encourages tribes and communities to censor outsiders who wish to come into their tribal areas to conduct ceremonies without permission from the tribe and/or spiritual leaders of that particular area (Navarro 1997).

The current popularity of New Age remedies, personal fulfillment, and spirituality borrows much from American Indian cosmology, as a casual perusal of magazine racks, bookstores, and the media discloses. This is true whether promoted by Indians themselves or non-Indians who have "studied" Indian lore and practices. This same perusal demonstrates the degree to which the New Age fever is exploitative of Indian medicine. The superficiality of much that passes for Indian medicine or even spirituality is in sharp contrast to the required years of apprenticeship and training. An important, largely unexplored, and little recognized aspect is that many Indian people believe that those who promulgate such activities, especially for payment, are violating, or plagiarizing, the intellectual property of the tribe. On the other hand, perhaps non-Indians, in their search for spiritual meaning, should not be deprived of the benefits of a sweat or vision quest. It is possible that there are circumstances in which the adoption of these practices may not be exploitative when done privately and unobtrusively. There is no question that much dissatisfaction arises from apparent cooption of Indian traditions by, for example, certain non-Indians who participate in a sun dance. It is this public popularization and the personal gain by those who publish books or articles or hold seminars about traditional Indian spirituality, especially those who may not have the support or backing of the tribe, that can pose a problem. Even if it does not represent expropriation of tribal intellectual (or other) property, the general feeling is that it corrupts Indian medicine.

Discussion

Like so much of Indian life, the role and significance of traditional Indian healing are continuing to evolve. We suggest that "true" traditional Indian

Figure 23.2. Mr. Atwater Aunko, a Kiowa elder, utilizing cedar smoke in praying for Mr. Gus Palmer, the leader of the Kiowa *Ton kon gaut* (black leggings) warrior society, in preparation for an annual ceremony of that organization.

healing consisted of a far more extensive and sophisticated profession than is generally acknowledged. While expressing credit to the field of psychiatry for perhaps providing the greatest understanding and acceptance of traditional medicine, we suggest that even the inexplicable powers exercised by certain traditional healers should be thought of as "metapsychiatric." In addition, the open and public application of cleansing, healing, and purifying techniques, such as the sweat lodge, and the ubiquitous "smoking" with a special material, such as cedar, sage, or sweetgrass, also tend to distinguish Indian ways of thinking from those embraced by most scientists. Smoking is often utilized in specific healing procedures or for spiritual protection and strengthening, always with prayer. It may also be employed for cleansing and blessing a home or building or for ending a formal period of mourning, as before a public ceremony. An example of the latter is shown in Figure 23.2.

The entire subject is presently muddled, with a considerable intrusion of what has been called "New Age" thinking and the many non-Indian "Wannabes" who seek personal spiritual fulfillment through Indian ways. The spiritual component of Indian healing, the benefit of certain practices that are not readily explained scientifically, and the inherent value of the Indian world view all suggest that caution should be exercised before intruding too abruptly into this realm. The concern that true traditional medicine is subject to easy corruption has considerable validity. It is recommended that one proceed with caution, keeping an open but skeptical mind and taking note that embracing something valuable too enthusiastically and superficially might in fact destroy it. Great care should be taken in promoting such "cures" to others. On the other hand, the practice of Western medicine would certainly gain immensely if physicians were more knowledgeable about the sociology of illness and health care. In the meantime, one should be very careful about promulgating Indian or putative Indian beliefs as universally applicable. For the general public, it would seem advisable to heed the advice of Rich (1993), who has pungently cautioned that one should be suspicious of adopted mysticism and "glib spirituality" and especially of the tendency to expropriate "exotic" ways of understanding.

REFERENCES

Ackerknecht EH. 1943. Psychopathology, primitive medicine and primitive culture. *Bull Hist Med* 14:30–67.
———. 1972. Introduction: An interview with Erwin H. Ackerknecht—ethnology and medicine. In: Walker HH, Koelbing HM, eds. *Medicine and Ethnology: Selected Essays.* Baltimore: Johns Hopkins Press.
Adair J. 1963. Physicians, medicine men and their Navaho patients. In: Galdston I, ed.

Man's Image in Medicine and Anthropology. Monograph IV. New York: New York Academy of Medicine.

Adair J, Deuschle K, Barnett CR. 1988. *The People's Health: Anthropology and Medicine in a Navajo Community.* Albuquerque: University of New Mexico Press.

Basso KH. 1967. Heavy with hatred: An ethnographic study of Western Apache witchcraft. Ph.D. diss., Stanford University.

Bergman RL. 1973. A school for medicine men. *Am J Psychiatry* 130:663–66.

Bourke JG. 1971. *The Medicine Man of the Apache.* Pasadena, Calif.: Socio-Technical Publications.

Boyer LB, Klopfer B, Brawer FB, et al. 1964. Comparisons of the shamans and pseudoshamans of the Mescalero Indian Reservation: A Rorschach study. *J Projective Techniques Personality Assessment* 28:173–80.

Brooks H. 1933. The medicine of the American Indian. *J Lab Clin Med* 19:1–23.

California Rural Indian Health Board. 1997. Seventeenth traditional Indian healing program successful. *Tribal Health Advisor* 28:1–3.

Corlett WT. 1935. *The Medicine Man of the American Indian and His Cultural Background.* Springfield, Ill.: Charles C Thomas.

Coulehan JL. 1976. Navajo Indian medicine: A dimension in healing. *Pharos* 39:93–96.

Densmore F. 1954. The importance of rhythm in songs for the treatment of the sick by American Indians. *Scientific Monthly* 79:109–12.

———. 1974. *How Indians Use Wild Plants for Food, Medicine and Crafts.* Dover ed. Toronto: General Publishing. (Reprint of "Uses of Plants by the Chippewa Indians" in the 44th Annual Report of the Bureau of American Ethnology to the Secretary of the Smithsonian Institution 1926–27, 275–397. Washington, D.C.: Government Printing Office.)

Driver HE. 1969. *Indians of North America.* 2d ed. Chicago: University of Chicago Press.

Eisenberg L. 1977. The search for care. *Daedalus* 106:235–46.

Eliade M. 1972. *Shamanism-Archaic Techniques of Ecstasy.* Bollingen Series 76. Princeton: Princeton University Press.

Fejos P. 1959. Man, magic and medicine. In: Galdston I, ed. *Medicine and Anthropology: Lectures to the Laity,* No. 21. New York: International Universities Press.

———. 1963. Magic, witchcraft and medical theory. In: Galdston I, ed. *Medicine and Anthropology: Lectures to the Laity,* No. 21. New York: International Universities Press.

Frazer JG. 1956. *The Golden Bough: A Study in Magic and Religion,* abridged ed. New York: Macmillan.

Gould HA. 1957. The implications of technological change for folk and scientific medicine. *Am Anthropologist* 59:507–16.

Grinnell F. 1874. The healing art as practiced by the Indians of the Plains. *Cincinnati Lancet Observer* 34:145–47.

Haile BOFM. 1938. Origin legend of the Navaho enemy way. *Publications in Anthropology* 17. New Haven: Yale University Press. In: Galdston I, ed. *Man's Image in Medicine and Anthropology,* Monograph IV. New York: New York Academy of Medicine.

Hallowell AI. 1963. Ojibwa world view and medicine. In: Galdston I, ed. *Man's Image in Medicine and Anthropology,* Monograph IV. New York: New York Academy of Medicine.

Hrdlicka A. 1932. Disease, medicine and surgery among the American aborigines. *JAMA* 99:1661–66.

Hultkrantz A. 1979. *The Religions of the American Indians.* Trans. Setterwall M. Berkeley: University of California Press.

———. 1989. Health, religion and medicine in Native North American traditions. In: Sullivan LE, ed. *Healing and Restoring Health and Medicine in the World's Religious Traditions.* New York: Macmillan.

Indian Health Service. 1993. A Roundtable Conference on the Traditional Cultural Advocacy Program — Final Report. Tucson: Indian Health Service.

Kleinman A. 1993. What is specific to Western medicine? In: Bynum WF, Porter R, eds. *Companion Encyclopedia of the History of Medicine,* 1:15–23. London: Routledge.

Kleinman A, Eisenberg L, Good B. 1978. Culture, illness, and care: Clinical lessons from anthropologic and cross-cultural research. *Ann Intern Med* 88:251–58.

Kluckhohn C. 1967. *Navajo Witchcraft.* Boston: Beacon Press.

Kluckhohn C, Leighton D. 1962. *The Navajo.* New York: Doubleday.

Kunitz SJ, Levy JE. 1997. Dances with doctors: Navajo encounters with the Indian Health Service. In: Cunningham A, Andrews B, eds. *Western Medicine as Contested Knowledge,* 94–123. Manchester: Manchester University Press.

La Barre W. 1980. Anthropological perspectives on hallucination, hallucinogens, and the shamanic origins of religion. In: *Culture in Context: Selected Writings of Weston La Barre,* 37–91. Durham: Duke University Press.

Landes R. 1963. Potawatomi medicine. *Trans Kansas Acad Sci* 66:553–99.

Last M. 1990. Professionalization of indigenous healers. In: Johnson TM, Sargent CF, eds. *Medical Anthropology: Contemporary Theory and Method,* 349–66. New York: Praeger.

Leighton AH, Leighton DC. 1941. Elements of psychotherapy and Navajo religion. *Psychiatry* 4:515–23.

———. 1944. *The Navajo Door.* Cambridge: Harvard University Press.

Martin M. 1981. Native American medicine: Thoughts for posttraditional healers. *JAMA* 245:141–43.

McDermott W, Deuschle K, Adair J, et al. 1960. Introducing modern medicine in a Navajo community. *Science* 131:280–87.

Melmer D. 1996a. Plastic Indians: The exploitation of American Indian culture — a culture stolen and sold. *Indian Country Today* 16(9):A3, A6.

———. 1996b. Plastic medicine man exposed. *Indian Country Today* 16(9).

———. 1996c. Become Indian, buy your own Indian name. *Indian Country Today* 16(10).

Mooney J. 1982. *Myths of the Cherokees and Sacred Formulas of the Cherokees.* Nashville: Charles & Randy Elder, Booksellers.

Navarro LD. 1997. Statement of the Committee for Traditional Indian Health. Sacramento: California Rural Indian Health Board.

Popper KR. 1959. *The Logic of Scientific Discovery,* 479. New York: Basic Books.

Porterfield KM. 1997a. The selling of the sun dance: Spiritual exploitation at Heart of Pine Ridge controversy. *Indian Country Today* 17(5):A1, A6.

———. 1997b. The selling of the sun dance. *Indian Country Today* 17(6):A1–A2.

Porvaznik J. 1988. Quoted in Wagner L. Blending of old traditions with modern medicine. *Modern Healthcare,* August 26, p. 22.

Rhoades ER. 1996. Two paths to healing: Can traditional and Western scientific medicine work together? *Winds of Change,* Summer, pp. 48–51.

Rich A. 1993. *What Is Found There: Notebooks on Poetry and Politics*. New York: W. W. Norton.

Stone E. 1932. *Clio Medica: Medicine among the American Indians*. New York: Paul Hoeber.

Task Force on Indian Health. 1976. Report on Indian Health — Final Report to the American Indian Policy Review Commission. Washington, D.C.: Government Printing Office.

Thomas L. 1978. Notes of a biology-watcher: On magic in medicine. *N Engl J Med* 299:461–63.

Toner JM. 1877. Some points in the practice of medicine among the North American Indians, with incidental reference to the antiquity of the office of the physician. *Va Med Monthly* 4:333–50.

Vogel V. 1970. *American Indian Medicine*. Norman: University of Oklahoma Press.

24

Raymond Reid, M.D., M.P.H., and
Everett R. Rhoades, M.D.

Cultural Considerations in Providing Care to American Indians

Cross-cultural medicine continues to receive increasing attention as the American population further diversifies and interest in alternative modes of therapy grows. Because of their relatively small numbers and because essentially all of their treatment has been within a single system, Indians have not always been a major focus of this attention. However, the number of Indian patients treated outside the Indian Health Service (IHS) or tribal systems is likely to continue to increase, and practitioners will find that attention to culturally related healing practices is important to their success in providing optimal care. This chapter presents an overview of the major considerations in dealing with Indian people, especially in the clinical setting.

The Ambience of the Interpersonal Encounter

Certain requirements for an ultimately successful interpersonal encounter seem to be universal. These include pleasantness, politeness, and general friendliness. However, in dealing with Indians, at least in therapeutic situations, two special considerations have been noted. The first is that, in public and sometimes private situations, Indians often appear unusually passive. The initial encounter for an Indian is always tentative and exploratory, testing first the general atmosphere for appropriateness (Rhoades 1990). Indians are often regarded as stoic and impassive, and perhaps in relation to U.S. Whites, generally this may be so. Indians, as a mark of respect, are often slow to express an opinion. However, this reticence is sometimes accompanied by a feeling that they are not really given a chance to talk. In a group, they may say nothing unless specifically invited to speak.

The second major consideration in Indian encounters is the necessity of establishing a satisfactory ambience. In most, perhaps all, instances, especially in situations such as a clinic visit, one should be aware that the encounter between an Indian and a non-Indian is, to some degree, uncomfortable, if not unpleasant, to the Indian person. Centuries of unsatisfactory encounters in which the Indian person has been almost always at a distinct disadvantage add an extra dimension, especially to a situation that already may require certain formalities. The establishment of a proper ambience accords with the general Indian principle of the desirability of harmonious relations. This is certainly operative in the clinical setting. Further, establishment of this ambience often takes precedence over the substance of the subject matter or content of the meeting. If the proper atmosphere is not established, the topic of concern to the individual may not even be brought up.

The initial encounter should always be conducted with decorum and dignity, even if the initial conversation is begun with some joking or bantering. The initial inquiry may be entirely indirect and deal with a neutral universal subject, such as "It's very hot" or "Sure had a hard time getting here." The responder will agree and add some personal note. In virtually all, if not all, tribes, a light handshake is the proper greeting. In earlier times, a person who came to another with a request always presented a small gift, often tobacco, upon arrival. Gifts of groceries are still considered a mark of respect and fellowship. If the occasion is of more than casual concern, a more prized gift is made; a blanket or, among women, a shawl remains the standard, as is the star quilt among Northern Plains tribes.

In the clinical setting, it is advisable to determine the language with which the patient is most comfortable. Those knowing very little or no English will require an interpreter but will often be accompanied by a family member who speaks both English and the native language. Even those who learned English as a second language will often feel more comfortable and will have a better understanding of the medical problem if the native language is used. Often, English-speaking Indians are intimidated by the use of medical terms, particularly terms that are not explained. The practitioner should speak slowly and use pictures when appropriate. The appearance of the physician is always important, with appropriate neatness of dress essential, especially for older Indians. The physician need not be unduly serious. The hallmark is respect and concern, which must be genuine. Movement should proceed at a deliberate pace.

It is always appropriate to extend one's hand in thanking or departing, and it may be insulting not to do so. However, there is a decorum to the handshake that should be kept in mind. It must not be "pushy" or intrusive. With women, particularly, it may be little more than a brushing of the fingertips. The businessman's vigorous pumping and jostling is inappropriate, as are back slapping and overfamiliarity of any kind. Although it may take more time than the busy physician feels is available, establishment of this rapport usually can be achieved reasonably quickly as part of the ongoing examination. Conversely, however, rapport may be destroyed in an instant, sometimes by something of which the physician is not aware.

In spite of the inherent discomfort, Indian persons will generally tend to be accommodating to the physician and, in an attempt to be cooperative, will often acquiesce to questions that they do not understand. There is, to a large extent, an intergenerational difference between Indians born before World War II and those born after, marked by the degree to which the latter possess varying degrees of hostility and anger as a defense mechanism in uncomfortable situations.

In contrast to the widespread idea of the stoic Indian, no group is more bantering, joking, and laughing than Indians — in the right circumstances. However, stoicism in most public encounters is indeed the case, arising from a desire to be dignified but also from simple respect for others. And there is often a stoic manner of dealing with illnesses. Taking one day at a time, maintaining the hope that the next day may bring improvement, is the usual method of bearing an illness. Living one day at a time without thinking about the future is consistent with the tradition of many Indians of not planning for the future.

Another seldom-discussed component of much present-day Indian life is the element of shame. This is often barely suppressed and colors a good deal of individual reaction, especially in the presence of non-Indians. Any sign of approbation or judgment on the part of the health-care provider is apt to stimulate this feeling, to the detriment of the interview. Indians are also extremely sensitive about references to them having high rates of poverty, alcoholism, and other diseases. Especially insulting is the manner in which others insensitively comment on or question poor home conditions, the sometimes unkempt appearance of many Indians, and the frequent visits to emergency rooms and clinics of those with illnesses that might be related to the so-called condition of poverty under which others say they live.

An aspect of the interpersonal encounter is that more than fleeting eye contact is a sign of great intrusion, if not outright disrespect. Staring is always obtrusive. To the Navajo, direct eye contact is believed to establish a path by which the evil spirits of the other person travel toward and enter a person. Even among groups where a discussion is taking place, it is not uncommon for those present to cast their gaze toward a middle, downward distance. Not infrequently, individuals will sit with their eyes closed. This does not denote disinterest or lack of awareness; it is part of proper respectful behavior.

Public Appearances

It is hard to imagine a situation in which a genuine effort to learn about local culture, customs, ceremonies, and beliefs would not be greatly appreciated by the Indian community. Again, a key is the manner in which this is undertaken. Being appropriately visible in the community and positively interacting demonstrate interest in the people and their culture. Invitations may be very casual, even secondhand, and may not be readily recognized as invitations. Even casual remarks, such as "come on out" (to, say, a celebration or powwow), should be given serious consideration. If one is asked to dance, this is always done in good humor and should be accepted graciously. If one receives a public gift, it is important to shake hands with the person bestowing the gift as well as accompanying family members.

When attending a public ceremony, one should observe unobtrusively and listen without asking questions in a forward manner. The timing and manner of questions should be carefully weighed, and interruptions should be avoided. At a celebration, if the group rises in respect for an individual for whom an honor song is sung, one should always rise, and men should remove their hats. If individuals are putting money on a blanket or in a hat or otherwise donating to a special person, it is always permissible to do likewise. If invited to someone's home or to a small family-type gathering, the presentation of a small gift is always appropriate and well received.

Great decorum and deference should always be exhibited in appearances before tribal councils. Each person should be addressed, unless the group is too large, in which case one addresses the group; use *Mister* or *Madam chair, president, members of the council, committee,* and so forth. The address *chief* is appropriate only in a situation in which *chief* is the actual designation of the leader. Some tribes have chiefs and principal chiefs, and others have chairmen or governors, and a few have presidents. One should take care to know and use the appropriate term.

An unsatisfactory clinic visit resulted when a well-meaning physician awkwardly addressed a young Indian boy as *chief.* The term *squaw* should never be used, nor should the term *redskin.* Among certain tribes, though, these terms are acceptable, *depending on the context in which they are used.* Navajos, for example, use *squaw dance* to refer in English to a commonly held summer ceremony which, in the Navajo language, has its own term that denotes a religious ceremony and makes no reference to women participants. On some reservations, the names of school teams often include names such as *Chieftains, Redskins, Warriors, Fighting Scouts,* and *Braves,* which among members of other tribes may be viewed with much disfavor. It is appropriate to ask "What tribe are you?" if it is done with genuine interest and not just curiosity. It is often hard for non-Indians to avoid talking about Indians as if the latter are novelties. One should be alert to the proper address of those with compound last names (e.g., one should not address, say, Mr. Flying Bird as Mr. Bird).

As in certain other cultures, much depends upon who is using the word and the circumstances in which the word is used. It is not uncommon for an Indian to refer to another Indian as a "Skin," as in "He looks like a Skin." However, the authors know of no situation in which a non-Indian could use the term appropriately.

In the Clinic

One of the keys to a successful encounter with an Indian and an attribute that the medical profession often lacks is the willingness to listen. With an Indian patient, listening may take more time than one is accustomed to, and one must learn how to listen and guide the Indian patient along the patient's story line to disclose ultimately what one wishes to know. The patient may or may not initially disclose crucial information. A common complaint of Indian patients is that the amount of time spent with them is very brief. Patients who come from traditional backgrounds and elderly persons often prefer to explain their medical problems in terms that go beyond just the physical ailment. Other aspects of their livelihood and personal universe are sometimes used to explain their illness. Mention of these is important to these patients. Other patients may feel the importance of mentioning how their own household and personal situations are affected by their illnesses. It may even be permissible to ask the patient to explain in Indian terms the cause of the patient's ailment, keeping in mind that witching and hexing and belief in evil spirits are often causes for illness for many Indian patients.

It is good to know topics that tribes consider taboo so that discussions of these are held with respect for the feelings of those who treat these topics as taboo. One such topic is death, which is dealt with differently by different tribes. Discussions regarding this topic are strongly discouraged. To speak at length about death is often believed to predict the death of the person being spoken about. Death is often associated with evil, and the direct cause of death to a person was traditionally thought to involve evil spirits. Evil spirits elicit fear, and the topic of death elicits fear. Individuals of tribes that have this taboo, such as the Navajo, formerly thought of hospitals as places where people went to die, since, when a patient was seriously ill, not much could be done to save the person, and, thus, the person died after reaching the hospital. Also, many Navajos still believe that any structure in which a person has died should be vacated or burned because the evil spirit causing death continues to reside in the structure. Deaths still occur in hospitals, and many traditional Navajos with an illness still resist the suggestion that they seek medical help at a hospital. Also, because of this taboo, traditional Navajos will many times not allow autopsies on deceased relatives, even when the clinician might think an autopsy would be useful. When it is necessary to discuss death with Indians of some tribes, the topic should be handled very delicately and only brief mention of it should be made.

On the other hand, the topic of death among some tribes is not as much of a taboo. These are tribes in which Christian religions and acculturation have largely dispelled the notion of the involvement of evil spirits in the death of people, especially those who die of illness. In some of these tribes, a wake in the home of the deceased is a common method of paying respect to the person.

Another practice considered foreign to many Indians, especially those who were brought up traditionally, is birth control and family planning. This concept is viewed in different ways among tribes and among individuals within the same tribe. The causes for these differences have their bases in population sizes, age, extent of traditional upbringing, and practice of traditional beliefs or assimilation into the lifestyle and thought of the mainstream U.S. population. On reservations, family planning efforts have had varied success as judged by persistently high birth rates and increasing population growth.

American Indians have not forgotten the grand-scale decimation of their forebears by White soldiers and settlers as they moved westward across the United States during the seventeenth, eighteenth, and nineteenth centuries. Population declines resulting from battles with soldiers and settlers over land disputes and from diseases of foreign origin have made many present-day Indians suspicious of any effort that might reduce the current populations of tribes. This is a view that Indians of smaller tribes, especially, often have of birth control and family planning. Tribal leaders never suggest that their tribes' population growth be limited by birth control. On the contrary, increases in their tribes' populations are desired.

For many Indians who had a traditional upbringing, birth control and family planning conflict with natural fecundity. Birth control, which is a human interruption of a natural occurrence, may violate traditional religious dictates. For many Indian women who live on reservations, birth control is not an alternative. Indian women without a traditional upbringing, especially those coming of age in urban surroundings, are much more open to using birth control and family planning. Indeed, fertility rates in some tribes seem to be falling, perhaps because of changes in use of contraceptives, such as repository parenteral hormones. In any case, the matter is dealt with very confidentially.

One should not feel awkward about asking whether the individual has been to, or would like to be seen by, an Indian healer. Among some, the term *Indian doctor* or *traditional healer* is more often used than the term *medicine man*. In conversing with a traditional healer, the health worker should feel comfortable offering to explain all that is being done and what the goals are and asking the Indian healer whether the physician should be alert to certain considerations. Simply asking how one can be of assistance is especially helpful in indicating respect for the Indian healer. This establishes a sense of respectful cooperation.

One should be alert to the fact that the responsible person, especially one accompanying a child, may not be the parents but, instead, may be the grandmother. Several family members, even members of the extended family, as with the Navajos, may attend the admittance of a seriously ill person, but one can usually readily identify the spokesperson. One should be prepared to spend more than a passing moment with the family. It is important to demonstrate that one is concerned with more than simply carrying out the technical aspects of treatment. One way to express this concern is to provide a mat or cot so that one family member, usually the mother, can stay overnight with the hospitalized child.

A great deal is made of the different ways in which Indians regard time. The time when something is to take place is when things are right for that event to take place, not necessarily a preset appointment time. A story is told of the arrival of a federal investigator looking for a Navajo man who had enlisted in the army but did not appear on the day of induction. His response, which flabbergasted the investigator, makes complete sense in the Indian community. When asked why he had not appeared at the appointed hour, he replied simply, "I wasn't ready" (R. McGilbray, pers. comm., 1994). This did not mean that the individual had changed his mind about entering the military service; it simply indicated that the proper preparations regarding self, family, and community had not been completed. The completion of these was entirely independent of a specific point in time. Another anecdote is told about a resident physician who complained that a patient had been seeing a medicine man for four years and that much could have been done for the patient if the four years had not been taken up with the medicine man. An Indian physician asked the medicine man about the situation, and he replied, "I've been trying for four years to get this patient to go to the hospital" (K. Annette, pers. comm., 1994).

The geriatrics program at the University of Oklahoma College of Medicine, in conjunction with the Creek Nation of Oklahoma, produced a video, *Grandma Goes to the Clinic,* that illustrates most of the situations that can result in an unsatisfactory clinical encounter. Another excellent video, *Communicating with Native Patients,* by Ellen Jackson, R.N., was produced by the Native American Research and Training Center of the University of Arizona. Hanley (1995) also discussed in detail considerations in dealing with Indian patients. Useful discussions were provided by Pachter (1994), Kramer (1992), Meleis and Jonsen (1983), Primeaux and Henderson (1981), and Primeaux (1977).

In one sense, there is no special mystique to an encounter with an Indian. Certain universals of human intercourse are always appropriate, even if sometimes overlooked by the clinician. The importance of respect cannot be overemphasized. In addition, friendliness and pleasantness, even in an uncomfortable situation, are always beneficial, as is the sine qua non of a healer, compassion. Treatment of all individuals who are ill requires certain basic principles, of which the Hippocratic oath remains an important cornerstone. These principles rest upon serious conduct befitting a professional person, who has some degree of power over the life and death of individuals. The dictum, *first do no harm*, stands in good stead in all therapeutic encounters.

REFERENCES

Hanley CE. Navajo Indians. 1995. In: Giger JN, Davidhizar RE, eds. *Transcultural Nursing: Assessment and Intervention*, 2d ed., pp. 236–60. St. Louis: Mosby.

Kramer BJ. 1992. Cross-cultural medicine a decade later: Health and aging of urban American Indians. *West J Med* 157:281–85.

Meleis AI, Jonsen AR. 1983. Medicine in perspective: Ethical crises and cultural differences. *West J Med* 138:889–93.

Pachter LM. 1994. Culture and clinical care: Folk illness beliefs and behaviors and their implications for health care delivery. *JAMA* 271:690–94.

Primeaux MH. 1977. American Indian health care practices: A cross-cultural perspective. *Nursing Clin North Am* 12:55–65.

Primeaux MH, Henderson G. 1981. American Indian patient care. In: Henderson G, Primeaux M, eds. *Transcultural Health Care*, 239–54. Menlo Park: Addison-Wesley.

Rhoades ER. 1990. Profile of American Indians and Alaska Natives. In: *Minority Aging: Essential Curricula Content for Selected Health and Allied Health Professions*. Publication No. HRS-P-DV 90-4. Rockville, Md.: Department of Health and Human Services.

25

Everett R. Rhoades, M.D.,
Dorothy A. Rhoades, M.D., M.P.H., and
William Freeman, M.D., M.P.H.

Research Ethics and the
American Indian

The differences in the patterns and manifestations of disease among American Indians compared with other population groups have an obvious attraction for investigators and, indeed, have proved to be an important source of knowledge about some disease processes. However, many special social, cultural, and political considerations, along with the long history of domination of and discrimination against Indian people dictate caution and sensitivity in all studies involving Indian people. Those with experience in Indian communities are well aware of instances of often egregious exploitation of Indian individuals, communities, and tribes by investigators. Sometimes these have resulted from overtly unethical behavior, sometimes from simple ignorance. In either case, Indians as a group remain vulnerable to insensitivity at best and outright exploitation at worst, a situation not ameliorated by the attractiveness of and desirability for more information about those conditions contributing to their excess morbidity and mortality. Most ethical issues affecting the general population are more acute for Indian people. Such issues are also, of course, profoundly influenced by the political sovereignty of the various tribes.

The Heightened Sensitivity Regarding
Human Experimentation

Many new considerations are forcing re-examination or refinement of not only requirements for ethical research conduct, but also what, indeed, constitutes research; what is informed consent and who should oversee it; and especially what is appropriate for the study of genetically determined diseases (Reiser 1993; Kerr-Wilson 1994; Robinson 1994; Kass et al. 1996; Sugarman et al. 1997; Foster and Freeman 1998). In particular, the mapping of the human genome raises additional issues, the end results of which cannot yet be fully comprehended.

An additional set of questions are being raised about the role of "the community" in research (Freeman 1998; Macaulay 1994; Macaulay et al. 1998, 1999). The community, not the individual members of it, may turn out to be the real subject of certain research (e.g., genetic research to determine the migratory history of American Indian tribes, or the "genealogy of groups"). Even when the community is not its direct focus, research involving members of a particular community may describe or identify that community. While recognizing that some Indian communities can and do benefit, at the same time research can be used by politicians, media persons, and the lay public to adversely affect American Indian people and communities and their political systems. Perhaps the biggest potential harm from such research, however, is disruption of the community (Foster et al. 1999).

The current U.S. federal government regulations to ensure ethical research cover the minimization of harms, maximization of benefits, and appropriate informed consent for only *individual people,* not *communities.* How can tribal governments minimize harms and maximize benefits to their communities? How can researchers minimize harms and maximize benefits to the communities involved in their studies? Should researchers seek the informed consent of communities potentially involved in research, not just of individual persons, and if so, how? Should regulations be modified to include harms, risks, and consent to and by communities? The National Bioethics Advisory Commission, appointed by the president in October 1995, is developing a final report dealing with these questions. The answers to such questions will have a profound influence on tribes and communities and, thus, on Indian people. Indian Health Service (IHS) policy dating to the 1960s has required tribal council approval of all research projects in which IHS facilities, records, or personnel are involved (E. A. Johnson, pers. comm., 1999).

Considerations in Conducting Research among Native Americans

Scholars in several countries continue to examine ethical questions involved in studies of aboriginal peoples. The Australian government's National Health and Medical Research Council (1991) has a detailed set of requirements for research involving Native peoples. Other guidelines include those by the Canadian Medical Research Council (1998) and Association of Canadian Universities for Northern Studies (1997). Macaulay (1994) addressed the central ethical questions involved in studies of Canadian Natives and listed considerations that are applicable to other aboriginal groups: an understanding that a community may be harmed by research, the need for true partnership, and recognition of the often highly political aspects of health care. Insofar as possible, the research should produce results of value to the community; subjects must participate freely and understand fully what is to be done; researchers must secure confidentiality; ownership of data and results must be clearly established from the beginning, and the decision adhered to at the very end; and results should be returned to the community in a meaningful way. "Safari" or "helicopter" research, in which investigators arrive, collect data, and depart, leaving the local community with no idea of outcomes, is to be condemned. Macaulay further noted the importance of resolving questions of ownership of data and publication of results. Both Mihesuah (1993) and Freeman (1993) provided extensive discussions of the various parameters involved in research in Indian communities, including the considerable good that may accrue to the community.

The subject of informed consent is increasingly complex (Kass et al. 1996). Often overlooked is the fact that the term itself implies that the investigator and subject "arrive at joint decisions, with subjects' choices ultimately receiving utmost respect" (Katz 1993, 31). Further, patients often provide personal information for purposes of medical care, not research (Jones, Murphy, and Crosland 1995). "Clinicians should be mindful of the tremendous influence they have over their patients, given that the mere suggestion of enrollment in research by a patient's personal physician was interpreted by many patients to be an endorsement" (Kass et al. 1996, 28). Assuring the proper acquisition and completeness of the consent form itself is at the heart of biomedical ethics (Beecher 1966; Katz 1993) and is one of the most important elements in obtaining appropriate tribal participation. "Whenever human subjects of research serve the ends of others, the morality of protecting their physical integrity, which continues to preoccupy the thinking of physician-investigators, is not the central issue. It is, first of all, *the morality with which the invitation to participation in research is extended so that the rights of subjects to be secure in their person and body remain sacrosanct*" (Katz 1993, 34). Guidelines regarding informed consent when dealing with Indian communities are available (Freeman 1994).

The Storage and Subsequent Use of Human Specimens

A growing consideration is the handling of specimens for future study, especially when genetic materials or permanent cell or tissue lines are established.

For many Indian people, the removal of any specimen from an Indian patient is a metaphysical act; that is, a part of the "self" is removed. This little-discussed topic is operative more often than would be supposed. It is reminiscent of the earlier fear that one's spirit was captured by photography. Despite widespread practice, the fundamental importance of this Indian point of view has not been controverted. As in so many aspects of Indian-ness, it isn't always the act itself that is forbidden, but the manner in which the act is carried out. That is, Indians may often feel more agreeable to the storage and disposition of specimens if this is carried out with appropriate respect and seriousness of purpose. The principle reflected in the concern of Indian people about the repatriation of human remains and cultural items also applies to considerations of the collection, storage, use, and ultimate disposal of all tissues and samples (Sugarman et al. 1997). The Strong Heart Study Group (Lee et al. 1990) formed a committee largely composed of Native Americans to guide it in this very subject.

The establishment of perpetual cell lines and tissue cultures and the storage of genetic materials are of special concern. Knoppers and Laberge (1995) identified several elements that should be considered in the use of such specimens, over and above the usual elements guiding research on humans. One is whether a new informed consent is required for the use of "extra" stored specimens not specifically covered in the original informed consent. Maintaining confidentiality and "anonymization" of specimens becomes even more critical. However, anonymization poses new problems (e.g., the possible inability to inform a participant of important findings) (Knoppers and Laberge 1995). The question of when or whether the institutional review board (IRB) or tribe, or both, should grant new permission in such circumstances is difficult and presently unsettled. Clayton et al. (1995) suggested that a determination by the IRB should include whether the proposed use is in conformity with the original consent or whether a new consent is required.

The IHS has developed a comprehensive set of guidelines for the collection and use of specimens for research, including genetic research (Indian Health Service 1997). These provide specific information regarding the collection of specimens, their storage, and their future use. Emphasized is the difficulty of maintaining confidentiality in small communities, the threat to anonymity by computerization, and potential harm to communities even when specimens are anonymous. The guidelines also emphasize that tribal governments legally control research done within their jurisdiction. The draft IHS guidelines make important points and provide useful background information (Indian Health Service 1997). They reflect both the seriousness with which Indian people regard research in general and the growing spiritual, cultural, social, and political concerns regarding such research.

Tribal Governing Bodies

Tribal councils are becoming far more involved in research activities, and as their knowledge increases, the questions posed become more penetrating, including such questions as exactly who will oversee the storage of specimens. It is not uncommon for tribes to disagree with the IHS or other IRBs, and indeed tribal members may disagree with their own council. A tribal council may approve a proposal, disapprove a proposal, or permit the investigation depending on individual choice. Although tribal councils are sovereign, they are subject to the same political pressures experienced by all elected representatives. Governance among tribes varies considerably. There is often a formal council, or committee, elected by the tribe and empowered to carry out certain functions. Among some tribes, this power is limited to business arrangements, and often the elected body is referred to as the business committee. In a number of tribes, the council represents all adult members of the tribe. Such an arrangement is not conducive to swift action; some such councils meet no more than twice a year. In such an arrangement the elected council or business committee is subservient to the tribal council, and the latter may overturn any action taken by the elected representatives. Tribes are not always opposed to research; on the contrary, they often want research carried out (R. Reid, pers. comm., 1996). However, they are often reluctant to turn matters over to outsiders. Ignorance and arrogance may lead some investigators to regard the community as uncooperative. In fact, the tribe rightly regards the investigator as uncooperative.

From time to time, certain occurrences or scientific findings excite the interest of the news media, posing an often even more delicate situation. Members of various media may be notoriously ignorant, even disdainful, of local customs and values. While researchers may have little or no influence on the boorishness of many media persons, they are wise to consider potential ethical lapses when dealing with the news media.

Protection of the anonymity of the community under study is often difficult and requires special care. During the early phases of hantavirus studies, the affected tribe made very clear that publication was not to identify any reservation community. However, when publications contained the names of communities within the tribe, the tribe viewed the event as a betrayal (R. Reid, pers. comm., 1996).

More than one insensitive investigator has been escorted off a reservation by a tribe unhappy with inappropriate conduct. Freeman (1994, 1998) and Macaulay (1994) discussed the importance of the sovereignty of Indian nations in conducting research and the importance of community control of research and publication. Many researchers may see tribal actions as restricting intellectual freedom, whereas the communities see them as ensuring that they are not harmed by research or by publications that could increase the prejudice against them. Having community members as co-investigators helps avoid some of these pitfalls.

The American Indian Law Center (1994) developed a Model Tribal Code governing research, which provides excellent guidance for researchers. As part of the process of obtaining political consent, researchers should fully inform the community and its government about the proposed research and the possible content of resulting publications and should negotiate respective roles. Although it is difficult to know how much information to present to the tribal group, ideally one should consult with the tribe in the design of the investigation itself. The provision of too little information may be seen as paternalistic, condescending, deliberately vague, or even deceitful. On the other hand, too much information may be viewed as a smokescreen designed to obfuscate the "true" purpose of the study. The investigator is well advised to seek the balance that will ensure proper involvement and understanding of the tribe. This frequently requires much more effort and longer time lines than many researchers and funding agencies anticipate. Indeed, the usual cycle of agency notice and request for proposals and funding is almost always unrealistically short from a tribal perspective, where far more deliberate and unhurried consideration is necessary.

The shift toward greater tribal involvement at all points is reflected in the assumption of IRB functions by tribes themselves. Presently, at least two tribes have established their own IRBs, and more are planning to do so. Attention to tribal needs is a highly complex and technical process, requiring great knowledge of the tribe, but also considerable art and judgment, skills not always possessed by highly skilled researchers. The Center for American Indian and Alaska Native Health of the Johns Hopkins School of Hygiene and Public Health employs a Native American physician whose primary responsibilities are ensuring that tribal concerns are fully met. Such personnel may become more necessary as research becomes ever more technical and threatening.

Discussion

Similarities and differences between various Indian groups, their social and cultural differences with the non-Indian population, and the high rates of certain diseases all combine to create a situation with many attractions for conducting biomedical and other research. Indeed, important biomedical advances have resulted from studies among Indian populations, including the use of sulfonamides in the treatment of trachoma, the chemotherapy of tuberculosis, the application of vaccines for hepatitis A and B and for *Haemophilus influenzae* type b, the development of improved pneumococcal vaccines, and understanding of the pathophysiology of type 2 diabetes.

While recognizing the important contributions made by Indian participation in biomedical research, it is well to be reminded that all concerns about individual and public safety are magnified and intensified for Indians. It will be generations before Indian people are able to more easily lay aside the results of centuries of exploitation and loss associated with interactions with non-Indians. Further, many investigators seem to disregard one of the fundamental aspects of Indian life: the sovereign nature of tribes and the resulting government-to-government relationship with the federal government. Although progress has been made in considering various requirements for proper Indian participation in research activities, a great deal remains to be done to avoid exploitation. Strict attention to rules of human research and the stimulation of further Indian interaction in the highly charged arena of genetic studies are strongly recommended.

REFERENCES

American Indian Law Center. 1994. *Model Tribal Research Code.* 2d ed. Albuquerque: American Indian Law Center (at www.BMJ.com/).
Association of Canadian Universities for Northern Studies. 1997. *Ethical Principles for the Conduct of Research in the North.* Ottawa: ACUNS (at http:/aixi.uottawa.ca/associations/aucan-acuns).
Beecher HK. 1966. Ethics and clinical research. *N Engl J Med* 274:1354–60.
Canadian Medical Research Council. 1998. Natural science and engineering research council. Tri-council policy statement: Ethical conduct for research involving humans. Ottawa: Public Works and Government Services Canada (at www.mrc.gc.ca/ethics/english/index.html).
Clayton EW, Steinberg KK, Khoury MJ, et al. 1995. Consensus statement: Informed consent for genetic research on stored tissue samples. *JAMA* 274:1786–92.
Foster MW, Freeman WL. 1998. Naming names in human genetic variation research. *Genome Res* 8:755–57.
Foster MW, Sharp RR, Freeman WL, et al. 1999. The role of community review in evaluating the risks of human genetic variation research. *Am J Hum Genet* 64:1719–27.
Freeman WL. 1993. Research in rural Native communities. In: Bass MJ, Dunn EV, Norton PG, et al., eds. *Conducting Research in the Practice Setting.* Vol 5, *Research Methods in Primary Care.* Newbury Park, Calif.: Sage Publications.
———. 1994. Making research consent forms informative and understandable: The experience of the Indian Health Service. *Camb Q Healthcare Ethics* 3:510–21.
———. 1998. The role of community in research with stored tissue samples. In: Weir R, ed. *Ethical and Legal Implications of Stored Tissue Samples.* Iowa City: University of Iowa Press.
Indian Health Service. 1997. *Guidelines about the Collection and Use of Research Speci-*

mens. Albuquerque, N.M.: Office of Research, Indian Health Service, Headquarters West.

Jones R, Murphy E, Crosland A. 1995. Primary care research ethics. *Br J General Practice* 45:623–26.

Kass NE, Sugarman J, Faden R, et al. 1996. Trust, the fragile foundation of contemporary biomedical research. *Hastings Cent Rep* 26(5):25–29.

Katz J. 1993. Ethics and clinical research revisited: A tribute to Henry K. Beecher. *Hastings Cent Rep* 23(5):31–39.

Kerr-Wilson R. 1994. Problems with the ethics of medical research [editorial]. *Br J Hosp Med* 52:495–96.

Knoppers BM, Laberge CM. 1995. Research and stored tissues: Persons as sources, samples as persons? *JAMA* 274:1806–7.

Lee ET, Welty TK, Fabsitz R, et al. 1990. The Strong Heart Study: A study of cardiovascular disease in American Indians. Design and methods. *Am J Epidemiol* 132:1141–55.

Macaulay AC. 1994. Ethics of research in Native communities [editorial]. *Can Fam Physician* 40:1888–90, 1894–97.

Macaulay AC, Commanda LE, Freeman WL, et al. 1999. Responsible research with communities: A review of participatory research in primary care. *Br Med J* 319:724–25.

Macaulay AC, Delormier T, McComber AM, et al. 1998. Participatory research with Native community of Kahnawake creates innovative code of research ethics. *Can J Public Health* 89:105–8.

Mihesuah DA. 1993. Suggested guidelines for institutions with scholars who conduct research on American Indians. *Am Indian Culture Res J* 17:131–39.

National Health and Medical Research Council. 1991. *NH&MRC Guidelines on Ethical Matters in Aboriginal and Torres Islander Health Research.* Brisbane, Australia: National Health and Medical Research Council (at www.health.gov.au/nhmrc/ethics/asti.pdf).

Reiser SJ. 1993. Overview: The ethics movement in the biological sciences. A new voyage of discovery. In: Bulger RE, Heitman E, Reiser SJ, eds. *The Ethical Dimensions of the Biological Sciences,* 294. New York: Cambridge University Press.

Robinson A. 1994. The ethics of gene research. *Can Med Assoc J* 150:721–27.

Sugarman J, Kaalund V, Kodish E, et al. 1997. Ethical issues in umbilical cord blood banking. Working Group on Ethical Issues in Umbilical Cord Blood Banking. *JAMA* 278:938–43.

26

Emery A. Johnson, M.D., M.P.H., and
Everett R. Rhoades, M.D.

The Future of Indian Health

The previous chapters have described the transformation of a struggling "colonial" health program, transferred from the Department of Interior to the U.S. Public Health Service in 1955, into a national system of comprehensive high-quality health care, with substantial improvements in both accessibility and health status. For example, all hospitals and health centers of the Indian Health Service (IHS) are fully accredited by the Joint Commission on Accreditation of Healthcare Organizations (Indian Health Service 1997). This has occurred in spite of inadequate resources, a situation acknowledged by independent studies (*President's Private Sector Survey on Cost Containment* 1982; Office of Technology Assessment 1986). Although these accomplishments have been impressive, much remains to be done, especially in certain situations in which the health of Indians remains unacceptably below that of the general population.

Principles of Indian Health

Any consideration of Indian health, including future developments, must keep uppermost in mind three unifying principles (Johnson 1993), firmly established in federal law: (1) the goal to be reached is the highest level of health status for American Indians and Alaska Native people (Indian Health Care Improvement Act, P.L. 94-437); (2) the federal government has a legal obligation to provide health services for Indian people (P.L. 94-437); and (3) Indian health programs must be carried out with the maximal participation of Indian people (Indian Self-Determination and Education Assistance Act, P.L. 93-638, as amended). The presence of a specific goal, at least of this nature, is unique and has proved invaluable in shaping Indian health policy.

The future of Indian health can be defined in terms of three categories of problems remaining to be solved: (1) specific diseases and human behaviors that cause illness, aggravate underlying conditions, or inhibit the treatment of illness (e.g., alcohol and substance abuse, diabetes); (2) special populations (children, disabled persons, and elderly persons); and (3) the organization and delivery of health services. Five health problems are the most critical for Indian people in the near future.

Alcohol Abuse

First in importance among the remaining health problems is alcoholism and its direct and indirect sequelae. It is not only directly related to the 5th leading cause of mortality in Indians but also a major contributor to at least 3 other of the 10 leading causes of death: accidents, homicide, and suicide. In addition, alcoholism is a major factor in child and spouse abuse, community and family disorganization, poor work and educational performance, and congenital mental retardation (fetal alcohol syndrome). In many Indian communities, alcohol abuse is assuming the dominance that in the 1950s was occupied by tuberculosis — so pervasive that it is considered to touch every Indian family in some way.

In spite of many seemingly intractable socioeconomic conditions, compounded by a lack of basic knowledge of etiologies, continued action must be taken using the latest information and applied across a number of fronts. Integrated studies such as those by the Scripps Institute group promise to expand basic knowledge of Indian alcohol abuse mechanisms (Ehlers et al. 1996, 1998; Wall et al. 1997, 2000). The growing determination of tribes and communities to deal with alcohol abuse and the increasing recognition that individual behavior modification is the most important factor in prevention represent important advances toward the prevention of alcohol abuse. The implementation of the many Indian programs and their diversity in the past two decades now provide a basis for careful comparison of the factors found useful in prevention and for identification of those associated with successful outcomes. Even without complete understanding of the etiology of alcoholism, it is still possible to make major inroads by careful observation of the results of these interventions to determine what works. In spite of the magnitude of the problem, there are reasonable bases for optimism over the long haul: the growth of empiric knowledge, continued epidemiologic studies, community determination to change, and the always possible biochemical, pharmacologic, or genetic breakthroughs.

Diabetes

As discussed in Chapter 13, the highest known incidence of diabetes in the world is found in certain Southwest Indian tribes. In addition to the high mortality (the fourth leading cause of death, with a rate 2.7 times that of the general population), morbidity in the forms of end-stage renal disease, amputations, and blindness are serious and are creating major and increasing demands on the health and social services resources of Indian communities.

The IHS Model Diabetes program discussed in Chapter 13 is a multifaceted, yet focused, approach to a complex problem. However, such projects do not cover all of the Indian diabetic population in need of special services. For the others, local initiatives in diabetes control are being carried out. In most of these, intensive nutrition education, obesity control, and exercise have been the main components.

Retrospective studies of comparable populations could identify control factors that seem to be most effective. The prospective efforts at prevention recently initiated by the National Institute of Diabetes and Digestive and Kidney Diseases should provide important information about possible prevention. Also promising are recent pharmacologic advances, such as the development of medications to facilitate insulin action at the cellular level and the application of angiotensin-converting enzyme inhibitors to ameliorate or postpone end-stage renal disease; these should improve the overall outlook for people with this modern scourge. A gathering momentum of federal and community efforts directed toward diabetes offers a basis for some optimism that this terrible epidemic will ultimately be controlled.

Cardiovascular Diseases

Any discussion of cardiovascular diseases (CVDs) must include the overwhelming contribution made by the epidemic of diabetes. As a result partly of previous successes in controlling contagious diseases and partly of an aging population, CVD has become the leading cause of death of Indian people. The prevalence of risk factors associated with hazardous lifestyles, including sedentism, improper diet, and especially tobacco use, has been discussed in Chapters 10, 12, 13, and 17. Under the leadership of the National Heart, Lung, and Blood Institute, data are being collected in a prospective and systematic manner. Perhaps more important, interventions directed at diet, exercise, tobacco use, and increased education about healthy living are beginning to be implemented. Whether these will be productive awaits analysis of carefully collected information. It is entirely likely that advancing pharmacologic, and perhaps genetic, studies will also prove to be of value in this population. The additional costs of newer antidiabetes and lipid-lowering agents are already placing strains on the overburdened IHS and tribal pharmacies.

Violence

Indians share with other Americans a propensity for violent death. Indeed, violent death rates among Indians of all age groups exceed those of the comparably aged general population. While very gratifying benefits continue to accrue in reducing mortality from unintentional injuries and suicide through the implementation of innovative community injury prevention efforts (Chapters 14 and 15), insufficient attention has been directed toward deliberate injuries caused by others. This is undoubtedly the result of regarding homicide primarily from a sociologic and legal rather than a public health perspective. While the trend for these causes of violent death is downward for the overall Indian population, the proportion of homicides committed against children under the age of four years is increasing. This situation is particularly tragic, given the history of infant and child nurturing that has characterized so much of Indian life.

A more systematic and public health approach to violence, especially intentional violence, with its great burden on the community of illness and disability, is warranted. The situation, of course, is intimately associated with the pervasiveness of alcohol abuse, and attention to the latter should produce benefits related to all injuries. However, it is generally acknowledged that the increasing number of youth without the usual social restraints associated with the concept of conscience poses a serious future threat for many Indian communities, as it does for the general population.

Malignancies

In contrast to a reduction in cancer death rates among the general population, cancer deaths seem to be increasing in the Indian population. Some of the same risk factors affecting CVD mortality, as noted above, may play the most important role among the Indian population, especially the use of tobacco. A particularly ironic situation exists with respect to malignancies among the Indian population. While most cancers seem to occur less frequently among Indian people, the survival rate once a diagnosis is made is also less, pointing to the need for increased screening and availability of vigorous therapies, in consultation with oncology specialists. The emphasis that continues to be placed on attention to women's health, especially in the post-child-bearing years, when they tend to encounter the health-care system less often, should prove to be beneficial. There is a need for intensification and implementation throughout the system.

Health Problems of Specific Populations

Infants and Children

While there has been a dramatic reduction in infant mortality over the past 40 years, Indian infant mortality remains about 10 percent higher than that of the general U.S. population (U.S. All Races). This is not a universal situation; many tribes have rates as low as or lower than those for the general population, while others have rates significantly higher. The major problem is in postneonatal mortality, where the Indian rate is 1.6 times the U.S. All Races rate. Causes of death in these later months are primarily sudden infant death syndrome and congenital anomalies, although factors related to the environment — infections and accidents — are important.

Disabling conditions and chronic disorders, especially among children, are another major concern. The latter were reviewed by Brenneman (1997). While complete documentation is not available, statistics from IHS and the Bureau of Indian Affairs indicate that 10 percent of the school-age Indian population may be afflicted with disabling conditions. Children with learning disabilities constitute the largest group. It is mandatory that the attention to children that has been the hallmark of IHS programs continue.

Aged Persons

The ravages of chronic diseases are the hallmark of afflictions of elderly persons. Compounding this are the limitations of the family and community in providing adequate housing, nutrition, and other support for their aged members. On too many reservations, the outlook for elderly persons who can no longer provide their own daily living support is bleak. Facilities for sheltered care and nursing homes are uncommon in Indian communities. Many elders are, by necessity, transported long distances from home and family and placed in an alien community's nursing home. The result is a tragedy not only for the aged but also for the Indian family and community, as the traditional contribution of the elders to the preservation of Indian culture is lost as well.

Further compounding these problems is the substantial and increasing cost of providing health services to elderly persons, which strains already marginal resources — health and social services, finances, housing — of the Indian community. The IHS and Indian communities are faced with the immediate problem of dealing effectively and humanely with the present and future elderly Indian population.

An example of one approach is the Laguna Pueblo, which has developed the Laguna Rainbow program with sheltered housing, an adjacent nursing home (which also provides dining facilities for the sheltered care residents), an elderly congregate meals program, and Meals on Wheels. In addition, Head Start children are included so the elders may continue to pass their culture on through teaching and working with the children. This also provides the elders with a continued presence in the community and a sense of remaining valuable members of their community.

The Challenges of Health Services Delivery

While substantial progress has been made, many Indian communities still have inadequate access to high-quality primary and specialty health services. Even for many who seem to have adequate services, these may be fragile; there is marginal funding, growing risk of further budget reductions, problems with recruitment and especially retention of health professionals, and problems of accessibility and acceptability of health services.

For many years, the objective of IHS and of the larger health services community as well has been to provide convenient access to high-quality and acceptable health services for all of the population. The rapidly escalating cost of health care threatens this objective. Cost containment has become the principal concern of government, the health-care industry, private businesses, and consumers. The Indian community, although having made great progress in obtaining access to appropriate health services, still lags behind in health status and is now being faced with the threat of actual reduction in their health services programs.

How to maintain, if not improve, access to high-quality and acceptable health services becomes one of the major unresolved Indian health problems. IHS is commonly thought to be a typical federal bureaucracy, with decisions made in headquarters and passed down through a chain of command implemented at field level. In fact, IHS can be more accurately defined as a rather loose affiliation of health programs linked by a common legislative authority, congressional appropriations, and national Indian health policies.

The spectrum of health delivery can extend from a health delivery system totally operated by the IHS to one totally operated by a tribal government. In fact, no entire health delivery system has been under IHS management since the late 1960s, when certain preventive services (e.g., community health representatives) began to be managed by the tribes. By fiscal year 1996, 76 of the 144 Indian health-care delivery systems were managed by the tribes, and that number is increasing; many delivery systems are a combination of IHS and tribal health delivery.

As a result, this great variety of health services delivery systems constitutes many natural experiments in the organization and delivery of health services in Indian communities. By carefully controlling significant variables, it should be possible to compare Indian health delivery systems to identify, for example, differences in outcome in health status, in costs, or in utilization of services according to specific organizational or delivery configurations. Both retrospective and prospective studies would prove to be instructive.

Another problem facing rural hospitals as well as Indian health delivery systems is how to remain financially viable in the face of current aggressive cost containment initiatives. Given the intensive effort by both government and the private sector to contain health-care costs, small rural hospitals will be increasingly stressed. Unless some method is found to lower health-care costs per unit and spread fixed costs over a larger workload, many of these facilities will be unable to survive. The small rural hospital has historically been modeled after the traditional large metropolitan hospital, a model that may no longer be appropriate for the rural community.

To deny a small community access to a local hospital without fully investigating potential options seems unreasonable. It should be possible to test alternative models of the organization and delivery of health care in the rural community and to obtain valid and objective data on these alternatives. One approach is to expand the services provided by the hospital beyond the typical bed-patient mode. Alternatives include supporting ambulatory care, hospice services, and skilled nursing (swing beds) and providing space or administrative and technical support for community health practitioners (e.g., physicians, dentists, pharmacists) or programs (e.g., public health nursing, environmental health, food and nutrition services). Tribes should have much greater latitude than the IHS in exploring such innovations.

In Indian communities, one finds integrated programs with all levels of health practitioners housed in a common facility under common management (IHS and/or tribal), providing inpatient, outpatient, and preventive services, including environmental services. In others, where the Indian community is more dependent on contract health services, one finds the more typical rural arrangement of freestanding hospitals and individual practitioners' offices with, at best, marginal coordination; there is almost every variation in between. No systematic study has compared, retrospectively, the advantages (cost, efficiency, effectiveness) of any of these models. An excellent opportunity exists to design prospective studies of alternative organization and management systems to determine the most cost-effective configurations for the small rural community. It may well be that a rationally organized, small, rural health delivery system can be cost-effective and economically viable, thus enhancing access to health services and promoting community-oriented primary care.

An alternative to more money is more efficient use of the resources already at hand (e.g., congregate feeding, facility maintenance, basic health services, social services), functions usually provided by a variety of agencies. For example, a recent study of a small northern Minnesota reservation found that seven different agencies were providing congregate feeding: the school, the hospital, the alcohol treatment center, the jail, Head Start, senior meals, and Meals on Wheels. Each had its own kitchen, staff, supplies, and overhead; the resulting excess cost to the community was substantial. Under the leadership of the tribal council, plans were developed to begin to centralize the purchase and preparation of food in one location — the hospital, which, incidentally, had the only registered dietician and public health nutritionist in the community. As this process is implemented, the community anticipates substantial savings, which can be shifted to other high-priority community needs. Such modeling could readily be replicated throughout the country.

Another finding was that there were at least four different maintenance organizations, frequently working over and around each other and with duplication of tools, machinery, and supplies. The community was also spending significant funds each year to place battered women in a shelter off the reservation while the hospital had sufficient space to accommodate this need. These are but a few examples of the kinds of inefficiencies that, if corrected, would enhance the viability of the small rural health services delivery system.

While there are many problems to be overcome in making these changes, the Indian community is an ideal location to test the validity of these concepts. The tribal government has the authority under federal law to direct most of these programs if it so chooses. In addition, state licensure often does not apply, so alternatives can be tested without that constraint. Of course, every effort is made to conform to state law if necessary to facilitate funding reimbursement.

Difficulty in the recruitment and, more important, retention of professional staff is likely to continue to be another major problem of health services delivery. The usual method for obtaining physicians is either through the Public Health Service (PHS) commissioned corps or by tribal or IHS direct hire. Both of these have their deficiencies. Alternative medical staffing arrangements could be tested (e.g., by creating an independent medical group similar to the Permanente group or by contractual arrangements with existing group practices). Design and comparison of these alternatives in carefully selected Indian health delivery systems could identify factors that are most important in obtaining and retaining a high-quality medical staff. Implementation of models in "experimental" and "control" Indian communities could be compared. It is essential, however, to preserve the authority of tribal health programs to use the PHS commissioned corps, which has been the mainstay of Indian health professional staff since 1955.

Finally, as pressure to contain the costs of medical care continues to mount, there is increasing concern that medical care will be rationed in unacceptable ways. Because of the fiscal constraints imposed by the federal budget, IHS since its inception has rationed medical care. The degree to which it has been successful can be debated (although the improvements in access, quality of health care, and health status of the Indian population cannot be disputed), but, again, there is in place a natural experiment that could be studied to determine not only the implications of various means of health-care rationing but also the mechanisms that are effective (or not effective) in providing health services under various restrictive conditions.

Scores of creative, effective, and exciting experiments in health services delivery are now being carried out in Indian communities. With appropriate technical support and funding, these could make major contributions to the understanding of effective community-oriented primary care and to the most efficient management of limited resources for health services delivery.

The Future Organization of Indian Health

To maintain and assure the continuation of the legal federal responsibility for Indian health services, some official federal agency must provide linkages between the federal government and the tribes; have a seat at the federal table when legislation, policy, and the president's budget requests are being debated and decided; and provide liaison with and obtain the collaboration and commitment of other federal agencies, such as the Centers for Disease Control and Prevention, the National Institutes of Health, the Social Security Administration, and the Health Care Financing Administration. Whatever this agency is called, these federal functions must be carried out. For the purpose of this discussion, we will continue to call it *IHS*.

In addition, activities such as health statistics, epidemiology, research, and training are all essential elements of an effective Indian health system that require aggregation, critical mass, synthesis, and coordination. Some of these efforts are best served by a central federal organization, even though most of the actual functions may be carried out at a local or regional level by tribes or tribal organizations. It is our view that many of the successes of Indian health, such as community health representatives, trachoma and tuberculosis control, and reduction in rates of infant mortality and chronic otitis media, would have been less timely and less certain without the central focus of the IHS.

Over the past four decades, IHS has developed a national system of health care, in essence an HMO/managed care system, which is far more comprehensive than any other and is uniquely designed to meet the special needs of the great diversity of Indian communities. Now, with the changed dynamics of managed care and cost containment, the national health-care scene is experiencing a consolidation of health facilities and programs. Small rural hospitals are closing or being absorbed by large regional or national health-care systems. At the same time, under Public Law 93-638 and other legislation, the IHS national health-care system is being broken up into small, self-contained reservation health facilities.

IHS was ahead of its time in its development of the national managed care system and in its commitment to the "healthy community" paradigm (Schlesinger and Gray 1998). In the healthy community model, the health-care organization promotes the capacity of the community to identify and respond to its own health needs, including the transfer of authority and resources for health-care services delivery to the community—the principle of Indian self-determination advanced by the IHS since the 1960s. The rest of the country has caught up with the concept of national managed care systems, although not with that of "healthy communities." If the national health-care wisdom of consolidation is correct, the delivery system for Indian health care is becoming out of touch and is going backward through the transfer of health-care management from IHS to individual tribal governments.

The issue is not the IHS as an institution but Indian health care as an organized system of care. Many of the successes of Indian health have been, in our view, the result of an organized and comprehensive approach to health that has gone beyond community-oriented primary care to embrace the "healthy communities" strategies. These initiatives can continue to be accomplished in a number of ways—through a national Indian tribal government-directed entity (e.g., the National Indian Health Board) and regional intertribal organizations (e.g., the Great Lakes Intertribal Council, the United South and Eastern Tribes, the California Rural Indian Health Board, the Alaska Native Tribal Health Consortium) or intertribal consortia (e.g., the Norton Sound Health Corp., the Southeast Alaska Regional Health Corp., United Indian Health Services). Individual tribally operated programs can join together in consortia or can share scarce or expensive services or services that are not feasible for a small workload while maintaining individual tribal clinical and preventive services. Health-care systems that are "virtually integrated," as in the current evolution of IHS from a "vertically integrated" mode, may actually be more appropriate (Robinson and Casalino 1996). Once again, IHS seems to have been ahead of its time.

The federal issue for the Indian health-care system is to continue to receive support through federal appropriations and the continued participation of other federal agencies in providing technical support, policy, funding, and services. The role of the federal Indian health agency is a key to these arrangements. A mandatory component is the assurance of accountability. Congress needs to know what is being accomplished with the federal funds being provided. For this reason, as well as for essential local planning and administrative needs, it is mandatory that certain data and information be provided (e.g., health statistics, workloads, services provided, health status indicators). It would be desirable for such a federal agency to avoid the movement in the rest of the country toward decision making by non-health-care workers and to strive to avoid rendering the federal leadership more political. The successes of the IHS have to a large extent been associated with leadership composed of experienced physicians (Bergman, Grossman, and Erdrich 1999).

The IHS has traditionally approached problems through pilot programs or demonstrations rather than through the initiation of nationwide programs. One notable example is the Community Health Representative (CHR) program. The initial CHR pilot project on the Pine Ridge Reservation in South Dakota was designed for the CHR to be an assistant to the IHS public health nurse. The second pilot project on the Northern Cheyenne Reservation in Montana was drastically changed at the recommendation of John Woodenlegs, president of the Northern Cheyenne. He believed that the CHRs would be more effective as tribal employees. The Northern Cheyenne model became the national CHR program, which initiated the movement toward tribal administration of their own health services. The evolution of Indian health care would have been far different and, in our view, much less successful without this modification of a federal initiative through tribal leadership.

Another critically important factor in the success of Indian health over the past 40 years has been the remarkable partnership among the Congress, the Indian tribal governments, and the IHS. The relationship between the tribes and their individual members of Congress has been key to this — their senators' and representatives' understanding of, support for, and willingness to be associated with successful tribal and IHS health programs.

Tribes also have the ability to make major contributions to health delivery in their respective states (GLITC Indian Health Programs 1998). If state governments, which are increasingly being required to assume more of the federal role in health services, are true to their responsibility for the health and well-being of all of their citizens, they will recognize that Indian health service delivery systems are among the most cost-effective and, in many instances, are the only potential for providing accessible and acceptable health services for this segment of the population.

Anticipated Political and Societal Changes

There are going to be substantial changes in overall Indian societies in the next few decades. One example is the continuing development in many Indian communities of gambling emporia, usually referred to as *gaming*. The full effects of this development have yet to be ascertained. On the one hand, anecdotes relate the newfound pride among individuals who for the first time have cash income readily at hand. Also, some tribes have made substantial contributions to health service delivery for their local communities. At the same time, in most communities one also hears concerns about possible adverse consequences of gaming upon both individuals and the community. One likely consequence is a widening of the gap between tribes with many resources and those with few, if any. Questions of the possible effect of this phenomenon on the level of federal support for tribes have already arisen.

It is almost certain that an examination of fundamental questions, such as the federal/tribal relationship discussed in Chapter 4, will continue. These include such basic questions as the definition of *Indian,* at least for the purposes of federal (and, therefore, other) programs; the question of individual eligibility for shrinking federal government programs; and the reciprocal relationship between federal trust responsibilities, on the one hand, and tribal sovereignty, on the other. As both the Indian and the larger society evolve into the "information age," it is almost certain that these questions, which have never been completely resolved to the satisfaction of all parties, will continue to be examined. It is likely that certain modifications in these definitions and relationships may be made.

The challenge in such eventualities will be the maintenance of the historically, legislatively, judicially, but also morally incurred obligations of U.S. society in respect to Indian people. Although these arrangements have always been fragile and marked by continued conflict regarding such matters as federal, local, and tribal jurisdiction and federal obligations, there is no compelling reason to believe that new accommodations will enhance the well-being of Indian people, still lagging behind the rest of the population. However, Indian tribal governments and tribal organizations, the IHS, and the Congress have demonstrated over the past 40 years that investment in Indian health care has positive results, that collaboration is successful, and that evolving change is not to be feared but is the indicator of success. If this collaboration can be maintained, the next 40 years should be no less productive.

REFERENCES

Bergman AB, Grossman DC, Erdrich AM. 1999. A political history of the Indian Health Service. *Milbank Q* 77(4, December).
Brenneman G. 1997. Chronic and disabling conditions among American Indian and Alaska Native children and youth. *Fam Syst Health* 15:263–74.
Ehlers CL, Garcia-Andrade C, Wall TL, et al. 1996. Determinants of P3 amplitude and

response to alcohol in Native American mission Indians. *Alcohol Clin Exp Res* 20:1438–42.

———. 1998. Electroencephalographic responses to alcohol challenge in Native American mission Indians. *Neuropsychopharmacology* 18:282–92.

GLITC Indian Health Programs. 1998. *IHS Staff, Tribes and State Work Together.* Lac du Flambeau: Great Lakes Intertribal Council.

Indian Health Service. 1997. *Trends in Indian Health, 1997.* Rockville, Md.: Indian Health Service, Program Statistics Team.

Johnson EA. 1993. National health care reform and Indian health. In: *Returning to a Natural State of Good Health: Report of the National Summit on Indian Health Care Reform, March 1993,* 48–49. Oakland, Calif.: American Indian Resources Institute.

Office of Technology Assessment, U.S. Congress. 1986. *Indian Health Care,* 190–93. Washington, D.C.: Government Printing Office.

President's Private Sector Survey on Cost Containment. 1982. Baltimore: Department of Health and Human Services, Health Care Financing Administration, p. 141.

Robinson JC, Casalino LP. 1996. Vertical integration and organizational networks in health care. *Health Aff (Project Hope)* 15(1):19–20

Schlesinger M, Gray B. 1998. Can managed care promote community health. *Health Aff (Project Hope)* 17(3):156.

Wall TL, Garcia-Andrade C, Thomasson HR, et al. 1997. Alcohol dehydrogenase polymorphisms in Native Americans: Identification of the ADH2* allele. *Alcohol Alcohol* 32:129–32.

———. 2000. Alcohol elimination in Native American Mission Indians: An investigation of interindividual variation. *Alcohol Clin Exp Res* 24:30–34.

Index

aboriginal peoples: of America, 3–16; research ethics and, 427–28

abuse. *See* violence; *specific type*

acanthosis nigricans, 224

accidents: alcohol and, 247–48, 254, 286; children in, 142, 146, 245; morbidity, 116–17; mortality, 97, 106–8, 111–13, 142, 146; paleoepidemiology, 31–33

accreditation of facilities, 80–81, 393, 434

acculturation: mental health and, 318–21; risks, 132, 167, 223, 265, 311; substance abuse and, 287–88, 291; suicide and, 267–69; variables, 21–23, 49–50, 167

acquired immune deficiency syndrome (AIDS), 358–59. *See also* human immunodeficiency virus

administrative perspectives: government relations, 61–73; health service systems, 74–92, 443–44; population data, 93–99

age: disease risks, 104–5, 166, 264–65; distributions, 42–43, 94

agriculture: demographics, 12–13, 15, 20; nutrition from, 212–13; paleoepidemiology, 24–29, 31

Alaska Native community health aide (ANCHA), 80, 84

Alaska Native Land Claims Settlement Act, 63

Alaska Natives, xxiii; cancer, 185–86, 188–89, 192; health, 168, 265, 301, 317, 397; infections, 348–50, 352, 354–55, 357, 359; origins, 4, 6, 9–12, 31, 124–25

albuminuria, 166–67, 233

alcohol dehydrogenase (ADH), 132, 289–90

alcohol use: abstinence rates, 283–84; accidents and, 247–48, 254; biological factors, 287, 289–90; psychosocial factors, 281–82, 286–89; risks from, 158, 167, 281–82, 304

alcoholism: in adults, 132–33, 283–87; age-adjusted, 281–85, 293; genetics, 131–32, 287, 289–90; mortality, 110–13, 281–82,

284–86, 294, 435; per gender, 282–86, 294; per geography, 284–86, 291, 293; prevention, 292–94; public policy, 292–93; recovery, 283–84, 291; risks, 132, 148, 158, 167, 285–87, 293; suicide, 269–71, 276, 290; time trends, 120, 281–82, 435; treatment, 290–91, 294, 435; in youth, 147–49, 282–83, 288–89, 314

aldehyde dehydrogenase (ALDH), 289–90

Aleuts, 9, 126–27, 188

alleles, as marker, 123–28, 130, 328–29

alpha-fetoprotein (AFP) screening, 356

alternative medicine, 401, 406, 410–12

ambulatory services: cultural aspects, 418–25; establishment, 76–77, 79; of IHS, 79, 83–84, 87–88; for injuries, 244–45, 250–51; utilization, 116–17, 145

American Indian Health Care Association (AIHCA), 81–82

American Indian Law Center, 431

American Indian Policy Review Commission, 67–69

American Indians: demographics, 3–57; as term, xvi, xxiii–xxiv

Amerindian language, 9, 127, 130

amputation, lower extremity, 234, 236

ancestral lineage, 63, 124–27

ancient cultures. *See* Paleo-Indians

anemia. *See* iron deficiency anemia

animal bites, 396

ankylosing spondylitis, 333–34, 336, 343

anomie, as health risk, 120, 267, 288

anonymity in research, 429–30

antibiotics, 357

antidiabetic agents, 222, 436

Anti–Drug Abuse Act (1986), 293

antigens, as markers, 123, 328

antinuclear antibodies (ANAs), 328–29, 332–33

anxiety disorders, 313–14, 317–18

Apache tribe, health status, 13–14, 201, 254, 262, 270, 348

Library of Congress Cataloging-in-Publication Data

American Indian health : innovations in health care,
promotion, and policy / edited by Everett R. Rhoades.
      p.   cm.
    Includes bibliographical references and index.
    ISBN 0-8018-6328-7 (hardcover : alk. paper)
    1. Indians of North America — Medical care.   2. Indians
of North America — Health and hygiene.   3. United States.
Indian Health Service.   I. Rhoades, Everett R.
RA448.5.I5 A597   2000
362.1'089'97073 — dc21   99-050740

LIBRARY-LRC
TEXAS HEART INSTITUTE